FOREWORD

I was a nineteen-year-old blushing bride when I became pregnant for the first time. That was in 1961. I would eventually give birth to nine children, although I had no inkling of what the future held back then. The mere thought would have given me acute heart failure.

I knew absolutely nothing about children. I can't remember ever so much as holding an infant in my arms until I had one of my own. No one could have been more clueless than I was when I learned I was to be a mother.

"So how do I do this?" I asked the nurse as soon as the pregnancy was confirmed.

"How do you do what?" the nurse replied blankly.

"How do I give birth?"

She looked at me indulgently.

"A lot of babies are born at this hospital. Let us take care of all that."

But I was young and stubborn. I wanted to know. I did not want to be treated like a passive vessel just waiting to be emptied. I wanted to give birth.

At a book sale I found a book entitled Giving Birth Without Pain, which gave me all the answers I was looking for. I read it and took its message to heart. What followed was fantastic. I did it. I gave birth without pain (although not without work).

"I'd do this every day if I could!" I gushed afterwards to a hollow-eyed couple in the room next door, the female half of which had been in labor for hours. They looked at me in stunned disbelief, but I meant every word.

Then came the next hurdle. How should I care for this little baby? There was no shortage of books on the subject, and I started to read. Like many a new mother before me, the more I read, the more confused I became. Complication piled on complication, guilt complex upon guilt complex. Not only was I useless, I was flat out harmful. The kid was going to be a basket case for life!

But I have a lot to thank my stubborn streak for. I refused to be cowed by all the fingers of moral opprobrium leveled at me by the psychological establishment. "The kid is made of the same stuff I am," I thought to myself.

Curiously, my greatest ally was my baby. There she was, alive and self-evident. She allowed herself to be observed. She allowed herself to be understood. She became my teacher. And what she gave me was nothing less than a fascinating insight into human development. I was allowed to accompany her on a million-year journey and observe the human species evolve from tadpoles into independent, thinking beings that walk upright.

Love crept up on me of course, but it was the opportunity to study with a view to understanding and learning, not just about young children but about people in general – about the human species – that set my soul on fire.

I have written this book for my children, but naturally also for anyone who might benefit from it, which is why I address you, the reader, directly. I wanted to write the book that I so sorely needed when I first became a mother.

This was, of course, rather presumptuous. I have no formal qualifications. My connections with the Ivory Tower are nil. I am a mother and a writer. I have never worked outside my own home. My children have been my job and my university. All I have to offer in defense of my presumptuousness is my experience as a mother, forty seven years of practical, hands on, daily (not to mention nightly) experience of living and working with my own and other people's children, some young, some not so young.

And this I do with a certain amount of pride. I am self-taught. Everything I have written is based on my own observations of flesh and blood children.

I remember what I was so desperately looking for: something along the lines of the book about childbirth, an instruction manual. This is how you do it! Alas, there I stood with my newborn bundle, and I had no idea what to do with it.

"Soon everything will be automatic," I was told. But where were all these supposedly "automatic" skills supposed to come from?

"Soon you'll be able to distinguish between different kinds of cries," I was told. But how was I supposed to respond to these various kinds of cries? I didn't have much faith in the "maternal instinct". Such ideas were hardly fashionable in the 1960s.

And I was young; the young are self-centered. No baby was going to dominate my life. She could take her place by my side and live with me, but she was not going to lord it over me. She was not going to obliterate me!

That proved to be the key.

My first child was – and is – a strong kid. I provided the resistance she craved, and I offered her the opportunity to participate in my life. The result was a structured day-to-day existence based on simple routines that could not be questioned (if they were, life soon became unbearable), in which working together was natural and mutual integrity was sacred.

This became my guiding principle of child-rearing.

In plain English, I brooked no argument about what my kids had to do, but I always kept my hands off who my kids were.

FOR THE LOVE OF CHILDREN

"All those degrees
– and what good are they now?"

Anna Wahlgren

FOR THE LOVE OF CHILDREN

FÖRLAG ANNA WAHLGREN AB

The opinions and advice in this book are just that – my opinions and advice. Some of these may be contrary to professional or government-endorsed advice that you receive on child rearing and parenting and so it is up to you – the parent, the carer, the reader, to decide how to use all of this information. In other words, any reliance upon any information in this book shall be taken at your own risk. The author and publisher cannot be held liable for any claims, actions or demands resulting from any person undertaking any or all of the recommendations, information, suggestions or advice in this book.

Anna Wahlgren
Author and International Publisher

(Förlag Anna Wahlgren AB)

© Anna Wahlgren
Illustrations: Gunnar Haglund
Swedish original title: Barnaboken
English translation: Bruce Junkin
Editing: Anna Wahlgren, Lisa Waldron
Cover: Christian von Essen
Publishing company: Förlag Anna Wahlgren AB
Typesetting and layout: Manne Svensson
Print: Swepo, Warsaw
ISBN: 978-91-977736-2-1

www.annawahlgren.com

Conversion Table	
1 kilogram	2.2 lb
1 liter	33.8 fl oz
1° Celsius	33.8° Fahrenheit
10° C	50° F
20° C	68° F
1 cm	0.39 inch

**People won't budge an inch
unless they think it's fun.**
Lars Bohman

People should be looked after
by people who love them.
Lars Danius

PART ONE

Pregnancy and childbirth

To parents: Stick to your guns.
To children: Be free from guilt.

Stockholm, Sweden, in July 2009
Anna Wahlgren

TO MY DEAR CHILDREN

My beloved children, I wrote this book for you, one for all and all for one. Don't misunderstand me. I don't for a moment think that you are all the same, any more than I think that all the young children whose upbringing is touched by the ideas outlined in this book are all the same. My point of departure has always been the qualities that all children, indeed all human beings, *share*, rather than specific individual traits.

When you read my book, I want you to react as you always have. I, your mother, have stated what I believe and what I stand for as clearly as I can. Read what I have to say, and then take what you like and leave the rest.

Not infrequently, you will feel a little lost in life. But remember that uncertainty is what compels you to seek answers. It forces you to think, draw conclusions and take action, and that's how you grow. That might not make uncertainty easy to bear, but it does perhaps make those times when you are not sure which path to take a little less frightening.

Your childhood has been chaotic. You have moved from school to school. Throughout your childhood and adolescence, you have had to cope with change and divorce. You yourselves are living proof that external changes don't necessarily mean internal fragmentation.

I can never know what has touched your heart of hearts or what the consequences might be. I can only tell you that what I see, and what everyone around you sees, are strong, fearless, loving people with clearly defined personalities who are more than equal to the task of wrestling with life and winning.

We human beings are infinitely adaptable. Our struggle for internal equilibrium is, to a large extent, our salvation. We are our own greatest hope.

You live in a culture that, in many respects, denies the fundamental human need for a sense of community. The generations have been segregated. In the name of economic growth, people are regarded as mere factors of production rather than the enigmatic, living organisms that they are. In such a culture, children are an impediment to production, all the lofty rhetoric notwithstanding.

I would like to highlight this sad state of affairs by telling you about a watershed event in my life.

After my first divorce, I found myself alone with the two of you who are the eldest. I had neither a job nor qualifications. The father of my two eldest, "Dada Lars" paid me support. His generosity gave me a year's breathing space. During this year, the plan was that I would get the qualifications I needed to land a sufficiently well-paying job. I would then have to make the mortgage payments on our house and support the three of us, as well as hire someone to look after the children. (Daycare was virtually non-existent in those days.)

This struck me as paradoxical. Why would I want to toil away at a job that I never really wanted in the first place – assuming I managed to get the necessary qualifications in only one year – if it meant *being separated from my children?*

For the first time in my young life, I began to question the system. After much desperate soul searching, politically naïve creature that I was, I did what I am still advocating today. I prioritized. I wanted to be available to my children, and I wanted them to be with me. Everything else would have to take a back seat.

To cut a long story short, I ended up living in a dilapidated old cottage in the middle of nowhere, where I tried to write short stories. Materially, our existence was primitive and daily life was simple, but my children thrived, and I could live and interact with them.

What's more, *I was free.* I had weighed assumptions that society took for granted in the balance and found them wanting. I had taken a stand, and I was living a life I could be proud of. That's what made firing up the ancient wood-stove and freezing my butt off in the outhouse on sub-zero mornings so easy!

Human beings possess a fundamental impulse that finds its clearest expression in a very young child. It is the impulse to explore, master and eventually change our reality, our conditions, our world.

You will have to do battle with a society that wants to smother that impulse. Don't let it be smothered! Keep it alive in yourselves, and in your children.

See the power in uncertainty! It is this uncertainty that forces you to think and to seek.

Don't sell your soul! The truth lies within you.

I love you.
Mom

THE GIFT OF LOVE

And here is my secret, a very simple secret:
It's only with the heart that one can really see –
What's important is invisible to the eye.

Antoine de Saint-Exupéry
The Happy Prince

All children are born with magic wands in their hands.

"My daughter gives my life meaning," says a well-known actress in an interview with a newspaper. Exulted, she describes how motherhood is the best thing that ever happened to her.

"It's so incredibly wonderful! I've become so unselfish. Suddenly another person has priority. I have difficulty comprehending that I ever had a life without her."

Naturally, she had heard from friends that having children was fantastic – that it was the ultimate love. But it was only when she became a mother herself that reality hit home. "This really is the meaning of life."

Fine words and somewhat astonishing ones when you think about it. The meaning of life? People have been searching for the meaning of life since the year dot. Have we been literally tripping over the answer all this time? After all, people are, or eventually become, parents. If the world is overflowing with people who have found the meaning of life, why aren't they saying anything?

Well, they are actually. The overwhelming majority of parents in this world, with so few exceptions that they are barely worth counting, are prepared to state unequivocally that having children is a luminously transforming, profoundly revelatory experience. It is a brush with the infinite. It really is the meaning of life.

But this meaning of life must be experienced. It cannot be conveyed or explained. It's impossible to imagine what it's like to have children if you haven't done it yourself.

Parents wax lyrical about little Lisa's first heart-stopping steps or little Carl's fantastic hand-eye coordination. Just look at how he managed to stick his finger right in the dog's eye! We listen and smile at the parents' happiness, but we don't understand the miracle. If the truth be told, maybe we think there's no way we would ever be that gushingly silly if we had children. Not in this lifetime anyway.

The silliness is just the crest on a tidal wave of joy.

People who have never had children don't understand because they can't feel what all these parents feel. They can't feel it until they're in that space themselves holding their own little children in their arms.

Feelings can't be translated into words and thoughts. All parents are brimming with strong emotions and want desperately to express them. But no matter how hard they try, the translation can never do justice to the original. Feelings don't lend themselves to description or dissection. Feelings can't be grasped by the intellect.

So the answer to that eternal question "What is the meaning of life?" is a way of feeling, not a way of thinking.

What is the feeling?

Love.

All children are born with magic wands in their hands. When this magic wand touches you, love's stardust falls over you. Actually, it may cover you from head to toe if you are close enough. You are transformed into a single pulsating feeling of love.

It's dust from a star that was already shining. You become a reflection of Love's starlight, a light that washes over the whole world, over all of humanity. It has always been there, and it always will be as long as there is life on Earth. As long as children are born into the world, Love's star will always sprinkle its shimmering dust over people's hearts.

People aren't eternal, but love is. Love is indestructible.

When a child lifts the magic wand and love's stardust falls over you, you suddenly feel that the insight that strikes you – which has to be your own before you can understand that this is the meaning of life – is not yours alone. Wherever you look, there are people who share this insight with you. They couldn't have explained it to you before you were ready to understand, and you weren't ready to understand until you had understood.

Suddenly and ultimately, it's love, love that must be your own. Love you have in common with all humankind, with all those who have been blessed with the ability to love. They recognize love in you, just as you recognize it in them. Suddenly, you all speak the same spiritual language.

When people congratulate you on the birth of your child, they are not congratulating you on the sleepless nights, the dirty diapers, the responsibility, or the economic hardships. They don't feel sorry for you! It's the love they're congratulating you on, your new membership in that exclusive club of timeless, limitless love, the love that has solved the riddle of the meaning of life. They are congratulating you on Love, which is life itself, life's meaning, and life's purpose.

Confirmation is everywhere. Parents, healthcare professionals, relatives – love's stardust falls over all of them, bringing a joyful smile to every face. At the birth of every child, everyone involved is united in common, genuine good will.

The love you feel for your child is deeply personal, but it's also a part of something bigger. Your love for your child is born when the child touches you with the magic wand, but the love has always been there too, just as the meaning of life has always been there.

Love and life are one and the same, a single universal soul, radiating its endless, glorious, indestructible light.

And everyone recognizes it. The soul's eternal love brings a smile to everyone's face, for it is benevolent, beautiful, pure, and it wants to do good.

When we fall in love, an experience that can turn our world upside down, we get a foretaste of the incredible effect that love's stardust has on us when we become parents.

"Because our old selves... are dead, we want to be genuine and pure... A man who is truly in love is renewed, unbearably light, and malleable. He is no longer greedy, miserly, or jealous, since the only thing he is interested in is his love... Precisely because he has glimpsed life's innermost secret, he cares nothing for obstacles. He feels he can triumph over all hardship, all deficiencies in understanding, all hate. This feeling of invulnerability does not dull his powers of reason. On the contrary, he is patient, alert and inventive." (Francesco Alberoni, Ti Amo, 1966).

The life you leave behind is gone forever, but you won't miss it. Time stands still, and a clear before-and-after demarcation line takes shape. Life after the birth of your child will never be as it was, and life before the birth of your child is but a dim memory on the border of a dream. "I have difficulty comprehending that I ever had a life without her..."

The child is not the only person who is born. The parents and everyone else the child touches with the magic wand are born too. Love's stardust glitters true and pure, open and honest, humble and responsible, patient, attentive, and creative.

Whoever is given a child to care for experiences the blessing of being born anew into a life whose meaning is perfectly clear.

Love is its own gift. It makes a present of itself to you.

You will see it in your child. You will see it in yourself. You will meet it in every thought, in every feeling that's covered with love's stardust when the child touches you with the magic wand.

You will see the testimony and proof wherever you look if you want to. And you will want to because that is love's great gift to you: to want to *live love*.

You will want to seek it, find it, express it, strengthen it, affirm it, be a part of it, duplicate it, extend its boundaries, help spread it, partake in its victorious march over the whole world. Love gives you the will to do all this.

You won't be content to simply wish and hope. "Now someone has to make sure that the child is taken care of, so the kid has a shot at the good life!" No, the buck stops with you. You personally will do whatever it takes to foster this child's happiness and well-being.

Including sacrificing your own life if that's what it takes to save the life of your child.

You want the best for someone and nothing but the best, and this is no idle wish. You have a purpose and you've made a decision. It is a quest whose path is graven in stone.

Your wish to live love sets in motion the powerful mechanism that prepares you for action.

Your will to act out of love comes from a steadfast conviction, a *faith* that you certainly didn't realize you had.

The moment the child touches you with the magic wand, an imperishable faith in love awakens inside you – not just as a glorious and beneficial spiritual condition that you succeed in attaining if you're lucky, if you believe in God, or happen to come across some other secret entrance to Happiness, but faith in love as a higher power.

When love's stardust falls over you, some of its singular power is bequeathed to you too. You burn with the desire to put your ability to use. Precisely that will, purpose, and decision; for love acts. It is an unyielding power, the strongest of them all.

Love puts you to work, and you want nothing more than to be its humble servant. You stand at love's beck and call.

Love is the meaning of life. It triumphs over death. Its power is infinite.

"I've become so unselfish," said our celebrity above. She no longer wanted to be a film star. She cared not one wit for fame. "Suddenly there's another human being who takes priority."

From having been the center of your own existence with only one real responsibility – you – you now stand ready, as a parent, to care for and take responsibility for another person's life.

The thought fills you with dread, and your dread calls forth caution, foresight and reflection.

But the feeling when you're faced with this incredible obligation, the feeling when you're ready to act in love's name now that you are a parent fills you with joy, pride, energy – and yes, happiness.

Every corner of your soul is ready to love as you have never loved in your life. With a love that doesn't seek its own reward, that reaches outside yourself, that is utterly dedicated to the welfare of another human being. Love's stardust is falling over you, and in your eagerness and joy, your pride and expectation, you feel that you will be allowed to experience Happiness.

The happiness of parenthood is born in and lives in the constant care you give a child – another human being. This is a happiness that is unselfish because it's so much greater than you.

You're getting close to the core of life itself. You will be allowed to hear love's voice, to see its signs, to be its tool, to act in this world, to live it.

Your life will have meaning, and that is the happiness. Your joy knows that love that seeks no reward is the meaning of life.

And the miracle never ends. Love's stardust renews itself forever and continues to fall over you. All you have to do is stand close enough.

A little boy, three years old, is looking at his father, who is stretched out on the sofa with a skull-crushing hangover. His face is a shade of yellowish green and he is in no shape to even stand up.

"Daddy, how are you today, really?" the child wonders, worried.

Dad tells the truth, albeit selectively.

"Daddy's a little tired... a little sick."

"Oh, well then, you need to rest," says the boy and pats him very gently on the forehead.

And Dad remembers this little event, tells everyone about it, rejoices over it, and keeps it in his heart.

It was love that stood in front of him in the guise of a little boy. It was love he heard speaking, and it expressed concern, empathy, tenderness and caring. It was selfless love that patted him so gently on the forehead.

The little boy could have promoted his own agenda. After all, Daddy was home for once. He had most probably promised that they would so something together on Sunday. That's what they usually did, wasn't it?

The boy could have yelled and screamed, tugged at Dad's sleeve and bugged him, reminded and demanded and recriminated. He could have gone to Mommy and tattled, and Mom would have read her hungover husband the riot act and reminded him in no uncertain terms of his paternal duties. It could have turned into a battle royal in the best tradition of family Sundays with arguing and carping, wailing and gnashing of teeth, accusations and threats, vitriolic parry and thrust – *war* in other words – if love hadn't interceded.

If love hadn't existed and lived and put forth its awesomely gentle power, Dad wouldn't have been able to go on sleeping for a while on the sofa, a smile on his face, the little boy wouldn't have been able to go on playing peacefully with his toys, a smile on his face, and Mom, whatever she would have thought about the situation, wouldn't have been able to tell herself that domestic peace reigned supreme, a smile on her face.

Everywhere the miracle happens. The weak overcome the strong. The weak only seemed to be weak. The strong only seemed to be strong.

And nothing is stronger than love. Nothing even comes close. Love conquers all.

Love is always the last thing left standing – now and forever.

When your child is born and touches you with its magic wand, you are born too.

You are born into happiness the instant your eternal longing for happiness is transformed into love's striving.

As a christening present you receive concern, empathy, tenderness, and caring – as well as the will to give these feelings the unlimited expression that is their due.

You received the happiness to enrich the world with your love, and the more you give – to your child, to the world, back to love itself – the more love you receive and the closer you come to your happiness.

You receive access to love. You receive authorization to act in its name. You receive the grace to teach your child to have faith in love's power.

We are not always able to live love's message. We don't always even see the happiness that surrounds us, the proof of love's existence and its never-ending triumphal march.

That doesn't mean it's not there.

Love and happiness exist. Once your little child waves the magic wand above you, you change forever. Never again will you doubt. Never again will you deny love's awesome power – its power over you.

Concern, empathy, tenderness, and caring are what love sprinkles over you with its stardust, and the will to live these feelings will never leave you, as long as you stay close enough.

That is love's gift to you.

The singular power of water is described in the Tao Te Ching, stanza 78. Exactly the same thing could be said about love.

There is nothing in all the world that is softer than water
But in any battle nothing that is hard and immoveable
can endure against water's strength.

In this respect, it has no equal.
The weak triumphs over the strong.
The soft triumphs over the hard.
There is no one who does not know this,
but no one is able to live accordingly.

The child with its magic wand will show you that the world is full of people who are trying to live accordingly.

PREGNANCY

HOW DO YOU KNOW YOU ARE PREGNANT?

The prerequisite is intercourse. There are guys who will tell you that you can't get pregnant if you only do it once, but of course they're fibbing. You can conceive at any time. "Safe" times of the month don't exist. I learned that early. I got my period on my wedding night (embarrassing under the circumstances), and twenty-four to forty-eight hours later, a seed found a field.

The classic sign of pregnancy is skipping a period. But you can be late for many reasons, not the least of which is worrying that you might skip a period. If you are a few days late, test kits are available, or you can of course contact your doctor.

Once your pregnancy is confirmed and you decide that motherhood is what you really want, you will embark on the adventure of a lifetime, and I am both delighted and proud to be able to accompany you on your journey towards a new life!

The next sign is tender and somewhat enlarged breasts. Within a couple of months, your breasts may leak semi-clear colostrum. Long before I began to show, my breasts were running like taps and were big enough to make Dolly Parton jealous. (This was also a little embarrassing. I was taking acting classes at the time, and as I stood on the stage declaiming for all I was worth, two dark, round spots slowly spread across my blouse.)

Eventually, your stomach will start to grow. How much can vary. Some mothers-to-be get by with a safety pin in their waist bands, while others have to start wearing maternity dresses by the third month. By the fifth month, people start asking them when they are due!

You will find yourself on a rollercoaster, both physically and mentally.

You may experience terrible morning sickness. There are people who maintain that morning sickness is a sign that the child is unwanted and the mother is trying to vomit it up. I have always regarded this as utter nonsense. Body and mind have to make enormous adjustments. It would be remarkable if the mother-to-be didn't react, and the fact that she does in no way indicates that she wishes the life out of her child.

At the beginning of your pregnancy, you will cry for no reason, get tired for no reason, and generally lose your groove. Don't despair. Everything will right itself eventually. Gallows humor can be the first sign that you have turned the corner.

Recently confirmed pregnancies can end in miscarriage, a so-called spontaneous abortion. This is very common in the second month. Nature has made a miscalculation – and corrected it. I know it's easier said than done, but try not to fall apart. You will soon be pregnant again.

At least one in ten pregnancies, and as many as one in five, ends in miscarriage. It has happened to me twice. There were some bloody lumps and then a menstrual bleeding. The first time it happened, I got pregnant again immediately. The second, it took me six months.

You may be utterly convinced that you are pregnant, but you then experience bleeding. This does not necessarily indicate a miscarriage. You may have small bleedings throughout your pregnancy. As a rule, these bleedings occur when you would have had your period or when you would have ovulated. (Ovulation normally occurs half-way between periods.) Just keep an eye on how much you bleed. These bleedings should be very moderate. If you bleed heavily, make a beeline for the nearest hospital. The baby can be saved.

Another classic sign of pregnancy is a feeling of disgust for certain things – cigarette smoke, coffee – and an intense craving for others – grapefruit, salty bisquits, chocolate – the list is endless.

Some of my cravings were expensive: smoked salmon and Alaska king crab. Others were easier on the family budget – warm cheese and ketchup sandwiches, eight to ten at a sitting. During one pregnancy, I couldn't face the day without a bunch of licorice twists, which I washed down with a soda pop.

You may be sullen, peevish, happy, dog tired, horny, frigid, or any combination thereof. You may feel generally on top of the world – or generally down in the dumps. Before the arrival of my first child, I moved down to the basement, locked the door, made up a cot for my unborn baby in the laundry basket and refused to speak to her father.

However you feel, trust me, it will pass!

A HUMAN BEING IS MADE

Incredible but true. A thimble full of sperm is enough to replace the world's current population. And the gentlemen manage to produce this small amount of sperm at very regular intervals… A woman, on the other hand, releases only a single egg each month for a limited period of her life. This egg is no larger than the head of a pin and has a life span of ten to twelve hours.

Extensive preparations are made to accommodate this egg, should it be fertilized. Menstruation is sometimes referred to as "the tears of the womb". All the preparations were in vain, and the womb received little for its trouble. The carefully prepared bed, which was awaiting the eagerly anticipated embryo, has to be thrown out.

It's the man who decides the sex. Male sperm swim faster but die more quickly. Female sperm swim more slowly but last longer. (So there!) If there is an egg already lodged in the fallopian tube when intercourse takes place, it will be a boy. If the egg doesn't materialize until the next day, all the male sperm will have died, and only the female sperm will remain. Thus, it will be a girl.

Finely tuned machinery now shifts into high gear in the soft darkness of your body.

What will one day be a human being spends its first twenty-four hours in the fallopian tube. Cell division begins immediately. The journey to the womb takes at least a week. The destination is the uterine wall. Once the docking procedure is complete, nourishment starts to flow, and a primitive placenta is formed, complete with amniotic sac and umbilical cord.

Four weeks after fertilization, the embryo is already six millimeters long. Tiny though it is, it has little knobs where the arms and legs will eventually sprout, and its heart is in its throat – literally. It has a little tail too!

The embryo grows at break-neck speed. In only a week, it doubles its length to eleven to twelve millimeters. The brain begins to form and forerunners of what will eventually be eyes are now discernable.

Six weeks after fertilization – and by now you have most certainly begun to suspect you are pregnant – this little human tadpole has reached the impressive length of one and a half centimeters. The small hands are beginning to sprout fingers. The liver is working at full throttle producing blood cells, but the skeleton remains rudimentary.

Your second month of pregnancy is drawing to a close and you are about to embark on your third. Pregnancy is reckoned to begin on the first day of your last menstruation, so you are eight weeks gone. Life for the embryo, however, did not begin until fertilization, so it is still only about six weeks old.

But in another two weeks, the embryo will not be an embryo any more, but a fetus. The basic components have been formed, and all that's left is the maturation process. The heart has been beating for a whole month!

At nine weeks, the fetus is five centimeters long. The uterus has grown and assumed the shape of a pear. For anyone who cares to look via ultrasound, the baby's sex is readily apparent.

At eleven weeks the heart is fully formed. The head accounts for a third of this little person's length, and the face has assumed recognizably human characteristics. He or she is starting to look like a child, with a rounded forehead, a little chin and a *retroussé* nose. The fetus's weight is still less than impressive: approximately twenty grams, about the weight of a letter.

By as early as the middle of the fifth month, the fetus is fifteen centimeters long, and in the next two weeks it will grow by another ten centimeters. That is about half the length the baby will be when it eventually arrives in this world.

Now the arms and legs are so well developed and the movements of the fetus so powerful that they can be felt through your abdominal wall.

The fetus has acute hearing – your voice, your cough, your laugh, the radio, the telephone... The mutual getting acquainted process has begun!

Inside the mother's womb, the fetus lives a pleasant life, even if conditions are a little cramped towards the end. It sucks its thumb, takes naps, wriggles about, exercises. It practices gripping things – the umbilical cord, its toes. It's never hungry. The supply of food and oxygen is constant. The mother's heart beat, the whispering of her lungs, the symphony of sounds from the placenta and the outside world, all make for easy listening as the fetus sways gently with the mother's movements, all the while surrounded by warm water.

From the seventh month on, the baby can survive a premature birth without too much difficulty, but it is only nine months and one week after the first day of the last menstruation that a child is reckoned to be fully developed.

The baby has been lying head down locked in position for some weeks now. What remains to be done is purely cosmetic – a few attractive curves added here and there, a little touching up on the baby's facial features. Mother Nature's aim is to melt the parents' hearts, thus guaranteeing that the baby will receive top notch care.

Dad will be reassured that he really is the father. All newborns have one or more of their father's very distinctive characteristics, but the resemblance, again thanks to a considerate Mother Nature, starts to fade during the first week.

Your body is being prepared for delivery. The vagina will be stretched to capacity, which requires a supplementary supply of hormones. This "afflicts" the baby, which is why all newborns come into this world with swollen genitals.

White fetal tallow provides the lubricant that enables the little body to force its way down and out of the incredibly narrow passage.

HOW SHOULD YOU LIVE?

Take care of yourself. Above all, be good to yourself!

You may feel on top of the world. If this is the case, count your blessings, sit back and enjoy the ride! It is just as likely, however, that you will not feel particularly chipper, especially at the beginning and the end of your pregnancy. Your body is undergoing a massive readjustment, and your mental state will reflect this.

Your body may suddenly seem to lose interest in *you*. It is devoting all its energy to the life growing inside you, and you are left to get on with things as best you can. You become a motel, an incubator, a larder... There is something wonderful in that if you think about it. As a woman, you will experience that your body is fulfilling the function that it was actually designed for. This can give rise to a feeling of profound harmony, of the circle being closed.

Fatigue will catch you unawares, as will tears. You will cry for nothing. You may start fights with your better half, throw vases against the wall and generally behave like an escaped lunatic. When the psychotic moment passes, you will look at yourself in the mirror, appalled at your behavior. "What kind of monster have I become?" you ask your reflection.

You may have the idea that you should be on cloud nine over this baby that you have waited for and dreamt of for so long – but all you feel is fear and loathing. Try to go easy on yourself! No matter how wretched you feel or how disappointed you are in yourself, you are not alone. Legions of mothers-to-be have walked the same road. Out of all this, a child will come, and this baby will be a happy, contented little soul, blissfully unaware of all the dark thoughts you have had these last few months! That is guaranteed.

Expecting a child has its positive sides too. When the first couple of months have passed and you have gotten used to the idea of becoming a mother, you will be eager to don that maternity dress. You will find yourself going about your business with a devout smile on your face, a smile that has caused people throughout the ages to wax lyrical about the "blessed condition"...

And when the little person you are carrying, who hitherto has been such an abstraction, suddenly starts to carry on in your stomach so that you actually *feel* it, you and your child enter into a covenant. You will feel a rush of tenderness and joyful expectation. Everything that is happening to your body has a purpose. You will start counting the months, the weeks and the days until your delivery. Everything will become easier and infinitely more exciting. A child will be born, and you are the one giving it life. You feel your baby's movements and you start to fantasize. What will your baby look like? What is he or she doing in there? You lay your hand on your stomach with love, devotion, tenderness and joy.

Women the world over are experiencing the same remarkable condition that you are. Life is growing inside them. More than two babies are born every second.

Anxiety attacks are not uncommon at this stage of the game. What kind of a world is your baby coming into? What kind of a mother will you be? "I can't even handle my own life," you anguish, "so what do I have to offer my baby?" Existential questions and mundane practical concerns will swirl around in your head.

Try to keep in mind that all your agonizing is part of Nature's plan. You are being prepared for what is to come. You can't very well shoulder your responsibility if you don't first understand it.

You will be impatient the last little while. You are tired and, above all, you are tired of being pregnant. Your stomach is always in the way and you are sick and tired of your wardrobe. You want things to get back to normal. The people around you add fuel to the fire by constantly asking you when you are due. "Haven't you gone to the hospital yet?" they ask. Obviously not, since you are sitting right in front of them with your stomach taking up half the room.

Expectant mothers are bone tired of being pregnant towards the end, and Nature has a finger in this pie too. The baby is soon to be born, and mother and child must be prepared for the dissolution of this union that has lasted so long.

As your delivery nears, try not to get fixated on a particular date. Every day around this date acquires such momentous significance. Some babies just don't feel like hurrying, while others have nothing but imperious contempt for the calendar and can't wait to get out.

All my children were at least three weeks late, and one kept me dangling for six! At the end of my first pregnancy, a neighbor rescued me from my slough of despondency with the laconic comment, "What's the kid gonna do? Stay in there forever?"

For most women, pregnancy is a psychological and physical roller coaster. You can minimize the instability by trying to cultivate good habits. Eat sensibly, take a walk every day, do things you really enjoy, and *sleep*. Demand to be allowed to sleep! Don't take no for an answer. Business as usual simply won't do. Body and soul are in overdrive, and you need your rest.

More often than not, following a sensible diet is easier said than done. All the jokes about pregnant women's cravings, which have to be satisfied immediately, are founded on fact. Attempts have been made to explain these bizarre cravings. The mother's body needs calcium so she munches chalk… There are also mothers who experience no cravings, only disgust for certain things such as cigarette smoke. If you are an expectant mother who stuffs herself with candy, or cookies or cheese sandwiches, or French fries drowning in ketchup, try to eat healthy foods *too* – fruit, vegetables and foods rich in iron.

If you gain too much weight, don't be downhearted. I gained between twenty-two and twenty-six kilos during each pregnancy. My children were all born large and chubby, but their weight soon stabilized at where it should be. Some of them even became downright thin. I got rid of my extra kilos too. (How? See "Afterwards".)

Obviously, I am not suggesting that gaining too much weight is beneficial, but don't despair over a few extra kilos! Some healthcare professionals make way too much of this.

If there is one thing you don't need when you are pregnant, it is moral lectures, and there is no shortage of people who are only too delighted to tell a pregnant woman what to do. You will hear things like smoking, if you happen to have such a foul habit, is strictly forbidden, as is drinking alcohol. If you smoke even one cigarette a day, you are guaranteed to have underweight, premature children, and if you consume so much as a drop of alcohol, your offspring will sustain irreparable damage.

I do not want to sound cavalier about these issues, but I am sick to death of listening to all these prophets of doom lay all the guilt and all the responsibility on the mother alone. The fact that the medical establishment has no idea what causes sixty percent of all birth defects is never mentioned. In certain quarters, Sudden Infant Death Syndrome has been blamed on the mothers' inappropriate lifestyles during pregnancy. This is as repugnant as it is scandalous.

It is the mother who has to live with a damaged child – or mourn a dead one – not the doomsday prophets. It's the mother who will always blame herself. "Was it the smoking? I tried so hard to quit. Was it the drinks I had at that party before I knew I was pregnant?" Giving birth to a child that has been developmentally damaged in utero is bad enough. Losing a child is unbearable. There is no other word.

The voice of common sense is heard seldom if at all. If the expectant mother feels OK during her pregnancy, in all likelihood the baby will too. The mother's well-being must be the number one priority.

With all the sympathy in the world, we should remember that even the most clean living parents give birth to children with defects. We can't protect ourselves one hundred percent against accidents or death, any more than we can stop living. Not all aspects of life can be controlled. Since the beginning of time, people in all cultures and under wildly varying living conditions have produced children with injuries, incurable illnesses and birth defects. For just as long, people have tried to discover the causes. Not everything can be explained however, and in life as in death, we sometimes have to resign ourselves to the fact that there are some things that are simply beyond our capacity to understand.

Thus humbled, we should not presume to condemn expectant mothers for their lifestyles during pregnancy, not as long as the pregnant woman is sensible enough and strong enough to see to her own well-being.

The hysterical attitude towards alcohol has always struck me as strange. Of course, drinking large amounts of hard liquor should be discouraged. It never did anyone any good. However, if it were true that moderate daily consumption of wine caused birth defects, half the children born in Mediterranean countries would suffer from them. Pregnant women in southern Europe have drunk wine (often diluted I grant you) with their meals since time immemorial.

All you can do is have a little faith and believe that God is in His heaven and everything is as it should be. If and when something goes seriously wrong, cross that bridge when you come to it – but leave the guilt on the other side of the river!

Let's look at some statistics.

For every birth, there is almost one pregnancy that is not carried to term. Thus, 100,000 births require 170,000 pregnancies. 20,000 of these pregnancies end at a very early stage through spontaneous abortion. Another 10,000 early spontaneous abortions are monitored. 8,000 are the result of "mistakes" by Mother Nature, 60 percent of which are the result of chromosomal disorders. Approximately 10,000 spontaneous abortions occur during the later stages of pregnancy. That leaves 130,000 pregnancies, 30,000 of which are legally terminated at the request of the mother. Of the 100,000 pregnancies that are carried to term, 300 are stillbirths. 2000 babies are born with some kind of defect, and this figure includes even the most insignificant deviation from the norm. As for the almost 98,000 remaining babies, they are all born perfect in every way.

Your body:
You can prevent stretch marks on your stomach and breasts by applying generous amounts of moisturizing cream. I and many other women know that this works, even if medical science claims otherwise. Apply the moisturizer and rub it in well every evening once your stomach begins to bulge and your breasts begin to grow. Pay special attention to your nipples. They will be sorely tried when you begin to breastfeed.

You can effectively prevent swollen legs and cramps by walking on tiptoe and stretching your whole body upwards for a total of ten minutes a day. *Don't forget!* It's easy, it feels great, and it does you a world of good.

At the beginning and at the end of your pregnancy, you will be running to the bathroom all day long and producing not very much for your trouble. Your bladder, like all your other long-suffering internal organs, is being literally pushed to the sidelines and has to make do with cramped conditions. As you approach the finish line, you may even have trouble breathing properly. Your ribs don't have much room to maneuver. Breathing deeply in front of an open window will help tremendously.

If you suffer from morning sickness, it will pass after the first three months. Try to eat something before you get up in the mornings. A little tea and some crisp bread should do the trick.

An irritating heartburn can set in, especially during the second half of your pregnancy. Soda water will take the edge off.

Leg cramps during the night? Stand up and they will fade away.

Fatigue is often your worst enemy. Keep an eye on your blood count and make sure you get enough iron. In acute cases, iron injections are available, and they are a godsend. Avoid prescription drugs. Question everything.

Beware of German measles (rubella) during pregnancy! I hope you have already checked to make sure you are immune. Protein in your urine is a bad sign. Get checked regularly. Protein in combination with swelling and high blood pressure may indicate toxaemia. This is not unusual and help *is* to be had.

Speaking of swelling, don't forget to remove your rings before it's too late!

Do your level best to avoid infections. Infections towards the end of a pregnancy can result in complications during delivery.

Colds can be hard to get rid of when you are pregnant, and coughing is certainly no fun with a baby inside you. Ten grams of pure ascorbic acid mixed with water will serve as both prevention and cure.

Your back will get tired. Try to keep the arch in your back, don't try to straighten it, and let your stomach muscles work to "lift" the baby. On the other hand, there is no need to waddle around like a drunken duck. Walk straight!

The fifth month can be dicey. Be careful! Certain movements, such as jumping, jolts and heavy lifting, can trigger a miscarriage. I was into classical ballet during my first pregnancy (business as usual I figured), and the lesson finished with a series of quick jumps in various positions. An hour later, I was doubled over in agony. For a while, it looked as though I had danced my way to a miscarriage. For the next week, I lay motionless in a fog of morphine. To the doctor's surprise, the baby was saved. Raising your arms above your head if you are holding something heavy, hanging curtains for example, is flat out dangerous, as is riding, jogging, anything that entails hard, jolting movements, and/or heavy lifting.

You will probably be constipated. Stay away from laxatives! Avoid milk and tea. (Yogurt can help however.) Drink mineral water and boiled water. Eat wholegrain bread instead of white. Eat fruit (except bananas), and, if you can, down some prunes. Baby food purée with prunes can help too.

Varicose veins are common. I have managed to avoid them, I think because I did my ten minutes of walking on tiptoe every day. Your veins will return to normal, or at least improve dramatically, after the delivery.

One thing has always struck me as rather odd. The body's center of gravity is pushed forward when you are carrying a baby in an overly large stomach, but the brain doesn't seem to grasp that fact. When you are walking down a flight of stairs for example, you instinctively calculate where you should put your feet. The problem is that these calculations are based your pre-pregnancy body. Thus, it is ridiculously easy to fall. Make it a habit always to hold the railing when you are going up or down a flight of stairs, even if there is only one step to negotiate! And lose the high-heeled shoes! If you can't avoid wearing them, pretend you are walking on ice and plan every step!

Avoid tensing your muscles. Don't pull up your shoulders or lock your neck in a backward leaning position. Do tension relieving exercises every now and then. Rotate your shoulders and neck a few times in both directions. One exercise you must avoid at all costs however is situps. Sticking your feet under something immoveable and then trying to raise your upper body off the floor is extremely dangerous.

You may develop liver spots on your hands and face. Some will disappear. Others, unfortunately, won't.

Being pregnant won't do your hair any good. Take vitamin B! You may experience some hair loss. This will right itself after the delivery, but it can take time.

Your teeth can give you trouble too, not because your baby is stealing all the calcium but because you are probably snacking on sweet stuff. Brush and rinse as often as you can, and be conscientious about using dental floss and toothpicks.

Keep moving. You can do anything that only involves soft movements: certain types of dancing, swimming, cycling, walking. Before the fifth month, you can do everything else as well.

You may have a lusty interest in sex (now that the "damage" is done) or you may be totally indifferent (the bun is in the oven, so what's the point?). Go with the flow. Nothing is permanent. Everything is shifting, so let it shift!

Your partner may react strangely too. Against his will, he might not dare lay a finger on you in bed. The equipment may go on general strike. Conversely, your swelling body may engender euphoric and seemingly endless desire in him. The winds of change are blowing through his soul too. Making love even at the very end of the pregnancy is not a problem, as long as you avoid the hardest jolting movements during the last month.

You should know that at the mouth of your uterus sits the world's most efficient security guard: the mucous membrane. The outside may be crawling with bacteria, but the inside is sterile. You can rest assured that nothing from the outside can get at the fetus.

You are now in the middle of the fifth month of your pregnancy, which means you are at the halfway point. It's time to start training for the delivery.

GIVING BIRTH: AN OLYMPIC MARATHON. START TRAINING!

I draw the analogy between a marathon and giving birth so that you will understand not only the importance of training but also the benefits, which are wonderful indeed.

No one runs a marathon without preparing for it properly. An untrained runner would have to endure the hell of pain and pulled muscles, and recovery would be long and hard. Giving birth requires training too if the strain on the body is to be minimized. A trained athlete runs faster than an untrained one and doesn't sustain injuries. Exactly the same could be said of a trained mother. Delivery is fast and injuries non-existent. She doesn't need anesthetic during delivery, she doesn't need stitches afterwards, and she avoids the agonizing after pains. She recovers far more quickly as well.

A trained mother works hard during her delivery, just as the athlete does. Just because she is exhausted at the end does not mean that she has been in pain. When the marathoner crosses the finish line, she is at the end of her rope too, but that doesn't mean she was in pain during the race. If she had not prepared for the event, however, pain would have been her constant companion.

Giving birth without pain is not the same as giving birth without work. Working hard is not the same as being in pain. The Good Book says, "Thou shalt bring forth children in sorrow." Men of course wrote the Bible. My message is just the opposite. Thou shalt *not* bring forth children in sorrow!

The sensible marathoner does not rely on willpower and good intentions. "I am going grit my teeth and do this. If I want to win badly enough, I will!" She knows that she has to train if she really wants to win gold. Nor does she think that someone is going to run the race for her. Once she is at the starting line, it's all up to her.

Sad to say, there are many mothers who do rely on willpower and good intentions. "If I want this baby badly enough, the delivery will go just fine," they surmise. And there are many mothers who think that as soon as they pass the hospital doors, the staff will somehow have the baby for them.

Unfortunately, passively suffering though a delivery can result in traumatic shock. Birth for the child is an ordeal in any case, so the delivery should not be prolonged unnecessarily. Proper training can reduce delivery time by at least a third and probably significantly more. The expulsion stage which places tremendous stress on the baby and which also poses a constant risk of oxygen deprivation can be reduced from an hour (or hours) to approximately fifteen minutes.

These days some form of anesthetic is the norm, but anesthetic of any kind always poses a risk to the baby. If you are properly trained, physically and mentally, you won't need any anesthetic at all.

The psycho-prophylactic Lamaze method is based on Pavlov's principle of conditioned reflexes. (Pavlov was the Russian scientist with the dogs. Ring the bell, and the dogs start to drool because they think they are going to get fed.) Lamaze, a French doctor, at first doubted reports coming out of Russia about women giving birth without pain. He traveled to Russia to see for himself and returned ecstatic. He could give firsthand accounts of women who had given birth smiling, relaxed, proud and radiantly happy without pain or anesthetic.

Lamaze died in 1953. His quest to bring the psycho-prophylactic method to French mothers was carried on by Dr. Pierre Vellay and his wife Aline, and they wrote a book on the subject "Giving Birth Without Pain" (*Témoignages sur l'accouchement sans doleur*, Les Editions du Seuil, 1956/Published in Swedish by Bonniers, 2nd edition 1985). This was the book I found on sale when I was expecting my first child.

When I take it upon myself to give you a physical training program, I must confess that I am in fact sinning egregiously against the basic idea behind the psycho-prophylactic method, which is holistic. Vellay specifically warned against this. The entire method might come into disrepute, and mothers would lose interest in it. Be that as it may, I can't resist the temptation to show you how simple it all is, how easy the exercises are and how little time they take. My goal is to dispel any doubts you might have and encourage you to learn more. Please do so – for your sake and the sake of your unborn child!

A birth consists of three stages: the opening phase, the expulsion phase and the afterbirth. You will play an active role in the first two.

The opening phase can be divided into two stages. The first is by far the longest, but it is also passive. All you have to do is relax. During the second stage of the opening phase, you are much more active. You will breathe in a way that you will have practiced, and this will support and facilitate the work of the uterus. As a result, you will experience no pain.

During the expulsion phase that follows, you will give birth. You will avail yourself of a pushing technique that you will have practiced so intensely that it will be purely reflexive.

• The first thing you will practice is *relaxing*.

Lie down and go through your body muscle by muscle. You may find your-self drifting off at the beginning, but the purpose is to be able to tell the difference between a tensed muscle and a relaxed one, so that during the delivery, you will instinctively react if you tense up anywhere. Make a mental note of everything. Start with your facial muscles and neck muscles, and work your way down. Tense and relax each muscle and feel the difference. You are going to use this relaxation technique during the opening phase, along with slow, deep breathing. This will enable the uterus to do its work undisturbed. You will notice how much good this relaxation training does you right from the first contraction. ("Pain" is a word that is foreign to the vocabulary of the psycho-prophylactic method.) You won't be afraid and you won't double over. Your body will not tense up – something that gravely impedes the work of the uterus and thereby lengthens the delivery. Quite the contrary, you will be calm, relaxed and mellow. And happy too, for now the adventure begins!

• The second thing you are going to practice is *shallow breathing*.

When you breathe normally or deeply, your diaphragm, which is a muscle, collides with the uterus, which is engaged in muscular work of its own, and pain is the result. This light, superficial breathing, rapid and almost fluttery, keeps your diaphragm immobile, which in turn enables the uterus to work undisturbed. By letting the uterus do its job, you shorten the last stage of the opening phase, which is when the real work begins. Shallow breathing is what helps you rise above it all, so to speak, and take control. This breathing technique is crucially important, and you must practice until it becomes automatic.

Lie down on the floor or half recline in a comfortable chair. Relax. Imagine a contraction as best you can (you can read more in the chapter devoted to the delivery itself). Keep your eye on the second hand of your watch. Now it's starting! Begin in neutral. Your lungs should be neither full nor empty. Start the shallow breathing, keeping it as light and superficial as you can. Breathe through your nose and keep your mouth closed. Try to keep your diaphragm as immobile as possible, which means taking small, rapid breaths.

Let's say the contraction peaks after thirty seconds. Now try to breathe even more rapidly, more lightly and more superficially for about five seconds. Hold it! Good! Now we'll pretend that the contraction starts to subside. Continue breathing lightly, rapidly and superficially, all the while keeping your diaphragm as immobile as possible. After approximately thirty seconds, the contraction ebbs and disappears. You have been practicing for just over a minute. A real contraction seldom lasts any longer. Now take a few deep breaths to replenish your oxygen supply and regain your strength!

When you first start practicing shallow breathing, you will feel a little dizzy, and you probably won't make the one-minute mark the first time you try. Most people cave in and take a deep breath after only twenty seconds. Take heart! You will improve! With every training session, you will feel a little less dizzy, and the dizziness will eventually disappear entirely. You will soon be able to shallow breathe for as long as ninety seconds. This is what you should be shooting for so that you have a comfortable margin.

Now that the "contraction" is over, rest for a while and try again. With mouth closed, eyes open and body completely relaxed, repeat the procedure! A daily ten-minute training session will do the trick. If you prefer two training sessions of five minutes apiece, that's fine too. The most important thing is that you are meticulous about practicing shallow breathing every day without fail. Regularity is what creates a habit, and habit is the prerequisite for the conditioned reflexes that will kick in when you need them.

In the end, after all your dedicated training, shallow breathing will become automatic. All you will have to do is go with the flow. You will sail through the end of the opening phase up to the transition to the expulsion phase, which is the most difficult part of the birthing process.

• The third thing you are going to practice for is the birth itself.

First, you have to know which muscles you will use for the expulsion stage, and then your task will be to strengthen them. It's not difficult! With daily training, these muscles will kick in when they are needed automatically, just as the shallow breathing will during the opening phase. (No other muscles should be in play however. That will only make the whole process more arduous.)

Lie comfortably on your back with a pillow under your head, knees drawn up and legs slightly parted. Your arms should be at your sides, palms up. Your whole body should be at rest. Take stock of every muscle, as you learned to do during the relaxation exercises. No tension in your neck, shoulders or thighs! Your lower abdomen should be completely relaxed. How do the areas around the urethra and anus feel? Soft as butter everywhere is the goal.

Now imagine you have a candle just in front of you. What you are going to do is very slowly blow at the flame. You are not trying to blow the candle out. You just want to make the flame continuously flutter a little. Start in neutral, lungs neither full nor empty. Breathe in, breathe out and begin. Blow at the flame regularly and slowly. Keep blowing until your lungs are completely empty.

Make a mental note of which muscles are working. Those are the muscles you will use when you give birth to your baby. Did the baby kick? Then you are doing everything right! (Don't worry. The exercise isn't dangerous. Babies aren't born until they are good and ready.) You were putting soft but steady pressure on your uterus from above and from the sides.

Now take a few deep breaths and replenish your oxygen supply. Then blow delicately at the imaginary candle again. Make sure all the areas below the pressure you are putting on your uterus are relaxed: thighs, vagina and anus. You can feel how the careful, gentle but steady pressure is controlled by you. This is how you will control the birth of your baby when the day comes. This is how you push. It's really that simple!

After three rounds of "blowing at the candle" and carefully monitoring the work your muscles do as you slowly empty your lungs, try pushing the *wrong* way and compare. Push as though you were having a bowel movement, an exhortation that can still be heard in today's supposedly enlightened delivery rooms. Inhale, tense your whole body and push until you are red as a beet. Imagine you are on the loo with a world-class case of constipation.

The difference between this technique and blowing at the candle is pretty obvious, isn't it? Entirely different muscles are at work, and these muscles work roughly and blindly, since the pressure is rigid and static. The uterus is being subjected to harsh cross-sectional pressure and even worse pressure from below, which means the vagina, the birth canal, is being squeezed shut. The net result of this appalling technique is that the baby has to fight to get out. The poor little person is met with resistance instead of assistance. For the woman, who is pushing as though she wants to expel a hard stool instead of a baby, this technique means pain and tearing.

After this little experiment, I'm sure you see the advantage in practicing the right way to push.

This is what you will do during the birth. (For simplicity's sake, we are going to assume that you will give birth in a semi-reclined position on your back. We will discuss alternative birthing positions later on.)

1. Lie down with your knees drawn up and your legs parted. Your eyes are open, your head is on the pillow, your palms are up, and your whole body is relaxed.

2. Let's pretend a contraction is beginning. Take a deep breath through your nose. Keep your mouth closed. Exhale immediately through your mouth. Close your mouth again, take a deep breath and hold it.

3. Now raise your head and place your chin softly against your chest. Close your hands around two imaginary handles, which are right beside you.

4. Push gently and carefully with those muscles you have learned to control by blowing at the candle. Direct the pressure gingerly from above.

Keep the muscles around the vagina, anus and groin area completely relaxed. Continue pushing gently until you need more air.

5. Breathe out through your mouth and immediately take another breath through your nose. (Stay in exactly the same position.) Push gently and carefully again for as long as you can hold your breath.

6. Now the pushing is over. The contraction is fading, and your stomach is becoming soft again. Let go of the handles, lay your head back on the pillow, take a few deep, even breaths and stock up on oxygen. You have one and a half to two minutes to rest before the next contraction comes. Once you have rested, practice once more.

As you can see, or rather feel, you don't have to put out that much effort, even if you do get dizzy the first few times. As I'm sure you have understood, it is not the *force* your muscles exert that counts, but the *direction* of the pressure.

There are mothers who push so hard that the blood vessels in their eyes literally burst, all in accordance with the exhortation to push as though they were having a bowel movement. That is *not* the way things are supposed to work.

The uterus itself exerts tremendous pressure. Your pushing exercise actually requires more work than the birth itself will. All you need to do is give the uterus a helping hand. It's enough to simply rest your chin against your chest and not resist. Every contraction will activate a conditioned reflex, so you will automatically relax and only those muscles that you have trained yourself to use will be in play.

When the pushing begins, you will also have decided which birthing position you prefer. Women give birth squatting, standing, hanging on to their husbands – anything goes these days. Whatever position you choose, let's hope you get the enthusiastic support you deserve!

Many mothers, however, still prefer to lie down and give birth on their backs, even though that position is male ordained and of relatively recent vintage. Be that as it may, I would advise you to do your exercises lying down, since this will enable you to relax most efficiently.

To sum up:
From the middle of the fifth month, make a ten-minute training session part of your daily routine. You can do it in the morning and/or in the evening while you are lying in bed. The program should include relaxation, shallow breathing and "blowing at the candle". In addition to this daily

session, practice the "correct" pushing technique once a week.

Let's assume that your delivery will take twelve hours. Your active participation will only be required for around two hours all told. There will be long intervals between contractions when not much happens.

You will apply the relaxation techniques you have learned for the first six to eight hours. You don't need to be lying down all this time. The technique works just as well standing up.

Shallow breathing is a godsend for the hours that remain, not least during the last stage of the opening phase. It is the transition from the opening phase to the expulsion phase that is the most demanding. It is the most arduous part of the entire delivery, and that is why you should be meticulous about practicing shallow breathing. Five minutes of every ten-minute training session should be devoted to this breathing technique.

The "blowing at the candle" exercise trains you for the birth itself, which will be gentle and short as a result – between ten and twenty minutes.

When the time finally comes, the various stages of the delivery will trigger a reflexive response in you. In an untrained woman, however, completely different reflexes would be triggered. She would instinctively resist what is happening inside her body, which she has no control over, and she would become frightened. The combination of fear and resistance is dangerous. The baby would be born anyway – but violently.

As I have already mentioned, I am doing an injustice to the spirit of the psycho-prophylaxis by giving you a description of only one part of its training program. As the name implies, there is more to this method than physical exercises. Try to learn more. There are courses you can take, and there are true believers who are only too happy to spread the gospel of psycho-prophylaxis. Ideally, you should go to the source and read the book I mentioned earlier, *Giving Birth Without Pain* by Pierre and Aline Vellay.

A MAN PREGNANT?

After four girls, I had my first boy. He was of course just as longed for as a little girl would have been after four boys. I kept looking under his diaper to make sure it was actually true. A boy!

And my favorite fantasy about this little guy was this: one day he would grow into a big, strong man with a hairy chest and a deep voice – and become a *daddy*! So I address these words to you, my son, and to all the men out there who might benefit from them.

You have grown up in a time when a hitherto closed woman's world has opened up for men. Can you imagine that when your eldest sister was born, at the beginning of the sixties, a man pushing a baby carriage was an object of ridicule? Now men participate in both the pregnancy and the delivery, and they are deeply engaged in caring for their newborn children. Paternal leave has been legislated, and even if some fathers don't take full advantage of it, attitudes have changed to such an extent that even men with careers think it is embarrassing *not* to take the opportunity to get to know their children and be a part of their lives for a time – a time that is all too fleeting.

The structure of the family has changed. The foundation of the nuclear family is emotional. You live with your woman because you want to, not because you have to. Neither of you (usually) is financially dependent on the other, so neither of you would be without means of support in the event of a break-up. Marriage is no longer a meal ticket, children no longer a pension plan. You must not bring children into the world to secure your old age. Parenthood is about emotions and, hopefully, love. Love, friendship and daily routines are what bind you and your woman together. And, obviously, in a relationship that is founded on and maintained by emotions, the baby that is about to born will occupy a special place.

Becoming a father is truly momentous. If you are not ready for the responsibility, take precautions *before*. Don't run away from your obligations after. It is not the woman's responsibility to ensure that you don't become a

41

father. You have no right to place the responsibility for something this important on anyone but yourself. A woman can't get pregnant all by herself. You fertilized the egg, not her.

You will participate in the pregnancy and the delivery, and you must prepare for it alongside your woman so that you can help her give birth. You will be involved in the care of your newborn baby, and you will on occasion be the primary caregiver. You also have upwards of twenty years of parenthood, child-rearing and financial support ahead of you...

Love wants children. A child is a confirmation. Your child is an expression of both of you, a symbol of your unity. You cannot stand by and pretend that none of this involves you.

Does a man get pregnant? The answer is probably yes. Not physically of course. That's impossible – unfortunately in my opinion. But emotionally.

You may well find yourself riding an emotional roller coaster with all its peaks and valleys of joy and despair along with your pregnant woman. If, on the other hand, everything is sweetness and light, thank your lucky stars and enjoy! There is nothing wrong with you.

You may have trouble wrapping your mind around the fact that you have a child on the way. You see your woman's stomach expand, you feel the baby kick, but it doesn't help. You still can't believe it. Don't worry. It will sink in eventually.

The feeling that something momentous has happened to your woman grows ever more intense. She's emotionally unstable, and you bear the brunt of this, since you are standing closest. Her behavior makes you feel that you have gone from beloved partner and friend to a dead rodent the cat dragged in. Be prepared for anything. Take a deep breath, count to ten and stay cool.

You may feel uneasy, afraid or antagonistic. You may have a vague feeling that an era is drawing to a close, namely the time in your life when you were just you. From now on you will not be just you; you will be a father as well. And because you feel that you will never be just you again, being just you, now and forever, becomes the most important thing in the world. There is no shortage of men who express a longing for children and then start screaming for an abortion as soon as the pregnancy is confirmed. But remember that even if your child will regard you as Dad throughout his/her life, you will still be you to everyone else. You don't have to say goodbye to your old, independent self!

Vaguely, or clearly, you may feel – to the point of having physical symptoms – that you are not prepared to give the world proof of your existence, which is what your child is. Your child is an extension of your life, undeniable physical evidence. Many a man has been frightened by the finality of it all. Your child is something you will always have to stand up for. Don't despair. Your child will help you find the maturity you need. Your child will draw you into a deep, enduring relationship. It is precisely through deep, enduring relationships that human beings mature and grow. Superficial relationships produce superficial people. Your child will not tolerate a superficial relationship. Be grateful for that. And your child won't be that demanding. He or she will be a superb little person, a pal who loves you – unconditionally. Is that really so bad?

You may experience a variety of bizarre physical sensations as a result of your deep emotional involvement. Men have described things in the mass media that once upon a time would have landed them in mental institutions. They talk of experiencing morning sickness during the first few months of their wives' pregnancies and of experiencing tenderness in their breasts. They talk of experiencing contractions in their non-existent wombs... Perhaps the classic caricature of the hollow-eyed father-to-be pacing back and forth in a smoke-filled room as he waits for reassuring news from the nurse will be replaced by an image of a frantic father trying to expel air from his swollen stomach.

If you experience such physical symptoms, don't panic. You are not in the throes of a spontaneous sex change! Your involvement in everything that has to do with your child is so intense that Nature is preparing you just as she is preparing your woman – and that goes for your body too. Be prepared for anything and everything in yourself, your woman and the relationship between you.

But remember that none of it is permanent. No matter how eagerly anticipated the pregnancy was, no matter how longed for the child is, both of you may feel regret and repugnance, and this can give rise to conflicts. It's hard to bear, but it's not unusual. Both of you are unstable.

Your relationship with your woman can change from one day to the next during the pregnancy – and from one night to the next for that matter. Subconsciously, you may feel left out in the cold, jealous before the baby is even born. This might cause you to want nothing to do with your woman sexually. Jealousy can also push you in the other direction. You have sex with her compulsively in an effort to "repossess" her, to "bring her back". A dim perception that she is in a blessed condition and therefore on a par with the Virgin Mary herself may take hold to the point that you can't bear the thought of "sullying" her. You may also find her wildly attractive. You make love like a newly wed, but your orgasm is no heftier than a vague blue string of smoke – and sometimes ejaculation doesn't happen at all. Impotence can strike without warning in spite of the fact you are so aroused your head is swimming. Nothing is too strange, and you have no control over any of it.

The fact that your woman is in crisis mode too doesn't help matters. She may reject you with disgust if you so much as give her a hug. She may feel utterly disoriented by the pregnancy and, deep down, think it is your "fault". She may turn frigid. Intercourse is for procreation and since the mission has been accomplished, what's the point? She may also go to the other extreme and want sex day in and day out. Now that the "damage" is done, what harm can it do?

She may be excessively needy and cling to you constantly. Your waking moments will be devoted to proving that you love her. She has to reassure herself that you will not leave her, now that she is carrying your child.

She may also feel so terrible physically that sex is the furthest thing from her mind. She has as little control over her reactions as you do.

Halfway through the pregnancy, if not before, your sex life will stabilize. You will, however, have to abandon your usual positions and find others that are more suitable. During the last month, you should not thrust too hard.

You should do your utmost to help your woman as far as everyday practicalities go. Above all, she has to sleep. (See "How should you live?") If you help her be good to herself, she will be good to you too!

The delivery training is supremely important.

Don't content yourself with being a passive follower. Take the initiative and encourage the mother to be. Don't be afraid to take the lead. (See "Giving Birth: An Olympic Marathon. Start Training!")

You should be the one to announce onset of the imaginary contractions during her training sessions. You should be the one who tells her when they peak and when they start to ebb. Keep an eye on her and make sure she does what she is supposed to, and do it with her.

Shallow breathing for example, which she will do during the most difficult part of the delivery (the last stage of the opening phase), will be much easier for her if you practice it with her.

Giving birth is a task for which you cannot prepare enough, and you must

44

take it seriously. The preparation involves you as much as it does your woman, but above all it involves your child. A good delivery, without pain or anesthetic, will give your child a wonderful start in life. Proper training means a delivery that is significantly shorter than the conventional variety, and it also means that the poor baby doesn't have to fight his or her way out inch by painful inch. This terrible ordeal – and make no mistake, being born *is* an ordeal – must be facilitated as much as possible.

And your input is invaluable.

You will see the results. After a good birth in accordance with the psycho-prophylactic method, the baby will put his or her lungs to use and cry spontaneously, and then fall into a peaceful silence. It is truly a beautiful sight.

Babies can't tell us what it feels like to be born without violence. That would be a beautiful tale indeed. So do what you can to make your child's untold tale as good as it can be! Give your child the opportunity to experience birth without violence.

During the delivery, you will play as active a part as you hopefully do now during the training. And, trust me, you will be needed. That you can count on. If and when you feel shut out or sidelined because everything seems to revolve around the baby your woman is carrying, remember that when the time comes for your child to come into the world, you will be more important than anything else for your woman – more important in fact than the baby.

The jealousy, the feeling that you have been shunted aside, will abate. You will realize just how important you are – if you only dare to. And you will!

You are going to be a father. What you are experiencing now is unique. Whatever you go on to experience in your life, nothing will ever match what you are experiencing right now. See it as an adventure, the greatest that life has to offer.

If you have to, comfort yourself with the thought that people have been having children for a long time.

Good luck, my beloved little big boy!

THE DELIVERY

IT'S TIME!
The following signs are an indication that your delivery is imminent:
- You are leaking amniotic fluid.
- The mucous plug comes loose.
- You feel regular and increasingly frequent contractions.

These signs can occur one at a time or simultaneously, but more often than not the delivery announces its arrival with contractions.

You have probably been experiencing something called Braxton-Hicks contractions for the last month, and they can be deceptive. They feel like the genuine article, strong and regular, so you pack your bags for the hospital – whereupon they disappear.

"Real" contractions are also regular, perhaps every twenty minutes for the first two or three hours, after which they become progressively more frequent. Finally, during the second and shorter stage of the opening phase, they are only two to three minutes apart. The rule of thumb is that you should be at the hospital (unless you decide to give birth at home of course) when the contractions are three minutes apart. This will give you time to deal with the necessary paperwork, which can be time consuming to say the least.

You will feel tension just above the groin area. You may also feel a dull ache in the small of your back, rather like the discomfort you feel during a period. This tension may spread to the groin proper and to the entire uterus, causing your stomach to harden. The contraction peaks with the stomach becoming so hard that it almost seems to come to a point, and then it subsides and disappears. The whole process takes about a minute and a half.

There is a respite when nothing happens, your stomach softens, and you no longer have to consciously practise relaxation. You can go on with whatever you were doing – packing your bag, vacuuming or having a shower.

As soon as you're sure that the game has begun in earnest, keep your eye on the clock. I usually go by the second hand, since that is the most reliable way to keep track of changes in the length of the intervals.

The uterus may tense and harden without your noticing. All you feel is a nagging, irritating pain in the small of your back when you lie down for a rest. You might also think that you have eaten something that didn't agree with you and that your guts are acting up. Babies have in fact been fished out of toilet bowls...

Be all that as it may, trained and prepared as you are, you know how to cope with contractions when you feel them coming on. You won't be afraid, and you won't double over. Fear accounts for half the pain, and resistance the other half. You are ready for this, your mental tolerance is high, and you feel nothing but joyous expectation. You may even have to say a few calming words to the people around you, who are trembling in their shoes and staring at you apprehensively. "Has it started? Oh, you poor, poor thing. Does it hurt a lot?"

Work on your technique during the opening phase! Relaxation-shallow breathing. (You don't need the shallow breathing at all yet, but it will give you a boost to see how effective it is. It is as though you are floating above the contractions. You have a feeling of complete control.)

The purpose of contractions is to efface the entrance to the uterus and dilate the cervix so that the baby can squeeze through the vagina and out into the world. The mucous plug, which acts as an effective barrier to bacteria, sits at the entrance to the uterus and loosens as the opening widens. As a rule, this happens during the delivery without your noticing, but it can also be a sign that your delivery has started. If this is the case, you will find a bloody clump of viscous material in your underpants.

The contractions put strong pressure on the uterus, and the baby, encased in the amniotic sac, is pushed downwards. (For the last little while, you have been able to feel how the baby has dropped.) When the amniotic sac finally breaks, the amniotic fluid pours out, and you should keep still. More common, however, is a small rupture that causes you to leak. This results in small puddles of clear or murky liquid in your underpants or on the sheet, and you will be able to tell from the odor that it is no ordinary discharge. You will know that the delivery has started, and in a few hours, the contractions will begin.

Your delivery can also sneak up on you. Hours of preliminary work may have gone on without you feeling a thing. One thing is certain: no two deliveries are the same, no matter how many children you have.

In my case, the first delivery was the best. (This goes against conventional wisdom, which claims that the first time is always the worst.)

I woke up on the morning of April 5 and saw a small damp stain on the sheet. The baby had been due on March 16. At this point, I had become numb to the endless waiting and had despaired of the child ever being born.

I got dressed and suffered through yet another depressing morning. Around one in the afternoon, I went to the bathroom and found another stain. I smelled it. Could it be amniotic fluid?

Then I began to feel something. There was a slight pull at the small of my back. My stomach hardened a touch. Could it be contractions? I didn't think so. By afternoon, my stomach was hardening at regular intervals. At first, it was every twenty minutes, then every fifteen. I still didn't believe it. Towards evening I began to time things methodically. My stomach hardened every ten minutes, then every seven, and finally every five. I decided that in all likelihood it was contractions, although I still had trouble believing it.

By 8.30 in the evening, I was at the hospital and duly signed in. I nagged the staff for information.

"Has it started?" I asked.

"You tell us," was the reply.

"How should I know?" I replied testily. "I've never had a baby before! I have no idea how it feels!"

"Tell us when the next pain comes then," said the obstetric nurse as she made notes.

I was irritated by her use of the word "pain". Whatever it was I was feeling, it didn't hurt.

When my stomach next hardened, I told her. She came over and felt my abdomen. To my surprise, she was mightily impressed.

"These are really strong!"

"So has it started?" I asked eagerly.

"You could say that," she answered. Then she examined me. It turned out I was halfway dilated. The baby was born two hours later.

It was my most perfect delivery. The training worked brilliantly, so brilliantly in fact that I wasn't even aware that I was using it. It looked after itself. It was a fantastic experience. What I had learned sat so deep in my marrow that I even argued with the nurse while I was pushing. She was exhorting me to push as though I was having a bowel movement. I couldn't believe that she, a medical professional, didn't know something that basic. It's simply not how babies are born! I regarded it as my duty to enlighten her.

Perhaps my naïveté contributed to the successful result. Why would having a baby be anything but a joy if one understood and applied the

Lamaze psycho-prophylactic method? The baby's father, who was present for the event, was just as enthusiastic.

After the birth, I was in superb shape – no pain, no stitches, and no after effects from anesthesia, since I hadn't needed any. The baby was in wonderful shape too.

Up in the maternity ward, however, I was made brutally aware of the fact that one didn't question the suffering that giving birth meant for most women lightly. Mothers who had torn and been stitched up, and who needed O-rings to protect their damaged genitalia tried to outdo each other with horror stories about the tortures of child birth. My airy assurances that giving birth didn't have to hurt and my enthusiastic endorsements of *Giving Birth Without Pain* (which I had with me) were met with ice cold silence and massive suspicion. I was regarded as a traitor to my very core.

I have become a little more humble since then. I have understood that suffering has to be justified. Suffering during childbirth has to somehow be turned into something legitimate. Women must be allowed to experience pain when we give birth. It gives us permission to complain without having to feel that we are somehow defective and without having to accept responsibility for changing anything. Legitimizing the suffering frees us from responsibility. This is the explanation for the cool reception that the psycho-prophylactic method still receives after half a century.

Widespread acceptance and use of psycho-prophylaxis will never become a reality until mothers themselves start talking about it, start expecting it, and start *demanding* it.

THE OPENING PHASE: PAVING THE WAY

The uterus is shaped like a large upside-down pear, broad at the top and narrowing towards the cervical canal and the cervix itself. The work you do during the opening phase is designed to widen and lift the cervical canal so that the uterus looks less like a pear and more like an apple open at one end, if you can visualize such a creation. The cervix merges with the uterus and disappears, leaving the way clear for the baby.

The uterus works slowly but inexorably. The cervical canal widens a little with each contraction. When the contraction subsides, the cervix contracts again, but there is a net gain. The principle of three steps forward, one step back applies here.

Vertical and horizontal muscle fibers are at work. The vertical fibers pull the cervix up, and the horizontal fibers exert pressure on the upper part of the uterus so that the baby, encased in the amniotic sac, is pushed downwards. During the first part of the opening phase, it is the vertical muscle fibers that will make themselves felt. The pressure will come from below, spread out towards your sides and across your back, and then over your stomach, which will harden. The pressure on the baby is enormous, and the poor little mite's heart rate will soar.

If the entire delivery takes twelve hours, the first part of the opening phase will account for nine of them. During these nine hours, you will remain passive, relaxed and calm, which will enable the uterus to work with maximum efficiency. You don't have to lie down if you don't feel like it, but if you opt to stand, keep still during the contractions.

Your task during the long pauses between contractions is to breathe properly in order to conserve your oxygen supply. Apart from that, conduct yourself as you normally do.

Before the second part of the opening phase, you will feel the horizontal muscle fibers at work. They push downwards. It may feel like the baby's arrival is imminent, but it's not – yet. These horizontal muscle fibers exert powerful pressure on the upper section of the uterus, the fundus, so that the baby, encased in the amniotic sac, is pushed downwards.

The second stage of the opening phase goes much more quickly than the first. If you are down to two and a half to three minutes between contractions, you can count on the baby being born within the next two hours.

During this second shorter stage, you will feel the downward pressure becoming ever stronger. It is during this stage that you will rely on shallow breathing to facilitate and shorten the work of the uterus tremendously. This light, superficial breathing will prevent your ribcage from locking, which in turn will ensure that pressure from your diaphragm will not counteract the muscular work being done by the uterus. There will be no resistance and therefore no pain.

When you are halfway dilated, the contractions are at their most intense and most frequent. This is as hard as the work gets. The amniotic membranes will probably burst when you are halfway dilated. The horizontal muscle fibers exert constant downward pressure causing them to bulge outwards in the vagina. Finally, the pressure is just too much. These membranes are tough however, and they don't always burst, in which case your obstetrician or midwife will puncture them. This does not hurt.

It is during the end of the opening phase, the most arduous part of the delivery, that your shallow breathing is most essential. You will finally feel the first urge to push. Don't give in to it! Not yet! Persevere with the shallow breathing for another couple of contractions.

THE EXPULSION PHASE: A CHILD IS BORN

The transition from the opening phase to the expulsion phase is difficult. It's short, but injuries can occur. This is when training and keeping a clear head really pay off.

Unfortunately, the urge to push kicks in *before* the cervix is completely effaced. The temptation to start pushing is well nigh irresistible, but you have to fight it. Persevere with the shallow breathing as long as you possibly can! If you start to push too early, violence will be the result. You are not fully dilated yet. The baby won't be injured, but you will tear, and you may require stitches both internally and externally – and all for nothing. Let shallow breathing be your friend in need through another two contractions. As long as your ribcage doesn't lock, you have no traction so to speak, and pushing is simply impossible. Hold out as long as you can! One contraction is good; two is even better. You can give in during the third, but by then the crisis will be over.

Now that the pushing has started, you will be astonished over how things seem to look after themselves, and all because you are not resisting. The idea is not to push for all your worth. It's the direction of the pressure that counts, not the force behind it.

If you are giving birth standing up or hanging on to something, you will also have gravity on your side. Listen to your body; you know better than anyone else how you should sit, stand or lie.

You feel the urge to push. You breathe in, breathe out, breathe in again, and hold your breath, your chin held softly against your chest. Gently direct pressure downwards and towards your sides, just as if you were blowing at the candle. When you need more air, maintain your position, inhale and work a little more. Keep your eyes open!

If you are asked to push a little more after the contraction has subsided, do so. Then rest, breathe, and gather your strength.

Very soon thereafter, the baby's head will be visible as it forces it way down. After each push, it recedes a little, but it gains ground every time. Since the pressure on the baby is horribly strong, an almost obscenely swollen artery on it head may be the first thing the onlookers see. Dad, be prepared!

Things are moving fast. You are working gently and precisely, but not hard. Soon the baby passes through the pelvic area and starts to emerge, probably after three or four contractions with two pushes apiece.

Now you may experience a sensation that you are about to tear. The pressure is enormous, and the fibers in the vagina and around the labia are being stretched to breaking point. These fibers are very elastic, and they are designed to take the pressure, but they will snap if you tense them even slightly. Tensing anything that is already stretched to capacity can only have one result.

When the baby's head is on the way through, you must not push. Tried and true shallow breathing will see you through this crisis. Any midwife or obstetrician worth his or her salt will tell you not to push. Breathe lightly and superficially for God and Country so that your ribcage doesn't lock! It only takes a few seconds for the head to get through, and the job will get done without any help from you.

The baby's father can be of tremendous help right now. If he has done his training too, he can breathe with you and be your coach during these short but crucial moments.

When the head is out, the midwife or obstetrician will take hold of the little shoulder joint and pull out one arm. The baby's body follows like a cork coming out of a bottle. This can happen so fast that it feels as though a little seal has slid out of you.

If your work has been arduous thus far – especially towards the end of the opening phase – it has been nothing compared to the ordeal that the baby has been through. The food and oxygen supply was cut off, and the baby had to force its way out to survive. The baby had to make its way down a canal so narrow that the pressure might have caused the two halves of its skull to overlap.

It was a brutal journey of no return. The baby was literally screwed downwards, doing a half rotation during the pushing contractions. Then the neck locked, and the face was forced outwards and upwards towards the light. Out comes an exhausted, crumpled little soul who has gone through an ordeal too agonizing for us to comprehend. There is yet another shock in store for the new arrival. Lungs that have never before been used expand and take in air, which the baby then expels in the form of a scream.

Giving birth according to the Lamaze method does not simply mean giving birth without pain. It also means providing a little wayfarer in need with the succor he or she needs to pass through the valley of death as gently as possible and emerge into the world of the living.

Covered in a blanket, your baby is laid at your warm, naked breast.

Your body becomes empty, silent and still. It's a remarkable stillness. The months of life inside you have come to an end. The powerful forces that were so recently in motion are now gone. All that is left is a large silent cavern below your navel where nothing happens at all.

Your reactions can be many and varied – happiness, lassitude, floods of tears, indifference...

Perhaps you have been so focused on working hard and working well that only now does it dawn on you that the point of the whole exercise was in fact a child. Or, conversely, you may have thought so long and fantasized so intently about this little mite that you are astonished to find a stranger at your breast.

Your first reaction is bewilderment, but this will soon change. You have accomplished an incredibly arduous feat. If all you want at first is to hear how brilliantly you have managed everything instead of listening to everyone heap praise on the baby, there is nothing strange about that. You are still most interested in what has happened to *you*. Don't be shy about saying so!

Now the umbilical cord joining you and your baby must be cut – perhaps by the baby's dad.

THE AFTERBIRTH: THE TREE OF LIFE

They are truly the tree of life, the placenta and the fetal membranes. The umbilical cord, which connected the placenta and the baby, branches off into an intricate root system.

Shortly after the baby is born, the placenta starts to dislodge from the wall of the uterus. You will push it out of you, while your obstetrician gently tugs the umbilical cord. Make sure you check to see that it is in one piece so that nothing is left inside you.

You are looking at a miracle. Under the placenta's tender care, your little baby has been supplied with oxygen and nourishment for nine months. It has watched over your child twenty-four hours a day. Do you see the membranes? They protected your baby. And the umbilical cord, blue, knotty and stringy, it was the connection to life itself.

For me, this was always a rather melancholy moment. The placenta's work was done. An era had passed, never to return. The care and toil were at an end. One of nature's miracles had done its work and been forfeited. It was when I saw the placenta that I usually realized that I had in fact had a baby. The torch had passed, and I had a responsibility to take over.

The placenta leaves a lesion on the wall of the uterus, so you will bleed for a few weeks. You are therefore susceptible to infections and should refrain from intercourse. The bleeding will stop once the uterus has contracted; this takes about six weeks. To ensure that the uterus has contracted normally, your gynaecologist or midwife should examine you.

And now, with the extraction of the placenta and the fetal membranes, the delivery's three phases – the opening phase, the expulsion phase and the afterbirth phase – are accomplished. Your body is your own again – and empty.

AFTERWARDS

A little baby has been born. This baby is unlike any other baby in the world. Let's say it's a little girl!

And this newborn little girl will have a miraculous effect on her surroundings. There isn't a midwife or a doctor alive, no matter how hardened by experience, who can suppress a smile at such a moment. A singular atmosphere of solemn exhilaration suffuses every delivery room when a baby is born. Every new human being is saluted for what she is: a miracle.

She is a new life. You bestowed that life. You will remember this moment for as long as you live.

You are tired, faint and hungry.

A tremendous feat of endurance is behind you. Your body is reacting. You may feel chilled to the bone. You may tremble and shake. You may giggle uncontrollably, cry rivers of tears, or just lie on your back in a daze. But at your breast is a little baby, and it's yours. She was what you were carrying in your belly. It will take a while for that to sink in!

Your little baby may now seek your nipple for the first time. She lifts her large, heavy head and nuzzles with pursed lips. She scrabbles her way over your skin with her little hands that open and close, open and close... It feels strange. This can be a disorienting moment, but you will lay your hand over your baby's head.

Her eyes are dark. Do you see? Most babies are born with dark blue eyes. That can change.

Her hair is dark, fair and downy or simply absent. "Real" hair will come later.

Ten fingers, ten toes, and the most beautiful nails in the world.

She may look a little on the pudgy side. You will soon know her weight, between three and half and four kilos probably. She will measure approximately half a meter.

Don't be concerned about her irregular breathing. It will be a while before it stabilizes. These little mites may desperately gasp for air or seem as though they are not breathing at all. (Sometimes they're not. Newborns can stop breathing for up to forty seconds several times a day.)

And the baby's father is with you – hopefully. Never is a man more handsome than when he sees his child for the first time.

A band will be fastened around your wrist with a number on it that corresponds with the number on a band around your baby's wrist. You can check for yourself that the numbers match.

You will be washed. Every now and then, you may feel a twinge in your stomach. When you lie down, blood from the lesion on the wall of the uterus where the placenta was attached collects and has to get out somehow.

The uterus begins to contract immediately, and it should be monitored continuously. You may be given an injection to accelerate this process in connection with the birth.

Eventually, you and the baby's father will have the opportunity to contemplate and admire the new arrival in private.

If this newly arrived little citizen of planet Earth starts to cry, there is no reason not to put her to your breast. Quite the contrary! You don't have much to offer, but there may be a couple of drops of colostrum to be had. The warmth of mother's skin and the familiar sound of her heartbeat are not to be sneezed at either.

This time with the baby belongs to you and the baby's dad.

Finally you are alone. I don't think you will be feeling particularly grown up or that you are much of a mother. Perhaps it feels as though the baby isn't actually yours. What has happened to you is too great, too overwhelming. You may feel as though none of it really has anything to do with you. If someone congratulates you, you may find yourself replying with a confused question. "What for?"

You need to sleep, but you might not be able to sleep at all. You should be over the moon, yet you have never felt sadder in your entire life. Be prepared for anything. None of it is permanent!

Whatever you are feeling right now, you will be hit with the mother of all depressions the third or fourth day after the delivery. Before and after that particular hammer falls, however, you will in all likelihood feel as strong as an ox and sleep like a log. Bear in mind that your body has undergone an enormous change! Such physical changes cannot take place without psychological repercussions following in their wake. And vice-versa.

Contradictory reactions are not only explicable but necessary.

It will take around six months before your body is completely your own again, and you feel like your old self.

You have become a mother. If your relationship with your parents has been bad up until now, you will find it very difficult to forgive them if they don't take an interest in you now. Such life transforming events give damaged relationships a chance to begin anew.

The support and presence of the baby's father is of vital importance to you as well. This is a time when you will be as close as you can be to each other, no matter how much bad blood there has been in the past – if you only let it happen.

Right from the start, this new little life lends a shimmer to her surroundings, a shimmer of hope, reconciliation and confidence. What's really important in life becomes clear, even through the humdrum of daily life. Do read "The Gift of Love"! Love's gift will be yours for many, many years to come – it will be given to all those around your child, if only they have eyes to see it.

You will be the first to be so blessed.

All children are born with a magic wand in their hands.

THE FIRST WEEK – AND ON

YOUR BODY

Eventually, you will be able to get out of bed. Be careful the first time. You can fall. You stagger off to the shower. Hopefully, your guts are settling down, but it can take a couple of days.

The shower feels divine. You are bleeding, and the discharge is less than fragrant. You are probably sweaty and feeling a little grungy. So far, so good. But your body...

I was dismayed the first time I saw myself. My stomach was not flat. I looked as though I was still pregnant. My labia hung and dangled like barn doors half off their hinges, and it looked as though kids could still roll out of me like quarters out of a slot machine (which is eventually what happened). I was nineteen years old, and this is what I was going to look like!?

I decided to lace myself up. I had gotten married in a corset and a starched dress, all in keeping with the fashions of the time, and I requested that my corset be brought to the hospital. It was an old-fashioned contraption, with hooks and eyes and steel supports, and I had a heck of a time getting into it. I nearly hemorrhaged with all the writhing and struggling, but I finally made it.

Ever since then, I have made a point of corseting myself from the second day after my deliveries – all nine of them. I wore the corset twenty-four hours a day for a month. The hooks and supports itched and chafed, so I took care to moisturize generously after every shower, and I wore a thin cotton T-shirt next to my skin. After nine enormous stomachs – I gained between twenty-two and twenty-six kilos during each pregnancy – I have wrinkled skin to be sure, but no stretch marks and no gut.

So, if you want to prevent stretch marks and get your flat stomach back, the prescription is to moisturize during your pregnancy and to corset yourself after the delivery (a strong, really tight-fitting girdle will do the trick too) and to do some exercises. (See below.)

Not all mothers gain as much weight as I did. Nor do all mothers have problems getting rid of the extra kilos. Indeed, some women drop so much weight while they are breast-feeding that they become ominously thin. If you belong to this group, you can rest assured that the problem will right itself, but it can take up to a year.

As a rule, however, five to eight kilos will disappear in connection with the delivery and your stay in hospital, and another three to four kilos will melt away during your first month at home. That leaves five kilos. Those five kilos can set the stage for a serious weight gain, and it's important to shed them – especially if you are planning to have more children. Otherwise, you risk gaining five kilos with every child. Breast-feeding helps your body get back to normal, but it won't take care of the extra weight.

Since women are psychologically fragile as long as they breast feed – a baby sucks the life out of you along with the milk – and since it takes six months for body and mind to return to normal, I usually waited six months before I started to diet. But if you don't do it then, there is a risk that you won't do it at all.

My method was simple. I didn't have the strength to follow a complicated dieting program, nor did I believe in miracle cures. So, for a couple of months, I simply skipped the meal I could most easily do without and substituted a liter of boiled, lukewarm water flavored with a little lemon. It doesn't sound particularly appetizing I know, but it gave me a pleasant full feeling. (Cold water is hard to drink in large quantities if you are not thirsty, and anything that is body temperature is better for you.) At the mealtime that I was hungriest, I would eat cooked food to my heart's content. At the third meal, I ate moderately, normally in other words, but I avoided bread and sugar. (Avoiding sugar is not always easy. Almost everything contains sugar today.) Following this regimen meant I didn't have to go hungry, I wasn't tempted to snack, and I didn't become fixated on food, a phenomenon that is the bane of many dieters. I achieved my goal – eight to ten kilos disappeared during those two months. I didn't weigh myself until I could get into my regular clothes again.

A few days after the delivery (if you have given birth at a hospital), you will be encouraged to do certain exercises. The most effective and the most important of them is simple and undetectable, so you can do it wherever and whenever you like. The exercise is the *vaginal squeeze*. You contract the muscles around the vagina as hard as you can and as many times as you can several times a day.

The uterus is still large and relatively heavy and rests against the floor of the pelvis on a sheet of soft muscles and cartilage that doesn't provide much support. There is a risk that the uterus might one day force its way down into the vagina, and you will have a condition known as "tilted womb". This is not imminent, but it can occur later in life after a number of children. This risk will be minimized if you do your vaginal squeezes faithfully now.

The more you train, the faster your labia will close and the more your vagina will contract. The man in your life won't feel like he has wandered into the Grand Canyon when he makes love to you, and he will thank you for it!

Other important exercises in the program are those that strengthen your legs and feet, which have been taking quite a beating for a while now. When you stop wearing the corset after a month at home (I usually stopped wearing it at night after one month but I wore it during the day for two), you can start doing sit-ups and side bends or anything else you enjoy to trim your waist. Devote a few minutes to it every morning! However, wait at least six months before doing anything that involves jumps or jolts.

And sleep as much as you can!

Make a point of writing down any questions you might have as they occur to you, so you won't forget them during your post-partum check ups. Once you get home, it's too late.

BREASTFEEDING

On the third day after the delivery, the milk usually starts to flow – all over the place. Your breasts will leak rivers at the beginning. You'll need something to soak up the excess. The expensive throw-away protection can be replaced with folded pieces of terry-towel that you can cut to order. These can easily be rinsed in cold water and reused.

Your breasts will be engorged and very tender, and they will swell dramatically. The swelling will pass however. When breastfeeding stabilizes after a few weeks, your breasts will have softened, but they will still be large.

The colostrum, which was all you had to offer for the first few days, was nourishing, but now comes the "real" milk. It will be watery at first, but after your baby has sucked for a while, it will become rich and yellow.

Female folk wisdom has a few tips for us:
• Keep your breasts warm.
• Never sit in a draught.
• Drink lots of liquids – water, milk, non-alcoholic beer.
• Wash your hands and nipples before you breast-feed, especially during the newborn period – "the honeymoon" – with soap and water or just luke-warm water. Air dry.
• Lumps and bumps should be massaged immediately and thoroughly, preferably while exposing the breast to a source of warmth – a hair dryer will do fine – and then your breasts should be insulated. Cotton wool works beautifully.
• Cracked nipples need rest. Wash them and let them air dry. The breast milk itself has a healing effect. Pump a little out and rub it in to your nipples.

If you are expelling milk by hand, grip your breast above the areola. Then milk yourself according to the tried and true cow-milking technique. (The milk squirts out through six or eight channels in all directions, a fascinating sight!) Hard, engorged breasts must have a little milk pumped out of them before the baby can eat.

The entire nipple must be inserted into the little mouth, right up to the border of the areola. The baby's sucking impulse is triggered when the nipple touches the little cheek. You can also stroke your baby on the cheek with your finger.

Decide whether your prefer sitting or standing. You will soon find a position that is right for you. Just make sure that the baby's nostrils aren't blocked by your breast. She needs air.

And hold her little hand with one finger! You will be able to feel how strong a baby's grip is. Newborns fear falling down, so let her take hold!

A newborn sucks hard. That causes the uterus to contract, and you will experience so-called after pains. If you have given birth without pain, according to Lamaze and psycho-prophylaxis, the after pains actually aren't painful. It feels as though a hand is gently squeezing your body, but from the inside.

Listen to your baby eating! She will suck powerfully and swallow regularly. Then the gurgling will cease. New milk is being sucked out. Your milk runs in fits and starts, but the baby will go on sucking between rounds. The milk starts to flow again and you feel it. The gurgling sound resumes. The baby closes her eyes in sheer delight and in an effort to keep up with the flow. Her eyes roll ecstatically under her eyelids.

Don't stop nursing, no matter how much the baby seems to be gorging herself. If she chokes, she will take a break.

Little newborns should be given as much food as they can take on board and then some. It is impossible to give them too much. It just comes out one end or the other anyway.

At the hospital, there are both nurses and mothers who suspect tummy trouble, colic and even milk allergies whenever a baby cries – especially if they refuse to eat because they are too busy crying. At this age, babies scream for one reason and one reason only: *survival anxiety*. There is only one way to alleviate this anxiety: food and lots of it.

If your baby is asleep when it's time to eat, stroke her gently over the head before you pick her up. Then put her to your breast. She will eat heartily, even though she seems to be asleep.

Newborns can suck until they are literally stuck to your breast even when they are not eating. To dispel the vacuum, pull the little cheek lightly and let some air in.

Don't panic if you experience sensual pleasure or even erotic stimulation. You are not abnormal, nor are you in danger of entering into a sexual relationship with your poor, innocent little baby. Breast-feeding is part of your sexuality. You are designed to procreate. To this end, Nature has made you a sexual being, and breastfeeding is a part of the package. The baby is the raison d'être of this complex sexual equation whose purpose is to ensure the continued existence of the human race. Human beings are not masochistic by nature. Pleasure is the fuel that drives the procreative engine. That's why the pleasure you take in breast-feeding your baby has a sexual undercurrent. It's perfectly normal, even if it is a little frightening for us cultivated westerners who consider ourselves above such animalistic urges.

My own first unsteady steps as a breastfeeding mother were a curious blend of tragedy and farce.

Back in those days, babies were weighed before and after meals and a record was kept of the amount of food they consumed. There were (and still are) special tables indicating how much food a baby needed at any given age. Wanting to err on the side of caution, I rented a set of scales when I got home from the hospital.

The baby was fed according to the table, and, in keeping with the custom of the times, I then sat down and pumped out my breasts by hand. The milk flowed, my fingers became encrusted and stiff, and all my clothes smelled of sour milk. The milk went into sterilized bottles for further delivery. Ill or premature babies would benefit from my milk, and I felt good about that.

The only problem was that my own child was wailing like a banshee. She screamed for hours on end. Her father and I took turns walking the floor with her during the night. We carried her, we took her on car rides, and we rocked her endlessly in her carriage. The days were just as bad.

Sometimes the baby's grandmother pitched in, laid the child over across her knees and patted her on the back for what seemed like an eternity. Finally, the baby would sleep, but slept with the air of one who has abandoned all hope, and her parents would stagger out of the house to gather their strength for the next onslaught.

Finally, my patience ran out. I was young and impulsive, and I had no desire to devote my life to an infant who rejected any and all attempts to comfort her. Could there be something wrong with the scales?

We rented a new set, only to discover that during the two weeks she had been home from the hospital, not only had she not gained any weight, she had actually *lost*.

At this point, I tossed all the scales and tables. I fed my baby until she literally choked, and peace descended on the house. In the weeks that followed, she did nothing but eat and sleep, eat and sleep, and there was not so much as a peep out of her.

Eventually, she bestowed a glorious smile on us that seemed to say, "So you two geniuses finally figured it out! Was it really that complicated?"

With that, I was on the right track – with the baby's help and a little common sense.

When all my other children came, I applied the same principle. I gave my newborns food, food, more food, and even more food!

HOME!

WHAT DO YOU NEED?

It's easy to fall into the trap of thinking that your baby needs a trainload of new stuff. Some parents make such an occasion out of the expected arrival that they refurnish their houses and buy enough equipment to outfit ten children for as many years. Other parents make no preparations at all. They even hold off buying a bed until after the delivery, by which time they know for sure that they are going to need it.

Whatever approach you decide to take, common sense dictates that anything you buy that has to do with the care of your baby should have a practical purpose, namely to make life easier for *you*.

The care you provide will be good and the equipment you buy will be sensible if you keep one overriding goal in mind: ensuring your baby is clean, warm, fed and dry.

You can get by on two or three changes of clothes if you wash them in the basin every evening, or you can buy a whole closet full of baby clothes complete with a specially designed washing machine. You can buy a change table with drawers, fitted shelves, a container with a lid for diapers, and, for good measure, an extension leaf so the change table can double as a desk at some point – or you can forego a change table altogether and just spread a terry towel wash cloth on a bed. You can buy a baby bath with a built in thermometer and a baby towel with a hood or bathe your baby in the sink (watch out for hot taps!) and simply wrap her in a regular towel when you are done. Babies that are cared for with only the basics do not fare worse than babies that are cared for with all the bells and whistles. There is no right or wrong here. What you are dealing with is *a little person whose needs are pretty much the same as yours.*

You probably have a lot of what you need already – things you have made yourself, inherited or bought on impulse. And decorations are fun! What follows is a list of a few things that I think are the most practical and the most necessary.

- Clothing:
  Cotton swaddling blankets: six.
  Snap-at-the-crotch or side snap T-shirts: six. (T-shirts that are pulled over the

head remind newborns of the journey down the birth canal and are thus to be avoided.)

Tight, stretchable baby pants: six. Invest in high quality! Good pants can be used for years.

Coveralls with feet: three.

A bonnet or a hat to protect the baby from draughts and direct sunshine (throughout the first year).

Booties: two pairs.

A sweater and/or cardigan

Cotton or wool mittens for outdoor use, depending on the climate.

• Care:

Diapers: Disposables, newborn size. (Reusable cloth diapers are too cumbersome for the baby in the beginning. They are, however, economical and more environmentally friendly.)

Washing bowls: two, one for the face, the other for the body.

Washcloths. A tip: buy some terry cotton fabric and cut it into smaller pieces. These work fine as washpads, towelettes, and little bibs. Rinse in cold water and reuse.

Mild soap.

Soft hairbrush for creating nice hairdos.

Baby cream or petroleum jelly.

Baby oil (for treating flaky skin and cradle cap).

Bath towels: two.

Small towels: three or four.

Plastic foam pad (for the change table, covered with a towel or a piece of terry-cloth).

A bottle and formula (mainly for psychological reasons).

Pacifier (dummy), anatomically designed (in case breastfeeding does not fulfill the total need for sucking; see details below).

A colorful plush animal with big, black eyes.

Hygiene! Keep the house clean, particularly the floors. Always wash your hands before touching your newborn, and tell others to do the same!

• Bedding

Baby carriage, sturdy and roomy with colorful inside lining, preferably brightly patterned.

Bassinet ("Moses Basket"), cradle or crib. A crib with slats can be used from the beginning; bumper padding is necessary.

Terry cotton with plastic backing for protecting the mattress, three pieces.

Sheets, baby-size, ten. Special baby sheets are expensive. You can make baby-size sheets simply by cutting your own into smaller pieces. No hemming is necessary at this early stage.

One sheet covers the mattress and another sheet can be folded in three and tucked in tightly at the head of the bed. It works as a "pillow" and stays in place when the little one is turning her head from side to side. And when the baby drools or spits up, you can simply unfold a new, clean segment.

Baby-size pillowcases: two. For the very first days, if and when the baby is sleeping on her side, a thin pillow is necessary to match the height of the little shoulder. Just fold a towel inside the pillowcase.

Crocheted blankets, shawls or quilts, two or three.

Something fun for the baby to look at. A mobile, for example, to dangle over the bed, the change table, and/or the baby carriage. Colorful pictures attached inside the bed with an extra picture at the head end will inspire babies who sleep on their stomach. Lifting the head is something your baby can do from day one.

A newborn's taste in art is less than sophisticated. Crude patterns and colors garish enough to inflict flash burns are what you're looking for. Cut up that Hawaiian shirt that you wouldn't dare wear outside the privacy of your own home. Your baby will be enchanted.

Just remember that once all these visual stimuli are in place, don't change anything for the first month!

(You will find more information about sleeping arrangements and bedding in "Sleep" in Part two of *For the Love of Children*.)

Apnea monitor (Baby Respiration Monitor). Rent or buy one.

Newborn children's breathing is irregular. They often stop breathing for as long as 40 seconds at a stretch. Few adults can hold their breath for that long.

As you know, tragically, during their deepest sleep, babies may stop breathing altogether. This monitor, which I recommend for the first ten to eleven months, will greatly reduce any fears you may have about Sudden Infant Death Syndrome (SIDS).

The baby respiration monitor comes with a thin sensory plate, which you place underneath the mattress, and an alarm unit. If and when the baby stops breathing, you will hear a sharp warning signal, comparable to household fire alarms. All you have to do is turn the baby over onto her back so that she sleeps more lightly (or wakes up). She will resume breathing and you can relax. Mercifully, the worst-case scenario, which can happen in only three minutes – and you can't watch your baby's breath 24 hours a day – has not happened.

Statistics show that SIDS decreased considerably after parents were advised to put their babies down to sleep on their back. The problem is that human babies are made for sleeping on their stomach, and they sleep more soundly. Obviously, one of the factors of the decrease in SIDS is due to the fact that babies who sleep on their back don't sleep as deeply, or as long, or as much as they need to (in other words, they don't sleep as well, or at all).

The baby respiration monitor allows both you and your child to have the best of both worlds. Your baby will sleep deeply, and you will have peace of mind. A little blinking light indicates that your baby is breathing continuously.

One other advantage to having your baby sleep in the prone position is that you won't have to worry about her choking if and when she spits up. On a flat surface, even a freshly minted newborn can lift and turn her heavy head.

WHAT DO YOU DO?

When you get home – if you have given birth at the hospital – throw out all the schedules. Let the little newborn decide when it's time to eat. She may already be a little cranky on the way home. It's nothing to apologize for. Just give her your breast.

If hunger strikes when you get home, friends and relatives who may have gathered will just have to wait. Your baby has to eat first. When she has been well fed and burped, you can get out of your coat, socialize and let everyone get acquainted with the little miracle.

If she is sound asleep when you get home, let her sleep! As soon as she so much as peeps, wash your nipple and put her to your breast.

You will have the baby's bed made and the house clean.

At my house, we seldom did fall and spring cleaning, but cleaning house before a new baby arrived was mandatory. Although breast milk offers excellent protection against infection, the world is still new and full of bacteria, dust and all manner of strange substances. If your newborn catches a cold and her nose gets stuffy, breastfeeding becomes a vale of tears.

When you sit down (or lie down) to breastfeed for the first time at home, choose a location that is comfortable and where you can relax your shoulder and arm. You will eventually decide on the spot that is best for you. You will need support for the arm that you have under the baby, and your baby needs support for her weak back and heavy head.

Hook one of the baby's arms around your back and hold her other hand.

Don't distract her while she is eating. If she makes eye contact, smile, but you don't need to speak.

This is a process that takes its own sweet time, and you are not a bad mother if you read, talk to someone or watch TV. Just be careful not to let your baby fall asleep! Every time she stops sucking, if you move your nipple in her mouth, you will stimulate her to resume eating. You can also try withdrawing your nipple a little. With a bit of luck, she'll come to, remember what she's there for and get back in the game!

Let her eat until she is stuffed to the gills. Burp her against your shoulder. You will help expel any excess air by patting her gently and steadily on the bottom with a loosely clenched fist. Start low and work your way up.

Many little angels sleep like logs after the first round. Don't be deceived! If you put her down now, she will be awake again in half an hour. Or fifteen minutes. Or five. So try to prevent her from sinking into a deep sleep.

After burping her, place her on her back in front of you (don't forget the blanket!). Newborns don't like lying flat and spread-eagled on their backs – it's too unlike life in the womb. Only babies who have eaten themselves into a stupor can fall asleep in that position. Half full ones soon wake up.

Give her the next round from the same breast. She won't take that much this time, but what she does take is nourishing. Coax her!

Burping her afterwards can take a while. She won't have swallowed that much air. Walk around with her and pat her little bottom steadily.

This first feeding, consisting of two portions with a burp after each takes about half an hour.

Now it's time for a diaper change, and you have a contented little soul to deal with!

A few prerequisites for changing a baby:
• Warm, clean hands.
• A warm draught-free room.
• A firm, confident grip; your baby is not as fragile as she seems. All newborns have an instinctive fear of falling. A loose, tentative grip makes them nervous.
• Stop whatever it is you are doing when the baby stretches. Don't lift or turn a newborn when she is having a good stretch! Wait.

Babies can be enigmatic introverts at times. Respect that. When you are changing your baby, when you are holding her, or in the middle of any other activity, you will see how she suddenly becomes immobile. Something strikes a cord deep within her soul. Her gaze becomes contemplative. It seems as though the world and time itself stops. Her meditations must be allowed to run their course.

What is actually happening? I don't know. Perhaps it's something like this:

Say you are reading a book and a sentence resonates with you so intensely that you stop reading, lift your eyes from the page and stare off into space. You contemplate the words and the feelings they have aroused within you. You are lost in the moment, off in your own private universe. If someone speaks to you, you don't hear. If someone were to intrude into your reverie with demands for attention, you would be both angry and confused.

From their first moments, several times a day, newborns become still and journey into themselves, and it feels as though an angel is passing through the room. At such moments, something will bid you to be still too.

Place your baby in front of you. A change is most comfortable on a soft baby blanket. To cut down on laundry, slip a piece of terry towel that you have cut for the occasion under your baby's bottom before you clean her.

Remove all her clothing except the little sweater. Then remove the diaper. Any excrement (which is yellow, loose, acidic and grainy as long as the baby is being breastfed) may have traces of dark meconium, which is still lodged in her intestines. Wipe it away with the dry part of the diaper and a piece of soft toilet paper or paper towel. Then wash with lukewarm water from a bowl or direct from the tap. Use your own hand as a washcloth or a piece of soft terry towel. If she has had a bowel movement, use soap, if she hasn't, water will suffice. Take hold of her feet with one hand and lift her bottom off the table and clean her underneath too.

Little girls have large labia, still swollen after being exposed to the mother's hormones during the delivery. Open them carefully. Inside you will probably find a large, white lump, a mixture of fetal tallow and ointment that was daubed on at the hospital. Don't remove all of it, but if the clump is very large, about half of it can go. Remove it carefully with the corner of a clean, lukewarm washcloth. Whatever is left will disappear in the next few days. Ultimately, the vagina will be clean and empty.

You should open the labia during every change to make sure that no ointment or excrement has become lodged there. But don't use soap, only water! Use a towel to pat dry the area outside and around the labia, especially the folds between the groin and the top of the thigh. Never use baby powder on a little girl's genitals!

Little boys differ from one another. Sometimes, the little testicles can't be felt in the scrotum. They will eventually descend, but it can take time. Your pediatrician will monitor this.

The foreskin can't be pulled back.

Boys are easier to change and clean than girls, but lift the scrotum and check in all those nooks and crannies to make sure that no excrement goes undetected. Pat dry when you have finished cleaning. (No baby powder on little boys either. Baby powder isn't necessary generally, although it does smell good. If you use it at all, save it for the fold in the neck and the armpits.)

Ointment. Apply a thin layer over a large area. This area should extend to the little buttocks, which will come into direct contact with the diaper.

Put on the new diaper. The front is usually decorated. Run your finger around the whole diaper to make sure that the plastic is not digging into the baby's skin. The diaper should not slide down the thighs. The legs should be completely free. It will take you a while to get your technique down pat, but since your baby is well fed and content, you have all the time in the world!

The diaper should not be touching the stump of the umbilical cord, which won't have fallen off yet (although it will any day now). Covering the stump with a compress will make life easier for you. If you fasten it with surgical tape, use very small pieces! There's really not much else you have to do with the umbilical cord stump. It will look after itself.

Once the diaper is on, dress the baby in a pair of short pants. Socks are a good idea. The tiny feet are probably ice cold, since the blood circulation has not really cranked into gear yet.

If the baby has had a little spit up (nothing to worry about, but babies with full tummies have to be handled with care), give her a new sweater. If you use wrap around sweaters – which, as previously mentioned, you should at this stage, since newborns don't like to be reminded of the journey down the narrow birth canal – the baby must be turned over so you can do the sweater up.

Rolling the baby over is simplest. Place your warm hands along the baby's sides and roll her over onto her stomach. You don't need to worry about the head. It will follow of its own accord. While you're about it, remove the piece of terry towel you placed under the baby before you cleaned her.

Untie the sweater, roll the baby onto her back again and pull the sweater off. Wipe off the baby's throat with a washcloth dipped in clean water. Wash her face too. It freshens up little people, just as it does big ones. Start at the top and work your way down with the wrung out washcloth. There's really nothing to it. The baby will have time to close her eyes.

Her face can air dry, but the neck should be patted dry. Pay special attention to the various skin folds.

Now it's time to put the clean sweater on. Place three fingers in the little arm of the sweater and take hold of the baby's entire hand, thumb included. Work crosswise. You right hand, the baby's right hand. Your left, the baby's left. Pull the baby's arm through and pull the sweater up to the shoulder. The sweater's sleeves will be too long, so roll them up. Roll the front of the sweater up too, since it will now be resting against the baby's knees. Smooth everything out and pull the pants over the sweater all the way up to the baby's armpits.

Time to turn the little package over. When you roll her, grip both baby and clothing so that nothing gets crumpled. Tie the strings all the way into the cloth with firmly knotted bows. Smooth and fold up the back of the sweater too, and then hitch the pants all the way up the baby's back. Turn her over again.

Now take a cotton blanket and fold down a third of the blanket. Place the folded blanket over the baby's stomach up to the armpits so that a shorter segment is on one side and a longer segment is on the other. Lift the baby by her feet and slide the shorter end of the blanket under her back so that it sticks out on the other side. Pull it over the stomach and hold it flat with your hand under the rest of the blanket. Then wrap the longer side of the blanket around the baby so that it fits snugly. Now you have a sturdy little parcel that is easy to handle. The baby is securely swaddled. The snug fit evokes the cosy pressure of the womb. The baby will also stay warm.

You can also dispense with the swaddling and be content with wrapping the blanket loosely around your baby. Lay out the blanket diagonally, fold down one corner (for the head) and place the baby on the blanket. Then fold the bottom corner over the feet and the side corners over the baby's body. She will stay warm as long as you keep the blanket wrapped over her, but a swaddled baby is easier to handle than a loosely wrapped one – especially for an inexperienced parent.

Whichever option you choose, a cotton blanket should always be wrapped around a newborn as soon as she is taken out of her bed and always when she is eating.

It's difficult, not to say impossible, for babies this young to stay warm. Of course, with central heating, it is highly unlikely that a newborn would freeze to death, but the fact is that newborns who do freeze to death expire without even a whimper of protest. They expend so much energy staying warm, they don't have enough left over for crying. So do whatever you can to help them conserve their strength! The temperature inside the uterus was 37 degrees Celsius. Now it's suddenly fifteen degrees cooler. That is a significant difference. *Never forget the blanket!*

Pick up your little package and install yourself somewhere with your baby facing you, her head resting in your hands. It's called socializing, and it is something you can do with a little baby from her first hours on the planet (as long as her stomach is full and she is not plagued by survival anxiety).

Try to lock eyes with her. Widen your own eyes. Make sure light is falling on your face. Say something. A simple "hi" or "hello" will do. If you think you are being a little ridiculous, rest assured your baby doesn't. She will answer you! Look closely. Your baby's eyes will dart hither and thither, but sooner or later you will capture her gaze.

Newborns can see. They are short-sighted to be sure, but at distances of 20 centimeters they see just fine. And your instincts are not entirely dead, however civilized you are. Without knowing it, you have positioned yourself so that your face is exactly 20 centimeters from your baby's eyes.

Once you have captured her gaze, widen your eyes, smile and repeat your greeting. Ask a question. "What did you say?" for example. You will receive an answer. Without making a sound, the baby seems to be preparing to speak. The little tongue flutters in and out, and the lips open and close. The "words" are many and complex – and what tales a newborn has to tell! Look into her expressive eyes. This is an elevated conversation indeed. It is an *encounter*.

Socializing ends when the baby's back gets tired or when she seems discontent for some reason. Then it's time for a refill. This you offer from the other breast. And the milk flows generously. The baby will eat, and she will really perk up if she was about to drop off during the socializing. Fresh produce is on sale!

The routine is the same. Sit comfortably, let the baby eat in peace. Don't interrupt her. Nursing newborns are sensitive to jolts, so move cautiously, but there is no reason why you shouldn't walk around or reach for something while you breastfeed. The most important thing is to ensure that your nipple stays in the baby's mouth. You may have to be a bit of an acrobat under certain circumstances.

Coax her gently to take more when she looks like giving up. Withdraw your nipple a touch and wait for the reaction. If she releases her grip, keeps her eyes closed and clamps her mouth shut (which may have a sucking blister from all the effort), then she is probably done. Don't give up however. Draw your nipple back and forth over her mouth.

Now you can feast your eyes on a fascinating performance. She will look utterly disgusted, as though your breast were the most repulsive thing in the world. She looks about the way you would if you had just eaten a seven-course gourmet meal, and someone then tried to serve you a bowl of cold oatmeal. That is how a full little baby should look! And if she doesn't, a little extra should be served.

Then it's time for another burp. Some babies decide that this is an ideal opportunity to relieve the pressure and so fill the diapers. A downhill burp is as good as an uphill one. Just change her and put her to your breast again.

More often than not, however, your baby will be resting so comfortably against your shoulder that she will doze off. Wait for the burp. Give it a little push. Then put the baby to your breast one last time – the same one – for one last little top up. The icing on the cake, so to speak.

There is no point in putting a newborn down before she is already asleep. (Don't get the idea that this is permanent. From what I call the true birth and on, at about three weeks, the baby can and should go to asleep under her own steam, which means putting her down when she is still awake.)

If she happens to wake up and protest when you put her down, one last sip is in order. We are talking a miniscule amount, perhaps not even five grams, just two or three pulls at the breast. She will go out like a light and sleep like a log.

You may be wondering when you should use a pacifier.

A pacifier – which in my opinion should not be called a pacifier but rather a "suckifier" – can be very useful for newborn babies that have an exceptionally strong sucking need that can't be satisfied by nursing alone. These babies refuse to sleep after meals, even though they are full to bursting and utterly exhausted. The will suck if they have anything to suck on, but they will literally spit out the nipple if any milk flows. They can't take any more food aboard, but they still need to suck. Pacifiers should be used in such situations – but *only* in such situations.

Newborns can start to panic if they are hungry, and panic can get a foothold if you don't give them your breast quickly enough or the bottle isn't ready. Don't fall into the habit of stuffing a pacifier in your baby's mouth under such circumstances. Offer her the knuckle of your finger or your lower lip. Newborns are partial to both. It's warm flesh at least, not plastic or rubber.

Your baby needs to be kept very warm during the first two weeks of her young life. Wrap her in a cotton blanket, lay her on her side, and put a quilt over her. Curled up in the foetal position, she will feel snug and comfortable. Just pull the arm she's lying on out from under her. Place a rolled up blanket behind her back for support. This will also help you remember which side she last slept on, so you can alternate.

You can also place a newborn on her stomach, umbilical rubber band and all. Tuck the blanket around her securely, but don't put it under her tummy. Then place the quilt over her. Pull the blanket right up to her ears. The helpless little mite is not so helpless that she can't wriggle up to the end of the crib or the cradle, by which time the blanket or quilt will be around her waist. It's touching to see these little tadpoles scrunched up in the upper left hand corner of their vast beds.

Activate the breathing alarm. Say good night and leave the door ajar.

Stick to your normal routine. Don't take any special precautions as far as light and sound go. Telephones, TV sets, vacuum cleaners, doorbells, music – your baby has been hearing all theses things ever since her ears first developed in the womb. She is used to them. Hunger is what wakes her up, or rather the survival anxiety does, and this cannot be allayed by silence. So don't accustom your baby to a silence that is difficult if not impossible for the family to maintain. You are complicating your life for nothing.

Straighten up the change table, so you are ready for next time.

The whole meal with all its various points should have taken around one and a half hours. (She may not be able to manage more than an hour, newborn that she is, but you should have been able to keep her wide awake for at least that long.) All her worldly needs were satisfied, and that is the prerequisite for a good sleep, which will last for around two and a half hours.

If she sleeps for longer than that, you can pick her up anyway. Prepare her by caressing her over the head, wrap her securely in a blanket, and immediately put her to your breast to begin the next meal.

She will probably only sleep for two and a half hours, but at this very early stage she may sleep significantly longer. If you let her sleep until she wakes up, be ready to swing into action!

Day:
1. Nurse from one breast without interruption until the baby calls it quits. Burp.
2. Continue nursing from the same breast, patiently coaxing the baby to take more, until she can't manage another drop.

3. Change.

4. Conversation – encounter.

5. Refill from the other breast, again until the baby stops eating. Burp.

6. A last top up before bed, also from the other breast.

7. Sleep.

The guidelines are as follows: *a one-and-a-half-hour meal, a two-and-a-half-hour sleep.*

If you take care of the former, the baby will do her part and take care of the latter.

Freshly minted newborns are awake a little less and sleep a little more. (See "Sleep".)

In the evening, it's time for a major clean and change. (Babies should not bathe before the navel has healed completely, i.e. approximately three weeks after the umbilical stump has fallen off.) As a rule, cleaning and changing should take place after the first two rounds of food.

Undress the baby completely and cover her with the blanket you have been using during the day. (After the major clean and change, it will be time for a new one.)

Moisten a washcloth in lukewarm water. You won't need any soap. Start with the baby's face. The eyes may be a little grungy. Clean them carefully. Start from the outer eye corner and work your way in. Rinse and moisten the cloth again and wipe her face. Then clean behind her ears, under her chin and in all the folds in her neck. Pat her dry with a small towel. Then draw the warm damp cloth over her head and hair (if there is any). Dry and brush perhaps!

Wash her little tummy, her arms, her hands, between her fingers, and the folds in her palms. Here you can use a tiny bit of mild baby soap. Rinse with a wrung out cloth and pat dry.

Continue down to her groin area, legs and feet. Is there any fluff between her toes?

Turn her over and clean her back and bottom, the folds in the back of her neck and the back of her knees.

Turn her over again. Smear a little baby ointment in all her various skin folds. I usually pay special attention to the folds in a baby's arms, the folds in her hands, the skin behind her ears (it can get a little chapped), the folds in the back of her knees, the folds in her neck and the folds in her feet. I also rub a little ointment on her bottom, especially her buttocks and the folds in her groin.

Is one of the little nails hanging askew? Bite it off. Her nails are very soft, but they will harden if they are clipped, and newborns have a tendency to scratch themselves.

Dress her in a clean diaper and clean clothes. A tie up sweater, pants and socks, a long nightshirt or pajamas with feet, whatever you prefer. Wrap her in her blanket and swaddle her securely. Isn't she lovely?

Continue with the program. Give her your other breast, burp her, and then it's time to socialize. You may have to cut socializing a little short, since the evening hygiene operation takes some time, and the baby is probably starting to fade at this point. When she can't keep her eyes open any longer, give her a final swig from the same breast.

Now it's sleep time. Activate the alarm and leave the door ajar.

She will sleep but not all night. Popular times for babies to wake up seem to be around 1.00 and 4.00 a.m., so you can count on two nocturnal feedings.

During the night, you will want to cheat and that is totally permissible! You mark the difference between night and day by cutting down the program considerably. Instead of one and a half hours, you're shooting for twenty minutes. That's all it takes to feed the baby from one breast, burp her, change her diaper (if absolutely necessary), and give her a second round from the other breast, where the milk is flowing in rivers. Burp her again – and then back to sleep.

You've dispensed with the second round of food from the first breast, the conversation, and the diaper change (as long as the baby hasn't had a bowel movement). You can cheat with the night-feedings, as long as you have followed the instructions above for the daytime meals and spent the required amount of time with a wide-awake baby.

A little newborn can scream herself into a blind panic very quickly. Survival anxiety is pure torture. To avoid this, *the newborn baby should not have to wait a single minute for food.*

Not that long ago, new mothers were told to put their babies in a separate room, the idea being to give the moms the rest they so desperately needed. For the babies, however, this solution was disastrous. If no one hears a newborn baby scream or the response is delayed, the little one falls victim to an all-consuming anxiety, and it can take a long time to calm a hysterical infant.

So keep your newborn in your bedroom during the night so that you will hear her the first time she cries and you can feed her immediately. This will mean short and tranquil night feedings.

With days managed properly, the nights don't have to be difficult. Still, you will soon feel the effects of broken sleep. You may be tempted to feed your baby lying in bed, and with that comes the risk you might fall asleep before the baby does.

It is said that the maternal instinct prevents mothers from lying on their babies and smothering them, but it has happened. Not burping a baby also entails risk. If your baby ends up on her back and she spits up, she may choke on her own vomit. And newborns have been known to suffocate under parental quilts, again because they have ended up lying on their back.

If you find that you just can't stay awake, you can eliminate the risk of suffocation as follows:

Prop up your newborn beside you with a pillow behind her back. This is better than your arm, since you may move while you are asleep. Then fold your arm under your head with no pillow so that your breast is exposed to the baby and your head is leant back away from the child. Put your nipple in the baby's mouth. Finally, if you are lying on your right side, stretch your left leg backwards away from the baby and your other leg. You should feel as though you are about to tip over onto your back. The only thing that is holding you on your side is the baby at your breast. Both you and the baby are lying on a flat foundation. The baby has your pillow firmly behind her back, and you have space behind you to roll over onto your back. (Your husband will have to make way!) If you both fall asleep, you will wake up on your back, and your baby will wake up on her stomach with two pools under her: one under her diaper, which never was changed, and another under her face where she has had a spit up.

Still, this is not something I would recommend. Remember that your baby is not a stuffed animal that you take to bed for your own convenience. My advice is stay awake during (the short) nightfeedings. Both of you. It's worth it!

Night:
1. Nurse the baby the second she so much as peeps.
2. Burp.
3. A quick diaper change without a cleaning (unless something important has happened) and without talking.

4. A refill from the other breast.

5. Burp and back to sleep.

The program for feeding and care that I have outlined is something I call *The Standard Model*, and it is tried, tested and true. (For more information on The Standard Model, see "Food".)

The Standard Model satisfies all the little newborn's needs at every meal during the day, and her basic needs during the night. Let it be your guide! As time goes on, you will no doubt evolve your own model for caring for your child.

As far as changing and cleaning go, parents develop their own routines in a few weeks. Some change their babies on their knees, others on a change table or a bed. Kneeling and changing the baby on the floor is another option. Some mothers breastfeed sitting down, while others prefer to lie down. (All parents, however, carry their kids on their left side...)

You might find it odd, but I usually prepared a spot in the kitchen for diaper changes and cleaning. Access to water and a garbage bag is practical, and things can be hung from the handles of the upper row of cupboards. The bottom shelves of these cupboards can be used to store all the things you need to care for your baby, and the counter height is perfect.

Another reason I preferred the kitchen is because it is the heart of the household. Right from the start, your baby is where the action is.

On a cautionary note, don't assume that instant, endless love is a cast iron obligation. If love doesn't blossom immediately, you're in no way unnatural. People need time to get to know one another. Love at first sight isn't for everyone. Cultivate something else, something that is easier to wrap your mind around. Curiosity!

The baby you see in front of you is what you yourself once were. Every being of woman born was once this tiny, this helpless and this hungry. What you see is a little person that will follow the developmental path that human beings have been following through millions of years. The little tadpole that swam in the ocean of your womb will grow and change into an independent, thinking being that will walk upright. It will become *human*, a representative of the species that has made itself master (mistress if you prefer!) of the planet, or at least tried to. How did such a miracle happen?

You will be able to watch this miracle unfold in front of you. In so doing, you will learn a good deal not only about your child but also about the human race – and, last but not least, yourself. It will be an odyssey like no other.

If you are puzzling over what I have written about how to care for a baby – *why* I have suggested certain strategies and what to do if they don't work – you will find detailed discussions, theories, practical advice and instructions, and generally a wider context in Part two of *For the Love of Children*.

DAD

If there's a father in the picture, and he wants to be a part of his child's life, don't shut him out, but rather make him feel that he is part of the team!

Be prepared for the possibility that strange things may happen when you come home with the baby.

As a new mother, you may find yourself looking at your baby and feeling nothing but confusion, helplessness and a gnawing sense of inadequacy. But when the child's father comes running and wants to hold his daughter, you discover a territorial streak you never knew you had. You snatch the baby from him as though you were afraid he might abuse her (or at least drop her). Suddenly, you are a mother to the max.

Your own behavior may astonish you. Perhaps part of the explanation is that, as a new mother, you are reverting back to cavewoman days. Real men don't lounge around the house. They go out hunting and get their families something to live on!

Many women, all too often and too intensely, reject their babies' father, only to regret it bitterly later on.

You may also go too far in the other direction and convince yourself that just because the father doesn't instantly melt and tearfully embrace his little daughter, it means that he is not interested. Thus, what should be an idyllic family moment degenerates into kitchen sink melodrama with all the requisite wailing and gnashing of teeth. "You should have told me that you didn't *want* a child!"

Becoming a dad isn't easy (See "A Man Pregnant?"). If you are having trouble grasping the fact that you are now a mother, it's not that surprising that he is having a hard time wrapping his mind around fatherhood. The sight of this little stranger may well fill him with conflicting feelings – or simply no feelings at all.

You have a head start. This head start is indisputable for very tangible reasons. You have carried this child inside you for nine months and given birth to her. You are breast-feeding. You have a physical connection with your child that seems unbreakable to a third party. No matter how confused and inadequate you feel at the prospect of mothering this little being, everyone else, the father of the child included, regards you as the expert. You have all the answers and can draw on a reservoir of knowledge that sits in your bones.

Even if the father has been your most enthusiastic supporter all through the pregnancy and the delivery, he has been banished to the margins now.

Being deprived of a sex life doesn't make things any easier for him. You might not give sex so much as a passing thought at this point, but he does. He can't make love to you for what seems like an eternity. And whose fault is that? The child's of course. It's a situation that provides fertile soil for jealousy and other less than noble sentiments.

Try to build some bridges to minimize his feeling of being shunted aside. It's not easy, but it's worth the effort. Don't neglect him sexually! Naturally, you shouldn't do anything that you're not completely comfortable with, but every attempt to give him something that at least approaches a sex life, even if it's only in the form of affectionate physical proximity, will make it that much easier for him to bond with the baby.

As far as the baby is concerned, you must allow him to take care of the little one every now and then – and make it plain that you trust him to do a good job.

This sounds easy, but it's not. The remarkable thing about a baby's cries is that they are so much more audible and so much more heart-rending when someone other than you responds to them. In such situations, you are going to have to cultivate a little *sang froid*. You just have to turn a deaf ear to your child's cries and resist the temptation to ride to the rescue and take over from the father.

I can't stress this enough. Think about it. Imagine how you would feel if you were trying to screw up the courage to attempt something that you found exceptionally difficult. Finally, you decide you're ready to take the plunge. You're down in the trenches when someone barges in and tells you how useless you are and how much better everyone else could do it. What little self-confidence you had would drain through the soles of your shoes, never to return. You would give up on the whole enterprise – permanently.

In the beginning, caring for and socializing with a little baby is pure joy. You'll be reluctant to withdraw, shut the door and miss all the fun. But that is exactly what you have to do. Leave the father in peace with his child. He has to build a relationship with his newborn child all by himself. Don't be constantly looking over his shoulder and giving him a running commentary on everything he's doing. Nor should you look on in joyful silence savoring the sense of togetherness, no matter how good it feels. You'll just make him nervous. Close the door and disappear. The three of you will have lots of time together, never fear.

Bear in mind that the father is definitely on the outside looking in as far as breast-feeding goes. He can hardly be expected to have the self-confidence to take the baby from you as soon as the little one lets go of the nipple. So give the baby to him! If he looks dazed and confused, tell him that you just have to have a quick lie down while he changes the baby (or whatever needs doing) and leave the room before he has a chance to object.

You'll prick up your ears the second the baby makes a sound, and you'll find yourself standing at the door, fingers curled around the handle, ready to ride to the rescue. Resist the temptation!

It's true that you are the baby's mother. But he is the baby's father.

If you've ever been irritated by someone looking over your shoulder when you've been tending to the baby in your own inexperienced way, you'll know how he feels.

Naturally, this goes beyond a father's right to his child. You are not hanging back for altruistic reasons. You're investing in your own future. The father will not be able to take up the slack for you later on if you deny him access to the baby now. You won't be breast-feeding forever, and a division of labor will be essential at some point. So think ahead. You are not being kind when you turn your baby over to the dad. You're being smart.

Dad is perfectly capable of taking care of burping, changing and socializing. If he tries to wriggle out of it, citing your superior expertise, disappear on some errand or other, but *disappear*. The major hygiene operation in the evenings for example can be turned over to him.

Don't comment on his input. Neither praise nor criticism is required. Even if he's red-faced and sweaty, and the baby he turns over to you is both ill clad and ticked off, act as though everything is as it should be. No one ever learned how to do anything without practice. Ask questions if you like. "Was it fun?" "Did you have as much trouble getting the baby into her top as I did?" But don't comment and even more important, don't criticize.

Right from the get go, give him at least one session a day with the baby all to himself. Regularity gives rise to habit, and habits impose order on everyday life.

When the father has gotten used to being alone with his child for a certain period every day, the foundation for a priceless relationship will have been laid.

The baby will have gotten herself a dad.

GIVING BIRTH ALONE

When I write about the baby's father, the man who should be at your side through the pregnancy, the delivery, the preparations for and the care of a brand new life, memories well up, memories that I don't want to pass over in silence. These memories encompass everything from minutes to years when I have had to give birth to, care for and raise children all by myself.

More and more women have children alone and raise them alone. No matter how much a woman wants a child, she will inevitably suffer from a profound sense of abandonment that eats away at her determination, her joy and her expectations.

It seems to me that we women are hard-wired to need protection and support while we are pregnant and when we give birth. Once the baby is born, it is much easier for us to manage on our own.

If, however, we don't have a man around during the long wait, loneliness gets its claws into us with a vengeance. Even if we don't want anything to do with the baby's father as an individual, our need for love, tenderness and attention is so strong that being alone becomes sheer torture. We feel like abandoned children ourselves sometimes.

Joy can be fleeting, dreams shattered, a loving and loved spouse snatched from us in an instant. He will live on in his child, but nothing can fill the shrieking void he leaves behind him. All we can do is hope that friends and relatives will step into the breach as best they can for the sake of the life that will soon be among them.

Single parenthood can also be a conscious choice. In a spirit of courage and hope (or hopelessness), thousands of women opt not to have an abortion, even though they can't or won't live with the baby's father.

Children are born under the most varying circumstances, and for the most varying reasons. Children come into the world as a cure for loneliness and feelings of futility. Children are born out of a yearning for love. Children are born and proudly displayed as badges of defiant independence. Children are brought into the world to compensate for a loss, to heal the wounds inflicted by an unhappy love affair, to be a companion to a solitary sibling. Children are also born, it must be said, for no other reason than pure chance.

There is no point in moralizing over the whys and wherefores. Human beings are not rational, and in any case they are compelled by nature to propagate themselves. At the end of the day, what you are left with is a little person who needs looking after. The purgatory of loneliness has to be endured.

Any man who thinks that he is not needed at times like these can rest assured that even if he doesn't so much as lift a finger during the delivery, the void he leaves behind him, should he leave the mother for only five minutes, is well nigh unbearable.

Giving birth alone is doable. Taking your baby home and caring for the child by yourself is doable. Being a single mother is doable. But it's not easy. No matter how much you want this child or how determined you are to raise it alone, you have chosen a road that is hardly strewn with roses.

If you're alone, it's a sad but inescapable truth that loneliness does not always confer strength. Loneliness does not always confer wisdom. Loneliness is, some days and some nights, despair. There's no getting away from it.

If you have decided to have a child on your own and you are resolved to stand by your decision, don't allow your despair to be tinged with regret. Give despair the space it needs. Your child will come into this world and she, or he, will come to you. With your child you will forge a bond far deeper than anything you long for or agonize over now.

There was a time when women who wanted a child more than anything had to accept a loveless marriage to fulfill their dreams. Other women had to accept remaining childless their whole lives because they never got married. Today this problem doesn't exist. Single mothers are not only accepted, they are socially respectable. Their children are not condemned and are given the same opportunities as other children. Children no longer have to suffer at school because they are fatherless. Nor do unmarried mothers have to suffer society's scorn – which is no mean accomplishment considering the not too distant past.

Such changes in attitude were not the result of humanitarian impulses but rather a changing social structure. Women work alongside men these days. As women gained access to the job market, they were freed from the oppression that had its roots in economic dependence on men, a dependence whose symbolic language permeated every aspect of existence and made the subjection of women a moral imperative.

Men can't bear children; women can. In the 21st century this ability is a strength, not a weakness.

Nevertheless, while this strength will carry you through your loneliness, it will not enable you to soar above it. What's most soul-destroying about loneliness is the bitter conviction that the way things are now is the way they will always be. I will never escape this isolation, you may think. And the baby will lock me in rather than set me free. But it's not true. You will see. To everything there is a season. None of what weighs so heavily on your heart now is forever.

I have been alone for three of my deliveries, one of my pregnancies, and, as far as the day-to-day grind of rearing children goes, I've had to fend for myself for many years. I have some bad memories, but I wouldn't want to be without them. They make the joy I take in my children that much more intense. Light is so much brighter when you step into it from the shadows.

What I found difficult was not being alone with the responsibility. What really hurt was being alone with the happiness. Having no one beside me to hear my child say her first words, to watch her take her first wobbly steps, to see her stretch out her little arms for her first hug, that was when loneliness cut the deepest. I ached not only for myself but also for my child. I couldn't turn to anyone and say, "Did you see that? Did you hear that? Look what she can do!"

I have missed out on the kind of happiness that's shared, which is the true kind. But loneliness also made me strong.

A profound and humble strength is born in anyone who must raise a child alone.

PART
TWO

Infant care.
Thoughts, theories and practice

INTRODUCTION: THE BEST LAID PLANS...

A mother:

"We dreamed about this baby for so long. We were over the moon when we found out that she was on the way. But all that happiness, all those joyous expectations turned into something that can be summed up in one word: hell."

A father:

"I'm going crazy. I don't know what to do. Every night is a descent into the inferno. Our every waking moment revolves around this baby. We have no time left over for each other or anything else. The worst of it is that our relationship is starting to fall apart. We just can't take the stress. We were talking about having two maybe three children, but now it looks as though we are heading for divorce court."

Love demands children. The human species wants to survive. In what is perhaps the best of all worlds, the Swedish welfare state, it is not uncommon to hear people describe being blessed with children as *hell*. How did we get here?

After the Second World War, sheltered Sweden, my home country, was gripped by gold fever. We found an insatiable market for our products in war ravaged Europe, and the money flowed in. We had it made in the shade. We bought houses and cars like there was no tomorrow. The future looked so bright it burned our eyes. We fantasized about moving pavements and private helicopters. We were rich. In fact, for one brief shining moment, Sweden was the richest country on the planet.

Women, who more or less willingly stayed home and took care of kids and old people, were called the invisible workforce. In this brave and affluent new world, however, they were to be put to work. Operation Slander was

87

initiated. Since the blessings of conspicuous consumption were deemed wanting – housewives managed family finances and households as they had always done, and there was a general perception that mothers were needed at home as long as the children were young – women who worked in the home were informed that they were social parasites. They were inadequate and blinkered (a popular expression in the sixties), stupid to put it bluntly, and to add insult to injury, they were also told that they were disloyal. Then came the coup de grace; they were told they were damaging their children, who, since they were exposed to their dull-witted mothers all day long, would grow up to be mentally deficient.

Operation Slander was a resounding success. Housewives lost their self-confidence. Willing or not, they were forced out into the job market to "realize themselves", which, for example, they would do on an assembly line or behind a cash register.

We became a materialistic people. Big Brother kept a watchful eye on us. He saw to it that we consumed more and more with each year that passed. Large parts of the country's productive capacity became ends in themselves. Few people had the time or the strength to question the status quo.

In the name of such lofty goals as time-saving and convenience, leisure and efficiency, Big Brother established a food industry that provided people with expensive, ready-to-eat food, concrete ghettos located close to the assembly lines and a network of institutions that took over more and more of the family's functions. School became a combination of educational institution and home with staff on hand to resolve diverse problems that mothers and fathers didn't have the time or the strength to cope with. Day care centers and aged care facilities were built so that children and old people could be warehoused on an industrial scale. The family was on the verge of extinction. It simply wasn't needed anymore.

With women becoming economically independent, men's stranglehold on power was broken. People divorced and lived "free". Swedish sin became renowned all over the world.

For children, the twentieth century was going to be the century of liberation. Child labor was abolished. Childhood became a concept. The cult of the teenager flourished. The decade of the 1950's was a golden time. Life was good, even in the shadow of the Cold War, and it was heaven to be young. The connection between past and future was broken, and all that mattered was the here and now. And Big Brother sat in his treasury counting his money.

As wealth and power increased, a new ailment spread throughout the land: loneliness. People had been cut loose from their roots to become cogs in a large-scale, centralized production machine. Clans and families had been shattered. The symptoms of underlying insecurity were obvious for those with eyes to see. Young people, having been left to raise each other, formed gangs, and substance abuse problems increased exponentially. Social workers and psychologists sprang up like dandelions. The ranks of the walking wounded swelled.

Big Brother was in denial for a long time. If there was something amiss, it must be *people* that were defective, not the brave new world that had been built! Every family has its black sheep, and Big Brother made sure that the marginalized had decent lives. But when children and adolescents began to lose their zest for life, or, even worse, rebel to the point where they refused to be inducted into the system, there were storm clouds on the horizon. Then Big Brother reacted, for that meant that the Holy Grail of economic growth and all the power that went with it was in danger.

At this point, Big Brother began to behave like any bad workman. He blamed his tools. "It's your fault!" Big Brother screamed at parents. He conveniently forgot that he was the one who had made it impossible for families to function as families.

His subsequent sermon was a thinly disguised guilt trip. Parents must pay a lot more attention to their children. They have to get involved! Parenting courses should be mandatory. "You have to be *taught* how to look after your children!" Big Brother thundered.

And his sermons have had the desired effect. There are very few parents today who are not plagued by their consciences. If you don't worry enough, you don't love... Big Brother's soaring evangel felt more like the shackles of guilt than the wings of love, and we have reason to ask why.

What was it that enabled people without specialized training to take care of their children perfectly adequately in the past? Or were parents incompetent before the truth was finally revealed to us after centuries of hypocrisy?

Over the last few decades, we have become more and more aware about childhood's importance. We have all become armchair psychologists. A ban on corporal punishment is enshrined in law, and children have every conceivable material advantage. Shouldn't children be a little happier than they used to be? Have they become happier at all? Shouldn't they at least look a little more cheerful than kids in countries where people barely have roofs over their heads and know nothing of child psychology?

What if going to parenting classes and becoming more involved in our children's lives makes not one iota of difference?

That is the problem that Big Brother, the Swedish welfare state and the entire industrialized world are facing.

A human being, big or small, has to be needed.

Being needed emotionally is not the only or even the most important part of being needed. Being needed means having a task to do. It means being part of a context. It means having a function to fulfil. It means making a contribution that benefits someone else. It means being able to say to yourself *"the others wouldn't manage as well without me"* and know it.

Anyone who is not needed practically and demonstrably will not be able to find anything but superficial meaning in life. Love can make meaninglessness easier to bear, but it can't – at least for long – compensate for it. If you were surrounded by people who hugged you, listened to you, caressed you and assured you, day in and day out, that they loved you, it would not be enough. You probably wouldn't even believe them. You have to be able to point to an accomplishment, large or small, important or relatively insignificant, and it has to be something that goes beyond you. "I'm needed. I'm part of a community and I make a contribution. The others wouldn't manage as well without me, regardless of whether they love me or not!"

Children, like old people, are not needed in a society in which the family has been separated from production. The old have been around too long to contribute to the productive process, and children haven't been around for long enough.

Every day, a child tries to commit suicide in Sweden. Every week, one of them succeeds. Is it a lack of love that causes these children to die by their own hands? There are of course no simple answers, but I think the most plausible explanation is *meaninglessness*.

Big Brother's evangel of love drips with guilt and smells of compensation. In the name of short-term profit, he has created a society where children are not needed and cannot be needed.

For example, if a couple of children are unable to come to day care because of illness, how do the staff react? "Good. Two less to worry about!" Their reaction doesn't make them bad people or even bad caregivers. It simply shows that the children aren't needed at the day care center. If they were needed, the reaction would be the opposite. "How are we going to get through the day with two of them absent?" Thus, *the others wouldn't manage as well without me*, is not something that these kids can say to themselves. Children have fun at daycare to be sure – but that is not the same as being needed.

In the industrialized world, a concept of childhood unique in human history has seen the light of day: *Adults make guest appearances in their children's worlds when they can or want to, instead of inducting their children into the adult world when their children can or want to.* This is tantamount to putting the world through the looking glass. Everything is backwards.

Let's go back to the desperate mother and father who were suffering through the "hell" of parenthood.

Every parent of an infant who has read up on child psychology and who gives the baby love and comfort twenty-four hours a day with endless patience knows that something is wrong. Instead of being serenely content, the baby becomes more and more persistent in her protests. The result is mounting problems instead of the peace that everyone hoped would descend on the household.

What are the poor parents doing – or not doing – that makes their baby so obviously dissatisfied?

They have taken advantage of their parental leaves to stay home and provide care for their child. In so doing, they effectively withdraw from their daily lives. They are at home for their child, and only for their child. The child is thus not inducted into a pre-existing social context, a pre-existing reality if you will. Instead, it is the child herself that constitutes reality. The child becomes the center of the universe, and the parents' lives revolve around her. This is how a "child world" is constructed within the walls of the home. The adults who spend their days in this world don't do so because it is necessary *for them*, by which I mean necessary for their survival. They are only there because they have had a child. And that is a situation no child can accept.

The best laid plans… Parental leave set the stage for excluding children from social participation. This exclusion continues at the day care center, which is little more than a glorified nursery, and at primary school, which is little more than a glorified day care center. Impenetrable barriers are set up between various categories of people. Children and the elderly are slotted into their respective pigeon-holes. Only adults in their productive years are allowed into the real world, where society's continued existence is ensured.

When production is separated from the family, adults have to make guest appearances in a child world, which exists outside the community, divorced from the struggle for survival. The looking-glass world becomes the real one. Mutual insecurity is the result. For a child, this can be catastrophic. Meaninglessness looms large. "I'm not needed. Everyone would manage just as well without me. Maybe they would even manage better."

If the despairing parents had something to occupy them during their parental leave that was necessary *for them*, something that set prerequisites for survival that everyone, the child included, had to accept, they would soon be liberated from the "hell" in which they were languishing. Not that long ago, parents who had seven other children, eighteen cows that needed milking and fields that had to be ploughed probably didn't complain of having to live through hell just because another baby was born. And whatever else their children might have suffered from, it wasn't a sense of meaninglessness.

The fact that today's parents don't know how to handle their infants and young children – problems with food, sleep and activities are enormous – doesn't mean that the parents are stupid or uninvolved, or that they need parenting courses. It means that the very foundation for human relationships has been undermined.

The fault doesn't lie with the people, Big Brother! It lies with the Brave New World that has stifled one of humankind's basic needs: the need for social participation in the daily collective struggle for survival. The human ecosystem has been thrown off balance. Nature has taken a back seat to profit – with obvious results.

Few significant social changes come from above. The most important changes come from below through the struggles of ordinary people. We can't expect a top-down revolution that will make children happy and easy to manage. We can, however, refuse to put child-phobic attitudes into practice in our everyday lives, attitudes that preserve and justify the exclusion of children from social participation.

This exclusion is a reality even in the home. If we need our children and make use of them according to their growing abilities, we will slowly but surely change a societal structure that is already crumbling.

Let's see how a little two-year-old wages *his* revolutionary struggle! Mom is trying to prepare a meal. Little Michael is clingy and wants to be carried. He stands amid a sea of toys, none of which interest him. He cries and whines and screams. Mom sighs and curses and finally starts to cry herself because it all seems so hopeless and she can't get anything done.

But then she resolutely lifts the boy up and puts him on the counter beside the stove. She gives him a sausage, holds out the frying pan and asks Michael to put the sausage in the pan. Michael does so, and Mom thanks him so very much for his help.

The effect is dramatic. Michael is pure sunshine. He looks at his mother triumphantly. "You see?" he would say if he could. "I'm needed. Without me you wouldn't ever be able to make dinner."

That's all it takes. It's as simple as that to enable Michael to feel that he is engaged in social participation, to realize his true worth, to make a contribution and thereby experience the satisfaction of being needed. He has done something that was necessary for other people and the struggle for survival the flock is engaged in. And now he can take a rest, kick back and relax for a while. *Now* he can contentedly play with his toys. He is on his own time!

This isn't complicated. The principle is as old as humanity itself: let the kids be part of the team! People have always gotten to know each other, benefited from each other, needed each other – even come to love each other – by working side by side.

Parents who go through "hell" with their infants and young children do so because they are giving their kids love and attention *instead of* social participation, rather than in addition to it. Their daily lives are not governed by conditions that pre-date the birth of their children and which should be all-encompassing. Children desperately seek clues about their parents' everyday lives. They want to understand it and be a part of it. The parents, however, persist in trying to demonstrate that everyday life – the struggle for survival – doesn't exist. "The only reason we are here is that you were born," is the message.

Just as Michael isn't satisfied (for very long anyway), no matter how many toys he is showered with or how willing Mom is to get down on the floor and play trains with him, so an infant isn't satisfied with being given more "love", hyper-attention, and comforting, being lugged around in a snugly, or being subjected to yet more symbiotic emotional bonding. Naturally, the answer is not indifference. But *children must be offered a place in the reality that the adults are involved with* and gradually, according to the children's wants and increasing ability, be made useful – needed – there. This is perfectly feasible – at least on a small scale in the home.

Thus can the revolution come from below with the help of those who are already waging a never-ending struggle: the children themselves.

This great social revolution doesn't force women back to the kitchen. Nor does it drive them out into the labor force without their children. It gives work back to the family. The whole family.

CARING FOR A NEWBORN

In Part one of *For the Love of Children* I gave you a brief introduction to primary care for a newborn.

Saying "Do it this way!" is simple enough. Common decency demands that I also tell you *why* it's appropriate to do this or that and what will happen if you do not do this or that, and so on. In Part Two, I am going to underpin my advice with theory, first hand accounts and examples. We will also take a look at the various problems that may crop up, what causes them, and how they can be remedied.

In the introductory chapter, "The best laid plans..." I tried to provide the socio-political background to why you, fresh from the hospital and on your own with your child, might have this vague feeling that endless love is demanded of you. (Dad will have to excuse me if I conjure him away – even though it is perfectly possible that it is a father, on his own with his child, who is reading these words.) You may believe that this little person's well-being somehow depends on your ability to give love. You may well be plagued by the fear that you don't have enough love to give. Perhaps you are terrified of not measuring up, of not being good enough. Since you are on parental leave, you have all the time in the world, and you are prepared to give your child all the time in the world – and all the love, comfort and care in the world, twenty-four hours a day, seven days a week. But you're scared anyway. Although your career as a parent has barely begun, you may already suspect that you are inadequate.

In the introductory chapter, I wanted to lay the guilt-laden love evangel to rest. This evangel offers love *instead of* social participation. It is a compensatory love, a love that says, "You can't be a part of my real life, but I'll love you to bits in my spare time."

When I use the phrase real life, I mean the collective struggle for survival, the struggle that all the members of the flock (you, your child, the family, the group) are engaged in but from which the child will be excluded. During your parental leave, you yourself are excluded from your own social participation, to which you will one day return – without your child. What I am trying to convey is that much of your feelings of inadequacy and fear stems from a gut instinct that this is wrong.

This is why the first commandment of good infant care is that you convince yourself and your baby that you are home because it is *necessary for you*. You are home because the struggle for survival demands it, not because you have a child. This may seem like a paradox, but if you look within yourself, I think you will see what I mean. You would not want people to devote all their time to you simply because you existed.

We won't worry about all this prematurely! You have had a child, and ahead of you is a time when this child will be inducted into the world, so you *should* put her or him at the center of things. Savor the experience and let everything else take a back seat. I refer to this time as the honeymoon and with good reason, as I think you will see!

What I am trying to coax you into is a resolute, de-dramatized, safe and sensible program of infant care that is free from the frenetic demand for love, which is not the socio-political panacea it is cracked up to be.

First of all, bear in mind that your baby is not a critic. This child has come to you to live and learn, not to judge you.

Even if you had never seen an infant before, you would know that food is what she or he needs above all else. You have instincts that civilization has not quite managed to stifle.

You have no doubt seen a bird's nest full of cheeping little chicks. The parents slave away to keep them supplied with food. The chicks barely swallow the food before they start to cry again, and there is real anxiety in those cries. It's survival anxiety.

Perhaps you have happened on a kitten that has been abandoned by its mother or separated from her. You wouldn't try to play or cuddle with this kitten before giving her a little milk, served in a doll's bottle perhaps. Nor would you put this kitten against your cheek and go to great lengths to comfort it. This is about life and death. The kitten has to be fed.

A newborn human is also ridden by survival anxiety, and nothing will allay this anxiety except food. No matter how much you comfort, rock, lull and cuddle, it will be to no avail. The child needs food before she or he can appreciate the other good things life has to offer.

You have a tremendous advantage. You can give your child food. You can allay the anxiety. Even if your breasts run dry or you happen to be a man, you can give your child food, as much as she or he wants, and in so doing guarantee your child's survival. Not all parents in this world have that luxury.

It is impossible to give a newborn too much to eat. Whatever you hear to the contrary, I beseech you not to believe it – in order to spare your baby survival anxiety.

Put yourself in your baby's place. If you were on the verge of starvation – and a newborn that has been expelled from the womb because the food supply has been cut off *is* on the verge of starvation – you would devote your every waking moment to figuring out how you could get hold of something to eat. The instinct to survive is the strongest instinct we have. Imagine you are hungry; if the larder is empty, you have no money to buy food with, and there is nothing but dust on the shelves at the grocery store anyway, believe me, you are hardly going to be interested in love, affection, clean clothes and tender words. Life has been reduced to physical survival, and that is as real as anything ever gets. You wouldn't be able to think about anything but food. And once you found it and you were certain that you would make it through *this* day, your thoughts would immediately turn to how you were going get enough food to make it through the next. Until survival is guaranteed, it's impossible to relax. It's impossible to think about anything else.

That is the kind of anxiety your little newborn has to contend with. "Will I survive, or won't I? If I do, for how long? There's food for the moment, but then what?"

Your first task as a mother or father to this baby is to allay that anxiety. Through your actions you say, "Yes, you are going to survive. I will make sure of that. You need have no fears on that score." And there is only one way to drive that message home: Food, food and more food. You would not want – or even tolerate – comforting small talk if famine was staring you in the face and you were frantically searching for food. Your newborn feels the same way. The little one will in no way benefit from being carried and comforted if survival anxiety is tearing her apart. She needs food, as much as she can possibly eat and then some, and she needs it immediately. *Then* there will be time for everything else.

This may seem obvious, but that doesn't mean that numerous sins aren't committed in this particular area. Cries of survival anxiety are misinterpreted. Babies are slapped with labels like "colic" or "lactose intolerant", or whatever the flavor of the month is. Such diagnoses are an insult to nature! They result in a baby being given water or medicine instead of food, a diet as frustrating as it is lacking in nutrients, and this in turn leads to a dramatic increase in anxiety.

It is also suggested in certain quarters that a baby should be changed before the meal, so she can fall asleep in peace afterwards. Changing a hungry baby, however, means waiting, crying and intensified anxiety, which can be a nightmare for both child and caregiver. When the change is complete, the baby has given up hope of ever getting fed. She is beyond anxiety. She attacks the breast and gulps down the milk as though her life depended on it, which of course it does. She swallows air along with the milk and so gets full too quickly.

She sleeps the sleep of the just, exhausted as she is – but she is awake again soon enough. She was never really full, and even more important, she wasn't at all convinced that she wouldn't starve to death at a moment's notice. And you, her caregiver, stand by helplessly, wondering whether she can really be hungry again, since she ate not half an hour ago. So you pick her up and try to comfort her. The baby then dares think that she might actually get food – but doesn't. Despair returns with a vengeance. Finally, the anxiety becomes too much to bear, and she slips mercifully into unconsciousness, only to awaken again as soon as she is put to bed. Hope is abandoned.

This is how real colic can come about in only a couple of days. Survival anxiety that is never allayed can soon morph into physical symptoms, and real stomach problems are the result. On the bright side, even an advanced case of so-called colic can be cured as soon as survival anxiety is allayed. (We'll come back to this in "If something goes wrong: Colic?")

Beyond the need for food, which stands for survival, and a good sound sleep of course, a newborn has the same basic human needs as the rest of us. These needs include belonging somewhere, security, bodily care, social participation and happiness.

Three things that do not appear on the list are love, comfort and silence. Let's begin with them:

• *Love* comes in its own time. It isn't delivered to your door ready to be unpacked, assembled and placed in your arms. It grows out of a shared life and out of a sense of belonging, and eventually out of a community where everyone works side by side. Liberate yourself from the demand for love! It is not *the child* that places this demand on you. Love will come when it comes. Nature has made your baby irresistible anyway. Love is not a competition, and in my opinion it's dangerous to turn it into one.

Allaying survival anxiety is the goal, not only so the child can enjoy the good things in life but so you can too. If your child cannot accept your love – and until she gets full, she can't, anymore than our kitten could play – there is a risk that the demand to love her that you place on yourself will turn into rejection, not to say hate.

• Let's ponder *comfort* for a moment. What exactly does an infant need to be comforted for? Why should she be so unhappy? Was she born unhappy? Have human beings outlived countless other species just so they can be miserable? Have they refused to die out because life is a drag? Does your baby *want* to live because she is sad, weak and tormented? Does she cling to life because she is forced to?

I believe that human beings live because they have a lust for life. Think about it! Once you stop assuming that your baby is in constant need of comfort, you will also stop assuming that she is unhappy every time she cries. You will come to regard her crying as a question, a question that you are there to answer. "Will I starve to death?" – "No, you won't." – "Will I survive?"- "Yes, you will." And since words don't mean much to little people, you will express yourself through your actions. Armed with this attitude, you will be able to stop worrying about whether you are a good mother or a good father, and whether your child likes you or not. *Every child's every cry is a question, and it is the duty of the caregiver to provide an answer.*

• Finally, *silence* is the product of anxiety and insecurity that no one, your baby least of all, will benefit from. It's consideration that is required, not silence. You would not of course expose your child to harsh sounds, any more than you would shine a bright light in her face. But you wouldn't do those things to an adult either.

I hope some of your fears – "do I love enough, do I comfort enough, and am I quiet enough when my baby is asleep?" – have been laid to rest. Free from such fears, you will see that looking after an infant really isn't that hard!

Your newborn's needs are few, clear and easy to fulfil.

• First comes the need for food. Food, food and more food, and then some.

• Then comes the need for *belonging,* which is there already. All you have to do is confirm it. It is you and the father who are responsible for the baby's survival, and she has an innate trust in you both. The imprinting process is in full swing. Her trust doesn't need to be built from scratch. The foundation is already there.

You fulfil this need to belong by being available for your baby in the form of a fixed point (the flock, the home), by not shutting her out, by not abandoning her, by not leaving her to her own helplessness. Survival depends on belonging somewhere, and this is something your baby knows instinctively. You also need to belong; you need a place to call home and people to call your own. The concept of *a fixed point* is an important one. Without a fixed point you would feel pretty helpless, even if, as an adult, you could physically survive. This fixed point is not only a person. It is also a home, a place on earth where there is always a rightful spot for you. I try to cover all these things with the concept of *the flock*.

Your baby is made of the same stuff you are.

• *Security* stands for leadership, answers, order and conviction. A newborn is helpless in the sense that she cannot acquire food for herself, but she is also helpless in the sense that she is totally defenceless. She wouldn't last very long among wild animals no matter how full her stomach was. The security you envelop her with will show her that she can rest easy, that she is protected from danger, that she is part of a flock that will stand guard over her twenty-four hours a day until she can manage on her own.

If she is to believe that the wolf won't come for her at any moment, you must convey an impression of complete confidence. Everything is in order. You know exactly what is going on. You are always on high alert, you foresee everything, and you take the necessary precautions. Nothing gets in under your radar. She will feel at ease because you do and because you are her guide. You know what it takes to survive in this world.

All this may require considerable acting talent, but it is worth the effort! If you have had a wild argument with your child's father, or you are in the middle of a vitriolic telephone conversation, or you are in the midst of a major depression when your baby wakes up and needs to eat, you will have to bring the curtain down on your own problems. It will be many years before your child is able to cope with your anxieties, insecurities, hesitation and despair without sensing danger. Take a couple of deep breaths, tap into your reserves of confidence, force yourself to smile and go into your baby. The more confidence you can muster, the calmer your child will be. That is what security means: the conviction that no danger threatens.

• *Bodily care* will be discussed later. We touched upon it in Part one of *For the Love of Children* (see "What do you do?").

• *Social participation* is another concept we will come back to and discuss in depth.

• Finally, *joy* is something that has been drowned in the chorus of complaints about how difficult children are. Not too long ago, people would say to their children: "You are punishment for my sins." Nowadays the refrain has become: "You are always in the way." (If you think for a moment that I am putting the blame on the parents, read "The best laid plans...".) Little children should be enjoyed, and once you have the hang of caring for them, the order of the day being food, food and more food, then life is pure joy. The icing on the cake is that your baby thinks so too.

Human beings love life. They love life because they think life is fun, exciting, fascinating, challenging, glorious, fruitful, and grand. Young children smile, regardless of whether anyone takes the trouble to coax a smile out of them. Young children smile because they genuinely love life. Once survival anxiety is allayed, the joy will come, along with the curiosity and the playfulness. Kids aren't that different from kittens.

Newborns need their joy confirmed. Otherwise, it may wither and die. So, *always smile when you lock eyes with a newborn*! Perhaps a little bit of acting talent is required here too. You might not feel you always have the strength to be happy. But can you really say with your hand over your heart that you don't live because you love life?

It's not me asking the question. It's your baby, a human being just like you!

FOOD

Food stands for survival. You have the food, so you stand for survival – literally. One of these days, your newborn will realize that *you* are the larder because you are the one with breasts! This is where every mother has an unassailable advantage: her breast status.

Consequently, you are going to feel like a larder on legs for the next little while. It is by no means a given that you will always think this is particularly desirable. Instead of your breasts being appendages attached to you, you are an appendage attached to your breasts. You are a means to an end. Who you are, what you feel, and your spiritual aspirations are of no consequence. You are a milk machine. Your existence is going to revolve around two things: your breasts and your baby. You might as well get used to it!

I usually regard the first two months after the birth as an extension of the pregnancy. This is a practical way of looking at things, since it will prevent you from falling into the trap of believing that things will always be this way.

It will take about two months for breastfeeding to function problem free (if problems occur at all, which is by no means certain). It will take about two months for vaginal discharges to disappear completely. It will take about two months before you are healed completely and can resume your sex life. It will take about two months for your body to resume proportions that you vaguely recognize and for you to feel more or less like a human being again psychologically after the experience of delivery. Last but not least, it will take about two months before you put together a timetable for the care of your child, which will give your daily existence a degree of predictability and thus create opportunities for other activities.

The two-month mark is significant for the baby too. By this time your newborn has come to terms with a good deal that has hitherto been a complete mystery to her. She has come to terms with her bodily functions – or at least she is used to them. She has been given all the food she needs and then some, so, since her survival anxiety has been stilled, she dares believe that she will make it though the day. She is beginning to treat herself to the good things in life, and she allows herself to be inducted into your daily existence under the conditions that you (the flock) operate under.

But the road can be long and winding sometimes. So that you can take each day as it comes without being constantly afraid that problems are just around the corner, it helps to view this time as an extension of your pregnancy.

This will also help you to allow the first month to be a true honeymoon, full of delight.

Your little newborn has come into what is perhaps the best of all possible worlds. She doesn't know that. She has no idea that the food supply is endless (at least for now). She is quite unaware that there is a vast social welfare apparatus ready to crank into gear to guarantee her right to live. She only knows that she has to survive at any price – and that her chances of getting food herself are non-existent.

As you will see, a direct line between your baby and your breasts is being set up. If the baby cries, the milk will start to flow, regardless of the fact that you each happen to be at opposite ends of the house. In a few weeks, you, or rather your breasts, will be working to a timetable. If you are away from your baby, your breasts will assume that you are going to nurse, since a certain amount of time has passed since the last feeding. The fact that you have pumped out your breasts thoroughly and there is a bottle of breast milk at home in the fridge is beside the point. Your breasts are what define you. The rest of you is just along for the ride.

Just as your body and uterus took care of the baby from conception to delivery, your breasts are prepared to take care of providing nourishment. The principle is simple. Your breasts produce nourishment ideally suited to your baby in the form of milk that has to be sucked out. The baby, for her part, comes equipped with a strong urge to suck. She will suck on everything, knuckles, lips, earlobes… And a newborn sucks hard. It is not simply a question of sucking the milk into her mouth; she has to suck it out of you too.

Your milk won't run in a steady stream during meals. It will come in fits and starts. At first it will flow in rivers, and the baby will swallow for all she is worth. She will gurgle lustily, and she will look almost ecstatic over all the manna that is raining down from heaven or rather flowing out of your breast. Then suddenly the flow stops. The baby will persevere but get nothing for her trouble. Eventually, the flow will restart, and the baby will again swallow at regular intervals. When the breast is nearly empty, the baby will suck out the richest milk.

The uneven, intermittent flow leads many to believe that the first round of milk – which takes a newborn about five minutes to extract – is sufficient and that from then on the baby is just nursing for fun. Nothing in my experience bears this out. The meal should not be interrupted. The baby should continue to suck until she has another round of food under her belt, which she needs.

You can count on the baby taking at least twenty minutes to eat her fill. After she has been burped, give her the same breast for a little while longer. Finally, give her a top up from breast number two. If, after this final round, she wants to nurse just for fun, by all means let her! Your baby suffers from the same survival anxiety that afflicted our little chicks crying for food in the nest. Your child's life hangs by the same fragile thread. By feeding her, you don't only keep her alive, you also allay her survival anxiety.

When she has done eating, she should be full to overflowing in every sense of the word.

If you break down your own meals into their component parts – and you know you are going to survive – they would probably look something like this: You eat the first portion because you are hungry. The second portion you eat to build up a little reserve, since it will be a while until the next meal. The third portion – a decadent dessert perhaps – you eat for purely sensual reasons. It just feels good. A baby's meals follow exactly the same principle.

The milk supply doesn't keep up with demand, any more than it flows at an even pace. Just as the baby has to suck out a new round of milk when the first has run its course, so must she call forth an increased overall supply as she gets bigger. And there's a time lag. You can expect three adjustment periods, and these periods can be critical. It takes time for your breasts to reach optimal production.

These adjustment periods don't have to be problematic. You may not even notice them. But if you do, don't think your career as a mom is over. Just let the baby keep on sucking! The worst thing that can happen is that you might have to give her a little formula to make up for the shortfall. Your baby's welfare comes first, and breastfeeding is not a competitive sport.

The first period starts about a week after birth. You should prepare yourself to sit (or lie) for fairly long periods, while the baby eats her fill.

The usual explanation for the drop in milk production – which actually isn't a drop at all but rather a time lag while supply cranks up to meet increased demand – is that the mother's body is out of sync because of all the changes involved in coming home, the responsibility of becoming a mother and so on. Now it is perfectly true that it is only when a new mother arrives home that she realizes that she does in fact have a child. However, I think it is unfortunate that people assume that this adjustment period bodes ill for a mother's ability to breastfeed. This creates anxiety. A new mother worries enough as it is. When her breasts don't produce enough milk to keep up with her child's increasing needs, she is likely to conclude that she isn't good enough to breastfeed because she is mentally unstable, has problems (who doesn't?) and is generally a lousy mother. A mom who can't even feed her baby...

If you are plagued by such doubts, think of all the mothers in countries where wars rage, famine is a part of daily life, and people believe they won't live long enough to see the next sunrise. Do you think these mothers can breastfeed their infants? Your sisters in these far off lands have probably never heard of the "expulsion reflex". There is no earthly reason why you should pay any attention to such things either.

The second period begins about three weeks after the birth. The meals will again be rather long and will require their share of sweat and endurance from both mother and child. Try not to despair if the milk is a long time coming. Instead, admire your feisty little baby who is doing her utmost to persuade your rather conservative breasts that the times they are a-changin'!

If your baby wakes up after only a very short snooze and wants to eat again, let her. She didn't get enough food, even if she nursed for an hour or an hour and a half. The reason she didn't get enough is that supplies ran out. But this is temporary. As early as the next day, the milk may start to flow again – and in record quantities. And once the milk factory ups production, the portions will be generous and dependable.

At the baby's age of seven or eight weeks, however, they won't be sufficient because you will be into the third adjustment period. Once you get through this, you can relax. Supply and demand will be in equilibrium, and your baby's appetite will have stabilized. She will consume an average of 200 grams per meal (five meals a day), about a liter all told, and she will stick to this ration for as long as you breastfeed. Her diet will later be supplemented with purées and baby porridge.

As I mentioned, it is by no means certain that you will notice these adjustment periods when your baby insists on a more lavishly stocked larder. If this is the case, count your blessings. They can, however, be critical, and they may cause you to throw in the towel.

Mothers who stop breastfeeding seldom do so on a whim, or because they are lazy or indifferent. Two months of breastfeeding is better than none at all. So is two weeks.

In Part one of *For the Love of Children* I introduced the guidelines for feeding that I call The Standard Model, which is the tried and true lynchpin of peaceful infant care (see "What do you do?").

I have systematized the natural way to feed babies, which is to feed them when they are hungry. According to this model, a meal – which includes as much food as your baby can take and then some, changing, socializing and a final top up, has to take its own sweet time. It should last as long as your baby does, which means about an hour and half with a margin for error of fifteen minutes, half an hour at the most, in either direction. After such a meal, a honeymoon baby will sleep for two and a half hours with the same margin for error.

You can set your watch by some babies right from the beginning.

Freshly minted newborns sleep longer and don't have the energy to stay awake as long. They are still exhausted from the birth, so the first week is usually peaceful. Many newborns just eat and sleep, eat and sleep. You might keep the meals short, twenty minutes to half an hour. Everything will be sweetness and light for a while. But soon enough, this way your little one becomes a night owl. If you introduce the Standard Model right at the beginning, with four or five large meals a day, (since the twenty-four-hour day and the schedule are not quite in sync) you will have relatively peaceful nights.

Two short night feedings of twenty minutes each for one month is bearable.

As you can see, my method occupies the middle ground between the old four-hour schedule and the somewhat anarchic own-rhythm method. A one and a half-hour meal and a two and a half-hour sleep make a total of four hours. Thus, every meal with all it entails starts every four hours. If your baby starts to eat at noon, she will be done by 1.30, and the next meal will begin at 4.00. Each meal will consist of three rounds of food, two large and one (or more) somewhat smaller.

Not only will your newborn's hunger be satisfied, but she will also build up a reserve to carry her through to the next feeding. The last little top up is just a feel-good exercise. Survival anxiety is allayed, not just after the fact but *preventively*. With this hefty reserve, your baby will sleep well.

The Standard Model has many advantages. It makes your day predictable. You can use the sleep periods productively because you know more or less how long they will last. You know that your baby is getting what she needs. You are on top of things and this will give you a healthy sense of security.

The greatest advantage of all of course is a calm, contented child. And this paves the way for mutual joy, mutual pleasure and a good life!

The Standard Model is a method, not a timetable that must be slavishly adhered to. During the honeymoon, it's your baby who calls the shots. Feed her the moment she wakes up, i.e. the moment she starts to cry. (Newborns often wake up without necessarily being hungry. They will "say" nothing and so should not be picked up.)

If you follow the whole program with two rounds of food, changing, socializing, a top up and one last bedtime sip, your baby will fall into a sound, fairly lengthy sleep, which will usually last for two and a half hours.

During the very first days, it might vary of course from as little as two hours to as much as four. By the same token, if your baby is too tired, the meal will have to be shortened. She may be happy enough during the change, but then the screaming will start and socializing will have to be left out – this time. Go straight to the top up. The whole meal can take as little as an hour sometimes. You should always bear in mind that at this early stage, it is the baby who makes all the important decisions. What the Standard Model does is provide the framework within which all your baby's needs are satisfied at every meal.

The nights can be unpredictable too. Since a twenty-four-hour day has the "wrong" number of hours for five large meals and two smaller ones, some nights will consist of three short meals, and some days will be restricted to four large ones. On occasion, four large meals and two night feedings will be sufficient. Take your cue from your baby and take notes, but don't cheat with the large meals! Do your best to make them last one and a half hours. If you cut corners, the whole edifice may come crashing down around your ears.

When the honeymoon draws to a close, dispense with the night feeding that is usually given around 1.00 am. Then the rule will be five large meals during the day.

The second month will be pretty much like the first, but it is now that with a little help from you, the days will take on a certain rhythm. Once your baby is two months old, the timetable that she has initiated becomes permanent. There will be four large meals during the day, and a nightcap just before bed. The nightcap is part of the last meal, which will have been lengthened to approximately two hours. But we will discuss this in greater detail when the time comes!

To sum up:
- Four or five large meals a day, each meal structured according to the Standard Model Program (see "What do you do?").
- Two night feedings of about twenty minutes each as per the minimalist program.
- Begin feeding as soon as your baby begins to cry.
- Flexibility is the name of the game. It's the baby who decides. Let your baby sleep for as long as she wants between meals, but never during!
- An extra night feeding is no problem every now and again, but never give fewer than four large meals a day.

Your honeymoon baby is the clock for now, but it doesn't hurt to time the various activities. You can keep a record of your baby's day, when she wakes up, how long she can stay awake, when she falls asleep, and then note the day-to-day (or night-to-night) variations. Her rhythms will eventually become discernable. Babies can be perky in the mornings, dozy in the afternoons, and tired troopers by the evening, they can be out for the count in the early part of the day but bursting with energy come afternoon, and they can insist on holding court at night but be dead to the world as long as the sun is up... (For this last group, the Standard Model is a superb recipe for aligning a little person's body clock. See "Sleep".)

The observations you make now will serve as the basis for drawing up the first timetable at the two-month mark.

At the risk of stating the obvious: *Always assume that when a newborn cries, she needs food!*

For a newborn, hunger is a hitherto unknown and intensely unpleasant sensation, and one which kick-starts her most powerful instinct: the instinct to survive. She knows only too well that she cannot feed herself. She has to carry a burden of gnawing insecurity, and this fills her with anxiety. "Will anyone hear me cry? Will I get fed? Will I be able to survive on what I get?" You answer these questions by doing the following:

• Picking her up immediately, "I hear you."
• Giving her food immediately, "I know what you need."
• Giving her as much food as she can hold, "Yes, you will survive."
• Giving her a refill or two after a change and some socializing, "There's lots more where that came from, so rest easy!"

Once the first two months have passed, you will have allayed your baby's survival anxiety to the point where she dares to trust another tomorrow is to come. It is towards the end of the second month that you put together a timetable, and in so doing, you introduce a fifth point:

• You know when your baby is going wake up, so you pick her up *just before*. You take the lead. Through your actions, you are saying, "I know what you need. I am looking out for your interests. Your survival is guaranteed. You no longer have to fear for your life. You can sit back, enjoy life, grow and develop."

Once the cries of survival anxiety are out of the picture, I can guarantee that there will be very little crying generally. In any given twenty-four-hour period, a Standard-Modelled two-month-old will cry for a total of five minutes at the most.

You can supplement breast milk with formula or go over to formula completely. No one stops breastfeeding without good reason, and few do so willingly. Most of those who stop do so because they have to. I will refrain, therefore, from recommendations and comparisons with regard to the various alternatives.

Your baby's sucking reflex will stimulate milk production. If you are considering giving your baby formula while continuing to breastfeed, ponder this. Human beings take the line of least resistance. Sucking milk out of a bottle is easier than sucking milk out of a breast. If your baby gets used to feeding without expending much effort, she may refuse your breast if there isn't a constant flow of milk.

If formula enters the picture at all, you run the risk of your milk production not increasing. You will be able to hold your milk supply steady – so much breast milk, so much formula – if you are consistent, but if you are planning to give your baby formula only every now and then – during those critical periods that we talked about for example – operate under the assumption that your own milk supply will be sufficient, but have the bottle as back-up.

Your baby will follow your lead. So make it difficult for your baby to suck milk from a bottle, not by interrupting the meal – still strictly forbidden – but by using a nipple with a small hole.

I usually breastfed until it became too much trouble for both of us. I never managed to get through the third and final breastfeeding crisis, which occurs at seven to eight weeks.

Today, society is in the grip of breastfeeding hysteria. Mothers are supposed to breastfeed around the clock. Cracked, bleeding, painful nipples are no excuse. ("Take some Tylenol and you'll be fine!") I would wager that these decrees issued by the people in the white coats will vanish as suddenly as they appeared if for no other reason than it is obviously impossible for babies to nurse around the clock. They need to sleep during the night.

Babies should have full tummies and calm mothers. That's all there is to it.

If your milk supply tapers off, it tapers off. You can't do more than your best. If you get to the point where there are more tears than milk, thank your lucky stars for formula! Having to give up breastfeeding is regrettable, but if it takes upwards of three hours for the baby to get herself a decent meal, socializing between a happy mother and a contented baby is all but impossible, and it's not worth it.

When I decided to stop nursing, I went over to the bottle. I didn't breastfeed at all that day. In the evening and the following morning, I was in pain, but I let the baby nurse and got some relief. Then I continued as follows: I relied primarily on the bottle, but gave my baby a meal, or half a meal, from my breasts in the morning and/or in the evening.

This method is as simple as it is effective. The milk flow will ebb eventually, but you will be able to give your baby a little breast milk every now and then for quite a while. The transition will be gentle. Psychologically, I primed my baby and myself for the bottle. The bottle was the norm, breast milk the exception and nothing that could be counted on.

If you are giving your baby formula but plan to continue breastfeeding, the exact opposite will be the order of the day: breast milk will be the rule and formula the unreliable exception – but it's an option in case of emergency.

Regular bottle-feeding of course requires its accessories. For simplicity's sake, let's assume that that you have opted for formula at every meal.

You will need five bottles and five nipples. The bottles can be glass, which holds heat more efficiently, or plastic, which doesn't break. The holes in the nipples should be as small as possible. You will need a saucepan big enough to boil all the bottles in, a wooden fork to fish them out of the water and empty them, a smaller saucepan to boil the water you add the formula to, a plastic container with a spout, and a whisk. These things are reserved for your baby and should not be used by other members of the household. Infants are susceptible to infections. Breast milk provides fairly solid protection, but formula doesn't, so *don't* skimp on hygiene!

There are various kinds of formulas. They are all expensive, but some are pricier than others. Price does not always equal quality. I tried many brands, but I usually let the baby decide. If your baby doesn't like your selection, it will come back up again, usually right after the meal. Just try another brand.

Make sure that whatever you buy is in fact intended for newborns (or whatever age category your baby falls into). Then follow the instructions carefully. The portions are important. No heaped measuring spoons. Little tummies can't handle them. If someone starts talking to you and breaks your concentration, and you can't remember whether you have taken six spoons or seven, err on the side of caution. Better too little than too much.

You should also change nipples during the feeding. You will notice that some of the nipples work better than others. Your baby will too. If you only use those that work best, or even worse only one, problems will arise when they have to be replaced. Your baby will object and feeding will become difficult. Try to have several nipples in circulation and pitch them as soon as they show any signs of wear.

Here is how you prepare the formula:

1. Sterilize the bottles. Place them in cold water in the large saucepan and let the water boil. Don't put the nipples in quite yet, but the bottle rings are fine. Let everything boil for ten to fifteen minutes. Turn off the heat and place the nipples, the whisk and the wooden fork (but not the handle) in the water.
2. Fish up the bottles with the wooden fork. Place the fork in the neck of the bottles and turn them upside down so that the water runs out. Place them on a clean dishtowel.
3. Look at the instructions on the formula label to see how much food a baby your little one's age needs and add fifty grams (the portions are usually on the cheap side). If your baby needs 150 grams per meal – I am assuming she or he is a newborn – multiply this amount by five. That makes 750 grams or seven and a half deciliters. Put the required amount of water in the small saucepan and bring it to a boil.

4. Rinse out the plastic container after washing it thoroughly. Use the water from the large saucepan.

5. Measure out the exact amount of powder required. Count carefully. If two level measures make 100 grams for example, then three level measures make 150 grams. Multiply that by five and you get fifteen level measures. Put it all into the plastic container after shaking any remaining water out of it. Be very careful handling the measuring spoon. It must be kept clean.

6. Pour the boiling water over the formula powder and use the whisk to mix it thoroughly. It's a good idea to let the water stand and cool for a minute or two so that the formula doesn't get lumpy.

7. Pour the formula into the bottles. There won't be quite enough to fill the last bottle all the way to the top. A little of the water has boiled away. If it is just a matter of five or ten grams, boil up a little more water and fill the bottle up to the full mark. If, on the other hand, you are thirty or fifty grams short, you will have to pour the contents of all the bottles back into the plastic container, boil up whatever amount of water is missing and blend it in with the whisk. The strength of the formula will be just right and you can then refill the bottles. If the water that has boiled away is not replaced, the mix will be too strong.

8. Fill the large saucepan to the halfway mark with cold water. Place the open, still hot bottles in the water. By all means let the cold water tap run beside the bottles so that they cool down more quickly. This cooling process is important.

9. Fish the nipples out of the hot water along with the rings and put them on the bottles, but don't tighten them. Let them sit loosely. They can be difficult to get off otherwise. When mealtimes roll around, then you can tighten them.

10. Put the bottles in the fridge as soon as the formula has cooled. Newly mixed formula attracts bacteria like a magnet. If you chill the bottles immediately and put them in the fridge, however, the formula will keep for twenty-four hours.

If you have travel plans, you can't use already mixed formula that has been out of the fridge for more than an hour. Put the powder in the bottle and have the boiled water in a clean thermos. Add the water to the bottle and shake thoroughly when it's time for a meal.

At home, when it's time to warm the formula up, put the bottle in the small saucepan that you have half-filled with water. (In my intuitive opinion, microwave heating of infants' foods should be avoided.) When small bubbles are visible at the bottom of the pan, the formula should be more or less the right temperature. Take the bottle out of the water without touching the nipple. Tighten the bottle ring and shake a couple of drops onto the front of your hand. If you feel nothing that means the formula is body temperature and you are ready to go.

Remember that a little too cool is better than even half a degree too hot! In case of emergencies, you can in fact give a catastrophically hungry baby formula straight from the fridge. Even newborns will accept ice-cold milk. And that is good to know if there is no other way out. Of course you can also emergency-warm the formula under the hot water tap while the baby sucks on your knuckle or lip.

Handle the feeding itself just as you did when you were breastfeeding. Sit comfortably and make sure the baby has support under her head and back. Hold her little hand in a reassuring grip and place her other arm behind your back. Don't forget the blanket!

Have a bib handy to catch any stray drops of milk. Position the bottle comfortably and make sure the nipple is full of milk. Half full won't cut it. Don't interrupt the meal.

After the first round and a burp, give the second portion. You don't have to warm up the bottle between rounds or after the change and the socializing, although you can of course hold it under the hot water tap for a while if you like.

If there's not enough to go round, you can pour a little milk from bott-le number two into the bottle you have just emptied without washing or sterilizing. If, however, there is anything left of what you take, it should be thrown away.

If the bottle is half full or more, it can be saved, but put it in the fridge immediately. This is not, however, something I would recommend if you are dealing with a newborn. In any event, *you should never warm formula up more than twice.* Fill the bottle and the nipple with cold water immediately after the meal. Wash them when time permits and sterilize as per the instructions given above.

As early as three or four weeks, you baby will be consuming 200 grams at every large meal. At night, the program is somewhat more condensed and she will eat less. In total, she will consume approximately a liter of formula every twenty-four-hour period.

At one month, you will dispense with one of the night-feedings. (Your baby may do it for you.) The second night feeding will eventually merge with the final evening meal or the first morning meal. Be a little careful here. The total amount of formula consumed should stay the same: approximately one liter every twenty-four hours. When the night feedings fall by the wayside, make sure you fill the bottles with 225 grams of formula instead of 200.

What if your baby refuses the bottle the first time it's offered? She won't. This is about survival!

But if you approach your baby fearing the worst and wondering "Is this really going to work?" or "What if she won't take the bottle?", you are committing a cardinal sin. You are transferring your own insecurity onto your baby, which will set off her internal alarm. *Something is wrong! Mommy isn't up for this! Danger threatens!* And immediately she is on a hunger strike.

This is a phenomenon that goes with childhood. All children sense danger when their parents are frightened, insecure or anxious.

The first bottle should be given with serene confidence. Just place the nipple firmly in the little mouth. Give the baby an encouraging smile. Your demeanour should convey the message that God is in his heaven and all is right with the world. It is not up to your baby to signal her approval of the menu to you. It is up to you to signal to your baby through your cheerful confidence that the food is good, that there is lots to go round, and that she can eat to her heart's content.

Here's a tip; if your baby stubbornly refuses to eat in spite of all the positive messages you send, you can trick her by giving her the bottle right after she has fallen asleep or just before she wakes up.

Finally, dear mom, if you have given yourself a failing grade as a mother because you cannot breastfeed and you regard having to give your baby a bottle as a defeat, try to bootstrap yourself, difficult though it might be. Deal with your anxiety and your sense of inadequacy as best you can, but *don't* transfer this negative energy to your baby!

Your job is to alleviate your baby's survival anxiety. Giving her formula instead of breast milk is not the end of the world. Your child needs your confident leadership far more than she needs your breast milk and the tears that go with the lack of it.

**It's impossible to give a newborn too much food.
It just comes out one end or the other.**

IF SOMETHING GOES WRONG: THE NEWBORN REFUSES TO EAT

There are babies who stray from the path when they are still at the hospital. Or more accurately, they never find their way onto the path in the first place. They just don't get the hang of eating. They suck half-heartedly for a little while, become anxious and start to scream. Their survival anxiety is so strong that they can't take a time-out to figure out what will soothe it: food.

They are a heart-breaking sight. They are suffering and so are their mothers.

So it happens that babies are sometimes labelled "colicky" when they are still at the hospital – especially if the family has already had a so-called colicky baby in their midst and lives in fear of being landed with another. But babies are not *born* with colic. There is in fact no such thing as a "colicky baby". Colic, like other psychosomatic ailments, with time becomes a physical reality. But we shouldn't talk about colicky babies any more than we talk about ulcery men or headachey women. The label must be done away with.

I would formulate the problem thus: there are children born with more survival anxiety than others. (See the passage about the chicks in the nest in "Caring for a newborn".) There is only one way to allay the anxiety these babies are feeling and that is to feed them. Trying to treat the problem with water, drops and TLC is a forlorn enterprise. There is nothing wrong with these babies. They just haven't understood that food is their passport to survival and life, and they must be helped to see the light. The only way they will learn is through experience. Rome was not built in a day – or during a feeding. It takes time and it takes experimentation. Gaining experience that leaves a permanent imprint requires long and systematic toil. This is as true for little people as it is for big ones.

There will come a day when this anxiety-ridden little baby will begin to grasp that it is *food* – the stuff that comes out her mother's breast, the stuff she so agonizingly sucks into herself, is what guarantees survival and a sense of well-being. Once the baby grasps this, she will have acquired the most important insight of her young life.

The path to salvation is methodical. Your task is to help your child understand what survival entails, not once but many times. Confidently, calmly and tirelessly, you must try to convince your baby that she will survive, and the only way to do this is to give her food. When your baby finally makes the connection between food and survival, when she finally understands that food means life, then, and only then, can you devote time to things like cuddling, playing and generally enjoying each other.

A newborn who nurses briefly and then breaks into a fit of hysterical crying has not understood the connection between food and life. This doesn't mean she or he has an upset stomach or "colic". It is true that babies come equipped with a sucking reflex, but they cannot know, once and for all, that sucking leads to a full tummy, which in turn results in a feeling of well-being. They experience the food, the milk that fills their little mouths, as something that exacerbates, rather than alleviates, their anxiety. Even the nipple being placed in their mouths can touch off a panic attack because it stops these babies from screaming. And screaming is the only thing they can – and indeed must – do in the valley of despair they find themselves in. Physically and mentally, life is now one long scream.

Not that long ago, your baby was inside you and received nourishment without having to lift a finger. The placenta provided her with everything she needed, and she wanted for nothing. It was like being fed by tube or an IV drip. She never needed to nurse, swallow or have her mouth full of milk. Survival anxiety was simply not an issue – until she was born.

The birth was a terrible ordeal. And before the newborn baby had time to recover from this first shock, another bomb dropped. Everything had changed. Nothing was recognizable. Her entire little body – and her soul – screamed for something that was gone forever – *a secure life*. How can a baby be expected to immediately figure out that it is milk, a substance that comes out of something she has to suck on, that will restore that secure life?

And, in truth, milk doesn't restore it; milk replaces it. A secure life is replaced by something else.

The whole breastfeeding procedure is an enigma for a baby who refuses to eat. Her anxiety, which overwhelms her anyway, is only made worse by this strange new phenomenon that she just can't fathom.

A little person who is plagued by unbearable anxiety cannot eat. She has to be calmed down first.

Calming is not the same as comforting. Calming a baby down has a clearly defined purpose, namely to get her into a condition in which she will be able to eat. Aimless comforting that entails wandering around the house with the baby in your arms soon results in the comforter her/himself falling prey to despair, worry and a feeling of powerlessness – a sad truth known to all who have tried this approach. And it isn't that surprising. The baby *wants* something, *needs* something. The little one is not crying because she is sad, which means that comforting won't work.

A hysterical newborn, completely overcome by survival anxiety, can be calmed in the following way.

- Stand up and take the baby in your arms. (Never forget the blanket.)
- Hold her as firmly as you can so that her little body is tight against yours.
- Her head and cheek should be placed against your cheek and held there.
- Now start walking, while you speak out loud.

Walk purposefully, as though you are going somewhere (towards a food source). This can be done even in a small room. Stride along as though you have a destination. You are taking the lead now, knowing exactly where to go. Your movements should be decisive and confident. Hold the baby firmly.

- As you walk, talk constantly. *Speak loudly enough to drown out your baby's cries.* Her ear is probably fairly close to your mouth, so don't yell. Your pitch should be deep, not shrill, but your voice should be loud and emphatic. Your baby is already terrified of her own screams, and that is why your voice should drown them out.

What you say doesn't matter, as long as there are no pauses. Keep the words coming. "Now we are just going to relax. Everything is going to be fine. You are going to eat soon. The sun is shining and grandma's coming to visit... " Try to make your speech rhythmic. You are aiming for a constantly recurring intonation pattern: "*Now* we are *just* going to re*lax*, *every*thing is going to be *fine*, you are going to *eat* soon, the *sun* is shining, and *grand*ma is coming to *vis*it..."

Tone of voice and rhythm are of course more important than what you say. You can recite recipes or pretend you are talking to some therapist about your marital problems; the baby won't know the difference. Don't change position. The baby's body is tense and resisting, but hold her tight to your own body. Don't look at her. Talk and walk continuously.

- As soon as you notice even a hint of diminishing tension, start rocking the baby but keep holding her tight. Short, quick rocking movements in your unwavering grip, light and tight, so that the baby's body vibrates. Keep walking and talking.

Some babies calm down after a few seconds, while other need a few minutes. You just have to wait your baby out. Keep your eyes on the prize. You are making it possible for the baby to eat. A side effect of all this is that you stay calm instead of becoming a basket case yourself.

- As soon as the hysterical screaming has shifted down to exhausted sobbing, sit down (as though you've reached your goal) and put the baby to your breast quickly and firmly. It is very important that you offer your breast immediately. No confusion must intrude. Keep talking. Stick to the recurring stress pattern and speak with conviction. Look optimistic. *Everything is as it should be,* is the message you want to communicate. Keep up the monologue until the baby has started to eat. Then you can lapse into silence and let her eat in peace.

116

• If your baby nurses calmly, and all is sweetness and light, the only thing you have to plan for is picking her up *before she wakes up* for her next meal. Then the vicious circle will be broken.

If, however, the baby lets go of the nipple and starts to scream again, instantly switch the monologue back on and resume rocking the baby in your arms. Don't change position, though; keep the baby at your breast. Talk, rock the baby and simultaneously stimulate the sucking reflex by touching the baby's cheek (the one nearest you) or by drawing your nipple over the baby's mouth until she – hopefully – starts to nurse again. Then stop talking and be still.

But if your baby still refuses to eat and works herself up into a panic again, you will have to repeat the whole walking and calming procedure. Then put her to your breast as soon as it is feasible – then, if necessary, calm her again, put her to your breast again, calm her again... Keep going until the job is done!

Do this throughout an entire meal. Remember the first time is the worst. If you are persistent, you will triumph. And so will your baby. Then the nightmare is over.

What I have just described is a worst-case scenario – a newborn that point blank refuses to eat. This is rare. What you are trying to do, if you have a newborn with an exceptionally bad case of survival anxiety on your hands, is to break the vicious circle. Intervene before panic has a chance to gain a foothold.

Hysteria has to be avoided at all costs – that goes as much for little people as it does for big ones. A hysterical newborn must *not* be abandoned but must be soothed. Her sense of security must be restored though all the means at your disposal.

A baby in distress, who can only be persuaded to eat in the way described above, sleeps fitfully. Anxiety plagues her even in her sleep. Break the vicious circle by taking her up after only an hour – or even less – when she is still sleeping deeply and apparently peacefully. Stroke her head gently a couple of times, wrap her in the blanket and place her gently and confidently to your breast. You should be alone in a quiet room. Smile and try to actually *feel* soft and tender. All worries should be parked at the door.

Of course, rousing your baby from her sleep after hours of crying hardly seems right. But this is about alleviating suffering and illuminating the path to life.

After (barely) an hour's sleep on top of a full meal as per the description above, your baby will not be that hungry, which means that survival anxiety is, for the moment, being kept at bay. Thus, she is capable of eating. Your baby's behavior will be your reward. Even if she is sleeping deeply when you pick her up, she will eat contentedly, her little face a picture of peace.

There is nothing more beautiful to behold.

SLEEP

Newborns sleep wonderfully. They are certainly wonderful to behold. You can handle sleeping newborns pretty much however you like, and they won't wake up. Their sleep is wonderful, but terrible too. A newborn's deepest sleep can be compared to falling into unconsciousness.

Birth was a traumatic experience. Life hung by a thread – literally. The child's head and body were compressed to the point that the two halves of the skull perhaps overlapped. The baby was forced out so that she would survive. Survival anxiety must have taken root already in the womb. The world that met her was terrifying. The protection, the warmth, the soft water, the familiar sounds of the mother's heart and lungs, the pulsating, murmuring, enveloping security – all gone. The baby was driven out into the cold, alien unknown knowing only one thing: *I have to survive!*

And life was waiting. Not as peaceful repose, but as toil. Life was not handed to her on a silver platter. It had to be conquered and re-conquered.

Sleep blots out this toil. Sleep liberates, just as unconsciousness protects a human being in an unbearable situation from enduring more than a human being can endure. A newborn's sleep is merciful, but even the deepest sleep is not free from toil. The child has to breathe. Breathing is not automatic at the beginning of life. Breathing has to be conquered too. The child filled her lungs for the first time at birth and then forced the air out in the form of a scream. The food supply via the placenta was cut off, and the child had to force her way out to survive, but the supply of oxygen was cut off too, and the child was forced to put her lungs to work in order to take in oxygen herself. This was certainly quite a shock too.

It takes many weeks, sometimes up to three months, for your baby to dare believe that she will survive. (Compare the erroneous concept of "three-month colic". Survival anxiety eventually yields to experience.) Similarly, it takes three months or more – I would go so far as to say as many as six – before breathing is reliably automatic.

Until then, breathing is also a struggle for survival. And there are babies

118

who give up. When sleep is deepest, it sometimes happens that small children stop breathing, and in a few minutes, life has passed.

The ability to breathe is not something that human beings are born with. It too is an art that must be conquered.

The deaths of these children are not completely meaningless. Their passing serves an important purpose: it engenders respect for the labor we call life. All children should grow up surrounded by this respect and should be accorded the reverence due to them for fighting for and constantly re-conquering life.

The irregular breathing will cause you worry. The baby alternates between gasping for air and seeming not to breathe at all. When a little newborn gasps for air, it doesn't mean that she is suffocating. It's simply the toil that breathing demands.

When she is lying motionless and you can't see any sign of the ribcage expanding or feel even a hint of breath, you can ensure that everything is as it should be by lifting one of the tiny fingers or touching the palm of the baby's hand. You will receive a reflexive movement in response.

The apnea monitor, a breathing alarm, which you can buy or rent, will spare you this kind of worry.

And newborns dream. There are those who believe that a human being comes into the world a blank slate, but I don't agree. A newborn has been through some traumatic experiences and has had a long life prior to birth, during which consciousness was gradually awakened. The impressions of the new world are obviously vivid. Infants react clearly to everything. It strikes me as unreasonable to claim that sensory perception only came into being at the moment of birth, as though someone had pushed a button and said, "From now on, you will react!"

Twitching, anxious spasms, trembling, agitated eye movements from side to side under the closed eyelids bear witness to a dream life that probably serves to help the newborn through the traumatic experience of birth, as well as helping her leave her old, secure and forever lost life behind her.

The baby may also emit sounds during sleep – sudden little noises, grunts and whimpers that remind you of a puppy. And these you can put down to her rich inner life! It is not just the past but also the disorienting present that must be noted, processed and inwardly digested.

On top of all this, there are her own bodily functions, all of which (or most) are hitherto unknown. She must now get acquainted with them, which doesn't happen in the twinkling of an eye. A blind adult who suddenly regains her sight halfway through her life, a previously active person who must suddenly learn to get around in a wheelchair, an individual who has undergone a bowel operation and must learn to cope with a colostomy bag could all attest to how their worlds had been turned upside down. This is what life is like for a newborn.

Sleep brings peace.

While awake, a newborn often falls into a state of drowsiness. Drowsiness is cute and endearing, and it's easy to sit with a drowsy baby. However, I think that this condition is traumatic. The baby withdraws from the world, screens off her senses and slides into a nothingness that postpones the inevitable – a confrontation with life as it is *now*.

Drowsy babies are neither asleep nor awake, and sleep's extinguishing darkness therefore does them no good and does not enable them to rest and recharge. A newborn that has slept has replenished her strength, both physical and mental, but a newborn that has dozed – even for several hours – shows no signs of renewed vigor.

This traumatic condition must be remedied. You should always try at any rate. And this doesn't only hold true for infants. If your little newborn starts to doze, put her down immediately and if necessary "rock" her – pull the carriage back and forth – to sleep. If she isn't full to the brim, she will wake up when you put her down. Once she is wide-awake again, the dozing cycle is broken.

Never sit with a dozing infant. Help the child either to sleep or stay awake!

Awakening from a deep sleep doesn't happen as quickly as you might think. There are many milestones to be passed along the way!

The child may initiate the process by turning her head – we will assume she is lying on her stomach – only to turn her head back to its original position ten minutes later.

Then nothing happens for a while.

Then a little arm is straightened and laid along her side. The little bottom rises and she draws her legs under her like a little frog, and then straightens them, simultaneously burrowing her face down into the bedclothes and showing her pretty (and often very red) neck. It all seems rather strange, but it isn't really. She is able to breathe. The head tilts to the side, the body becomes still and nothing happens for a while. Eventually, a little eye opens. Or two. And then they close again. And open and close.

Again nothing happens for a while.

Then perhaps a little hand with delicate nails begins to scrabble against the sheet. Once again, she becomes still.

Then there is a succession of facial expressions. The little mouth pouts, and she yawns so wide you think her jaw will crack. Then she falls back to sleep again. And then – boom!

A cry from deep within her, from hunger, from the survival anxiety itself, bursts forth. The first cry seems to say, "I don't have the strength – *I want to live*!" It's as though she is reminding herself of the conditions that are in force now – conditions of anxiety and struggle. In her sleep, she perhaps thought she was back in that soft, hungerless world, where everything was simple and secure. She has been brutally reminded that she isn't. Panic can sink its claws into her in less than thirty seconds.

The awakening process itself must not be interrupted. During the night as well as during sleep periods during the day, you will notice if you observe your baby closely that she often seems wide awake. Her eyes are open and she can even lift her head and hold it up for long periods. All the diverse sounds she makes can also dupe you into picking her up in the belief that she is awake.

But just as you would dislike being disturbed before you are "properly awake" – even though you might talk in your sleep, sit up, open your eyes and generally sleep so lightly that people actually start talking to you – so a newborn is unprepared to eat, socialize or be confronted with the world around her immediately. Let her wake up at her own speed and don't disturb her even if she is sleeping only lightly. Wait for the cry – and be prepared.

Soon you will learn to recognize the signs in your baby that immediately precede her crying, so you will be able to intervene at exactly the right moment.

Still, sometimes picking up a sleeping infant can't be avoided, especially if you are dealing with a newborn who is afflicted with such overwhelming survival anxiety that she refuses to eat – we discussed such cases in the preceding chapter – and the vicious circle has to be broken. Even babies who eat well sometimes have their meals rescheduled for practical reasons.

Choose a moment when the baby is sleeping soundly, her face smooth and her eyes immovably shut.

It's easier – and better – to pick up a newborn who is deeply asleep and put her to your breast (or give her the bottle) then it is to interrupt the awakening process.

Always give a sleeping newborn a warning by stroking her over the head and temples with your warm hand a couple of times before you wrap the blanket around her and pick her up.

Sleep for a newborn is beneficial and necessary.

Newborns sleep because they have to, not because their surroundings encourage them to. Newborns sleep because they are exhausted. Whether they are surrounded by noise, light, voices, music or absolute silence makes no difference. You can no more rouse a little newborn out of a deep sleep by talking, laughing or carrying her around than you can induce her to go to sleep or to stay asleep by observing a rule of silence. (I hope that what I said earlier about letting a baby wake up at her own speed won't mislead you into going too far in the other direction. The problems start if you *pick the child up* and interrupt the awakening routine.)

A newborn is so touchingly tiny and seems so helpless and weak that one can easily fall into the trap of thinking that she needs to be handled with kid gloves even in her sleep. There are more than a few parents who disconnect doorbells, put foam pads under telephones and tiptoe around the house speaking in whispers. Unfortunately, all this solicitude is pointless. In the beginning none of it makes much difference one way or the other. But after a few months, these parents manage to create a living hell for the baby. She has gotten used to total silence and the most insignificant sound wakes her up. Her sleep is constantly disturbed. In many families, evenings especially are a nightmare. The other family members are virtual prisoners in their own home, and they don't dare flush the toilet, fill the coffee pot or use the microwave.

Let silence and noise coexist naturally so that nothing becomes alien or frightening!

From my own experience, I can attest that you can err on the side of noise. When my first baby, a couple of weeks old, had been fed, changed and gotten her top-ups, I put her down to sleep in the baby carriage, which I had in the house. I put it in a corner of the living room and then I put on a record. I was young and liked music, and so I wanted to have something to listen to while I puttered around in the kitchen. I was especially fond of classical music, crashing symphonies that oozed world-weariness and anomie. The magnificent stereo system that the baby's father had bought was the perfect medium. The speakers were over three feet tall, the volume was cranked up and the effect was stunning.

It wasn't until the baby was about three months old that I registered where I had parked the carriage. Right in front of one of the speakers! The child grew up to have a taste for classical music and the ability to sleep like a log...

As has already been pointed out, newborns sleep anyhow and anywhere. Once they have fallen asleep, nothing wakes them until hunger and survival anxiety set in. For the first little while, there is no risk of her falling to the floor if you have put her on a bed or something similar. This happy state of affairs does not last long however – about two weeks.

At this point, if you have not already done so, it might be wise to choose a permanent sleeping spot for the baby. There should be barriers – a crib or a cradle/carriage with high sides.

You will also have to be careful during diaper changes. You can no longer leave the baby on the change table, not even for a second. You never know when an infant will turn over for the first time or simply "flounder" her way over the edge of the table. *A newborn must never be at risk of falling.* If you have to leave the room and you can't take the baby with you, put her on the floor!

The sleeping spot should be chosen carefully. Cradles and wicker baskets are cute but soon become too short. The problem with cradles is that the runners are usually so small that rocking is impossible. (In addition to being too small, they usually run sidewise.) But they look nice and make great family heirlooms, and they can be used as a bed for dolls and teddy bears. Or cars for that matter!

You can use a crib from day one if you like – and for a long time after that. A crib should last your baby at least three years, preferably four (until the terrible twos have passed), so investing in quality pays off. Padding around the sides will be needed for the first six months so that there is no way she can push her head through the slats. Wicker cradles and baskets should also be equipped with padding so that your baby doesn't lacerate her scalp.

You can also use a baby carriage as a sleeping spot, but you will bring in dirt with you when you have been out. Some parents buy a sturdy, roomy second-hand carriage for exclusive indoor use.

The carriage will come in useful if and when the baby needs help sleeping through the night meal(s). A carriage rocks better than the most expensive cradle, since pushing a carriage back and forth is much more efficient than rocking a cradle from side to side.

Very young babies sleep between sixteen and twenty hours a day, often closer to twenty than sixteen. This lasts for a week or two.

Most parents who have been regaled with horror stories about how hard it is to have a baby in the house are pleasantly surprised by how easy things are the first couple of weeks after the birth. The baby sleeps and eats, sleeps and eats, and everything is sweetness and light.

All this changes drastically at the end of the second week of life or the beginning of the third. (All ages given in this book presuppose that the baby was not born prematurely. In terms of development, the age of very premature babies should be calculated according to the date on which they should have been born. This holds true throughout the first year of life.) At this point, little babies who have hitherto slept angelically through the day start partying at night. (For information on how to help them separate day from night, see the following chapter.)

The transition at the end of the second week/beginning of the third is pronounced.

I have a theory that the pregnancy is repeated in a different form, by which I mean that mother and child have to separate from each other in a way that mirrors the pregnancy. In other words, the pregnancy is repeated but outside the mother's body. It takes about as long for the fertilized egg to migrate down the fallopian tube and attach itself to the uterine wall as it does for the newborn baby to "migrate" out of the womb – after the traumatic experience of birth – and find her place outside it and live a life of her own. Only then is the baby ready to start living, to look out into the world and accept it – in short, to leave the womb once and for all.

• The appetite increases (the first nursing crisis).
• The sleeping pattern changes (sleep isn't "unconsciousness" anymore).
• Efforts to socialize begin.
• The influence of the mother's hormones disappears, the swelling of the sex organs subsides and the baby starts to function under her own steam.
• The baby's appearance changes, which, if nothing else, manifests itself in the reactions of the people around her. A freshly minted newborn elicits reverence with her air of introspection, profound wisdom and grave otherworldliness, while a three-week-old baby elicits emotional, delighted reactions from each and every one.

The fact that people will often spontaneously want to hold and schmooze with a three-week-old but will lapse into devout silence in the presence a newborn is not solely the result of the two to three-week age difference. (I will come back to this theory of the "repeated" pregnancy later in the book.)

It is useful to anticipate the change that will take place in connection with what I call *the true birth*. As already mentioned, the sleep pattern changes. Sleep no longer only serves to blot out the memory of a traumatic event – birth – and to provide relief from the back-breaking toil. A new kind of sleep enters the picture, the kind that we all need, not only to heal the wounds from things past but also to gather strength for what is to come. Anyone who goes to bed to sleep that kind of sleep – let's call it *normal* sleep – must be not only tired but also reasonably calm and relaxed. Conversely, anyone who falls unconscious from sheer exhaustion because neither body nor soul can take any more sleeps the sleep of a newborn.

A newborn can fall into such a sleep on meagre rations of both food and socializing, but a three-week-old definitely cannot. At this stage, the baby should get as much food as she can hold and stay awake for as long as she can at every meal. She should fall asleep in peace and contentment, not exhaustion. Other forces have come into play. Tiring out a three-week-old is a tall order! She needs her sustenance in ever increasing amounts as well as her social participation, her awake time and her induction into the world that, as a newborn, she screened herself off from. And she has unimagined resources with which to back up her demands – above all endurance.

It is now, with the true birth, that the problems can start. The "package" period is over. If you continue to treat the baby like a newborn package, she may play along during the day, but she will rebel during the night.

A three-week-old's sleep needs are down to around sixteen hours a day. That in itself is a big change, but the quality of her sleep is different too – healthier, pleasanter and more strengthening, as "normal" sleep should be.

You can now put the baby down before she has fallen asleep, which was more or less impossible before. There may be protests of course, and, as usual, check to see if she wants a few more drops of milk. If she doesn't, you will have to help her achieve the peaceful state of mind that normal sleep demands. The baby's condition is not unlike your own when you are drowsy and both want and need to sleep but can't. It's not that you are worried or have unpleasant thoughts swirling around in your head. You just can't switch off.

This is when something I call *buffing* can be useful. Sit on the baby's left, either on a chair or on your haunches. It's simplest to have the baby lying on her stomach. Make a loose fist with your right hand and buff the baby's diapered little bottom through the blanket, with an upward movement. This buffing should be firm but gentle, almost like shoving. You are not hitting or banging. There must be nothing hard about your movements. Buff with the same energy and the same rhythm you would use if you were chopping parsley on a carving board where you guide the tip of the knife from the handle.

While you firmly but delicately buff the baby's bottom so that the little body moves slightly with each tap, spread out your left hand over the baby's back, still outside the bed covers. With every fourth tap, as though you were keeping time with a rhythmic song, press your outspread left hand against the little back just for an instant. The pressure should be gentle and steady, just short of real pressure, a soft "push" for every fourth tap. Practise the technique in advance – on your own thighs for example. Your outer right thigh is the baby's bottom and the upper side of your left thigh is her back. It is not as difficult as it sounds once your get the rhythm down!

(This method is just as effective in calming older babies who are shrieking at the top of their lungs. After you have positioned them correctly with a firm touch: arms up, legs out-stretched, head to the right, this buffing also works on babies who are on the point of scrambling out of their carriages or beds. My all time record was with an eight-month-old baby who was visiting me and whose parents were considering both medication and hospitalization for the child. I had a magazine spread out in front me and read as I buffed. I had time to read the whole thing from cover to cover, but it worked.)

You should not talk while you buff (young children will try and find the face the voice is coming from and this will distract the baby). If you are dealing with an older baby, make sure the room is dark. A little three-week-old on the verge of sleep, however, needs only a few minutes of buffing or rocking to drift off, and this with all the lights on and the usual hustle and bustle going on around her.

A three-week-old baby who has left the womb once and for all no longer has anything like the need or the inclination to be warm and snug that the newborn has. Circulation has improved. The baby conserves heat more efficiently. She has also adapted to the usual indoor temperature which is about 17 degrees Celsius lower than that of the uterus.

Now, after approximately two weeks of life (for children of normal weight), it is time to dispense with the quilt under the bedspread. If you have been using a set of neck-to-toe heavy pyjamas, switch to lighter sleeping attire! A thin cotton sweater with matching shorts will combine beautifully with a blanket. Continue to wrap the baby in the blanket as soon as you pick her up from her bed. It is also time to lower the temperature in the room where the baby sleeps and to open the window at night. Now a cautious toughening process begins. *The baby* should not be cold, but the air around her should be kept cool.

During the first two weeks of life, you should avoid taking the baby out if it's rainy, windy or exceptionally cold. If the weather is reasonably clement, a baby less than a week old can sleep outside provided she is dressed warmly and tucked in securely. Even in summer, a newborn should be securely tucked in.

A three-week-old, however, can and should sleep outside no matter what the weather. Dress the baby the way you would like to be dressed if you had to sleep on a park bench. Cover her with a blanket or quilt or whatever covering you would want if you were her. It is easy to overdo the bundling up out of sheer habit. It is tempting to regard the baby as being fresh from the womb, cast out into a cold world, but a three-week-old has acclimatized. From now on, as far as clothing and bedding go, you should consistently use yourself as the benchmark. If it is very cold, you can insulate the bottom of the baby carriage by putting newspapers, a blanket or a sheepskin under the thin mattress.

From three weeks on, the hood of the carriage should *not* be up – I usually removed it – unless it is raining, snowing or very windy. The hood isn't much use as protection against the sun either. It turns the carriage into a sauna. During the summer months, the carriage must be parked in the shade, and however closely you stand guard, a mosquito net is recommended. A lone wasp can cause a catastrophe.

An infant should always wear a hat, no matter what the season, for the first year of life.

The toughening process, which begins in the third week, is beneficial. Don't be nervous. The baby can take it! She also needs it for health reasons. It toughens her immune system. It is a fact that babies, like adults, sleep better in a cool environment as long as they have as much clothing as we adults would need. It is not the *baby* that should be kept cool. This toughening process is sadly neglected these days.

A three-week-old is fast approaching the one-month mark, and one night feeding – the most ungodly one – drops out of the picture. Not a few one-month-olds sleep through this meal all by themselves. One night goes by, then another. On the third night the baby wakes up and asks to be fed, and so it continues. The night feeding doesn't vanish for good all at once. There will be relapses every now and again. However, many one-month-old babies do *not* sleep through this feeding of their own accord, and they are probably in the majority. They need some help.

Parents who try to help young children and infants to sleep, to become accustomed to an unbroken night's rest, to tell the difference between night and day and *not* to require feeding, carrying and "comforting" twenty-four hours a day easily fall prey to feelings of guilt (with no small amount of assistance from their surroundings). They feel that they are inadequate, egotistical parents. Their defence is that they need to sleep themselves so they can get up and go to work in the morning and have some hope of getting through the day, but there is a tacit acceptance of the idea that this takes a terrible toll on the baby!

But it doesn't take a terrible toll on the baby. On the contrary, what takes a toll on young children is constantly having their sleep interrupted. It is hardly sportsmanship to deprive infants and young children of the sleep they so desperately need, developing at break-neck speed as they are.

Children suffer just as much as adults do if they don't get their quota of continuous sleep. Probably they suffer more. Their impressions are brutally strong and their struggle to develop unceasing. An adult is a veteran. For a baby everything is new and unsoftened by experience or hindsight.

Only during the honeymoon should the night sleep be broken, since the baby's survival anxiety must be immediately allayed. *At one month, a baby of normal weight is perfectly capable of sleeping for at least six hours straight without food.* The prerequisite of course is that the baby is given a full day's activities according to the Standard Model with all the food she needs during at least four meals (plus a goodnight snack) in addition to having all her other needs satisfied.

After another month, the remaining night meal will merge with either the evening or the morning feeding, which ever you think is best, and the baby's night sleep will increase to eight hours. With (or without) a little help from you, the baby will then be sleeping ten hours a night at three months and twelve hours a night at four months without a feeding. We will go through all this chronologically.

Around the one-month mark, observe your baby for a few nights to see if she shows any tendencies towards sleeping through one of the night feedings. If she doesn't, decide which night feeding should go. Decide in the morning so that your baby's day will be a full one in every sense of the word!

When evening comes, put her down to sleep in the baby carriage rather than a cradle or crib. When she wakes up and cries for food, start to rock her immediately. Don't speak and avoid touching her.

Pull the carriage back and forth, back and forth in long, rapid, steady movements. Extend your arm fully when you push the carriage away from you and maintain the tempo. Cautious, hesitant movements will not have the desired result (unless you want to keep her up all night. The baby will think it's great fun, but the goal here is to get the little angel to fall back to sleep all by herself.) If the baby screams lustily, respond in kind through your movements. Yank the carriage hard when you start to pull it back towards you. Imagine the carriage is about to go over a cliff and you have managed to grab it at the last second. The first time, it may take a while before the baby drops off, since it is the very first time in her little life that she hasn't been given food the second she asked for it. Her surprise is greater than her hunger.

Keep pushing the carriage back and forth steadily and rhythmically. Stay the course! Her cries may cut you to the quick, but console yourself with the thought that an infant that does not sleep through on her own at the one-month-mark seldom does so later. The baby's nocturnal vigils will stretch into eternity because *the baby will continue to wait for your help.*

This first time, the baby will fall asleep in about twenty minutes, and you will have stopped rocking *just before* she drops off. Wind the rocking down and finish by giving the handle of the carriage a few rapid little shakes.

Babies who are barely one month old *can* be rocked to sleep, but it's not a good idea. When they wake up, which all people do more or less consciously several times a night, they are likely to jump to the conclusion that something is wrong because the carriage isn't moving. So make sure the baby isn't completely out for the count when you stop! The older the child, the more important this rule is.

Then go lie down. You have a fair amount of time. When the baby has fallen back to sleep, she will think that she has eaten.

The first night you will get up to rock the carriage at least two and probably three times. After that, things will move more quickly (provided your technique is sound). Come morning, you may feel you've been a bit of tyrant, but your baby will behave as though nothing has happened. *She* won't be complaining!

The second night, you will have to rock the carriage once and probably twice, the third night once or not at all.

Then silence will descend.

The Three-Night Cure. A Little Memo:
- Follow the Standard Model Program to the letter throughout the day. Splice in an extra half an hour for the one-month-old so that the all-encompassing meals last for two hours instead of one and a half. If infants are to sleep at least six hours at a stretch at three weeks to a month, eight hours at two months, ten hours at three months and twelve hours at four months, they must be properly full and content at the end of the day.
- Start pushing the carriage back and forth the instant you hear your baby's first cry. If you hold off in the hope that she will go back to sleep all by herself during the cure, survival anxiety will have time to get its claws into her, and once the damage is done, it will take you so much longer to get her to go to sleep. So don't dither! An immediate response is required.
- The child's cries should be regarded as questions. Your job is to provide the answers. *At night, people sleep.* Your little baby will not be able to take this message to heart immediately, since she obviously doesn't have a clear idea of what night actually is, but the penny will soon drop. As soon as you get the "rocking" technique down pat, the crying will stop within two minutes (after the first time).
- If you find her crying unbearable – because you haven't been able to perfect your rocking technique – and you discontinue the three-day cure on the first or second night, and pick her up to feed her, the next attempt will take a week or more. You are giving the baby contradictory messages and she doesn't know what to believe. This sounds harsh, but contradictory messages undermine trust and credibility. Your anxiety has let in the wolf.

IF SOMETHING GOES WRONG: THE NEWBORN REFUSES TO SLEEP

There are newborns who find it exceptionally difficult to settle down.

Just as certain newborns refuse to eat because they don't understand the connection between food and survival (See "If something goes wrong: the newborn refuses to eat"), there are babies who are plagued by survival anxiety so strong that death seems imminent. They get no peace even from deep, almost unconscious sleep, which otherwise knocks out an anxiety-ridden baby. Their survival anxiety must be allayed, and only food and more food can accomplish that.

You might think it impossible that the baby would still be hungry. She has eaten only recently and she practically eats continuously, eats and screams, eats and screams… Could she be sick? Does she have stomach problems or colic? No, there is nothing wrong with the baby. *Your point of departure should always be that newborns who scream need food.* Food is the path to life.

A baby who is plagued by survival anxiety so intense that she is staring death in the face has been transported back to that traumatic, agonizing moment of birth, when life literally hung by a thread. And that thread has been cut.

You should concentrate primarily on giving the baby such huge quantities of food that it actually seems *unreasonable* that she should want or need so much. A pair of avian parents who spend their days shuttling worms and insects to their shrilly peeping brood probably also think that it seems unreasonable that their young should require so much fodder – if they have time to think at all, struggling as they are to supply all those gaping mouths with sustenance.

Read "What do you do?" in Part one of *For the Love of Children* and follow the Standard Model as described. Your little newborn, who is refusing to sleep, will not be calmed with only one such meal. A one and a half-hour meal, followed by a two and a half-hour sleep will not become standard

130

operating procedure all at once. A single meal will not allay survival anxiety so strong it has escalated to mortal fear, even if you follow the program to the letter (which is essential if you are to succeed). You will have to be patient. You can't give up after one attempt because the baby doesn't immediately fall asleep after one and a half hours.

Put yourself in her position. You are on the brink of starvation, you think you are literally staring death in the face, and then someone offers you a lavish dinner. Would that be enough to make you believe that life would go on *after* you had finished eating?

After a meal with all the trimmings, in keeping with the Standard Model, a newborn is at least calm, even if she is awake. And that is no mean feat. Your lavish dinner would calm you down too. So make that work for you! Let the baby stay awake but in a restful way. Don't excite her and don't carry her around. The meal, including the socializing, is officially over, even if she doesn't fall asleep.

Take her out for a walk in the carriage, for example, and let her lie on her back and look at the sky (take down the hood). Don't try to attract her attention. Or if you want to stay home, wrap her in a blanket as always and lay her down on a bed or on a soft carpet where you can keep an eye on her without disturbing her. Put her down on her back, since she is so wide-awake. Put out something pleasant to look at: a book with a colourful cover (lean it against something or open it so that it stands up), a vase of flowers (preferably red or yellow, a newborn's favorite colours), or a brightly patterned blouse or towel which you can hang over a chair beside her. She can lie where she is for quite a long time. Don't do anything until she does.

Either she will fall asleep, in which case all you have to do is leave her where she is on her back. Just put an extra blanket over her. But keep watch. There is always the risk of potentially suffocating spit-ups when a newborn is on her back.

Or she will become anxious after a while and start to cry. You will hear from her crying how tired she is. Go to her immediately, pick her up gently and put her to whichever of your breasts is fullest.

Let her eat with no interruptions. Sit (or lie) still and say nothing. Try to *feel* tender and confident. Everything is going to be fine now! As you will have realized, this little portion is extracurricular. It's an emergency ration. The baby will close her eyes and continue eating, albeit slowly. Stimulate her every now and then by moving your nipple in her mouth. Hold one little hand with your finger and make sure she is bundled snugly in her blanket.

Finally, sleep comes. She releases her grip on your nipple, which slides out of her mouth. Put her carefully against your shoulder and burp her.

When you take her off your shoulder and hold her in your hands as she rests against your arms, you will see how marvellously deep her sleep is. Whatever you do, however you handle her, she will go on sleeping. Nothing in the world can wake her until survival anxiety does.

Put the baby down on her stomach and tuck her in. The blanket should be loose on top but tight around the little body. And peace descends. The baby will not sleep for long, though. A newborn who thinks she is staring death in the face does not dare sleep for long, even if her anxiety is not acute.

You would feel bloated and dozy after your lavish dinner, but you would not dare to close your eyes for very long either. The dinner was merely the exception that proves the rule.

Regardless of where the baby fell asleep – the bed, the carpet or out in the carriage and regardless of whether or not she needed a crisis ration, she will start crying again relatively soon – in an hour or less. (If she sleeps longer, count your blessings. Maybe you have solved the problem in one fell swoop!) Now you just follow the program again.

As soon as the baby starts to cry, put her to your breast and start another meal. Follow the one and a half-hour Standard Model routine to the letter. Even if you think it seems impossible, or even downright insane, to stuff her with so much food and keep her awake for so long when she has already eaten enormous quantities and stayed awake for hours (except for the little nap), trust me. This is the only way, and it is an effective way, to allay the anxiety that so plagues a child that she doesn't dare sleep because she is afraid that she will die.

As soon as the conviction that death is imminent turns into normal survival anxiety, which you will alleviate continuously by following the Standard Model, your child will sleep. And sleep well.

In the section entitled "Sleep", we discussed little people who get day and night backwards. They need help setting their internal clocks.

Jerry, two weeks old, is a perfect baby. All he does is eat and sleep, eat and sleep. Feedings take half an hour at the most, Mom or Dad changes his diaper before or after the meal, and then Jerry is off to dreamland again. And his parents have heard all these horror stories about how difficult it is to have a baby in the house! Mom and Dad, and everyone else who happens to be around Jerry are utterly enchanted by this "good" baby. The nights are a little up and down, but nothing serious. Sometimes Jerry eats two or three times, but good baby that he is, he falls back to sleep – until he hits three weeks that is.

Then storm clouds start gathering on the horizon. Little Jerry, who sleeps like an angel during the day, starts holding court at night. His night sleep is but a memory. He keeps waking up and wanting to be fed, and then he sleeps for half an hour and screams for two. He refuses to sleep. Soon a pattern emerges. Jerry starts using his mom as a pacifier, but he is still not satisfied. He does not sleep any better just because he is glued to his mother's breast.

His parents are hollow-eyed zombies, but Jerry is wide-awake. No one wants to socialize, turn on the lights and present the world. If there is nothing else to do, I might as well scream, Jerry seems to reason. Then the night comes when he not only refuses to sleep, he refuses to eat too. But scream he does. And with that, the circus has come to town. Mom and Dad carry him endlessly, hour and hour, and Jerry of course cooperates – until someone tries to put him back to bed...

Little Jerry won't be able to set his internal clock all by himself. He needs help to schedule his social activities so that they coincide with the daytime hours. For that is just what Jerry has become: social.

A child's efforts to participate socially are as determined as they are fascinating. Not only the people around him, but things, the world, culture, time, reality, the whole range of dimensions and concepts are encompassed by his desire to learn, understand, partake and participate. A human child's striving becomes evident at a tender age indeed, from the end of the second week of life or the beginning of the third, when what I call the true birth occurs. It is then that young babies' innate, inexorable instinct to *participate socially* makes itself known.

This instinct is just as strong as – and inextricably linked to – the instinct to survive. For human beings are flock animals. Until they are old enough to fend for themselves, their lives depend on their membership in a flock that protects them and schools them in the art of survival. So little Jerry is not simply in need of "company". Nor does he need comfort (which he wouldn't accept anyway). He is on a voyage of discovery. He wants to learn how to live. That is why Mom and Dad can't expect any leadership from *him*. He is expecting leadership from *them*. And he will allow them to assume a leadership role without a murmur of protest if only they will step up to the plate! For in Jerry's eyes, they are the ones who know how this world works. Jerry looks to them not only to ensure he stays alive but also to ensure that he is inducted into the flock community that guarantees survival.

Therefore, Jerry's parents have to give their three-week-old baby his first *social* cue. "Out here in the world, we sleep at night and save social activities for the day."

The method is the tried and true – and infallible – Standard Model. The parents pick a certain morning to begin and then follow the program religiously. Jerry, for whom the difference between day and night remains a mystery, is of course very sleepy during the day, so mom and dad have to employ all manner of ruses to keep him awake through the whole program, meal by meal. They are aiming for two-hour waking periods. Jerry is to be thoroughly entertained during socializing through concentrated direct contact. Demonstrations of earthly wonders are on the agenda: mirrors, windows, lamps to name but a few, in addition to abundant rations of talking, laughing, cuddling and playing. And if it should happen that one of the day's meals – which are designed for the express purpose of giving Jerry all he can handle in terms of food, sensory input and socializing – pushes him over the edge into overtiredness, he may have to be buffed for a little while to regain his equilibrium.

When night falls, no quarter is given. *At night, people sleep.*

Jerry is placed in the carriage. The carriage will be pulled back and forth with steady movements to send him back to sleep as soon as he wakes up during what will be a six-hour night (at least) without food. See "Sleep" for techniques to wean babies off night feedings! If he is under a month old, he should be given one night-feeding, but only a quick refill to fall back to sleep on, and six uninterrupted hours is the bare minimum.

After three days of this methodical cure according to the Standard Model, night court has been shut down and internal clocks have been adjusted.

But there is evening court too. We should perhaps say a word or two about this, even if it doesn't really fall under the heading of children who refuse to sleep.

Babies who hold evening court need to be helped to take a little nap.

The evening fuss, which I and many other mothers usually call it, is a very common phenomenon. It is part and parcel of the baby's arduous struggle for social participation. This evening fuss is sometimes labelled evening colic, or simply colic. I can only shake my head in disbelief. The fact that little newborns, who have just begun their terrestrial odyssey with an unshakeable determination to be inducted into a community, to belong somewhere and to learn how life is lived on Planet Earth should be over-tired by evening is no more bizarre than adults feeling like dish rags after a day touring the Vatican Museum in Rome. How else would we feel after wandering slack-jawed through hundreds of galleries and being overloaded with sensory input in the form of *objets d'art* and trying desperately to make sense of what we were seeing, even though we lacked the expertise or even sufficient elementary knowledge to even come close to understanding all this art, culture and history? How would we react when we staggered down the steps of the museum only to be met by someone who sympathetically asked us if we were suffering from colic?

Here is how the evening fuss can look: You have looked after your newborn just as the program says you should for the whole day. She has slept when she is supposed to and been awake when she is supposed to, and the evening feeding is drawing near. The meal starts. She eats, is changed, socializes, "converses", and gets the requisite dose of impressions and encounters. All is as it should be. Just over an hour goes by, an hour and a half perhaps if she has started having baths. Now it's time for a top up, as specified by the program.

In a panic, the baby refuses. What's going on? You are confused. You try to coax her to eat. Refusal!

Your baby can go on strike at any time in the late afternoon or evening; it can happen in the middle of the meal, in the bath, during changes, or during socializing. And food will *not* help. If nine out of every ten cries are due to survival anxiety, then the tenth is due to over-exertion – mental exhaustion. The remedy is a very short nap.

This nap – twenty minutes will do it – corresponds to the "mental" nap you, as an adult, would take (hopefully) if your circuits were overloaded with new input. "I have to be alone for a while," you say and withdraw. You perhaps lie on your bed for a while or just lean against a closed door and shut your eyes. Locking yourself in the bathroom with a newspaper is a good time-out, as is sneaking out into the garden under some pretext. After this little mental holiday, you feel renewed and ready to grapple with the world again. You have recovered your strength, cleared your head and caught your breath.

Infants don't have the privilege of taking such mental holidays. Infants don't have access to any escape hatches. Newborns have no ruses, as you and I do, to enable them to withdraw from the world. Newborns must be helped to sleep, since it is only through sleep that they can get a little mental relief, a sorely needed spiritual pause.

Under such circumstances, putting the baby down in her bed or in the carriage will have a less than successful outcome. She associates bed and carriage with sleep and her despair may worsen because she doesn't *want* to sleep. She *wants* to be a part of the action. She has to be because that is how she is programmed. Her striving for social participation is as undiminished as it is necessary. But she doesn't have the strength. Right at this moment, she is just not up to it. Instinct is strong but ability is fading.

So put the baby on a blanket on the floor and let her stay with you, wherever you happen to be. Don't banish her from the community. Let her remain at the center of things. Help her to sleep by buffing her a little. Speak to her soothingly if she has so worked herself up that her little body is tense. Buff calmly, confidently and continuously. Tense little evening fussers are few and far between. As a rule, they are mentally and physically exhausted, and they are more than happy to take a break from things and rest.

Put a blanket over the baby when she has fallen asleep and keep an eye on the clock. If she doesn't wake up by herself after exactly twenty minutes, wake her. If she sleeps longer than twenty minutes, this will result in confusion for the rest of the evening, and both of you will be out of sync.

Caress her gently over the head, wrap her in the blanket and pick her up. Then take up exactly where you left off and continue the meal. You will witness a metamorphosis. The little baby who was at the end of her rope is sunny and full of curiosity again, and in full and tireless pursuit of social participation.

As you no doubt have gathered, the evening meal can take its own sweet time as a result. The baby has recharged her batteries, so the last meal will be extended by a significantly larger margin than the twenty minutes that were lost during her brief nap. A good deal of food will go down the hatch! This extended meal makes a perfect end to the day, before a long and good night's sleep.

Naturally, you can carry a baby who is in evening-fuss mode around and let her nap in your arms, or sit down and let her drop off on your knee. However, there are two reasons why I think neither of these options is a good idea.

For one thing, you risk being regarded as a walking bed – or a sitting one – for a long time to come and under all circumstances. For another, you are also denying your baby the right to her own life, now that she has left the womb once and for all. In so doing, you make it more difficult for her to step out into the world, which is where she has to live now. A symbiosis, which should have ended with the true birth at around three weeks, is thus prolonged.

Of course the baby longs back to that state. Of course, she loves sleeping in your arms. Your movements, your warmth, the beating of your heart are all sweet reminders of her familiar past life in the womb. But there is no going back, and your baby knows it. A human cub's stubborn struggle to participate socially is courageous and inexorable. However, given the chance to return to what is safe and familiar, she will, in weak moments, want to do so – just as we adults try to hide from life's challenges and somehow avoid having to deal with them when we are weak and insecure. But we *must* deal with them if we want to grow, develop and learn.

Don't misunderstand me! I am not for a moment suggesting that you should never carry your child around in your arms. But I do think that you should only do so in three contexts and three contexts only (unless of course you are comforting a child who has hurt herself and is sad):

1. To get a newborn into a *certain state of mind* so that she can eat or sleep. In the latter case, the baby is in such distress she is on the verge of hysteria. Thus, you must avail yourself of the same calming techniques that you use on a baby that refuses to eat so that she can be put down at all (see "If some-

thing goes wrong: the newborn refuses to eat").

2. To *transport* her from one place to another.

3. For *fun* when you cuddle and play.

The third scenario would fall under the rubric of socialization, according to the Standard Model. Carrying thus signifies a mutually enjoyable activity, which presupposes that Mom or Dad *wants* to carry the baby around and don't feel obliged to for whatever reason. It is a meeting that both parties want, need and get a kick out of. Give and take in other words. It is here that tenderness and loving physical affection are born. Two people who are curious about each other and who arouse joyous expectation in each other have the chance to interact. And that is a meeting between a little person and a big person that is worth being wide-awake for!

PSYCHOLOGICAL WELL-BEING

We come into this world tiny, naked and defenceless. A newborn with nowhere to belong wouldn't last a day.

To compensate for her defencelessness, a newborn arouses a protective instinct in her parents. A father was telling me about the birth of his child:

"Suddenly, there was a cry – a cry that seemed to break through everything. It kind of woke me up. I was bowled over. Not by *her* cry, but the baby's. It wasn't like anything I had ever heard before. It was so weak and helpless. It was like he was pleading with me. I felt my chest tighten. *She* had had a rough time, and I wasn't feeling so great myself. But the baby... the baby had suffered the most. In that second, I understood. At the same time, I was overwhelmed by a feeling that was so new, so unfamiliar, a feeling that I didn't know I had in me – a feeling of responsibility, a desire to come to the rescue of this helpless little being. I wanted to support him and protect him, no matter what. Here was a human being so dependent, so exposed, so defenceless... and his cries were so despairing. It was almost as though he knew how helpless he was as soon as he took his first breath. 'A boy,' said the mid-wife and she smiled at me, but it was so much more than that I remember thinking to myself, much, much more. It shook me to the core. It was a turning point. My world suddenly acquired another dimension, a new depth. Ever since then, I've felt my responsibility as a father twenty-four seven. It's not a heavy burden, but I take it seriously."

A man can perhaps remain unmoved by his woman's pregnancy, but he can't help but be deeply moved at the sight of his child being born.

The mother, for her part, is prepared both physically and emotionally to bond with the child that has just emerged from her womb.

It is not only a protective instinct that is awakened in the parents, but joy and pride too. A mother who shows off her baby, or a father who offers cigars to all his friends are not only experiencing profound feelings of tenderness and responsibility. If producing a child isn't an accomplishment, I would like to know what is! And the result should be displayed. However civilized and open-minded we think we are, there is still a primitive hunter-gatherer within all of us that jumps up and down and pounds its chest. "I did it! I did it! I propagated the species! I am one of the fittest, so my genes will live on! Just look!"

Say what you like, but the tender delight that new parents – the flock – take in their recently arrived child is palpable. One only wishes that such delight would endure.

Why doesn't it always? Naturally, the reason is that newborns are demanding. A baby cannot be abandoned. The need for nourishment is bottomless and continuous. The need for protection against every conceivable danger is constant.

An element of inadequacy soon creeps into the parenting experience in our time and culture, which is a paradox indeed. For in our time and culture, with all the material means that we have at our disposal in the so-called developed world, we are superbly equipped to provide our newborns with everything they need in terms of sustenance and protection. Instead of being happy, grateful and proud over our good fortune, we stagger under a mountain of guilt. We will come back to this paradox a little later.

A human cub immediately seeks its *belonging* – just as a cub of any species that must be taken care of in its infant years seeks its mother and its flock. The newborn's life depends on his or her community. The community provides food, but also protection. A human cub is dependent on both for a very long time. Everyone knows how important it is that a newborn receive love, tenderness and security. We have all been enslaved to the insight that the first year, the first year's first months, even the first moments after birth can set the tone for a baby's psychological health. It is a crushing responsibility, and many parents are terrified of it before the child is even born. How can they ever be good enough? How will they ever be able to give their children all the emotional contact they need?

I wish I could just snap my fingers and free you of your terror. For everything that needs to be given is at your fingertips, and it is a wonderful relief to *know* that it is at your fingertips. Parents should not be filled with dread, but instead should feel nothing but joy and natural pride.

You can give sustenance and protection. You can provide belonging. And belonging is what human cubs seek.

It is there that love is born.

It is not difficult to become attached to a newborn. Nature has thoroughly prepared the way. However, you would have to be a saint, or at least inordinately virtuous, to maintain your enthusiasm for a baby that does nothing but scream. Few are the parents who have not at some point had murderous thoughts towards their infants. Feelings of powerlessness, despondency, desperation – it's a continuum with many stages – afflict parents, but in the end, self-preservation kicks in and all that's left is a single enormous black hole of *refusal*. And the baby screams and screams and screams.

So, my advice to you, when you are tending to your baby's psychological well-being, is to give her food, more food, and then more food after that! Follow the Standard Model, which stipulates that food shall be given not only to alleviate hunger, but also to *prevent* hunger from occurring in the first place. For just as you are unable to feel joy or pride – or love – during those times when your baby does nothing but scream, so is your baby unable to accept your love when survival anxiety is ripping her to bits. Give her food. Give her food until she really can't take any more – not until you don't feel like giving her any more.

Physical well-being will come. Then, and only then, will psychological well-being be possible. And once your baby achieves psychological well-being, you will too. And you don't have to be either saint or superhuman to joyfully take to your heart in every conceivable way a newborn who is calm and satisfied. On the contrary, it would require superhuman effort *not* to fall head over heels in love!

So, at the top of the list – as usual – is food. Then comes care, protection and personal connection. The point in the Standard Model program that I call socializing – a high-level conversation – involves direct contact, *an encounter*, between you and your baby. Socializing confirms the fact that she belongs, and provides that vital connection to the flock into which the baby has been born.

Even today, in spite of (or perhaps because of) all my years parenting infants, I can't resist trying to kindle the merest twinkling of socializing with every little newborn I come across. Those social moments with infants have been the high points of my life. Certain encounters one remembers – those moments when your soul enters into a union with another human being's in a conversation, a glance, a feeling. Fleeting though these encounters may be, they are unforgettable because they are pure, open and genuine. They confirm a profound commonality. An encounter with a newborn is just that – your soul opens to another and there is a mutuality that involves complete union just then and there.

You can catch the gaze of a newborn, even a very young one, even if it does take a little time and effort. And what a gaze it is! The eyes wander where they will – the eye muscles are still not fully operational – but once the eyes coordinate and you capture her gaze and hold it, time stands still. And if you say something, anything, a question, a greeting, or simply a vowel with a smile and some warmth in your voice, a miracle happens. You receive an answer. Even if you don't say anything, but merely capture the baby's gaze, she "talks" to you.

This socializing, this *encounter*, confirms that she belongs.

A little person who feels good should have fun too. And all it takes is a little organization.

I think that, apart from survival anxiety, which must constantly be allayed, we are born to live joyfully. Babies love life and expect it to be fun. It takes very little to amuse a little baby! Consequently, it doesn't require much artistry on your part to awaken a *joie de vivre* that is already there. All you have to do is make sure that your baby doesn't sink into a malaise that takes the edge off her lust for life.

Always smile at an infant when you make eye contact with her, regardless of how you feel yourself!

Position her bed so that she can see what's going on rather than having to stare at a blank wall.

Make a habit of leaving the hood of the baby carriage down when you are out for walks and take it away completely as soon as the weather permits. Even if a newborn can't see much else besides the sky – if she is on her back and awake – a wide open sky beats an obscured one any day. And a newborn who is lying on her stomach in the carriage will soon start to struggle up high enough to peek over the side. Her efforts are touchingly determined and they should be facilitated whenever possible.

Make sure the carriage, the wall and/or the crib is decorated with brightly patterned textiles or pictures. The classic Disney characters are always popular with a newborn because of the prominent black eyes and bright colors. Your baby should also have something to look at on both sides when she is on her change table. Colorful postcards or book jackets are perfect. Place them at the baby's eye height so all she has to do is turn her head from side to side. These pictures, patterns, colors and similar refinements require a certain amount of effort on the baby's part to contemplate *and should not be replaced during the first month.* (Thereafter, however, they should be replaced at regular intervals.)

Newborns like yellow and red. They like eyes too; a stuffed animal with large eyes and bright colours is usually appreciated. Position it so that the animal's eyes "meet" the baby's.

One of my eldest children was once given a cotton rabbit with long ears. The body was red, the arms were yellow, and the eyes were black as coal. She was given this rabbit before we even left the hospital, and I had no doubt that she was way too young to play with it. Once we got home, I put it up on the wall at the head of her bed, and there it stayed. I promptly forgot about it and didn't notice when it ended up on the floor.

But the baby did. She was one month old, and the evening that the rabbit fell to the floor, she cried for an hour.

I did everything I could think of. I fed her, put her back down, picked her up, changed her, tried feeding her again, put her back to bed, and felt myself slowly going insane. Her screams continued unabated. I was about to leave the room, catch my breath and count to ten, when I suddenly caught sight of the rabbit, which was sticking out from under the bed. The poor rabbit had to bear the brunt of my frustration. "Bloody rabbit! As though *you'd* be of any help!" Angrily I put the smugly grinning rabbit back on its perch. The baby fell silent. For the longest time, she supported herself on her arms with her head up and looked at the rabbit. Then she put her head down and fell asleep.

The world has to be little before it can be big.

The baby's struggle to orient herself in the world, to know, to recognize, to grasp, to understand is admirable, ceaseless, courageous and implacable. Over-exertion is an ever-present danger. Over-exertion finds expression in new cries that, in conjunction with the true birth, are added to the cries of survival anxiety. These cries signify over-tiredness. Such cries are most noticeable during the evening fuss, which we discussed in "If something goes wrong: the newborn refuses to sleep". The risk of over-exertion can be minimized if you present the world to your baby in manageable chunks rather than throwing the entire Vatican Museum at her in one afternoon.

Give her certain bases within the home from which she can orient herself and which she can recognize. The bed or the cradle, which is a fixed point, the change table, which is another fixed point, a corner of the sofa that you have designated for breastfeeding, the place where you always begin socializing, a spot on the carpet where she always takes her nap during the evening fuss, and, from one month on, a particular place in the house where the baby lies every day on her blanket, looks around and stays awake! Designated, recognizable points that are used for some purpose regularly provide beneficial stability. Naturally, you ensure that everything *within* these reoccurring locations is agreeable, but don't move them unless it is necessary.

Against this background, you will understand why I maintain that it is less taxing for a baby to be carted around to friends and relatives for inspection when she is a freshly minted newborn *before* the true birth rather than after, since it is at that point that the baby starts to take in her surroundings in earnest.

Don't allow yourself to be stressed into believing that infants need a multitude of stressful activities on what is an already stressful agenda! Ideally, the baby's world should remain more or less unchanged during the second month of life.

Attachment is vital for a baby's psychological well-being.

A large part of this attachment is there already. A baby nurses at her mother's breast, and during the honeymoon, especially before the three-week mark, she is in the world physically, but mentally the baby is still in the womb.

In conjunction with the true birth, this attachment must be affirmed. This happens during breastfeeding, but also during socializing, *the encounter*. And, naturally, it happens during those moments of tender cuddling that become warmer and more frequent as the baby's survival anxiety recedes.

What must not be forgotten, however, is that the baby is establishing – and was born with a powerful instinct to establish – an attachment to her environment, to the flock as a whole, and all that the flock signifies in terms of a firm foothold and a place on earth to call home.

A baby's sense of belonging is not restricted to one person. Your own sense of belonging is not restricted to one person either, or even to a group of people. You live somewhere, surrounded by familiar objects, signs and symbols that confirm you are where you belong. You have a place in the universe that is yours. Even if you live alone and you are your own flock, you still have a nest, a fixed point. You can move your nest, just as an office or a factory can change premises – but the signs and symbols of what you call home move with you, and when a child forges her attachment, such things are just as vital as the people in her life.

At the risk of sounding less than respectful, I would argue that the people in the nest, the flock members, constitute a category of symbols in the child's eyes. Belonging encompasses everything, the people *and* the nest. The whole package constitutes the flock and it is the flock that provides the very belonging.

This I hope will go some way towards putting to rest the misconception that you are inadequate. You are not solely responsible for ensuring that your baby feels secure and attached to her home and hearth!

I also hope to liberate you from the flip side of this misconception, namely that you are the only one who can give your baby what she needs. ("Everything will be all right now. *Mommy* is here!") Within the fixed point, within the flock, other people can confirm to the child that she belongs.

Of course, this doesn't mean that a newborn should be exposed to a constant stream of strangers who take turns spending the day looking after her within the nest. Nor should mother and child be shunted around from flock to flock, where they make guest appearances in environments that change from one day to the next. In both cases, the baby's psychological well-being is jeopardized.

Let me repeat: let the world be small before it becomes large – this goes for people as much as for environments! The more constant and predictable the base, the more extensive and secure the area of operations.

The baby strives to belong, and attachment only needs to be confirmed, not built from scratch.

By the same token, a child is also born with an innate sense of trust that only has to be confirmed, not conjured up out of thin air. To confirm trust, all you have to do is prove yourself worthy of it, and your baby's demands are more than reasonable. All that is required is a guarantee of survival and protection.

Older children also require leadership. "What do I have to know in order to live in this particular place? What do I have to learn to manage life in the best possible way?"

To forfeit a trust is to betray it, and to betray a child is to reject it.

However, the baby's innate sense of trust is so strong, and having it confirmed so vital to survival, that she will spare no effort to win the parents' – primarily the mother's, with whom the baby has her prime connection – love, attention and care. This innate sense of trust must be confirmed and responded to not just once, but time after time, day after day.

The good news is that this trust is not easily forfeited either. However bad your parenting, whatever your sins, you have a generous margin for error. Your baby will give you another chance. Magnanimous to a fault, children will stretch out their hands to their parents a hundred, a thousand, ten thousand times as they grow up.

The well-known Harlow experiments tell how baby monkeys behave in their attempts to establish contact with mothers who systematically reject them, mothers who themselves have never had maternal contact and are therefore indifferent, or even abusive, to their children:

"One of the things that tore at the heartstrings of the people in charge of the experiment was the desperate attempts of the young monkeys to make contact with the abnormal mother. She hit them and knocked them down. Again and again they would approach her. The mother would grind the faces of the young monkeys against the floor. They would wriggle loose and again try to make contact with her. The strength, the stubbornness, the endurance that the youngsters exhibited in their attempts to make contact and

144

the punishment they received affected strong men to such an extent that they could barely bring themselves to observe this unnatural behavior."

Eventually, the young monkeys developed the technique of going behind the mother, climbing up on her back and working their way around to her front, tells Harlow.

To accept and embrace, rather than reject, is to respond to trust, affirm belonging and maintain attachment. This is what cultivating an infant's psychological well-being is all about.

In our time and culture, a feeling of inadequacy soon insinuates itself into parents' lives. In the chapter "The Best Laid Plans...", I talked about an exaggerated emphasis on love to compensate children for their exclusion from their social participation.

A mother or father who takes parental leave must overcome resistance that is built in to the structure of parental leave itself.

Adults who are excluded from their own communities, be that exclusion ever so voluntary, know full well that their children will never be a part of those communities. The flock will be broken up and depleted. The common struggle for survival that should be the flock's goal isn't really common at all. Certain flock members will be excluded while the struggle is actually going on and will only be granted entry when everyone else takes time off.

This is how the situation might be explained to the human cubs: "There is no place for you in my struggle for survival, I have no use for you, and I don't need you. But I will love you to pieces in my spare time."

So the world is upside down: adults make guest appearances in their children's world when they can and want to instead of inducting children into the adult world when the children can and want to.

Therefore, the first commandment of good infant care, which in turn is the prerequisite for an infant's psychological well-being, is to ensure that *both you and your baby operate under the assumption that you are at home because it is necessary for you, and not because you have had a child.*

All the love in the world cannot compensate children for their exclusion from social participation, from the struggle for survival that so engages *you*, the flock – and deep down in their heart of hearts, parents still know it.

Let's take a look at how young children behave when they learn to iron clothes.
- They look at what the adults do.
- They try themselves.
- They succeed.
- They are put to work with the goal of making sure that what needs to be ironed gets ironed. For everyone. They have a task within the flock. *(The others wouldn't manage as well without me.)*
- They evolve their own method of ironing. Maybe later on, they will develop a new and better iron. They will in any event be in a position to pass on the art of ironing, which they will have developed from personal experience.

This is social participation. It is one of thousands of examples of children's methodology, which is common to the entire human species. Children are born to explore, master and eventually change reality, the human condition and the world. It is difficult to explore, even more difficult to master, and quite impossible to change a reality from which one is excluded.

And to soften the blow and to justify the systematic exclusion of children from social participation, kids are given toy irons to iron doll's clothes with. The parents get a consolation prize too. They don't have to feel guilty about "forcing" their children to "help out". And love is *compensatory*.

Many parents stay home with their children, even though they want to work outside the home and indeed have to in order to make ends meet.

They do not do so because they love their children so much that they can't bear to be away from them. Nor do they stay home because they distrust all other kinds of supervision as a matter of general principle. They stay home because they think it is wrong to exclude children from the reality that is valid for the parents, namely the struggle for survival that involves all the flock's members.

They therefore transfer this reality, their own activities, to the home, where they can construct an existence that includes their children and in which their young can be put to work when they request it (as dictated by their social instincts). The parents want to keep the adult world accessible, even though this world is relatively isolated. They construct a community within the flock, where the young are protected and *needed*.

The home is one of the few workplaces where children are given the chance to participate socially, to contribute and to be needed. (*The others wouldn't manage as well without me.*) The work that is done in the home is limited to be sure, but it is for the good of, and necessary for, all the flock members. It is in the interests of the flock's collective existence. It is reality, not therapy. In a home, the cleaning, cooking and laundry have to be done, whether anyone feels like it or not.

The institutions that take care of children have to overcome resistance that is predetermined by their structure. The adults who work in these institutions would have to find things for children to do that were necessary for the *adults* in order to offer the children socialization. The adults must participate socially if they are to offer children social participation. Children cannot create social participation from nothing.

And creating the pre-conditions isn't easy. Parents who work at home, and who maintain that doing so is not only economically defensible but also necessary, pull off this *tour de force* without even thinking about it. They do what they do not just for the child or children, but for the flock as a whole, whose members are engaged in a common struggle for survival.

Thus, making use of the children is the most natural thing in the world. The kids are needed. And within the confines of the flock, socialization takes place.

Parents on parental leave, who feel that they have more or less been condemned to staying at home with the child, are not as successful.

However, it is the staff at institutions that are least successful, since they are under strict orders from on high never to do anything that is necessary for *them*. The opportunities for socialization that society's institutions have to offer children are negligible to non-existent.

These are places where young children are not needed and never will be.

Human beings are born with three primary instincts that dictate their goals from the moment they are born to the moment they die.
- *The instinct to survive.*
- *The instinct to participate socially* – to belong to a flock and to contribute to the common struggle for survival.
- *The instinct to develop.*

On the first point, this New World is without sin. If it is humanly possible, our children's physical survival is guaranteed.

Transgressions with regard to the third point are also few and far between (although often enough, restrictions are imposed).

It is the second point against which sins are committed as a matter of principle and to enthusiastic acclaim. With much ideological fanfare, children are expelled from the flock and left to themselves in a hermetically sealed children's world. They are refused participation in every task that relates to the struggle for survival, a struggle that should be the whole flock's business. They are then trotted out like some kind of leisure accessory and showered with compensatory love.

With industrialization, work was separated from leisure, the workplace from the home, and the productive from the non-productive. The result was as bizarre as it was logical; emotional life was separated from work life. We were to love in one place and work in another.

With this parting of the ways, the word need took on a purely emotional connotation as far as children were concerned.

But real community goes beyond loving and being loved. Being a part of a community also means being needed in a concrete way. It means having tasks that contribute to the common good; it means functioning in a social context where we serve interests other than our own.

Every adult knows full well that a purely emotional community is not enough. The instinct to participate socially demands so much more of us.

If a purely emotional community were enough, adults home on parental leave would be completely content just being with their children, being needed by them, being loved by them and loving them back. They would not feel the urge to do anything (except housework while the child slept; see "Mary and her mom" in Part five of *For the Love of Children*).

Children, in turn, would be completely satisfied with loving and being loved by their mother and father, who would be constantly hovering around them. But children are not satisfied with this arrangement. This purely emotional community is not enough. The instinct to participate socially demands so much more.

Human beings are constructive and adaptable animals. When they divide the concept of community into an emotional part and a work-related part, they begin to think that if one is strengthened, the other can be eliminated without making a whole lot of difference. In keeping with industrial society's all-encompassing trajectory towards centralized production, the message of love's necessity is trumpeted ever more loudly and intensely.

Emotional hysteria, however, does no one any good. Nor does material abundance – Swedish pre-school children today have over 500 toys apiece

– make for a meaningful existence. Children must be inducted into a community. The barriers that society has put up must be torn down, and it is ordinary people like us, not the elites, who will do the job.

I want to believe that our motivation will be that most important of instincts, the instinct to survive. We must take back our lives, and our lives include our children. When the day comes, we will not do what has to be done out of charity or because our consciousness has been raised or because we have been gripped by a new trend. We will do it because it is necessary.

Children should be at the center of things.

But children should not be the center of things.

IF SOMETHING GOES WRONG: THE NEWBORN IS UNHAPPY

A mother wrote:

"As a new first-time mother, I have often thought about you. You have managed to bear and raise so many children. I have thought about you because I feel like such a clueless failure as a mother.

Marcus, our son, is now four months old. He is such a beautiful child, and I am so terrified of damaging him mentally – of destroying him.

Marcus was planned and wanted (I am 35 years old), and I was so looking forward to being home and looking after him. Things went pretty smoothly for the first two months, in spite of colic and sleepless nights. But the anxiety was there. I was – and still am – so worried about doing something wrong. I so want Marcus to be happy. I love him so much and would never do anything to hurt him. I was alone with him during the day and in the evenings, and even on weekends. My husband travels on business a lot, and my mother and mother-in-law live out of town.

Two months after giving birth the fear hit me. Everything seemed so hopeless. I had to psych myself up to look after Marcus. It was like trying to run under water. It was sheer hell.

I eventually got some help from my mom and mother-in-law, and things were really looking up, but when I was alone with Marcus again, the dread and the sleepless nights returned. My condition is called 'post partum neurosis' and is not unusual. Not everyone ends up in a psychiatric unit, as I have. As you can understand, I am forever trying to figure out why things turned out the way they did. Of course, one reason is that I worry so much about Marcus, which, funnily enough, probably has something to do with the fact that I work in a day care center…

I have learned that children have to be listened to, that they should never just be left to cry. I have read everything I could lay my hands on about child care and child rearing, and the more I read, the more confused I got. Now I'm at the stage where I regard Marcus as a gigantic problem. I don't dare, I don't want to be around him. It is such a terrible feeling. My fondest wish is to be a good, have-it-all-together mother to Marcus, but how? Maybe they can help me here. I'm told the prognosis is good…"

Anxiety over a child is necessary and right. But the word has negative connotations. Perhaps seeking is a better way of putting it. If there were no anxiety at all, our senses would not function up to par.

Anxiety crushes so many parents, Marcus's mother being a case in point. This anxiety is something that parents should feel but not suffer from. It is a constructive force. It is related to curiosity, and a willingness to learn and develop. Without this anxiety, this seeking, human beings would simply have stopped developing and the species would have died out.

Our anxiety about our children is what gives rise to our feelings of responsibility for them. A pregnancy is a psychological jolt. It involves much more than an ever-expanding abdomen that eventually squeezes out a baby. Assuming responsibility for another life is a momentous undertaking and not one that human beings embark upon lightly, but as parents we do it willingly. Behind the scenes, Nature is putting us through a profound preparation process.

Why is having children so difficult today? "I'm at the stage where I regard Marcus as a gigantic problem. I don't dare, I don't want to be around him."

The pressure on families with children is tremendous, and newborns feel it too. Parents, especially the mother, since she is the one who is still expected to hold the family together, convey to the child that life is hard. "But here at home, you can be happy. Mommy will protect you from everything bad." The burden placed on the mother is heavy indeed. No human being, all by herself, can guarantee another's happiness. The community, a feeling of social solidarity and life itself are part of the mix too. A man can't imprison his wife in a tower and expect her to be happy, no matter how much he assures her of his undying love.

Mothers often crack under the strain. Marcus's mother despaired over her own inadequacy to the point where she was unable to do the only thing that is really necessary: to be *available* to Marcus. Simple availability within the flock – being in physical proximity to her child in a shared world – was made impossible by demands for love and happiness. The baby cracked under the pressure too.

Today, the family by and large no longer produces anything. It consumes, maintains its existence and recovers. The only thing it still does produce is offspring. Around this one product, the parents come together in a community that weighs heavier than emotions because it is fulfilled and complete. (About the division of this community into an emotional part and a work-related part, see the preceding chapter.) This puts a newborn baby at the center of the family in a unique way. It has its advantages to be sure. The child receives attention and consideration, and is given a voice. On the other hand, since the family has been deprived of its economically productive function, the child's community is so limited that socialization is barely possible. In reality, the community is outside the family, and the child plays no part in it and is assigned no tasks. The net result is that the child's only mission in life is to feel good and be happy in the bosom of her family. The child is expected to be happy in spite of the fact she is not needed and does nothing that is necessary or even vaguely beneficial for the flock. She in no way participates in the struggle for survival, which, if she did, would enable her to say, "The others would not manage quite as well without me."

And since it is the child that is the only "product" the family produces, she becomes the focal point of everything. In the end, the child *is* the community. Many parents hold a long dead relationship together for the sake of the child – and there is nothing wrong with that, provided those involved understand what a burden it is for a child to carry the weight of the entire family on her infant shoulders.

So, after all that, here is a memo from me to you:
  • Don't make the child the permanent focal point!
  • Don't feel sorry for a child because she has been born into this cruel world!
  • Don't assume that your child needs constant comforting!
You are the means, not the end. The child is not the end either. We are people who have been born into a world that we share. It must be *explored – mastered – changed.*
  • The first task you offer.
  • The second task you permit.
  • The third task you leave to the child herself.

Although I am of the opinion that the demand for love must be examined, this does not mean that the love between parents and child, which manifests itself in closeness, physical affection, warmth, care, consideration and interest, isn't indispensable.

But the love that is necessary for life is not the same as the love that is given as a consolation prize. Genuine love is something we all need, and we suffer horribly if we are deprived of it. But it doesn't arrive in the mail in an envelope addressed to "occupant". It doesn't arrive with the stork together with the baby. It grows out of a shared life, out of the solidarity that arises from shared burdens, not because it is demanded or wished for.

A newborn needs (in addition to food and sleep) tender physical affection and warmth, and an *attachment* to the members of the flock. This is the soil in which love slowly but surely grows.

And even if this love takes its own sweet time to develop – whereas attachment must happen immediately – its quality is assured, once it develops in the child's heart. Children's love for their parents is sublime. We parents can never expect from other adults the same steadfast loyalty, the same selfless devotion, the same unwavering love that we receive from our children!

Unfortunately, we often take it for granted and don't recognize it for the gift, the miraculous asset that it is.

We must dispense with this exaggerated demand for love and allow love to develop naturally in its own good time. We have to understand what attachment really means, since, while love can take its time, attachment has to occur immediately.

A depressed infant lacks a *positive attachment*.

Imagine you found yourself in an alien world. A Bedouin camp, let's say.

This is where you must live. You have never laid eyes on a Bedouin camp before. You know nothing of life within it. All you know is that this is your world from here on in. You were never given a choice. The decision was made for you. You have to leave your old life behind you – forever.

You're terrified but also curious. And since you don't have a choice, you might just as well make the best of things. You want to live, and this is your only option. You're going to have to do your best to live like a Bedouin.

So, who is going to greet you when you arrive in the camp? Let's call him – we will assume it's a he – your contact man. Without him, you are done for. Someone has to take you under his wing. Someone has to show you around, guide you and help you. How else would you manage? Would you even be allowed to enter the camp without him? You need someone you can pose questions to, someone who can explain how things work, someone who knows at least a few words of your language. You are in an alien environment, surrounded by a bunch of strange people in strange clothes. Their language and customs are incomprehensible. You know nothing of life in a tent or how to survive in the desert generally. All you know is that this is going to be your life. It's the only life on offer.

What if you had no contact man? What if no one greeted you, no one let you into the camp, and no one showed you the ropes? You're just left standing outside the tent until everyone packs up and moves on. You realize you are going to be abandoned in the desert. You would of course run after the Bedouin. You wouldn't have a choice. The alternative is certain death. But what if they rejected you? What if they didn't let you follow them? You would not survive, let alone live in the full sense of the word. You would never be one of them. You would never belong. And the curiosity you felt initially would give way to a bottomless depression. You would be alone, and this would result in your death. The desert would be the end of you, and you know it.

There are researchers who are convinced that all forms of depression have their roots in depressions that occur during infancy. These depressions in turn can be traced to infantile survival anxiety. We have all been helpless and tormented by survival anxiety. We have all been utterly dependent on an adult and a flock that gave us life – literally – from the womb to the day when we were capable of fending for ourselves.

Let's return to the Bedouin camp. We will assume that your contact man is where he should be. He greets you and welcomes you. He shows you the tent. He takes you around and introduces you to the other people in the camp. You greet your new fellow travellers and they all smile at you. The contact man shows you where people sleep, where food is prepared, and what provisions are kept where. He shows you what you can cover yourself with when you get cold at night and where you will sleep.

Outside the tent, he shows you the camels, what they eat and where they are housed. One camel is especially gentle and you are allowed to ride him.

The contact man helps you up onto the camel's back and holds on to you and your mount. You and your contact man laugh together.

Evening comes and you participate in all that is going on. The women are mending clothes and blankets. You have no idea what these things are used for. You scratch your head and ask questions. Everyone laughs and shows you. You leave your contact man and sit down among the women. You watch them work. They show you what they are doing and they let you try your hand at it. You smile at one another.

All the while, your contact man is available to you. He is the only one who understands a little of your language. You can more or less explain your wants and needs to him. Above all, he is very anxious to understand you and help you get what you want as efficiently as possible. He is the one who inducted you into the group. It is his task to make sure you learn to live like the other people in the camp, adjust well and are generally happy.

And he is proud of what he has to show you. He thinks he has a pretty good life. There are problems to be sure, but he doesn't burden you with them. He only wants to acquaint you with the good things in life. It makes it that much easier for you to settle in well. As far as he is concerned, difficulties can wait until you are mature enough and experienced enough to deal with them – and perhaps do something about them.

All the people in the camp do their level best to make sure that your existence is as pleasant, secure and joyous as possible.

The contact man makes sure of that.

That is positive attachment.

In our analogy, a *negative attachment* would look something like this:

You have a contact man, but he is not particularly interested in you. He has taken you in, but his heart is not in his work. He feels he has been co-erced. You were dumped on him. It just happened to be his turn to look after a stranger. He regards you as a burden. He has much better things to do.

But he figures he might as well make the best of a bad deal, so he does what he is supposed to do. He shows you around and explains things, but his enthusiasm is lukewarm to say the least. When you seek him out for guidance on something, he doesn't always have time for you.

And above all, he doesn't like being with you. You're a disturbance. You're in the way. You're irritating. You're a pain. You pick up the vibes. He isn't very subtle about his attitude either. He sighs and rolls his eyes when you ask him questions, so you finally stop asking.

It takes you a long time to feel at home in the camp – if you ever do. You are sad a lot of the time. You feel lonely, rejected, superfluous and in the way.

Eventually, you try to make yourself invisible. You wish you could just disappear. Everyone would be better off.

Your survival is not at stake, not in a physical sense. There is food, and of course you are allowed to eat just like everyone else. But your zest for life is failing. Your depressions become deeper and more frequent.

In the end, depression becomes a permanent state. You can't bootstrap yourself anymore. No one smiles at you, no one takes you under an affectionate wing. You are allowed to participate, but at the same time you are shut out. You are not alone in the literal sense, yet you are as lonely as a human being can be.

Your life is meaningless. There is nothing for you to do in the camp. You don't belong.

You might very possibly leave the camp and head out into the desert, into the darkness that is your constant companion anyway – this time to die.

An infant who is saddled with such a negative attachment eventually turns in on herself and sinks into depression. No matter how well she is cared for physically, she loses her zest for life, and this zest for life is the same as the life force itself.

Infants can commit suicide. If they lose their zest for life, they stop eating. They eat maybe, but they do not keep the food down or derive nourishment from it. They wither away and eventually die.

Fatal depression in infants was not uncommon in orphanages around Europe until quite recently. It should be noted that depression can harvest babies' lives even if material, hygienic and medical standards are very high.

In this regard, there is not much difference between infants and adults. If I am bone weary and just tired of living, all the luxury and medical attention in the world won't save me.

A strange story is told about an orphanage. As was usually the case, infant mortality at this orphanage was high.

The babies slept in a large dormitory with the beds arranged in rows. The strange thing was that the baby who happened to end up in the last bed beside the door survived. This happened time and time again. What was it that was so remarkable about this bed?

The doctors spied one night.

It turned out that the little old woman who cleaned the dormitory was responsible for the miracle. When she had mopped the floor in the evening while the children were asleep, she would sit down beside the last bed to rest her back. While she rested, she would pick up the baby in the last bed and cuddle with it for a while. Once her backache receded, she would kiss the baby, put it back to bed and be on her way.

That is what was saving the lives of the babies who slept in the last bed by the door.

If you take a hard look at depression in adults – your own for example – the common thread that runs through everything is loneliness. Even if loneliness is not literal in the sense of your being physically isolated, it is still a crushing reality for a depressed person.

The well-meaning advice from friends and acquaintances echoes hollowly in the frozen void that imprisons the afflicted. It is difficult to reach someone who has fallen into a deep depression. Conversely, it is difficult for a severely depressed person to reach out to other people.

It is probable that depression in infants and adults has its roots in a feeling of loneliness that is perceived as a threat to survival. Infants are not alone physically. They would not survive alone, any more than you would if you were left to your own devices in the desert in our scenario on the previous page. Infants know, just as you would, that surviving alone is not an option.

From their first moments of life, infants seek out the attachment that will guarantee survival. Throughout their lives, human beings continue to search for a sense of belonging, a place where they fit, a place where everyone's attitude says *you are one of us*.

And just as you would arrive in the Bedouin camp with the positive conviction that your contact man, the one who brought you there in the first place, would look after you, your child is born with an innate sense of trust. Your child counts on the fact that the flock into which she is born will accept her. She has the same positive conviction.

Your baby wants to live and is ready to get on with the business of living in a spirit of curiosity and joy, under the protection and guidance of the flock.

In adults, the same sense of innate trust is awakened when we fall in love and prepare to share our lives with the object of our affections. We don't sit down and draw up a list of demands. We *believe* that the person we love wants what is best for us. We depend upon him/her. We trust completely.

Love makes us just as prepared to *give* trust and understanding.

It takes a lot to erode that trust. We are willing to go a long way to understand and love, to forgive and start over. Kids are too. Their innate sense of trust will survive some hard knocks indeed before that trust is forfeited. It is a trust that forgives and understands.

Infants are hardwired to trust. A normal abandonment – Mom or Dad disappears and then returns – will have not the slightest effect. Your contact man in the camp could be away for days on end without your losing confidence in him. You miss him, but you manage. You know he is coming back. You know he is out there somewhere. Far worse things are required to shake that innate sense of trust.

It is difficult, not to say impossible, to predict what will damage a child.

On the other hand, it is possible to seek explanations after the fact for why things happened the way they did. But even those explanations can be wrong or insufficient. We can never really know since it is impossible to compare a child who, for example, loses her mother with what the same child would have been like if she *hadn't* lost her mother.

What is obvious is that *it is essential for every newborn to immediately forge an attachment* when she or he enters this strange, alien world to carve out a life.

This attachment should of course be positive.

Without this attachment, the child will not survive.

A negative attachment will damage a child.

And this is all predictable.

The contact man in the camp must welcome you with joy, enthusiasm and good will.

Without such an attachment – without a positive attitude from the contact man – life in the camp would become impossible for you. The environment would strike you as *hostile* as the unknown or the concealed always does. You would sink into a depression, into loneliness so intense that it might compromise your instinct to survive.

An infant with a negative attachment or no attachment at all sinks into just such a depression. The threat posed by depression is as great to an infant as it is to you, as you stand alone outside the camp, because it can affect the survival instinct to the point where it is put out of operation entirely.

Depressed infants behave like adults. We adults don't go out into the street and scream. We don't cry for help. We don't demand what is rightfully ours. Instead we withdraw. We keep ourselves to ourselves. We think, we brood, and in the end we wall ourselves off. We may seek comfort in oblivion through drugs, whether prescription or the other variety. The protection that a sense of belonging gives us must be replaced with the false protection that we manufacture ourselves.

Depressed infants retreat into a dream-like drowsiness. They slip into silence, and the light in their eyes and souls flickers and dies. Infants who scream the house down are seldom depressed. Quite the opposite. The most dangerous depressions are also the quietest ones. Infants whose zest for life is ebbing away don't eat, or if they do, they don't gain weight. They don't cry, apart from the odd whimper. They entomb themselves in solitude until all contact is broken and they are unreachable.

Grave neglect, loveless treatment, complete indifference surrounding them can produce such results in infants. They feel totally rejected.

It is very rare that a parent, however little love she or he might feel towards a child, completely rejects it. And infants are prepared to wait a long time for that vital attachment, and they will fight long and hard for it before they finally succumb to depression.

And even after depression has taken hold, you, however wretched a parent you have been, can still repair the damage. We will discuss this further below.

Do you have to resolve all your difficulties and personal problems in order to give your newborn a positive attachment?

My answer is *no*.

Let's take a look at some specific cases of infant depression and the struggle of these infants for attachment. In a book of the 1950's, the Swiss child psychologist, Jacques Berna, relates the following:

"On the advice of a pediatrician, a mother contacted a psychotherapist. Her three-month-old son was suffering from digestive problems. The child accepted the bottle unwillingly and invariably spat out the contents. The baby cried constantly and rarely slept. The pediatrician could find no physical reason for the child's problems.

The therapist was confronted with a closed, emotionally cold woman who discussed her relationship with her child and husband most unwillingly. It turned out that the only reason the marriage had taken place was her pregnancy. The woman felt no connection to her husband or her child. She had been working as a bookkeeper in a store and was well-regarded by her employer. It was her dearest wish to go back to work. All appeals to her maternal instincts had fallen on stony ground and she was completely uninterested in working on her relationship with her husband.

An emergency solution had to be found. As a result, a nanny was employed to take care of the baby, and the woman returned to work. A few days later, the baby was symptom free. Feeding took place without incident, the digestion problems disappeared, and sleep patterns were normal. The baby had found the security he craved with the nanny."

I would like to widen "security" to include "positive attachment". The nanny did not reject the baby. The fact that the baby was comfortable with the nanny indicates that she was good at her job, probably because she liked it. But if the baby had been comfortable with the mother, then the mother would not have been able to return to work (obviously), and returning to work was what she wanted. Her child prevented her from pursuing her career, so she rejected the child.

"Another mother had breastfed her child for four months without any difficulties. Suddenly, she could not breastfeed anymore. At the same time, her child started behaving strangely. The baby cried often, showed signs of anxiety and had physical symptoms. These problems continued for some weeks until the young mother contacted the psychotherapist on the advice of a friend. She unburdened herself to the therapist and admitted that the same day all the trouble started, she had discovered that her husband was being unfaithful. Because she was afraid of him and his relatives, she could not talk to him about it. The therapist saw the couple together with the result that they spoke to each other frankly and the extra-marital affair ended. Shortly thereafter, mother and child were back in equilibrium. The mother's emotional crisis had so disturbed her inner harmony that both mother and child were thrown off balance psychologically."

"A doctor had come across a case of an infant who periodically suffered from bouts of vomiting that could last for several days. No physical causes could be found. It turned out that the baby exhibited these symptoms whenever the father went on a drinking binge and disappeared from the home. The mother was depressed and bitter during these absences and rejected the child. It hardly needs to be said that such a child cannot be successfully treated until the parents sort out their own problems."

With all due respect to the child psychologist, noble though his actions were, I do not agree with his conclusion.

In keeping with the socio-political conditions that prevailed at the time, he placed the burden of guilt on the mother. He encouraged a phoney happiness between mother and child, where the child's well-being would depend on the well-being of the mother.

I would maintain that this demand for love lacks relevance *for the child*. The child does not demand that Mom and Dad live together in idyllic harmony and be blissfully happy.

The child's psychological well-being stands or falls with a positive attachment. This you can give your child without being particularly happy yourself. I know this only too well from personal experience.

As you stand outside the Bedouin camp waiting to start your new life, would you demand that your contact man be totally harmonious and capable of solving all his personal problems? Does he have to be happy? Or would you expect him to be reasonably content and cheerful *when he is with you*? You would know nothing about his personal problems, and I doubt they would strike you as being particularly important. What you would demand – and be positively convinced of – is that he likes showing you the ropes in

159

this incomprehensible Bedouin environment and that he likes you so that you can accept his guidance without feeling that you are in his debt or that you are inadvertently causing him trouble. During those times when he is with you, you would want him to focus on *you* and help *you*, and enjoy himself while doing so. Whatever is going on in his private life, whether he is happy, whether his wife is cheating on him (however these things happen in Bedouin camps!), whether a camel has gone missing, whatever might be worrying him, the important thing is that he not let it worry him just *now*. He doesn't reject *you* because he has personal problems.

As we know, children can live happy, "normal" lives under the most difficult circumstances. In times of war, tribulation and grinding poverty, children can laugh, sleep well at night and eat with a healthy appetite. They can literally play among bombed out ruins and create a world that is, well, normal.

That is not possible, however, if the adults in their lives reject them or abandon them. As Berna points out, it was the rejecting attitude of the mothers that caused problems for their children.

Two things have to be kept separate: *Personal happiness is not the same as positive attachment; personal problems don't necessarily translate into negative attachment; your child's happiness doesn't stand or fall with your own.*

I repeat: all this guilt must be lifted off the mothers' shoulders!

During all my years as a mother, my personal life was a train wreck. As a child, I was abandoned by both my parents, and they rejected me as long as they were alive.

Loneliness, deep depressions and suicidal thoughts have plagued me all my life.

My unhappiness became manageable when I lived in a little village in Egypt not much different from the Bedouin camp. Life there revolved around very tangible things. If you spend a whole week desperately trying to get hold of a bar of soap and you finally find one in a crummy little basement store at an exorbitant price, once you have run home and hidden it under your mattress so no one will steal it, possessing soap really makes you happy.

Anxiety evaporates when physical survival takes up all your energy.

Although my personal life has been a shambles, I have been able to give my children a positive attachment. I know it, and I think anyone else who is exposed to my children's openness, zest for life and striking social competence knows it too.

I have never tried to pull the wool over their eyes or deceive them. I have simply made *them*, rather than myself, the focal point when I have been with them, and shouldered my responsibility as leader and protector. Just as the contact man in the Bedouin camp, I understood that if my children were going to function adequately and get something out of life, it was my responsibility to welcome them into this world and to show them how it worked in a positive and inspiring way. That is really all there is to it, and I don't think for a moment that children demand anything more.

So, once and for all, I want to categorically state that you, mother or father, don't have to be happy yourself to give your little ones a good start in life. All you have to do is not reject them; all you have to do is try to understand them and enjoy guiding and protecting them *while you are doing it.*

I have gone through so many divorces and have had so many children that I have had to provide for more or less alone that I know perhaps better than most that few accusations burden a mother with more guilt than this one: "You're a bad mother because you're not happy."

I know that it is possible for you to be a good parent even if you are very unhappy.

Your child expects you to be capable of living – in the literal sense of the word – and obviously you are. For a child, life is an adventure. The only prerequisite for a child to live this adventure is the opportunity to do so.

And this is where the contact man and the flock come in. They provide such an opportunity.

Children's expectations are positive. A positive attachment says, "Jump in! The water's warm!"

A negative attachment says, "I'm not sure. Actually, I don't much feel like showing you anything. I don't think taking care of you is much fun. I only do it because I have to."

As Berna says, even if you are not capable of sorting out your own problems, you can still function as a tool, a guide and a positive contact man for your child. *The only requirement is that you want to do all these things while you are actually doing them.*

And you do!

Even if the contact man in our Bedouin camp thinks life is hard sometimes, and he probably does, he is still proud to show you, a novice, around the camp. He has skills that he wants to pass on. He has his life. He can try to see the world through your interested eyes – which is an asset for him.

It is interesting to note that the child that became symptom free after being handed over to the nanny obviously didn't suffer from being without her mother. It wasn't the mother per se that the child needed most. The child was seeking a positive attachment and that was something the nanny could give – without even being particularly involved emotionally with the child.

Through her attitude and her actions, the nanny said, "Jump in! The water's warm!" And the child was content with that.

Without this "Jump in! The water's warm! The world is yours. All you have to do is explore it!" in combination with loving protection, without this fundamental attachment that corresponds perfectly with the child's positive expectations and innate trust, an infant ends up in a terrifying no-man's land.

That doesn't mean that the child simply lies down to die without further ado. Infants can protect themselves. They seek out silent solace, just as we adults do. They create a dream world for themselves and there they take refuge from a cruel reality. They turn in on themselves until they become unreachable.

During the time that the child enters a mental bunker, you, the caregiver, "the contact man" can take a breather. There is a grace period. An infant who sinks into a depression does not become unreachable for a long time. Like adults, infants can return to the light after a lengthy sojourn in the dark. The power of love is infinite and infants can be lifted out of depression, just as you and I can.

Depression becomes dangerous only when it is allowed to settle and penetrates so deeply that the soul itself begins to suffocate.

Superficial depressions in infants are not unusual. They can manifest themselves in various ways. We saw in Berna's example involving the alcoholic father how the child despaired. Children are sensitive and take in everything that happens, sometimes in advance. If the family is planning to move the following week, an infant can start to show signs of distress a couple of days before the moving van arrives. When change is in the offing, young children react like animals that sense something in the wind.

A temporary depression, when your baby seems to retreat and becomes more difficult to reach than usual, is nothing to worry about. Infants, again like adults, take a mental holiday from a demanding world and withdraw.

On such days, make an effort to have as much direct contact with your baby as possible. Try to be as positive, happy, friendly and tender as you can be. Thus you are giving your child confirmation that you are there, that you are not worried, and that you are waiting calmly.

Socializing, as per the Standard Model program, is an effective preventive measure. As always, an ounce of prevention is worth a pound of cure.

In the event of a serious infant depression however, which is the result of a directly negative attachment or no attachment at all, there is no time to lose.

Rejecting mothers exist, and they are easy to spot. Like everyone else, they end up in a maternity ward, and they reject their children before they go home. If they spend time with their babies at all, it is only because they have to, and an observer might well speculate on what will happen when these women are no longer subject to pressure from their surroundings.

The following anecdote concerns one of my own children and I relate it because I want to show that this problem can strike any parent under any circumstances. Common sense does not always trump the refusal to connect, the inability to accept that rejecting mothers suffer from just as much as their children.

Any mother and any father can reject certain children at certain times *without wanting to*.

The solution is to swallow your pride and turn the job over to someone else.

Let's go back to the Bedouin camp. You arrive at the perimeter and the person that you expected to be your contact man either cannot or will not step up to the plate. Someone else has to – and must want to – step into the breach. You can transfer the trust that you have arrived with to a new contact man. You can focus your expectations and trust on the second contact man instead, even if you were originally primed to focus them on the first.

If you are allowed to choose, which we hope you are, you naturally place yourself in the hands of the contact man who receives you warmly and happily rather than in the contact man who just drags you around like a piece of unwanted baggage.

The important thing is that the initial attachment is forged quickly and positively, and that it doesn't end in disappointment. The fact that you personally don't do the forging is far less significant.

A positive attachment, where innate trust is answered and affirmed, can be transferred at a later date. If you and your contact man have a solid, trusting relationship, your trust will eventually expand to include the other members of the tribe. You will cooperate with them, and your sense of belonging will come to embrace them until you become "one of us".

Then you will have been socialized. Then you will have become a fully-fledged member of the camp, capable of collaborating, contributing, influencing – and loving.

If, on the other hand, your connection with the contact man ends in disappointment, if he rejects you and abandons you, after welcoming you and affirming your trust, your confidence in him will have been severely shaken. Your innate sense of trust will have taken a hard knock indeed. The next person who tries to establish a connection with you will need considerably more time than he would have needed had your ties with the contact man not ended in disappointment.

Your own attempts to establish a new connection within the camp after your disappointment with the rejecting contact man will also be that much more tentative and fearful. You will tend to wait for someone else to take the initiative. Should someone do so, he will need both time and patience to repair the damage done to your ability to trust. You would no doubt test the person's good faith by testing him from day one and by being unequivocally rejecting yourself to guard against another disappointment.

That is how infants whose innate trust has been damaged react. And there are many of us in that boat.

If, therefore, you are a parent in such a deep depression that you cannot accept your child and give it that vital positive attachment, you must allow someone else to take the reins so that this attachment is established and confirmed.

This does not mean that you will lose your child forever. Attachment can be transferred and it will be. A child's innate trust seeks confirmation first from the person who stands for physical and psychological survival and expands from there. As long as it is not constrained by disappointment, it can encompass anything. The pre-requisite is a fundamental positive attachment.

So, if you know in your heart that you are a terrible mother or a terrible father, and in spite of all the good will in the world, you find yourself incapable of liking this little newborn who has been placed in your care, if you are so indifferent to your own child that it frightens you and you think you must be at best deficient and at worst evil, swallow your pride, activate your common sense and think of the baby as a person!

This little person's life depends on attachment. You can't provide it, so find someone who can! Turn to the child's other parent. Turn to your own parents. Seek until you find. Stop condemning yourself. Treat your child the way you would like to be treated.

Your child is every bit as human as you are. She needs to belong somewhere, just as you do. Like you, she wants to live, and like you, she strives to be happy. This step is not irrevocable. You will not lose your child. If her innate sense of trust finds a secure foothold, she will come to trust you too. She will always give you another chance.

So don't fixate on your own feelings of guilt. Focus instead on your child's ability to live!

Not all developmental theories in the world can predict the course a child's life will take or how a child's personality will turn out. Human beings are simply too richly enigmatic, too gloriously multi-faceted.

This much, however, *is* predictable: there is one thing that causes damage so severe that the child's life may be placed in danger or, if the child survives, it causes such psychological damage that the child may end up emotionally paralysed. That one thing is denying a child any possibility of attachment.

I had a difficult time bonding with one of my children for a simple, albeit incredible, reason; the child was a carbon copy of a person – not the father I hasten to add – that I disliked intensely. It made no difference that common sense told me I was being totally irrational. When I looked at my newborn baby, I could not help my feelings.

Once home from the hospital, there were times when I even avoided looking at my child while I was changing her. How well *that* worked I will leave to your imagination... The child was not the most beautiful baby in the world, but I had had other less than photogenic children. I found it hard to look at this baby for emotional rather than aesthetic reasons. All I could see was this person I hated, this person's eyes, this person's mouth. I expected the same malevolent words to pop out this poor innocent infant's mouth as emerged from the mouth of her double.

This came on top of a personal crisis. I was on the brink of my first divorce. I was young and, to cut a long story short, everything that could go wrong had gone wrong.

This baby was given an attachment that was weak and relatively negative during her early infancy. She had to exist on very lean portions of joy, of direct contact during socializing, of *connection*. I understood that the baby was suffering, as was I. But I had a flaw that was greater than all the others combined – pride. No one was going to care for that baby except me. I was too young and defiant to grasp that the baby's father could have taken care of the initial attachment without any help from me. Since our relationship was falling apart, I gave him a failing grade in this area. He was smart enough not to take no for an answer, and I allowed him to become involved. But I could not, or would not, see, how important *that* connection was to the baby.

This child retreated into her bunker. At a very early age, she created her own little dream world. She seemed content, but she was a thousand miles away as she lay there and dozed. As soon as she was big enough to drag a pillow with her, she would place it in a corner of the sofa or on the rug and lie down, cut off from everything in her dream world. She slept a great deal, but dozed even more.

With the divorce, my misery was complete, and I handed the child over to the father and his housekeeper for a period of time. Although my visits were frequent and regular, they provoked little, if any, reaction in her.

During this time, I was overwhelmed by one of the two great sorrows of my life. I had never imagined that I would miss my children as much as I did, this baby and her sister. I had never regarded myself as their mother. I never called myself Mom. I was Anna, their friend, and they were little people. Now that I was without them, my whole world collapsed.

At the same time, I was mourning my marriage. I had been deprived of *my* protection and *my* security, and I was adrift in a world that terrified *me*. I developed anorexia and more or less fell apart. Intense anguish made it impossible for me to sleep, and I would wander the streets at night sobbing.

On one occasion, when this little child was spending the weekend with me, I became frightened. In the midst of my own sorrow and despair, I was able to see hers.

She was eighteen months old now, and she was sitting at the dinner table. But she didn't eat. I tried encouraging her. No reaction. I tried to feed her. No reaction. She didn't open her mouth in any sense of the word. I looked at her, but she wouldn't look at me. I took her by her tiny shoulders and tried to make eye contact. She looked right through me, and her eyes were dead.

I was seized with terror, the tears streamed down my cheeks and I called her name. I shook her. No reaction. Along with a feeling of utter powerlessness, rage welled up inside me and I screamed at her furiously. No reaction. I don't know how long this went on. Finally, I took her in my arms and sat with her, crying my eyes out. I sat rocking her for a long, long time, beside myself with despair.

Thus began the long, hard road back to mutual trust.

She held on to her dream world, that protective drowsiness for a long while. When she eventually began to return to me, there were two things that made it possible for me to slowly get close to her.

The first was that I refused to accept that she was unreachable. I yelled, I cried, I shook her, I forced her to see me as soon as she began to retreat into her bunker and those invisible shields went up. I stood outside and banged on the door of her bunker. I was going to get in one way or the other. I had to take some drastic measures over the years and, not infrequently, I lost my temper.

It was, however, just in those moments that I spied a certain sense of satisfaction in her. She reacted. She not only had proof that she meant something to me but also that she could influence her environment. She *was* someone.

The second thing that enabled us to connect was laughter – humor – a gift from the Creator that heals the human soul.

The importance of laughter is underestimated in our culture. If you can still laugh, you can still live! Laughter bestows more than health. It bestows a zest for life. And that in its turn is the life force itself.

Feelings of guilt and powerlessness rise to the surface in relationships like the one I experienced with this child. All that constant striving to reach her, which often ended in mute failure, provoked in me feelings of disappointment and antipathy that had to be directed somewhere. I felt outrage towards this child that was so full of distrust. It is not easy to foist love on someone who doesn't want it. No matter how firmly my common sense told me that I had to persevere with patience, prudence and fixity of purpose, my rational side ultimately foundered on the shoals of emotion – as usual. My love would sometimes morph into hate.

But life-giving laughter sweeps aside all the guilt and powerlessness in the world. Disappointment, weariness, resignation, everything gives way to laughter. Every peal of laughter rips a little hole in the cloud cover, and the day comes when the sun shines so bright, it hurts your eyes.

Every child is a little comedian. Human beings are born with a sense of humor; it's just a question of making sure it becomes a habit!

This little child – who stayed locked in the bunker of her dream world and didn't come back to me until she started school – could not maintain her drowsy isolation when she laughed. I spared no effort to bring a smile to her lips. I tickled her and made faces – two habits I have clung to through all the years and all the children – and was utterly silly. Making faces, doing impressions, behaving like a defiant two-year-old, squealing like a stuck pig, sulking theatrically, pretending to be overly sensitive, playing stupid, feigning surprise in completely mundane situations – all these things are "open sesames" when socializing with unhappy or depressed children.

And very often, it is much easier to get a laugh out of a child than to live up to that ideal of patient, unshakeable love that no human being is saintly enough to achieve every waking moment.

Contact is the password.

Tenderness is the path.

Happiness is the goal.

Little Marcus, whom we met at the beginning, was obviously not the one who suffered the most, even if the so-called colic bore witness to a severe case of survival anxiety. His mother was depressed.

With dashed hopes, crushing guilt, terrible feelings of inadequacy, and paralysing dread, she labelled herself a bad mother who was so lacking in inner harmony that she might damage – "destroy" – her son. The hospital labelled her neurotic but also told her the prognosis was good.

Marcus's mother fell victim to exaggerated demands for love. She believed that the fault lay with her, a perception that was confirmed by the institution she turned to for help.

Eventually, she came home to her son, happily but with lower and more realistic expectations on herself and her surroundings. Life went on in a way that was *necessary for her* and which did not involve making her son the constant center of attention.

Let us return to our Bedouin camp. Your contact man took you in when you wandered into the camp. Everything was as it should be. He came out of his tent to welcome you.

Then he took you into the tent and exposed you to life there: objects, activities and people.

He then gradually introduced you to the work that was done in the camp, and gave you the opportunity to try your hand at it. He offered you amusement and relaxation too of course!

All this was regarded as perfectly natural, and eventually you were socialized. You were "one of us".

What *didn't* the contact man do? He didn't come to meet you and then sit down with you in the sand with his back to the tent, his life and his work. He didn't spend twenty-four hours a day with you and stop taking part in the life of his camp – which would have meant that the camp was no longer his.

If he *had* done all this, you would never have learned anything. And that was what you had come for – to learn.

You wanted to be "one of us". How would you accomplish that sitting out there in the sand in the charge of your contact man, who was kind to you to be sure, but who had turned his back on his daily life?

You would point to the camp to show him you wanted to go in, and you would try to make him understand that *that* was what you really needed him for – to be a means, a guide, a leader, a teacher, someone who would smooth the path and open all the locked doors that separated you from the unknown life.

Infants protest too.

Infants need social participation.

No matter how much parental love you lavish on your children, no matter how eagerly you place yourself at your children's disposal out there in the sand, they will never be satisfied. Not as long as the tent is closed to them.

The honeymoon is the welcome reception. Then the child wants to move on, into the tent, to look and learn, to understand and test, and to gradually be made useful.

If you don't let your child, there is a risk that you will end up as one of those parents who bear witness to living in "hell".

If you were the one out there in the sand, yelling and screaming, and pointing to the camp that you so desperately wanted to get into, but your contact man did everything in his power to keep you out, you would not be very easy to live with either!

To end the chapter, a final word about unhappy newborns:

There is a story about a Caliph in Baghdad, who was a powerful and curious man. He pondered the riddle of the language that human beings originally spoke.

Could he not discover this by seeing what language young children spoke to each other if no one spoke to them?

No sooner said than done. The Caliph gathered together a large number of newborn babies and housed them in his palace. They would be given the best possible care. The Empire's most eminent doctors and nurses would take care of them, and naturally their births went off without a hitch.

Clear instructions were given. No one was permitted to speak to these children. They would develop a language for use amongst themselves – humanity's original language.

Nor was anyone allowed to cuddle these children or play with them. Avoiding small talk in such situations would be difficult. Physical contact was to be restricted to what was necessary for daily care.

And so the Caliph eagerly awaited the answer to the question that he had ruminated over for so long.

But the answer never came. Not a single child survived long enough to reach the age when children usually begin to talk.

All their babbling ceased. Every one of them died.

DEVELOPMENT. BABIES ARE BORN UNFINISHED

I don't claim that this chapter covers every eventuality. I just want to inspire you take a wait-and-see approach so that you don't cause yourself any unnecessary anguish.

Little newborns are not really finished when they come into the world. Much will change and change again. Wait six months before drawing any conclusions and assuming that something is wrong!

Babies are born with reserves. Nature guards them at the beginning. During the first two or three weeks of life, there are seldom any problems.

After that, the skin reacts. Babies are immersed in water until birth. Their skin was protected by foetal fat, but outside the fat was water, not air. When infant skin is exposed to air, dry clothes and so on, eventually there is a reaction. Adaptation takes time – over a month (although seldom more than three).

Tiny so-called heat spots appear on most infants, primarily over the chest and cheeks.

Large, red, chapped, ulcerous rashes can break out on the face and it takes a long time for them to clear up. Little bottoms are irritated by prolonged exposure to acidic urine and excrement and sores may appear. The best cure for all kinds of skin problems is good hygiene and air. Pat with luke-warm water and leave to air dry. Then apply a thin layer of salve. In my experience, cocoa butter is a good one.

As a rule, I do not apply ointment to the face, unless the skin is unusually dry.

Rashes on the face are persistent, and you can't do much more than keep the affected area clean and ensure that whatever your baby lies on is clean and very soft. Milk spit ups are acidic. A bottom sheet topped with a sheet folded in three and spread out smoothly at the head of the bed and tucked in under the sides of the mattress is a practical solution. Your baby can drool and spit up without you having to change the bed every time. All you have to do is refold the sheet so her face rests against one of the clean segments. (Little angels who sleep on their sides for the first little while should have a terry-cotton towel or something similar inside a pillowcase under their heads. It adds a little height, which compensates for the shoulder joint.)

Newborns easily develop rashes from foods the mother eats that make their way into the milk. Chocolate, strawberries and eggs belong in this category. These rashes are not allergic reactions, they don't cause the child any grief, and they vanish as quickly as they appear.

Some skin problems are present from birth. Birthmarks come in all shapes and sizes. They can be large and dark, covering a whole thigh or half the abdomen, or spotty and light. So-called "stork bites" may be visible on the forehead or nape of the neck, left by the stork's beak during the long flight to earth... Both birthmarks and stork bites fade with time, although it may take years for them to disappear completely. Some birthmarks have to be removed later, but there is usually no reason to worry about such things during the first six months of life.

Rashes that look infected because there are blisters in the middle of the spots are not necessarily infected at all. These blisters burst and it may look as though your baby has come down with something, but it's normal. The pores are not yet functioning as they should. Air-dry and wait! Such rashes can take a few weeks to clear up.

Little infections in the cuticles can occur. They are not dangerous. Newborns develop infections easily, but they also recover quickly.

That is why it is sad that many doctors are so quick to prescribe antibiotics. Once you start to give newborns penicillin or sulpha, infections have a depressing habit of popping up one after the other. The immune system – which is still under construction – is weakened.

Do not give antibiotics to a child under the age of one unless the illness is life threatening!

By the same token, you should be on the lookout for ointments that contain penicillin or sulpha.

Chapped, flaky skin is common among newborns and is caused by the tremendous adjustment process they are going through. The stomach, chest and upper back are especially sensitive, as well as all folds in the skin. A little baby oil will soften things up.

Small sores can erupt behind the ears, between the fingers and between the toes. Dry these areas carefully after washing and bathing, and apply a reliable baby ointment.

Chaffed skin on the scalp is common. It looks less than appetising after a while. Large yellow flakes accumulate. Wash normally for as long as you can. Don't use too much soap and make sure the soap is mild. Rinse thoroughly and dry. If the flakes keep piling up, schedule an evening treatment. Massage the scalp generously with baby oil and let it sit over night. In the morning, comb away the flakes with a clean, fine comb.

You can read the section entitled "Sleep" if and when your baby's irregular breathing is worrying you.

A few additional points about the body and general appearance: The shape of the baby's head may strike you as strange – pointed or slanted – after the pressure applied during birth. The head will assume an attractive round shape in a couple of weeks. As you will have noticed, the skull is malleable (and will remain so for a long time). Consequently, if you leave a baby lying on its back 24/7, he or she will soon develop a so-called flat skull.

The skull is divided into two halves, which can be pressed together until they overlap during the delivery. Just above the forehead, which is whole and undivided, is an opening in the seam between the skull halves: the main fontanel. This fontanel seems unprotected and delicate, but it is covered by very strong membranes (which should be flat, not convex). Sometimes the pulse is visible there, which is just as it should be.

Babies who are born with any hair at all are more often than not brunettes. Some babies are born blond, but their hair is downy. New hair will grow in eventually. Some babies lose all their hair and become little baldies. Many months go by before they develop a head of hair worthy of the name. Other babies get their new hair gradually as the old hair falls out, and the change is barely discernible while it is going on.

Little newborns who lie on their backs for long periods rub off some of their hair and look as though they have fringes on the wrong side of their heads. Babies who sleep on their stomachs and turn their heads from side to side can develop bald patches over their temples. New hair comes towards the end of the first year, if not before.

All babies are born with dark eyes. You will be able to make out their real, permanent eye colour after two or three months. The eyes, more specifically the irises, are the only things that are full-sized from the moment we are born. That is why newborns seem to have such huge eyes.

As a rule, all newborns resemble their father or a male relative. Nature carries fatherhood insurance. A baby's ears, for example, are and remain miniature copies of Dad's. If your child's father is not the handsomest man ever to walk the earth, you can comfort yourself with the thought that your own characteristics will shine through by the time your child turns three, if not earlier. Until then, you will be able to detect the beginnings of an encouraging compromise. Thereafter, your child will gradually develop his or her own highly individual appearance.

"All babies look the same," some people say disparagingly, but seldom those who have had children. Whatever happens, facial features will change very quickly. Above all, they smooth out. The grim fold between Dad's eyebrows, the drooping corners of Granddad's mouth, the pensive wrinkles on cousin Bill's forehead will disappear during the first week, and your baby's face will be rosy and smooth.

Babies don't have much of a neck. Their heads are way too big – and way too heavy – for their little bodies.

Seven months ago, when your baby lay in the womb two months after conception, the head accounted for half her length and the body the other half. A newborn's head accounts for a quarter of her body length. If the same proportions were applied to you, your head would reach down to your nipples. In an adult, the head accounts for only an eighth of total body length.

A newborn's shoulders are straight and pliable, the chest is elevated, the stomach is round, and the hips are narrow. Newborns are also extremely bow-legged. For a long time to come, the skeleton will be more cartilage than bone.

Oftentimes, the stomach is tight as a drum skin and protrudes at the sides. It's nothing to worry about and will pass.

The sex organs are swollen after birth, as is the face sometimes, the former condition being the result of the influx of the mother's sex hormones before the birth, the latter the result of the pressure applied during delivery. Both will subside in a couple of weeks.

In children born face first, the swelling takes longer to disappear. A remarkable detail: children who are born face first sleep with their heads tilted back and up for many years. They stubbornly grind their faces back and up against the pillow for approximately six years…

173

The mother's sex hormones can transfer a small amount of milk into the little breasts of the child, even if the child is a boy. The milk, like swollen nipples, disappears after two to three weeks.

A newborn male can have a scrotum that would not look out of place on an adolescent, but the testicles are not always where they should be. One or both of them may not have dropped yet. They make their way down eventually. No corrective measures need be taken for a couple of years.

The foreskin cannot be drawn back. That also is normal.

Little Don Juans start practicing early. Newborn baby boys often have erections.

Discharges, mixed with blood, are not uncommon among little girls during the first few weeks of life. Again, this is completely normal.

Navel ruptures are not uncommon. As the abdominal wall is still weak, the intestines can press themselves through it, forming a lump that causes the skin to swell on either side. The whole navel area can turn into quite an impressive knob. Navel ruptures look worse than they actually are. Not that they are anything that a newborn "should" have, but they will clear up by themselves. Just wait and see!

A newborn's hands and feet are often ice-cold. Blood circulation is running at half power.

The eye muscles also need time to rev up. A newborn's gaze wanders in all directions, and the eyes can cross or swivel out. It takes time and effort for the baby to coordinate them.

The little mouth also has to adapt to the changed circumstances. All the sucking gives newborns blisters on their lips. They subside after meals however.

The tongue is often chalk white. Also normal.

Already at three to four weeks, your baby will have grown phenomenally. The first wardrobe has to be retired. The heart is now functioning more or less the way it should. Breathing should be more or less regular and even, and blood circulation dependable. The muscles are at work too. Your three-week-old tenses her muscles to ready her body when you pick her up.

And while a newborn speaks soundlessly, a one-month-old can make sounds. All kinds of interesting combinations are possible with a speech apparatus that is coming on line and a tongue that is cooperative.

All the organs require a relatively long period of development and adaptation before your baby is really "finished". As a rule, regard the first six months as a continuation of the work Nature began during the fetal stage – work that isn't complete yet!

Your own body is going through its own changes. You won't feel completely yourself again until at least six months after the birth.

Children are delivered unfinished. What has yet to be done is pre-programmed. Teeth come at a certain time, as does menstruation in girls and beard growth in boys…

Mother Nature knows what she's doing. It is a miracle that should be observed with wonder and admiration, not worry and mistrust!

Children are born with reflexes. The gripping reflex you will already be familiar with if you are in the habit of holding your baby's little hand while you breastfeed. A baby's grip is hard and very strong. A newborn can hang from a bar and support her entire weight. This is not worth putting to the test however. The ability can disappear from one day to the next, and it is invariably gone after two to three weeks.

Another reflex comes to life if you run your finger along the sole of your baby's foot. All the little toes spread instantly like a Japanese fan. This reflex lasts a while – eight to nine months – after which children react like adults. The toes curl instead of spreading.

The walking reflex is fascinating. It indicates that human beings are designed to walk upright. A newborn can't hold her head up, but she can walk! If you hold your baby under her arms over a firm, smooth surface, her legs will start to whir in perfect walking movements. This walking reflex will last a couple of months.

The sucking reflex has already been mentioned. It is activated by touching your baby's cheek or lips with your nipple or your knuckle. If you want to test how hard your baby can suck, give her your lower lip. It won't be the same after a while, I can tell you!

The embracing reflex is heart-warming. Loud noises cause a baby to throw out her arms in a desperate appeal. "Help! Hold me!" It is a circular, gripping movement. The baby is seeking a pelt to hang onto with all her might. After about three months, the embracing reflex disappears.

What can a newborn do?

Lift and turn her head. Make crawling movements. Newborns who are placed in incubators seem to want to crawl out of them. Newborns on their backs, however, are not much more capable of movement than turtles in the same position.

Eye sight. Newborns are near-sighted, but they can see very well at up to twenty centimeters. At longer distances, their vision is reasonable too.

Hearing. Your baby will already be used to many sounds, since she heard them while still in the womb. No newborn is startled by the sound of the phone ringing. Even though it is sharp and sudden, it is all too familiar.

Newborns can "turn off" their hearing. If you make a sharp, penetrating sound, your baby will react strongly the first time she hears it, but if you make it again a little later, it will produce no response.

A beating heart is a sound that always goes over well. Tapes of heartbeats send anxious infants off the sleep. Not surprising, since they have lain for months underneath a beating heart, surrounded by the whisper of circulating blood and breathing lungs. Back home!

Newborns can do other things about which we know very little. I don't think people are blank slates when they are born, ready to be written on by anyone who happens to be in the vicinity with a pen. I think people are born familiar with a world, a dimension that we all know but forget over the course of our lives, only to remember it again as our lives draw to a close.

A mother wrote to me: "I experienced something very special when she was born, something I have trouble putting a name to. It was as though time and space slowed down and became still. It wasn't her newborn helplessness, her obvious need for protection and care, or her forlorn, frail nakedness that moved me. Nor was it all that much talked about cutesy stuff that is supposed to awaken maternal instincts, family pride and feelings of continuity. It was something quite different, something completely unexpected. It was her intelligence. I would even call it wisdom. She carried a secret with her. It seemed to me that she knew that answer to the riddle, the nature of God, the meaning of life, everything. Looking into her eyes was like looking into all the insights that humanity has ever had. It was like seeing the face of God. The earthly curtain had parted. I was looking right into the infinite."

IF SOMETHING GOES WRONG: THE CHILD IS NOT NORMAL

As a new parent, especially if it is your first child, you will take attentiveness to the absurd. Attentive can cross the line into obsessive. No comment about your child, no observation, however casual, escapes your notice. Everything takes root. And grows.

Nature has prepared you for parenthood and equipped you with all you need in terms of a sense of responsibility, protective instincts and empathy, and, as a result, you are overly sensitive both to the positive and the negative. Your common sense is not working the way it should, and you take supremely idiotic remarks to heart.

And there are quite a few people who are happy to make such remarks. On top of thoughtless relatives who remark that your baby has "a very low fore-head" or "weird eyes" or "a harelip" and then forget what they have said the minute the words are out of their mouths, there are the people in the white coats, who are sometimes not only thoughtless, but flat-out irresponsible.

The health care horror stories are legion. "Your baby is gaining too much weight. She should not be this heavy!" So what should you do? Put her on a diet?

"His head is too big," a friend of mine was told about her son. What was she supposed to do? Operate? Drain his head?

The latter child was also not permitted to eat as much as he wanted. He was gaining "too much" weight. He was only allowed so much milk, and from then on nothing but water in the bottle. Constantly racked by survival anxiety, the baby screamed his head off and was diagnosed with colic. Treatment: less food. At three months, this baby was on a starvation diet: one hundred and fifty grams per meal.

Time passed. The hospital machinery clicked into gear over the size of the child's head, which someone had seen fit to label "too big". After a battery of examinations, the little boy's mother got a telephone call (!) from the hospital. "We have been looking at your son's records. Either he is mentally challenged or he has water on the brain."

I will leave the mother's anguish, tears and sleepless nights to your imagination.

CAT scans, MRIs and more examinations followed. In the end, the baby would start crying at the mere sight of a white coat. (It should be said that today's ultra sound techniques make head examinations so much easier.)

He now was plagued by constant diarrhoea. Treatment: fasting.

At one and a half, this little boy was still not even within striking distance of a normal diet. Now surgery was discussed. A biopsy would be taken from his intestine to see what was wrong.

After nearly two years of agony, the boy's mother had had enough, and she turned her back on the hospital. I managed to convince her to give her son regular food: meat, potatoes and vegetables and *as much of them as he wanted*. The diarrhoea disappeared the following day. Apart from the odd case of loose stools, his bowels functioned normally.

Now that the boy was finally allowed to eat as much real food as he wanted, he tucked into all the goodies with such gusto that he was soon the size of the Good Year blimp. At just over two years, he was still obsessed with food. It wasn't until he turned three that he finally shook off his survival anxiety. Only then did he dare start to believe that the food that was put in front of him would not be snatched away and that there would be more of it every day. Only then did he leave the table without devouring everything in sight and then asking for more. He had escaped from the white coats. He now had a happy mother and regular food, which transformed him into a happy, trusting child.

His head, which was supposedly too big, proved to suit the rest of his body just fine.

Another child in my circle of acquaintances had cramps as a newborn on two occasions. This is not unusual and is seldom dangerous, but naturally cramps are frightening while they last. The parents were terrified and made a beeline for the hospital. There they were told that cramps could be an indication of developmental problems. "But we won't be able to tell for sure for another couple of years."

The parents were distraught at the prospect of "a couple of years" of uncertainty. "I see there is nothing I can say to comfort you," said the doctor apologetically. And the audience was over.

When you are looking after a newborn, the absence of routines and habits permeates your whole existence. Every day is new territory, long, hard and uncertain. Every day is a law unto itself. You don't think six months, three months, or even one month ahead. You think in terms of days, at most weeks. Any further into the future than that is as remote as outer space.

There was nothing wrong with that little boy.

I am not out to demonize the medical profession, but I wish medical practitioners would wake up to the fact that their tendency to engage in idle speculation has devastating results. As sensitive as new parents are, they take every word an expert utters as gospel, and their anguish is so unbearable that they end up in a place where they almost wish their child *was* developmentally challenged so that at least they would know where they stand.

It is difficult, if not impossible, to take the seeds of worry that doctors and healthcare workers so casually sow with the pinch of sceptical salt they deserve when the soil these seeds fall on is so fertile.

A Little Memo:

Be sceptical about every observation made about your child. If you go to a doctor or a clinic to ask about something that is worrying you, you should resign yourself to the fact that you may come away from the consultation feeling even more worried.

Don't look for problems. If something really is wrong, your instincts will sound the alarm. Then the doctor's diagnosis will simply be confirmation of what you already suspected.

Trust your instincts and your own good sense more than the hypothesizing of doctors. Few developmental problems can be confirmed before a child can walk and talk. Trust Mother Nature. The variations are infinite.

Don't blame yourself. Life always has a value for the person who is living it.

Always get several medical opinions. Don't allow yourself to be passed from one doctor to another. Don't consider the diagnosis confirmed until several doctors come to the same conclusion independently!

Confirmation that your child has an abnormality or an injury is of course devastating. In the face of such tragedy, you react defensively. In your despair, you deny the unbearable.

Then, resigned, paralyzed and even desperately hopeful, you accept the inevitable. You reconcile yourself to the irreconcilable, even though the process is bitter and excruciatingly long.

You will spend a lot of time in hospitals. Doctors are only human, and it is not always possible to educate them in the art of being humble and compassionate. It is more difficult to cure a troubled soul than a broken finger. Illness and death don't seem to bother all doctors, but suffering does.

If you are lucky enough to have a compassionate doctor, someone who is not frightened of suffering but recognizes it and is capable of helping you bear it without succumbing to hopelessness, hang on to him/her! Such doctors are willing to move mountains to help their patients. Try to seek out such a person to help and care for your child.

I will say it again. Double check. Seek out specialists who don't have access to earlier diagnoses. Once a child has been diagnosed, the new doctor will assume the diagnosis is correct. Think about it. If you were told that a particular individual was mentally ill, you would treat him differently than you would if you had not been informed that he was mentally ill. Whether he actually *is* mentally ill is a separate question…

Challenging conventional wisdom requires time and effort. Don't place all your trust in one doctor. Get as many opinions as you can!

If your child has been diagnosed with brain damage, and you are absolutely satisfied that this is the cold, hard truth, ask your neurologist about IAHP, *The Institutes for the Achievement of Human Potential* in Philadelphia, U.S.A.

There is always hope. The human brain is a miracle.

Then make contact with other parents in the same situation. They are the only people who understand what you are going through. Just knowing that you are not alone can rekindle hope and optimism, which will lead to more constructive thinking. You are suffering through an ordeal that others have experienced and transcended. When people unite to reach a common goal, wonderful things are happening. With the help of your brothers and sisters in sorrow, you will climb out of the darkness that perhaps prevents you from seeing your child's true value. All life is precious. The only person entitled to assess the value of an individual life is the person living it.

A mother wrote to me:

"I was pregnant and we were overjoyed. We had a little boy. When he was three weeks old, the nightmare that I am now living through began. He suddenly became ill, and when we went to the hospital, we were told that he had a serious heart defect. Since then, we have been commuting to and from the hospital and our son has been diagnosed with one illness after another, several of them fatal. Most of his life – he is ten months old now – has been spent at the hospital. We care for him at home for a few weeks, and then it's back to the hospital for a week so he can be given a check-up and more tests, and we can rest.

He is incurably handicapped and terminally ill, and we don't know how long he is going to live. My greatest problem is that I have such poor emotional contact with him. I have trouble grasping the fact that he is actually my child! It often feels like he has destroyed my life. I know how horrible that sounds, but if he had never been born, I could live happily with my wonderful husband. I feel so guilty for feeling the way I do. And I am so exhausted. I take pills to sleep and pills to stay functional when I am awake.

I am fond of my son. He is a lovely baby and he shows that he likes *me*. But my love for him is so tainted by feelings of powerlessness, exhaustion and despair. Can you give some advice on how I should deal with my little boy and his handicap, and how I can prepare myself for the day when I lose him?

I live with death every day. It took a lot of courage for me to write these lines."

I tried to answer:

"Life itself has betrayed you. Your child is going to die. How could you feel anything but powerlessness, exhaustion and despair? When a woman conceives and bears a child, she stands ready to ensure that child's survival. Now all that preparation was for nothing. You can do nothing to guarantee your child's survival. It's as though Nature has violated her own laws. Your unimaginable disappointment has to be directed at something. Your son is a concrete symbol of the meaninglessness of it all. He is the one who has to bear the brunt of your disappointment. Don't feel guilty! Life has knocked you to your knees. You have to strike back to get to your feet again.

Waiting for a child to die is the worst thing in the world. Like you, many parents just want it to be over. It's unbearable. Your child is suffering, and you have to endure his torment as well as your own. You have blocked out your urge to bond whether you wanted to or not. 'How can I prepare myself for the day that I lose him?' you ask. That is precisely what you are doing. You don't dare love what you are about to lose. It is not your fault that you can't love your dying child. It is Nature's. Nature has equipped you with a survival instinct. Death can never be your friend. We live to live, not to die.

In the face of imminent death, something tremendous happens. The day will come when you are reconciled to your son's fate and your own. That is the day when you will be able to take him to you, in the valley of the shadow of death. A terminally ill person – and this goes for the very young as well as the very old – has the ability to open a new, and forgotten, dimension in the rest of us, we who operate in the day-to-day world in all its simplicity. Every person who lives on the border of death, even a little baby, knows on some level that he is going to die. In that twilight land, he touches love far more profound than the earthly variety and reconciles himself to his fate in a way that transcends everything else. You will be able to get close to your son, if not through a mother's love, then through a fellow human being's respect and admiration for something beyond human comprehension.

Your son is reaching out to you. You feel betrayed. But somewhere, beyond the guilt and paralysing bitterness, you will meet him. He is waiting for you, and he will enrich you."

Finally: Two straws to grasp at. Two miracle cures whose effectiveness has been confirmed by science.

One is vitamin C. The other is laughter.

What Linus Pauling has long asserted has been proven right. Large doses of vitamin C cure or alleviate the symptoms of a host of illnesses. It has been documented that women with breast cancer and lung cancer have very low levels of vitamin C in their blood. Pauling has demonstrated that patients that have been diagnosed with terminal diseases have benefited greatly from large doses of pure ascorbic acid (between 5 to 10 grams a day). The progression of these diseases was delayed and the patients lived longer. In contrast to other vitamins, which in high doses can be poisonous, a large intake of vitamin C is risk free. Nothing to lose, but the gains are immeasurable!

Today we know that all that stuff about a good laugh prolonging your life is more than just a folktale. There is the famous case of Norman Cousins, who was so gravely ill that he was given only a one in five hundred chance of surviving. When he received his death sentence, he locked himself in a hotel room. He decided that since the end was nigh, he would do nothing but read funny books and watch funny movies.

After a while, he discovered that laughter functioned as a painkiller. He found he could cut back on his medications and that he could sleep.

Cousins recovered. In a few years, he was completely healthy, which led to laughter being prescribed for many other medical conditions. A little girl with schizophrenia was cured after having a good laugh at a clown. A life-threatening tumor shrank and disappeared with no medication other than laughter. The examples are legion. Here again, there is everything to gain – and nothing to lose.

If you feel compelled to tickle your little one until he laughs because you yourself feel as far from a smile as life is from death, laughter must have a beneficial effect. "Little things amuse little children." Parents have always known this. They swing their children, toss them up and down, blow raspberries on their tummies, make faces and pretend to be monkeys. Children's bubbling laughter is so unbearably sweet, the mere sound should cause the entire medical profession to tip their hats.

A laughing child is a happy child. A happy person is a healthy person – or at least has good prospects of being one.

EVERY CHILD'S EVERY CRY IS A QUESTION

Children cry. A newborn that didn't cry would be as much cause for concern as a newborn who screamed constantly. A child who cries is seldom in serious danger, or indeed any danger at all.

As a new mother, I read a number of tracts on childcare. It was the parts about crying that I always read first. Crying has been an enduring interest, and this has enabled me to acquire a certain perspective over the years.

At the beginning of the 1960s, when my first child was born, there were, as now, lists of things that caused children to cry. At the top was: *too little food*.

Fifteen years later, when my last child was born, topping the same lists was: *too much food*.

Conventional wisdom changes according to trends, the meanderings of research into childcare and the various edicts issued by social services. What remains constant through time, trends, and socio-political wanderings and misconceptions, however, is the child itself – with a newborn's universal needs.

Newborn humans, like all other animals, are tormented by survival anxiety. This anxiety is both good and bad. The instinct to survive is linked to an imperative that is both wonderful and horrifying. A newborn's cry arises out of anxiety but leads to life. A crying child gets fed.

This anxiety asks a question in the form of a scream. "Will I survive?" Food gives the answer. "Yes."

Earlier we made an analogy with newborn chicks ("Caring for a newborn"). The cheeping and crying in the nest is heart-rending, and one doesn't have to be an ornithologist to detect the frantic anguish in the chicks' cries. The parents search for food as though their own lives depended on it, but still their young never seem to have enough.

Newborn humans cry in the same way, and their survival anxiety must be allayed in the same way – through food, food and more food, and then some.

Swedish children are perhaps born into the best of all possible worlds, but they are unaware of their good fortune, since they are hardly receptive to sophisticated economic arguments. Because they are not born literate, they are unable to decipher the brochures and articles on diet and subsidized children's health programs put out by Social Services. They have no way of knowing that no one has starved to death in Sweden for the last 150 years. Their survival anxiety can only be allayed through repeated experience. The *only* thing that will help a newborn who is crying out of survival anxiety is food.

Naturally, I don't recommend this, but if you were to pick up a screaming newborn in a soiled diaper and dirty clothes, feed her and put her back down again without tending to any of her other needs, she would fall back to sleep.

According to my own observations, when a newborn cries, survival anxiety is the cause nine times out of ten. The tenth is due to over-tiredness. The tenth cry asks: "Is life too tough for me? Is it going to crush me?"

And the answer is: "No. I will get you through this until you are strong enough to make it on your own, just as I will see to your survival until you can fend for yourself. I always have your back."

There are "cranky" babies and there are "good" babies. I put these words in quotation marks because we should be careful about labelling children. Let's just say that some babies ask more questions than others!

Every child's every cry is a question.

In every nest, there is a chick in the brood that cries less than the others and gets forgotten every now and then, but survives anyway. Conversely, there are always a couple of chicks that barge to the head of the line and swipe the juiciest morsels.

Human beings are not born generous or greedy, although in the struggle for survival, they may develop traits that strike their siblings as less than agreeable. But the instinct to survive is the strongest drive we have, and newborns don't cry to be difficult, to make unreasonable demands, or to hog more of the action than they have a right to. Newborns cry out of survival anxiety and nothing else, and what we have to do is guarantee their survival and thereby allay this anxiety. A newborn cannot be "spoiled".

An experienced member of the National Association of Ornithologists (if there is such a thing) would be able to work out exactly how many calories a chick needs for its physical survival. And, in a purely mathematical sense, he would be right. But providing enough calories for physical survival and allaying survival anxiety are two completely different things.

Babies, like chicks, cry desperately and the parents are told that their young have colic and stomach ailments, and that they are allergic to the milk they live on. They are given drops for cramps and meticulously measured amounts of food that ensure they don't starve, but that don't allay survival anxiety. How can they be expected to sleep peacefully? How would they dare believe that they were going to make it through the day?

Every child's every cry is a question. A human newborn asks, "Am I going to survive?" You know the answer.

The Standard Model stipulates four, sometimes five rounds of food at every meal, which should take one and a half hours. "Cranky" babies, babies that ask questions more often and more urgently than their "good" counterparts, do particularly well on the Standard Model because it operates *preventively*.

184

The Standard Model meets a baby's every need at every meal: food, food and more food, diaper change and hygiene, socializing so that vital attachment is formed, and finally a refill or two, a reserve to go to sleep on. (The only other requirement is fresh air, something that can be tended to while the baby is asleep.)

The Standard Model is founded on the principle that an ounce of prevention is worth a pound of cure. A baby's needs are satisfied continuously and before they become acute, or more precisely before the *absence* of satisfaction becomes acute.

You would not put off eating until starvation set in. Nor would you wait until hunger pangs actually made you feel ill. You eat at noon (say) because that is when you usually eat, because you know you need food at that hour, and because food is available. You would eat even if you were not ravenously hungry. Experience has taught you that if you don't eat at noon, by one your stomach is rumbling, by two it is hurting, by three you are having dizzy spells, by four you feel nauseous, by five you can't work any longer, and by six you are not even hungry any more, just exhausted. Perhaps you would not be able to eat even if food were offered to you.

Babies function in exactly the same way.

The same principle applies to their other needs.

The list of reasons that babies cry – which I would instantly reject if food, food and more food didn't stand right at the top – usually includes things like "lack of contact", "feels isolated" etc. The Standard Model includes that vital element of "socializing", during which a positive attachment is forged and affirmed, and an interesting, if wordless, conversation is carried on. If babies are given the opportunity to socialize at regular intervals, before any urgent needs, or, even worse, acute shortfalls, arise, they will react the same way you would if you were granted the opportunity to socialize with pleasant people. They are content and think life is fun.

If, however, loneliness has gotten its claws into you and had time to work its evil magic, it becomes harder for you to accept social contact when it is offered, and it becomes more difficult to just sit back and enjoy life. Little people do not function any differently. Providing contact, tenderness, intimacy, love, and "company" to a little newborn who is crying precisely because she *lacks* those things is far more difficult than giving them preventively.

If you follow the Standard Model, you will not wait for your baby to start crying before you try to remedy the situation by various means in the hope of hitting the target eventually. You will fulfil your baby's needs continuously and preventively. In so doing, you answer her questions before your baby even has the chance to ask them. And the crying will cease.

The Standard Model doesn't just have advantages for a newborn. For you, Mom or Dad, it means long, unbroken periods of sleep between meals and the ability to plan your day. Your nocturnal sleep will be relatively undisturbed too. If you have satisfied all your baby's needs to the hilt during the day, you can skip them with impunity during the night – except for food. A couple of twenty-minute feedings are bearable.

In time, other advantages will become apparent. And they are to be treasured!

From day one, you will believe in yourself as a parent, and this will become a self-fulfilling prophecy. If you *know* that your baby is getting what she needs, continuously and preventively, you will not worry over the odd fit of *tristesse* that all newborns fall victim to occasionally. We adults, after all, have been known to whine when things don't go our way. Instead of having the common sense to go to bed with a good book, we take out our ill humor on innocent bystanders.

If you know you have met your child's needs, not just once, but many times at every meal and she is still crying, you can close the door and be on your way – angry or sad, ticked off or resigned though you may be – and your baby will sleep. *You will dare to leave your baby in peace.*

This is an effective antidote against the insecurity that you have, and must have, as a new parent – an insecurity that impels you to be responsible, alert and understanding. This sense of security also means that you will be able to have confidence in your child. "I am giving you what I know you need. The rest you can take care of yourself."

No one can take total responsibility for another human being's happiness. Little people – like big ones – can manage more than they are given credit for, and they are not well served by being declared incompetent. All people, big and small, who have had all their essential needs satisfied can live their lives under their own steam and they should be encouraged if they doubt their own abilities.

The other advantage, which will not become apparent until later, is something that will serve you well during your entire career as a parent. It is the habit of thinking preventively, planning ahead, foreseeing consequences and putting yourself in your child's shoes with the help of your own experience – staying one step ahead of the game in other words.

Needs are constant. All human beings have them. If they are not satisfied, a shortfall occurs.

Rectifying shortfalls is more difficult than satisfying needs, and normal, latent needs are easier to satisfy than acute ones.

The Standard Model is, as you can see, structured. What happens if you, as the mother or father of a newborn, don't structure your days at all?

This is how life might look: Your baby wakes up, cries and gets food. You burp her and change her, and then sit with her for a little while, tenderly cradling her in your arms. She gets drowsy and drops off. You put her back to bed. After thirty minutes or an hour, she starts crying again and needs more food. She was given enough food to alleviate the worst of her hunger, but she didn't get enough to build up a reserve. Now she is out of fuel and needs to tank up. Another feeding, a clean diaper if she needs it, a burp and a cuddling session. She falls asleep and you put her to bed. Twenty minutes later, it's time for another feed. Or she cries, but she doesn't want to take your breast. Something is wrong. But what?

The risk with this completely "free" variety of child rearing is that this food-sleep-food-sleep pattern leaves little time for awake-time and socializing.

On top of that, you may find the situation untenable because of the constant demands placed upon you.

This free model, where the baby eats for fifteen minutes, sleeps for half an hour, eats for fifteen minutes, sleeps for an hour, cries for fifteen minutes, eats for five minutes, is changed periodically, eats for ten minutes, sleeps for half an hour and so on – may work during the honeymoon (which should be a honeymoon, not one long tribulation, mind you), but it soon becomes problematic for all concerned. Such an arrangement rests on the principle that you fulfil needs after the fact, needs that have been neglected or allowed to become acute. Your baby cries, you react, and then she tells you through her behavior whether or not you have done the right thing. You are always one step behind.

As a result, your baby is compelled to scream. It's the only way to get any dire attention.

Making a newborn responsible for how life should be structured is hardly reasonable.

Remember our Bedouin camp? You arrive at the perimeter knowing nothing about camp life. All you know is that you have to live there, whatever that entails. How would you react if the whole tribe sat there in the sand, staring at you expectantly, waiting for you to take over and run things?

Some newborns who are cared for according to this free, fulfil-needs-after-the-fact model set up their own structure towards the end of the first month. Most of them do not.

There are very few babies that don't need any help or support at all. Now is the time that your belief in yourself comes into play. Sooner or later, you will be forced to show some leadership, whether you want to or not. Your child will demand it of you.

Never expect leadership from an infant!

For information on how to deal with a newborn who is so worked up that she can't eat or who is on the verge of hysteria, read "If something goes wrong: the newborn refuses to eat". Buffing, which helps newborns and older infants to relax, is described in "Sleep", where you can also find instructions on effective rocking.

IF SOMETHING GOES WRONG: COLIC?

What is colic?

Babies can bawl for hours on end. Their stomachs are tense, their bodies contorted, intestinal gas extensive and clearly painful, and the attack obviously serious. When it's over, these babies sniffle and shiver. Carrying these babies around only provides short-term relief.

Colic strikes primarily in the evenings or at night and continues until they turn three months. Then it disappears.

There are many theories about what causes colic and I will present one more.

Colic is supposedly caused by too much food, too much gas, too little burping, various possible ailments and a poor diet on the part of the nursing mother. These mothers are told to avoid all dairy products and to eat a protein-free breakfast, neither of which is easy (nor particularly pleasant). Often enough, they are also told to seek help for their personal problems.

To combat colic, a combination of drops that counteract gas formation in the intestine, and anti-cramping medication is prescribed. Some parents claim these remedies help, while others dismiss them as worthless. Many find solace in the knowledge that help is out there. They thereby transfer to their children, along with the drops, an optimism that, sporadically at least, makes life easier for everyone. *Worry is the biggest villain in childcare.* If worry can be alleviated, you can automatically expect improvement.

Colic was long regarded as a psychosomatic ailment, and I'm sure you can guess who got the blame for transferring psychological problems to babies! Then there was a shift. Colic became something that certain babies were more or less born with. You have "a colicky baby". Distressed pregnant women tell tales about how they have already had one colicky baby and how much they fear having another one.

Parents are regarded as powerless. They are condemned to three months of torment, and there is nothing anyone can do about it.

It has always been glaringly obvious to me that *colic is unalleviated survival anxiety.*

Children are no more born with colic than males are born with ulcers or females are born with headaches. Children *get* colic. As soon as their survival anxiety is allayed, the colic disappears.

If you have turned directly to this page because your child has colic, I would like to refer you to the fundamentally important chapter "Caring for a newborn", where colic as a manifestation of survival anxiety is dealt with.

Three-month colic and evening colic are frequently mentioned. So-called evening colic has nothing to do with colic but is a symptom of over-tiredness – psychological exhaustion. I and many other mothers refer to it as "the evening fuss". For information on why little angels fuss in the evenings and how the problem can be dealt with, see "If something goes wrong: the newborn refuses to sleep".

Three-month colic, like other psychosomatic illnesses, produces such obvious and painful physical symptoms that it cannot be dismissed as imagination. This type of colic disappears at three months, sometimes earlier. It occurs in connection with the so-called true birth at about three weeks, when a child recovers from the trauma of birth and turns outward into the world, hungry in every sense of the word.

After three months, the baby has learned through painful and repeated experience that her daily survival is assured. This experience finally allays her survival anxiety. Other factors contribute to the baby's confidence. At three months, she is introduced (or at least she should be) to food that is either mashed or puréed and which supplements the breast milk or formula which has hitherto been her only source of sustenance and which has been given in all too skimpy portions. Furthermore, the baby can attract the attention of her surroundings by means other than crying. She can do something or indicate something. She can, for example, gurgle while she stares at a banana and tries to reach for it. Helplessness is a bitter pill for someone who suffers from survival anxiety. A three-month-old is no longer completely helpless.

Not everything that is called colic *is* colic, by which I mean that physical symptoms and pain are not always part of the picture. Symptom free so-called colic is hunger pure and simple, and hunger and survival anxiety are the same thing in a newborn. There is one cure. Give your baby *as much food as she can possibly take* and then some, without messing around with water or drops.

It is hard to believe how much a newborn can actually get down, once she is allowed to eat to her heart's content during one of these "cures". If the tables say a feeding should consist of 120 grams, you can be sure that a baby can consume double that. Thereafter, she drops into a deep sleep.

For about twenty-four hours, the baby will eat double the "normal" ration at all meals and sleep in the meantime.

During the next twenty-four-hour period, her intake will drop, but the portions will remain way above the table average, i.e. the recommended starvation ration. Waking time will increase, but now the baby will be calm and content. The crying, the "colic" is gone.

An infant who has had time to develop real colic is stuck fast in survival anxiety that plagues her more or less constantly. An infant with real, physical colic also suffers pain that must be soothed.

In dealing with colic, you will have to arm yourself with fixity of purpose, prudence, caution and an air of confidence – which will do much to calm your baby. The most urgent goal is to get your baby into a condition that will enable her to eat.

A baby with a real case of colic will protest immediately. A baby with colic is tormented with unimaginable survival anxiety. Panic grips her time and time again, even when she is eating. Because of survival anxiety, your baby is incapable of experiencing the sense of well being that food should give. The tension and resistance in the little body also causes abdominal pain. Interrupt the meal and get the panic under control! Calm your baby using the technique that is described in "If something goes wrong: the newborn refuses to eat". The goal is to calm her so that she is in a condition to eat, and as soon as her little body relaxes and her cries begin to subside, put her to your breast or give her the bottle without delay. If necessary, you will have to alternate between feeding and calming throughout the meal. The baby has to eat at all costs.

Nothing but food, food and more food will convince her that she is going to survive. (Time will. But three months is a long way off.)

Persevere! Your baby is crying as if she were in pain, and she *is* in pain. The pain has its roots in the survival anxiety that has reached such a fever pitch it is unbearable.

You can't make the symptoms disappear immediately, but you can attack the cause.

A human being, big or small, who has lived in a state of constant anxiety for a long time will not be comforted in a day. Her distrust will dissipate only gradually. She will be walking on eggshells for a long time.

And she is perfectly justified in hanging on to her negative expectations.

A baby with colic must be handled with the utmost care, and her trust must be systematically rebuilt. Panic will be waiting in the wings for a long time to come.

If you declare victory too soon, colic, with its pain, gas, cramps and screams, may return with a vengeance.

If you are caring for a baby with colic, you should initiate a methodical three-day 'cure'. From here on in, you should try to satisfy your baby's needs *preventively*. (See "Every child's every scream is a question".)

Begin the cure in the morning, when newborns, even the ones with colic, are sound asleep. Don't wait until the baby starts to cry.

Caress her over the head to prepare her, wrap her in a blanket and take her firmly into your arms. Put her gently but insistently to your breast, or give her the bottle. Look her in the eye and smile. Stimulate the sucking reflex if necessary by touching her cheek (the one closest to you) with your nipple, your finger or the nipple of the bottle. Sit comfortably and be prepared to hold your position for quite a while.

Hold her little hand. Make sure she is not subjected to any jolts or tugs. Keep her tightly wrapped. If there is any fussing at all, react calmly. Hold her fast and say something in a firm, confident voice.

If panic takes hold in spite of your efforts, get up with the baby held tightly in your arms and comfort her. (See "If something goes wrong: the newborn refuses to eat".) Resume the meal as soon as possible.

Just getting your nipple in her mouth can be a sweaty and demanding job – she may refuse it, and then both of you will be close to panicking. Make sure that the nipple is not so tense that the baby can't get a grip. Pump out a few drops of milk with your hand.

Make sure that the milk is flowing as it should. A baby with the dark butterflies of anxiety in her tummy is easily led to believe that food won't be coming. And it won't if it has to be sucked out first. "Suck" the milk out yourself by pumping a little. While doing so, place the baby over your knees on her stomach and rock her gently from side to side. Then try again and persevere.

If you become uneasy, get up and walk for a little while with the baby up on your shoulder, as if a burp had to be coaxed out of her right now (whether or not she has eaten anything) Think about something else until you are able to focus on what matters. You are the one who needs to soothe yourself now. Take all the time you need.

Put the baby to your breast again. A stubborn little one will take the nipple more easily if you hold her neck and the back of her head, and aim her mouth at your nipple at a ninety-degree angle. You can relax your grip when she begins to nurse. Make sure the soft breast tissue doesn't block the little nostrils.

Let her eat as much as she wants for as long as she wants. Do not interrupt the meal under any circumstances!

As you know, your milk does not flow steadily but in fits and starts. The baby will suck for quite a while without swallowing, so she is not ingesting anything. Don't be deceived into believing that she is full and the meal is over. She is just waiting for the next round.

If she gets tired and starts to doze off with the nipple in her mouth, coax her to continue by moving your nipple or by withdrawing it a little so she locks back on and starts to suck again. You can also tickle or rub her a little on the jaw or under the ear.

When she is definitely full, and she lets go of the nipple, purses her lips, closes her eyes and looks as though she is about to pass out, burp her thoroughly. Don't be too gentle. It's a wake up call! Then follow the rest of the Standard Model program to the letter.

The meal should last at least an hour and a half, longer if the baby has the strength. (The socializing and/or the refill can be extended.)

A nap will follow, which you should interrupt after approximately two hours.

Caress her over the head, wrap her in the blanket and repeat the whole procedure as per the Standard Model.

The first night will probably be uneventful if you have organized the day *preventively* in the prescribed manner. But old habits die hard, and if your baby starts her usual melancholy routine towards evening or at night, you have two cards up your sleeve.

During the evening fuss, you can buff the baby into a twenty-minute nap – right in the middle of all the family action – which will give her a little mental holiday. (See "Sleep".) Then see the program through to a conclusion. It will be somewhat extended and a couple of extra top-ups may be needed.

During the night, you will give her one or two short feedings, depending on whether or not she has passed the one-month mark.

Put the baby down *on her stomach*, which will soothe her abdominal pains, in the carriage beside you. Pick her up and feed her as soon as she wakes up. Change her if she needs it, give her a refill and a burp, and put her back down. The whole procedure takes about twenty minutes. Skip the other points in the program.

Pull the carriage back and forth if she can't settle down, using the highly effective method described in "Sleep". Give her one night feeding, two at the most. Apart from that, if and when she cries, rock her back to sleep.

Don't pick her up and walk around with her.

In the morning, follow the cure as per the Standard Model throughout the day. Don't let naps between meals last for longer than two hours.

Applying this cure meticulously for three days will crack even the toughest case of colic. That I can promise you.

If you care for your baby continuously according to the Standard Model, whose guiding principle is food, food and more food, *non multa sed multum*, freely translated, and if you give her lavish meals that last an hour and a half while she is really awake, rather than skimpy snacks at odd hours, you will be satisfying your baby's needs preventively and thereby allaying her survival anxiety as much as is humanly possible. Peace will descend.

If you are so overwhelmed by feelings of powerlessness and despair that you don't even have the strength to contemplate implementing such a cure, and your baby's crying torments you to the point that you no longer feel you can take responsibility for your actions, swallow your pride and recognize your limitations. Ask for help!

You are not the be all and end all for your child. You are, or you should be, the guarantor of her survival. If, for whatever reason, you are not up to the task, you must hand it over to someone else. When all is said and done, no matter how essential you think you are, you are less important to your child than her own survival.

There are other people around. You don't have to do everything yourself. The baby has a father and relatives. You have friends or at least acquaintances. Use them! Someone must be able to devote a couple of days or a weekend to your baby and to a cure with such a wonderful outcome.

You can then return and reap the harvest.

When your baby has been liberated from her survival anxiety, she will embrace the whole world – and especially you – with her trust, which has finally been affirmed. Then you will actually be able to enjoy your child.

And your child will be able to enjoy life – she will *dare* to throw herself into it.

If you have colic medication for your baby, throw it away.

Every single infant that I have come across in my life – and there are quite a few of them – who has been diagnosed with colic, or has actually been afflicted by it, has been cured by food, food and more food.

All according to the Standard Model.

THREE WEEKS

A LITTLE MEMO

For the first little while, your newborn will not be difficult to look after provided she gets all the food she wants. But there may be the odd problem in connection with what I call *the true birth*, which occurs towards the end of the second or the beginning of the third week of life. This little memo will sum the situation up.

The true birth means that the trauma of the delivery is fading. Your newborn is ready to face the world and start living. The so-called "package period" is over. The first signs of the baby's desire for social participation are clearly discernible, and this desire must be met.

So:

• Do not consign your baby to isolation or silence if that is what you have been doing up to now!

• Broaden her horizons. Be careful not to limit your baby to one particular room or, even worse, your own bed.

• Make sure that your baby always has something interesting to look at, and preferably something interesting to listen to as well, all the time she is awake.

• Expand the Standard Model by adding another point to the program: lying on a blanket on the floor and being awake. This sets the stage for *passive social participation*. Your baby is a part of things.

While the trauma of delivery lasted, you provided protection and warmth. You were, figuratively speaking, a protective cocoon, just as your body literally was a few weeks earlier. Now that is no longer enough. Your baby needs more. If you continue to handle her like a helpless package – and there is a risk that you will, since she is still so tiny – distress and discontent are just around the corner. Don't be afraid to present the world within the flock with all the appropriate fanfare! Music, voices, sights, sounds, light and people – life is swirling around you and your baby wants to join in.

Separate night from day. When night falls, peace, darkness and silence should reign. But during the day, there should be life and movement, yells, bells and smells, always something to see and hear.

Now, when your baby sits on your knee, she doesn't have to be facing you, as was the case during those vital socializing periods. When you are talking animatedly to someone, for example, she can face away from you and look out into the world. And you will see that when you are talking, laughing, twisting, turning and gesticulating, all the while with your baby in your arms facing outwards, your little one will be so interested you will *feel* it.

Now your baby can and should lie beside you as you work, and not just on the floor, but on a bench or a table right at your elbow. Change positions for her when need be and keep a hand on her back. She must never be exposed to the risk of falling.

But solitary periods on the floor, baby on stomach, should also be included in the program – although there should always be something to look at and listen to. Don't take unnecessary precautions. Crank up the stereo – newborns like the thundering drums, the falling stars and the crashing planets of dramatic classical pieces – and they like it played so they can hear it, not as bland background music.

If you haven't done so already, decorate the designated spots for changing with things that are fun to look at. Things that dangle and swing are almost a must at this stage.

Waking time will increase, and if you want to make sure that your baby doesn't engage in any late night partying, extend the meals during the day appropriately. If Standard Model meals with all they entail have hitherto lasted an hour and a half followed by approximately two and a half hours of sleep, you should now be shooting for a two-hour meal instead (followed by a two-hour sleep).

Follow the program as before, but that newly instituted thirty minutes should be jam-packed with all the entertainment that you and the flock can come up with. (Stick to one and a half hours for feeding. Your baby no longer needs to be "knocked out" with a top-up before bed.)

The entertainment should not be connected to your person, but to the world and the life going on around you.

And pull out all the stops. Nothing exceeds like excess!

THE FIRST BATH

It's time for the first bath when the laceration around the navel has healed. That usually happens around three weeks after the umbilical stump has fallen off. You can tell by opening the navel. If there is no coagulated (or fresh) blood and everything is dry with a rosy hue, the healing process is probably complete. Wait a couple of days just to be sure.

The first bath is a big event. It is a relief of course to be spared the elaborate cleaning routine every evening, but it is an exciting milestone in your baby's life too.

Water is the element that human beings are first exposed to and the exposure should continue. I don't think human beings bathe just to keep clean. People, not least newborns, need to bathe in order to feel good.

Even if an infant's skin is often dry, with or without a daily bath, there is reason to believe that the skin needs to be supplied with external moisture other than the internal milk. Perhaps not in spite of the dryness but precisely because of it.

A daily bath also lays the foundation for good habits. It becomes natural for a growing child to take a daily bath or shower and thereby keep clean.

A bath at the end of the day will also soon become associated with going to sleep for the night.

We have discussed the so-called evening fuss in "If something goes wrong: the newborn refuses to sleep". The little nap during the evening fuss will extend the last meal, which in turn sets the stage for a long, unbroken night's sleep.

This is a good place to splice in a bath, in which case the program for the big evening meal would look like this:

1. Food. Burp and more food from the same breast.
2. Socializing. (Skip hygiene since you are going to give the baby a bath.)
3. Passive social participation – which in plain English means that your baby, who is now one month old, can lie on a blanket on the floor or "crawl" barefoot on the table (your hand on her back), as long as she is where the action is.
4. Short nap because of the evening fuss, when sudden distress sets in. Put the baby on her stomach, still at the center of family activity and buff her to a little twenty-minute nap, no more.

197

5. Wake her up if she doesn't wake up by herself and feed her immediately from the other breast. One round will do it. Burp.
6. Undress her and bathe her.
7. Dress her for the night.
8. Yet another portion from the same breast as last time. Burp.
9. Socialize for a little while if she is still alert.
10. A last top-up – the night-cap – when she starts to fade. Bed for the night.

To begin the bathing, fill the tub and make sure the water is warm enough. Imagine you are the one taking the bath. (Unless you are into bathing Japanese style of course. You will have to acclimatize your child gradually later on!) Hands are a little too insensitive for testing the temperature, so use your elbow or forearm.

Place the tub high enough so you don't have to bend over. You will be standing for a while.

The tub should be properly filled. A puddle at the bottom is no use.

Equip yourself with a towel, some mild soap and possibly a washcloth, although your hand will do just as well. Undress your baby and let the fun begin!

Hold her under the armpits so that her head rests against your wrist. Place your other hand around the little bottom and thighs. Look her in the eye and smile. Lower her very slowly into the water bottom first. Release your grip on her thighs so her legs can float free. She will probably gasp a little and look a tad surprised, her face a dismayed question mark, when she first makes contact with the water. Answer her by looking confident and encouraging.

Stay still. Don't start washing her yet. Let her slowly remember this once familiar element, lost and now rediscovered! Remain motionless as long as the baby does.

If, against expectations, she starts to cry when you lower her into the water, don't worry. Continue as though nothing is amiss. Place her in the water, wash her, and pick her up again. Speak to her soothingly over her screams and remember that every cry is a question. If you yank her out of the water immediately, you are answering her question in the affirmative. "You are absolutely right! Bathing is very dangerous, so I won't expose you to it." Repeat the bathing procedure calmly and quickly, evening after evening, and the protests will soon cease.

When the baby decides that the moment of stillness is over and she starts to move a little in the water, you can gently start to wash her. Rinse her face (or run the cloth over it without soap). Hold her head up a little so that water doesn't get into her nose, fill your hand with water and draw your hand over her face from top to bottom a couple of times. That may sound a little frightening, but your baby will not react with fear. She will just close her eyes. Children who have their faces washed this way right from the beginning develop a natural relationship with water.

Now soap your hand and wash the little body as it lies under the water. Don't forget to wash between the fingers and toes as chapped skin particles can collect there.

An important tip: See that her ears are under the surface of the water!

When I started bathing my first child, I thought that memories of the womb would be that much clearer if her ears were submerged, so I tried it. Only her face was above the water. She became very still as though she was listening. Then I began to speak loudly and launched into quite a harangue. I imagined that my voice would sound muffled and diffuse, as it must have done when she was in utero. Our eyes met and a surprised look came over her face. I thought I could see sweet satisfaction in her expression. It so fascinated me that her immersion lasted quite a while.

Now, after nine babies, I have come to understand that what I did was precisely the right treatment for infant ears. Not one of my children ever had any ear problems when they were young. Perhaps they were just lucky. Yet, for young children *clean ears are just as important as clean teeth*.

The bath should end *before* the baby starts to complain. If you are alone, spread the towel over your breast, pick the baby up, put her to the towel with her back against you and wrap her. If any problems occur, there is nothing to stop you from giving her a little snack immediately. Just wrap a blanket around the towel for good measure.

Place the baby on the change table, or whatever you use for such things, and rub her dry. Babies love having their tummies rubbed! Then get a diaper and dress her, after dabbing on a little ointment in all the strategic places, and wrap her in a cotton blanket. Scrubbed and fragrant, she is ready for supper!

A word of warning. Newborns don't drown. They instinctively close their air passages if they are submerged in water. Many babies can "dive" when they are a few months old. They can be placed in those nowadays oh-so-popular baby pools without getting water in their lungs.

At around one year, however, these instincts disappear. And with them goes a fair chunk of their survival instinct. I have seen babies of eighteen months slide under the water and remain lying there without making a move, even though they are perfectly capable of sitting up. Catastrophe can strike in the space of a couple of minutes without any telltale splashing. Babies this age just lie motionless in the tub. Young children can drown in puddles, ditches, brooks, fountains, inflatable pools and plastic tubs in as little as twenty centimeters of water. Keep your eyes open!

THE PACIFIER. IF, WHEN AND FOR HOW LONG?

We discussed pacifiers – which are aptly named suckifiers – in "What do you do?" in Part one of *For the Love of Children*.

The word pacifier would seem to imply that the child is worked up about something. The pacifier has come to serve a purpose that has nothing to do with satisfying the sucking reflex, which is so strong that nursing alone is not sufficient. It is used to keep children quiet.

I once watched a pathetic scene play itself out at a railway station. The child, a four or five year-old little girl, tripped and fell on the stone floor, hurt herself and screamed her head off. Her father put a pacifier in her mouth. The child spat the pacifier out and resumed screaming. Her father, visibly distressed, put it right back in. And the child spat it out. And Father put it back. This went on for five minutes. What was Dad to do? A pacifier pacifies. So the kid should be given a pacifier. But the child wanted to scream out her pain and be comforted because she had hurt herself, and she wanted to be comforted not by a pacifier but by her *father* – who was underestimating his own importance.

You can and should give a pacifier to a newborn if nursing is not sufficient to satisfy the sucking instinct. How you determine that is explained in "What do you do". You can give a child a pacifier to send her off to sleep but never to "pacify". Nor should you give a child a pacifier before a meal. That will come as a disappointment to a hungry child. If you can't give her your breast or the bottle immediately, your knuckle or lip is a better substitute.

In my experience, a pacifier that is contoured to the gums is to be preferred, since it doesn't slip out of the child's mouth so easily.

A newborn's pacifier should be sterilized in boiling water every day. Have two or three in circulation at a time, and test them regularly by pulling them hard!

If the pacifier ends up on the floor, you can suck it clean yourself as a stopgap measure.

At the very latest, pacifiers should be thrown away when your child turns six months. The earlier the better. (See "Away with the pacifier" in Part three of *For the Love of Children*.)

TWO MONTHS

DAILY LIFE

Only you know what a normal day looks like. Perhaps you have forgotten what normalcy is.

Perhaps every day is uncharted territory, your entire existence is utterly chaotic, and the future is both terrifying and incomprehensible. Then again, your days may be all peace and contentment, and you take joy in every moment, full of gratitude for the life you have.

The sky may be azure blue and cloud free, or dark and threatening.

You may be sobbing and exhausted, or you may be feeling stronger and happier than you ever have in your life.

You may feel as carefree and playful as the child you once were, or you may feel so weighed down by the responsibility you have taken on, you fear it will crush you.

You may look to the future with nothing but tranquil optimism – after all things have gone swimmingly so far – or you may be languishing in a slough of depression so deep, you think you will never see sunlight again. Like little Marcus's mother, who was prostrate with despair after just two months: "Everything seemed to cave in on me. Looking after Marcus was such an effort. I felt as though everything was against me. My life was a living hell."

Whatever you are feeling, you are not alone. There are always others who are experiencing the same solitude, the same questions, the same joy, the same fatigue, the same hope and the same despair that you are.

Having children is earth shattering. Having children is an experience that suffuses and radically alters your world, now and forever. There is perhaps only one generalization that holds true for everyone: Whatever expectations you had about parenthood, the reality was different.

But however things turned out, they are what they are. You have to take care of a little person that didn't exist a year ago.

Your days of being the proverbial island are gone for good. You no longer stand alone. If you journey to the ends of the earth, you will never be able to expunge this child from your consciousness. There is a bond between you that distance can't break. As long as you live, your child will walk by your side, invisible perhaps, but there nonetheless.

That an upheaval so profound could leave you unaffected is impossible.

The proposition that you should simply get on with life the way you always have is totally unreasonable.

Yet that's precisely what you have to do.

There is a little person that can't cope with your existence being turned upside down. There is a little person that cannot cope with the knowledge that everything has changed and that you are no longer the person you once were, and that the life you lead is not the life you have always led. That little person is your baby.

The baby is in the situation you would be in when you arrived at a Bedouin camp and your contact man abandoned his life in the camp to sit out in the desert with you, instead of taking you into the tent and showing you around. The fact that he had left his old life behind would bother you intensely. A burden would be imposed on you to compensate him for what he had lost: his niche, his everyday life, and his place among his peers. Sitting out in the desert, you would be deprived of all this too – you who had come to the camp to learn the Bedouin way of life and to share in their struggle for survival.

What would you do? Would you love your contact man? Yes, and he would love you. But would that be enough? How would you ever learn how to live among the Bedouin if you were never granted access to the tent? The day would come when you would no longer be particularly cooperative, but would become ill tempered and demanding. Maybe you would become aggressive with your contact man who was keeping you so isolated and would try to force your way into the tent.

"My entire existence out here in the desert revolves around you, doesn't it?" your contact man might ask. "Why aren't you happy?"

"Because you're ripping me off!" you might reply. "You're supposed to teach me how things work in the camp. You're supposed to show me the ropes. How am I supposed to learn to live like a Bedouin?"

We have already talked about the frenetic demand for love, the kind of love that is supposed to compensate children for being excluded from their social community. We have talked about the inexorable human instinct to participate socially that kicks in with the true birth at approximately three weeks. We have talked about the fact the prerequisite for socialization is a social context that is necessary for *the adults* (the flock's collective struggle for survival).

Now after two months, things reach critical mass. The child can no longer occupy center stage. It is no longer feasible to separate the baby from the life that is pulsating all around her. Your contact man (if he's doing his job) welcomed you and inducted you into camp life. Now you have to familiarize yourself with his life – the life that will one day be yours. You, as a parent, must not keep your metaphorical tent closed and sit out in the desert with your baby. No matter how much love and attention you lavish on her, if you fail to provide her with an opportunity to participate socially, you will notice one or several of the following phenomena.

1. The baby will become demanding and difficult to please, and she will seem to always be seeking something. She will cry a lot, seem to want to be carried and exhibit anxiety. She won't like playing by herself and will not develop independence. She will have trouble sleeping, seemingly preferring to spend her nights stuck to her mother's breast.

2. You will find yourself proclaiming that looking after an infant is a full-time job, "fun but demanding...". You will announce to all within earshot that there is no way you could ever find the time or the energy to have another child, as you had perhaps planned. Everything you had intended to do during your parental leave is but a dimly remembered mirage.

3. You will feel frustration, pangs of conscience, and mental fatigue. You will feel like you're being "eaten alive" and will have trouble keeping pace with the daily grind. You will have a vague sense that the love you feel for your baby, or the baby herself, should compensate you for what you've lost – but it doesn't. As a result, you feel guilty, egotistical and utterly inadequate as a parent.

The baby's behavior will clearly indicate discontent too.

Why isn't she happy, no matter how much comfort, nursing, carrying, or cuddling you shower her with during the night? You are prepared to sacrifice anything and everything, just as a good mother or father should, so why is your baby so ticked?

Because what she wants is social participation. She wants to get a handle on the existence experienced by you, the adults, the flock. She wants into the tent.

Why do parents usually say that the second child is much easier than the first? It's not because they have more confidence in themselves as parents or because with time and experience they worry less. It's rather because the second child is born into a reality *that is already up and running.* The first child is already there. The second has to be inducted into a pre-existing context, the parameters of which, though they can be modified, are already securely fixed in place. The household cannot be turned upside down because of the new arrival. It has to keep functioning smoothly for the benefit of all its members.

Thus, the second child is automatically offered a chance to participate socially in a pre-existing little community. Just as automatically, a large number of problems disappear – or never occur in the first place.

So how can you create such a community out of thin air for the one child we will assume you have?

If you have ever entertained thoughts of running a business out of your home or taking up a new hobby, now would be a good time to take the plunge! In all earnest, *you have to convey the impression that you operate in a context that would exist with or without the baby.*

The baby is seeking to participate, first passively and later actively, in a social context under conditions that apply to *you.* From two months and up, this instinct cannot be suppressed (See "Social participation systematized" in Part three of *For the Love of Children*).

The baby expects you to operate in a community, so if no community exists, you will have to invent one. The struggle for survival does not revolve around a child. The struggle for survival takes place in a hectic, not to say sometimes hostile, world, and it is your task to provide leadership and protection to your offspring as you wage this struggle until your young are able to fend for themselves.

No infant will accept being the center of her parent's existence, other than during the first two or three weeks of life.

She will not accept being isolated in the desert with you, while the tent you should both be living in remains closed to her.

So what can you do? Renovate the house, study, paint pictures, make clothes, work from home, exchange services, work with others, do anything that is pleasant and possible, and pretend that it is absolutely necessary, whether it actually is or not!

You are the only one who can decide what will work for you. Only you can decide how you will structure your days, your life, your world, now and in the future, so that they will constitute an existence that *is necessary for you* and in which you can offer your child a place, first as a passive observer and later as an active participant.

At approximately two months, an infant's increasing desire to participate socially finds its counterpart in the mother's equally inexorable need to re-establish some sort of order, to return to a life that does not revolve *solely* around her child but of which her child is a natural part.

In accordance with my theory of the "repeated" pregnancy, I draw certain parallels.

An expectant mother goes through tremendous changes during the first two months of her pregnancy. Nausea and mood swings are the usual signs. Nor are spontaneous abortions uncommon during this period.

When the mother-to-be enters her third month, things stabilize. She adapts to the status quo. The nausea usually disappears, and the woman is able to wrap her mind around the fact that she is going to be a mother.

In a similar vein, a two-month-old has lived through a period of enormous upheaval and basically come to terms with her new world and her bodily functions. The baby begins to wrap her mind around the conditions that life on earth imposes on her. Both parties want stability at this point. Daily life starts to solidify into a routine – or at least efforts are made in that direction.

A two-month-old baby is a little creature of habit who gratefully accepts a fairly static existence, and the mother for her part longs to "be herself again" and "get back to normal".

In my opinion, this need for "normalcy" is part of the natural order of things, and as such it should not be condemned but rather respected and affirmed. Try to plan your daily routine in a way that suits you. Find something that you want to do, can do, and "must" do. Try to build yourself a life in which the baby can be at the center of the action, without being the action itself!

But what if you have to go back to work, and you only share your life with your baby evenings and weekends?

There is a risk that you will erect a barrier. You are in effect permitting the baby to participate passively but not actively. You are routinely relegating your child to a separate children's world within the confines of the home very early on because you know that her need to participate socially will not be satisfied.

And you will get a lot of assistance from the prevailing socio-political ideology.

No book on children is going to revolutionize society, so I can only make this appeal:

Try to save at least the first three years. *Prioritize!*

Give your baby the opportunity to live and participate with you, the parent(s), within the flock she has been born into.

A LITTLE MEMO

- A two-month-old is perfectly capable of amusing herself for fairly long periods if she has been given enough food and socializing, and has something pleasing to look at and listen to. *Little people need a little time to themselves as well.*
- A two-month-old obviously enjoys life – as long as her surroundings are reasonably positive and her caregivers aren't stingy with food and smiles. No one who lives a good life needs comfort.
- A two-month-old not only accepts a bustle of activity that would go on whether she was there or not, she expects it. *Children always accept whatever is necessary for the adults* (i.e. activities that contribute to the flock's struggle for survival).
- A two-month-old will accept any routine that satisfies her basic needs as long as this routine is set up and followed as though it were self-evident.
- On the other hand, a two-month-old will not accept being the flock's (read adults') *raison d'être.*

No human being can be the sole source of another human being's happiness.

This is as true for little ones as it is for big ones.

LITTLE HUGO, TWO AND A HALF MONTHS

Hugo was born into a large family: five brothers ranging in age from preschool to high school. Hugo's mother has been a homemaker ever since her first child was born and her experience of children and childcare is vast. I asked her to tell me how she cared for Hugo and how his day was organized.

Monday

1. Hugo wakes up at 7.30. He is fed immediately and eats for 25 minutes. Hugo is breastfed. After a change, some socializing and a cuddle he is put down to sleep at 9.30. He sleeps for 50 minutes. He was awake for two hours during that meal, and he slept for just under one.

2. At 10.20 it's time to eat again and Hugo does so for 35 minutes. At 11.30 Hugo is put down to sleep again. He has been awake for an hour and ten minutes during this meal. Now he sleeps for two and a half hours, which takes us to 2.00.

3. At 2.00 he eats for half an hour, and is up and about until 4.20. He is then put down to sleep again. He was awake for two hours and twenty minutes this time, and that was followed by a one-hour nap.

4. At 5.20 he eats again, this time for 35 minutes. He stays up until 7.00. He was awake for one hour and 40 minutes during the fourth meal.

5. That was followed by a sleep that lasted until 1.00 a.m., when his mother woke him up and fed him.

During this twenty-four hour period, Hugo was awake for 7 hours and 10 minutes. The sleep periods during the day were fairly short, since Hugo's day was short. He decided that the curtain should come down at 7.00 p.m. After the first meal, he slept less than one hour and after the third, one hour only. He did not indulge in any evening fussing.

His mom had to wake him at 1.00 a.m. She obviously thought that he would not get through the night on the rations he had received during the day. And every time little Hugo ate, he nursed for at least half an hour.

That day Hugo was active during all of the first three meals. His personal best was during the third meal when he was up doing his thing for as long as two hours and twenty minutes. During the fourth meal, however, he began to fade after only an hour and a half. The night meal was McDonald's drive-thru, very fast indeed.

Tuesday

1. Today little Hugo wakes up at 6.00 a.m. He eats for half an hour and is up until 8.30, so he's awake for two and a half hours – whereupon he sleeps for an hour and a half.

2. His second breakfast is served at 10.00. Hugo nurses for 45 minutes. He is up until 12.00 – that's two hours. He then takes a quick nap – a mere 30 minutes.

3. At 1.00 he wants food again. He eats for half an hour and stays awake

for another hour. He is then put down to sleep in a carriage outside, but he doesn't really settle down. He is still too peppy. He doesn't fall asleep properly until 3.00 and he sleeps until 5.00.

4. The fourth meal is served at 5.00 and Hugo is out for the count an hour later. Now he sleeps through the night until six the next morning – and, *mirabile dictu,* he has to be woken! He could have gone on sleeping it would seem.

Over this twenty-four-hour period, Hugo was awake for a grand total of seven and a half hours. He started earlier than he did the previous day, and therefore slept longer in the morning after his first meal. After his second meal, however, he perked up royally and only slept for half an hour. He overdid things a bit, since at the third meal he was a little out of sorts. It took him a while to get to sleep, and he was less than happy. After the fourth meal, he slept like a log, and his mother decided that the fourth meal was to be the last one. In spite of the fact that Hugo is still too young to manage a whole night on only four meals, she let him sleep, and it turned out to be the right decision.

Wednesday

1. Hugo is woken up at 6.00 a.m., is up for one and a half hours and falls back to sleep at 7.30. He logs as much sleep time as waking time and comes to at 9.00.

2. Breakfast number two is served at 10.00, which means Hugo waits an hour for his food. He is now old enough to wait for food without getting anxious. After nursing for half an hour, he is given a change, he has a "chat" and a cuddle with mom, and he is put back to bed at 12.00. He has been awake for three hours, but he still only sleeps for one.

3. Food is served again at 1.00. But there is a little play-cuddle session first. The meal doesn't start until 1.20, and it lasts for 40 minutes. After the meal, Hugo goes into town with his mom. Again, he has been awake for three whole hours in connection with this meal, and then, as he did last time, he sleeps for only one hour.

4. At five, the last meal is served. Hugo is up until 6.30 p.m., which makes one and a half hours.

5. He sleeps for five and half hours, until 1.00 a.m., when he is given a top-up.

During this third twenty-four hour period, little Hugo has been awake a grand total of nine hours – which is quite a lot of "up" time. But he still woke up during the night and wanted more to eat. One might think that he would sleep through the night after having been awake for so long, but the previous night Hugo slept for twelve hours straight, and this reserve has yet to be depleted. If his mother had woken him up and fed him that night, he would probably have slept straight through the next one instead – in which case he would have built up a reserve of food instead of a reserve of sleep.

Like the day before, Hugo slept one and a half hours after the first morning meal, but was really on the ball during the two meals that followed. He was awake for as long as three hours at a stretch. The fourth meal was a somewhat truncated affair. Evidently, Hugo thinks that one and a half hours of being socially active is enough in the late afternoon or early evening. The lad is not one for burning the midnight oil.

Thursday
1. After a nocturnal refuelling, Hugo sleeps until 7.30. Now the previous day's social exertions take their toll, and Hugo hits the hay again right after being fed. He was only awake for half an hour during this meal, and he sleeps until 9.00.
2. Breakfast number two is served at 10.20. Hugo has been awake and easy to get along with since 9.00. He eats for half an hour, and at 12.00 he is put to bed. Hugo has been awake for as long as three hours at a stretch. He then sleeps for only one hour.
3. At 1.00 p.m. he is given food again and he eats for forty minutes. After a change, a cleanup and some socializing, he falls asleep at 3.00. He has been up for two hours, and the sleep that follows lasts one hour.
4. At 4.00 Hugo wakes up hungry, eats and is up for one and a half hours. Then he grabs himself a half-hour nap.
5. He wakes up hungry at 6.00. After more food, followed by one and a half hours of socializing, he checks out for the night at 8.00 p.m. This was in fact neither one meal nor two but something in between. All told, Hugo was up for close to four hours, but slotted in a little nap. The night's sleep that followed was ten and a half hours long.

During this last twenty-four hour period, Hugo was awake for a total of nine hours. That's no mean feat for a person that little. When Hugo got his five meals – or four and a half – he slept the whole night, close to twelve hours. Such a long unbroken night's sleep is unusual for a baby that is just over two months old. (On the Thursday, Hugo was two months and ten days old.)

That day, it was in connection with the second and fourth meals that Hugo partied hardest: three and almost four hours respectively. He maybe was a touch out of step with his own rhythm, since during the fourth meal he fussed a little in the evening, which is unusual for him. He had to take a little nap to recharge his batteries.

Friday
1. After his long sleep, Hugo wakes up at 6.30 and is ravenous. He eats for nearly 45 minutes. At 7.30 he's back to sleep again. He was awake for one hour, and he slept for an hour and a half.
2. The clock strikes 9.00 and Hugo is awake again. Food is served at 10.00. Hugo again nurses for 45 minutes. He stays up until 12.00. So he was awake for three hours and then slept for one and a half.
3. At 1.30 it's time for another feeding. Hugo eats for half an hour and is up until 3.30. He's been awake for two hours. He then sleeps for two and a half hours.
4. At 6.00 the fourth meal is served, and Hugo is awake until 7.30, for a total of one and a half hours. He falls asleep quickly but doesn't sleep through the night.
5. He wakes up at midnight. After a quick nosh, he sleeps until 6.00 the next morning.

During this twenty-four-hour period, Hugo was only awake for seven and a half hours all told. He probably thought that this was a little cheap, which is why he woke up at midnight. Then he got that fifth meal that he didn't have time for during the day.

Otherwise, both the early morning meal and the evening meal were, as usual, lean, mean and business-like. During the second and third, Hugo was at his most active and awake for the longest – again the norm. Active days, lazy mornings and evenings are evidently the lifestyle that suits Hugo best.

Saturday
1. Hugo wakes up at 6.00, and he is so perky that, once he's eaten breakfast, he stays up until 8.30, which makes a total of two and a half hours. This is followed by a one and a half hour sleep.
2. He eats his second meal at 10.00. He eats for half an hour and stays up until 11.30. After having been awake for one and a half hours, he then sleeps for two, and doesn't wake up until 1.30.

3. Meal number three is offered at 2.00. Hugo is changed and entertained for half an hour before being fed. He eats for half an hour and continues socializing until 3.30. He's up for two hours during this meal, whereupon he sleeps for one and a half.

4. Hugo next wakes up at 5.00, but he doesn't eat before 6.00. After eating, he takes a quick nap. His mom and dad have been invited to a friend's house for dinner, and they take Hugo with them. Once there, he fusses a little. Hugo stays awake until 10.30 that evening – very rare for him – but he is over-excited by all the activity taking place around him. This isn't surprising, since even though Hugo is a curious fellow, he is not at his best in the evenings.

5. At 10.00 p.m. Hugo is fed and finally gets to sleep. But he doesn't sleep through the night, as we shall soon see. Hugo has been up for almost four hours in connection with the evening meal, but he only sleeps for one and a half hours.

6. At midnight, he has to be fed again, so he is up to six meals during this twenty-four-hour period – again an unusual state of affairs. And now he finally settles down. He sleeps until 7.00 the next morning.

This Saturday Hugo was up for eleven and a half hours. That' s too much. Hugo's schedule was thrown out of sync by the dinner invitation, and he became over-tired. It's worth noting that even when he is over-tired, Hugo doesn't sleep that long – in spite of the fact that he really needs to. Exhausted infants never sleep longer or better just because they are exhausted – quite the opposite in fact.

Sunday
1. Hugo wakes up at 7.00 and is his usual sunny self. He eats and stays awake for one and a half hours. Still tired after the exertions of the previous day, he sleeps for two and a half hours after this meal, not waking up until 11.00.

2. At 11.00 it's time to eat, and this Hugo does for half an hour. He is awake for two and a half hours until 1.30. He's clearly back on the beam. He then sleeps for one and a half hours.

3. At 3.00 he is fed again and stays up until 5.00. He has been awake for two hours, after which he sleeps for two.

4. At 7.00 the fourth meal is served, and Hugo is out for the count one hour later.

5. At midnight mom wakes him and gives him a top-up.

Hugo was only awake for seven hours during this last twenty-four hour period. He was exhausted by the previous day's social whirl. At midnight he had to be woken up. His mother felt he had not eaten enough or been awake for long enough to sleep through the night.

Otherwise, Hugo's pattern was as per normal: he was awake and doing his thing during the day and afternoon, but mornings and evenings were a lot less active.

His mother's notes show that Hugo is no night owl. He's fairly chipper in the mornings, but he really hits his stride during the day.

His night sleep is fabulous, and he is already showing signs of wanting to sleep twelve hours at a stretch.

Furthermore, we are clearly dealing with a young man who regards fussing in the evening as not something a gentleman does. His falls from grace are few and far between, and when they do occur, it's usually during the afternoon when the risk of becoming over-tired (at least for him) is at its greatest.

He can wait for his food, which means his survival anxiety is but a pale shadow of its former self. Experience has taught him that an unlimited amount of food is there for the taking and that he can take his sweet time while he eats it.

As we can see, his mother tries to keep to the four-hour schedule even if she is not obsessed with sticking to specific times. If Hugo wakes up at 7.00 in the morning, the meals start at 7.00, 10.00, 2.00 and 7.00. If, on the other hand, he wakes up at 6.00, she sticks to the old classics 6.00, 10.00, 2.00 and 6.00. The problem – if we can really call it a problem – is that there is no room for the fifth meal, and Hugo still needs it. Hugo wants to go down for the night after the fourth meal, but he's still too young for that. His mother therefore has to wake him approximately every other night.

Would a parent gain anything by establishing a schedule for Hugo with hard and fast meal times?

If he or she were *inexperienced*, the answer is yes.

We took a look at this in the section entitled "Every child's every cry is a question". When I summed up, I said that parents have to be *very confident*

– just as Hugo's mother was – if they are going to successfully apply such a free wheeling approach to child rearing. You have to know your craft intuitively; it has to sit in your bone marrow.

Let's take a look at how a schedule for Hugo might look! I am going to "borrow" him, since we know him a little after having observed him for a week.

First, there has to be room for five meals – four big ones and a nocturnal top up. Second, the risk of over-exertion during the afternoons has to be eliminated. Third, the activities of the other members of the family have to be taken into account. These would be our points of departure, if we were charged with the task of setting up a schedule. And naturally, all Hugo's needs have to be satisfied continuously and preventively according to the Standard Model Program.

Let's ponder our options in more detail. First, we have to set meal times. If we are going to squeeze in five meals, we are going to have to start early. Six in the morning perhaps? With four-hour intervals, the last meal would begin at ten in the evening. Unfortunately, we are dealing with a rare breed. Our borrowed model, Hugo, dear lad that he is, gets tired in the evenings and exhibits tendencies to sleep through the night. The last meal should therefore be scheduled earlier. So our meal timetable should perhaps look something like this: 6.00, 10.00, 2.00, 5.00 and 8.00.

This sounds better, but there is another problem. The four-hour gap between the meal at 6.00 and the meal at 10.00 might not be to Hugo's liking, since he prefers to eat a second breakfast after about three hours. On the other hand, he doesn't mind waiting for his food. Would 9.30 be better?

We have seen that Hugo is full of pep and very active during the late afternoon and sometimes during the earlier part of the afternoon as well. He is so active in fact that he sometimes over-exerts himself. Would a proper midday sleep be in order? With that extra gust of wind in his sails, Hugo would be able to enjoy his afternoons with gusto. Furthermore, a habitual, solid rest period in the middle of the day would certainly be beneficial several years down the road.

Clearly, this child was born to be active during the day, and a timeout to recharge his batteries might be just what he will need. How does two to two and a half hours sound? If he is going to sleep that long, he will of course have to stay up and be thoroughly entertained during the first two meals. So, if the first meal is served at 6.00 and Hugo stays awake for two hours, and then the second meal is served at around 9.30, and he is up for two hours during this meal too, he will have to marshal his strength to be fit for duty by the early afternoon. We should therefore schedule the midday sleep between 12.00 and 2.00. The third meal will be served at 2.00 sharp.

If the fourth meal is offered at 5.00 p.m. and the fifth at 8.00 p.m. there won't be much time for sleep between rounds of food. This suits our purposes rather well. After the long sleep in the middle of the day, Hugo will be full of beans, and after the last meal it will be time for him to check out for the night. Thus, a one and a half-hour nap after meal number two is enough. During the second meal, Hugo will be awake for two hours. This should suit his constitution without over-exerting him. The fourth meal would then be served at five after a one and a half-hour nap, and now Hugo can be expected to last all the way to the last evening meal – if he gets a twenty-minute nap as and when he needs it. Here we have to be flexible. Every schedule should have a margin for error of fifteen minutes in each direction. In any case, the last meal should be served at 8.00 – perhaps even 7.30. Hugo's evening habits being what they are, he should probably be put down for the night at 9.00 after one last top-up.

How much waking time and how much sleep time would Hugo log under such a regimen? The night would last from 9.00 p.m. to 6.00 a.m. That's nine hours. Is it fair to expect a baby of barely two months to sleep nine hours at a stretch? Actually, it is, provided that the baby has been adequately fed and amused during the day.

Then we have a midday nap of two and a half hours. To that we can add a one and a half-hour morning nap, a one and a half-hour afternoon nap, as well as one (or possibly two) little twenty-minute naps towards the late afternoon/evening peak. That makes a total of six to six and a half hours of sleep during the day. All in all, Hugo would be sleeping between fifteen and sixteen hours per day. According to his mother's notes, Hugo needs to square between fifteen and sixteen hours of sleep per day.

In the schedule we are putting together, Hugo's waking hours would add up to between eight and eight and a half hours a day. Thus, in terms of the number of hours spent asleep and the number of hours spent awake, our timetable meets all the criteria.

Beyond the Standard Model various program points, outings and baths for Hugo have to be spliced in. How shall we tackle this?

He can take his midday nap outside. He is big enough to sleep outside in any weather if he is clad for it. But he also has to get out and take in the sights while he is awake. Perhaps the best time for this would be in the morning after the 9.30 feeding before the midday sleep. If we decide on this option, we will have to keep him amused and alert so that he doesn't fall asleep before the appointed time.

In connection with which meal should we bathe him? When the 8.00 meal rolls around, everyone will have eaten and be winding down for the day, so the house will be fairly quiet. At 5.00 the house will be a little chaotic with food preparation in full swing and family members getting home from work. However, Hugo will be perkier at 5.00 than he will at the end of the day.

What's more, a bath at this time is a good habit and will come to be associated with going to sleep for the night. Perhaps the last meal should be moved up a little so that the bath can be savored at a more leisurely pace.

Our schedule is beginning to take shape. We have set the times, and now we have to decide the content.

We have to make room for social participation and solitary play (see "Solitary play in the mornings" in Part three of *For the Love of Children*). Solitary play should be scheduled for the mornings. Hugo has had a long sleep, a big meal, and he's chipper in the mornings anyway, so he can certainly amuse himself for a while as long as he has something interesting to look at and to listen to.

Social participation – i.e. Hugo is where all the action is but not the action itself – should be spliced in during the fourth meal between 5.00 and 6.30 p.m., when the house hums with activity. He can lie on the floor on his blanket in the middle of everything and take part passively by simply watching the world go by, and actively by being passed from lap to lap, lying on the table, being talked to and generally being made to feel a part of the proceedings.

Once we have a finished product, it should be written out and taped to the wall where everyone who looks after Hugo can see it.

This is how it would look:

6.00   Food, change, socializing
7.00   Solitary play
8.00   Morning nap
9.30   Food etc., play and cuddle, outing while awake
11.30   Midday sleep in the carriage outside
2.00   Food, change, socializing, lying on the blanket, talking/playing
3.30   Afternoon nap
5.00   Food. Social participation while the house is a hive of activity
6.30   (or when needed) Twenty-minute nap
8.00   Bath, socializing, top-up before bed
9.00   Down for the night.

Will the dear lad go along with all this?

He may need a little help to come to terms with the long midday sleep, since he's not used to it. In the beginning, he might need some rocking in the carriage now and again.

We might also have to tempt him a little by scheduling something fun in connection with the last meal at 8.00. He will probably think it's time to go down for the night after the fourth meal at 5.00, so we may have to make it worth his while to stay awake.

These caveats aside, the schedule shouldn't pose any problems. It's based on Hugo's rhythms and it satisfies his needs. He is also big enough to wait for his food, which facilitates things immensely.

Once you plan and decide on a schedule of your own, you should adhere to it very strictly until you see how it works for everyone. There should be a fifteen-minute margin of error each way, but not more. It will take three days to establish the routine and at least a week for everyone to get used to it.

If there are problems, you can make adjustments later. You will, of course, have to make adjustments to keep pace with the baby's development and changing needs anyway. But bear in mind that you will have to give your baby time to get a handle on any innovations or adjustments, and, like the building of Rome, this is not done in a day.

The greatest impending changes concern sleep. In Hugo's case, the afternoon nap between 3.30 and 5.00 p.m. is the first sleep period to fall by the wayside. The next nap to disappear is the twenty-minute time out before the last meal of the evening. The last two meals of the day will merge naturally in another month and a half, and Hugo's nights will be twelve hours long.

The midday nap, however, can stay on the agenda for a long time to come, and solitary play in the mornings can be gradually extended (more about that later).

Finally – but this won't happen until he is over a year old – the morning nap between the first and second meals will be phased out. Solitary play is also practical in that the baby himself can decide if and when this little morning nap should be taken. Otherwise, a one-year-old can be difficult since some days he'll need it and some days he won't. Young children who are used to solitary play can make this decision for themselves.

Generally speaking, it's never a bad idea to keep half an eye on the future when you are putting a schedule together. As I already mentioned, the midday nap can be kept as is for a long time yet, and sleeping outdoors does babies a world of good. Later, you might have your baby sleep indoors but in front of an open window, which fosters a good habit. The evening bath lays the foundation for another good habit: daily attention to hygiene. Solitary play enables the baby to start the day in peace, but also implies respect and confidence in the baby's ability on your part.

A structured, organized day also gives you time for all kinds of other activities, and a timetable means the day ends at a pre-determined time.

Since we've been discussing Hugo, both descriptively and prescriptively, let's take a look at what else his mom said about him when I asked her.

"Hugo is now two and a half months old and weighs 6.230 grams," she says.

"Between the ages of six weeks and two months, he began to discover his arms. At first, he caught sight of them by accident when they happened to cross his field of vision. Now he consciously holds up his arm and studies it long and hard. He was exactly two months old when he began to feel things that were within reach. A face held close, a toy on the edge of his bed, for example. Until then, he just looked at things intently. He likes being carried and looks eagerly around him. Now he can see things at a distance. He follows people with his eyes as they walk past his bed. He can recognize my breasts from six to seven feet away and uses his arms and legs to express his excitement."

"If I asked you to describe Hugo as a person, what would you say?"

"He's sensible, understanding, good-hearted and has a great sense of humor."

"Did you love him the minute you laid eyes on him?"

"Yes."

"How do you think he feels about you?"

"He trusts me."

"What are his likes and dislikes?"

"He likes it when people talk to him. He uses his whole body to respond at great length. He doesn't like to be left lying in a wet diaper. If I'm not quick off the mark, he screams his head off. He doesn't like interruptions during changing and feeding either. I never answer the phone when I'm breastfeeding for example. That's why he's never startled or bothered when it rings. If I just ignore it, so does he."

"Any eccentricities that you've had to learn to cope with?"

"He sleeps longest and deepest on his stomach, but sometimes, especially right after meals, he likes to fall asleep on his side. Once he's really out, I lay him on his stomach. If he surfaces and starts rubbing his face against the mattress, I give him a pacifier for a little while."

"You have a great deal of experience in caring for infants. Do you have a system?"

"Feeding, changing, hygiene have to be done routinely, so a system develops all by itself. I've never bothered to schedule things like walks or baths. Now that he is two and a half months old, feeding times and the care that goes with them are pretty fixed. They don't really vary by more than an hour. When and if we go out depends on the weather. Bath times can vary too. If he poos in the morning, I'll give him a bath then. If we don't have time for a bath during the day, he'll get one in the evening instead. When he was really little, he would get the odd bath at night, all very peaceful, no pressure."

"What's the routine at mealtimes?"

"When I pick him up, I hold him close and we cuddle for a while. The joy of reunion. Whether I change him first or feed him first depends on how hungry he is and how wet he is. I always talk to him when I change him. 'It must feel good to get that diaper off... now we'll just put a little oil on...Does it feel cold?' and so on. After he eats, we just hang out together, sit for a while and rest, and he has a burp. Then he's up with me for a while on a blanket. He socializes a bit with his brothers, watches while I iron or work in the kitchen... After about half an hour, when I see he's getting tired, I usually put him down to sleep in his bed and it usually doesn't take him long to drop off."

"How much time does Hugo spend crying on any given day? Or night?"

"Five minutes a day at the most. Nothing at all at night."

"What have his nights been like since you got him home? Have you tried to extend his night sleep?"

"Hugo was smart enough to sleep through the night-feeding before we even left the hospital, and that continued when we got home. But a couple of times he would fuss in connection with a very late feeding round about midnight. He would fuss for a couple of hours. Change-food, change-food, spit up, rock to sleep. Then he would sleep until five or six o'clock. If he had a meal earlier in the evening, he would sometimes sleep until four. When he was one month old, he stopped fussing at night and slept from eleven or midnight to five pretty well every night. Now that he's two and a half months old, I wake him for a late evening meal, but he doesn't eat as long as he does during the other meals, and he usually sleeps like a log when I put him back down. He doesn't wake up until six or seven in the morning. He's extended his night sleep all by himself. If he hadn't, I'd have moved the late evening meal back. If he had still woken up at around two or three o'clock, at one or two months I would have tried to get him to go back to sleep with some rocking. Preferably on his stomach and with a warm blanket over him."

"How long do you usually breastfeed?"

"Varies. Anything from six weeks to six months. Depends on what everyone wants and has the energy for. Fashion too, I suppose. When my second child was born, I breastfed him exclusively for only six weeks. That had a lot to do with the fact that his elder brother, who was just over eighteen months, demanded a lot of time and attention. On top of that attitudes towards breastfeeding were hardly enthusiastic at the time. If that was what you wanted, no one would stop you, but 'the bottle is just as good and at least you can see what you're feeding the kid'."

"Did you have any problems breastfeeding?"

"It's absolutely phenomenal that your breasts can produce as much milk as the baby needs. If you just leave everything to nature, everything works just fine. But you have a lot to contend with both at home and with all the professional advice. As soon as the baby cries, everyone assumes that the baby is hungry and it's my fault because I'm not producing enough milk. Just one thoughtless comment those first few weeks can destroy your self-confidence and suddenly your breasts seem to jam. My advice to expectant mothers is to tell everyone a good while before you deliver that you need support while you are breastfeeding and that there can be times, no matter how long you've breastfed, when mothers feel they're not producing enough milk for their babies and they become terrified that their infants will starve to death... I remember once I was tired and didn't think I had enough milk, so I expelled my milk into a bottle just so I could see with my own eyes that my baby was getting enough to eat and he wasn't going to die of malnutrition. I mean, it's great that there is all this information about breastfeeding, but why does everyone assume that breastfeeding is so difficult? I get brochures with titles like *'How to make breastfeeding easier'*. You see stuff like this and you think that breastfeeding must be really hard. You're leafing through one of these brochures and you read that 'the expulsion reflex is easily disrupted'. And the vicious circle starts.

"How did you look after your breasts before and after the delivery?"

"I rubbed moisturizer into the nipples and 'test stretched' the nipple every day during the last month. After the delivery, it's important not to let the baby suck for a long time the first few days. That can cause painful lesions on you nipples that will last for weeks."

"As far as infant care goes, what's your guiding principle?"

"Empathy. And the baby's reactions. Experience. Last but not least, intuition."

"What do you think your husband goes by?"

"The baby's reactions."

"Do you think it's possible to spoil an infant?"

"No. Doing everything you can to make sure babies are happy isn't spoiling them. It's just giving them their basic human rights."

"What do you enjoy most about infant care?"

"Being around for the first contacts the baby makes in life!"

"What have you learned by caring for infants?"

"To forget myself... to put myself in another person's shoes... Compassion."

"Why do you think so many parents of infants complain over how difficult it is to have children?"

"The conflict between work and kids. The isolation and over-concentration on the baby during parental leave. I think continuing with your former life as best you can makes everything a lot easier. Boot-strapping yourself, getting a baby-sitter and going out and having some fun helps too."

"Finally, what have you gained by having children?"

"I've been enriched. Emotionally. I've developed. Matured."

"What have you lost?"

"I've lost the freedom to do whatever I want, whenever I want, but is that really that big a loss? I've also lost my ability to be petty and germophobic!"

"You have six children. Why so many?"

"Because I believe in having a lot of close relationships. It gives you a great start in life. It gives you security. It's good for kids to grow up with a ton of people who really care about them."

"What personal qualities have you developed by becoming a mother? What qualities would you have developed if you hadn't become a mother?"

"I've become softer, more tender, more humble. The quality I would have developed above all others if I hadn't become a mother is self-absorption."

PART THREE

Little People.
A Practical Guide

NEVER, HUMANHEART,
shall you find peace for your dream of eternity. Never shall life be large enough for you. Create you must, seek something else, something beyond. Incessantly, we must give the imperishable what belongs to it. We must dream, long and battle for the cause of our ultimate victory. Because within us, there are powers born that want to break open the imprisonment of life; that cannot find room in it – that wants the walls to tumble down and the shackles to cast off our feet, and that wants us to walk towards our destiny – towards complete elucidation.

Pär Lagerkvist: *The Conquered Life (Det besegrade livet)*

ABCs FOR LITTLE PEOPLE: LOVE, ROUTINES, PARTICIPATION

The ABCs for infants consist of three components that dominate daily life: love, routines and social participation.

Love denotes the direct contact between you and your child, a seamless connection, a perfect alignment, a total involvement here and now.

The routines denote the practical side of life: essential care, habits, schedules – all the daily rituals that take place around the child.

Social participation denotes activity within the flock – a reality that would exist with or without the infant. To begin with the baby's participation is passive.

In "Little Hugo, two and a half months old", Hugo's mother described how a meal would run:

"When I pick him up, I hold him close and we cuddle for a while. The joy of reunion."

That's love.

"Whether I change him first or feed him first depends on how hungry he is and how wet he is."

That's the routines.

"Then he's up with me for a while on a blanket. He socializes a bit with

223

his brothers, watches while I iron or work in the kitchen...

That's social participation.

Unfortunately, socio-political misconceptions have crept into this very simple formula. This was touched upon in Part two ("The best laid plans...").

The first misconception involves confusing A and B. The second involves eradicating C all together.

The first misconception mixes up love and routines. If I love my baby, this misconception goes, I can't decide when the day is over and it's time for bed. If I love my baby, I can't say, "NO, you can't use my breasts as pacifiers all night long." If I love my baby, I can't dress her in a red jacket if she wants to wear a blue jacket or fishnet stockings or nothing. You can no doubt list examples of your own. What they all have in common is the outlandish notion that routines have something to do with love. If you "force" a child to conform to certain routines, you are thwarting your child's will and are thereby smothering her independence. This is proof positive that you don't love her and are an authoritarian parent.

If we take this argument to its logical conclusion, companies who insist that their employees begin work at a certain time rather than whenever the employees feel like it would be smothering their independence. Journalists would be considered professionally stunted if they had to sit at the same computer all day long rather than being able to use any computer in the building. Farmers would feel that their independence was compromised because the seasons force them to plant and harvest their crops at certain times.

The routines are a tool. Having to conform to certain routines has no effect on an individual's personality or development other than that of freeing up energy which would have been wasted on trivia such as when to eat, when to sleep, what color clothes to wear, and whether the head of the bed should be facing east or west. An infant has no routines, so of course, you, the adult, have to introduce them.

The second misconception has led to the disappearance of social participation.

Parental leave itself is a deceptive creation. A mother or father on parental leave is isolated and is thus precluded from social participation in a wider society. It is of course true that there are many things to do around the house that offer the child the chance to participate socially, and the reality goes a long way towards satisfying *the child* because the world has to be little before it can be large. But because you are on parental leave from employment outside the home, you know that your own social participation in society comes at the cost of your child being excluded from your world.

Very early on, you separate your child's reality from your own.

Very early on, within the walls of the home, you may find yourself constructing a child-world, where you make guest appearances instead of inducting the child into your world – all perfectly in accordance with generally accepted practice. Your child will never be put to good use.

Most children are allowed to participate *passively* but that's as far as it goes. Reality is replaced with toys.

Activities that adults participate in and that are necessary for them are closed to children. Instead parents play with their children, read them stories and roll around on the floor with them – not that there is anything wrong with rolling around on the floor. Playing with kids is fun. But necessary, it's not. Children can play perfectly well without adults. Social participation, on the other hand, does require adult involvement. Children can't do it alone.

All the love in the world can't make up for a lack of meaning in life. If human beings don't feel that they are needed on some level – *the others wouldn't manage as well without me* – they are dangerously close to an existential void.

You might think all this is irrelevant for a two to three month old infant. I would beg to differ. It is precisely at this stage that these three components, this simple ABC formula, become an ongoing concern.

As a mother or father, you do it automatically. You have certain routines that you stick to. You have moments of love and intimacy with your baby, you also have household duties you have to perform, and it strikes you as perfectly natural that your baby should lie beside you and watch what you're doing because you want to keep an eye on her or him while you work.

If these three components can work their magic, if the first and the second aren't confused with one another and the third isn't tossed out completely, if love is allowed to reign and the routines are recognized for the tools they are, and *if passive social participation is allowed to become active* at a time and to a degree of your child's choosing – then your daughter or son is one lucky child.

And you are a revolutionary!

THREE AND FOUR MONTHS

Let's take a look at what's been happening!

During the first two or three weeks of life, before the trauma of birth begins to fade, you, the baby's mother, gave your newborn meticulous and constant protection. Your care was a warm, loving cocoon, just as your body was during your pregnancy. You supported your baby through the transition from the soft, liquid darkness of the womb to the cold light of a world where we all have to breathe under our own steam.

At the end of the third week of life, the baby, ready to begin her new life, began to look out into the world. You were still at your baby's disposal, night and day, but you gradually extended the radius of the circle. The periods on the floor and the change table, the conversations, and the socializing sessions were extended little by little, and you became more than a protector. You became a companion eager to show your baby her new environment, a big person showing a little person how to get by in this world.

You would certainly have noticed a change at the two-month mark. The baby's increased familiarity with the world would have been noticeable, and at the same time you would have felt the urge to get back to normal. (And if there wasn't a "normal" to get back to, you hopefully created one. See "Daily life" in Part two of *For the Love of Children*.)

Now you are following a more or less fixed schedule that ensures your baby's needs are continuously and preventively being met, and you are back to your everyday life where you occupy yourself (or pretend to) with *activities that are necessary for you*. It is these activities that so fascinate your child.

226

Three to four-month-old babies have some idea about how the world looks, sounds and feels. The focus of the baby's attention now is how the world actually functions. What happens? What do I do? Where do I fit into all this?

This relentless desire to be inducted into the community and to be put to work there is at the root of your baby's ceaseless efforts *to learn and understand*.

Your baby, at the beginning of her sojourn on Planet Earth, behaves pretty much like you or I would on our first day in a new job.

First, we find our desks and get settled in. Then we have to get a handle on our duties. To help us, we have co-workers who train us, be that training theoretical or hands-on. We also have our own education and work experience to draw on. Just watching others is an effective way to learn too. Since a baby lacks experience and education, she learns a lot through observation and hands-on training.

A human child is born to investigate, master, and eventually change her world. For a child to be able to investigate and later master her world, the world that is presented must be one which functions according to principles that would pertain whether the child was around or not.

For new employees to learn their job, the workplace has to exist and function according to is own internal logic. Few people start a new job with no skills at all, but not even the most qualified new employees would try to toss all established procedures overboard at their first day on the job.

If an infant is forced to operate in a workplace where all established procedures have been thrown overboard for no other reason than a baby has been born, the little one will react with anxiety and confusion.

Your baby will follow your lead and learn from you whether you like it or not. If, however, you follow the baby's lead, the baby will very quickly protest – just as you or I would do if the boss handed us the keys to his office and told us to run the company five minutes after we were hired.

Show the baby your world as a loving teacher would! And don't fall into the trap of thinking there isn't much worth showing. Even if you think your existence is a bit on the sorry side, it's still a slice of reality. Your reality, the activities *that are necessary for you* are synonymous with the flock's struggle for survival as far as the baby is concerned. That's the venue where the baby participates socially. That's the venue where the baby develops her ability to investigate, master and eventually change the world into which she has been born.

A three to four-month-old baby is an extroverted, curious and lovable person. (We still assume the baby is a girl.) She has two passions: how the world functions and her own endlessly fascinating abilities.

Her body is round, solid and stable. It is a tool to play with, and an asset to enjoy, even if at this age she's not sure where her body begins and ends – or even that it's really hers. It doesn't matter. She can rock, wriggle and bend, and she can raise her body off the ground if someone holds her hands. And she can turn over. If she really tries, she can flip from her back to her stomach. And to flip from stomach to back is done in a flash. (So be careful about leaving her anywhere near the edge of anything!)

Your baby has gained three kilos since birth, maybe more. Her eyes have taken on their true colour. And for little bald people with chaffed scalps better times are coming, but they haven't arrived quite yet.

Conversations are no longer mute. On the contrary, your baby can make a number of vowel sounds most eloquently. As a parent, you will be treated to flights of oratorical genius emanating from the depths of the crib in the early morning, all those odes to pure joy... Perhaps, once upon a time, all humans began their day with a song to express their happiness over just being alive.

Survival anxiety is a thing of the past. Little people this age can wait for their grub. While they wait, they can play with their fingers, these curious UFOs that float across their field of vision and sometimes land in their mouth.

Three and four-month-old babies are strong and patient, alert and on occasion bored to death. Once the world is more or less familiar, not being able to make it work for you is a heavy burden to bear. A third kind of cry, in addition to cries of hunger and cries of over-tiredness, (cries of pain are not included) may be added to the list: cries of boredom.

Amusing activities and various kinds of entertainment are of course effective antidotes to boredom. For little people this age, this often means THINGS. Soon your baby will be fascinated by the strangest odds and ends. This materialistic obsession hasn't reached its peak yet, but it soon will. The tendencies, however, are crystal clear: things, things, things.

Things to look at and things to try and grab. Things to try and knock over and things to follow with your eyes. Things to study carefully and things to grin at. Things to laugh out loud at and things to talk to. Things to listen to and things to suck on. Things to bite with toothless gums and things to recognize. Things to sing for and things to get tired of. Things to discover again and again and again, and things to say hello to. The lamp in the kitchen for example. A baby this age can find a lot to say to such an entity.

As soon as the baby can grip and hold, she should always have something in her hands.

The evening fuss – if it was ever an issue – has gone for good. (At least we hope so. If it hasn't, see "If something goes wrong: the newborn refuses to sleep".) The evenings are shortened and waking periods during the day are extended.

However, the need for sleep remains more or less constant. A baby of three to four months logs the same number of sleeping hours as a two-month-old – between fifteen and sixteen hours a day. This means the total time spent awake comes to between eight and nine hours.

And during these hours, you will be treated to smiles as beautiful as sunlight spreading over a field of flowers. No heart, however frozen, can help but melt.

INNOVATIONS IN THE ROUTINES: SOLID FOOD

Mashed fruits and vegetables can be placed on the menu after three months to supplement breastmilk or formula.

Such supplements should be served with the mid-morning or afternoon meal. The puréed food should be offered first, followed by the milk. I usually started my babies off on banana, a reliably tempting fruit.

Mash the banana on a clean plate with a clean fork until you have a purée that's almost runny. With the baby on your lap, the purée on the table and something to wipe with in your hand, you are set to go. The small spoon should be half full with the food gathered on the tip. Put half the spoon in the baby's mouth and scrape off the purée against the tooth ridge on the upper gum. Banana will run down one or both corners of the baby's mouth, and your little lady (or lord) will look very surprised.

Gather up the run off with the spoon and offer it again. Eyes wide with astonishment, your baby is asking herself if all this is actually possible. Try to look encouraging and confident and don't betray even a shred of doubt in your facial expression or your tone of voice. Your baby is not going to be of much help to you I'm afraid. She is not going to tell you how delicious bananas are and that she wants them served every day at two in the afternoon. If you simply continue feeding her with a confident, steady hand, you will convey to her that bananas are one of life's great pleasures and they have been eaten by all and sundry for as long as anyone can remember.

You may have to administer the same spoonful several times. It's nothing to worry about. It certainly doesn't mean that your baby doesn't like bananas. Your baby has a lot of innovations to contend with: the spoon, the act of eating (as opposed to sucking), the different consistency, the intermittent way the food is served, the absence of the breast or the bottle. Her mind is probably a bit of a blank, since she's so busy trying to learn.

You can continue giving your baby banana for two or three days at the same time during the same meal. The next sample can be apple purée or tomato purée, both sure winners. Blueberry purées are also popular with babies. You should bear in mind that blueberry purées are good for loose bowels and thus can cause constipation in babies whose digestive systems are functioning normally. (Prune purée has the opposite effect. It will loosen that which was tight!) Carrot purée is often not very well received, whereas cauliflower and corn purées usually hit the spot.

It's probably a good idea to start with sure winners. At the beginning, pretty well everything will go down because everything is new. After a few weeks, however, preferences will develop. All fruit purées are usually popular. Pears and peaches top the list. Babies raised on breastmilk are used to sweet things.

Store-bought purées don't need to be heated as long as the jar hasn't been opened. The first round can be served from a plate or right out of the jar. During the first few days one to four half teaspoons will be enough. Soon the baby will get a taste for the novelty and will scoff down half a jar. You should draw the line at half a jar, however, or there will be no room for breastmilk.

Store-bought baby food should be tossed out after four days, five at most, even if you've only used one teaspoonful. As soon as the jar is opened, it has to be kept in the fridge with the lid on. When you take it out the next day, whether you have to heat it or not will depend on the consistency. Fruit purées stay loose and the entire contents of the jar can be served cold. Vegetable purées harden in the fridge, so you'll have to heat them until they are pleasantly soft. Put the appropriate amount on a plate and place the plate over a saucepan of boiling water until the consistency feels right. Test the temperature with the knuckle on your index finger. Make sure the food isn't too hot! (To be on the safe side, don't microwave baby food for the first year.)

I've had nothing but good experiences with baby food in a jar apart from the price (although some people claim it's tasteless and too sweet). If you want to make your own purées, it's just a question of doing the necessary cooking, peeling, blending etc. Just be selective in your choice of raw materials and pay careful attention to hygiene. There are specialized cookbooks on this subject.

Food for infants should not be salted for the first year. *Sugar should be banned for the first two years* for the sake of the baby's teeth if nothing else.

Be careful with red beets and remember they will turn the baby's stools blood red. Personally, I steered clear of strawberries, red beets, eggs in any form, celery, spinach, mangel-silverbeet (mangold) and chocolate (cacao) during the first year. I also avoided regular milk for the first six months.

A three to four-month-old does not need to drink anything other than breastmilk or formula, as long as the temperature doesn't soar. Then boiled water that's been cooled may be in order. The risk of hyperthermia and dehydration is always present with an infant. Infants and heat are a very bad combination, so be very attentive on hot days. Give your baby water and *always* keep her in the shade.

During feeding, it's not necessary to wait for your baby to swallow one spoonful before you give her the next. Feedings should not take forever. It doesn't take long for babies to learn to swallow. Letting the baby suck the food from the tip of a spoon that's held to the baby's lips is a time-consuming and unnecessary detour, so introduce her to the correct way of eating from day one. She can handle it!

Don't be afraid to take the lead, and cultivate the art of looking as though you know exactly what you are doing. This is what your baby expects.

If in spite of your best efforts, every ounce of food you put into the baby's mouth simply runs out again, try to get her to swallow at least *one* spoonful and then quit. Tomorrow is another day!

Don't jump to the conclusion that the baby doesn't like or can't tolerate the food. It's the process of eating that's the stumbling block. Imagine how you would feel if, after a lifetime on a liquid diet, you were suddenly presented with a hamburger, something you didn't even know existed. *The taste* would be of secondary importance, but the mechanics of actually eating it might be problematic.

When you have finished serving the purée, go directly to the breast or bottle, all the while maintaining an attitude that all is well with the world.

Vary the menu. You should have six or seven flavours of purée in your arsenal. Vary the temperature of the food too. Don't restrict the baby to lukewarm food. Let her get a taste for a little more extreme in both directions. Do, however, decide on one particular meal (or two) when you are going to supplement the baby's diet and stick to it.

SLEEPING THROUGH THE NIGHT

Babies need help to sleep through the night – that's to say a twelve-hour stretch – fairly often. Decide on a cut-off point.

Four months is a good time for two reasons. First, a healthy four-month-old of normal weight is perfectly capable of getting through the night without food. Second, if you are giving your baby gruel or the thicker formula (see "A day with Sophie" below), the contents are filling and night-sleep inspiring.

If you are breastfeeding, you might want to consider giving your baby breastmilk during the day, and gruel or porridge as a good-night snack before the last breastmilk night cap.

The prerequisite for your baby sleeping through the night is a surfeit of food, as well as a sufficient number of hours of waking time packed with activities, joy and fresh air. So once you have decided on a particular night, make sure these conditions are fulfilled to the max during the day.

You will also have to adjust the schedule you have been following. Food and waking time in the evening disappear, so this shortfall has to be compensated for during the day.

The total number of sleep hours will remain unchanged (between fifteen and sixteen hours per day). If twelve of them will be accounted for by night sleep, that leaves only three or four hours of sleep that the baby has to log during the day. A long midday sleep, a shorter sleep period in the morning, and an even shorter time out in the afternoon should do it.

Let's assume your schedule has looked like this: 5.00, 9.00, 1.00, 5.00, 9.00. In the morning, your baby has certainly been falling back to sleep. Between the second and third meal, it's been party time. After the third meal comes the midday sleep, and finally the fourth and fifth meals have merged with a short twenty-minute time out spliced in as needed. The baby has also had a bath, interacted with everybody and participated socially in all the activities of the household. This is a fairly standard pattern.

Over time, the midday sleep is often moved up a little however, and the third meal maybe starts at 2.00 instead. The last meal of the evening is often over and done with by 9.00, rather than just beginning. The two last meals have a tendency to merge into one towards the end of the third month.

At any rate, it's now time to take the bull by the horns and put together a new schedule around four meals (plus a bedtime snack; see below). You'll need a pencil and paper for this! Provisional times might look something like this: 5.00, 9.00, 2.00, 6.00 – with a solid midday sleep spliced in between 12.00 and 2.00. 6.00, 10.00, 2.00, 6.00 are also good candidates.

If you think that a somewhat longer pause during the day is preferable to an evening full of socializing, you don't have to insist on a twelve-hour sleep at night but can choose the following times: 6.00, 10.00, 3.00 and 7.00. The midday sleep can be three hours long – between 12.00 and 3.00 preferably – and the evening meal can last until 8.00 or 9.00. A schedule for little people should always take your own schedule and other household activities into account – the day-to-day business of the flock in other words.

The point is that little angels this age – four-month-olds are definitely creatures of habit – will dutifully accept any schedule as long as it is consistent – *very* consistent. There's actually nothing to stop you from scheduling the night sleep between midnight and noon if that's what everyone fancies!

For now, let's go with 5.00, 9.00, 1.00 and 5.00. Let's say you have decided that the last meal should end at 6.00 and that a twelve-hour night sleep is your goal. That means the day will start at 6.00 am rather than 5.00 am from now on.

Our first adjustment then is: 6.00, 9.00, 1.00, 5.00. Work out the total number of sleep hours. There will be twelve during the night and two during the midday sleep; that makes fourteen hours. How long should the morning and afternoon naps be then? There's not much to play with as you can see. If your baby is used to sleeping properly in the morning after the early meal, there won't be much left over for the afternoon nap. You might decide to ditch the afternoon nap altogether and simply splice in an optional five-minute time out, given the long night sleep that will follow.

Our next adjustment is: 6.00, 9.00, 1.00, and 4.00. These times might look a little strange, but the last meal is going to *start* at 4.00 and won't finish before 6.00.

Once you've decided on meal times and nap times, you're ready for D-day!

D-day will start at 5.00 am as usual. Keep your eye on the time so that the morning nap doesn't drag on too long. This is one day when you are going to have to ensure that the party never stops. Your baby's waking hours should be packed with social participation, fun and laughter.

Naturally, your baby should eat like there's no tomorrow and at least one expedition out in the fresh air should be on the agenda. Prolong the late morning meal and the afternoon meal as per your schedule (by which I mean the number of waking hours; the time spent eating two to four rounds of food should not be taking more than one hour these days), and make sure the midday sleep ends at the appointed time.

As you know, little people this age can be woken up with absolutely no ill effects (especially if it's timed to coincide with the baby's natural sleep rhythm i.e. after a sleep lasting *five minutes, twenty minutes, forty five minutes, one and a half hours, two hours* or *three hours*).

It's during the final meal in the afternoon/early evening that the big push comes. Stuff your baby with food, and give her all the entertainment and social stimulation in all its various forms that you can. She should be laughing all the way to her date with the Sandman. Spare no effort. Remember that a little baby who has snoozed most of the day and who still has room in her tummy for more food will never sleep for twelve hours – any more than you would.

After her bath but before bed, give her a last little nightcap. Make sure she is stuffed to the gills, but don't let her fall asleep at your breast or with the bottle in her mouth. She has to be conscious when she is put down for the night. Awake and happy!

Put her down on her stomach in the carriage – preferable with a little good-night jingle. Place the carriage somewhere dark, quiet and cool. (Don't forget to activate the breathing alarm.) Open a window. Fresh air brings a good sleep.

When you tuck her in, there is no room for even a hint of equivocation. You have decided that this is when the night begins and you have also decided when it will end. Don't budge on the times. If you have decided that the day should not begin until 6.00 am, stick to your guns and don't pick her up her before then.

Just as with a one-month-old who was being trained to sleep through the night-feeding, you can now expect your baby to take one, two, or at the most three nights to adapt to the new routine.

Do what you did then. See "Sleep" in Part two of *For the Love of Children*, where you will find effective techniques for rocking described in detail.

If and when your baby wakes up and it's any other time but 6.00 am, get up and rock the carriage. Don't speak to her or touch her. Do nothing to reveal your presence. Pull and push the carriage back and forth, extending your arm fully, and give the carriage a fairly strong jerk each time.

Your baby will lift her head in an effort to see what's going on, but since there's nothing to see or hear, she will soon lay her head back down. Angry, anxious and generally astonished, your baby is asking, "Aren't you going to give me something to eat?" And you answer, not with words but with your confident attitude and energetic rocking, "No, the kitchen's closed. It's time to sleep now." *Nights are for sleeping* is the message.

Your baby will eventually go back to sleep. Stop rocking *before* she drops off. Otherwise, you run the risk of getting stuck in a rut. You don't want to teach her that she has to be rocked in order to sleep well or she will wake up as soon as the carriage stops moving. For this reason, rocking shouldn't be too pleasant an experience, but an unambiguous message about the rules in force.

The first night you will probably have to get up and rock her three or four times. It's important that you rock her *immediately* – and that you stop as soon as she is calm and quiet but before she falls asleep. Rock a little more gently towards the end, finish by shaking the handle of the carriage a few times, and leave.

If for any reason, your baby does see you, you can use words to back up the message you have sent through your actions. "It's night and time to sleep. Good-night, good-night." Or whatever good-night jingle you have decided upon. Say it loud and rhythmically *four times over* while leaving the carriage.

Never apologize for anything you do. Your voice should be friendly but firm. This is not a debating society you're running. What you say goes. Don't let a hesitant demeanour undermine your actions.

At 6.00 the next morning – if that was what you decided – the ordeal is finally over, but, be warned, things can get intense towards morning. You can allow yourself a margin of half an hour, if things get *too* hard to bear, especially if your baby is used to getting food at 5.00 (as in our example).

Still, you should pick her up when she is calm or even still sleeping, *not* after she starts to cry. If she is crying, she should be calmed in the carriage with rocking or a jingle, or both.

The second night and on, you should keep strictly to the timetable. The margin of error is down to fifteen minutes, no more.

The second night you will have to rock the carriage once, twice or at the most, three times (provided that before the "cure", your baby was accommodated to at least eight-hour-long nights of unbroken sleep).

The third night you shouldn't need to be up more than once if at all. And peace descends.

Again, all you have to do – apart from ensuring the baby's well-being according to the instructions given above – is:
• Rock with sufficiently drawn-out movements, a firm grip and a steady rhythm, and stop *before* the baby falls back to sleep, so she does the job her-

self. Make the rocking sessions ever shorter. Always *leave* between rounds.

• Adopt an attitude that brooks no argument and radiates confidence. Set your baby free from any worries. Spare her your over-concentration.

• Don't discontinue this "cure" until the habit has begun to take root, which takes three nights. If you quit on the first or second night, it will take not three, but seven nights the next time you try, since you will have given your baby contradictory messages.

If you harbor any doubts about your ability and determination and you take these doubts with you to the baby carriage, you will fail. It might be better under those circumstances if you recognized your own limitations and asked a more resolute person to see this three-night-cure through for you. Keep in mind that this is not about your comfort and convenience. This is about making sure your baby gets a solid, restful, continuous, energy-giving night's sleep. It's the *baby* that needs to sleep after such a disorienting and lightning fast developmental spurt.

If you have trouble developing an effective rocking technique, you can of course go for buffing instead from the very start. (See "Sleep" in Part two of *For the Love of Children*.)

What should you do if there's a relapse?

Once your baby starts sleeping peacefully through the night, she will continue to do so. *If you or those in your surroundings don't question the baby's unbroken night sleep, the baby certainly won't.*

There will of course be the odd blip on the radar screen. "Once is a coincidence, twice is a habit, three times is a lifestyle" should be your motto.

A little baby who normally sleeps through the night but who out of the blue wakes up crying wildly of course needs attention and comfort. Babies can dream, and sometimes their dreams are less than pleasant. And if you think the origins of the problem may lie elsewhere, it should be investigated. But don't make more of the problem than is necessary.

The idea is *not* to upset your upset baby even more.

So, *don't pick her up,* but rather calm her where she is, in her bed. If you pick her up, she may think that obviously, the day has begun – or she may get the idea that just as obviously, it has become dangerous to lie in bed, since you appear to be saving her from it.

It's easy to inculcate habits in three to four-month-olds, but it's just as easy to break them.

If it happens a second time, try to resist the temptation to rush into the baby's room. Content yourself with standing outside the door while chanting your clear and convincing goodnight jingle out loud times four.

If you have to physically remind the little one that the twelve-hour night sleep is not negotiable, you will have to resort to rocking the baby in the carriage again. If you have put her down to sleep in her crib or cradle, quickly transfer her to the carriage, move the carriage to a dark and quiet spot where you have room to manoeuvre and start rocking.

Stop when it feels far too early to quit, shake the handle a few rapid times, and leave.

As you go, serve an affirming good-night jingle times four. End of discussion!

SOLITARY PLAY IN THE MORNINGS

The baby herself will take the initiative in this area, so say a prayer to whatever god new parents worship and be appropriately grateful!

Three and four-month-olds have reached the stage where they can enjoy their own company, and they seem to get an extra kick out of it in the mornings. Once your baby has had her hunger satisfied and her diaper changed, and she has been treated to a healthy dose of affectionate attention, all she needs is a little daylight to enjoy lying in her bed or cradle and checking out her universe. She has her arms and legs to play with, and all manner of curiosities to contemplate. This will keep her amused for quite a while, and she will sing into the bargain!

An infant doesn't need entertaining at six in the morning. There is no reason for you, loving mother or father that you are, to shift into entertainment mode. That may be fun for a while, but it will become less so as time goes by. Trust me, in six months to a year, you will be willing to sell one of your internal organs for an extra half hour in bed or a chance to eat breakfast and read the paper in peace.

Introducing solitary play as part of the morning routine is a walk in the park at this stage because the baby has already decided that that is what she wants. There is not a shred of doubt in my mind that you will come to realize that not looking this particular gift horse in the mouth was one of the smartest things you ever did! Anyone with kids would agree with me.

First, some background.

I was young and very tired in the mornings after the birth of my first child. At three months, she was only too happy to be put back to bed in spite of the fact that she wasn't tired. She would while away her time babbling to herself and fencing with her arms and legs. This was a situation I gratefully accepted. If she was this content with her own company, why should I haul myself out of bed at six in the morning to attend a party that I wasn't invited to?

I supplied her with what I hoped were inspiring things to look at and left her to her own devices. When she got tired, she just fell back to sleep.

Soon a habit developed, one that I wasn't about to break.

Time passed, and she learned to grasp things and sit up. Her toys became more and more advanced. The day came when she was playing by herself for two hours, a little nap included sometimes.

I spied on her through the keyhole, absolutely fascinated. She was in fact working. Methodically, she would try to place one block on another, a puzzle piece in the right spot, a ring over a stick. Periodically, she would produce sound on a mouth organ. Sometimes she would just sit for a while, deep in thought, before tackling a new problem.

When one of her endeavours failed, no one comforted her. No one helped her. I wondered how she would react. No one praised her when she succeeded either. I wondered if that would cause her to lose her enthusiasm for problem solving.

In fact, she handled her successes just as independently as she handled her failures. Disappointment would occasionally cause her to lose her temper, throw aside the recalcitrant toy or object, and stare off into space – but then she would try again.

Her successes inspired her to look for new challenges, higher mountains to climb.

There was only one situation that caused her to look helplessly at the door or cry for me. She would sometimes drop all her toys on the floor and then realize that she couldn't reach them and that she no longer had anything to work with. Then I would go in and retrieve her tools.

Her tenacity and her constant attempts at innovative problem solving impressed me, as did her constructive, carefully thought-out solutions.

A certain rhythm was also discernible. After intense effort that resulted in success, she would take some time off and amuse herself with something that didn't require much effort. She might blow a few notes on her mouth organ or poke at one of the slats of her crib with her toes. If her efforts had resulted in failure, however, she couldn't relax but had to try again.

Her behavior taught me that human beings have trouble accepting that something is impossible, and when they eventually have to bow to the inevitable, they do so only grudgingly.

I used to listen to Billie Holiday back then:

> *"The difficult I'll do right now*
> *The impossible*
> *Will take a little while…"*

From this a system of sorts evolved. All my children have "learnt" to play by themselves. These play sessions have also been the only times during the day that they have had access to toys.

While I would never draw any universally applicable conclusions from any of this, it is a fact that all my kids developed excellent powers of concentration. They take failure philosophically – and then they get back in the game and try again without any prodding from me or anyone else. They don't seem to need kudos from their surroundings to bolster their self-esteem, even though, obviously, they appreciate being appreciated.

I think that these solitary morning hours devoted to concentrated, uninterrupted work paved the way for their self-reliance, and their attitude towards work and life in general – a job well done is its own reward and obstacles are there to be overcome.

Of course, I have to confess I was grateful for these morning hours because they meant that I could wake up at my own pace… a not insignificant blessing!

Over the years, many parents have asked me how you get children to occupy themselves in the mornings. The best way, as usual, is to hitch a ride on the child's own initiative, and three to four months is the ideal time to establish a habit that will redound greatly to the benefit of all parties involved. But if you have accustomed your child to being entertained from the second she opens her eyes, and you are tearing your hair out because the kid is now two and in the habit of attempting to demolish the house on those morning-after-the-night before Saturdays, it's not too late for a regime change. (See "Problems? Keeping busy" in Part five of *For the Love of Children*.)

The primary directive for a three to four-month-old, creature of habit that she is, is regularity. One day should be like any other.

From time to time, you can break with tradition of course. A vacation, for example, can turn everything on its head, as can unexpected events that require a flexible response. Such exceptions will do no damage provided that there is, generally speaking, a routine to disrupt, a basic framework.

Young children who live in a predictable environment with fixed routines adapt far more easily to the unexpected than kids who are confronted with the "new" every day of their lives. Thus, once you have decided that solitary play is to be a regular part of the morning routine, be as good as your word. Don't deviate. Your baby will soon get used to it, and it's a habit that will be as much a boon in the future as it is now.

As your baby grows, you can extend this morning play session. By the age of one, it can be as long as two hours (nap included sometimes). The prerequisite is that you continually challenge your child with interesting, demanding toys and that you keep the toys organized.

But back to three and four-month-olds:

1. Feed your baby as soon as she wakes up. Change her and burp her thoroughly.

2. Put her down on her back in the crib, cradle or carriage.

3. Take stock of the temperature in the room, the baby's clothing, and the lighting. Is everything as it should be?

4. Place something overhead that's interesting to look at and grab for. There are any number of interesting mobiles on the market, but if you prefer putting something together yourself, so much the better. A cord or a piece of string, securely attached to each side of the crib can be hung with strings of beads, rattles, brightly coloured stuffed animals or various innocuous but interesting kitchen utensils. You can use clothespins to attach soft, light objects that won't hurt the baby if they fall down. The only caveat is that you must pay attention to the height and position of the bar, cord or whatever it is you are hanging these objects on. It should be placed over the baby's face/upper body so that she doesn't have to sink her chin into her chest or stretch her neck back and up, and she must be able to reach the objects but not the bar or cord itself. At least one, preferably more, of the objects should make a sound when the baby swats it/them.

5. On each side of the crib, on a level with the baby's head, you can place

eye-catching book covers, dolls (not so heavy that they will hurt the baby if they fall over) with clearly discernible eyes.

6. If it's winter and still dark, make sure the room is lit in such a way that all the objects are clearly visible, but no light shines directly in the baby's face.

7. Music is always appreciated. But remember that if you leave the radio on, the baby will be distracted by human voices. Instrumental music or silence is best.

8. Finally, put something in the baby's hands. It should be something she can really grip. Dumbbell-shaped rattles are ideal.

9. Check everything carefully before you leave. Everything the baby can reach will eventually end up in her mouth. Everything soluble will eventually be dissolved by the baby's saliva. Book covers must therefore be very firmly attached. Postcards, pictures and posters that she was content to simply admire a month or two ago are now history. She will chew on them the minute she gets hold of them. If, for example, you have been decorating the crib or cradle with self-adhesive pictures, your baby will now claw at them methodically, pieces will stick to her hand, and she will immediately put the pieces in her mouth. While such a diet is not poisonous, it is certainly not recommended since choking poses a very real threat. (It pays to check your baby's mouth. You can find all sorts of interesting things stuck to a four-month-old's upper gums, and once she starts to crawl the assortment will become even more diverse.) Bear in mind that anything that can wrap it-self around the baby's throat is exceptionally dangerous. Check and double check to make sure that nothing can come loose that isn't supposed to come loose. Get into the habit of thinking ahead. What would happen *if*...?

10. Leave the baby to her own delightful company after a kiss and an encouraging smile. Take your leave properly. Don't sneak out of the room. Say, "Bye for now. See you soon!" and make sure she gets your waving-goodbye message.

If you're not using a crib but a cradle or carriage, you'll have to use your imagination. The half-raised hood of a baby carriage can be used as a surface to attach things to. If your baby is in a cradle, the surrounding furniture or walls will have to do. Beds are moveable. During solitary play, you can refurnish!

It's practical (and fun!) to position the bed so that you can see your little researcher without being seen yourself.

The things you give your baby to attempt to reach and study should be redisplayed every morning – but *only then*. She should not have access to them around the clock. Nor should they be taken out during those times she is on her blanket on the floor during the day. They are reserved for solitary play and when that's over, they should be put away.

You won't have to vary the repertoire for many weeks to come, provided all these fascinating objects are linked in the baby's mind to solitary play-time.

At the beginning, solitary play should not be a drawn-out affair: fifteen minutes, half an hour, forty five minutes under exceptional circumstances.

At that point one of two things will happen. In the first scenario, the baby will make sounds indicating frustration born of fatigue. She will want to sleep, but since she usually sleeps on her stomach, you will have to go in and turn her over. In the second, silence will descend, which means she has simply flaked out on her back after a hard morning's work. All you have to do is remove the solitary play objects and put a blanket over her.

General frustration that isn't rooted in fatigue is not something that should be remedied too swiftly – if at all. The baby may very well take care of the problem – whatever it might be – herself. When all is said and done, the underlying principle of solitary play is self-reliance, so you have to be prepared to rely on your baby's ability!

Solitary play should be gradually extended, but a two-hour session is not on the cards until the baby's second year. You should aim for not more than half an hour for some months to come. An incurably happy little lass or lad can play alone for significantly longer than that, but you shouldn't tempt fate.

Solitary play should end when the baby is still content (which affirms for the baby that everything is as it should be) *not when she becomes frustrated* (which sends the message that something is wrong and that she has to be "rescued").

The important thing for the baby at this stage is not how long solitary play is, but that this blissful little interlude, which is hers and hers alone, is a regular morning fixture.

SOCIAL PARTICIPATION SYSTEMATIZED

To the casual observer, a three to four-month-old's social participation would appear to be passive. In fact, the baby is processing information at break-neck speed.

Let's return to our Bedouin camp. On your arrival, you would know nothing of the language, customs, or day-to-day life in the camp, but you would be able to grasp that these were the people among whom you would have to live for the foreseeable future.

Your social participation might *seem* passive, but in reality all your senses would be working overtime. You would be trying to process everything at once: the unfamiliar language, the incomprehensible customs, the techniques of food preparation, the uses of the various tools, the care of the animals, the daily ceremonies, all the sights, sounds, dangers and pleasures... Your efforts would be more or less invisible, but that wouldn't make them any less real – or any less exhausting.

You would of course receive a great deal of essential help from your positive contact man, who would be showing you the ropes, instructing, demonstrating, and generally making himself available. And he would do all this gladly out of devotion to you and out of understanding for your plight. You are completely clueless, but you are trying so hard to learn.

An infant is in exactly the same situation. Your baby is not a tourist, any more than you would be a tourist in the camp. She is here to stay, she needs to be initiated into the mysteries of life on earth, and there is one overriding imperative: the group's, the flock's, the camp's survival.

This initiation process is called *social participation*.

The prerequisite for social participation is that the adult world be accessible. The baby needs a social context, a community, in which a place will be prepared for her and where she will eventually be put to good use.

This community can consist of only one adult. Solitary or not, all the adult has to do is to engage in activities that are (or appear to be) *necessary for you*, activities that you would have engaged in whether the baby was around or not. The baby participates, seemingly passively, in these activities, but she is not the focal point. The activities themselves are.

Social participation occurs naturally, since the adults want their babies close by so that they can keep an eye on them while they work, do the dishes, make meals etc. Unfortunately, the natural element disappears at about the time that children start pushing for *active* social participation (when they start to grip and grasp, sit and crawl).

Because of the socio-political distortions and misconceptions that we discussed in Part two of *For the Love of Children*, the adults are manipulated into excluding the children from their reality and banishing them to a segregated children's world, where they make guest appearances when time permits.

Let's look at an example.

Little Lisa's mom has gotten the rather odd idea that love, real love, demands that she focus all her attention on Lisa all the time. She can only do the dishes when Lisa is asleep. If Lisa wakes up while her mother is working in her vegetable garden or doing household chores, she must immediately stop what she is doing and devote herself to her daughter. She goes down into Lisa's world instead of drawing Lisa up into her own.

Lisa's mother is taking her cue from one of the bad contact men in our Bedouin camp, the one who dropped everything he was doing when you, the stranger, arrived. He took you out into the desert, while the tent and the camp where you were actually supposed to live remained off limits.

Lisa is about as happy with her situation as you would be with yours.

Lisa knows what she has to learn. She has to learn about what's essential for the adults, the flock's struggle for survival. You, the stranger in the Bedouin camp, also know what you have to learn. You have to learn about desert life so that you are not completely helpless if the day ever comes when the Bedouin strike camp and you are left to fend for yourself.

Lisa's mother should not feel guilty about continuing to wash dishes, tend to her plants, weave carpets or whatever she happens to be doing. Quite the contrary. An activity that is necessary for her, for the flock's struggle for survival, is *the prerequisite for Lisa's socialization* and thus for her happiness.

Lisa's mother must of course meet all Lisa's needs – the Standard Model is a reliable guide – but when it comes to activities that are necessary for Lisa's mother, Lisa has to bite the bullet. A farmer has to milk his cows at a certain time. The whole farm can't stop just because a baby wakes up – even if she's unhappy. An infant learns from experience that some activities are essential for the flock's survival, and everything else has to take a backseat.

This is why the most common phrase to come out of a parent's mouth is "I don't have time." Although it is rooted in something wholesome and right, it could be reformulated so that it doesn't smack of rejection:

"What I am doing now is essential for all us. Come and work with me!"

To sum up:

• Ensure that you have an activity that is essential for you, preferably an activity where something is actually produced. If you don't have such an activity, find one!

• Pursue this activity with steadfast determination as though it was literally a matter of life and death. If you didn't study, paint walls, screw in light fixtures, lift weights or build card houses, civilization would end.

• Expand the Standard Model's program by adding *social participation*. It is just as essential a part of the program as diaper changes and feeding. It should be the last point during every meal.

• Work with your baby next to you. Place her so that she is at the same height as whatever it is you are working on. Don't place her at your feet.

• Concentrate on what you are doing. Don't look at your baby, apart from stealing the odd glance in her direction. Convey through your body language and attitude that you are well aware of your baby's presence and you're glad she's there but that this is work that's so essential, it would have to be done whether she was around or not. It's about staying alive! But look happy. It's great to be alive!

• Put something in your baby's hands, preferably an object that is connected to your work. By all means talk about what this object is used for, but concentrate on the task at hand and don't feel obliged to speak if you don't want to. The important thing is that the baby is getting a glimpse of something that is essential for you.

• Stop what you're doing when the baby gets tired, but try to be a little subtle. Don't suddenly transfer all your attention to her. She'll smell a rat. Put her down to sleep and return immediately to your work. You are conveying the idea that she is not the center of the universe and life goes on whether she's awake or not.

• If social participation is discontinued for reasons other than the baby being tired, clearly and enthusiastically indicate that work is done. "All done for the day. Let's eat!" (Or play, or go out, or whatever is next on the agenda.)

• Bear in mind that your baby's apparently passive social participation will become *active*. Be on the lookout for any indication that she is ready to make the transition. If your "work" is building a house of cards (nothing is impossible!) and your little one reaches for a card, finally manages to pick one up and of course immediately puts it in her mouth, gently take it from her and thank her profusely for her contribution to the project. Your attitude should be business like. You are not thanking her because you think she's nice or good, you are thanking her because she has made a contribution to your work i.e. the flock's survival, thereby making life that much easier for everyone. Your baby has in effect been put to work for the common good.

• Try to avoid disrupting your social/work schedule even if the baby is unhappy and seems to want you to. Try to find ways of bringing her "up" to your world rather than going "down" to hers. If you are doing the dishes for example, and your baby begins to fuss, let her come nearer, feel the water, immerse her whole arm if she wants, even suck on the dish brush (being excluded from social participation is worse than getting a little soap in your mouth!). If you are vacuuming and the baby becomes frightened and starts to protest, don't shut the vacuum off. Pick her up and carry on working. Let her touch the handle and show her how to vacuum. Concentrate on your work.

• Your attitude should convey the idea that work takes time, but it has to be done whatever happens. Draw her in, don't shut her out. Let your child be a part of what you do, passively first, actively later. You are planting a seed that will eventually sprout into a conviction so essential for human happiness: "I'm needed. *The others wouldn't manage quite as well without me.*"

A DAY WITH SOPHIE, FOUR MONTHS

Sophie has been cared for in accordance with the splendid advice offered on the pages of this book, so I am delighted to present a day in her young life as a demo model!

Sophie's mother has stopped breastfeeding, and her dad is looking after her. On this particular day, her dad has started her on "valling" – the thicker formula we have in Sweden. (For a recipe of homemade valling, go to the end of this chapter.) She has been sleeping through the night (eleven hours) for the last two weeks.

What follows is the schedule that her parents have drawn up with a fifteen-minute margin of error in both directions.

Meal one 6.00 a.m.
Food, change, more food, a cuddle, talk and laughter.
   Approximately 225 grams of formula.

A thorough burping.

Solitary play in the carriage.

Sophie's dad is using a chest of drawers and the outside of the hood to attach the braided cord that he has festooned with rattles, a cloth elephant with ears you can tie a knot with, an unused hair brush with plastic bristles and a hole in the handle, a post card with a monkey's picture on the front (prominent eyes!) that has had a hole punched through it, a shoe-lace threaded with wooden beads, a whisk with a metal handle, and a cluster of little bells bound together with thread. He's attached clothes pegs in strategic places so everything doesn't bunch in the middle. The lamp on the chest of drawers is lit and music is playing on the radio.

Sophie's solitary playtime lasts half an hour. She then gets a little weary and is turned on to her stomach. She is sometimes rocked briefly in the carriage. Her dad turns off the light, tucks her in and takes away the cord, but he leaves the radio on.

Waking time: 1 hour and 30 minutes. Sleep that follows: 1 hour and 30 minutes.

Meal two 9.00 a.m.

The whole nine yards according to the Standard Model

Food, change, food again, and socializing. Sometimes Sophie gets a little more food down after the socializing. Her dad usually tries to get her to eat a bit more after the socializing.

Approximately 225 grams at this meal too.

At 10.30 a ration of social participation. In addition to housework, Sophie's dad is involved in two projects that are necessary for him. He is taking a course in architectural technology, and he is building a cabinet with drawers. Right now, he is studying. Sophie is lying on her blanket beside him. He has sacrificed a book for her to manipulate, rip and suck on.

When she gets tired, he picks her up and puts her on the desk on her stomach, so that she gets a change of scenery but can still watch what he is doing. He devotes all his attention (or at least seems to) to his studies. He makes sure Sophie is comfortable, but he doesn't make her the center of attention. He is careful to always keep one hand on her back so that she doesn't fall.

By 11.10, Sophie is tired of it all. Her dad interrupts his studies to put her down to sleep in the carriage after putting a hat and a sweater on her. It's a little nippy out, so he covers her with a couple of warm blankets. Sophie sleeps on the balcony.

As he goes back to his books, Dad finds comfort in the fact that even if he hasn't learned much during the first part of his study session, his daughter certainly has.

Waking time: 2 hours and 30 minutes. Sleep that follows (midday sleep) 2 hours.

Meal three 1.15 p.m.
Half a jar of tomato purée (home made) today (and tomorrow), followed by formula.

A first round of 100 grams.

After a change and some attention to personal hygiene another 50 grams for a total of 150 grams. Unusually small portions, thinks Sophie's dad. Normally she gulps down 200 grams after the purée.

Now comes socialization. Sophie's dad has been cracking the books while she slept so he's in a good mood. That's how the day usually pans out, so the early afternoon meal has evolved into a session with lots of laughing and fooling around. Sophie loves it when her dad makes faces as long as they are punctuated with smiles. She is developing into a mischievous soul herself.

After a socializing session packed with fun and giggling, Sophie goes down to the floor on her blanket to be by herself for a while.

She has three spots around the house that are permanently "hers". One is her bed, where she sleeps at night. The second is the carriage, where she plays in the mornings. The third is her place on her blanket in the living room, where she lies on her stomach among objects that vary according to a three old, one new, six old, two new system devised by her dad. (An object becomes "new" once it's been out of circulation for a week or so.) Everything is placed around her. Some objects are within reach and some are beyond. Today, she has also been given a piece of crisp bread, which is lying close to her on the blanket.

Sophie's dad waves to his daughter, "Bye-bye Soph! I'll be back soon!" And he leaves. At regular intervals he checks on her without her noticing. He monitors what she's up to and makes sure everything is as it should be.

The room is quiet apart from Sophie's breathing and cooing. But she soon ends up on her back and starts to get cranky. She cries somewhat sulkily. Her dad goes in and turns her back onto her stomach, makes sure she is facing a different direction and tries to reengage her interest by re-arranging the objects.

When he leaves, he again says, "Bye-bye Soph! Back soon!"

He has decided that she is going to spend at least 20 minutes and at most 30 minutes thus occupied. During this time, he does his utmost to avoid disturbing her. Then he returns to her while she is still contented and happy.

The last program point for this meal is a walk outdoors at around 3.00. Sophie's dad usually carries her unless there's something he has to do that requires the use of his arms. If that's the case, Sophie, propped up by cushions, rides in the carriage until her back gets tired and she wants to sleep.

But as a rule, he carries her, so he can wander freely up and down the slopes surrounding the house. He shows her the trees, the leaves and the bushes. He stops beside everything, so Sophie can touch.

By four in the afternoon, Sophie is so satiated with new experiences that she drops off on her dad's shoulder. When they get home, Dad puts her down to sleep in the carriage. Since she is already dressed for the outdoors, she sleeps on the balcony again. If the weather is really vile, he undresses her and puts her to bed inside. Sometimes he has to rock her in the carriage if she wakes up while he's undressing her.

Waking time: 2 hours and 45 minutes. Sleep that follows: 45 minutes.

Meal four 5.00 p.m.

Food. The new, thicker formula is presented – and accepted with the enthusiasm of a true *gourmand*.

The first round consists of 175 grams.

Burp.

But no change or refill. Sophie is going to have a bath. She'll get a refill last thing before bed, so she's ready for a good night's sleep.

Then comes some socializing. Sophie's mother comes home. The reunion is intense. Little Sophie lies on top of her mom who has gotten down on the floor, and the idyll is complete.

The clock strikes six. Social participation follows.

Now Sophie's dad gets busy with his carpentry. Sophie is on her blanket beside him. He passes "safe" tools to her. She looks at them and babbles. He answers her prattling by telling her what he is doing, but he rarely looks at her. While all this is going on, Sophie's mother is making dinner.

Today Sophie is not in top form. Her dad's plan is to make social participation last half an hour, but Sophie doesn't cooperate. He lets her whine and protest. Work comes before everything is the message he wants to get across to her. Only when she starts to get really upset does he change her position and bring her closer to the work at hand. He tries to capture her interest by showing her a large piece of white sandpaper that feels so rough to the touch. When things reach crisis point, he bribes her with a piece of crisp bread, but he refuses to leave his work before half an hour has elapsed.

Then he draws a bath with his little girl on his arm, undresses her and bathes her. The operation is carried out with the little plastic tub perched on the kitchen counter, so Dad doesn't have to bend too much. The bath takes a good twenty minutes, and both Dad and kitchen floor get a good drenching. Sophie looks happy. She's having the time of her life!

On the change table, she is thoroughly rubbed and patted dry with the towel, a process that Sophie thinks is just heavenly. Newly bathed and dry, dressed for the night and wrapped in a warm blanket, Sophie gets her last round of food warmed in a bottle under the tap.

Once she's eating properly, Dad interrupts her feeding to pop a spoon with vitamin A drops into her mouth, and then immediately gives her the bottle again. Sophie is then burped, gets a warm kiss, has a last little giggle before bed and is put down to sleep.

During this last little feeding session, she ate another 75 grams of food for a total consumption of 250 grams.

Waking time: 2 hours. Sleep that follows: 11 hours.

During this 24-hour period, young Miss Sophie was awake for a little more than 8.5 hours and slept for a little less than 15.5 hours.

Sophie weighs 6.460 grams.

Sophie's day is a simple illustration of infant care the way it should be – simple, peaceful and joyful.

Let's take a closer look at how Sophie's dad solved the "problem" of social participation!

Many parents, especially fathers, reason like Sophie's dad. "When I am home on parental leave, I'll have time for all kinds of things…" However, they make the mistake of thinking that important or desirable activities have to be scheduled for those periods when their baby is sleeping. As soon as the baby wakes up they think – like Lisa's mother, who stopped her weaving – that they have to focus all their attention on the child, who usually ends up glued to Dad's arm.

As we have seen, the amount of time the baby spends sleeping during the day becomes less and less. Sophie takes a nap in the morning that lasts for one and a half hours. That's a reasonable length of time, but hardly more than is needed to do the essential housework. The next nap is at midday, and it lasts for two hours. This is not an eternity either especially if you use the time to go shopping with the baby asleep in the carriage. Finally, the afternoon nap only lasts for forty five minutes, and when the baby wakes up, it's usually time to make dinner. When evening comes, you hopefully have an opportunity to socialize with your better half if you have one, or at least to feel that you're alive. If even that requires too much energy, sinking into a quasi-vegetative state in front of television can be therapeutic too. Nothing has come of all those grandiose plans.

Sophie's dad, like many a father before him, had decided he was going to build a cabinet and take a course. The problem was that all these good intentions to study and build were not really regarded as necessary (for the struggle to survive), but were relegated to the status of hobbies and recreation.

A farmer, however, who has seven cows that must be milked, can't keep them waiting until their udders burst just because a baby is crying, nor can he reschedule the milking for a time that suits the baby on that particular day and then change the time again the next. The cows have to be milked, and the baby has to adapt to the reality she has been born into. The farmer of course does his best to make sure that the baby is content while he goes about his work, but he can't devote himself exclusively to the child. He has to milk his cows and the baby has to understand that. He sees to it that his child is well taken care of and is properly supervised, but life goes on. If he did not tend to the running of his farm, his own existence would be in jeopardy and, by extension, so would the child's.

This is the basic attitude that Sophie's father is trying to cultivate as he pursues his goals, however "unnecessary" they might seem.

Within the framework of this basic attitude, Sophie's father can permit himself a number of improvisations. For example, he doesn't have to study in the morning and build his cabinet in the evening. He can very easily reverse the order. He can also devote the evening ration of social participation to food preparation, something that is necessary for the adults' (the flock's) survival. This doesn't revolve around Sophie, but is an activity that would have gone on with or without her, so making dinner is a perfectly legitimate context within which to offer social participation. All Sophie's parents have to do is include her. Dad doesn't hesitate to put Sophie on the table while he and his wife are eating. This also counts as social participation because Sophie's parents are doing something that is necessary *for them*.

In fact, virtually all household activities can be regarded as necessary, since they would have to be done whether the child was around or not.

Homemakers of both sexes are good at offering social participation – at least homemakers who regard housework as beneficial and necessary rather than as a burden they have to bear as punishment because their wives/husbands don't do their share or because children have come into the world. The fact is that if we are doing something we know is essential, we have a tendency to like or to at least learn to like it, as an act of mental self-defence if nothing else. It feels so much more natural and is practically speaking so much simpler to gradually put a child to work alongside you if you're involved in something essential than if you don't really believe in what you are doing.

In the latter case, there tends to be a latent discontent that causes you to reject involvement from the outside, even your child's. I'm arguing that if parents deny a child access to their reality, their everyday life, they are making a mistake that their child will suffer for.

Sophie's dad would study a lot more effectively if he were alone without Sophie on his desk. The half hour he studies with her is perhaps utterly fruitless for him, but it isn't for her. She is getting a glimpse into *his* reality. That is *social participation*. And that is just as important as food, sleep and love.

Of course, offering a three or four-month-old baby social participation is not all champagne and roses. Even if we are only talking about relatively short periods – Sophie's dad devotes two half-hour periods a day to that end – it requires no small amount of mental endurance from the baby. Her powers of concentration are not always up to scratch. You too would have a tough time keeping your enthusiasm at fever pitch in the Bedouin camp. Learning is exhausting, especially things that you find fascinating but don't really understand.

Some people claim that three to four months is too early to expose a baby to a reality that doesn't constantly revolve around her and that the baby plays second fiddle to. However, the baby's behavior contradicts this assertion. If the instinct to participate socially was not as inexorably powerful as it is – I think it's comparable to the instinct to survive – infants who were constantly the center of attention and the objects of assiduous emotional attention every minute of their waking lives would sleep superbly at night and exhibit every sign of serene contentment during the day.

But they don't.

In reality, it is precisely those parents who give and do "everything" for their babies that complain (quite correctly) about how difficult and exhausting parenting is. They can't sleep at night, and their days are pretty lousy too. They treat their kids like Barbie and Ken dolls, which children will not accept. The parents put their own lives on hold and devote themselves exclusively to their children and never do anything that is necessary for the *parents* as long as their children are awake (and they're awake pretty well all the time). It is precisely these parents who bear witness to the "hell" they have to live in. (See "The best laid plans…" in Part two of *For the Love of Children*.)

A young child (or an older one for that matter) who is never offered the chance to participate socially is often unhappy. A child who is allowed to participate socially seldom is.

During these short periods that you set aside for social participation, you should try to behave like our farmer. The cows have to be milked even if the baby is ticked off about something. Soothe the baby as best you can, but the farm is your livelihood and business is business.

Sophie's day, as described above with all its various program points, meets all Sophie's needs.

Thus far, the only person she needs is her dad. Thus far, the social contact her dad offers is enough. Thus far, she still needs a limited world, which must be allowed to be little before it becomes big.

An adult, one person, by offering access to his environment and his activities, is perfectly capable of providing a child with all the social participation she needs. From the time a child first begins to explore the world up to the two-year mark, isolation in a single flock is absolutely no problem for the child – although it is sometimes a problem for the adult(s).

Valling
1 portion (one bottle)

1 dl (deciliter) water
2 dl milk (3% fat)
1 tablespoon flour (wheat)
1 teaspoon sugar
½ teaspoon butter

In a small saucepan mix water, milk, flour and sugar together and bring to the boil.
   Add the butter, bring back to the boil then simmer mixture slowly for about 5 minutes.
   To cool, place saucepan in the sink or a large bowl filled with cold water.
   Serve warm.

The mixture can be stored in the refrigerator for 24 hours so for convenience you may wish to multiply the quantities of the ingredients and make 2 or 3 portions at one time.

HAS DAILY LIFE GONE OFF THE RAILS?
If everything that can go wrong has gone wrong, and if you – against your will (as if you would go through all this voluntarily!) – have become one of those parents who bear witness to "hell", what should you do?

Let's take a look at the adults: two people who love each other dearly

253

and want nothing else but what's best for each other – yet their relationship is collapsing around their ears. Why is this happening? In all the confusion, one thing has gone missing: perspective.

Human beings have a tendency to shrink their world. If the world is too big they become confused, and if things progress far enough, they are overwhelmed by a feeling of paralysing helplessness. As long as the world can be surveyed, and as long as it's limited, it's controllable, but if our vision is distorted and we no longer see clearly, we lose perspective – and sometimes our sanity.

People who claim they have "hell" to contend with and who almost seem to enjoy lamenting the fact that they have been condemned to the inferno through no fault of their own are in fact ensuring that the flames that are consuming them will continue to burn. Legitimate suffering is one thing. The suffering involved in delivery is an example of legitimate suffering. Suffering has to be endured even though there is nothing wrong with the sufferer. It's also perfectly legitimate to complain. The victim of legitimate suffering bears no responsibility for his or her plight. "What happened happened. It wasn't my fault."

If certain kinds of suffering were not regarded as legitimate, the responsibility would be too heavy a burden to bear and freedom would be too demanding.

But the idea that young children, who never asked to be a burden or a bother to anyone, should be labelled as a source of legitimate suffering is a bitter pill to swallow.

It is difficult, if not impossible, to encourage or inspire people to change if deep down they don't want to. Change and fear often go together. Parents can talk for hours about what hell they have to go through. They haven't had a decent night's sleep for two years, they never get out of the house, the baby has turned their whole existence upside down, and divorce is imminent. There is no end to all this misery in sight, and everything is impossible.

If anyone makes a suggestion, "But if you did so and so... If you tried such and such," any and all advice is immediately discredited and the status quo confirmed.

"Oh, you don't know Leo!"

"Stephan would never go along with that!"

"That might work for other kids, but not Dorothy!"

"Oh no. Julie is way past that. Thank God we have an appointment with a child psychologist on Monday."

It's pointless to try and convince these parents, who cling so desperately to their status as victims of legitimate suffering, that little Leo doesn't *want* to wake up thirteen times per night, that Stephan doesn't *want* to cry for hours on end, that Dorothy doesn't *want* to be carried around all day long, and that Julie doesn't *want* her parents to have to live through hell.

The parents I am appealing to are those parents who are genuinely searching for solutions to a problem, who realize that they have lost their perspective, and who understand that they have lost their way somehow and want to get back on the right track.

If daily life has gone off the rails, the first thing you have to do is step back and look at the big picture. All your notions about how complicated everything is or will be should be consigned to the dustbin, and the void that has been left behind should be refilled with common sense.

There are millions, billions of children. Two or three children are born every second. Kids are as numerous as leaves in the forest. It's not like you're all alone. Your child is of course the most important thing in the world for *you*. That doesn't mean that your daughter or son isn't made of exactly the same stuff as every other child on the planet.

Put paid to the misconception that what works for other kids couldn't possibly work for yours because she/he is way too special, sensitive, idiosyncratic etc. We're all special, sensitive and idiosyncratic. That doesn't change the fact that we all have to sleep well at night and eat well during the day. This goes for professors and cleaners, vegetarians and cannibals. Your little girl or boy is a miracle – but human nonetheless.

You have to set up routines and show leadership. To a large extent, children manage their personal development very nicely on their own. In this area, you are not as important as you think you are. That may be poor consolation, but it's a true one.

There is no limit to how complicated you can make infant care. Whatever your situation, you have company.

For example, little Maurice's mother is trying to feed Maurice some purée. She is constantly bombarding the poor boy with questions. She may not express all these questions in words, but her attitude and actions step ably into the breach when words fail.

Does he like the purée? Is it too cold? Would he have preferred another flavor? Does he want to suck the purée off the spoon? Should she put the spoon into his mouth? Would he be afraid if she did that? Is it gross? Is he going to throw up? Does he want another spoon? Is the spoon too sharp? Too cold? Too big? Too small? Is he sitting comfortably? Does he want to sit somewhere else? Does he want to sit on Mom's lap? Does he want to face the other way? Does he want to sit in another chair? Is he full now? Does he want more? Has he swallowed everything? Is she giving him too much? Too little? Is she feeding him too fast? Too slowly?

Once the meal is finished, Maurice has eight open jars of purée in front of him, a plate of mashed banana and a plate of mashed potatoes; he also has four spoons, two of which are plastic, each a different color. There is a plastic cup with a spout on the table, plus a mug of boiled water to thin the purée with, since it might have been too thick and Maurice might have preferred a thinner variety in the cup with a spout. There are also three chairs, and Maurice has sat in all of them at some point during the meal. The stove is awash with pots and pans for warming food in.

You don't have to be Sigmund Freud to figure out that all these questions eventually drove Maurice right up the wall, and he started to squeal like a stuck pig. How is *he* supposed to know all this stuff?

Maurice's mother loves her son and wants the best for him. Thus, she is meticulous about trying to satisfy his every need. But she risks doing the polar opposite. There is a risk that Maurice will become rather nasty before she's done. He is defending himself against his mother's solicitude because he finds it utterly confusing, and it complicates his life immensely. His mother is met with screaming rejection and "ingratitude". Maurice can't stand the routines constantly being changed or challenged – if there ever was a routine in the first place.

What Maurice's mother has to do is stop asking questions. Just serve the purée. Period. End of sentence.

Just as she decided to give Maurice purée in the first place without in-dulging in an orgy of self-doubt – and the whole thing was her idea after all – she also has to carry through her decision without equivocating. She has to stop second-guessing herself and apologizing the whole time. She has to stop seeking Maurice's approval of a decision he was never involved in.

If she doesn't feel she can stand by her decision, she shouldn't give him purée in the first place. Maurice is not going to take responsibility for a de-cision his mother made or help her implement it. He will simply eat what is put in front of him in the belief that *she knows what she's doing*.

The more firmly his mother stands by her decision, the more she comes across as confident and experienced, the easier it will be for Maurice to eat his purée and feel good about it. Even as we speak, somewhere in the world, there are mothers who are serving their kids puréed grubs without giving it a thought if that's any comfort to you!

An infant who has gone off the rails – or never gotten onto them in the first place – cries because so many questions are going unanswered. Babies don't cry because they think their surroundings – or their parents – are somehow inadequate. Kids this age have nothing to compare them with. They could live in an igloo in Nunuvut just as happily as they could live in a tent in the Sahara.

But wherever babies live and to whomever they have been born, they, like all other human beings, need their questions answered. "How am I supposed to live? What do I have to do? How do I manage this particular task?" As children strive for social participation, emotional belonging and physical survival, they have their eyes fixed on one overriding, if distant, goal: to be able to survive and thrive by themselves outside the flock one day.

Thus, your task as an adult member of the flock is not simply to love and protect. Your task is also to lead. Your child knows this and expects it of you.

So: *Never expect leadership from an infant.* It takes many years – about twelve! – before children, by virtue of their common sense and experience, can accept anxiety, doubt or insecurity in their parents without fearing for their lives.

1. *Structure the day*
   In a quiet moment, take pencil and paper and write everything down.
   The day should have a scheduled beginning.
   The day should have a scheduled end.
   Mealtimes are fixed and your baby should sleep through the night.

2. *As soon as you are able to create a little order out of the chaos, decide on something that you want to do.*
   You don't live for your baby.
   Your baby does not live for you.
   It's about both of you having lives.
   What do you want to do? What is your deepest longing?
   You will find the time.
   You will find the strength.
   You just have to give yourself the possibility.

3. *Implement a three-day cure*
   • Serve food in the morning. Follow the Standard Model calmly and methodically, point by point, including social participation (but no solitary play for now).
   Let the "meal" last for two hours.
   Your baby is perhaps tired after a stressful night, and you are probably

anxious and tense yourself. In spite of all this, let the meal take its time, and comfort yourself with the knowledge that things are going to get better. Coax your baby to stay awake so that the program can be completed.

Finish the meal with more food, as much as the baby can get down, and then some.

Social participation towards the end of the program can be provided simply by having the baby in her chair on the kitchen counter while you do the dishes or by reading the newspaper with her beside you with something in her hands. What's important is that you do something that is (seemingly at least) necessary for you, and that you *devote yourself whole-heartedly to it.*

Put her down to sleep.

If she doesn't fall asleep right away, don't let it get to you. Leave the baby to her own devices. Don't spread anxiety. If you have followed the Standard Model, you have met all your baby's needs. You've done all you can. Leave the rest to her.

• Keep an eye on the clock and stick to your timetable. There may well be a lot of crying this day, but don't lose courage. The baby needs time to figure out what the rules of the game are. If you have not provided answers, leadership and instructions until now, you can't expect your baby to immediately understand that there has been a regime change. The process is going to take its three days.

Don't disturb the baby until the next meal. If she cries, see to it that there is sound: music, life, movement. But stay in the background. The world does not begin and end with you. You may find it helpful to watch the clock when the baby cries. What seems like an eternity is in fact only a couple of minutes.

Serve food at the appointed time. Stay calm, follow the program, and try to look happy and confident. The universe is unfolding as it should. At least it soon will be! This "meal" is going to last two hours as well. You might want to consider substituting a walk outdoors for social participation during this meal, weather permitting. The baby should sit propped up with cushions in the carriage so she can see properly – or you can simply carry her. The walk should focus on the world – houses, trees, cars – not on your relationship. This focus on the outer material world will help quiet the emotional turmoil that is tormenting you both.

Stick to the timetable. Put her down to sleep when the "meal" is finished, preferably out in the fresh air.

• Again, stick to the timetable. Serve purée at the third meal, followed by breast or bottle. Follow the Standard Model.

Social participation is next on the agenda. Perhaps you are making dinner now. Include the baby in the proceedings. Let her watch, but don't look at her so that she notices. Concentrate on your work. The impression you want to convey is that even if there were ten babies screaming their lungs out in your kitchen, you would not bat an eye. This is work that has to be done.

Steel yourself against any protests. Don't get uptight. Remember that ninety percent of the screaming is caused by confusion over the new regime you are instituting. The baby is no longer the center of attention. Babies are no different from adults in this regard. A man who suddenly discovers that his woman is in the process of building a life for herself that doesn't necessarily include him doesn't always nod with approval either. Put your baby to bed with an air of indefatigable calm. Keep an eye on the clock. Twenty minutes, or forty-five minutes (max). After the next meal, night falls.

• Put everything aside so you can focus on giving your baby all the love, tenderness, joy and support you can muster. Give her food, talk to her, cuddle with her and try to coax as many laughs and giggles as you can out of her. Make bath time a soft, languid, sensual delight. Food again. Hugs, conversation, and love. This is the Standard Model at its most beautiful. It's as though your baby had just come into the world. She's brand spanking new!

And use every ploy in the book, as well as a few that aren't, to make her laugh. Try to feel what's germinating: the hope and joy beyond the despair.

Put the baby down for the night in the carriage, again at the time that you have chosen. During the night, which will also end at a time you have scheduled, you can get up and rock the carriage if necessary, but keep the rocking rounds as short as possible (see "Sleep" in Part two of *For the Love of Children*).

• The next day – and night – will follow the same pattern. The first day may have been pure terror. You feel like a traitor. You are convinced that your baby hates you, and that you have inflicted psychological wounds that will scar her for life… Trust me, things are nowhere near that bad! On the morning of the second day, your baby will be her usual sunny self – or even sunnier! Do you really need any more convincing? The second day will go much better. Keep up the attitude. Stick to the routine you have set up as though it is simply a part of the natural order of things and thus eternal and immutable. Now is not the time for deviation. You introduce little variations and improvisations when the routine has solidified, not before.

Pull yourself up short if you feel tempted to slip back into old habits by expecting guidance from the baby instead of providing it yourself. That is filed under love, not routines. (See "ABCs for little people".) Take charge!

The night of day two is a carbon copy of the night of day one.

Once you are through the third day and night, daily life will be back on track for good.

It is often very difficult for you, as a parent, to get help and support from those around you if you aren't sure of yourself. People will be only too happy to undermine and criticize the care and upbringing you are giving your child if they catch the faintest whiff of self-doubt.

Nothing confirms people in their own superiority more than making someone else feel inadequate.

How different would life be if we got a pat on the head for what we do right as often as we get a kick in the butt for what we do wrong?

Unfortunately, praise is a commodity in very short supply. If you give your infant superb care, you'll most likely be told how "lucky" you are to have such a "good" baby... The idea that there might be a carefully thought out, ambitious plan behind this "good" baby never occurs to anyone. You are supposed to go down on your knees and thank God for your (undeserved!) good fortune.

A modicum of self-doubt is healthy. It keeps you sharp. But perhaps a better term for this kind of anxious doubt is *seeking*. A mental flexibility, a sensitivity, a desire to understand and empathize is essential for anyone who lives with children. Without this seeking, you never really see your children; you never reach them or understand them.

But this perfectly healthy reticence is what makes you an easy target for any number of crafty snipers: "Is this right?" – "Are you sure you know what you're doing?" – "This is none of my business, but I'd be careful if I were you."

Under such circumstances, you can always fall back on the classic ploy of agreeing with everyone, nodding sagely and saying, "You know, that's a good point. I'll think about that." Then do what you want. No one will notice. People don't criticize you because they expect it to have any effect. They do it because for some personal, irrelevant reason, they enjoy it.

So, a dash of self-doubt is necessary, productive and inevitable, but – and this is a big "but" – it is absolutely forbidden as far as the *routines* are concerned.

Some things are innate. We all know people who are handy around the house and can fix virtually anything, and others who have to call an electrician to change a light bulb. The ability to deal with small children is a gift too. Some people have it "innate", and some people don't.

What we can see in parents who have a way with kids is precisely this unsentimental attitude to routines. They don't think that love is being jeopardized every time they give unequivocal instructions in either word or deed – quite the opposite in fact. They don't live in constant fear of making mistakes, and they don't bow down in trembling obeisance before their children. They may be humbly curious and more than a little reticent when they approach their children as *people* – but they are not insecure about their guiding and protective role as parents. They don't confuse love with routines.

It is also very seldom that anyone tries to ride roughshod over such parents because they know what they're doing. Implicit in the whole concept of routines is the idea that it is better to be confidently wrong than hesitantly right. And doing something wrong is better than doing nothing at all!

A ROUTINE MEMO

• Your child is not interested in complicating your life. Quite the contrary, your child is a big fan of simplicity.

• Your child doesn't think you are inadequate. Your child is simply asking you questions – and the longer the reply is in coming, the more pressing the questions will become.

• Your child will not be damaged by having to follow certain routines any more than you will. Your personality does not suddenly become distorted just because you have to follow a daily schedule. If routines do anything, they free up energy.

• For both your child's sake and your own, you have to try and find an activity that is necessary and desirable *for you*, and which you can pursue with your child at your side.

• Implement every change with an air of *serene self-assurance*.

FIVE AND SIX MONTHS

I am regularly in touch with a girlfriend who recently had a baby. We call each other every week or so.

"How's it going?"

"Oh, OK, I guess. Except for the evenings... and breastfeeding... and he has a sore bottom... and a rash... and he's always got the hiccups ..."

One day, when the little boy was around five months old, the reports suddenly changed. She no longer talked about the humdrum routine of daily life. Now she would say, "So much is happening!"

Whereupon I would get a detailed description of what kind of a *person* her baby was. His personality had emerged into the light of day.

So what was happening? Well, how do you describe that transformation that takes place when a baby is no longer just a little baby but a *person*?

A five-month-old is not a baby that you have to care for to the best of your ability. He's a little buddy. (We are now going to assume that your baby is a little boy.) He's a friend, a fully-fledged personality with very clear characteristics and a soul that is reaching for the stars. It's a metamorphosis.

Five months, like two months, is a turning point. The child's personality blooms. My theory of the so-called repeated pregnancy draws a parallel between the transformation that takes place in a five-month-old and the first movements of the fetus, when the child suddenly becomes a reality for the mother-to-be. The anonymously growing stomach actually contains a human being that can be named. There is a person in there with a life of his or her own. The five-month-old acquires a life of his or her own too. In terms of personality, the baby "quickens".

Let's take a look at what has happened thus far!

After the shock of birth, there followed a traumatic transitional stage. The baby was physically out of the womb, but needed an environment that was just as protective.

You said through your actions, "I'm here. My arms are your womb, and my breasts are your survival."

After the real birth, the baby turned outwards to face the world and strove to participate socially. The baby struggled hard during the last part of the first month and all of the second month to come to terms with his bodily functions and to acquire an elementary familiarity with the world.

You said, "This is the world you will be living in, and I am here with you."

In the two months that followed, the baby became relatively accustomed to life on Planet Earth, and began to demand a place in the community into which he had been born and the right to participate passively in a pre-existing social order.

You said, "This is how you do it in this particular world, and you are with me."

Now, as the baby nears the half-year mark you say, "How do *you* do it in this particular world? And I am with you!"

When we discussed three to four-month-olds we drew a parallel that we shall now take a little further.

You or I, or a little five-month-old starts a new highly skilled job at an office. For the first little while, the new employee familiarizes himself with his new environment. After all, he doesn't know where in the building he'll be working, who his co-workers are, or what he is supposed to be doing. This initial orientation is stressful, and our new employee has to be very observant. In the end, however, he finds his desk, learns the drill, and pretty soon everything becomes routine. He discharges his duties faithfully and makes a name for himself as a model employee.

Automaticity has entered the picture, and this is where the five-month-old is.

But now things start to happen! Our new employee, who thinks he knows everything he needs to know, decides he wants to improve himself. He starts to learn more about the company. He begins to see things in a somewhat broader context. He takes a course. Then he takes another. And another. He wants to change, revitalize and improve. He begins to arouse enthusiasm in a few people, and he becomes bolder. "If we did so-and-so or such-and-such, the company would be so much more profitable!"

He becomes a wellspring of ideas. He starts to question all the old assumptions and has so many innovative ideas. He's on fire he's so passionate about his work. He is not afraid of change. On the contrary, he makes a point of thinking outside the box.

This is the mindset of a five to six-month-old (and he has kindred spirits in kids at the crawling stage and on).

So how do the others react?

Thus far, our new employee hasn't made too many waves. Outwardly, he just plods along and does his job. A lot of people don't even know his name. But then he suddenly emerges from anonymity as a man with a mission. He wants to get somewhere and make a name for himself. He has definite ideas about how things should be done, and he's not afraid to put his money where his mouth is. A fellow like this stands out. Our once quiet new employee has found his feet, and his days of being just another face in the crowd are gone.

A child of five to six months emerges from anonymity and takes his place in the world as his own person in precisely the same way.

But other people in the office are getting nervous. This new guy is rocking too many boats. The status quo is threatened.

"Someone should shut him up," some employees start muttering darkly to each other.

Our new employee wants to innovate, but innovation means change, and change threatens those who have long been lounging around in their comfortable little sinecures. Better one bird in the hand than two in the bush, such people reason.

On the other hand, most employees know that without new ideas, the company is probably going to go belly up anyway. The competition is stiff. So when our new employee holds meetings to discuss his various proposals, there are a lot of people who react very enthusiastically – but the enthusiasm doesn't always translate into action. Others who come to the meetings are non-committal. They adopt a wait-and-see attitude.

Does our new employee let that get him down? Absolutely not. He has too much energy for that. He doesn't need other people to pave the way for him. He has discovered too much all by himself for that. He doesn't announce to the world, "I have an idea," and then expect someone else to make the idea a reality. He is fully prepared to push the envelope as far as it will go.

All he really wants other people to do is *not to get in his way*.

Six-month-olds, babies who have started to crawl, and one-year-olds make the same modest request.

Does our new employee have a competent boss? We have to hope so.

An incompetent boss would react the way mediocrity always does when faced with innovation: "AND JUST WHO DO YOU THINK YOU ARE? KEEP YOUR MOUTH SHUT AND BE GRATEFUL YOU HAVE A JOB

BECAUSE YOU MAY NOT HAVE ONE FOR MUCH LONGER!"

A competent boss, however, would give the new employee his time and listen very carefully to his suggestions. A competent boss knows his own limitations and makes sure his company stays profitable. A competent boss knows that if he and anyone else on the company payroll are going to get anything out of their jobs – indeed if the company is going to survive at all – regular infusions of new blood are essential.

What follows is a little memo to *incompetent* bosses/parents of five to six-month-olds (and older). If you follow these rules to the letter, you can expect very bad times indeed:

- Believe you are indispensable to your child.
- Never leave your child in peace.
- Institute no routines, schedules or habits.
- Refrain from engaging in activities that could provide your child with a venue for socialization.
- Constantly admonish your child with such gems as "No!" "Don't touch!" "Bad!"

If you want a flourishing business/child, do the following:

- Regard yourself as a tool and a guide.
- Facilitate your child's work rather than hindering it.
- Institute routines, schedules and habits.
- Pursue your own essential activities to which your child is allowed to contribute.
- Never put obstacles in your child's way unless *mortal danger* threatens.

A STAR IS BORN

As carefree or as exciting as it is now, life will never be.
As glorious as it is now, the world will never be.
As luminous or sweet as it is now, love will never be.

A five to six month-old is fabulous company. Now is the time to parade all your long lost relatives before your baby and wait for his charming indications of affection. You can then exclaim, "Well, you were certainly a hit!" (This will provide emotional insulation against the inevitable day a few months hence when the mere sight of the same relative will elicit nothing but wails of revulsion – which will of course damage your poor relative for life.)

This is the time to enjoy interactive activities – and more than a little good-natured mischief!

A six-month-old is a combination of researcher, worker bee and flirt. Research requires peace and quiet, work requires social participation, and flirting requires – someone to flirt with! The last item on the list makes falling in love so easy!

A six-month-old's natural flirting partner is Mom or Dad, but it's perfectly possible that your baby finds his own reflection the one most unbearably charming.

Six-month-olds like flirting under the covers, kissing in door openings, and exchanging adoring looks with you wherever you happen to be. He can lark about with you endlessly, as people in love tend to do, and of course he is loveable, not least in his own eyes.

If you have followed the instructions in the book you are holding, your five to six-month-old is a little person who:
- Sleeps soundly and continuously through the night.
- Likes his own company.
- Knows you will always come back and so never cries when you go.
- Has stopped crying (a long time ago) because he knows that he will get food without crying and that he will be able to rest before he gets too tired.
- Has great trust in his surroundings because he knows *there is someone always looking out for his interests.*
- Is familiar with the life that you and the flock lead and participates socially in that life.
- Can predict his day and therefore feels secure.

If you have *not* followed the instructions and not one item in the list above can be applied to your baby, then there is a button marked *reboot.* You can in fact go back to the beginning and start again. (For one illustrative example, read "Marie and Samuel – an email correspondence" in Part five of *For the Love of Children.*)

You can count on it taking one week for every month of life to reprogram.

Five to six-month-olds can grip and hold on to things, and so should always have something in their hands.

When lying on his stomach, your baby can lift his head and ribcage high off the mattress, and on his back he can lift his head. He can roll from side to side, from back to stomach, as well as from stomach to back. He can also sit up if he has some support, and he can raise himself against your legs if you hold him by the hands.

Your baby has mastered both consonants and vowels and the saliva flows copiously. Teeth are on the way or have come, the first two probably in the front of the lower jaw. (Gnawing on crisp bread will alleviate the itching.)

Your baby is also capable of moving things from one hand to the other, of holding things in both hands at the same time and banging them together, and of pounding them on the table.

Soon the baby will be able to sit propped up on his own hands and will start to crawl or slither or wriggle his way forward (or backwards or sideways) along the floor.

Encourage his creeping by letting him enjoy the combination of bare feet, prone position, and floor entertainment!

Little humans' creeping and cross-wise crawling are vital prerequisites for proper neurological development.

At this point, he will have doubled his birth weight or more.

As has already been observed, his disposition is sunny, but that doesn't mean that five and six-month-olds, just like everyone else on the planet, don't have their bad days. The thing to remember about little people this age is that, more often than not, they solve their problems themselves.

Little Alfie, for example, is out of sorts and is whimpering. Nothing seems to please him. His mom tries to interest him in various things, but to no avail. Finally, his mom gives up and goes about her business.

Alfie continues his fussing for a while. Then, much to her surprise, Mom hears Alfie heave a deep sigh. Then he energetically tries to get a grip on an old lampshade that his mom has placed on the floor. At the same time, he spies the piece of crisp bread he so recently turned up his nose at. With an ecstatic "Giii", he grabs at it, and suddenly the sun is shining again.

If he were able to talk, he probably would have said, "I'm bored with being bored! I want to amuse myself!"

A six-month-old has a remarkable and constructive independent streak that should not be underestimated. Take my advice, don't glue yourself to your baby in the belief that he is completely helpless without you. Give the enthusiastic and determined independence that's making itself known the room it deserves!

You are no longer the demonstrator: "This is how you do it in this particular world."

Now you are above all an *observer*: "How do *you* do it in this particular world?"

Stick to the routines as resolutely as you always have but give your baby space to take any off-routine initiative. Encourage him and support him in his endeavours.

You must have seen what parents usually do when their kids take their first steps. They squat down, stretch out their arms and smile encouragingly. It would never occur to them to organize walking classes. "Today I am going to teach you to walk, son!"

Nor would anyone dream of hindering the child by saying, "Oh, sit down! It's too dangerous!"

Let a child's first steps symbolize the change that is taking place now.

Offer social participation. Watch for and encourage your child's every attempt to progress from *passive* participation to *active* participation.

Think of yourself as the fixed point in your child's universe, a base of operations to which he always returns. Be as passively observant as your child has been these last few months. Don't make demands – don't set up roadblocks.

This striking independence, this desire for autonomy is not just something to be respected. It is also something to be exploited.

This is the most appropriate time to move your baby out of your bedroom. You can also see the move as symbolic. It's less about you being free of the baby, and more about you letting him be free!

There are a lot of parents who complain bitterly over a little baby that requires all their time, day and night. These parents are zombies. They haven't had time to read the paper for an eternity, they barely have time to go to the toilet in peace, and as for taking a shower – what is a shower anyway? But oddly enough, when little babies born to such parents show tendencies to go their own way and manage very nicely thank you without the tender ministrations of Mom and Dad, it is precisely these parents who are the most reticent to relinquish the privilege of being indispensable.

It's a bit like a man complaining about how helpless his wife is without him. She can't even drive into town by herself, he moans. But when his wife takes it into her head to work full-time, take courses or go travelling by herself, he goes ballistic. Now she is not *allowed* to drive into town. He *forbids* it!

Your child is developing into a person who wants to push the boundaries back and explore the unknown. You are no longer indispensable. Accept it.

You are a human being, and your child will interact with you as a human being.

268

You have a friend, and friends aren't helpless.

My theory of repeated pregnancy comes into play again here. If I so choose (and of course I do!), I could draw another parallel with life in the womb.

A fetus is regarded as viable from the seventh month on, which means it could survive outside the mother's body. Until the seventh month, surface tension in the pulmonary alveoli makes it impossible for the baby to draw air into them, which is why very premature babies need a respirator. In the seventh month, however, certain cells are produced in pulmonary alveoli, which release a substance that lowers the surface pressure, and lung function is normal in the event of a premature birth. The baby can breathe under his own steam.

You could say that a six-month-old, figuratively speaking, starts to breathe by himself.

NOVELTIES IN THE ROUTINES: OUT OF THE BEDROOM

As I said, this is the ideal time to move the baby out of the bedroom. You shouldn't wait more than six months to regain your nocturnal privacy – and to give your baby his.

A six-month-old is stable and independent. An eight-month-old, however, suffers from an anxiety that can manifest itself at night, so it is a little cruel to wait until then to make the move. A one-year-old goes along with most things, but as a rule, a child of one is constantly longing for company and may interpret the move as rejection. This is not a problem at half a year. For the six-month-old, all news is good news!

Up to five months, however, I think your baby should sleep in your room during the night. We talked about this in connection with the newborn's survival anxiety, which has to be soothed immediately. After the baby is weaned off the night feeding(s), it's prudent to have him under supervision, in case of spit ups and the like. When he starts sleeping through the night at three or four months, it's still a good idea to be able to keep an eye on him. He can end up on his back and start to cry, lose his pacifier (if he has one), or get all tangled up in his nightshirt and/or bedclothes. So that the baby isn't disturbed by light (sound doesn't matter), putting up a screen or attaching a curtain from the ceiling is – was! – a good idea.

But now, when the baby's night sleep is rock solid, he's developing independence, and he is full of enthusiasm for everything new, is the perfect time to make the move.

The baby doesn't necessarily have to have his own room. A screened off nook will do. The point of the exercise is that the baby gets a quiet little spot where he can be left in peace that's not in the parents' bedroom.

It is of course practical if there is a door you can shut, but as long as the baby can't see what is going on in the rest of the house during the evening, night and early morning, that's sufficient.

If there are siblings in the family, move the newcomer's bed into their room and let him bunk with them! It's an investment for everyone.

It is now that a crib becomes essential if you haven't bought one already. The bottom should be at the lowest level. The pads shouldn't be needed anymore, but play that by ear.

You can include a little cushion in the bedding. Liven up the sleeping quarters with inspiring pictures, a music box perhaps, a new teddy bear, a quilt with bright patterns...

The transfer itself is simple. Prepare the new sleeping quarters during the day. Go about the task with an air of affectionate expectation, baby there to share.

In the evening, place the baby in his new bed and give him the grand tour of his new home with joyful enthusiasm. Act as though you were presenting the eighth wonder of the world – whether the baby exhibits any scepticism or not.

When you actually put the baby down to sleep, do as you always do. All is right with the world. Your demeanour should not betray even a shred of doubt.

Indulge in a little mischievous play – try to get a laugh out of the wee lad so he will go off to dreamland with a smile on his face. Then put out the light, say a friendly but firm goodnight and leave. The door should be left ajar. Go about your business as usual so that the baby knows the house is chugging along as per normal.

If, against all expectations, problems arise, just repeat the procedure. It should take less than a minute. Go in to the baby's room, but don't turn on the lights; put him in go-to-sleep position – arms up, legs straightened out down and head turned away from you – and mark the message with a two-hand final little pressure over the package. Leave the room while saying your goodnight jingle calmly and convincingly, times four.

Don't linger at the door. Leave the door ajar, and let the household go about its evening business with all the usual light and sound.

If the baby has only recently begun to sleep through the night, he may wake up and cry, in which case you simply repeat the procedure described above without delay. After the first night, try to stick to the reminder good-night jingle times four from outside the door. Without disturbing the baby, you can then check on him and even lift him right if need be, when he has been sleeping for ten minutes (not twenty).

Bear in mind that you are in the process of introducing new, reliable routines that will give your baby a sense of security. To inspire a feeling of security in others, you have to be secure yourself. If you send contradictory signals, you will soon have an unhappy, confused child on your hands.

You've decided to move. Stand by your decision and make life easy for him!

AWAY WITH THE PACIFIER

This is also a good time to say goodbye to the pacifier if you haven't already done so.

The need to suck is mild now, since the baby is living on more than just breastmilk. Little people this age are often not that interested in breastfeeding either. They need the nourishment from either the breast or the bottle, but sucking is no longer a joy in itself. They've moved on to bigger and better things you might say.

If your baby's sucking urge is still so strong that it needs an outlet over and above breastfeeding, bear in mind that five and six-month-olds, quite in keeping with the independence so characteristic of this age, can find creative solutions themselves.

No child more than four months old needs a pacifier.

Certain children just stop using a pacifier of their own volition. They simply lose interest in it. More often than not, this happens at four months, when the sucking urge decreases significantly.

There are of course also children who never get interested in pacifiers in the first place.

If it's time to lose the pacifier, the procedure is simple: just take it away. The baby will probably protest. If his cries go unheeded, a six-month-old, constructive little fellow that he is, will take a leaf out of Nike's book and "just do it". Thumbs, fingers, sheet and cushion corners are all acceptable substitutes as far as he's concerned.

Thumbs and fingers are preferable, since they are used for so many other things; they can't sit in his mouth all day long. A pacifier can, however, and this impedes tasting the rest of the world as well as the beginnings of talking about it.

A baby of half a year is nothing if not innovative, and he expects the rest of the world to be as well. So if your baby decides to object, let him! He'll have forgotten all about it by the next morning.

If you find that the thought of taking away the pacifier makes you uncomfortable, step back and examine your own motives. Is your baby using the pacifier to satisfy his need to suck, or are you sticking the pacifier in his mouth to keep him quiet?

"It's time to sleep. Here's the pacifier."

"I don't know what to do with you. Here's the pacifier."

"Did you hurt yourself? Here's the pacifier."

"Are you scared? Here's the pacifier."

"Please sweetheart, Mommy's tired. Here's the pacifier. I can't cope right now."

The greatest resistance to tossing the pacifier overboard often comes from the parents, not the baby.

Obviously, a six-month-old who has had a pacifier in his mouth more or less round the clock all his very short life will miss it once it's gone. There will be objections and confusion, rending of hair and gnashing of teeth – half a day. Or half a night. At the most.

But think about it. If you were the one who introduced a bad habit, it's only fair that you assume the task of breaking it. If you were the one who decided to use the pacifier in all manner of situations as a kind of cork, you made your baby into a little "pacifier junkie". If you dance, eventually you have to pay the piper. You can't offer people cigarettes and encourage them to smoke, and then take the moral high ground when they refuse to quit.

So just take the pacifier away and don't make life more complicated than it already is. For a five to six-month-old, nothing is complicated anyway!

BATHING IN THE BATHTUB

Baths in plastic kiddie tubs usually get so wild at this age that most parents realize they might just as well bathe themselves. Since they get soaked to the skin anyway, why not kill two birds with one stone?

And taking a bath with a six-month-old is an experience. There is nothing more relaxing, fun, tender and surprising on God's green earth. All you have to do is set aside time, run the bath and place yourself in the tub at your baby's disposal.

The consequences of bathing your baby in a real tub without getting in yourself are twofold:

1. You will get a sore back.

2. Your baby may slip under the water.

If you take a bath with your baby, both these problems are solved, but bathing with your kids is not always feasible. To spare my back, I delayed bathing my kids in the tub until they could sit up by themselves, and as a simple safety precaution, I placed a little towel under their bottom.

We have already discussed the risk of drowning (see "The first bath" in Part two of *For the Love of Children*). However stably your baby can sit, however certain you are of his ability to reflexively close all his air passages, you must not leave your baby unattended in the tub for a second!

So make sure you have everything you need within reach before you start. You will of course need a dry towel. Six-month-olds like playing with things in the bathtub, so he will cast himself over the soap. Soap is hardly healthy, but it's not particularly dangerous either, and since you shouldn't hinder your baby unless mortal danger threatens, don't make an exception for soap. However, you can through your facial expressions indicate to the baby that soap is not exactly a dish lauded by gourmets the world over. Some little people just aren't satisfied until they've taken a bite out of a bar of soap. Needless to say, their gastronomic delight is short-lived. You will have to dip a corner of the towel in the water, and thoroughly clean out the little mouth. All very tragic, but since a lesson hard learned is a lesson well learned, soap will be off the menu for good.

Children who sit or are held half reclining keep their ears above water. Don't neglect this detail.

"Wash your ears!" was once upon a time a parental command as ubiquitous as "Don't forget to brush your teeth!" is today. And with good reason.

To make sure your baby's ears are properly immersed, you can avail yourself of a tried and true technique. Hold your baby under the armpits and back with one hand and under his bottom with the other, and introduce a new game by "swooshing" the baby back and forth, immersing his ears as you go. It will be much appreciated! The ears should then be cleaned with soap.

This technique works equally well for hair washing (if there's anything to wash!). Shampoo and then rinse by tipping the baby backwards.

A little baby who has been bathed every day from the age of one month won't be afraid of water. If you have also gotten him used to having his face washed with a wash cloth or handfuls of water, he won't be leery of getting water in his face or eyes.

The bath should be ended while your baby is still enjoying himself, *not* when he starts to fret.

While we are on this subject, let's look ahead.

Somewhat older children refuse to allow themselves to be "swooshed" when they are being rinsed off or shampooed, and you might not be strong enough anyway. Once this day arrives, you will have to put one hand under the baby's neck and gently lean him backwards. If that doesn't work – and it usually doesn't until the child is old enough (around three) to grasp intellectually that the purpose of leaning backwards during a hair rinse is to make sure no soap gets in the eyes – you'll just have to take the bull by the horns by pouring water over his face and being quick off the mark with a towel. Press the towel gently into the baby's eyes, all the while, cooing encouragingly "There we go! All done!".

Baths and hair washing are part of the routines and cannot be questioned. I would never recommend skipping hair washing, much less baths.

But very few young children like having their hair rinsed after a shampoo. It's hard for them to shut their eyes tight, since with eyes shut tight they know even less about what is going on around them.

They also have trouble grasping that they would avoid all this unpleasantness simply by leaning backwards. Just the position can cause panic. Some things *are* unpleasant, and that can't be helped. Getting shots at the doctor's is no fun either, but there is no way around it.

It's your job as a parent to keep your cool and make sure that:
• Anything unpleasant is announced immediately before it happens.
• It's over and done with as quickly as possible.
• The child is comforted as soon as the deed is done.
• It's not dwelt upon. Over and out!

Some young children are afraid of water, or the bathtub, or both. This fear, whatever its origins, has to be overcome by any and all means at your disposal.

Kids are water animals because water is a human being's primordial element. I happen to think that children should not be allowed to forget this. Bathing is more than pleasant. It's essential. Since we all emerge from water when we are born and we largely consist of water, water is where we find peace and equilibrium.

The best way to help young children overcome their fear of water is to bathe with them. You can, as usual, embark upon a little three-day "cure" if you so wish.

Undress the baby and yourself, talk about this and that, look happy and expectant, and then get into the tub with your baby in your arms. Wash and rinse yourself, and conduct yourself as though your bath, rather than the child's, was the main event. Then climb out of the tub, still with an attitude that everything is as it should be.

If your baby starts to tremble, it is very important that you don't comfort him and thereby send a message that something terrible has happened. Your demeanour is one of happy-happy, joy-joy.

Repeat the procedure each evening. Bath time is gradually extended. Remember to end the bath *before* your baby starts to cry, or you will find yourself back at square one.

The best antidote to fear is laughter. If you have to contend with a baby who is frightened of water, spare no effort to make him crack a smile. Make faces, pretend to eat the soap and look grossed out, anything to get a laugh!

On the fourth day, fill the tub as usual, drop some toys into the water, undress the baby and put him in the tub. Look as though you are going to join him. Putter around in the bathroom. Look for something in the bathroom cabinet, hang up towels, and generally look busy without really doing anything... You are not undressed yourself, and you are not going to join him. Watch him out of the corner of your eye, but be discreet. He mustn't know he is being observed. The fact that you are busying yourself with various things and perhaps talking to yourself as though nothing is amiss will take the edge off any remaining fear.

Follow-up is as simple as it is necessary. Give your baby a bath every evening, no exceptions, for many weeks to come. So as not to tempt fate, remember to end the bath while he is still enjoying himself.

Be careful of hot bath fixtures! Run the cold water first and last.

MORE FOOD – AND HOW

At five months there are usually some dietary changes, and since five-month-olds are keen on novelties, these changes will be received with enthusiasm.

Otherwise, one might expect some protests. After all, the breastmilk that has sustained them all their lives, may be out of the picture for good only to be replaced by rather dull, grey stuff called porridge… Purées, which were soft and brightly colored are now bumped in favor of grey, rather heavy stuff that has an entirely different taste. The world as been turned upside down!

But since five and six-month-olds are constantly searching for new experiences, they will take menu changes in their stride.

A five to six-month-old's stomach is designed to digest all kinds of food. On the other hand, he can't chew. His food must therefore be mashed or whipped in a blender, or possible to loosen up with saliva (crisp bread for example). The problem is not in the stomach, but one floor up, so to speak.

It is now that two breastmilk free meals consisting of other foods are introduced. The mid-morning meal and the afternoon meal are good candidates. The day's menu might look something like this:

6.00 a.m.   Formula/breast.
9.00 a.m.   Porridge with milk and/or fruit juice.
1.00 p.m.   Puréed meat, fish, potatoes, and/or other vegetables. Water.
5.00 p.m.   Dinner. Puréed food as above plus dessert.
6.00 or the likes Night cap (formula/breast).

Interesting leftovers from family dinners can be chopped fine and mixed with mashed potatoes and served the next day (if the baby doesn't eat dinner with the rest of the family). Watch the salt though. An infant's diet should not include any salt.

There are some great books on the preparation of food for infants on the market for those who don't want to buy mass-produced baby food.

Different kinds of porridge in powder form are available. All you have to do is mix them with water. I think we go overboard with pre-prepared infant food. There is nothing easier than whipping up some oatmeal porridge (well, mashing a banana is). The big problem with pre-prepared baby porridge today is that it contains large quantities of sugar. This causes infants to retain their taste for sweet stuff (breastmilk is sweet). Such products sell well. If things get to the point where your baby refuses to eat anything that isn't sweet, you have a serious problem on your hands.

The overwhelming majority of babies like (real) oatmeal porridge if they are exposed to it from the start. They retain their taste for it year after year right up into adulthood. It's nutritious food and a good habit.

Mix half a cup of rolled oats and one cup of water, and bring to a boil. Let it simmer for three minutes and stir. Then pour it into a bowl, add a bit of butter (the real stuff) and mix it with 3% milk. Stir until all the lumps are gone. Then let it cool until it's the right temperature for the baby. No sugar of course.

It's rather unappetizing to look at, but you'll be surprised how well it goes down. The first time you serve it though, the baby will leave half or even more. Just behave as you did when you introduced your three-month-old to purées (see "Solid food"). The first few times you serve oatmeal, you can tempt the baby's taste buds by offering a little bribe in the form of fruit purée at the very tip of the spoon.

And how are you supposed to feed your baby?

Think twice before you have him on your lap. In another two or three months, he will be eating meals with the family. If you've gotten him used to sitting on your knee, you will have trouble getting at your own food. Babies that age also have the charming habit of stealing food off other people's plates.

Since five and six-month-olds are so focused on independence, this is a good time to introduce the high chair. You can prop the baby up with a pillow or two as soon as he can sit upright.

The baby will love feeding himself – an art that must be mastered sooner or later anyway. It's a pleasure too. Some babies sink both fingers and hands into the porridge to check its consistency. Others attack it with a spoon as though their lives depended on it, and sometimes succeed in splattering porridge on the ceiling before they're through. Burying one's face in the porridge is also a popular pastime. You might want to take the precaution of holding the bowl.

Cleaning up the mess afterwards leaves a lot to be desired, but it's for a good cause. A baby who starts learning to feed himself at this stage (while you are feeding him as well) will be able to eat soup at ten months without spilling a drop.

So that the orgies don't get too wild, you can also have the baby half reclining in a rocker while feeding him. This won't stop him from digging his hands down into his food or using his spoon as a slingshot, but it will make the graver transgressions a little more difficult. His clothes will need washing frequently and bibs aren't adequate protection. You'll need towels!

Lunch and dinner should be served with the baby in his high chair. Give your baby a spoon and take one yourself. There will be a lot of exploratory digging and a lot of debris to clear up after these meals too, but the food is at least a little more solid.

If you don't like food fights, give your baby a piece of crisp bread, or anything else interesting, edible and sugar-free, to hold while you feed him. If he puts it in his mouth, just remove it with one hand while you pop

277

in the spoon with the other. The crisp bread will go right back in again. Peace will reign and no plates will fly.

There is a great deal of paranoia about infants not being able to tolerate certain things.

Negative expectations are as self-fulfilling as positive ones. If you get worried because your baby might be allergic to certain foods or doesn't like something, refuses to take the bottle, protests against sleeping in another room, is frightened of changes overall or whatever it is, you can be certain that problems will arise. Babies are just as suggestible as adults.

If, for example, you are constantly told that the job you've just gotten is way too difficult for you, you are not going to approach your duties with much enthusiasm or self-confidence. You might even refuse to go to work at all.

If everyone around you is terrified you might become ill because your work environment is so dangerous, it won't be long before you break out in a rash or develop flu symptoms.

You will do yourself and your baby a big favor if you put paid to all your fears about what the baby can and can not tolerate.

When caring for infants or children in general, your default attitude is: *everything is fine and it's going to stay that way.* This is your golden rule, your point of departure.

If you look for trouble, you will find it.

If you honestly believe there is a problem, rely on your own instincts and look for proof.

Suffocation through choking while eating is a much greater risk than not being able to tolerate certain foods.

Choking is an ever-present danger for little people who can't chew. Very small objects can lodge in the windpipe and since food is not the only thing that goes into a baby's mouth, you've got to be constantly on the look out for anything small enough to be dangerous. Inspect your baby's bed, the floor, the toys, everything!

If your baby does get something caught in his throat, turn him upside down and thump him firmly on the back just below the shoulder blades.

Before we leave the subject of food and worry, let me issue two caveats: first, egg yolks really can cause problems, so no eggs before your baby passes the one-year mark. Second, your baby should not know what sugar is until he is two at the earliest. Candy, cookies, cake, sodas and the like should be avoided like the plague.

Six-month-olds have very healthy appetites (if they sleep well at night, that is), and are enthusiastic about pretty well everything. You need have no reservations. Just shovel in the food.

If it's too much for his little mouth, the worst that will happen is that the baby will spit it out. Little people this age will, however, become irritated if you feed them too slowly or if meals take too long, or, naturally, if the portions are too cheap. Healthy appetites claim their due!

As always, give your baby as much food as he can take on board. An infant will treble his weight in one year. You can imagine how much food is required for such an accomplishment!

A six-month-old should be packing on the pounds. His appetite must be satisfied. Anything else is indefensible.

He should also have crisp bread, apple segments and bananas to chew on between meals.

It is only during this period and again during the teen years that snacking does not spoil appetites for meals. Snacks and meals are enjoyed with the same lip-smacking appreciation. You should do nothing to short-circuit this. Just enjoy it for all its worth. It's a time that won't come back for another thirteen, fourteen years, a time of boundless, life affirming, lusty appetite!

No foundation for obesity will be laid during the first year. During the second year, however, your child's appetite will decrease significantly, since his growth rate will taper off. If it didn't, your child would weigh 108 kilos by the time he was three if he weighed 12 kilos by the time he turned one.

When your child's appetite takes a nose dive during the second year, there is a risk that you will worry and start stuffing him with ice cream cones and cake because you reason that the poor kid has to eat *something*. And that's when the foundation for obesity in later life is laid.

Finally, a few words on weaning.

The instructions on weaning are just as voluminous as those on continuing to breastfeed forever. My advice is simple. Rather than drawing up elaborate timetables, just quit cold turkey and only nurse when you feel your breasts are about to explode. This will usually happen in the mornings, which is convenient, and in the evenings when a little breastmilk and the warm intimacy that goes with it marks a sweet end to the day.

Milk production will decline in tandem with the decreased demand and finally, after four to eight weeks (it varies from individual to individual and also depends on how long your baby has been breastfeeding and how much milk he has been consuming) the weaning process will be complete, no muss, no fuss. You have just been serving breastmilk as a side dish.

Perhaps it should be mentioned that you shouldn't use your breasts as pacifiers. Only nurse when your breasts are so full it's uncomfortable – never breastfeed to comfort your baby. There are not a few two-year-olds who suck at their mothers' breasts at night. If you put yourself and your baby into such a situation, you may find yourself resenting your child and that of course is grossly unfair.

THE SIX-MONTH-OLD RESEARCHER, WORKER AND FLIRT

THE RESEARCHER

This is the age of exploration and inquiry. People and animals, things and places, food and lodgings, as well as his own ability – all these things are potential targets for a scientific Researcher.

A fixation on inanimate objects is another hallmark of the six-month-old. Many a Researcher this age would be only too willing to swap a loving mother or father for a drawer full of cutlery.

Researchers should never be hindered. They should not be steered in any particular direction either, for that would entail transforming genuine research into an empty exercise with a predetermined outcome.

A Researcher who knows where he is going before he starts his journey has sold a piece of his soul.

The true Researcher never lets himself be steered. He walks his own road. He is a trailblazer. He investigates and surveys virgin territory. His research consumes him. He is driven by relentless determination to discover, to understand and to illuminate the unknown.

If you were a housewife in the traditional mould and your husband was a Researcher, you would be bringing him his meals on trays, shielding him from visitors and telemarketers or anything else that might distract him, and of course paying the bills so that he wouldn't have to concern himself with such sordid, earthly matters. After six months or a year, he would stagger out of his study or laboratory and yell, "Eureka!"

Luckily, six-month-olds have other interests besides research, but while they are engaged in it, they should not be disturbed. All interventions should be very carefully considered. The rule is: *Never hinder a child under the age of one unless mortal danger threatens!*

If you are really adroit, you can delay interfering until your child is eighteen months (this age being a foretaste of the "terrible twos") and, after that, right up until the terrible twos begin in earnest.

Let's look at some concrete examples.

Your Researcher has made his way into the kitchen and become interested in what's in your dog's bowl. He is about to plunge his hand into the dog food. Should you stop him from having a taste?

No mortal danger threatens. Observe. What does he do with his discovery? How does the dog food taste? Awful? Interesting?

When your Researcher then crawls off in search of new challenges, you can remove the dog's bowl if you don't want dog food to become a regular part of your baby's diet, which it probably shouldn't.

A door is standing ajar. Outside there is a downward flight of stairs. Your little Researcher is slithering/sliding/wriggling towards the door, over the threshold and out on the other side.

Is intervention necessary? Does mortal danger threaten?

Yes, if the baby falls down the stairs. But is it certain that the baby will actually wriggle all the way to the staircase? You don't know yet. If he does, is it certain that he will fall down the stairs instead of turning around when he gets to the top step and refraining from the further exploration in that direction? You don't know that either.

Observe. Without touching or intervening in any way, you can stand right behind him, a hand at the ready. Wait until the last possible moment and when it's obvious that the baby is going to fall down the stairs, then step in and turn the little optimist in another direction.

A typical day in the life of a Researcher is rife with such episodes. And there is the risk that these episodes may provoke knee-jerk reactions.

Friends of Order dictate that young children shouldn't be allowed to touch scissors or knives. They are on the official list of Dangerous Things. As soon as the Researcher has gotten hold of a pair of scissors that some careless individual has left within reach, the Friend of Order says that you must immediately rush to the rescue and take the scissors away. "Sweetheart, you mustn't play with scissors!"

If this reprimand is repeated often enough, scissors become irresistibly fascinating and conducting research on scissors becomes absolutely imperative. This particular line of inquiry, your Researcher has learned, must be pursued in haste and secrecy, since there is a constant risk of interference. This may well eventually lead to your baby injuring himself quite seriously.

A Researcher who is never hindered handles objects calmly and investigates them thoroughly and carefully. He's not under pressure. If you have steady nerves, hold off. What is the baby going to do with the scissors?

Your Researcher is lying on his stomach looking at the scissors. He turns them over and around. He tastes the handles and sucks on them. No mortal danger threatens – yet.

But now he opens them, points the sharp ends towards himself and looks as though he is about to put one of the blades in his mouth. You have been standing quietly in the background, watching him like a hawk and poised to pounce. You quickly but delicately turn the scissors around so it is the finger and thumb loops that end up in his mouth. No reproaches or exhortations accompany the intervention, so your Researcher doesn't feel harassed or steered. The finger and thumb loops on the scissors are accepted.

Once the examination is complete, the Researcher abandons the scissors, which you then put away. You can then give yourself a couple of minutes while your heart descends from your throat and resumes its customary position.

A young child who is allowed to explore the world without interference develops a serene self-confidence and familiarity with the things that surround him. This, in turn, means that accidents will be few and far between. The whole house won't need to be refurnished. The child won't have an urge to "destroy", and things won't get broken.

And I am of the opinion that it should be possible to have a child in a room that hasn't been "child-proofed". You might want to contemplate what it means for a little person to not have to contend with fear and obstacles right from the start.

All this sounds fine in theory, but the practice can be problematic. You have to fight knee-jerk reactions. You have to ruthlessly train yourself to always keep this prime directive in mind: Don't interfere unless it is absolutely necessary!

The other thing you have to do is maintain an iron control over your surroundings. Not many adults could idly look on while an eight-month-old sat on the counter beside the stove and stirred a stew simmering in a saucepan. (This sort of activity isn't really research and should be filed under "shared work", which is really social participation; see "The Worker".)

You might be thinking that living by this non-interference principle is very time-consuming. You're quite right.

But hindering and distracting a child is time-consuming too. Distracting a six-month-old Researcher is easy, true enough, but the research task remains, and so distracting your child becomes a full-time occupation. And endless ingenuity is required to constantly come up with new distractions.

If your baby wants to investigate the garbage, why not let him? Unappetizing certainly, but is it really dangerous? If there is broken glass or cigarette butts in the garbage bag, fair enough, stay alert, but don't interfere until it is absolutely necessary. I actually waited until one of my babies got a cigarette butt all the way to her mouth before I took it away. I still wasn't completely sure she would actually try and eat it. It was perfectly possible that she would simply put it between her lips just as I did (used to do). And if the cigarette butt didn't end up in her mouth but just fell from her lips to the floor when she launched into a monologue about something else that had caught her interest, then I could pick up the butt and garbage (with my heart in my throat to be sure) without her noticing.

You need nerves of steel, it's true. But your baby's inner harmony – your Researcher's satisfaction at being able to work under such benign conditions – is a wonderful reward.

The examples I have given are of the worst-case scenario variety. Your baby will not be inducing heart attacks his every waking moment. His activities will, more often than not, focus on relatively innocent things. The main thing is that your baby is allowed to work in peace and that *your supervision is discreet, sensitive and positive.*

A Researcher must not be steered, and any attempt to "activate" a six-month-old Researcher is a grave insult.

You should treat a six-month-old Researcher just as you would an adult one. Scholars and artists are eccentric. Everyone knows that. One doesn't bother them when they're at work. Bothering them is difficult anyway, since they live in their own little worlds. Everyone has a right to be happy in his own way, so try to respect what your little one is engaged in, no matter how incomprehensible or pointless it might seem to you.

Some pointers:

• Don't try to substitute things for the objects that your little Researcher is interested in. Don't give him toys that he "should" be playing with.

• Don't interpose yourself between your baby and the world, between your baby and objects. Don't demand attention.

• Don't lift your baby up and carry him around out of habit. Believe that he can in fact do things. Don't glue yourself to your child.

Let's go back to the Researcher with the traditional wife. If his wife plopped herself down on his lap and said, "But darling, what exactly is the point of all this?"

Or, "I know something you could do that's a lot more fun!"

Or, "Can't you pay a little more attention to *me*?"

Unless the adult Researcher was dependent on his wife for groceries and clean shirts, divorce would not be long coming...

THE WORKER

Unlike the six-month-old Researcher, who works alone, the six-month-old Worker functions in a group.

This little person is team player. His built-in desire to participate socially has long seemed to be passive. Passive social participation was hopefully systematized when your baby was three to four months old. It's now time for social participation to become active.

From here on in, the baby is given something useful to do. He is needed by his community.

Of course, the activities of the Researcher and the Worker intersect. The big difference is how you, the adult, conduct yourself. While intervention is to be avoided while the Researcher is gathering his data and drawing his conclusions, leadership and guidance is permitted, desirable and necessary when the Worker is engaged in active social participation.

You are the leader in that you decide upon the activity and put your child to work within that framework – but on your child's initiative.

A concrete example: If you are vacuuming, and your little lad hastens into the room to watch the show and looks interested, pick him up, place his hand on the handle of the vacuum and go on with the vacuuming. Then thank him for his help and put him down as soon as he glimpses something more interesting.

All a Researcher needs is his research. He is sufficient unto himself. Work, on the other hand, involves an activity that is necessary *for you*. The child's participation in that activity means that he is being inducted into his community. This is why intervention is permitted, desirable and necessary. The child's actions within this community must be steered so that they contribute to the over-arching purpose of ensuring the flock's survival.

If you are painting a wall and your child wants to get involved, put him to work. The little lad will try and take your brush. Now is the time to make a clear distinction between work and research. Painting the wall – let's pretend – is an activity that is necessary for the family's, the flock's

285

survival. Your child wants to put in his two cents worth and thereby contribute to this survival.

If you are working (in order to survive), the child will view the activity as work too. Don't shut him out, but rather lead and show him what has to be done to survive in this world.

If the child takes your brush, you can't work. We have established that the work you are doing is vital for the flock's survival and therefore must be seen through to the end. The child should be put to good use within his community, not excluded from it. Exclusion is the last thing the child wants. Quite the contrary, he wants to join in.

So, get yourself an extra brush and give it to the child. Take his hand and dip the brush in the paint and let him paint with your hand held gently but firmly over his. Tell him what a good job he is doing. Your tone of voice and your words will send the message that your child is relieving the pressure on you. He is facilitating work that is essential to his community's survival. Two heads are better than one.

After another round of practice painting, your little Worker will want to try and paint himself.

"What's going to happen to the wall?" cries the Friend of Order.

The wall will be just fine. Your little Worker will soon tire of painting (or try to stick the brush in his mouth, which at all costs must be prevented. Mortal danger threatens. Furthermore, that is not the way the work should be done. Steer your child in the right direction. This is not a game; this is about survival). Your child will work with you for two to five minutes. You can retouch the wall a little later, when he won't see you. The Worker and Researcher are always taking turns so when the Worker is resting and the little Researcher has emerged to investigate the world, you will then have time to repair any "damage" the Worker has done.

There's a minor miracle hidden in all this. Children of all ages who are put to work in this way by the adults – the flock – and included in activities necessary for the flock's survival for as long as they want (never less, but more when they get older) feel a tremendous sense of satisfaction afterwards. This feeling of satisfaction enables them to contentedly amuse themselves for a good while.

We adults experience exactly the same feeling of profound satisfaction after a particularly productive workday. We feel inspired to pursue a hobby or are simply content to kick back, relax and enjoy being alive. The five minutes you spend making a serious effort to put your child to good use will result in fifteen minutes to a half hour's worth of peace and quiet, when your child will take a little "vacation" after a job well done.

If you sit down and think about it, you will realize that there are in fact very few activities where a child can't be put to good use. Anything that is necessary *for you* is an opportunity to make your child feel he is really a part of his community.

If you're a man and you happen to be shaving, it's perhaps not work, but it is still necessary for you. I can guarantee that the Worker will want to have a go at helping you shave too. Is this possible? Of course it is! The child can in fact "shave" you if you hold his hand on the handle of the razor. His input is mercifully brief at this stage, and you will then be able to finish the job yourself.

As usual, thank the lad extravagantly so as to let the Worker know that shaving would have been impossible without his timely and inspired assistance. He has not been "kind", but has made life easier for you by doing a good job and making a contribution to something necessary.

⤙∴⁚○⁚∴⤚

Let's move out to the kitchen. A well-known source of all kinds of grief is the stove.

Little people have a habit of playing with the knobs, opening and climbing up on oven doors, thus causing the whole stove to tip. Range guards are regarded as an absolute necessity, and the stove has to be securely attached to the wall or floor.

Whether it's the Researcher or the Worker who is attacking the stove, it is worth asking oneself what it is the child is really after.

The stove symbolizes food and is the heart of the household. The child wants up, so he can investigate, learn and work. It's a perfectly logical reaction, and I don't think it should be prevented.

Rather than preventing a child from investigating the stove through elaborate security measures, it would be simpler – and more sensible – to lift the child up and demonstrate how everything works.

How would an adult who had never seen a stove be treated?

No one would try and deter this individual from learning how a stove worked. Everyone would take for granted that this individual would one day have to use modern appliances. If this person were deaf or blind, he would still have to learn how to use a stove. Someone would hold the blind or deaf person's hand above the burner to demonstrate that the burners produce heat, as well as the connection between the dial settings and how much heat is produced. The same helpful contact person would bring a saucepan of water to the boil and let the blind or deaf person feel the heat rising from the saucepan, turn the burners on and off, and so on.

You should treat a young child in exactly the same way.

Young children who are allowed to familiarize themselves with stoves early and are allowed to participate in work that involves using the stove tend not to regard it as a toy or a jungle gym. Thus, all the security measures are unnecessary.

It is in fact more difficult and time consuming to be forever keeping a child away from something than it is to respect a child's ability and intelligence and show him.

Cooking is the little Worker's dream job. He can make a contribution to his community within the context of the collective struggle for survival – literally! – and he also gets to taste things. Whether you are cooking with a Researcher or a Worker, I can guarantee you a memorable experience.

Some parents object that their own work is made more difficult and more time consuming by allowing a young child to take part in it all the time. They think it would be better to hold off giving a child something to do until they are old enough to do something that's really useful.

As one father asked, "How old do they have to be before you can send them on simple errands?" (Four!)

It's relatively rare for parents to make much of an effort to put their children to work at the tender age of six months or during the months that follow. Instead they give their children toys, and the kids play unobtrusively beside the parents while they work.

For a while, all is right with the world. But the need to be inducted into a community is so powerful that it soon demands its due.

Parents who have neglected this vital part of their children's socialization usually have tremendous problems keeping them occupied when they reach the age of seven to eight months. Even six-month-olds are sometimes so upset at being prevented from participating socially that they stick to their mother/father/primary caregiver like glue.

So-called AP-parents (attachment parenting) tend to interpret this as meaning that their children need to "fill up on intimacy". (This "fill up" is a twenty four-hour-a-day affair, which is brutally ended when the child starts day care.)

This is how a six-month-old is described by one of today's child psychologists:

"Your child has gotten to know and love you more than anyone else, and wants to have you all to himself all the time. He doesn't want to share you with anyone or anything, and you must not devote any time or attention to anything else. Your child's fondest wish is to be enveloped by you and your attention."

Apart from the fact this exhortation places an insanely heavy burden on you, the mother or the father, it is patently untrue. Children who participate socially (albeit passively) from three weeks on and then make the jump from passive to active social participation from five to six months and up do *not* exhibit such behavior.

You, as a mother or father, both personally and in your activities must be available to your child – just as the contact man in the Bedouin camp was for the newcomer. You must be your child's fixed point, his support and his guide – his contact man.

But your child definitely does not require you to be available exclusively for him twenty-four hours a day or that you refrain from devoting time and attention to anything else. Your child is ill served by such an arrangement anyway, just as you would be if your Bedouin contact man dropped all his duties, left the camp and sat in the desert with you, completely cut off from the tent, the camp, the community where you are both supposed to live.

A five to six-month-old's clinginess and demands for attention have their roots in social exclusion, and this condition won't be cured by love alone.

If a person feels he is good for nothing except being loved by another person, of course he will be devastated when that person disappears. But if he feels he is of value to his flock in the collective struggle for survival that everyone is engaged in, he can bear and accept that this other person might disappear from time to time. He knows he has value because he contributes, and that has nothing to do with whether or not other people love him. He will naturally seek out this person when he needs her or him and wants to be with her or him for whatever reason, but he doesn't seek the "contact man" out because he is helpless without the contact man.

The time and effort you expend to enable your child to join in and help out will pay for itself many times over. Show me a child who is inducted into his community and made useful in tasks that are necessary for you, the adults, be these tasks ever so simple and limited (or imaginary!), and I will show you a child who has a rock solid sense of self-worth.

You are making an investment that will pay huge dividends.

Contented children are calm. Discontented children are demanding. Just like their larger counterparts in the adult world!

A Little Memo
• Be on the look out for initiative. Take appropriate action as soon as your child shows the slightest desire to take part in activities that are necessary *for you*.
• Don't confuse initiative with a need for emotional attention. Don't stop what you're doing. Make your child a part of it.

• Let your child work exactly as you do and don't let work turn into play (by for example having your child paint with a kiddie brush on a pad while you paint a wall).

• Thank your child for his input as though he has really helped. Avoid excessively emotional praise. Anyone who participates in the struggle for survival is not being "kind" but is contributing to his community. "Congratulations to us on a job well done!" should be your attitude.

• Don't make demands that don't coincide with the child's desire to help (until he is quite a bit older). No demands and no obstacles!

• Even if you are engaged in a "make-believe" activity, it should be presented as essential for survival. Don't present it as a game. Don't say, "Let's have some fun and paint the wall!" Survival is a serious business. With your attitude, say rather, "Now this wall has got to be painted. We've left it far too long."

THE FLIRT

No memos or instructions are necessary for interacting with a six-month-old Flirt. Just enjoy him!

The Flirt is a divinely inspired comedian who throws himself body and soul into uninhibited cuddling and mischievous joy. A six-month-old Flirt adores physical contact – and himself for that matter, which of course is not surprising. He can fall helplessly in love if he catches sight of himself in a mirror. The Flirt discovers this breathtakingly beautiful, utterly enchanting child in the looking glass and is overcome by blissful, unreserved adulation. The Flirt then discovers that Mom or Dad, or whoever is holding him has a double. Remarkable! Love blossoms. The Flirt stares enraptured at the guest of honor, this delightful person all of six months old, and kisses the miracle in the mirror full on the lips. Their romance thus sealed, their union is complete. If the Flirt could propose to himself, he would! (A Flirt can be so insanely in love with his own reflection, he may go overboard and start hitting the mirror. Then it's time to take the little hand and gently stroke the mirror together.)

The Flirt doesn't only flirt with himself, but also with you, his loving parents. You, as a mother or father, now have an opportunity to toss inhibitions to the wind for once in your life. You can shower the Flirt with kisses all over his body – he'll be ecstatic. You can let him explore your own body in minute detail – without so much as the merest hint of shame or obscenity. For the Flirt, nudity is the most natural thing in the world. If you are the bashful type, the Flirt is an ideal audience before which to become comfortable with your body. If you have never grasped the difference between sensuality and sexuality, now's your chance. Time spent in bed or in the bath is a pure joy. Make hay while the sun shines, because the day will come when your Flirt will call for a fig leaf, and both nudity and bodily contact will be far more strictly rationed.

The Flirt, loving little soul that he is, loves encounters. Every time he sees you, he falls in love with you all over again. You, of course, should respond in kind, and if you make a grand affair of your reunion every morning, the Flirt will be delirious with ecstasy. So when you enter the room where the Flirt resides at night, shout HELLOOOO as though you hadn't seen each other for ten years and you'll make his day.

After solitary play in his bed, when it is time to give the Flirt his porridge perhaps, repeat the procedure. The Prodigal Son has returned and it's time to kill the fatted calf. The Flirt lives for these encounters.

Peek-a-boo and give-and-take are integral parts of any love affair worthy of the name. When the Flirt offers you a bite of his crisp bread, well gnawed, and grey with age and wisdom, don't make the mistake of declining. Always take what the Flirt offers you. Even if you don't like well-gnawed crisp bread, half rotten bananas or somewhat grubby apple cores, at least pretend to taste whatever is offered, thank him profusely, and hand it back. (But if he offers you something you actually like, don't eat all of it. You are courting disaster!) None of this really has anything to do with food or hunger. What the Flirt is offering you is love. He has endless amounts of it, and he is dying to share it.

If the Flirt (and his twin the Worker) is helping you make dinner, and you ask for something you need, a spatula say, that's right *there,* it may take a while before the Flirt understands what it is you actually want. You may have to wrap the little hand around the handle and virtually give the spatula to yourself and thank him for his help before he finally gets the message.

But immediately thereafter the Flirt will bombard you with every object he can lay his hands on. You must of course pretend that you actually need all the pens, keys, potholders, and bottle caps, thank him from the bottom of your heart, place all these objects to one side, and act as though it's only a matter of time before you throw all this stuff into the pan and fry it in butter.

Give-and-take is an act of love (while food preparation signifies work and the community to which the child belongs). During give-and-take sessions, the same button or clothespin can change hands fifty times. It may not look like much to the outside world, but the love between the Flirt and his partner is so intense that the button or clothespin almost glows.

A tip: if you consistently say "please" and "thank you" on the child's behalf during the give-and-take sessions, you will find he will soon use these words of his own accord. In fact, he'll be in the habit of saying "thank you" before he can even talk properly, which will mightily impress your friends and relatives!

On a more serious note, courtesy is a virtue that still opens doors even in our rather uncivil age.

The Flirt doesn't just love you as mother or father or "contact man". The Flirt loves the whole world and shows it. The most grumpy, wizened, sour old geezer in your entire clan is interesting, huggable and loveable as far as the Flirt is concerned.

And that is a precious gift indeed. Everyone who has a little Flirt in the house should do the grand tour among those acquaintances who aren't so lucky and give them the blessing of being encircled by a little child's endless love. Not everyone has the chance to experience it.

And it lasts such a short time. With the eight-month anxiety, fear of strangers kicks in and this fear may include people the child knows relatively well.

Soon thereafter, the child goes through a stand-offish phase and up until the age of five young children may refuse to greet or hug people. So treasure this brief time of endless love!

The Flirt and your older relatives will have a very special connection, and whenever I witness it, I wonder if the separation of the very young from the very old is not as great a crime against human ecology as our ravaging of the planet is against Nature.

A very old person and a very young child have something in common that the parents and other people of the parents' generation are excluded from. It's a bond, a mutual understanding, a shared serenity, a oneness.

That's not much of a description, probably because I'm not even sure I know what it is I am trying to describe, but with an old person, a very young child will suddenly become still in a pure, trusting, intimacy that is a joy and fascination to observe.

THE CRAWLER

PREPARATIONS

Once a child can get around under his own steam, the house has to be meticulously inspected.

All windows have to be childproofed so that they can't be opened more than a crack. It will be a while before your child can crawl up on furniture, get on to the windowsill, and figure out how to open the window, but you never know from one day to the next when he'll develop the craft.

I was once looking after a little one and a half year-old who, God only knows how, managed to access a high window from his crib, open it wide and climb out on to the ledge, where he proceeded to study the traffic four stories below... Nerves of steel are a must in such situations, since a scream or a sudden movement might have frightened the child and caused him to fall. I had to creep soundlessly across the room to the window and finally, after what seemed an eternity, I managed to grab hold of the little body and lift him back in.

I learned my lesson. An ounce of prevention is worth a pound of cure.

All chemicals and medications must be out of reach and preferably under lock and key. Even small amounts of ammonia, for example, can endanger a young child's life. Vitamins, pills of any kind are dangerous. As few as three iron capsules, for example, can be lethal if swallowed by a child this age, and immediate stomach pumping would be necessary.

Take stock of what you have in the cupboards under the kitchen counter and storage closets. Don't forget the bathroom. The toilet is a great stepladder, and very often, young children can reach the bathroom cabinet from there. The effects of medications commonly kept in bathroom cabinets can be catastrophic if they find their way into the hands of a young child.

The best strategy is to simply get rid of as much as you can. Set aside an evening and go through all the medicines and chemicals you have in your home and pitch everything you don't really need. You have to make sure that there is absolutely no way, even if he has a ladder, that your child can get at whatever potentially dangerous substances you decide to keep. This is regardless of whether you actually own a ladder or not!

All plugs, sockets, wires etc. must be secured. It's worth the trouble to lead all wires over doorframes and somehow hide all extension cord sockets, so you can put them out of your mind once and for all. A more serious problem is wall sockets, which are placed at the worst possible height. Those not in use can be kiddie proofed, while those that are essential must be hidden – preferably by placing heavy furniture in front of them. There is nothing simpler, or sadly more tempting, than pulling the plug out of a wall socket and trying to stuff something else in. Accidents happen in the blink of an eye, and mouth-to-mouth resuscitation won't work on a young child whose heart has stopped – and that's exactly what will happen if he gets a jolt of electricity through his body. Hard blows to the chest over the heart are required to get the heart going again – but this is a dicey proposition. Do everything to prevent accidents like this.

Naturally, show your child the correct way to plug something in, and that the lamp lights with the plug in and doesn't with the plug out so that he knows what these tempting little apertures are actually for. Your child will not get the procedure for plugging and unplugging things down pat for a good many years though, at least not to the point where he gets it right every time.

All ashtrays and cigarettes in the house must in future be stored safely. Cigarettes should be placed high up and all ashtrays must close over the butts. Cigarette butts must *not* be accessible. Ashtrays should also be placed on high shelves. A quarter of a cigarette won't kill a child, but a whole one will. Give milk and induce vomiting in the first case, call an ambulance and have the child's stomach pumped at the hospital in the second. You might want to pray hard too. Don't take the risk!

Cigarettes are attractive. Even two and three-year-olds love playing with them, even if they usually content themselves with breaking them up. If you try to stop a crawler from moving around, you are tempting fate. It's an exercise in futility too. So, make sure that cigarettes and tobacco products are simply not part of the child's environment.

In this context it should be mentioned that the sulfur on matches and matchboxes is for some strange reason regarded as particularly tasty by young children. As far as I know, it hasn't hurt anyone, and I usually don't interfere, although you must naturally intervene if there is a fire hazard. Matches and the tasting thereof belong to a category of investigative work which, like the examination of knives and scissors, must be monitored closely.

The handles of all saucepans, frying pans etc must be pointed inwards towards the back of the stove. A crawler who manages to raise himself against the stove can't even see that the handles are attached to anything. Babies that age see handles that stick out as just that: handles.

The best way to avoid accidents around the stove is to show your child how the stove works – and to put him to work while you make dinner.

You should spare a thought for the glass panel in the oven door. Unless there is an outer sheet that stays cool, the crawler has to be warned time and time again that the glass can be hot when the light inside the oven is on. Hold the little hand close to the hot glass so he gets the message, and then be vigilant! The crawler can develop the ability to stand literally from one day to the next, and if the oven light is on and good smells are wafting in your child's direction, little hands can eagerly be laid against the glass.

Minor burns you can treat with cold running water until the skin no longer feels warm. When the skin is cool and stays cool, apply ointment and an airtight bandage. The burn won't hurt.

At the launch of the crawler's career, the carpets have to be shampooed and then vacuumed daily. Bare floors should be mopped every day too. If there is grime on the kid, it should come from food and research projects (it will of course be bathed away every evening anyhow), but it should not come from the floor.

A clean floor or carpet won't automatically make your child healthy, but it will help! Clean floors will do a child with a cold more good than medicine will.

The crawler should be allowed to wander barefoot – cold feet are better than restrictions on movement. Crawling pants made of something soft, preferably not knitted, will protect his knees.

Finally, tour the house once more and keep an eye out for things you really love. Family heirlooms, articles of great sentimental value should be stored away. Things can get broken – even if it's not inevitable. We'll see how to avoid such tragedies a little further on.

You must never take your eyes off your crawler. There's just no getting around that.

On the other hand, by this time you have probably grown a third eye, a layer of teflon on your nerves and an extra arm... The time that is to come won't be more challenging than that which has already passed. *Be available when your child needs you, but when he doesn't, leave him be.*

The only goal of a crawler who is exploring the world is... exploring the world. The crawler doesn't defy, provoke or intentionally frazzle the nerves of his tender caregiver.

The crawler isn't that interested in relationships generally. The crawler thinks in very concrete terms. The crawler is out to explore the world, and if that irritates or disturbs you, it's your problem, not the child's.

We have already talked about the perils of intervening, especially if it's unnecessary, in "The six-month-old: the researcher". However, mortal dangers do exist, and accidents can happen very quickly indeed. Among the many extra organs the parents of infants grow is a third ear. There is nothing more ominous than silence.

But constant supervision is not only to guard. It's also to help. You can protect your child from disappointment by helping him. You can help by opening a cupboard door, by moving a piece of furniture, by supplying him with that one extra ounce of momentum he needs to cross a threshold by giving the diapered bottom a little shove.

You are entering new territory. Once your child just stayed where you put him. Now he's mobile. A new world is opening up for both of you. As this new adventure beckons, you are probably contemplating it with somewhat more trepidation than your child is. It's perfectly natural for a loving parent to worry – before it's really necessary. But if you can restrain yourself and close your ears to everything except real danger, you will have mastered a talent that will serve you well until your son or daughter moves out.

Nothing is more insulting to a young child (or an older one) as distrust, hasty conclusions, and premature interventions.

If you as a parent try to clear potential disappointments from your little crawler's path and do your best to function as reservoir of ability that your child can draw on when his own runs dry, you will hear protests from your surroundings sooner or later.

"You can't just let him do whatever he likes!" says the Friend of Order. "You'll spoil him!"

That statement is not only inaccurate, it's backwards.

A spoiled kid, as everyone knows, is an insufferable little being who can barely be allowed into civilized society because of his whiny demands, his ill temper and his complete inability to take the initiative. A young child who is happy, courageous and self-confident isn't spoiled. A crawler who can move around freely and is spared disappointment will be happy, courageous and self-confident as a result. Any apprehensions you have about spoiling your child should be laid to rest.

A little child who is allowed to roam is a free little person. A little child who is hindered is an oppressed little person. It's that simple and that serious.

But Friends of Order die hard. "You must give him a proper upbringing!" you will hear by the time your child is one if not before.

No you don't.

You shouldn't start "bringing up" your child until he reaches the terrible twos, which will happen at around two and a half (little girls) or three (little boys). The exception is a short period – it will last approximately two months – at the eighteen-month mark, a foretaste of the terrible twos, when you will have to say NO both in word and deed (because the child does).

I know there are many people who disagree with my opinion about when "upbringing" should begin and who condemn my ideas, just as I condemn theirs, but here I side shamelessly with the children.

It is simply a fact that a crawler who is hindered, steered and resisted, whether the obstacles are people or things, will react with despair, rage and feelings of powerlessness. The child can become inconsolable. This demonstrates that resistance, which is what upbringing usually means in practice, is too overwhelming for young children.

Thus, the assertions of the Friend of Order are indefensible.

A child going through the terrible twos on the other hand is, through his actions, asking to be hindered, steered (by boundaries) and resisted, and so reacts with blessed relief.

And that's when a child's upbringing begins – on the child's own initiative.

THREE GOLDEN RULES

Let's take a look at some everyday situations. We can relate them to three rules, which should be your point of departure when you decide how to act and react to any given situation.

1. Don't hinder.
2. Remove potential sources of disappointment.
3. Function as a tool and a guide.

In many situations, you will combine two or all three.

1. Don't hinder

Adam, nine months old, is on his way to a staircase leading downwards. His mother watches and waits. When it's completely obvious that he plans on crawling over the top stair, she lifts him up, but she doesn't take him into her arms, or show any concern or dismay. She does not link the intervention to her personally. Instead, she turns Adam in a direction that leads away from the stairs and places a spool of thread that she happened to have handy a short distance away from him. When Adam has crawled back into safer territory, she closes the door to the stairs without his noticing.

Alice, six months, is lying on her stomach next to a kitchen drawer that her dad has pulled out for her to examine. The drawer contains whisks, ladles and various small dishes, but also a sharp knife that Dad hadn't noticed. Both catch sight of it at the same time. Alice's dad stays close and waits. When Alice is about to clutch the sharp blade, he quickly turns the knife around and places the handle in her hands. He says nothing but proceeds to lay out the most interesting whisk. When Alice has finished examining the knife handle, she moves on to the whisk. Discreetly, Dad removes the knife.

Max, seven months is wriggling his way towards the fridge, which goes right down to the floor. Mom is getting something from the fridge. When she shuts the fridge door, Max howls with disappointment. He had time to see how bright the fridge light was and that there was a host of interesting things in there. The cold air was exciting too. Mom opens the door again. Max is allowed to look into the fridge, grab what he can reach and pull it out onto the floor. When it looks as though the eggs might be in danger, her patience begins to flag, so Mom takes out a package of ham that Max couldn't reach and gives it to him to examine. She then quickly picks up the food and puts it back in the fridge and shuts the door. When Max has finished examining the ham and has set off on a new adventure, she puts the ham away without Max seeing.

Victoria, eight months, is sitting in her highchair at the dining table. Her parents have invited guests and the table is laid festively complete with candles. Victoria happens to have a candle right opposite her. She stretches her hand towards the flame and tries to crawl out of her high chair and onto the table so she can reach the candle. Victoria's dad doesn't remove the candle, but rather moves it closer to her. He then takes her hand and places it close enough to the flame that Victoria can feel the heat but not so close that she runs the risk of getting burned. "Hot," he explains. He looks at her to see if she has understood. He demonstrates with his own hand and shows her how you can "burn" yourself on the flame. Finally, Dad returns the candle to its original position and studies Victoria. Was she satisfied with her examination of the candle? If so, she won't try to reach it again. If not, Dad will repeat the procedure.

William, nine months, has, against all odds, managed to get hold of a chocolate cake. William has never eaten chocolate before, and his dad has no plans to let him start. With an exceptionally loving smile, Dad says, "Oh thank you so much!" Whereupon he gently but firmly takes the cake away from William as though William had given it to him. William looks a little startled, but, being an affable little fellow, he's delighted by the appreciation. Before he has time to mourn his loss, his dad breaks off a tiny piece and gives it to him. While William puts the piece of cake into his mouth, Dad hides the rest of the cake. When William remembers that it was a pretty big cake and twigs to the fact that he actually wants some more, Dad shares his son's disappointment and with a gesture of non-comprehension he says, "Gone!"

Violetta, seven months, has gotten hold of a tube of adhesive paste. She has four sharp little teeth, and she has gotten the cap of the tube off. Violetta's mom thanks her profusely, takes the tube from her, squeezes a miniscule drop out onto Violetta's finger and then hides the tube. "Gone!"

Eric, six months, has found a pile of poo that the cat deposited in the wrong place. Dad doesn't think that this particular line of research should be a priority in Eric's life. He grabs little Eric, puts him under his arm and rushes out to the kitchen to fetch some paper towel. He then brings Eric back to the pile of cat poo with him and as he cleans it up, he makes all kinds of disgusted sounds. An expression of revulsion fixed firmly on his face he takes the paper towel and its contents into the bathroom and flushes it down the toilet, still with Eric under his arm. He conveys the impression that this is absolutely the grossest job he has ever had to do. Eric doesn't understand much about all this, but he does know that *he* hasn't done anything wrong. It's not Eric's behavior that is condemned. The fact that he was planning to put cat poo in his mouth is not met with dismay. It's the poo (or the cat!) that is at fault.

Little Angelina, eight months, is out playing in the sandbox and she puts sand in her mouth. It's Angelina's first encounter with sand. Her mom lets her be. When Mom decides Angelina has learned all she needs to know about sand, she lifts her out of the sandbox and tries to interest her in other facets of life on earth.

Elliot, seven months, finds a large roll of tape that was fairly expensive and is in the process of smothering it with drool. Elliot's dad needs the tape, and it's the only roll he's got. Dad peels off a decent length of tape and places it in Elliot's hand and discreetly places the rest of the roll out of reach.

Emmy, nine months, is moving at full speed towards a rose on her mom's night table. Mother is unobtrusively tailing her. Emmy raises herself against the table and reaches for the flower. Emmy's mother brings the rose, vase and all, down to Emmy's level. She squats down, takes Emmy's hand and has her stroke the rose gently. "Stroke the flower," she says tenderly. "Smell," she says and smells the rose thoroughly herself. "Ooh, it smells so good!" She places the flower close to Emmy's nose. Emmy tries to smell it and makes a sound similar to mother's "Ooh". Emmy's mom keeps holding the rose close to her daughter's nose until she has touched and smelled to her heart's content. Mom then puts the rose back in its place, waves goodbye to it, and leaves the room. And Emmy, who was not prevented from examining the rose, can leave it in peace too.

Philip's dad has a bookcase in the living room, and Philip, eight months, wriggles over and drags a couple of books out onto the floor. Dad stands discreetly behind him ready to intervene, but for the moment he just watches and waits. Philip now takes hold of the dust cover of one of the books and seems to be getting ready to pull it off or rip it up. Dad leans forward quickly and takes the little hand. With his own hand on Philip's, he lets Philip open the book, leaf through it, and stroke the text and the pictures – and finally close the book. Then he takes away his hand.

Philip then examines the book again, but correctly. His behavior is exemplary.

But then he suddenly takes it into his head to grab a page and scrunch it up. Philip's dad immediately takes hold of the little hand again. "Oh-oh," he says. The tone is not reproachful. He sounds as though he was afraid an accident was going to happen. He takes Philip's hand and smoothes out the page. Then he lets Philip continue leafing through the book and stroking the pages until he finally closes the book with Philip's hand. Only then does he let go.

Dad waits to see whether Philip wants to examine the book yet again. If he does, he's more than welcome to. Philip's dad waits patiently until Philip is finished with the book, and then he puts it away.

Philip will come back to his book and Emmy to her rose, not once but many times. They will do so partly because they want to examine them again, and partly because they want to test their ability to manipulate these objects. Their prudent parents stay in the background. They don't automatically assume that everything will go well, but they don't automatically assume that everything will go badly either.

If Emmy pats the rose and tries to smell it, her mother expresses tenderness and appreciation that is directed towards *the rose*. "Oh yes, pat the little flower. It's so pretty and smells so good."

If, on the other hand, Emmy doesn't pat the flower gently but tries to grab it like she did the first time, her mother behaves as through it really was the first time. Without a hint of reproach, she gives Emmy exactly the same little lesson she did before. If Emmy behaves as though she had never examined the rose (which she did ten minutes ago), Mom plays along and makes as though Emmy had never even been near the flower. There are no demands and no expectations.

Philip's reactions will be more or less the same. He will pull out a book again, the same book or another one, in fifteen minutes, tomorrow, or next week, grab the dust jacket in exactly the same way and try to rip it. His father will behave as though it were the first time that Philip had encountered a book and teach him the right way to do it, while he rhapsodises about the book. "What a beautiful book, so many lovely pages, pat them gently..."

It may well be that Philip will take the first lesson to heart and, not mindful of Dad's watchful presence, will treat the book the way he did when Dad's hand was on top of his. He will leaf gently through the book, stroke the text and pictures, close the book, and crawl away. If this doesn't happen on the second attempt, it will on the fifth.

Philip has no interest in destroying anything. He only wants to investigate.

Young children who are taught how to handle things properly and are not prevented from getting anywhere near them very quickly learn the drill, and do in fact learn the right way to handle things – but that doesn't mean they will get it right every time. It's a mistake to assume that just because they can do something right they always will.

"But why do they do that when they know they're not supposed to?" I hear you cry – and come to the conclusion that your young child is yanking your chain, if you'll pardon the expression. But I imagine you would behave exactly the same way if, for example, you were confronted with an electric stove for the first time after having spent your whole life on a deserted island.

Someone would demonstrate the stove for you and teach you how to boil water to make tea. It would only take you a few minutes to learn. Your teacher would be pleased with you and would go home secure in the knowledge that you had mastered the art of using a stove (although we have restricted ourselves to one of the stove's simpler functions). But what then?

Yes, you can boil water for tea, but what is to stop you from using the stove for a thousand other things too? It's the world's most exciting apparatus! Lots of dials and knobs, and heat that comes and goes. What happens if there's no saucepan on the burner, and what happens if you have an empty saucepan on the burner, and what happens if you pour water directly on to the burner, and what happens if you put butter or a scarf on the burner, and what happens if you turn the stove upside down?

The next day, your teacher surveys the devastation and exclaims, "But you know how to boil water! What did you do all this for? There's no point in trying to teach you anything!"

If we draw a parallel with little Philip and his books, it becomes obvious that accidents can happen. Philip's dad is perhaps not quite fast enough turning the pages. Philip investigates in the "wrong" way, and one of the pages is torn. But Philip didn't mean any harm any more than you, the stove apprentice, did. The stove apprentice knew how to boil water perfectly well. Little Philip knew perfectly well how to leaf through a book – but both you and he wanted to try other things too – and that's when it all went wrong.

Reproach is not only pointless but also counterproductive. It provokes sulkiness, anger and distress. (If we were flies on the wall when our imaginary stove apprentice was bawled out by his teacher, we would witness quite a scene. Our apprentice would have told his teacher that he wasn't going to boil water for tea or anything else in the future. In fact, he was going back to cooking everything over an open fire on the balcony.)

Behave instead as though an accident has happened. Something just "went wrong".

"Oh dear!" says Philip's father. "Did the book rip? Poor, poor book!"

He looks unhappy for the book's sake, but he doesn't accuse Philip of anything. In fact, he makes no connection between Philip and the book. Philip understands from his father that something bad happened to the book – not that he, Philip had done something bad to the book. All that remains to be done is to try and remedy the misfortune that has somehow befallen the book. Philip's dad gets some scotch tape and repairs the torn pages. Both Philip and his father are happy once the book is as good as new. "The book is happy again," says Dad, as though the book had a life of its own – which, after all, was how it got damaged in the first place. "It's all fixed."

Alternatively, if the book is so badly damaged, it can't be repaired then and there, if at all, Dad then puts the book on a high shelf and says in an apologetic, sorrowful tone, "The poor book will have to stay up there, it's so ripped." By appearing to go into mourning, you can save things from further destruction without the child feeling hindered, harassed and misunderstood.

2. Remove potential sources of disappointment

For the crawler, the world is often impossible. There are doors that can't be opened, thresholds that can't be crossed, chairs that fall over, cabinets that are locked... If all that wasn't enough, the crawler's own abilities are so depressingly limited. He can't reach the things he wants to reach. He can't crawl fast enough, or even in the direction that he'd planned to. He can't sit down, once he's succeeded in raising himself against something. Above all, he's just too short. Literally and figuratively, he is the underdog.

Disappointments lurk everywhere. Removing potential sources of disappointment then is going to require a little more effort on your part than simply not hindering does. You have to think ahead of the game if you want to get ahead of the game.

Olivia's mom, for example, sees that Olivia is on her way towards the sofa set. She knows that Olivia can't get between the coffee table and the sofa, so she beats Olivia to the punch and moves the table a tad.

The same thing happens when Olivia heads for a closed door. Mom opens it and leaves it slightly ajar. When Olivia eventually reaches the door, she can push it open herself.

All parents have ridden in an elevator with their own or other people's children and have pushed the buttons themselves. "*I* wanted to push!" says the child (with or without words depending on his or her age). Do the manoeuvre over again! Go back down to the ground floor and let the child push the button.

At first, Olivia's mother was too helpful. She opened the door all the way when she saw that Olivia was heading in that direction. Major tantrum. Olivia wanted to open the door herself. The door had to be closed so that it was ajar just a crack, and Olivia had to be taken back to the place on the floor from which she had begun her expedition. Now Olivia can do what she had originally intended to do.

Children are generous. They are always more than happy to cut clumsy adults some slack.

When little Olivia begins to stand up by raising herself against things, she practices on a rickety stool. One of these days, it's going to fall. Olivia's mother makes sure she holds the stool for her. She doesn't take the stool away, nor does she try to steer Olivia towards another piece of furniture that's perhaps a little more stable. She respects Olivia's choice and supports her. Mom has no idea why Olivia likes that particular stool, or what she hopes to achieve by raising herself against that particular piece of furniture, but her daughter has made a decision and that decision must be respected.

If you are faced with potential sources of disappointments that seem impossible to remove, you can wholly or partially neutralize them by sharing them.

Little William has gotten hold of some chocolate – a textbook problem. The child has had time to taste it, figure out that it's good, and then of course he wants more. If his dad were to just snatch the chocolate or cookie or whatever it is from the child's hand, he would unleash a perfect storm of disappointment. Instead, William's dad breaks off a tiny piece and gives it to William, but the rest mysteriously disappears. William's dad is just as surprised as William over how the chocolate vanished. "Gone!" he says and looks perplexed.

This is a useful little ruse that enables you to hitch a ride on the fact that objects are alive as far as young children are concerned. Furthermore, they know nothing of logic. Or more precisely, they apply their own. Chocolate has a life of its own, just like everything else. If a cat can disappear under its own steam, so can a chocolate bar.

When they're a few months older and wiser, they know that things don't just disappear willy-nilly. Little angels also learn to root around behind cushions and under rugs, or wherever you are in the habit of hiding candy, glue, pearl necklaces, or whatever it is you are trying to hide or save with your "Gone!". Once your child twigs to the fact that inanimate objects don't just run off into the wild blue yonder, you will have to tell him the naked truth. "There's no more!" But the principle is the same. The chocolate, candy, cake, ice cream that the child had time to taste is finished, and you are just as surprised as the child. You regret the fact that there's no more of whatever it is, and you would have loved to have another mouthful too, just like the child. As this lamentable situation affects you as well as the child, his disappointment will be mild or non-existent.

If, on the other hand, you add a personal element by saying, "You can't eat as much ice cream as you want. You are too little. So, you can't have any more!", what you are doing is limiting the child rather than the ice cream. You must then be prepared for the child's protests against you because he was not at all done with the ice cream. You are misjudging the child, you are failing to understand him, and the child will be disappointed in *you*. The child has to forego ice cream because you are refusing to give it to him, not because there is no more.

Inanimate objects have a life of their own, and ice cream disappears when it feels like it. If you had a couple of liters of ice cream ten seconds ago and now you suddenly have none at all, the child will accept it and be only mildly disappointed. All you have to do is be apologetic rather than critical. The ice cream abandoned you too.

You can also make disappointments work in your favor. Victor, ten months old, has a loving, imaginative mother who excels at this. Victor was on his mother's knee in a café eating baby food from a jar, while Mom had a coffee and some cookies. Suddenly, Victor got hold of one of the cookies, tasted it and thought it beat the hell out of baby food. A minute later, he noticed there was a plate on the table that was positively overflowing with such delicacies, and he decided to crawl up on to the table to get at them.

306

Someone tried to take the plate away, but Victor's mother warned them off. She didn't try to hold Victor on her knee to stop him from getting up onto the table, but she distracted him by quickly putting a cookie between her teeth and turning him around so he was facing her. Victor was not keen on this idea at first and looked as though he was getting ready to make his disappointment known, but then he saw the cookie between his mom's teeth, and it was a sight he appreciated mightily. Mom bent down towards him and let him taste the cookie. At the same time, she took a big bite herself. When they had eaten up the cookie between them, Victor opened his mother's mouth and inspected it thoroughly to see if there was any more of the cookie to be had. There wasn't. The whole business ended in a flurry of kisses, and the plate was discreetly removed without Victor noticing.

The net result was that instead of disappointment, Victor got a mini love-in with his mother.

Disappointment is the polar opposite of empowerment. Not even adults with all their accumulated knowledge and common sense always have the strength to wrestle with disappointment and win. Common sense is based to a large degree on experience. Young children lack experience generally, and there are large gaps in the little they do possess.

Aurore's dad is leaving the house. Her mother goes out into the hall with Aurore on her arm. Dad kisses Aurore and tells her that he is going now. He also tells her that they will wave to each other through the window, and he carries her over to the window to show her. "That's where Daddy is going. You are going to wave to me and I am going to wave to you." Back in the hall, Mom takes Aurore into her arms again, Dad kisses his daughter once more, and then he leaves. Aurore then waves to her dad through the window.

Aurore's father can't go out into the hall with Aurore toddling after him and shut the door on his way out without her becoming disappointed. Nor can he simply disappear while Aurore is playing without her becoming disappointed once she finds out he's gone. And he certainly can't forget to turn around and wave to her, whether or not he can see her or even see the window.

So many unthinking adults disappoint so many young children on so many occasions. A good rule is to always adopt a wait-and-see attitude until you know exactly what the child's frame of mind is.

Little Julia, one year old, has taken a piece of bread from the breadbasket. The family is sitting at the table and Grandpa is over for dinner. Now Julia takes another piece of bread. Her mother interrupts this little enterprise and puts back the piece of bread and says, "Julia has already has a piece of bread. Eat it first." – whereupon Julia starts crying in despair.

Her mother has jumped to conclusions. The next time Julia is offered the breadbasket, it becomes apparent that Julia wasn't going to take another piece of bread for herself, but was going to offer one to Grandpa who hadn't gotten any. Julia was making a gesture of affectionate generosity – which was misunderstood. Julia felt misunderstood to the depths of her soul with the result that her trust in her surroundings was a little bit eroded.

The keyword is respect. The path to respect is empathy.

Anton, eight months, with no small amount of effort, has managed to raise himself against his dad's legs. Dad is standing at the kitchen counter rinsing salad greens. Anton is standing straight, but he still isn't satisfied. Dad assumes that he wants up onto the counter. He probably wants to see what Dad is doing. Perhaps Anton thinks it's time for a little social participation/work? Anton's dad lifts him up onto the counter and gives him a lettuce leaf. He puts his hand over Anton's and shows him how to rinse the leaf under the tap. But Anton doesn't think it's much fun. He's still not satisfied. He stretches his arms out to Dad as though he wants down. Dad is wondering what Anton wants, and only Anton can tell him. So he lifts him down and then sits on the floor beside him and simply waits. Then Anton snuggles up to his father and sits between his legs with his back to him. Nothing happens for a long while. "What did you want?" his dad asks tenderly. Still no response. Finally, Anton crawls away, his usual affable self again.

What Anton was looking for was confirmation of his belonging. He returned to his dad – his fixed point, his operational base – and took a little time out. He was tired. He had worked hard, researched assiduously, borne several disappointments, none of which were serious but that weighed him down nonetheless. He wanted to have a little peace and a rest from his labors, but that didn't mean that there was anything necessarily wrong.

A stressed father could easily have become irritated and rushed off in search of a toy. Anton's dad took the time to try and understand.

3. Function as a tool and a guide

For all that your little crawler doesn't know about the world, there is one thing he does know. You have the abilities that he lacks. For one thing, you are tall and can reach everything. For another, you are strong and you can lift everything. And last but not least, you are familiar with all the peculiar contradictions in this bizarre world, and you know everything.

As a tool you extend the child's physical abilities. You have long arms and legs. You can lift him up so he can see and touch. You possess digital dexterity. You can open doors and drawers. You can unlock and extract. You are also an essential tool during the child's sojourns out of doors (and of course during social participation). He needs you to get outside, and outside there are stone steps and grass, gravel paths and sandboxes. He needs you to push him on the swing.

Your child will use you because you're there and you're willing. It is difficult, not to say impossible, to convince a crawler that a tool as versatile as you doesn't always want to do the things you can. Whatever you *can* do, of course you *do* do, reads the little crawler's resolute attitude towards life.

Being a guide to a young child is like being a guide to anyone else. A guide (let's say it's a man) whose task is to show people around a church doesn't stand outside and haul people in off the street. He waits until the tourists come in and show some interest. Then he takes them around.

If the tourist asks for detailed information about a particular triptych or painting, he answers the tourist's questions as best he can. A guide makes himself available, but he doesn't force information on people. He only informs and demonstrates if he is asked to.

And naturally he doesn't force himself personally on visitors to the church. He knows that it's the church that draws the tourists, not him.

A father takes his son, Fredrick, thirteen months, to the playground. He carries him in his arms and demonstrates the swing. Does Fredrick show any interest? Definitely.

Now Fredrick's dad morphs from guide into tool and puts Fredrick in the swing. Then the guide takes over and shows Fredrick what to do. "Hold tight!" says the guide. Dad slips back into tool mode and starts to push the swing.

You, the adult, are now being put to work as a guide and tool within the community in which the child is now taking an active part. Just as the guide in the church knows that the tourist is there to learn about the church, not the individual who is showing him around it, you are aware that in this particular context your person is hardly a priority for your child. You are, however, indispensable as a tool and a guide.

A friend of mine who desperately wanted children once asked me up to what age can you treat a young child like a pet. I couldn't help laughing, but he was dead serious. If by pet, he meant cuddle with, play with, enjoy, even seek comfort in, I would say the proverbial line in the sand is drawn when the child starts to crawl. Thereafter, expressions of love will take place under conditions set by the child. Any pushiness on your part can be distressing for a child this age, even if it's naturally not always the case.

From now on, it will be the child who terminates your tender expressions of love – not you. The time when your child was an infant and would simply lie there passively and eagerly accept all the love and attention you could throw at him is long gone. So, once your children begin to crawl, they can no longer be treated like pets...

In a time of frenetic demands for love, where smothering children with affection is a popular adult leisure activity to compensate children for never being included in anything that smacks of social participation (see "Psychological well-being" in Part two of *For the Love of Children*), it may be liberating for parents who have a tendency towards guilt complexes to remember that the crawler is not really into deep, meaningful relationships, but is an insatiable little materialist who always wants to be doing things, and who would quite happily swap his progenitors for a used cash register that rang every time he pressed the right key and the drawer opened.

To sum up:
• Never hinder a crawler unless mortal danger threatens!
• If there is a risk that something might break, place your hand over the child's and demonstrate the right way to handle the object in question.
• If something does get broken, react as though it was an accident. Inanimate objects have a life of their own.

A crawler who is allowed to conduct research under such favorable conditions is fit to keep company within a furnished room – and in the most Baroque of salons. One is treated to any number of captivating sights. Fourteen-month-olds who can barely walk will handle Grandma's fragile antique porcelain coffee cup and the equally fragile antique porcelain saucer with the utmost care instead of smashing everything to bits with a flick of their wrists. They will gently stroke a cat over its back instead of pulling its tail or ears. They will approach an elaborate flower arrangement in a crystal vase and draw in its fragrance with a delicacy and grace that verges on the ethereal instead of lunging for the most beautiful flower and sending all that meticulously created splendor crashing to the floor.

So, always treat a young child with trust and respect! What goes around comes around.

EIGHT AND NINE MONTHS

EIGHT-MONTH ANXIETY. BORN TO THE SELF

At around eight or nine months, the child changes. Sometimes this change is not particularly striking; often it's very dramatic.

Psychologists call it separation anxiety.

Parents can tell tales of eight and nine-month-old children who burst into tears at the sight of someone they merrily babbled to only a couple of days previously. Parents can also attest to children who had always preferred to be comforted by their mothers if they had hurt themselves or were disappointed, but who now stretch out their arms to Dad, even when they are securely ensconced on Mom's lap – which of course wounds and worries any mother.

Parents have described physical symptoms: trembling, strange rashes, violent movements at regular intervals – the sight of a child banging his or her head against the crib or the wall can be terrifying – all of which are expressions of anxiety. Sudden physical fragility that manifests itself in fevers, cramps, vomiting etc. is also characteristic of this age. (A child with a high fever should always be kept cool. He should be lightly dressed without even a blanket. Massaging with hands that have been held under the cold tap for a while usually cures fever cramps.)

Parents have also told horror stories about children who, after sleeping soundly through the night for months, suddenly start to wake up, cry, fuss, and generally show signs of distress night after night. Nights become disrupted and increasingly difficult to cope with.

According to my theory of repeated pregnancy, there is another birth at eight to nine months of age – not a physical birth, but a psychological one. The physical birth, when the child had to confront the world, was a painful, disorienting traumatic transformation. The psychological birth, when the child has to confront itself, is no less dramatic. Something irrevocable happens. The Self is born, and the world is changed forever.

The child is no longer a part of the space that surrounds him and with which he has become familiar. The child now stands as a separate entity in that space and directs his gaze towards it and towards his own newly acquired self. This gives rise to agonizing uncertainty – as facing the unknown always does.

The change can be compared to that which a new mother experiences. The newborn baby is suddenly there, living and visible, outside the womb. The child is no longer a part of the mother's body.

The new mother of course was able to grasp intellectually that the child within her had a life of its own, but until this child was born, it was a part of her. Her reaction to this change is multifaceted and complex. She also sees herself through new eyes. The reactions of a child who suddenly becomes an entity separate from its surroundings at eight or nine months of age are comparable to those a mother experiences when the child in her womb becomes an entity separate from her.

A new mother's reactions are many and varied. So are a child's. The entire range of emotions and behavior is represented. One new mother might feel nothing but joy, pure and simple. She experiences the new life she holds in her arms as the most natural thing in the world and she is untroubled by the transformation in herself. Another mother might find her new baby utterly alien and might feel an impulse to injure or even kill her child – an impulse that is as common as it is agonizing and terrifying for those who experience it.

When faced with profound change, children are as unpredictable as new mothers. Many children show no signs of eight-month anxiety, but some go to the other extreme.

Just as the people who are close to a woman who has just given birth understand that she needs attention, care and consideration – regardless of whether or not she asks for it – you as a mother or father must pay heed to the inescapable fact that your child of eight or nine months has been reborn with a "self". Even if this "birth" is not announced by a choir of angels, it still requires a response. An eight to nine-month-old is unstable, just as a new mother is unstable, and just because this instability is neither noticeable nor particularly painful, that doesn't mean it's not there.

People experiencing great change need peace, quiet, consideration and patience. An eight to nine-month-old child, however loving, harmonious and sociable he was at six to seven months, who suddenly begins to fuss in every conceivable way is reacting to a change that is just as radical as a woman's delivery. This might be a comforting thought if you find the changes in your child frightening.

Instability appears suddenly, as it does in a new mother. It might have already been there – as it might be in a pregnant woman – but it manifested itself differently. It will be followed by balance and stability – just as a new mother radiates calm assurance once she has reconciled herself to her altered station in life. And just like a new mother, a child who has been reborn with a "self" is sensitive to stress and any demand that is out of the ordinary. Eight to nine months is not the time to place demands and expectations on your child.

If, for example, Grandma comes over and stretches out her arms towards a child who is perched on his dad's arm, and he starts to cry and buries his face in Dad's shirt, Dad should give him his loving protection. Grandma's feelings will be hurt, but it can't be helped. Dad might actually be doing both Grandma and the baby a favor if he scheduled social events with relatives to the time before and after this period, which is relatively brief (usually about a month).

Needless to say, this is the worst possible time to move the child to a new environment. If children and their developmental needs were the decisive factors rather than ideological and economic considerations, no one would dream of placing a child of eight to nine months in day care – which was quite common in Sweden until relatively recently (and still is in some parts of the Western world). Placing a child this age in day care is on par with moving a woman fresh from the delivery room into a new home and foisting a new husband on her.

To be reborn with a self is to become conscious of one's separateness. I am someone. Dad is someone else, and Mom is someone else. I am a person. Mom and Dad are other people. I am not like them. I am like me, unique. My hands, my arms, my legs, my mouth, my knees, my body, my sensations and perceptions, all my tools, belongings and means to live, all this combines to form "I". This "I" signifies a human being: "I" the person. I think. I feel. I am.

What does the child do with this knowledge? He severs himself from the rest of the world. He is irrevocably detached. He is in the world, but as an "I", not as a part.

When a woman gives birth, her child is no longer a part of her. The baby lies beside her, the umbilical cord cut. The baby is of her, as it was before the birth, but it is no longer in her. The eight-month-old still belongs to his surroundings, his home, his mother, his father, his flock, but he is no longer a part of all these things. He is present but detached.

A new mother feels joy over her child, but she also feels emptiness. She can no longer feel the baby kicking, the familiar is now unfamiliar, her womb is silent, her body is mute. Instead, there is a child. New mothers unanimously bear witness to the fact that it takes time before they can wrap their minds around a change that is so basic yet so subtle, so simple yet so complex, so in-your-face yet so elusive. Making sense of it all can take days, weeks, or even months.

A child needs time to grasp and adjust to the change that occurs when the Self is born. A sense of unreality, and a vague feeling of emptiness and loss afflict the child as intensely as the new mother. But unlike the new mother, a child does not have a fully developed intellect to fall back on. A baby can't reason and say to itself, "My Self has been born. That is why I feel so strange. Soon I will feel better. All the other babies who have suddenly acquired Selves tell me so." Women, however, can reason. "I have had a baby. That's why I feel strange. I'll get used to it."

In the absence of intellect and the common sense born of experience, children this age very easily become frightened. There is simply nothing in their experience to use as a basis for comparison.

This fear can find its expression in any number of ways. What was once familiar can, at certain times and under certain conditions, become terrifying for the child. It might be anything: mother's laugh, father's beard, the sound from a music box, a much loved teddy bear... and, not least, the child's own sense of self. The sense of self can become odious precisely because it is an unknown entity.

Eight to nine-month-old babies can exhibit behavior that is mildly or extremely aggressive. Masochistic rituals are not unusual. Children this age sometimes bang their heads against the wall rhythmically and so frighteningly hard that you have to put your hand in between wall and child to cushion the blows. Some children bang their heads against the crib slats and wake themselves up, and then get upset because they're awake. Crib padding may be required.

The child's environment may cause him to explode. The Self has been born and the environment is thereby changed. The child feels compelled to defend himself not only by withdrawing but also by fighting. An apparently sweet-natured little soul, who is compliantly lying on his change table, can, after a dry diaper and a kiss, suddenly take it into his head to punch his loving parent in the face with astonishing force. No remorse should be expected either. The aggressive outbursts are as stress relieving as the masochistic rituals.

You will be able to detect a triumphant gleam in your child's eye when the worm turns and he takes charge of his unknown self and in so doing takes charge of his environment. "It's me against you. I can hit you. I am master of myself now, and I have power!" (Rending of hair and gnashing of teeth serve no good purpose, even though a punch in the face is painful in more ways than one. Gently grasp the tiny hands and hold them down, kiss your child as you had originally intended and generally try to project an understanding that you don't feel.)

For a child who has given birth to the Self, understanding from the people around him is far more beneficial than condemnation. Dismay would be catastrophic – just as it would be for a new mother. No one has to bow and scrape, but in difficult times, the child, as well as the new mother, needs to be able to count on support from a non-judgemental environment.

A few final words to sum up:
- Don't interpret unexpected changes and problems that seem to come out of nowhere as indications that something is seriously wrong. Watch and wait. Remember the symptoms can also be physical. The eight-month anxiety will diminish and disappear after approximately one month. Soon the child will be on his way to becoming a tough little one-year-old who likes himself, even if he still isn't sure exactly who this new found "self" is.
- Nights that have been peacefully somnolent can become wakeful. Your rule of thumb should be: once is a coincidence, twice is a habit. Leave the door ajar and speak reassuringly from outside the child's room. "Now it's time to sleep. Everything is fine. I'll see you in the morning." Leave a light on outside the child's room, but don't go inside. Don't give your child a pacifier, and don't pick him up. (See "Problems? Sleep" in Part five in *For the Love of Children*.)
- A fear of strangers is often very pronounced. Respect it! Children this age will in no way be negatively affected by not associating with adults (or other children). Don't fall prey to fear mongering by the people around you. "He has to be around other people, or he'll be scared of them for the rest of his life!" No, he absolutely will not. Your child is experiencing no small amount of internal turbulence. Try to make his external environment as placidly familiar as possible.
- Swallow your pride if and when your child prefers someone else over you. You can be rejected in ways that will cut you to the quick. Give your child a hug or a kiss all the same to show him he can count on you and your love, but don't make an issue out of the rejection. Wait for better times. A new mother can harbor feelings of both love and hate, and wish both life and death on her baby. Such contradictory feelings plague a child who has given birth to a self.
- Don't be afraid if your child becomes aggressive. A child must be allowed to react to a change that is this terrifying. But don't let your child

hit you, or anyone else for that matter. Violence and destructive tendencies must be fought with love. Take the little hands that are hitting and make them stroke instead, or gently hold them down and kiss and stroke your child. Calmly and clearly show him you love him no matter what, and then leave him in peace. Stop your child from hurting himself. If he's banging his head against the sides of his crib, don't skimp on the padding, but don't try to stop the banging itself.

• Abandon any plans you might have to introduce new people or new environments into the child's life during this period. Find other less traumatic solutions. Your highest priority should be the maintenance of a peaceful, stable external environment in order to offset the brutally chaotic internal environment that your child is coping with.

• Treat your child as you always have – don't express disapproval, but don't smother him with sympathy either. Don't try to "comfort" him. Treat your child the way you would treat a new mother. A new mother needs attention but not pity. The people around her should be prepared to ensure the demands placed on her are kept to a minimum, but they shouldn't declare her mentally incompetent. Just like the new mother, a child who has given birth to a self benefits most from a familiar and fairly simple daily routine and an environment that offers affectionate support and peace, not aggravation.

What psychologists call separation anxiety is, in my opinion, the reaction on the part of the child to the birth of its self out of the old and familiar, where the child was a part of an enveloping whole, just as he was a part of the mother's body when he was in the womb.

I don't think the child's psychological fragility has its origins in a fear of losing his mother any more than a new mother's psychological fragility has its origins in a fear of losing her newborn child.

MARRY YOUR CHILD OR PREPARE THE CHILD FOR A LIFE WITHOUT YOU?
The title is hardly realistic. Nobody (one hopes) has any desire to marry his or her children. In spite of changes in the definition of marriage in re-

cent years, marrying one's child isn't going to be legal any time soon.

What I'm trying to highlight is an emotional bond that in some respects can be compared to the bond that unites two people in a marriage. This is not so much about love in and of itself. Love is of paramount importance. Without love, human beings are poorly prepared for life, and the lives they do have are impoverished. It's more the *kind* of love you show a child. Now that your child's first year of life is drawing to a close, you should ask yourself what path you, as parent and caregiver, are going to choose. Are you going to "marry" your child in the sense of "Till death do us part" – or are you going to *prepare your child for a life without you?*

Contemporary society has been thrown off balance. Like everyone else who doesn't produce anything of tangible economic value by the end of every financial quarter, children are superfluous.

Once upon a time children were put to work in their communities – they still are in many parts of the world – not to socialize them or to give them a "good" upbringing, but because their contributions to the collective struggle for survival were necessary. Naturally, no one wants to reintroduce child labor. Not that long ago Swedish children suffered appalling privation and hardship, and many were literally worked to death. It's no exaggeration to say that the road to the modern welfare state is strewn with their bodies.

Nonetheless, in spite of all the suffering, all the grinding poverty, all the backbreaking labor, these children would have been aware of one thing: They were needed. They were useful. Whatever other torments they had to endure, a sense of being superfluous was not one of them.

We have tried to gloss over the fact that children are no longer needed by virtually suffocating them with love, sensitivity and trainloads of material goods. This, so the theory went, would result in a happy and carefree childhood. As we all know, things didn't exactly work out as planned.

The twentieth century, which was supposed to have been the century of the child, instead put a meaningful life, in the sense that one's contributions mean something to other people (*The others wouldn't manage as well without me*), out of reach for children. Hopefully, we in the Western world are beginning to realize that we have to find a middle road. Children need to be needed, just as every human being needs to know on some level that she or he has a task to perform that will benefit others in the collective struggle for survival. If this doesn't happen, children – all the love, attention, money, and material goods notwithstanding – will experience life as more or less meaningless.

What *For the Love of Children* tries to show is how, with a very modest investment, we all can instil in children from infancy and on the knowledge that they are needed. Unfortunately, in our time and culture, where work and family life have been separated, the social context within which this will take place must be built from the ground up. Not everyone has a family business, or a farm, or some form of self-employment where a child can be offered a place and put to work in a natural – necessary – way.

We have a very different family structure to contend with. The number of only children is increasing, as is the number of single parents. More and more families consist of one parent and one child. An overly intense – not to say unhealthy – emotional bond between parent and child is a distinct possibility, and that is what I was trying to draw attention to with my somewhat outlandish title for this chapter.

As our society changed, the family became an emotional hothouse. An ideology of the family evolved. If children were not needed in a concrete, practical way, all the more reason to need them emotionally.

Children were to be made privy to all the adults' problems. At a very early stage, children would, for example, be made aware of the family's economic situation. Family meetings would be held at which revenues and expenditures would be discussed, and the children's opinions would be as highly valued as those of the adults. Children would also participate in important decisions such as moves, divorce, the purchase of capital goods, the creation of siblings, vacations, leisure activities and daily consumption.

The parents' anxieties and problems as well as the children's would be aired in public, and the parents would stand humbly before their children as flawed human beings of flesh and blood, rather than infallible authority figures. (Actually, authority was to be written out of the equation completely.)

Naturally, parents would tolerate – even support and encourage – their children expressing opinions about the parents' friends and acquaintances. There are a lot of single mothers out there who have had their lovers and boyfriends trashed by jealous little kids who behave like dictators.

I once witnessed a telling scene on a train. A mother and her son, who would have been about seven, were sitting opposite each other beside the window. After a while, an older gentleman got on the train and sat down beside the boy's mother. An innocent conversation about the weather ensued. Suddenly, the boy burst out, "I don't want him sitting beside you! Tell him to go away!"

The mother was confused, but she "respected" her son's point of view. She apologetically asked the man to move. And he did, probably too astonished to refuse (which he could have done through his actions by calmly remaining where he was).

The spirit of these strange, emotionally overheated times, where logic and proportion have gone out the window, has paralyzed parents. (There are exceptions to prove every rule of course.) The cardinal sin is to say NO.

If you tell off an innocent child, whose only job in life is to be happy, you're a sadist. And if you forbid or force a child to do something, not only are you a sadist, but a fascist too.

Absolute authority is of course nothing to be desired. Authority without responsibility or accountability requires blind obedience, and children aren't that stupid. They refuse, they protest, they revolt. Good child rearing can only take place in an atmosphere of trust.

Children are more outspoken than they used to be, and they question more than they used to. That's good. But when parents renounce absolute authority to free children from a subordination that is purely arbitrary, they should present themselves as human beings worthy of respect because they are possessed of a wealth of life experience, not as insecure, ignorant, confused little kids themselves.

They should respect their children's opinions, but they should not place what are after all parental responsibilities on their children's shoulders.

They should offer their children friendship and trust, but they should not use them as problem solvers, confidantes, or emotional punching bags. Those are roles reserved for other adults.

Parents should see their children as human beings, but at the end of the day, they are children not spouses.

What we are really doing in this day and age is robbing children of their childhood.

At one, they are to be called pupils and placed in "pre-schools" and learn the law of the jungle.

At two, they are to take responsibility for choosing their clothing. "Do you want the blue or the red socks?"

At three, they are to take responsibility for their daily routines.

At four, they can decide whether or not they want any siblings.

At five, they are placed in charge of their leisure activities.

At six, they can decide whether they want to live with mother or father.

At seven, they are to take responsibility for the family finances.

At eight, for the parents' private lives.

At nine, for the family's leisure activities.

At ten, for their circle of friends and whose houses they sleep over at.

At eleven, for their evening entertainment.

At twelve, for their alcohol consumption.

At thirteen, for their sexual debut…

A fifteen-year-old that I knew derailed her family's trip to the USA, for which her parents had been saving for three years. They had rented a house and planned to tour towns originally colonized by Swedes for a couple of months. The fifteen-year-old didn't think she could be away from her friends for that long. If there was going to be any travelling at all, it would be a short trip to California. The result was that the trip of a lifetime was down the tubes.

The moral of the story is this: The fifteen-year-old didn't torpedo the trip for the rest of the family because she was mean, but because she lacked the experience that would have told her that a trip abroad does far more to enrich a young woman's life and broaden her horizons than hanging around with a bunch of people she has known all her life. Thus, she did not understand what she and the rest of the family were missing. The bitter realization would probably have set in at some point, but twenty-twenty hindsight is cold comfort…

Can we expect a fifteen-year-old to have the experience to make a good decision in such a situation? If not, where is she going to acquire it? From her friends? People who are as inexperienced as she is?

Should the parents have forced her to come with them? Would that have been the right thing to do? Or would it have been authoritarian? Or would it have been both?

How should the mother on the train have reacted? What do you think?

Good upbringing is based on trust. The child must be able to rely on the parents and the flock having the desire and the ability to act in his best interest. The child must be able to rely not only on the parents' willing-ness to shoulder responsibility, but also on their judgement, judgement that is rooted in experience.

Every child comes into the world with a built-in ability to trust. It doesn't have to be established. It's just there. You affirm and strengthen this trust by never giving your child reason to doubt your judgement or your ability. At the end of the day, it's about your ability to survive, which requires you to cooperate with others. Your job is to instil this ability in your offspring so that your children will one day master the art of survival and be able to function effectively independently of you and the flock.

If you want to appear as a person of sound judgement in the eyes of your child, you should be very careful about conveying the impression that you are a little boy or little girl lost in the forest yourself. Think very carefully before you set up a sham democracy that gives the child the idea that you really have no idea what you're doing.

We drew a parallel between a young child's introduction to the adult world and a new employee's orientation in the work place (see "Five and six months"). Every enterprise demands leadership. This of course does not preclude respect for the opinions of the employees, cooperation or team spirit – quite the contrary. But all these things are the product of trust.

A competent manager has good judgement, which in turn is based on extensive knowledge. Such a manager is respected for the simple reason that she (or he) has respect for herself as well as other people.

If, however, she were to admit in front of all her employees that she had no idea how the company should be run and on top of that pour her heart out about all her personal problems, some employees might feel sympathy, but a fair number would feel contempt. She would be vulnerable to manipulation by unscrupulous subordinates.

Let's face it, people aren't saints, and the desire for power corrupts. A kid who takes over his mother's life is no more fun to be around than a new employee who declares the manager unfit to lead. The manager becomes an object of ridicule, the mother an object of pity.

Even if you, as a mother or father, have no idea how to run your life, you must behave as though you do in front of your child. You have to be able to answer your child's questions, give explanations, and justify yourself. Don't apologize for your decisions, don't be constantly changing your mind, and never ask your child for advice – at least not until your children have the experience and maturity to view you as a human being rather than a parent. This maturation process takes many years. Only then can you drop the façade.

We can continue our workplace analogy. It's only when our new employee has acquired sufficient knowledge, maturity and insight into the manager's duties, working conditions and responsibilities that he (or she) can criticize her and question her methods in a constructive way, while retaining respect for her as a supervisor and understanding for her as a fellow human being.

Naturally, children seek to liberate themselves from their parents, but this liberation process should not manifest itself as condemnation or contempt. Condescension has never improved anyone's character or provided any useful experience. Genuine respect has nothing to do with arbitrary authority. Arbitrary authority has never elicited anything except fear. Genuine respect is humble, insightful and empathetic.

No parents ever won respect by banging their fists on the table and yelling "Do what you're told!" Parents win respect by living their lives the way they think their lives ought to be lived even when it costs them dearly. To live such a life, you have to know what you are doing and why you are doing it. If you don't know what you are doing or why you are doing it, you will inevitably sail into very troubled waters.

It has always been my view that parents should give their children the illusion that they do know what they are doing and why – just as they should give young children, who actually aren't needed in the struggle for survival, the illusion that they are, even if it means constructing the illusion from the ground up.

Society has changed in a third way. The world of adults and the world of children have been separated. The vast majority of parents with very young children in Sweden work full-time outside the home. The children are deposited in day care and looked after by municipal employees or by some other third party by private arrangement. Parent-child time is scarce, and the demand for love great.

This is both positive and negative. The separation during the day results in a mutually joyful reunion in the evening, and this is tremendously satisfying for both parent and child – hopefully. Unfortunately, the leisure time available to compensate for the daily life that never was offers little room for upbringing or social participation – or indeed for those things, positive and negative, that occasionally transpire between adults and which are none of the child's business.

"We have so little time," says Alexander's mother. "What's the point in arguing with him? I just let him do what he wants."

And what does Alexander want? That his mother doesn't meet her boyfriend for one thing. Alexander and his mom have so little time together. And that she doesn't go out with her girlfriends. So little time. And that she doesn't read a book, watch TV, or soak in the bathtub. So little time.

Alexander has twigged to the fact that if he kicks up a fuss about something, his mother will be the first to blink, and this of course gives him power over her. Is this good or bad?

I would argue that it's bad because Alexander, who is after all just a little boy, lacks the wisdom and experience to handle power. Since it takes a steady hand to carry a full cup, he will very probably misuse it – with the result that he will, sooner or later, disrespect, belittle and eventually terrorize his mother.

He has also twigged to the fact that he doesn't have to overly exert himself to get what he wants – a misconception that will cost Alexander dearly when he discovers that this path called life is strewn with thorns as often as it is with roses.

But doesn't Alexander grow into the responsibility? No, he doesn't. In practice, all he does is take over his mother's life. He calls all the shots, but that is not the same as taking responsibility. The only thing growing is Alexander's megalomania. There are very few activities that his mother can engage in without Alexander expressing an opinion, an objection, or a prohibition. If she is weak, unwary, insecure, or simply lonely, she will fall into the role she is allowing him to assign her without so much as a murmur of protest.

In effect, she is "marrying" Alexander. She is developing a relationship with him that is not unlike that which pertains between husband and wife in marriages of the more toxic variety. The endless mind games between the weak and the strong, complete with silent treatments, tantrums, omnipresent disapproval expressed or implied, and constant wheedling demands soon become daily fare.

And what Alexander loses is his childhood. He loses the framework that his mother and his flock should have given him by providing confident guidance so that he can develop his personality, his thoughts and feelings, his hopes and dreams, his games and fantasies. Instead, he is burdened with his mother's problems without having to assume responsibility for her life.

Back to the title! Preparing a child for life – what does that mean?

It means never losing sight of the fact that one day your child will leave the flock for the outside world, and to act accordingly.

This means your task as a parent is to prepare your child for a life without you.

Your relationship with your spouse is hopefully forever – "to have and to hold in sickness and in health till death us do part." Your relationship with your child is quite different – "You and I will be together until you can manage on your own, and I will help you prepare for that day as best I can."

I am your leader, your guide, and your contact man. I have the knowledge and the experience. I have been a child and I have been an adult. I have survived. I get by because I know the rules of the game, and I know where the rattlesnakes are. With all this knowledge, experience and ability, I will guide and protect you until you can stand on your own two feet. Then you will leave me and move on to bigger and better things. I am not married to you. It's not your job to make me happy. Your job is to discover, master and eventually change your conditions, your reality, your world. My overriding goal is to make sure you have the skill, strength, and free-thinking independence to do all that – without me.

What you as a parent have to do is scrutinize your own motives. And that's not always easy. The most wonderful thing in the world is having a trusting little person at your side who loves you.

But it takes steady nerves, courage and foresight – and perhaps even pain – to differentiate between love that promotes freedom and love that encourages dependency.

Far too many parents try to keep their kids at home for far too long, and some want them to stay forever. "Children" today live at home until they are twenty-five and thirty, and when the "divorce" comes, it is as painful and protracted as its marital counterpart. Some parents speak of an emotional void as devastating as that created by a death in the family. Therapy and Prozac are commonly prescribed. Instead of booting their kids out the door and forcing them to move, parents who have "married" their children keep their offspring in the nest for as long as they possibly can. This can result in the kid being incapable of moving out of the parental abode even when he or she tries.

So what do we have kids for? To marry them or prepare them for life?

A child shows tendencies towards independence from the tender age of six months. He strives for the kind of freedom that is not dependent. This striving for independence results in the birth of the "self" a couple of months later (see the previous chapter). A child separates himself from the surroundings of which he has hitherto been a part. He still belongs, but as his Self. A few months further down the road, this self, which at first was an unknown, rather frightening entity that sometimes made everything else frightening, has been transformed into an asset, a source of growth and enrichment, just as parenthood is a source of growth and enrichment for adults.

And here we come to the proverbial fork in the road. If you have ever heard yourself say, "Mommy's here. Everything will be OK now!" you should rein yourself in and think very hard. Why not say/think instead, "Everything *is* OK. I'll just keep an eye on things."

What I am saying may seem contradictory. At the same time as I encourage support for a child's striving for freedom, I am absolutely opposed to placing children under the age of three in day care.

A common argument in favor of day care is that it helps the child separate from the parents. Wonderful! We park our children at a day care facility and thus avoid any unhealthy bonding, and the socialization process is taken over by the children's peers!

This argument simply doesn't fly. Children leave their relationship with their parents at home and go to day care without it. When they come home, everything goes on as it always has. Depending on – or blaming – arrangements outside the fixed point, which is the parents and home, the flock, is cheating. Only you can decide what kind of relationship you are going to have with your offspring. Are you going to "marry" your child, or prepare him for life?

Whether you have one hour or twelve hours a day to put your decision into practice doesn't matter much, as we saw with Alexander and this vexing problem of "too little time".

I fear that the current generation will have tremendous difficulties in understanding the meaning of the word *freedom* and in serving and acting for the freedom of others.

TOILET TRAINING?

From the time a child can sit up properly, toilet training becomes an issue.

Many parents toilet train their kids and do so successfully. I never have. Toilet training involves a certain risk. What I want to call your attention to are the unintended consequences, which of course are by no means the inevitable consequence of toilet training, any more than eating disorders necessarily follow because ambitious parents try to teach their children table manners at a very young age.

There is a risk that your child might get the idea that emptying bladder and bowels in the right place is important for *you*. Doing it in the wrong place, on the other hand, is a slap in the face for Mom and Dad, and the ability to slap their parents in the face is something that young children can and do put to good use on occasion. Young children who are ticked off about something will express their anger by peeing on the sofa or the carpet, just as an angry dog might.

There are other more serious aspects to all this which you might want to think about. If bodily functions become associated with expectations – "I hope something happens!" – your child will also place expectations on himself in this area. For something to happen, the machinery has to work, but in trying situations probably it won't.

Children's inner equilibrium is sometimes thrown off. Children sometimes have problems just like everyone else. It's inevitable. If bowel and bladder functions are not regarded as things that simply take care of themselves, but become associated with conscious expectation – "I can!" – they may well be thrown out of sync if a child's confidence or self-esteem is thrown out of sync. An anxious child can become constipated. A child who has never harbored any expectations about his bodily functions, however, even if he is upset about something, will likely have no digestive problems at all.

The same principle can be applied to food. If food has to be eaten in a certain way to satisfy you, Mother or Father, you have placed a weapon in your child's hands – and he will use it. Because of the expectations you have placed on your child, run-of-the-mill psychological stress can throw a spanner in his digestive works, and he may suddenly start to vomit, get stomach aches, have difficulty swallowing and become more prone to allergies.

Your goal should be to do everything in your power to encourage your child to express psychological pain directly by crying or protesting to your face, rather than taking detours via toilet training or food to make his point.

Human beings consume nourishment and the body disposes of the waste products; this should be the most natural thing in the world and not something to be directed or fretted over.

Will your child eventually be able to use the toilet if you do nothing? Of course. Human beings are hardly enamoured of their own waste products.

Children with no toilet training at all will no longer need diapers by the age of three. There are parents who have shown that it is possible to throw out the diapers when a baby is only a few weeks old. A newborn gives indications that something is about to happen, and some parents have learned how to interpret the signs. They then take down the baby's pants and hold him or her over a suitable spot. Reading these signs is not a craft that I have ever been engaged in.

Boys are toilet trained later than girls. This is true of development generally.

If you just let your child go solo on toilet training, one or several of the

following things will happen:
- He will refuse a diaper at around the age of two and will be clean and dry from then on.
- He will be dry during the night, but need a diaper during the day.
- He will by dry during the day, but need a diaper at night.
- He will announce that something is on the way – and so it was, already.
- He will show interest in the toilet, clamber up with the help of a stool a couple of times – then lose interest and continue wearing a diaper.

The variations are legion. All of them, however, are indications that the child has attained the physical and psychological maturity to control his bladder and bowel functions.

Curiously enough, today's expensive "underwear" diapers are so comfortable and thin, so incredibly absorbent that a fair number of children don't want to get out of diapers. They think they are being robbed of something pleasant instead of being liberated from something that is unpleasant.

What's important is that you keep your eyes peeled for signs that your child is ready to get out of diapers. Make it possible for him to take care of his own business! A kiddie stool by the toilet is a good idea as is a kiddie toilet ring to go with it. (Make sure you put the stool back in position and leave the ring on when you have used the toilet yourself.)

You can of course buy a potty and position it accessibly and present it to your child as a suitable place to offload whatever needs offloading. Place the potty in its appointed spot with the toilet paper beside it so that things are as "realistic" as possible.

If your child has been dry for five or six nights in a row, stop putting a night diaper on him without making a big deal out of it. "You probably don't need a diaper anymore," you can say with the stress on "probably". You don't want to burden the poor child with parental expectations.

Once you have dispensed with the night diaper (or the day diaper if you child is dry during the day), don't go back to it even if there are accidents. If you do, you are saying one of two things: "You couldn't handle it" or "I was wrong". Both messages are very risky.

Since I am less than enthusiastic about toilet training in general, it will come as no surprise that I strongly advise against using potties that come in the form of little chairs with belts. The child is parked on the chair and has to stay there until the desired result is achieved. This is inappropriate to say the least, and you are asking for trouble. The classic result is that the poor little mite sits patiently on the potty chair for an hour without anything happening. He is then released from his prison, and right on cue he pees – on the floor.

By the time your child can sit properly, if not before, bowel movements should be coming once a day at about the same time. Once regularity is established, you might want to make a point of being on hand with the potty at zero hour. Not to have to contend with soiled diapers is a relief for everyone, and this method works brilliantly for many families. Just don't make a big deal out of what happens (or doesn't happen). If your child gets wind of the fact that you care more about the results than he does, he will sense demands being placed upon him and that spells trouble.

The first time your child uses the potty is of course a milestone, and I'm not suggesting that you ignore what is for you and your child such an important event. His declaration in word or deed that he is bidding farewell to diapers should be accorded the appreciation it deserves. But show your appreciation in a way that makes it clear to the child that it is above all a question of practicality. "You peed in the potty! It's goodbye to the diaper!" Then throw the diaper away together.

The child is not being rewarded for performing well. He is not "clever" or "good". Emptying one's bladder or bowels is not clever. It's just necessary.

Accidents are to be expected, and this will cause your child some anxiety. Not a lot, but some. It's a sign of the child's innate desire to be clean, and is a further indication that human beings are clean animals.

Help your child bear the burden. "Oh-oh, is there pee in your pants? Isn't the pee silly. Let's get you a new pair of pants."

It's the pee that's at fault, not the child. Sharing the burden is far better than blowing it off with an "Oh, it doesn't matter". And anything that smacks of reproach is of course forbidden.

Even if you have allowed your child to toilet train himself, he may still react to stress by wetting his bed. He may also wet himself simply because the machinery isn't fully operational yet.

Some children who have been sleeping dry for some time can suddenly start wetting the bed every night, and this can go on for weeks or even months. Do not go back to the diaper. Once it's gone, it should stay gone. Instead, put a plastic tablecloth over the mattress, and cover it with a piece of terry towel and a regular bed sheet, and most important of all, make like the proverbial cracked record at bedtime. "We pee in the potty, not in the bed. We pee in the potty..." Make sure the "positive" potty, not the "negative" bed has the last word. Say it at the child's bedside two or three times in a neutral tone of voice, so that through mere repetition the message penetrates the child's subconscious and connects with whatever mechanism regulates the child's bladder and bowels. Make sure that the potty is easily accessible so that the child can use it during the night if he has to.

Diapers for children older than three are not recommended, since this may short circuit their built-in desire for cleanliness. A child this age in a diaper doesn't have to answer the call of nature, and the alarm system that controls bodily functions may deactivate.

By three at the latest, children with no formal toilet training at all will be dry and clean with few, if any, relapses. You should give everything a year to settle.

I was so paranoid about disturbing the natural process that I would pull down my kids' pants in the middle of the street rather than suggest a visit to the toilet before we went out...

Bedwetting among older children is a serious problem and difficult to fix. I lack the medical competence to go into this in any depth, and it falls outside the scope of this chapter anyway. That said, I feel qualified to give some advice in this area since I have been a bed wetter myself.

From what I have been able to gather, bedwetting in older children has its origins in a reaction to a past event or anxiety about a future one, or both. It becomes a habit, the dial that controls bladder functions is adjusted to the wrong setting, and everything is out of joint.

A little boy I knew fell out a window at the age of six, and his injuries were so serious they required a lengthy stay in hospital. He wet his bed for the next ten years.

My own son, who had been sleeping dry for a long time, wet his bed night after night before the journey from which he would not return alive.

I also know of a twelve-year-old who had wet the bed his whole life. His father lost patience and gave him a severe beating and threatened the boy with more of the same if didn't stop immediately. He stopped wetting the bed, but began to stutter to compensate.

I myself wet the bed when I was little and this continued until several years after I started school. I remember I would dream that I was going to the bathroom, and when I woke up and realized the dream had tricked me, I wept bitterly. The dream had seemed so real.

I felt profoundly ashamed. I don't remember my mother (for as long as she was around) or any of the other people I used to be parked with ever bawling me out for wetting the bed, but I felt ashamed anyway. I would get up and place a towel over the wet spot. If the towel was still there when I got home from school the next day, I felt a surge of relief. If it was gone and the sheet had been changed, I was so mortified I would become nauseous. I didn't want to put anyone to any trouble. I felt so unclean, and this feeling plagued me endlessly. I didn't want to feel dirty. Being dirty felt so unnatural, but I seemed powerless to do anything about it. It was a difficult time.

If I had a little – or a not so little – bed wetter, my primary goal would be to enable the child to do something about the problem so that others didn't have to concern themselves with it.

I would take a pragmatic approach. "This is what we will do – if you wet the bed." I would be business like and give clear instructions. "Put the wet sheet in the washing machine. I do a laundry every day. Then get a towel and a clean sheet, you know where they are, and make your bed. Does that sound reasonable?"

I would indicate that I fully realized that the problem was not much fun for the kid. But I would also point out that it's tough all over. I would tell the child about something bad that had happened to me. (Subtext: I know how you feel. Life is harsh. We just have to do our best and wait for better times.) I would emphasize that even though I had gone through hard times, I grew up and turned into a decent adult. Bad things happen, but they pass. I would not blow the problem off as though it were nothing, but I wouldn't turn it into a life-and-death issue either, and I would certainly not mention it to anyone else.

I would, however, kick up a fuss if the youngster did not look after the practical side of things as agreed, even though I was the one who suggested it. It's a household chore like any other, and it has to be done.

Hopefully, one day the child would come to view the problem as a purely practical matter and not a shameful personal failing. That might not solve the problem, but at least it would depersonalize it.

And I would also make a point of ensuring that the child got at least one good laugh a day, especially in the evenings.

ELEVEN MONTHS TO ONE YEAR

MAINTAINING GOOD HABITS

Little people on the verge of turning one are a delight to be around. As long as they don't have to listen to sob stories about how difficult they are and how their sensitive parents are being punished for sins committed in a past life, they are the best little buddies anyone could wish for.

Their personalities are blossoming. As they approach the end of their first year, little people are developing so intensely, the spectacle is as interesting for them as it is for those around them. They learn to crawl, stand and finally walk. Some kids limit the crawling stage to a minimum either because they are lazy or in a hurry, but all kids have to crawl (and develop depth perception among other things) before they can walk. Most develop their own special techniques for propelling themselves across the floor before taking those first decisive, if uncertain, steps. Little people like baby walkers – well worth introducing to kids who have made it plain that they plan on moving up in the world – and they shoot across rooms at breakneck speed displaying a familiarity with their vehicles that would be the envy of any professional driver. A baby walker race would be a world-class sporting event! (Do not overdo it, though. A baby walker is a toy, not a parking place. As crawling is so important at this stage, I would suggest a maximum of two twenty minute sessions in the baby walker each day.)

And they talk. Babies this age live a rich inner life, which manifests itself in imaginary telephone conversations and heated debates with teddy bears. They like themselves, as people of all ages should, and they talk about it. By the age of one, human beings have mastered approximately fifteen words, including their own names, although the way they pronounce their names is creative to say the least. *Hi, look, lamp, car* can be among the first words, before or after *mamma* and *dadda*.

Little people this age make fabulous family members. They stand tall and proud in the center of things exuding life. They are sociable, loving and industrious. They kiss, wave, love and work, all with the same soulful joy. They also begin to show impressive (and at times tedious) stamina at this age. A mother or father who politely offers a little social participation can have trouble understanding why one and the same fork has to be dipped into the water twenty times, slathered in dish detergent, scrubbed with a brush and then rinsed under the tap for twenty minutes before it can be considered properly washed. Children this age investigate the world, all things animate and inanimate, and are forever trying to deepen their knowledge. They will pull people's hair for example to see if hair is removable. Ditto for noses and teeth. Little babies and unsuspecting animals have to be discreetly rescued. Eleven-month-olds don't mean any harm. They're just exploring the world, and they are thrilled with the results. Many people can't say that about their lives.

Rarely are people as positive to change, innovation, and new discoveries as children who are about to turn one. Little people this age are constructive, creative and imaginative, and they will blossom even further over the year that is to come. Enjoy it while it lasts because soon enough it will be gone forever. Never again will your child be as open minded, unabashedly curious, or as suffused with such unadulterated joie de vivre as he is now.

One thing I would like to emphasize about the time that is to come is the maintenance of the good habits that your child has hopefully acquired. I'm thinking primarily about the routines:

• Night sleep – unbroken night sleep for a predetermined period lasting eleven, eleven and a half or twelve hours, which ever you think is appropriate, and regularly so.

• Meals – four meals a day at fixed times (approximately three and a half hours apart) and an evening snack or night cap.

• Solitary play of a predetermined duration that is long enough to include an optional morning nap. Solitary play can last as long as two hours after the age of one provided that the conditions are sufficiently inspiring. (See "Problems? Keeping busy" in Part five of *For the Love of Children*.)

• Midday nap – this depends on the length of the night sleep. A one-year old should sleep for thirteen to fourteen hours over any given twenty-four-hour period.

• Excursions out of doors – this should not be restricted to naps outside. Take your child outside when he is awake for at least one predetermined period each day.

• Social participation – in two predetermined contexts every day. When your child wants to do other things that don't fall within the parameters of the "work" program, that's fine.

• A good laugh before bed.

It's practical to draw up a schedule. Even if you are an experienced caregiver and have everything in your head, there is always the possibility that someone else might have to take over if you are away for a few hours or a few days. If you have something down on paper, life is less stressful for everyone. Anyone who has to spell you for whatever reason will know what needs to be done and won't constantly be second-guessing him/herself.

If your child stays at someone else's house for a day or more, write out a detailed schedule. It facilitates things tremendously – not least for the child who can still predict his day (and night). It will give him a great sense of security.

Let's look at each good habit on the list in a little more detail.

Night sleep

An unbroken night's sleep is a must. Not being able to sleep properly is as vexing for young children as it is for adults, but not getting enough sleep is way more dangerous for your child than it is for you. If your child is having trouble sleeping, learn to help him find the peace he needs! (See "Problems? Sleep" in Part five of *For the Love of Children*.)

Decide when you want the night to begin. There is absolutely no reason to "wind down" and wait until your child is keeling over from exhaustion. Some parents do this, but it drains any reserves the child might have. Imagine how you would feel if you put off going to bed until you were on the verge of fainting. You would not be able to cope with the odd late party night or emergency phone call at four in the morning. Young children who are put down to sleep while they are still more or less in the world of the living build up such reserves. They can be charming right up until midnight on the odd occasion if there is no way around it, and they won't be too tired the next day either. After an agreeable day and a merry bedtime routine – more about that below – don't be afraid to let your child lie awake until the Sandman comes for him. Leave him in peace! Generally speaking, parents would be well advised not to glue themselves to their kids when they are going to sleep. If parents give indications that they don't think that

333

a baby who will soon be one can go to sleep by himself, the child may get the idea that it is dangerous to sleep alone. If that happens, complications won't be long in coming.

Night sleep should end at the same time every morning. If you have taken on a leadership role as far as the routines are concerned (which I fervently hope you have), take charge in the mornings too. Your child is counting on it. As long as he knows on some level that there is someone looking out for his interests, he won't start the day by howling anxiously or frantically trying to scramble out of bed. (This will happen sooner or later, but the later the better; with improved motor skills, the child is far less likely to fall.) As long as he knows that you are on the job, he will calmly await food, a diaper change and some attention. This frame of mind – *someone is looking after my interests* – must not be placed at risk by waiting until your child starts to cry before you go into him in the morning. Then you are back where you started. Your child thinks he has to scream if he wants anything done, and you can kiss your hard won domestic tranquillity goodbye. If your child is an early bird, get yourself an alarm clock to avoid eroding the trust that has been built up.

Bear in mind that you don't have to take any special precautions when the child is asleep. Don't bang around on purpose, but there is no need to tiptoe around shushing everyone who speaks above a whisper. The business of the household should carry on as normal. Silence doesn't promote sound sleep any more than sound does.

Fresh air is to be desired however. Children, like adults, sleep better in cool rooms than in hot ones. By all means leave a window open all night as long as it doesn't mean exposing your child to bitter cold or gale force winds. In any event, your child's room should be allowed to air for a couple of hours after you put him down for the night.

Children who sleep in cool rooms don't kick the covers off.

Young children can wake up, as can adults, and we all dream. I think it's perfectly possible that children have bad dreams after peaceful, happy days more often than after difficult ones. It wouldn't surprise me to learn that human beings need their quota of misery! If they're happy during the day, they have to suffer a little adversity in their dreams – and vice versa. Whether that's science or not is of course highly debatable, but if a loving, harmonious, happy little eleven-month-old suddenly emits a heart-rending scream in the dead of night, it's only natural that you, his mother or father, should be terrified. When you rush in to comfort and soothe, keep in mind that there is no point in frightening the little lad even more – you are there to *calm* him. Keep your own fear under control! Remember those nights when you have sat bolt upright in bed with a pounding heart, only to lie down again and go back to sleep a couple of minutes later. Don't turn on the lights or start walking the floor with your child in your arms. Don't pour fuel on the fire! It may well be that he is not even awake.

A tender hug while the baby is still in bed, some kind words, a caress over the head, a kiss and a good tucking in, followed by some audible pottering around for a little while will help uneasy little dreamers back to sleep.

Meals

Food makes for contented little people. Children who are approaching the one-year mark have a salutary, uncomplicated relationship with food and eating that you can hitch a ride on. The simpler the better is their attitude.

Just bear in mind that their appetites decline significantly at around this time. Growth slows down. If it didn't, your child, with a birth weight of three kilos, would weigh 7,290 kilos by the time he was seven! A baby's weight trebles during the first year of life, which of course is unsustainable.

Portions should thus be smaller, and you should be cheap with "bribes", crisp bread, bananas, crackers, or whatever you have been giving him between meals. They are no longer as necessary as they once were because your child is bigger and has developed other interests that don't necessarily have anything to do with putting things in his mouth.

Don't give him water like there is no tomorrow either. It will make him feel full.

Stick to a simple menu, and do your best to de-dramatize mealtimes. If you serve elaborate meals with much pomp and circumstance and your child is less than appreciative of the trouble you go to, you wouldn't be human if you weren't disappointed. Keep everything simple for now and for a fairly long time to come. The thicker formula – for a recipe of homemade valling, go to the end of the chapter "A day with Sophie, four months" – in the mornings and evenings will be good enough for your child for the next few years. The bottle is practical. From one year onwards, you can give your child a bottle in his crib just before you say goodnight and just before solitary play. Just make sure that this formula or valling is sugar free.

Good old-fashioned oatmeal porridge, wholegrain cereals, or for that matter semolina, or rice pudding, without sugar but with milk and a dab of butter can be served every day for years to come. A little sandwich on the side – the filling may disappear but not the bread – and a little cup of fruit juice makes the meal a veritable orgy of nutrition.

In Sweden we give rosehip or blueberry soup in a bottle, which is greatly appreciated before or after the afternoon nap. A little plate of buttermilk with crushed crisp bread (without sugar) can be served instead, or yogurt with sugar-free cornflakes, pureed fruit, or sliced banana with milk. Whatever you choose can be served day after day – and in my opinion should be for the second and third years of life on a regular basis.

In my opinion, canned baby food or any other type of food specifically aimed at children should be dispensed with at around one year. From then on, the baby can take meals with the family and eat pretty much what he wants. You don't have to worry about nutrition. The baby's nutritional needs are taken care of with the base meals.

Solitary play

If you introduced solitary play from the beginning, it is now a firmly established institution and greatly appreciated by all concerned. That of course doesn't mean that it looks after itself. The conditions under which solitary play takes place must be exceptionally entertaining, so aim high! If you get lazy – which is easy to do when everything is running like clockwork – what took you months to build can disappear in a matter of days.

Solitary play is supposed to be an inspiring period of *undisturbed work* that challenges your child's tenacity and abilities, and provides a stimulating start to his day. It also allows for a nap if necessary. But if you notice that your child sleeps more than he works, plays or amuses himself, then ennui has crept into the picture and that was never the idea. The toys must be put away every day and presented anew the next morning. Your child should really use them and *want* to use them.

And when you put them away after solitary play, inspect them carefully. It's not solely a question of safety, although that of course is important. Ask yourself whether the toys are fun too. Are they whole and pretty to look at? Does the stock need replenishing? Has your child grown out of them? Is he bored with some of the toys? Is there anything that should be included in the stock but isn't?

A musical instrument of some kind should be included. As should a "secret bag" – always popular! Take an ordinary little bag made of paper or fabric and fill it with an assortment of small items that you can vary every day: dinky cars, a little box, an old pumice stone, a little measuring cup, some interesting pieces of fabric, a plastic clock, a couple of pieces of non-toxic chalk (unless you're worried about the wall), a children's card game, anything you can find in drawers and cupboards as long as they aren't too small. Close the bag so that effort and perseverance will be required to open it and place it in the bed with a secretive and enthusiastic expression on your face.

Before solitary play begins, be conscientious about marking the difference between night and day. Turn on the lights if necessary, pull the curtains, clear the bed of blankets and stuffed animals, and of course leave no stone unturned when you check for anything that might injure your child. Double check *everything*. Always wave and say a cheery goodbye.

You should not disturb your child until a predetermined period of time has elapsed (and at a point when the baby is *not* unhappy). If you hear indications of the common garden variety of disappointment, resist the temptation to get involved. The idea behind solitary play is to encourage the baby to overcome problems. Children this age should be allowed to react negatively when things don't go their way. And positively when they do.

If you really have to go into the child's room and intervene, procure something especially intriguing before you leave so that the baby doesn't think that your presence signals the end of solitary play and the beginning of the next program point. So don't show yourself unless you absolutely have to. You should position the bed so you can keep an eye on your child without being seen yourself. You will worry less and will have a ringside seat from which to study human behavior!

Let me repeat: solitary play is a resource for your child, not a form of banishment. The child gains something from solitary play, the caregiver is not relieved of a burden (i.e. the child). And as with everything else, solitary play ends at a moment when the child is content.

Midday nap

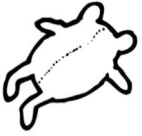

The midday or early afternoon nap is another habit that should be retained for a long time – preferably out of doors in all kinds of weather. Kids this age sometimes fall out of baby carriages so some kind of harness might be indicated. Failing that, just take the cot off the wheels and put it on the ground. Young children who take naps outside should always be positioned out of the wind and in the shade. In the summer, use a mosquito net, and of course keep a sharp eye on the little one.

Little thumb suckers have problems in winter. Cut the thumb off a mitten; the sacrifice is for a good cause! If the carriage basket is going to stand directly on snow or stone, newspapers make excellent insulation.

If you live in an apartment with a balcony, this is both a curse and a blessing. I once lived on the eighth floor of a high rise. I had decided that my ten-month-old would take her afternoon nap on the balcony. I had attached a six-foot-high length of steel mesh to the railing, so I felt secure. I put the carriage basket out on the balcony, waved good-bye to the baby and closed the balcony door. It was a cold winter's day, and there was snow on the balcony (and newspapers too of course). A few minutes later, when I looked out the balcony window, my little angel, clad in her winter zip suit, was sitting in the snow meditating intently. I was astonished. She hadn't fallen asleep! What would she do now? She sat where she was for a while. Eventually, when she was done with her quiet contemplations, she scrambled back into the carriage basket, lay down and went to sleep. Children *can*.

The midday (or afternoon) nap is a wonderful break. If you don't question it, neither will your child. There is no more reason to expect whiny, clingy over-tiredness at afternoon naptime than there is at night. Just let the baby drop off. *Fixed times lead to fixed habits.*

As in the morning after a good night's sleep, something fun should be scheduled for immediately after the afternoon nap – a joyful reunion with much fanfare and something to eat or something to do that is more or less the same each day.

Outings

Every single day, come rain or shine, the baby must get out of the house. The prospect may not always thrill you, but if you are cultivating routines for your baby's sake, you have to do your bit. An outing will be a shot in the arm for you too! (Never did I feel so guilty as on those few occasions when I didn't manage to get out of the house. I needed it as much as the baby.)

Before you set off, sit down and ask yourself whether you are going out with your baby or your baby is going out with you. Irritation is guaranteed if you think you can combine the two. Taking a toddler on an outing is like taking a puppy for a walk. Every bush, lamppost, flight of steps and pathway has to be investigated. The process takes its own sweet time. "Oh look, what a pretty lamppost… bye-bye lamppost!"

Everything has to be waved at. The world is full of friends. A walk of perhaps a hundred feet can take an hour. So, if you have an errand to run, take the baby out in the carriage or carry her. Up to the age of three, "Come on! We have to hurry!" is an exhortation that falls on deaf ears. If you try it on a one-year-old, you are wearing out your vocal cords for no good reason.

I have never used a harness when out for a walk with a one-year-old. Puppies have to be on a leash, but a one-year-old human will never leave you! Strollers I have always regarded as a means of transporting babies from A to B, not equipment you take on a walk. When young children are out for a walk with me, they *walk*. I am their companion and tool. If and when they see fit to use me, I am at their disposal.

So, take your child out for at least an hour and a half every day. And when I say out, I mean out as in *outside*. Stores and shopping malls don't count.

Social Participation

Social participation should also be a planned, recurrent activity. At least twice a day, you should allow your child to take part in something that could be described as work – something that is for the good of the other members of the family, the flock, not something that is connected to the child.

The older and more able your child becomes, the more he should be put to use and the less you should wait for him to take the initiative. If it's time to make dinner (for the flock, you *and* the child), put the baby on the kitchen counter and start working. *Whether* the child will take part in the process is your decision. *The form* of the contribution the child makes, within the framework of food preparation, is the child's.

Food preparation is a superb venue for social participation, which will pay huge dividends in the future. Your child will learn things that will stand him in good stead when he is older. But there are other forms of work. The most important thing is that the activities you choose as contexts for social participation are activities that recur day after day and that are *necessary* for you, the flock.

Your child will also want to participate in essential activities that fall outside the program so to speak. When this happens, all you have to do is welcome the child's input and go with the flow. He may want to turn the page of the newspaper you are reading ("Thank you!"), or fetch you your shoes one at a time, or pick up a letter you have dropped on the floor in the hall ("Where can that letter be! I can't find it anywhere! Oh, you've found it! Thank you so much!").

After every contribution the child makes that benefits *you* (the flock), he will take himself a well-earned rest, and a period of peace and contentment will ensue.

Laughter

A goodnight laugh is indeed a blessing. Happy little people sleep well. And it doesn't take much to make them crack a smile. Tickling, funny faces, hiding behind a curtain, pretending to trip, butting heads with a teddy bear are all things that kids this age find hugely amusing. A laugh a day keeps the doctor away and inoculates children against most of life's cares.

Laughter isn't just pleasant. It's necessary. Laughter is a wonderful way to end the day and the harbinger of a good night's sleep.

A few tips on daily dealings with your little comedian:

• Changing diapers on a frisky eleven-month-old, as you have no doubt noticed, is a bit like trying to straighten out an eel. Don't underestimate the power of bribery! An apple to gnaw on or an interesting object to twist and turn will prevent the little angel from twisting and turning himself.

• Children who have just mastered the art of crawling or who have just learned to walk have a habit of suddenly disappearing on you when you are trying to dress them. You then have to chase them all over the house brandishing their clothes, your exhortations to stand still punctuated by less than appropriate language. To save yourself all this anguish, put the child up on something high such as a chest of drawers or a dauntingly high bench and dress him there.

• When he grabs your hair – a throw back to our monkey days probably – resist the temptation to tug at the little arms and hands. Gently pry his fingers open instead.

Let's get back to the routines. The routines provide a skeleton plan for daily life. They give the day structure. You know – *and your child knows* – when the day begins, when it ends, and what happens in between.

Perhaps only people who have experienced daily life *without* structure with a one-year-old can fully grasp how much easier everything gets if the day is predictable. Allowing a young child to freely explore the world may seem like a full-time job, but the routines provide a framework.

If, for example, you know that the midday nap comes one and a half hours after the porridge meal, you can give your child all the freedom in the world for the one hour between the end of the meal and the beginning of the nap. You serenely put yourself at your child's disposal and function as tool, guide and ability extension. You know that it's for a limited time and that when he goes to sleep, you can do the things that have to be done.

If the day lacks structure, however, you can find yourself in the situation that one mother described to me in a letter:

"I wake up and see before me an endless day that I don't know how I am going to get through. I don't want to get up. It will be at least sixteen hours before I can go back to bed I think to myself. Sixteen hours, and then I will be even more tired than I am now. That's my life. Day in and day out. What should I do?"

Structure!

Structure and routines create a clear distinction between being alone and being together. As a result, you, the adult, will have the strength to get through the day. *And so will your child.*

You put the routines together and then follow them as though they were self-evident. In a nutshell, you take the lead. Your child will support you for the simple reason that he expects you to take the lead.

If little Daniel is digging through a drawer examining its contents, and nap time rolls around, his dad says without a trace of diffidence in his voice, "Nap time Danny. Bye-bye drawer!" and picks Daniel up. Together Dad and Daniel wave goodbye to the drawer, but Dad shows not a trace of regret for having interrupted Daniel's drawer investigations.

The Friend of Order now protests and says that it is absolutely forbidden to interrupt a child's play. In a time when kids are banished to a closed children's world cut off from adult leadership in the collective struggle for survival, Daniel's dad interrupting his son's play can seem like a terrible violation.

But Daniel's play is not a *substitute* for social participation. Daniel's play takes place within the framework of the flock's struggle for survival. Daniel isn't playing because he has been banished from the community, and therefore he isn't chained to his game.

The routines that Daniel's dad has set up and is following determine the outer *form*, i.e. the duration, of Daniel's play, but it is Daniel who decides the *content,* i.e. whether – and how – he will play with the drawer. Within the framework laid down by the community, Daniel chooses his activity. Daniel is playing freely. He has not been forced to play with the drawer (nor is his play being steered, which is even worse).

Children's play consists of two more or less equal elements: using their own abilities and adaptation to the surrounding adult world in which they (hopefully) participate. Daniel's game is not therapeutic compensation. His game reflects (and alters) reality. It doesn't replace reality.

Thus, it is perfectly acceptable for reality to interrupt it, and Daniel doesn't protest.

If the most important thing for six-month-olds and crawlers is not to be hindered, the most important thing for one-year-olds is that their zest for life not be dimmed.

One-year-olds think it is great to be alive. And if you watch how little people this age throw themselves into life with such unaffected joy, love and curiosity, you can't but realize that human beings as a species did not survive out of a sense of duty or pity. Life isn't a burden to be borne. Life is a feast to be savored. Children between eleven months and a year are the best proof there is of this (with two-year-olds running a close second).

So, forget "upbringing" for now, and let the good times roll! Always greet your child with a smile. Respond to and confirm his zest for life, the sparkling joy he takes in just being on the planet. This joy will never again be as pure, as solid, or as certain as it is now. So share in it! It's worth it.

The world is new and fascinating, even for a one-year-old that has already catalogued a wealth of experience. A dog that shows up during a walk evokes rapturous interest (and sometimes fear). A bush with buds, a branch laden with snow, a stone stairway, the pavement's edge, an old lady with chubby legs, a pile of gravel, a baby in a stroller, a bag that someone has tossed on the ground are all objects worthy of ecstatic contemplation.

All this was new to you too once back in the days when you looked at the world with fresh eyes.

If you think that a one-year-old or a two-year-old should be able to walk to the store without pausing to investigate things on the way, ask yourself if you would be able to walk through the Louvre or the Vatican Museum without stopping to look at the art. It's hardly a reasonable request!

At the railway station the other day, I saw a father buying a train ticket to foreign parts. His son was stretching out his arms to his father because he wanted up on the counter. "There's nothing to see up here", said the father.

I suppose there was nothing to see on Dad's trip abroad either.

The whole second year, which is now beginning, is a time of frenetic investigation that lasts until the mastery era at around two and beyond.

Even though your child seems able to do a great deal and operates confidently at home with his flock, much remains to be investigated and learned. His eagerness and enthusiasm will keep pace with the growth in his abilities, and a one-year-old is only too happy to take a walk on the wild side to the point of risking his life in the process. But you still have to try to apply the same principle you always have: don't hinder and don't steer.

It takes nerves of steel to let a one-year-old climb a ladder for example, so try to cultivate them. Climb up after him ready to catch him if he starts to fall, but avoid touching him unless it's a matter of life and death – and try to look unflaggingly optimistic. God is in his heaven and all is right with the world.

And *if* your child loses his footing, take him to you with an insouciant "whoops" as if it's a mishap of no consequence rather than a close call. Your child should not perceive the world as dangerous, and just like the crawler, your one-year-old has to test his abilities.

But doesn't this result in rash behavior? No. Quite the opposite in fact. Little people this age indulge in rash behavior when they think the only way they are going to get to climb a ladder is if they do it when no one can see them. A child that has been forbidden something is always in a great hurry to try it, and things done quickly and secretly often end badly.

Of course your patience will be tested! All the more so since you have to pretend that something you have seen more times than you can count is happening for the first time. But refraining from criticism and correction is worth the effort.

Your child has wonderful self-confidence. If he gets the support he needs during this period, you will be laying a foundation that will enable him to become a courageous, genuinely self-reliant adult. Accidents should be regarded as accidents, no matter how many times the same "accident" happens. "Oh, the flowers fell on the floor! How can we help them?" instead of

"You KNOW you have to be careful with flowers. Otherwise, you shouldn't touch."

As your child's tool and guide, you should conduct demonstrations as though for the first time in a completely unexplored world. Even if your bedside table drawer has been investigated a hundred times before, pretend it's the first time (again). Yes, your patience will be tested… The nail clippers have to be examined and tasted as though your child had never seen them before. All the objects in the drawer have to be strewn on the floor and studied, twisted, turned, manipulated, put down and picked up again. Ultimately, the investigator has to be persuaded to put everything back in its appointed place (with your hand over your child's: "This goes here and that goes there… perfect."). Then he should put the drawer back in the bedside table and close it – whereupon it has to be pulled out again and re-examined, and on it goes…

Of course, you'll feel your temper rising. If you didn't, you would be a saint or an idiot. If you can't be easy going and happy through all this, then get angry – at yourself. Cut irritation off at the source *before* it bubbles to the surface. You have two alternatives. Either you accept your fate and patiently allow your child to examine the contents of the drawer again, and again, and again until the day comes when it's no longer interesting (that happy day will arrive!). Or, you quite simply take the drawer away when your child is momentarily distracted, and answer his surprise with "It's gone!". You are of course just as disappointed as your child is over this remarkable disappearance. (Remember the wandering chocolate cake?)

You, Mother or Father, are the child's most understanding friend, and you also extend your child's abilities. If you feel you don't always measure up – you will inevitably be faced with situations that push you just a little too far or that simply have no satisfactory solution – try to change the external conditions instead of trying to change your child. The rule is: *move the thing, not the child!* Change the circumstances, not the child!

Transform the reproach, irritation and dismay that well up in you into amiable patience. It can be done. There is usually a way out of most "impossible" situations. Instead of snatching something from a young child's hand, you can take it from him gently, and thank him profusely for the magnificent present. He will be so pleasantly surprised by your gratitude that he will willingly let whatever it is go. You then acknowledge the child's good deed by giving him something else instead. *Never leave a young child empty handed once you have taken something from him!*

This applies metaphorically as well as literally. If you say no to a child or tell him something is impossible, don't leave him "empty handed". If you have taken away a wish, a desire, an initiative, you must give something in return – a suggestion, an alternative, a solution.

If you leave a child in a state of mute negativity, he will be overwhelmed with a sense of powerlessness. Let me give you a few examples.

"No, you can't come along. Daddy has to work." That is powerlessness.

"But tonight, when Daddy comes home, we'll go out into the backyard and throw a ball around." That's empowerment.

Empowerment is forward looking. Empowerment provides a way out. The child receives something in exchange and is not left "empty-handed".

"No, you can't go and see Grandpa. He's sick. He can't see anyone right now." Powerlessness.

"But in a few days, when he's feeling better, *then* we can go visit Grandpa. He'll be so glad to see you!" Empowerment.

"You mustn't fight. I don't care how angry you get, you just can't hit people." Powerlessness.

"But you can say whatever you want, and you can hit *things*. Hit the table as hard as you like if you are so angry you have to hit something. Hit the wall! I'll hit it with you." Empowerment.

"You're too small. You can't do it." Powerlessness.

"But next year, when you're bigger, *then* you'll be able to." Empowerment.

Children around a year old understand a good many words, even if they don't talk that much (if at all). Adults are sometimes tempted to rely on words rather than actions. They order and they forbid. They *talk* instead of showing.

And that's sad. The world becomes a rather dreary place when words take over. Enthusiastic demonstrations trump words any day! *Words are no substitute for actions.* Words have meaning, but for now – and for a long time to come – they take a back seat to actions. If you want a hairbrush that's lying beside a one-year-old, you have to reach for it and at the same time say, "May I have the hairbrush, please?" Not until your child reaches the age of three can you simply sit with your hands folded on your lap and expect mere words to do the trick.

There are a lot of one-year-olds in the world who have been talked to and admonished half to death. There are a lot of two-year-olds who are bombarded with words. What they all have in common is that their zest for life has been all but extinguished, and this becomes obvious when they stop listening and smiling when you speak.

Words should be considered carefully and used sparingly. For young children, words are not the be all and end all. They act first and speak later – a sequence that wouldn't be entirely out of place for adults to imitate.

All parents develop a special talent – a talent for worrying. It would be strange indeed if it were otherwise. This tendency to worry must, however, be hidden from your child. Worry is the evil spirit that haunts all childcare. The anxiety that adults transfer to children opens the door for the "wolf" and exacerbates their survival anxiety.

Even when something disastrous happens – your child hurts himself, bleeds, or is in any kind of danger – you have to try and keep your emotions in check even if you are numb with terror. Screaming or losing your head is like pouring gasoline on a fire. Your own terror is more dangerous than anything else. It plants fear in your child, and this fear leaves scars much deeper, I think, than physical injuries do. For if you, the flock, can't protect your child when he is in danger, who can? The threat is doubled if you show fear, and what is threatened are the very foundations of your child's world.

One of my kids fell off a jungle gym when she was five. It was a fairly long drop, and she split her forehead open. I picked her up, pressed a diaper to the wound, sent my other kids home, and began to walk. Where I was going I had no idea. I walked aimlessly with a purpose, if such a thing is possible, all the while talking reassuringly to my daughter. I had a vague idea that I should somehow get hold of a cab, but I was so dazed with shock I couldn't figure out how to go about it. I sat down on the steps of a convenience store. My lips kept moving. I talked and talked, holding my bleeding daughter in my arms, and she didn't cry. After what seemed like an eternity, it occurred to me that I could call a cab from the convenience store. The taxi driver was concerned about the blood, I remember, and I discussed the matter in depth with him, although I have no idea what I said. The diaper was saturated with blood by this time. We got to the emergency room, and my daughter still wasn't crying. Not even when the doctor began to probe the edge of the wound looking for a suitable spot to inject anaesthetic did she utter a sound. She just looked at me trustingly. But once others had taken over, I was the one to faint from fear...

Children are frightened sometimes. Whatever happens, try to bear in mind that your child turns to you because he wants you to alleviate his fear, not make it worse.

That doesn't mean pretending his fear isn't well founded. The flock knows how to deal with threats, true, but danger is clear and present on occasion. The archetypal "wolf at the door" is real enough.

Whether your child's fear stems from thunderstorms, vacuum cleaners, stomach aches, thieves under the bed, monsters in the closet, or bad dreams, try to convey to him that you are familiar with these dangers – you were little once and you've been afraid too – but also try to make him understand most things are *not* dangerous. There is nothing in the dark that isn't there during the day.

The younger the child is, the less he will respond to logic and the more important laughter is. Nothing makes monsters vanish like a good laugh. Don't dismiss your child's fear, "Oh that's nothing to be scared of!" Recognize it respectfully and then help him put things in perspective. "You don't have to be afraid. I'm here. I'm standing guard. I will make sure nothing happens to you. You can count on that." If you can then coax a timely laugh out of him, the healing is complete.

Fear can strike even the most confident one-year-old without warning, so respect it and try to alleviate it constructively. If, for example, your child is frightened of the vacuum cleaner one day, pick him up and hold him in your arms, but don't turn off the vacuum cleaner. If a mean looking dog crosses your child's path and frightens him, pick him up and stand there looking at the dog. Naturally, you shouldn't force him to confront the dog, but don't make him more scared than he is already by getting as far away from the dog as you can.

Protect him, but let him contemplate whatever it is that is frightening him from the security of your arms.

Little Paul has always enjoyed the swings, but suddenly he's frightened. "I'm scared."

Dad sits on the swing with Paul on his lap. "Come on," he says. "We'll swing together."

A child who falls when he jumps from something for example will be gripped by fear, and this fear should be overcome as quickly as possible. He should be encouraged to repeat the performance, but this time under the protection of Mom or Dad. "You CAN do it!"

Some parents rush into their children's room if they so much as peep, pick them up, turn on the light, walk the floor with them, comfort them, and anxiously study their every change of expression. They tell them everything is going to be fine, but words mean nothing. Their actions speak far more loudly. Their actions say, "I am just as frightened as you are. We're all in mortal danger! I have no idea what to do. Do you?" Their actions and words *should* say, "There is nothing to worry about. I'm here. I will make sure nothing happens. Whatever you are afraid of, I won't let it hurt you." A gentle soothing hug, a caress, a kiss – that's all you need.

Allowing a young child to explore the world freely, without fear, obstacles or steering is no mean feat. My recommendations for dealing with infants and toddlers may seem overly ambitious. It's not merely a question of supervision. If it were, we could simply put our kids in a playpen (or in a day care center for that matter). This is about opening the world for children and placing ourselves at their disposal. It's about offering the chance to participate freely and joyfully in all that's going on around them. It *is* ambitious, but the result is a trusting, courageous, secure, happy little person who is well equipped to meet life, love and work head on.

Here is the program in a nutshell: *Open the world. Place it at your child's disposal. Offer your child things, activities and yourself, all in a spirit of constructive enthusiasm.*

Put into practice, this directive might result in the following scenario: Your child pulls the cat's tail.

The first four times it happens, you think it's fun to show him how you pat a cat to make it happy. (The cat of course is doing its best to get away, which is why you have to hold it so tightly while you show the kid the correct way to treat a cat. Since the cat is hissing and spitting, the happiness being patted engenders is conspicuous by its absence.)

When you have shown your child the correct way to pat a cat ten times and he still pulls its tail, your temperature starts to rise and your palm starts to itch. You then count to ten while you look in another direction (still holding the cat in a vice-like grip). After a few deep breaths, you show your child yet again how to pat a cat and make it happy.

And hallelujah! He actually pats the cat the way he is supposed to – which you more or less force him to do with your hand on his. Meanwhile, the poor cat is so happy, it tries to express its ecstasy by sinking its teeth into your flesh. You joyously acclaim your child's achievement on behalf of the cat. With burning enthusiasm, you express your appreciation for your child's somewhat absent-minded efforts to pat the cat and pull its tail *simultaneously*. Naturally, he keeps trying to pull the cat's tail. How could he do anything else? Nature has equipped cats with handles, so it's only reasonable to use them.

Gently and patiently, a smile frozen to your face, you persist in your attempts to demonstrate the proper way to treat a cat. "*There* we go! That's how we pat a cat! See? Now the cat is sooo happy!"

Of course, you could also destroy the cat. This option however falls a bit outside the scope of this book...

PART FOUR

Little Becomes Big
1–16 years

INTRODUCTION: FROM MY LIFE THEORIES FOR COMFORT

Development theories do not predict how a child will eventually turn out. Perhaps with twenty-twenty hindsight, they might partially explain it.

I was an abandoned child. I was seven when my father, my four half-siblings and my brain-damaged little sister disappeared from my life, and nine when my mother and my only full-brother followed suit. I was alone. My flock had dissolved into its constituent parts. The following years, when various "aunts" looked after me, were a nightmare. If I ever laughed like a child, I don't remember it. I only remember crying silently every evening, being beaten up at school (and beating back), being sick often, and being *alone*, constantly.

At various times in my life, I have been a dysfunctional, disharmonious person, and in many ways, I still am. To this day, even though I am now over sixty-five, I fall prey to bouts of loneliness for which there is no cure. It's the loneliness of an abandoned child.

My children haven't made me happy. That would have been impossible, and it's not their job anyway. Yet they have given my life meaning.

I have seven crashed marriages behind me. Being in love brought out my inner child's primordial trust. (See "The gift of love" in Part one of *For the Love of Children*.) Each time I fell in love, the child I once was thought that Anna had finally come home and she would be a part of a family with all the warmth and security a family can give. Unfortunately, it didn't work out that way.

Nevertheless, I have been a good mother. That's why I want to say to all the parents out there that even if you think you are less than perfect human beings, suffer from feelings of inferiority, or are wracked with unhappiness to the core of your beings, remember this:

You don't need to be happy, harmonious, or satisfied with your own lives to raise children who grow up to be vigorous, loving, good people.

The opposite has been said so often and so emphatically that it's become a truism. If you are not in balance yourself and can't handle your own problems, you won't be able to provide your children with the conscientious care and love that they need to develop all their abilities and become well-adjusted adults themselves – which of course is the prerequisite for their being able to raise well-adjusted children when the time comes…

I know that this is not necessarily so.

There are many parents like me. We all carry so much pain within us, so much sorrow, so many problems in our psychological baggage as we journey though life. All of us are damaged to some extent. We shouldn't disqualify ourselves as parents because of that.

"I don't want my kids to have to go through what I went through." This has been the refrain of parents since forever. Society has worked so that children would receive better education, better material and emotional environments and an improved existence generally. We wanted to give our kids a better start in life than we had.

I wanted to give my children that sense of belonging that I never had. They would grow up in a family that was stronger than anything. They would develop bonds of sibling solidarity that would last their whole lives. They would always have each other, and I would always be there for them.

At the beginning, I probably wasn't thinking consciously in those terms. I just knew what I wanted in some vague way. But maybe I wouldn't have worked so hard to give my kids a sense of family if I hadn't been without it myself.

As new parents, even as parents-to-be, we all have such doubts about ourselves. We are insecure and fearful. The world is the way it is, and it hardly inspires confidence. We have no idea what the future holds, and the fact that preceding generations of parents were flying equally blindly is cold comfort. We are all aware on some level that we really don't measure up. In our time and place, the lack of traditions, the virtual disappearance of knowledge that's handed down from one generation to the next, and the absence of personal support and role models make everything that much worse. Our insecurities and fears eat away at us, and the little faith we do have in ourselves evaporates.

I write these words to comfort and support you, not to extol my own virtues. Abandoned children are not particularly prone to overestimate themselves.

Not only was I unable to transfer any of my own nonexistent inner harmony to my children, I was also unable to provide them with the things that our society deems so important for healthy development. My kids have been through several divorces. They have moved often, every one or two years. They have lost friends and changed schools as often as they have moved. Father figures have come and gone. Extended family members have been thin on the ground to say the least. Death has touched my children through the loss of a dearly loved little brother.

I have painted my children's lives in broad strokes thus far, but the devil found his way into the details too. For example, I have seldom read them stories. I have always found read stories deadly dull (possibly because I am a writer myself). I didn't provide them much else in the way of stimulation. They didn't go to libraries or get involved in other "activities" until they were able to manage on their own and help each other. Their careers at play school, three hours a day at the age of four, were short.

Of course, I felt guilty about not giving them more stimulation, stimulation being the clarion call of the day. I tried to comfort myself with the fact that at least my many kids had each other.

During the sixties and seventies, the evangel of "stimulation" was preached with revivalist fervor. At demonstrations people would chant HEED THE CALL, DAY CARE FOR ALL. Those parents who managed to enrol their eight and nine-month-old children in stimulation paradise considered themselves very lucky. During the fifties, when women were needed in the labor market, the caricature of the listless housewife gained currency (see "The best laid plans..." in Part two of *For the Love of Children*). She was castigated as an out-of-touch social parasite. Isolated in the suburbs, she flopped around the house in worn out slippers and a slovenly dressing gown with curlers in her hair. She was accused of depriving her children of the stimulation they so desperately needed through a combination of stupidity and incompetence.

Like most people, I bought into this and felt appropriately guilty. It was only during my sojourn in an Arabic country, where I lived for six months with my children as wife to the eldest son of a merchant family, that I began to suspect socio-political manipulation. Here I was, living in this godforsaken hole in the wall of a village where nothing much had changed since the Middle Ages, where toys, at least those of the pedagogical variety, were unheard of, and where few adults would dream of actually playing with children. Yet it was here that I was first exposed to poor, filthy little kids with a stunning capacity to play independently. At the risk of sounding nostalgically romantic, I honestly believe that many Swedish children would have envied them. They had fun. They knew how to play. And they played together, rather than each child retreating into his or her own little "mini-home".

Kids develop whether they are organized and stimulated or not. Human beings are programmed to develop, to grow and to move forward. They will inevitably investigate, master and eventually change their environments.

"What a man can be, he must be," says A.H. Maslow, master of humanist psychology. When human beings have the maturity and the capacity to grow, they will.

I know I'm on thin ice when I claim that my children are harmonious people. There have been times when not all of them would have agreed with me!

But harmony is not an easy concept to define. Generally speaking, I would say that a harmonious person, big or small, is someone who sleeps well at night, eats with a good appetite, is healthy most of the time, is happy more often than sad, is capable of feeling tenderness and empathy, has integrity, can concentrate on both work and play, has self-confidence, and contemplates the future more or less optimistically.

My children's lives have not been a bed of roses. On occasion, they had to walk a hard road – and sometimes they stumbled and fell. But life, like music, is complex. It's composed of major and minor keys, light and darkness, laughter and tears, but the contradictions offset each other so that the overall effect is melodic rather than dissonant. Human beings have never had the luxury of floating through life grinning moronically at everything fortune throws at them. They laugh and they cry, they hope and they despair, on some days they stand firm and on others they yield. They live because they want to and because it's necessary – not because it's easy.

Human beings are their own greatest hope. I also think that, when all is said and done, they have the power to heal themselves.

What I have done for my children is be available. I have stuck to routines and insisted on a certain outward conformity, but my motives were hardly noble. If a throng of people are going to live together without going crazy, a simple, reasonably hassle-free daily existence is essential. My children always went to sleep fairly quickly because for obvious reasons I couldn't spend two hours at every bedside. I didn't have time to change clothes on six kids three times a day either. If they didn't like the clothes I put out, they just had to grin and bear it. What I said went.

But apart from the established routines, I basically left them in peace and interfered as little as possible. This too was more the result of everyday necessity than conscious planning. I just didn't have time to put toys in their hands and plan their days for them. I never helped my kids with their homework either, or even asked if they had done it. The truth is that I sometimes had trouble figuring out who was in what grade... I'm not bragging about my shortcomings, but I think I can justify them. It wasn't indifference that lay behind my lack of involvement in their schoolwork. Time was a problem, true, but my primary motivation was respect and trust. I believed in their ability to shoulder their responsibilities. They, in turn, could count on me to shoulder mine.

As a matter of general principle, I was also unwilling to poke my nose into what I regarded as their business. I could therefore expect that they would show respect for my personal integrity.

What I'm getting at with all this is somewhat provocative. I think that the only thing a child needs to develop into a reasonably harmonious adult is *a fixed point, a center in the form of one accessible person (or more) and one accessible home,* a flock in other words. Through membership in this flock the child participates in the collective struggle for survival and receives leadership and protection when the *child* wants it or needs it.

Human beings are born to investigate, master, and eventually change their reality, their living conditions, their world.

A newborn establishes its primary connection with the mother, who guarantees survival and thereby fulfils the newborn's most basic need. Under her protection, the child begins to become acquainted with its surroundings, which, in addition to the mother, constitute the flock. This connection, this sense of belonging is not established only with a person. "Belonging" is a package deal. It encompasses the people and the dwelling. Everything taken together is the flock.

Remember that we single adults need to belong too. We have homes, fixed points that we always return to, where we keep our possessions, clothes and the things that identify us. We don't wander the streets and sleep on park benches (hopefully). We belong somewhere.

With the true birth, which happens at about three weeks, the baby begins to look out into the world and away from Mother, as the urge to participate socially makes itself felt. The child's courageous struggle to be inducted into his community and to become "crew", so to speak, begins. Up to the age of two, the child investigates his flock with its adult members and their activities (and experiments with transferring his primary connection from one adult to another).

Two years marks the beginning of a period of dominance. The child knows he belongs and he is the master of his own fate within the flock – at least he *thinks* he is. Then the "terrible twos" kick in, and new and terrifying vistas open up. (See "The terrible twos: I want to, I don't want to!") When he comes out the other end of that ordeal, he will be able to operate outside his own flock secure in the knowledge that it will be waiting for him when he decides to return. He will also have developed sufficiently to realize that other flocks exist and that they have a right to do so. At three or three and a half, having learned to conduct himself with a judicious blend of assertiveness and consideration, a child can play *with* other children rather than just *beside* them, without interaction.

A young child operates from a base, a center. For a long while, this center is a person. Every parent knows that this center has to be immoveable. If you stay in the kitchen, your child will play contentedly. If, on the other hand, you are constantly running from one end of the apartment to the other, the little one will immediately get nervous.

Let's say you stagger home exhausted, but you still have a lot to do. Your child clings desperately to your skirts and does nothing but whimper and whine. You tell him that as soon as you are done doing whatever it is you are doing, you will sit down with him, read a story or just cuddle. As soon as you finish your chores and you are free to devote yourself to him, you sit down. Now he's happy. Suddenly, he has a thousand things to occupy him and he is more than happy to play by himself. Your presence is no longer a priority!

The center has to be stationary and unchanging. As long as the center is where it is supposed to be, the child can operate unperturbed.

The much maligned housewives, castigated in the fifties as "out-of-touch social parasites" who had never taken a course to improve themselves and for whom "self realization" was an alien concept, weren't quite as useless as everyone claimed. Actually, they weren't useless at all. They ensured their children were clean and fed and nurtured, and they made themselves *available*. They were – and are – enduring, connected, immutable centers.

Little Christine, two years old, is off to the playground with her dad.

When they arrive at the park, Dad sits down on a bench and gets out his newspaper, and Christine makes a beeline for the playground, where she contents herself with just watching the other kids for a little while. She then trots back to her dad, although she doesn't seem to actually want anything from him. She turns around almost immediately and goes back to the playground and begins to tentatively explore its possibilities. Dad looks up from his paper every now and then, but as far as he can see, Christine is taking no notice of him, so he continues reading.

A few minutes pass, and Christine comes trotting over to her father again, stands beside him with her hands on his knees, and looks towards the other end of the park. She then embarks on a little expedition in that direction. Christine wanders a fair bit away from her father, but as long as he can see her, he doesn't feel it's necessary to interfere. Dad goes on reading his paper.

Twenty minutes later, Christine returns and now Dad gets a kiss. Immediately thereafter, Christine is off on a new adventure, this time in the opposite direction towards a part of the park that is as yet *terra incognita*.

Dad starts to think that maybe it's time to head home. He has trouble keeping visual contact with his daughter in that section of the park. He gets up and calls her.

Christine hears him, and she picks up speed – but she runs *away* from her dad. Dad gets up and calls her again. Alas, to no avail. But then he sees she has stopped running and is standing beside a sandbox studying some other children as they play. Then she gets into the sandbox and sits down beside them. Dad decides that she can play a little longer. He spies a bench that faces in his daughter's direction and sits down.

Now Christine stands up in the sandbox and looks for her dad. She sees that he has changed benches. Very purposefully, she trots over to the bench where her dad is sitting and rests her arms and head on his knees. Dad strokes her hair, and she lifts her head and looks at him. Then she heads back over to the sandbox.

When Dad has finished reading his newspaper, he looks at his watch and decides it really is time to go home. He gets up and calls Christine. She appears not to hear him, so he starts moving in the direction of the sandbox.

Christine catches sight of him, and he stretches out his arms towards her. "Time to go home," he says. Christine doesn't move.

"Come on, sweetheart," says Dad and stretches out his hand. Christine turns on her heel and starts to walk in the opposite direction.

Dad gets a tad irritated. "Come on, Christine! We're going home! Come here!"

Then Christine starts to run as fast as she can. Dad has to break into a run himself to catch up with her.

"What do you think you are doing? I said come here!" But in the end, he has to pick Christine up and carry her home.

Christine was operating from a base. As long as her dad was sitting on the bench, all was sweetness and light. Christine could roam as she pleased, explore the park and acquaint herself with everything the park had to offer. Every time she decided to move in another direction, she went back to the bench and her father to check in with base camp. Then she could embark upon a new voyage of discovery.

When Dad moved to another bench, her base of operations changed. She had to check in with her new base camp and reorient herself from there. Her lines with base camp secure, she operated within a radius of 150 to 200 feet. She never moved further than that from her father.

But when Dad got up and called her, and simultaneously started to walk, her operational area began to disintegrate. Her center was no longer immoveable. Her base camp was no longer a fixed point from which she could operate. She became disoriented. As a result, Dad couldn't get her to come to him, take his hand and follow him home. He had to pick her up and carry her.

A moving center confuses young children. In their confusion, they either stay rooted to the spot when you call them or they turn and run. *It is pointless to try and call a young child if you are moving yourself.* The best way for Christine's dad to get her to come home with him would have been to seize the chance when she came to him to orient herself. Then he could very easily have put her in the stroller or taken her by the hand. As it was, the only solution was to go and get her.

Children orient themselves with reference to a center for quite a long time, especially when they are visiting other flocks. One father I discussed this with remarked on how his ten-year-old son came out to us in the kitchen where we were sitting around the table talking. Father and son were visiting me for the first time. The boy didn't seem to want anything in particular. He just stood beside his dad for a little while without saying anything. Then he wandered off to check things out in another part of the house.

This young man was operating from a base camp, just as little Christine was.

Employees at day care centers can testify to how confused children become when they discover that the people who work there don't actually live there.

"Why don't you have a bathtub?" asked a three-year-old little boy named Herman. In the washroom, there were five kid-sized toilets but no shower or bathtub.

"We have bathtubs at home," replied the day care worker. "We don't live here, you see. We go home after work and have our baths."

For poor little Herman, this was a bolt from the clear blue sky. Suddenly, his world was out of joint. The day care center and the people who worked there constituted a flock that he was visiting, but in this flock, there seemed to be no center. Everyone was a visitor!

That staff turnover at day care centers is high, and the people, male and female, have constantly changing schedules so that the children never know *who* is available or *when*, all this is confusing enough. But that no one actually belongs there – that no one is there when the children are not – that is quite incomprehensible. There must be an accessible center, and this center must exist whether or not the child happens to be physically present. That is the little flock member's starting point – "point" being the operative word!

I believe that young children who are deprived of an accessible center are plunged into such anxious confusion that their development is affected. To put it another way, I believe that children who do have an accessible center can pretty much look after their own development unperturbed by the helpless anxiety that confusion brings.

Anything can happen outside the flock without a child feeling threatened. It's only when a threat is directed at the person or people that constitute the flock's center that children feel that their very existence is at stake. (This is why newborns and infants get so upset when adults let their own insecurities show.)

Children can contend with external changes, moves, financial uncertainty, even all out war, as long as the flock with its fixed, human center remains accessible. Children can play and laugh among smoking ruins.

Many of the Finnish "war children", who were sent to Sweden during the Second World War, have said that coming to live with strangers in a strange land, even though it was temporary and Sweden represented security and survival, was far worse than having to suffer deprivation and nightly air raids with their parents.

Without a sense of belonging, children are as unable to survive as the abandoned young of any species. It frankly wouldn't surprise me if people with a good sense of direction have had access to a dependable flock with a fixed human center. Conversely, people with a bad sense of direction or none at all (my own is non-existent) have never had such access or the center has been unclear. Access to the flock has been limited or absent. As a result, their disorientation has been complete and literal.

These days joint custody of children after a separation or a divorce is fairly common. In practice, what happens is that the child has to divide his time equally between the two parents – one week with Mom, one week with Dad. This is a solution that is designed for the benefit of the parents, not the child. The child is caught between two flocks. He can't put down roots and feel he really belongs in either. This holds true even if the parents live close by to each other, and friends, neighbourhood, schools etc don't change. According to the theory of the indispensable center (the center being the base the child operates from and always returns to), it's impossible for a child to orient himself from two centers. There must be one and only one. A child can *visit* as many flocks as he likes, but he can only belong to one. No matter how much children interact with friends (which even newborns are encouraged to do nowadays), nothing can compensate for a severed or dysfunctional connection to a flock.

This introductory section to Part four of *For the Love of Children*, which deals with development, is meant to comfort you. I want you to understand that, even if you sometimes stagger under feelings of inadequacy, you should keep one thought in mind: *just being there is enough*. A good deal of what is trumpeted as being so beneficial and so necessary for children – organized activities, stimulation, an unchanging environment outside the flock (same day care, same school etc.), friends and more friends – is in reality a substitute for a missing human center, for limited access to a flock.

On the other hand, I know my words offer little comfort for those parents who for easily explained socio-political and economic reasons are convinced that staying home with their children for the first three years is impossible. All I can say is that they are wanting in the one area that is essential: being there and forming the center of a flock that is always accessible.

If people who fall in love can crash their respective marriages, give up opulent houses, sacrifice in terms of both salary and prestige and squeeze into a bachelor apartment in one of the less desirable areas of town, all so that they can live together, why can't they do it for their little child?

It's called prioritizing.

You *can* save the first three years!

PEOPLE SHOULD BE LOOKED AFTER BY PEOPLE WHO LOVE THEM

Lars Danius

Children are not obstacles. The obstacles are in your mind and in the society that surrounds you. Your child can help you, indeed *force* you, to surmount these obstacles. Your child can force you to prioritize.

Your child can force you to contribute in your own small way to the transformation of society, to the humanization of society.

Your child will enable you to look at the world with new eyes and distinguish the important from the irrelevant.

Your child can help you take stock of your own life, which for so long has been controlled by profoundly manipulative commercial and socio-political forces you never intended to submit to.

Your child will enable you to take back your life, your autonomy, your judgement, your freedom.

Your child will show you a new world, the world the *child* will have to live in, and into which you will guide your child.

Your child will give you insights into other people and yourself.

Your child will give you the truth, and the truth will set you free.

Children are not obstacles, and if that's what you believe, you are kidding yourself. Children are development in every sense of the word.

THE CYCLE OF LIFE: SOMETHING ABOUT DEVELOPMENT

Just as the earth is programmed to pass through its seasons, a newborn baby is programmed to pass through the various stages of life. Teeth appear, the little body grows, matures, passes through puberty, and reproductive mechanisms switch on – everything kicks into gear at its appointed time.

And as summer turns to fall and fall to winter, hair turns grey, the flame of life begins to flicker and eventually goes out.

Over the course of a lifetime, from conception to death, every human being mirrors the development of the entire species. From a tiny amphibious creature – the beginnings of gills are clearly discernable in a fetus, as is a tail – a human being becomes an independent, thinking being who walks upright on two legs and who speaks, creates, explores, masters and changes. The story of evolution and the entire human species is contained in the blueprint that we all carry within us. Little becomes big, stage follows stage, all according to this blueprint.

Developmental stages are not necessarily bound to particular ages, but they are regular in the sense that they follow certain rules. Lisa may start to walk as much as a year earlier than Karl, who is the same age but can barely crawl. Nature does not dictate that Lisa and Karl are going to walk at fifteen months, but she does dictate that both will stand before they take their first steps – and before they stand, they will wriggle and crawl. Certain prerequisites have to be met before progressing to the next rung is possible. Progress requires a specific set of physical and mental skills to overcome the resistance offered at each stage of the long, hard climb.

If the behavior of young children is anything to go by, human beings create this resistance for themselves if nothing else does. Something within Lisa compels her to start walking, even though she gets around just fine by crawling. Something within little Karl, who is a bit slower off the mark, will eventually impel him to start walking too. What is this mysterious force?

It is certainly not logic or common sense. "If I can learn to walk, I will be able to open the fridge."

Nor is it distaste for the way things are. "Crawling is a drag. I'm sick of it. I want to learn to walk."

Nor is it observation or experience. "Everyone who can walk has a lot of fun."

Nor circumstances. "Great. Here's a smooth, flat surface. I think I'll learn to walk."

Nor people. "They all think I should start walking, so I guess I'll learn."

Why does a bank teller who has toed the line in immaculately shined shoes and lived a life that his colleagues could set their watches by suddenly decide to become an aid worker in Africa? What is it that makes him take that leap into the unknown? Why does he defy the outraged appeals to common sense and leave his predictable, stable, comfortable life for parts unknown?

Whatever his motivation, he would not have been particularly happy *before* he made his decision. A gnawing dissatisfaction would have plagued him for perhaps years. Not that there was anything wrong with the life he was leading; it just wasn't enough. Something was driving him forward. *What a man can be, he must be.*

Development is not a choice. It's a law that's written into our DNA.

And even if most of us don't move to Africa to become aid workers or indeed do anything that could be described as drastic, life impels us to change and develop at regular intervals, even if we can't put our finger on what it is that's lacking. Something makes us stand up and walk, no matter how well we crawl.

And, like our banker, before we decide to walk, we suffer through a more or less painful period of dissatisfaction, as a persistent yet strangely mute force within us compels us to search for something that we can sense but cannot quite define. I call this stage the *changing* phase, which is followed by the *explorative* phase, which in turn matures and culminates in the *mastery* phase. The serene contentment of the mastery phase is eventually broken by a new urge to move forward, which ushers in a new innovation stage, followed by another cycle of experimentation and mastery.

Children don't need anyone to tell them to walk. Children don't need anyone to teach them to walk. They do it of their own accord. If anyone tried to stop them from walking, they would walk anyhow. *Something within them impels them to walk, no matter how well they crawl.*

Development doesn't stop once adulthood is reached at eighteen or twenty years of age. We develop all our lives. We learn to walk all our lives, no matter how well we crawl.

Young children follow a simple, predictable trajectory without questioning it. Adults, however, live in a manifestly rational world and as a result, this urge to develop poses problems. The people around us demand explanations, plans and guarantees, and so do we. A bird in the hand is better than two in the bush after all. We fight against our vague longings for change and brush them off because we don't want to – or don't dare to – succumb to them.

The changing phase is not easy to deal with. It throws children off balance too. Just before a child begins to stand up and walk, there are clear signs of restlessness and dissatisfaction.

But something fascinating happens on the border of the explorative phase. Children – like adults – make a decision. In that fog of vague, barely articulated yet insistent feelings of dissatisfaction, human beings suddenly choose a path. They decide to take action. They see a possibility and they accept the challenge. Once a child decides to get to her feet and take her first step, nothing can stop her. Once our bank teller decides to be an aid worker in Africa, his resolve is unshakeable. Objections simply bounce off him. He's picked the road less travelled and he will walk it.

Something truly inspiring happens when the craving for change calls forth a decision. When human beings accept a challenge, they take a step into the unknown. They then explore that unknown quantity and thereby explore their own abilities as well. Finally, they take charge of their new world.

An individual human life follows the same pattern: Childhood and youth are characterized by exploration, young adulthood by mastery, and middle age by change ("Life begins at forty"). This is followed by another explorative phase, and life ends with the mastery of old age.

This general framework can be divided into shorter intervals. With an infant, these intervals are measured in weeks, with a young child months, and with an adult years. Human beings follow their own rhythms that are as predictable as the seasons. Life is indeed cyclical – and perhaps this cycle continues even after death.

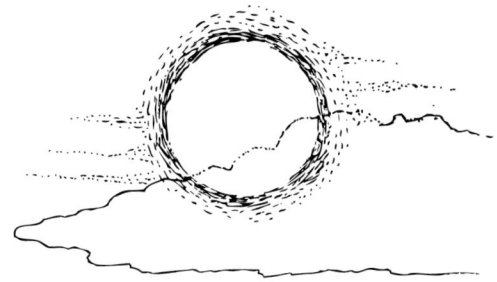

Mastery phases during childhood occur at two, five and ten. Interspersed between them are changing phases, which occur during the terrible twos, at six – the so-called six-year crisis – and at eleven. They are followed by explorative phases, and the circle closes with a new mastery phase.

Any attempt to pin development to age is a risky undertaking. Little Lisa and Karl, you remember, didn't walk at anything like the same age. What I am trying to get across is that development follows a pattern, a rhythm.

Let's begin with the balanced, harmonious mastery phase. It recurs between ever lengthening intervals and lasts longer each time. The two-year-old is lord of all he surveys for about six months. The five-year-old is peace and contentment itself for about nine months. The ten-year-old enjoys mastery for about a year.

If we extend these recurring cycles to cover an entire lifetime, we end up with the following overview:

MASTERY PHASES

Age	Duration
Around two	lasts around six months
Around five	lasts around nine months
Around ten	lasts around a year
Around seventeen	lasts around eighteen months
Around twenty-six	lasts around two years
Around thirty-seven	lasts around three years
Around fifty	lasts around four years
Around sixty-five	lasts around six years

For those who hang in this long, the final mastery phase occurs at around eighty-two and lasts for approximately eight years.

During the mastery phases of life, little people (and big ones) can crawl, figuratively speaking. They crawl superlatively well and they enjoy crawling. They have zero desire to do anything else. Our bank employee is content with the status quo. He is in control of his life and satisfied with his accomplishments. Never in his wildest dreams would he imagine himself pulling up stakes and heading to Africa to be an aid worker.

But something compels both babies and bank tellers to walk, even though they crawl brilliantly. This mysterious, irresistible urge to move forward takes hold, and it manifests itself in discontent.

CHANGING PHASES

Around two and a half
Around six
Around eleven
Around eighteen and a half
Around twenty-eight
Around forty
Around fifty-four
Around seventy-one
Around ninety...

The duration of each of these phases tends to decrease with age and there is tremendous variation from individual to individual.

Children going through the terrible twos must endure a long, drawn out ordeal. Their lack of experience makes it more or less impossible for them to find solutions to their problems. They lack alternatives – or the knowledge that alternatives exist – as well as the maturity to choose between them.

Adolescents and adults, on the other hand, can actively change their situation – or consciously choose not to.

This painful changing phase is succeeded by an active, decisive explorative phase. Those frustrated crawlers, once so content over having acquired the ability to crawl finally stand and start to walk – only to fall and hurt themselves. And get up again. And again. And again. And one day they stay on their feet. Like our bank teller, the child is setting off on the journey of a lifetime. He has only the vaguest idea of where he's bound, but come hell or high water he will get there!

EXPLORATIVE PHASES

Around one
Around four
Around eight
Around fourteen
Around twenty-two
Around thirty-two
Around forty-four
Around fifty-six
Around sixty-two

Children who are exploring are alert, eager to learn, willing to experiment and contemptuous of obstacles. With adventurous curiosity, they set off on their own voyage of discovery, determined to extend the boundaries of the known world. That leap out into the unknown is exhilarating but seldom frightening. Necessity gives rise to certainty.

Strength, decisiveness and courage are all hallmarks of explorative phases, but so is recklessness. A willingness to try anything once and circumspection would be strange bedfellows indeed. Young children going through an explorative phase rarely think ahead, easily overestimate their ability and often over-exert themselves. They push the envelope just a little too far.

The explorative phases are positive, flexible and stimulating for both the children and their surroundings. The action never stops!

Children in a mastery phase are calm, sensible, balanced and mature for their age. They are also serenely unperturbed by obstacles that crop up. The mastery phase is characterized by patience, a capacity for sober second thoughts, well-adjusted contentment, and confidence. The world is exactly as big as it should be. Boundaries don't have to be pushed, since what there is within them is sufficient.

Children in a mastery phase know exactly where all the lines go, and they seldom step over them. They are in equilibrium both with themselves and their environment. The mastery phases are delightful – and provide a much needed vacation for weary parents, who then make the mistake of believing that this happy state of affairs is permanent. The kid is basically "finished". All that's needed is a little parental polishing here and there. Life is unfolding as it should, and the child is right in the middle of it, steady as a rock.

The changing phases bring such idylls to an abrupt end.

Children who are going through a changing phase lose their balance both literally and metaphorically. They fall and hurt themselves, have growing pains and are generally miserable. They may start to stutter, wet their beds, or have trouble with their eyesight. Hypersensitivity, extreme mood swings and temper tantrums are also common.

Children who are "changing" are demanding, impatient, provocative and generally hard to handle. The world that was recently just the right size is now too big *and* too small. Most capricious of all are the child's own abilities – or rather their absence. Delusions of grandeur segue into inferiority complexes at bewildering speed, and mental anguish is never a commodity in short supply.

Children in the midst of a changing phase are often labelled hopeless cases, and comparing them to the wonderful persons they were only a year ago becomes a parental hobby – which of course does little to improve the situation.

368

All this is trying for everyone, but it is unquestionably the child who suffers most.

The agonizing alienation from self and surroundings that is so clearly manifested in the child's behavior during the changing phase begins to loosen its grip when the child is finally able to take the appropriate action to find a way out of the maze he is stuck in, so that the painful process of maturation can move forward. The explorative phase takes over. After having taken their confusing and terrifying leap in the dark, the children land, find their feet and begin to boldly and purposefully navigate what were hitherto unknown waters.

What follows is an attempt to provide a more detailed description of the various phases children and adolescents go through.

Three weeks to approximately five months (overall): explorative
Five, six, seven months: mastery
Eight, nine months: changing
Ten to twelve months: explorative
One to one and a half: mastery
Eighteen to twenty months: changing
Twenty to twenty-four months: explorative
Two to two and a half years: mastery
Two and a half to three and a half (overall): changing
(Three: mastery)
Three and a half to five (overall): explorative
Five to six: mastery
Six to seven: changing
Seven to ten (overall): explorative
Ten to eleven: mastery
Eleven to twelve: changing
Twelve to seventeen: explorative
(Thirteen: mastery)
Fourteen: changing)
Seventeen to eighteen and a half: mastery
Eighteen and a half to twenty: changing

When you are dealing with children going through any of the three stages, the most important thing to bear in mind is that *nothing is necessarily wrong* if their behavior is radically different from what it was six months or a year ago. The younger the children are, the more radical the changes. The older the children are, the more their personalities have developed, and consequently they remain at least recognizable as they move from phase to phase.

• Little persons in a mastery phase can cope with most things. They will take external changes in their stride, and common sense has fertile soil to grow in.

• Little persons who are "changing" should be subjected to as few external changes as possible. Because of their inner turmoil, they need to be able to depend on fixed routines, sufficient sleep, predictable days and a reasonably stable environment – an external calm to counterbalance or at least alleviate to some degree the chaos that roils within.

• Above all, little persons who are "exploring" should be left in peace. They should be allowed to walk their own path and break new ground in their own way. Obstacles are obviously not desirable, but good supervision is. The world mustn't become too big too quickly. Our bank teller can't save Africa all by himself!

SOMETHING ABOUT PERSONALITY

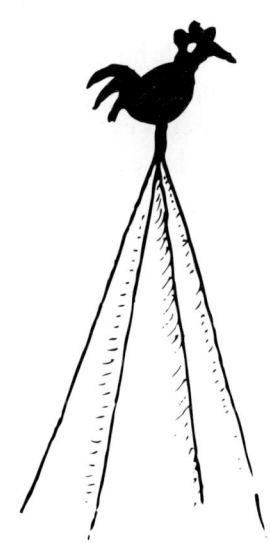

Personality is unique, it makes us all individuals, and, in my opinion, it can't be much influenced.

As distinct as it is beautiful, a child's personality is in full bloom by the age of five months. If the loving parents still haven't figured out what to name their child, a name usually comes to mind then. The babies themselves probably put in their two cents worth somehow or other!

How exactly does personality manifest itself? You might as well pose the same question about the human soul. If a person's behavior is what he *does*, then his personality is what he *is*. But, of course, what he is finds its expression in what he does.

Let's take a peek at a married couple. We find a man who sleeps as late as he can in the morning. Furthermore, if he has to get up before nine, he is in a pretty foul mood. His wife, on the other hand, bounces out of bed at six in the morning.

She is a loving wife, so she suggests that her husband go to bed a little earlier. Perhaps he would learn to appreciate getting up with the sunrise? He does as she asks. He goes to bed early and stares at the ceiling for hours on end, while his wife sleeps like the dead. To the wife's chagrin, her husband is his usual cantankerous self come morning. It would seem that no matter how early he goes to bed, mornings are a heavy cross to bear.

Conversely, if the wife breaks her routine and stays up late, she still wakes up feeling chipper as you please at six in the morning. Obviously, change is not an option.

Consequently, as good spouses and friends should, they give up trying to change each other and accept what are obviously personality traits. No sensible wife would try and haul her night-owl husband out of bed at first light, and no sensible husband would try to force his early bird wife to stay up until the wee small hours. They simply accept each other the way they are.

Wise parents extend the same courtesy to their children.

Children have personalities just like adults do. We all feel more in tune with some people than with others. We find some people appealing and others less so. Some people just seem to "belong" together. It's the same with parents and children. Some personalities attract, others repel.

I have many children, and I adore each and every one of them, but now that they are adults (middle-aged adults in some cases), if I met them for the first time, I'm not entirely sure that I would seek out their company (nor they mine) with a view to forming lasting friendships. Some of them have personalities that just don't fit very well with mine – and vice-versa.

Extrovert, active, intense parents who lead frenetic lives can have a child who is so laid back he's barely conscious. Conversely, the most phlegmatic of couples can produce a little prima donna. Life is a strange business sometimes, but it is what it is!

Human beings, big or small, who have the freedom to be who they are can feel, think and dream whatever they want – and talk about it. (However, they cannot *behave* however they want.)

You may have to bite your tongue when your little angel informs you: "Last night I dreamt I killed you, cut you up, and made you into a hamburger. Then I fed you to the cat."

Or: "You know what? I dreamt that Dad kissed a lady in a store and I got an ice-cream cone for promising not to tell you."

Or: "I saw a red elephant with green spots."

Or more briefly and to the point: "You're stupid."

All these pronouncements are a trifle unnerving, but the only suitable response is an interested "Really?!"

Resist the temptation to retort: "How could you dream something so horrible about me?"

"Dad would never do that!"

"Don't be silly. There's no such thing as a red elephant with green spots."

"Don't you take that tone with me, young lady!"

Does this have anything to do with the personality? It has to do with *the free expression* of the personality.

For now, little Leo wants to be a train driver when he grows up.

When he gives voice to his ambition, what he doesn't need to hear is that he's not suited for the job, it's a precarious profession, he is going to change his mind, he'd be better at computer programming and that the era of train travel is drawing to a close anyhow since everyone prefers to fly. In all probability, Leo *will* want to be something quite different next year, but that's not the point. What's important is that *while* Leo wants to be a train driver, he must feel free to express his desire, which means his ambition must be respected.

Here's a tip: An enthusiastic "Really?" (after you catch your breath) followed by some interested questions will carry you through most situations.

I usually whispered to guests whom my communicative offspring found interesting, "Just agree with everything!"

Little Annabel mumbles something incomprehensible, but it sounds as though she is making a prediction or an assertion. The Friend of Order seems concerned. "I don't understand, sweetheart. What do you mean?"

The correct answer is, *"Really?"*

What Annabel did was share something. All the Friend of Order has to do is say thank you and accept whatever it is she is sharing.

But fantasies, out and out lies, red elephants with green spots? Is *"Really?"* the appropriate response?

I think so. Think about it. How much damage can a red elephant with green spots do?

How many times have you seen things that weren't there?

The difference between "I saw" and "I thought I saw" is dictated by adult reason. The child honestly believes he saw a red elephant with green spots, and that's what should be respected.

"I can count to ten," an optimistic little person announces.

"Alright, let's hear you!"

"One, two, fifteen, feven, ten."

"Oh, that's amazing!"

Will the child always count like that? Will she or he grow up proclaiming that "feven" is a number or that red elephants along with all manner of exotic animals actually exist?

Of course not. Parents can rest assured that development will follow its appointed course. Children correct themselves. What your child thinks he sees and what is actually there will converge. Your child will become more objective – and probably a little sadder – often to the point of pedantic officiousness. (This is something that "perfectionist" five-year-olds excel at!)

There's no need to hurry this happy day. It will come soon enough.

The same tedious scene is played out every summer on family beaches.

Little children in a wading pool or in the lake, their feet firmly planted on the bottom, flail their arms around wildly and imagine they're "swimming".

"Look! I can swim," they shout. Their delighted parents approach preparing to lavish praise upon them. When they realize that "swim" is a misnomer, their disappointment shows.

"You can't swim! You're cheating!"

And what then? The children know perfectly well that they can't swim perfectly, but almost. Anyway, they look like they're swimming, don't they? Next summer they won't be content with "almost". Next summer, they will be able to swim – for real!

If it's worth trying that is. If Mom and Dad don't give the thumbs down on *the way* they swim, or find fault with something else.

It doesn't take much to snuff out a child's happiness. As a parent, you shouldn't be nervous about your young (or not so young) child's fantasies, nor should you be so quick to condemn them as falsehoods – at least not if your goal is to promote honesty. Human beings lie because for whatever reason they *can't* tell the truth. There are always reasons for that. No one is born a liar. We can always tell the truth when we feel free to be the people we are in front of those who love us, wish us well and really try to understand us.

Children tell the truth *as they see it*. Every time a child's perception of the truth is dismissed as a lie or a fantasy, yet another brick is laid in that wall that hinders a child from being truthful.

I have done exactly what young children do. I have told detailed "lies" about the elves, and of course about the Swedish little house brownie – this invisible mini-Santa, who silently and secretly protected the home and the family all year round. Mr. Brownie had to be gratefully rewarded on Christmas Eve. Rice pudding and cookies had to be laid out so he could snack after having finished his hard work for the Holy Night. When the children had gone to sleep, I emptied the bowl, removed the cookies and made miniature footsteps in the snow.

One of my daughters, at the ripe old age of nine, wrote a letter to Mr. Brownie telling him how kind he was and wondering if the rice pudding, lovingly homemade by her, was good. She begged for a reply and provided an extra sheet of paper and a pencil as an incentive.

I was in a terrible bind. Finally, I actually went so far as to cobble together a reply. My daughter was overjoyed, while I was both happy and ashamed.

The years went by, more children came along, and they became acquainted with our personal protector the brownie man too. Sometimes one of them would ask me if there really was a Mr. Brownie. I always assured them that there was and managed to come up with even more convincing details.

But the day of reckoning finally came. My eldest daughter informed me triumphantly that she had figured out the truth. "There is no House Brownie. You're the one who empties the bowl and makes the footsteps in the snow with your finger, right?"

I hesitated, but she smiled. There were no accusations and no disappointment. So, I came clean and admitted she was right.

"But if you say anything to your brothers or sisters, you're toast!" I admonished her.

One after the other, they all figured out that the brownie wasn't real. Nobody reacted negatively to the fact that I had "lied". Nobody was upset. They all took it with a smile – except one. She had had the truth revealed to her by someone else. She hadn't been allowed to figure it out for herself *in her own time and her own way.*

She was so sad that I almost really did make toast out of someone that day.

Children figure things out all by themselves. The path to enlightenment is circuitous on occasion, but they get there in the end.

Parents are admonished by the powers that be not to use "baby talk" with their kids. Correct usage is the order of the day. The result is endless correction.

"Don't say 'eated'. It's 'eaten'. Can you say 'eaten'?"

"Eaten," says the child obligingly. "Have *you* eated?"

You can speak baby talk with a good conscience. Children are hard wired to acquire language. In fact, kids are hard wired to develop generally. You can leave them to their own devices more than you think.

The human personality is rich and varied, a complex kaleidoscope of light and darkness. Children who in their mastery phases are the epitome of phlegmatic common sense can morph into bundles of almost neurotic anxiety during their explorative phases with the result that many parents jump to the conclusion that something is wrong.

Being observant is one thing. Looking for problems where none exist is something else. In all likelihood, nothing is wrong. Different facets of a child's personality are seeing the light of day, nothing more.

That's why I think you should think twice before giving voice to your concerns. If there's one thing a child does not need to be told, it's how much she or he's "changed", especially if it's done in a way that makes the children feel they're being criticized or rejected. Put yourself in the child's shoes and ask yourself how you would react.

"What do you mean I've 'changed'?" you might say. "*Aren't I allowed to just be myself?*"

During the onerous changing phases, hitherto hidden personality traits bubble to the surface. We all know how adults react when they are subjected to severe stress. Some exhibit extraordinary strength and tenacity, some exude a quiet determination that has a calming effect on everyone around them, and some succumb to wild-eyed, screaming hysteria. There are children who burst into tears at the mildest rebuke, while a brother or a sister reacts to the same rebuke with a resigned shrug.

Strategies for dealing with adversity vary as much in children as they do in adults. Some kids retreat, others hurl themselves into the fray. Some kids are jello, others are bullet proof. Tact and finesse are required if you find yourself having to deal with less admirable personality traits in a little person. Bear in mind that personality traits are indelible. They're there for the duration.

Timid children will not become brave by being forced into situations where bravery is required. They can, however, become a little less timid if they are having fun. Little Sarah, for example, timid to the point of being reclusive, dares to swing high one day because her dad coaxes a laugh out of her, but she would never swing high just because her father ridiculed her for swinging too low.

The changing phases in children's development create space for the less attractive, "trying" aspects of their personality because they are off balance. How this imbalance manifests itself says a lot about them. Children of the so-called terrible twos, of six, or of eleven who are on the offensive, pushing the boundaries, yelling and screaming, battling enemies real and imagined, are displaying personality traits. They are going to get ahead. They won't necessarily have an easy life – who does? – but they will fight for what they see as their due, and they won't bow to authority. They are strong.

On the other hand, those little ones that are dissolving into tears, who mistrust everyone and everything, who despair of anyone ever liking them, who simply retreat into themselves during these changing phases are displaying a sensitivity and an emotional fragility that, in my opinion, is also a personality trait. They will be prone to depression. They won't fight for their due – not unless their very lives are threatened. They will react to setbacks with sadness rather than anger. They will crack under the strain and take refuge in isolation.

It has always seemed to me that sensitive children are equipped with a greater capacity for humor than the so-called strong ones. Humor is perhaps their salvation… If the so-called strong little persons decide that they are going to get ahead because life is about survival of the fittest, their more sensitive counterparts make their way in the world by making life fun. And funny!

At the risk of over-generalizing wildly, I am going to present three personality types with the caveat that there are of course a myriad of ways in which these types can combine.
- *The strong type*
- *The fragile type* and
- *The little eel* (why will become clear below).

The Strong Type can take as much conflict, rage and ill will as the world can throw at him (we'll assume it's a he), but he cannot abide scorn, contempt or ridicule.

He tests every limit there is. If you give an inch on the rules or the routines, he'll take a mile before he's through. When you run out of arguments and fall back on parental authority of the BECAUSE-I-SAY-SO variety, then he's happy. He thrives on opposition. Your willpower has to match his – and surpass it. There will be arguments that leave you exhausted and him feeling pretty good about life.

Subterfuge and low blows are intolerable however, and mere irritation gets under his skin. His sense of fair play is highly developed and seemingly innate. Appeals to common sense are successful at a surprisingly young age – except when he is being deliberately provocative.

Since the strong type cannot cope with contempt when it's directed at him, he finds feeling contempt for others very upsetting, so be prepared to say what you mean and mean what you say in all your dealings with him.

Above all, the strong type craves a *comrade* who never walks away from a fight. All attempts to manipulate him by giving him the silent treatment or playing the martyr are doomed to failure. He will just get annoyed and turn his back on you. The key to dealing with the strong type is straight talk. Whatever you have to say, say it to his face. Don't equivocate. Give him the plain, unvarnished truth. He can take it. He is loyal to a fault and has a strong sense of justice.

The strong type never retreats in the face of inner demands for change. He just draws his sword and charges up the hill, which is perhaps a fitting metaphor for his whole life.

His Achilles heel is sadness. When the strong type falls silent – in word and deed – you have to move fast. His zest for life hangs in the balance the moment he turns inward and locks himself away with nothing but his own despair for company.

The Sensitive Type is very dependent on domestic harmony. He needs a pleasant atmosphere to function. As long as sweetness and light reign, he can live and work, and he would just as soon do so by himself. If his surroundings become too trying, he retreats unhappily into his shell.

The sensitive type can laugh until it hurts one minute and cry rivers the next. He rarely stands up for himself, and as a result he can be stricken with a bad case of the blues without his parents noticing. Getting close to him again can be a torturous business indeed. Even as an adult, he has trouble standing his ground. Sadness comes far more easily than anger. Aggression is not part of his universe, but hysteria is.

The sensitive type avoids conflict like the plague, and there is little point in trying to change him. The world needs more peaceniks anyway!

The sensitive type needs to be told he is doing the right thing, not that he is weak. His right to be who he is has to be constantly affirmed. Try to listen to him, even when he is speaking softly – which he does frequently, and try to see things from his side of the fence, even when you don't agree with him.

Making yourself understood is just as important as understanding. You need to put the sensitive type on your lap and explain things carefully.

"Do you think this means that I don't love you? – "No…well…Maybe. I don't know." Get set to give a marathon explanation!

The sensitive type needs tenderness and a daily laugh more than anyone. As far as the routines go, he's fairly good at sticking to schedules. This makes him easy to take care of – at least on the surface. What's lethal for the sensitive type is being distrusted, misunderstood, misjudged and generally condemned without trial. He will not protest in the face of rejection and disapproval, but he will suffer. He won't lose faith in you, but any joy he takes in being alive will be smothered, and he may plunge into a deep depression.

The sensitive type has a wonderful capacity to give of himself. Although being distrusted cuts him to the quick, he very rarely distrusts other people. If he is allowed to be who he is, he will develop into an irresistibly charming child who will enchant everyone he meets with his kindness and consideration.

The Little Eel glides through life with few mood swings or emotional outbursts. Elegant and flexible, he walks his own road.

The little eel doesn't erupt into peals of laughter or burst into heart-rending tears. He's balanced. Either he's content, which he doesn't make a big deal of (actually, he doesn't make a big deal out of anything), or he's whiny.

The little eel is elusive. Anything parents (or anyone else) say to him runs off him like water off a duck's back. Or an eel's. There may be occasions when the little eel will work himself up into an emotional frenzy, and then a door might slam, but these episodes are few and far between. The world could literally crumble around him without provoking much of a reaction other than mild puzzlement over where his toothbrush went.

The little eel is by and large careful with his possessions and his predilection for order sometimes tips into obsession. Yet from one day to the next supposedly ingrained habits can be tossed to the four winds without so much as a backward glance.

The eel is a bit of a player and has a talent for manipulating his environment. When you finally realize you've been had, and you slam your fist on the table and say "THAT'S ENOUGH!", he will just look astonished. "Enough of what?" he replies innocently. He has no idea what you're talking about. Or so he wants you to think. (Perhaps he really doesn't know what I'm talking about, you wonder. Unanswered questions go with the territory when you call a little eel's bluff.)

The little eel has a rich inner life, but life out in the world is somewhat banal. He makes friends with kids who are pretty much like him, and what they do when they're together is a bit of a mystery. Little eels and their friends can sit and read comics together for ten hours at a stretch without saying a word. One can imagine little eels growing up to be typical English gentlemen who observe the world with amused detachment.

The little eel can be lazy, secretive and generally enigmatic. When it comes to the crunch however, his integrity is rock solid. As a rule, he is pleasant to be around and seldom causes trouble, but, as I've said, he will confuse you sometimes.

Knocking a little eel off balance is difficult. He is a natural survivor. The only thing you have to remember is that he needs to be left in peace every now and then.

A child's body type can provide clues about personality. Body types too fall into three main categories: the endomorph, the ectomorph, and the mezomorph. (Body type does not stabilize until the third year.)

The butterball (the endomorph) is soft and sensual, a dedicated little hedonist. Her body – we'll assume it's a she – has a beautiful rondeur. No sharp edges here! Her facial features are agreeably gentle.

The butterball loves food. She doesn't need to be plied with food. She'll happily clean her plate more than once.

The butterball sleeps deeply and sweetly. She loves to sleep and seldom fusses at bedtime. And she sleeps long too.

The butterball loves people and hates conflict. She is sociable and entertaining, and she has a rich inner life that she is more than happy to share. She talks, tells stories, fantasizes and dreams out loud. The people around her find her unbearably charming.

The butterball throws love around like a drunken sailor spends money, but the object of her love can change from one day to the next. She is uncritical, warm and welcoming.

A little butterball in a bad mood tends to sulk rather than get angry. She can be sentimental to a fault and is easily moved to tears.

The little butterball loves everything that is beautiful, soft and pleasurable, but she doesn't put much effort into imbuing her surroundings with these qualities. Curiously enough, she doesn't seem to notice the unlovely and is content to enjoy the beautiful.

The butterball is anything but petty. Life is too short.

The butterball is profoundly sensual. She seldom has tummy trouble and eats just about anything. She's also a patient, persistent, adaptable little soul. The little butterball is a joy to take care of, but she needs love and joy in her everyday life like a flower needs sunshine and rain. Simply put, living well is an art, and the butterball is an accomplished artist!

Butterballs and eels rarely overlap. Butterballs are mostly to be found among the sensitive and the strong types, or combinations thereof.

The Little Asparagus (ectomorph) is thin and lanky, often with a flat ribcage and less than impressive musculature on her arms and legs. Her facial features are tightly bunched and her chin is pointed. She's fine boned, not to say flat out skinny.

Oftentimes, the little asparagus has problems falling asleep. She can toss and turn for what seems an eternity complaining about one thing or another. She sometimes gets out of the wrong side of the bed and can sulk for hours.

Her appetite is often terrible, especially during her first year. The asparagus hangs on to life by her fingernails. Luscious desserts and aromatic stews arouse little enthusiasm. The asparagus eats because her body needs fuel not because she loves food.

The little asparagus seldom talks loudly, and she needs her solitude. Most of the time, she has the air of one occupied with vitally important matters of state. The asparagus is often strikingly advanced intellectually. She is eager to learn and has an excellent memory. She thinks constructively and has a knack for the theoretical.

The asparagus is an orderly and organized young lady, and she hates chaos and dirt. She is meticulous about keeping her environment tidy, not only for herself but for others as well.

The asparagus knows exactly where she stands and is not shy about letting her surroundings know. She organizes relationships, clears up misunderstandings and will always give a straight answer to a straight question. This need for order runs deep, and it encompasses every facet of her life.

The little asparagus is deeply loyal, and words left unsaid can affect her badly. Depressions, however, are rare. She has a talent for finding constructive ways to deal with life's problems. The asparagus is above all a realist. She is conscious of her responsibilities and ambitious.

The asparagus has a sensitive stomach – especially during the first year – and scrupulously avoids foods (or anything else for that matter) that might disagree with her. Headaches and stomach aches are common when life gets stressful.

Keeping up appearances is important for the asparagus.

The asparagus might well be a little eel, but she is found among the strong type too. She rarely combines with the sensitive type however.

The Little Body Builder (the mezomorph) is big, strong, lithe and beautifully proportioned. She is neither fat nor thin. Her flesh is firm, and she often has large pores. She has prominent, "spread out" facial features.

The little body builder is a natural born competitor. She gives whatever she does everything she's got and feels good about it afterwards. She's a good loser and a gracious winner. She's a generally well-balanced person.

The body builder loves food, but she eats with lip-smacking gusto rather than the dreamy sensuality so characteristic of the butterball. More often than not, the body builder is a big eater, always hungry.

She sleeps well, but in a true competitive spirit, she pushes herself to the limit and goes without sleep for far too long. She recuperates by sleeping round the clock for a couple of days.

The body builder is goal oriented. While the butterball talks a good fight without actually *doing* that much, and the asparagus engages in much soul-searching about how things should be, the body builder jumps into the fray and takes the bull by the horns. She walks her own road, and she acts. The butterball has a lot of irons in the fire, but most of them are imaginary. The asparagus has a lot of irons in the fire, but they are real. The body builder only has one iron in the fire at a time, but while it's there, she gives it her all.

The body builder has a positive outlook and loves life, but like all competitors, she realizes that there are some tasks she's just not up to. Like the good loser she is, she withdraws and suffers her defeat in silence. Depression lurks, and this can be dangerous.

The body builder is a good comrade, happy and enthusiastic, with both feet on the ground. Her devotion is ironclad. Yet, she has a sensitive side, and she's uncomfortable with it. It can take a lot of persuading to get her to show this facet of herself. She's not always as strong as she looks.

The body builder needs attention from her surroundings, and she needs to feel she's *needed*. She doesn't like the sidelines. Loneliness is the body builder's Achilles heel.

The little body builder is found mostly among the strong and the sensitive types.

What follows is a typical example of how the body builder deals with the world.

Little Felicia is learning to walk. She's using a stool for support, and she's pushing it in front of her. The stool meets the wall, and Felicia finds herself at a dead end, but, little body builder that she is, she wants to go through the wall, stool and all.

A butterball faced with a similar situation – assuming she had exerted herself sufficiently to get this far – would have abandoned the entire project. Stools and walls are just too much effort! There are so many other ways to amuse oneself.

The little asparagus would have stared imploringly at whichever of her progenitors happened to be in the vicinity as if to say, "There is a wall in the way. What are you going to do about it? Get rid of it! What are you waiting for?"

The body builder, however, grits her teeth and struggles in silence. She is going through that wall, and she's going to do it her way. Live free or die!

When Felicia's doting parents turn both her and the stool around, Felicia marches doggedly across the room until she hits the opposite wall. The performance is repeated. Now she wants to go through *that* wall. Silent, resolute and goal oriented, she struggles to force her way, stool and all, through yet another wall. Again the parents turn their daughter and the stool around. Off Felicia plods towards new walls and new battles.

This scenario repeats itself ten more times. A fight isn't over until a body builder says it's over. Failure is not an option. The asparagus would have heeded the voice of common sense – either her own or that of her surroundings. The butterball would have abandoned the whole enterprise for a more diverting temptation. The body builder, however, pays little, if any, attention to anything but her own stubbornly explored experience.

ONE YEAR: THE GOOD LIFE

(Throughout the rest of Part four, we are going to assume that the child is a boy.)

The one-year-old is an exceedingly pleasant little person. Social and sunny, he greets every new day as though the adventure of a lifetime beckoned with the dawn – which, as a rule, it does. If by any chance it doesn't, the one-year-old has ways of remedying the situation.

The one-year-old loves his freedom. You won't be able to hold him on your lap against his will, no matter how huggable or affectionate you are. If he doesn't feel like being cuddled, it isn't going to happen.

The one-year-old walks his own road in every sense, and if he can't walk, he'll crawl.

That little people this age are so loveable is probably part of Nature's plan. Mind you, one-year-olds and furnished rooms sometimes don't mix. Children this age use everyday objects with imagination and more vigor than one might wish. They cheerily pull tablecloths off heavily laden dining tables, drop food on the floor and turn bottles of shampoo upside down, fully expecting everyone else to enjoy the spectacle as much as they do.

If there is one thing the one-year-old understands, it's showmanship. If you laugh at something he does, you will be rewarded with at least fifteen encores. The one-year-old never gets enough. Peek-a-boo in a doorway is great fun. Hiding behind the furniture is even better. If you get tired after two hours, don't expect the one-year-old to give up!

The one-year-old is a ray of light on two legs. He's fearless, up for anything and almost always happy. His imagination is inexhaustible. He loves to play, listen to nursery rhymes, count fingers and toes, sing, dance and generally test the limits of his world. He's robust in both body and soul, and he loves life.

The one-year-old blithely assumes that he is the center of the universe, and that everyone and everything else takes a backseat. His wants and needs are all that count. He likes people that are like him: other one-year-olds and infants. He is all over them. Consideration is not part of his reality, but he doesn't mean any harm. He just can't resist treating other people as though they were furniture or food. Why should he? What's the difference anyway?

Life is for living, so make hay while the sun shines!

The one-year-old passes through all three developmental stages on his way to his second birthday.

At the beginning of his career, he is an explorer, and this is followed by a wonderful period of mastery. At around eighteen months, he enters a changing phase, but this doesn't have to be that traumatic. I have always regarded it as a foretaste of the terrible twos. For a couple of months, a one-year-old can be a tad on the contrary side. Saying NO to everything becomes something of a hobby.

During the three or four months before he turns two, he goes back to being an assiduous little explorer. Around his second birthday, he enters another mastery phase and is harmony personified.

By and large, the second year of life is explorative, which means that the one-year-old is best served by being allowed to roam free. (Consequently, this is the worst possible time to lock him into the kind of no-freedom-of-movement regimen that day care centers are famous for.)

This of course does not mean that you should let your one-year-old out of your sight. Close supervision is not merely desirable but essential.

If anyone has a talent for biting off more than he can chew, it's the one-year-old! He is so convinced of his own brilliance that he believes that tiresome little constraints like the law of gravity don't apply to him. If he clambers out a third-storey window, he really thinks he can clamber back in just as easily. Pleas for caution fall on deaf ears, as is usually the case with explorers. It's like telling someone who is intent on skiing across Antarctica to avoid harsh climates.

You will just have to intervene when a one-year-old gets too far ahead of himself, but try to be as discreet and as tactful as possible. Ideally, he shouldn't see your intervention as a barrier.

You can avoid insulting a one-year-old (or boring him stiff) by trying to divert his attention to other things. For example, you might want to shout enthusiastically, "Look at the DOG!" – then hope that a dog conveniently materializes... If one doesn't, the one-year-old will soon find something else to occupy his time.

Words are things that the one-year-old files under "recreation". Admonitions, explanations, and other long-winded flights of rhetoric he finds stupefyingly dull, and he can't fathom how people can blather on and use words, which are actually so much fun, in such a dreary way. Orders are an almost sacrilegious misuse of the power of speech in his book, and he duly ignores them – with sensitivity and finesse of course.

He is, however, more than adept at *playing* with words.

You should learn the art of avoiding any utterances that could conceivably be answered with the word NO. (Especially if you are dealing with a little fellow who is passing the eighteen-month mark.)

Don't say, "Shall we go out now?" or "Let's go out!"

Say rather, "Where are your shoes?"

You will learn (among many other things) a whole new mode of communication from keeping company with a one-year-old.

I hope I don't need to point out that resorting to such gems as "Bad boy!", "Naughty!" and "Ah-ah-aah, shame on you!" is about as low as you can sink. Burdening a one-year-old with shame and guilt is unsporting and just plain mean.

It's also about as pointless as shaking your fist at the sun because you're sweating.

Any plans you might have drawn up with a view to "bringing up" your one-year-old can be consigned to the nearest wastepaper basket.

Upbringing will not be an ongoing concern until the terrible twos.

It is an inescapable fact that eighteen-month-olds are difficult to handle and unpleasant to be around sometimes, but this is true for all kids (and adults) who are going through a changing phase. They are not always at their best. During the third quarter of the second year of life, a one-year-old goes through such a phase.

Research has shown that eighteen-month-old children are over-represented in abuse statistics.

It's easy to condemn the parents, and corporal punishment can never be justified, but parents usually hit their children because they feel powerless, not because they are cruel. We have already discussed the devastating effect that feelings of powerlessness can have on young children (see "Eleven months to one year. Maintaining good habits"). Such feelings are no less devastating for adults.

If and when impotence, despair and rage close in on you, and you feel you are about to really lose it, pick the kid up, put him in bed, close the door, take a deep breath and count to ten. *But don't under any circumstances hit him.* Your child can rant and rave to his heart's content. There is a closed door between you, and it should stay closed until you both calm down.

When your child is quiet and you have regained your self-control, open the door a crack and ask him calmly and friendly (if you can't keep a challenging edge out of your voice, wait a little longer) if he is ready to join in. If the reply is a howl of protest, shut the door. Silence, even if it's a little sullen, is a peace offering.

If you have to open the door and ask ten times, so be it. The closed door stays between you as long as the response is hostile.

Persistence is vital. *You must not leave your post at the door.* The last thing you want to do is give the child the impression that you are rejecting him for good.

Ostracism indicates that you disapprove of the child's behavior, not the child himself (See "The terrible twos. I want to, I don't want to!"). As soon as the behavior changes for the better – that is as soon as the child stops howling, kicking, biting, tearing the house apart and generally going berserk – the ostracism ends. Then it's back to business as usual.

Anything that smacks of malicious triumph on your part is strictly forbidden. The same goes for threats of another round of ostracism.

And, since the behavior that caused you to explode in the first place has now come to an end, you should show supportive appreciation and, decently enough, look happy!

For more information about routines, food, sleep, social participation etc, see "Eleven months to one year: Maintaining good habits" in Part three of *For the Love of Children*.

I would like to stress yet again that a child's appetite diminishes drastically during the second year. Snacks at all hours will have a significant impact at meal times.

This can be somewhat troublesome, since the odd "bribe" is still required. Bribes are particularly useful during diaper changes. One-year-olds are up for just about anything – except lying still. That is boring unless you can wriggle like an eel and generally play to the gallery. An apple is a bribe that lasts for a while and isn't too filling.

Watching your one-year-old, with his four to six teeth, eat an apple is rather an interesting spectacle.

He'll nibble off little bits of the skin, which he will then spit out. The apple is then abandoned in a corner of the living room, on a book case or under a heating element. Two days later, when the apple is rediscovered, he will happily pick up where he left off – only to discard it yet again, this time in one of your shoes. When the remains of the apple have had time to gather dust and rot properly, he will realize that a well matured apple makes an ideal present. Your one-year-old will then graciously give it to you, knowing full well that it's something you have always wanted.

Generous as he is, the one-year-old will be utterly baffled if you reject this token of his affection, but he will hardly be deterred. He would never stoop so low as to use mere words to show his displeasure, but he will quite happily take action and try to stuff the moth-eaten remains of the apple into your mouth (or anyone else's).

If however the child offers you something more appetizing than an apple core that's seen better days, such as a cookie fresh from the box, it is strictly forbidden to eat the whole thing.

Cowed by the Friend of Order, visiting relatives often make that mistake. "Thank you sweetheart," says Aunt Mary as she scoffs it down, "that was delicious." The one-year-old immediately goes to pieces. He was offering to let Aunt Mary *taste* the cookie. She wasn't supposed to *steal* it!

Aunt Mary feels like a criminal who has just deprived a defenceless child of his cookie, but at the same time she is bewildered, since it was the child who came up with the idea of giving away cookies in the first place. It's an experience that gives rise to so-called mixed feelings. (By the way, children under two shouldn't eat cookies.)

A tip: Encourage the one-year-old to use his superbly honed abilities – and not only during systematic social participation but whenever the opportunity presents itself and imagination inspires. He will be over the moon if you can convince him that you need him not only for practical, work-related reasons, but also for personal support!

If for example your glasses are lying in full view on the table right in front of you both, look helpless, fumble your way searching for them and ask, in proper despair, "*Where* are my glasses? Oh, I can't find my *glasses*! Where can they be? My my, *where* are my *glasses*?"

The one-year-old will eventually get the message, "find" them for you and hand them over, whereupon you thank him profusely. Blessed contentment will ensue.

If you hurt your finger, scream your head off and let the one-year-old kiss your finger better. You will make his day.

If he gets to put a band aid on your finger too, so much the better. It may take him half an hour, mind you, but by investing that half hour, you are making a little person feel wonderfully indispensable.

To ensure that he doesn't try to affix a band aid to every square millimeter of exposed flesh, hide the box when he is momentarily distracted and exclaim, "Gone!" as though you were utterly mystified. Your little buddy knows exactly how fickle life can be. Things disappear sometimes. What can you do?

388

One simply has to rise above life's tribulations, keep the aspidistra flying and do the best one can. We have each other at least!

A SAFE HAVEN

Happy days, full of laughter and sunshine, that's the good life. It's good to listen to a little man, fresh from his midday nap, lying in his crib talking to himself. "Nuh, nuh, nuh," he seems to be saying. I don't know what he is protesting against, but it is a gentle protest indeed.

The second year of a human being's life is probably the richest. It should somehow be recorded, videotaped, archived and used as teaching material in every conceivable context. It's the year that has everything. There's love that asks for no reward and self-confidence that replenishes itself. There's an almost reckless courage that doesn't fail in the face of unfamiliar cookies offered by unfamiliar old ladies, or at the top of a flight of harsh stone steps. There's happiness that doesn't require reciprocity. There's rich delight in one's own ability. And this ability knows no bounds. Its proud possessor, armed only with a plate of spaghetti and any flat implement, can transform a pristine kitchen into a work of grunge art. He can stuff toothbrushes into faucets with uncanny dexterity and conduct erudite conversations with ladybugs.

One-year-olds sleep because they want to, eat because they want to and love as they pass by. They don't have time to worry. Life is too interesting.

Being four, for example, is a lot more complicated. If as a four-year-old you accidentally knock over a beloved sibling, you'll try to smooth things over with a hug. Since sometimes people who have recently been knocked to the floor don't take kindly to being hugged by the person who put them there, they don't return the hug but continue to howl. You, cut to the quick, will sadly observe, "He doesn't want me to love him!" What do you do then?

At my now respectable age, I find myself locked into a distressingly complicated pattern when it comes to socializing. If I see an older couple sitting on a park bench enjoying the sunshine and tenderly holding hands, I can't go up to them, like Baby, my one-year-old could, look at them and get a pat on the head as I stand in the warm circle of their affection. There is an intricate web of social conventions that I have to adhere to. It makes life so dull. Love and affection should not be shackled. So many of us are starved of it.

But the good life is good anyway. There was a big reunion yesterday. All six children back in their mother's arms – which seem to have opened wider and wider as the years have gone by. Everyone is home in a safe haven. Safe havens are not built of steel or stone but of somewhat more abstract materials. Still, that doesn't make them any less durable.

And the worry that has caused me to stay up all too late all too many black nights is stilled and becomes but a far distant dream, like the memory of the dead chill of winter on a lazy summer's day. I feel as though I'm holding the warm, life-giving sun in my arms. I laugh again, I run around like a kid myself, and I play with them. And I think to myself, as I have done so many times over the years, that as long as I can run and laugh, I still have some living to do.

Life is brief, but joy is powerful. Happiness spreads like rings on the water. It can't be shut in. It bursts forth and spreads. We must accept it, embrace it, and pass it on. We need it, just as the soil needs sun and rain to bring forth life.

I hear Baby protesting – real protests now – that it's time for him to join in. His three-year-old big brother indignantly informs me, "He's sad, don't you hear? Give him a hem and chief sandwich!"

TWO YEARS:
MASTER OF ALL HE SURVEYS

If the one-year-old regards himself as the center of the universe with an absolute right to dispose of both man and beast as he sees fit, the two-year-old has realized that he has a capital-R responsibility, which of course he unilaterally assumes.

This responsibility is both a burden and a joy, and the two-year-old is always conscious of it. As Louis XIV put it, *L'état, c'est moi!* Without the two-year-old at the helm, the ship of state would founder on the rocks and all hands would be lost.

He is the linchpin of the family unit. It rises or falls with him. He knows full well that without him, meals would not be served, the other family members would not get up or go to bed when they were supposed to, and no one would clean or spruce the house up when company was coming. He's also noticed how people skimp on their personal hygiene. They have to be washed, their teeth have to be brushed, and their hair has to be combed.

Everyone is disorganized too. His shipmates seem to have no idea where their clothes or papers are. The two-year-old is forever reorganizing the possessions of his chaotic fellow travellers only to see them ruin his meticulous work. Shouldering responsibility for absolutely everything that goes on in the home is a tough job, but someone's got to do it.

At two years of age, a human being's sense of self-worth and independence is at its zenith. The two-year-old is truly master (or mistress!) of all he or she surveys.

In a true spirit of *la noblesse oblige*, he graciously sees to the fortunes of his vassals. His ministrations are as officious as they are tender. Anyone who bursts into tears in front of a two-year-old can expect solicitude above and beyond the call of duty. A blanket and pillow will materialize, and water, milk or whatever other beverages come to hand will be served.

The afflicted will then be stroked over the forehead and comforted with a stuffed animal deemed to have explicit healing properties.

Through all the years and all the children, I have always thought that no household should be without a two-year-old.

The two-year-old is a cooperative, helpful, loving soul who radiates well being and harmony. He is filled with a joyful benevolence. He will gladly do whatever you, Mom or Dad, tell him. He is up for anything that seems like fun. He comes when you call him. He will hold your hand when you are out with him (usually). He will even put candy back on the shelf at the store and wave goodbye to it – if only you let him have candy on another occasion.

He is fearless, happy and positive. Animals, new people and new environments are all interesting. He meets the world and life with tranquil optimism.

And he's courageous – but not to the point of recklessness. He has the dogged, unpretentious courage that truly responsible people tend to have.

He can manage a great deal. He understands the day-to-day lives of his parents. He understands the mechanics of cleaning, cooking and dressing. He can find his way around the house in his sleep if he has to. What was so foreign to him only a short time ago, he knows like the back of his hand now. It's really quite an achievement. He has become familiar with literally thousands of things. He understands how they are used and what they are for – and he knows exactly how his own ability fits into the equation. He is as balanced and secure as it's possible for a human being to be. He knows what he needs to know.

Or so he thinks. Life isn't that simple of course, but in his own estimation he's perfect. He is on the verge of life's most horrendous changing phase – the terrible twos. It is during this phase that he will discover his shortcomings, and he will have to face terrors beyond his wildest dreams.

But he is blissfully unaware of all this.

For now, he is master of all he surveys.

The mastery phase that a little person goes through at the age of two is one of the most wonderful periods in all of childhood. A sense of calm, stability, security and happiness are the hallmarks of all mastery phases, and the two-year-old embodies them perfectly. He is so secure that he can gladly cope with anything that comes out of the blue. If there is a party, he can keep going until midnight or more. If you're away from home with him, he will take radically different (or non-existent) routines in his stride and even thrive on them. He is flexible, adaptable and gloriously positive. He is a pure delight both for himself and his surroundings.

All his talents must be put to good use. The one-year-old regarded himself as an existential *sine qua non* and the rest of the universe as an optional appendage. If there is one thing the two-year-old can't bear however, it's being shut out of his community.

Clingy, whiny, insecure two-year-olds do exist, but the root cause is lack of social participation. The child has simply not been put to work. The all-important conviction that he is needed in some practical, concrete way and that he is a participant in the flock's daily struggle for existence is missing.

The knowledge that he is indispensable is the source of the two-year-old's self-confidence.

This knowledge should ideally be inculcated at three to four months (See "ABCs for little people" in Part three of *For the Love of Children*), but if that has not happened for some reason, it's not too late to repair the damage. The two-year-old is grateful for any sign that he is needed and that he has a worthwhile contribution to make. Naturally, the two-year-old needs love just like the rest of us, but he also needs tasks to carry out that *do not revolve around him*.

If you offer him systematic participation in the activities that are necessary for you (the flock), no matter how brief or seemingly insignificant, you will make his day. If, on the other hand, you effectively expel him from the community by fobbing him off with toys (in your own home or somewhere else), you are depriving his life of meaning.

A two-year-old who is not needed for anything and who is not allowed to contribute to the collective struggle for survival will often try to compensate for a life devoid of meaning by taking control over his own little slice of reality. This results in an obsession with ritual. Cut off from social participation, the two-year-old will try to convince himself and his surroundings that he is in control of his life – and life's rituals "need" him.

Thus, going to bed can take hours. Stories have to be read in a certain order, and his room has to be arranged just so. The bed has to be made a certain way, and Mom or Dad has to sit in a certain spot. He has to pee, drink three glasses of water, and plump his pillows. Then stuffed animals have to be arranged, each animal having his or her predetermined place. The blanket has to be smoothed out and folded back at a forty-five degree angle, and the pattern cannot vary by so much as a millimeter.

There are experts who claim that this kind of behavior is normal for children that age. I vehemently disagree. Quite the contrary, this kind of behavior should set off alarm bells. A two-year-old who deep down knows that *the others wouldn't manage as well without me* (See "Psychological well-being" in Part two of *For the Love of Children*), who is needed, put to good use and allowed to contribute will *not* develop this almost hysterical obsession with ritual.

Two-year-olds talk. Sentences now comprise three or four words, and he knows his own name. His comprehension skills are even more impressive. Because he understands so much, you might be tempted to overestimate the power of words and underestimate the importance of actions.

I strongly advise against this. If you want the child to hand you a newspaper, you should – for quite a while to come – stretch out your hand towards the paper and simultaneously ask for it.

Be prepared for the possibility that your two-year-old still won't understand you. He may hand you the letter from the collection agency threatening to repossess your car instead of The New York Times.

It's not easy for people who are perfect (at least in their own estimation) to be told they have made a mistake. Sensitive parents refrain therefore from saying things like, "Why are you giving me letters from people who are out to wreck my life? I asked for the newspaper!"

Instead, sensitive parents thank their offspring profusely for handing them the charming missive from the collection agency and add, "May I have the newspaper *too* please?"

Words are good; words are important – but words are not an essential part of a two-year-old's life.

Over the years, many parents have expressed their concerns to me over the fact that their two-year-olds have not begun to speak or speak badly. But there are so many ways to communicate! The spoken word is just one option. A two-year-old who knows he is understood without actually having to speak doesn't attach much importance to words. An understanding atmosphere in the home is far more important than words.

Or, to put it another way, all the words in the language cannot compensate for a lack of understanding except superficially.

My little boy, who had five older siblings, was still not talking at three. Just after his third birthday, I went on vacation with a girlfriend, and my son stayed with her parents. He had never met them before, and I was worried because he still had not started to talk. But when I returned to bring him back home, he was talking a blue streak. He had realized that he had to talk if he was going to be understood.

It's just that when we got home, he *stopped* talking again…

The two-year-old possesses practical knowledge about people, things and life generally. He has devoted his brief existence to exploring the world he was born into, and he has now reached the apex of the mastery phase.

He can do a lot and he knows a lot, but he lacks judgement. He doesn't have the experience to weigh the pros and cons of a course of action and make an informed decision. His knowledge of the world is restricted to the concrete and the demonstrable.

He sleeps in his bed because it's his and that is where he has always slept. He knows that the other people in the household have their own beds, and that's where *they* sleep. (Speaking of beds, it should be mentioned that the fashionable idea of throwing out the crib and giving a two-year-old a regular bed is a bad one. Depriving him of his familiar, lived-in crib and casting him adrift in a vast, unfamiliar twin mattress is best left until after the terrible twos.)

It is during the terrible twos that the abyss opens at the two-year-old's feet, and he begins to ask questions like: "Why should I sleep in this particular bed? What would happen if I slept in another bed – or didn't sleep at all?"

Being able to pronounce all the letters in the Hebrew alphabet doesn't mean you can understand the Torah. That in a nutshell is the two-year-old's dilemma. He grasps the form but not the content.

In fact, he doesn't even know that there is such a thing as "content".

Still, mastering the Hebrew alphabet is no mean feat. The two-year-old regards himself as highly competent – and his competence should be given the admiration it deserves.

Competence, however, should not be confused with judgement. He has lots of the former but none of the latter. You can't count on him or place demands on him, but you can make him happy by allowing him to enjoy his matchless overestimation of himself for as long as it lasts. Soon enough, he will realize that his Hebrew isn't as good as he thought it was. When that day arrives, his self-confidence will evaporate.

But for now, he's perfect (in his opinion), and thus sensitive to criticism, as people who think they're perfect always are. He knows, for example, how to read a book. If you, ambitious parent that you are, point out that he's holding the book upside down (a fairly common occurrence) and turn it the right way up, he will be deeply wounded. He knows how to read a book. You hold it and turn the pages!

If he dresses himself and puts his pants on back to front, ridicule is, needless to say, a dagger in the heart.

Even kind encouragement and offers of help are offensive. A well-meant "Can I help you?" will cause the two-year-old to look at you as though you had just violated every single provision in the UN Convention on the Rights of the Child. The situation demands that you wax poetic over his unparalleled ability to dress himself.

You then notice quite by chance that his pants are on backwards.

"Look at your pants!" you cry. "They've turned themselves backwards. Let's turn them around."

It is the *pants* that are at fault, not the two-year-old.

For information on routines, food, sleep, social participation etc., see "Eleven months to one year. Maintaining good habits" in Part three of *For the Love of Children*.

THE TWO-YEAR-OLD AND LIFE

You have a lot of business to take care of when you're two. There are things that have to be mixed together for example. There is orange juice that has to be poured on cereal, and there is cheese that has to be washed in the dishwasher. You just have to remember to put the detergent in first. There are hats that have to be tried on – and slept in. Shoes need to be checked. All kids need shoes. With no shoes to put on, how would you know when it was time to go outside?

And it's nice to have company when you go out. Mom can wear her slippers. When you're two, you have no qualms about commandeering Mom's boots. Mom's friend, a tall round person, will manage fine in white stilettos. The seventeen-year-old visitor can have your worn-out blue sandals. It's nice to dispense things you like to people you like.

Once you're out of the house, sometimes a car is waiting. Doors have to be opened and closed, and buttons have to be pushed. Most fun are the windshield wipers. They glide and whisper over the glass until four-year-old big brother comes and removes them. Well, a lot of things come loose like knobs on the stove. If it isn't one thing, it's another. And then there's bathtub faucets that have to be turned on. The water just runs and runs. And phone calls must be administered. "Hello, goodbye! Hello, goodbye!" Same format every time. Never-ending job, but someone's got to do it.

There are also hedgehogs that sneak into the outhouse and have to be looked after, and at two you are only too happy to step up to the plate. But you're not stupid. Let big brother have first dibs. Big sister fetches milk in a bowl. It sloshes around and you have to run your legs off if the hedgehog is going to get anything to eat.

Animals are fun. Starlings sometimes nest under the boards in the ceiling. People think that you can't climb a ladder, but what do they know? You just have to shut the door first so that you're left in peace. Some things you just have to do alone.

Food can be a problem. There's never enough to eat. With a variety of discreet gestures, you try and catch the attention of your surroundings. You drag a high chair up to the table, climb into it and wait. And wait and wait. Not a soul pays a blind bit of attention. So you just have to raid the fridge on your own. There are some empty bottles in the cupboard. They'll do to pour milk into. Then you can retire to a quiet sofa corner, have a drink and munch whatever you've managed to snaffle. It's not the same as a real meal though.

Spiders and worms make great presents for Mom. She just loves them. You can also pick flowers, but it's best to tear off the pretty part and leave the stem. What good are stems anyway? Clay has to be transported too. It can be placed in shoes, on the kitchen floor or in the oven. It depends. Variety is the spice of life. Clay is at its best when it's wet. It's squishy and sticks to things.

The world is full of people who need help blowing their noses. You have to grab yourself a couple of yards of paper towel and make the rounds. Then everyone has to be kissed. That's almost a full-time job in itself. But when you're the stanchion that holds up the universe, you have to make concessions. Give the peasants their due. Then take what you like and leave the rest.

When evening comes, you have to go downstairs twenty times to see what everyone is up to. And you're put to bed again… and again and again.

The end of another tough day. But tomorrow's another breakfast.

THE TERRIBLE TWOS: "I WANT TO, I DON'T WANT TO!"

The agonizing changing phase, popularly known as the terrible twos, begins at approximately two and a half if the child is a girl. As is usually the case, boys develop a little more slowly, so the phase begins later, at around three.

The terrible twos last around a year. In the middle of this period, the child will take a break lasting two to three months and enjoy an interlude of mastery and equilibrium. Then comes the second half of the match. How the child behaves during the second half will depend on how you dealt with her or him during the first.

Little children can try your patience in all sorts of ways – see "Something about personality" – but generally speaking, the most common pattern is one or two tough days followed by a few days of relative (or total) peace.

When children eventually emerge from the terrible twos, they possess maturity and insight that are quite beyond the ability of two-year-olds – emperors with no clothes that they tend to be. Once kids cross this Rubicon, they are capable of *interacting* with other people, big and small, and possess genuine consideration, understanding and generosity. They are both willing and able to make concessions to avoid being expelled from their communities. The existence they thought they understood so well now reveals itself as the multi-faceted marvel it really is, and they rise to the challenge with their newly acquired self-knowledge.

If the two-year-old could pronounce Hebrew words perfectly without grasping their content, as well as being unaware that something called "content" even existed, a child going through the terrible twos is immersing himself in the text. Once the process is complete, he is on his way to understanding what he's been reading.

The two-year-old was happy as long as he thought he had mastered his art. He thought he understood Hebrew, to continue with the analogy. Now he realizes that things aren't that simple, and it's a painful discovery. He has been forced to face that fact that being able to pronounce the alphabet is not the same as being able to understand the language. His whole conceptual universe has been turned upside down, and this plunges him into despair.

How is he going to surmount the formidable obstacles that have been placed in his path? He thought the journey was more or less over, and now he realizes that it's barely begun.

Changing phases are never pleasant. They are characterized by restless dissatisfaction. Something within a little (or big) person prods him towards further development, but this inner demand is vague and directionless. We all go through periods in our lives where something compels us to change, but a child in the throes of the terrible twos is experiencing this ordeal for the first time.

We all know how pivotal events such as a marriage breakdown or a mid-life crisis force us to evolve. We resist the inevitable for as long as we can, because we don't know where change will take us, but everyone succumbs in the end. Once we realize that it's sink or swim, we find the courage and the strength to propel ourselves forward. We pick a path and follow it. Our dissatisfaction morphs into decisiveness and we are empowered.

A child going through the terrible twos is still so young. He has so few tools to deal with the changes taking place in his life. Lacking the intellect, experience and maturity to cope with it all, he's caught between a rock and a hard place. This changing phase is agonizing, and there seems to be no way out. His unbalanced behavior is a protest against the impossible situation he finds himself in. The urge to develop inexorably impels him forward, only to hurl him against an immoveable wall.

As a one-year-old, he enjoyed himself and his own company. He quite shamelessly adored himself. At two, his self-esteem was at its peak, and his sense of mastery over his environment was total. Now the rug has been pulled out from under him, and he's in free fall. What is he? What can he do? What if the answer is *nothing*?

He's adrift on a cold, grey sea of doubt, distrust and despair.

Throughout the ordeal of the terrible twos, the child is delving ever deeper into the world he has been born into. He knows his abilities are inadequate and that terrifies him, but he wrings all he can out of the few resources he does have to draw on. He challenges his surroundings, just as they challenge him. He resists change even as he fights so ferociously to achieve it. He is utterly incapable of taking charge of his own life, but that doesn't stop him from trying. For the first time, he is at war with himself.

There are many similarities between the terrible twos and an adult's mid-life crisis. "What was the point? What became of all my hopes and dreams? Is this all there is to life?"

It's not surprising that the forty-something man of our imagination does his utmost to avoid these vague but probing questions, and when they eventually hit home, he blames his wife.

"You've never understood me!" he rages. "It's your fault I'm unhappy!"

Equally predictably, the wife defends herself. "Easy to blame everything on me," she says, "but you're hardly perfect yourself."

Let's assume our mid-lifer divorces his wife, convinced that everything was her fault. It wouldn't be long before he discovered that no matter how far or how fast he runs, he can't escape from himself. The battle raging inside him is his and his alone. Nothing has changed. He still has to come to grips with his own life. He realizes that the dissatisfaction he experienced in his marriage had nothing to do with his wife and everything to do with him. The marriage got stuck in a rut because he got stuck in a rut. He would have had a mid-life crisis if he had been single.

Now let's assume that the wife, instead of rejecting his accusations, gives her husband a hug and says, "Of course, sweetheart, it is my fault that you're not happy. I'll change. What do you want me to do?"

Now our mid-lifer starts making demands. His wife is to change her habits, her appearance and her behavior. She complies with his every whim, but no matter how hard she tries, there is no pleasing him. Quite the contrary, the more she tries to mollify him, the more outrageously idiotic his demands become. He becomes jealous, tyrannical and generally impossible to live with.

As the icing on the cake, he starts to physically abuse her. His wife finally draws the line.

"Enough!" she screams. "No matter what I do, it's never good enough!"

And he is back to square one. She leaves him and he is alone with himself again.

Deep down he knew the truth all along. It wasn't her "fault". It wasn't about her at all. It was about him.

He drove both her and himself to the point of no return. He was forced to face the demand for change – a demand that came from inside him.

Sooner or later, we all meet ourselves.

The child going through the terrible twos is in the same boat. To stave off the demand for change, he attacks his surroundings. No matter how hard you try to meet his increasingly absurd demands, he's never satisfied. He will push you until you lash out – and then he's alone with himself again.

Unpleasant tendencies will rise to the surface. Like our forty-something, a terrible two can be tyrannical, wildly jealous and even physically violent. Just like our mid-lifer, a child this age is ill served by parents who cater to his every whim and who blame themselves for his problems, problems that are born of the battle raging inside him.

No one, big or small, a terrible two or a grown man going though a mid-life crisis, matured into a better person by being allowed to blame everyone but himself, manipulate his surroundings and elude his inner demons by pretending they don't exist.

The terrible two, like the mid-lifer, on some level, knows this. And that's where guilt enters the picture.

Whether I am a two-and-a-half-year-old or a mid-lifer, if I am dissatisfied with myself and my life and I know I should be moving forward, and I turn my dissatisfaction outwards towards you and you acquiesce, I will punish you for humoring me in my delusion and enabling me to put off the inevitable day of reckoning, since I know in my heart of hearts that the problem is with me not you.

I will certainly not be content, loving and grateful. Quite the contrary, I will be hostile, contemptuous and demanding.

A child going through the terrible twos, like our mid-lifer, is a trial sometimes. Temper tantrums come with the territory.

The harrowing description that follows is taken from a wide-spread manual on children:

"More than half of all two-year-olds have tantrums at least once or twice a week, and very few children reach their third birthday without having had such an attack. Children behave differently during tantrums, but your child will in all probability behave in a similar way each time. Children can run around the room screaming. They have no control over themselves and may therefore knock over anything moveable that happens to be in their path. If you don't protect children who are in the midst of a tantrum, they can easily hurl themselves against walls or heavy furniture. They may fall to the floor, writhe, scream and kick, as though they were possessed. They sometimes scream until they begin to turn blue. This means they have exhaled so violently that they are momentarily incapable of inhaling. Temper tantrums during which children hold their breath are particularly distressing for parents. Children can stop breathing for such long periods that they begin to go grey in the face and are on the point of losing consciousness. They will sustain no lasting harm however. Their reflexes take over and force air into the lungs before these children are in any real danger."

The assertion that more than half of all two-year-olds behave this way once or twice a week is perhaps true, but that does not make the situation any less horrifying.

Why don't we ask why children have tantrums in the first place? We ask why alcoholics drink, don't we?

The kind of behavior described above is unacceptable. It has to be prevented!

The Friend of Order recommends that the parents show love and affection to comfort their children in such situations. The terrible two who is so beside himself with rage he almost passes out should be stroked and hugged tenderly.

The result is, more often than not, more rage not less, and ultimately children can lose consciousness.

I would argue that empathy is hardly appropriate during tantrums, and loss of consciousness should never be accepted as a "normal" part of the terrible twos. Children who have temper tantrums are suffering mightily from inner chaos, and our duty as parents is to impose order on chaos, not give chaos our seal of approval.

How would you react to a hysterical adult who was rolling around on the floor in a paroxysm of fury? Would you really smile tenderly, put your arms around him and empathize with his plight?

Opposition and leadership are required to put an end to what is clearly an unbearable situation. Children going through the terrible twos have been known to whimper "*Help me!*" in the middle of a tantrum.

Love can only be given to someone who is capable of accepting it.

Tantrums, be they aggressive, despairing or hysterical, must be met with firm leadership, a way out, an alternative, a new direction, the net result of which is *an end to the cycle of helplessness.*

Your terrible two, who has trusted you implicitly since birth, is really asking for your support and help if you look beneath all the provocation and disharmony.

Some parents offer no resistance and fail to provide leadership during tantrums out of a misplaced fear of being cruel. After all, the poor kid is suffering enough, and fighting fire with fire seems unduly harsh. But if a child discovers that he can't depend on the one person he trusts above all others, a terrible burden is laid on his shoulders. The burden he already has to carry – the inexorable urge to develop which forces him forward on a path strewn with thorns – is heavy enough. That goes for big people as well as little ones.

The responsibility for his own relief, his own liberation, his own release from inner chaos is way too much for a young child. Forcing such a responsibility on him is a betrayal.

Some terrible twos do nothing but fight you tooth and nail, and others never have a tantrum of the kind described above.

You might think that parents whose children sail through the terrible twos with relatively little trouble – and some kids do – should count themselves lucky. But there's a danger here. Without realizing it, some parents circumvent the terrible twos by acquiescing to the child's every whim – rather like our mid-lifer's wife.

And that is a mistake. The terrible twos is a maturation process that has to be lived through – and expressed. If this stage is skipped or skimped on, the child will be ill prepared to deal with an ever more demanding world. And himself for that matter.

"Kate is never a problem," asserts her mother. "She's good as gold."

Unfortunately, Kate's mother has become her daughter's doormat without even realizing it. Since Kate's mother never puts up any resistance, her daughter doesn't need to defy her.

"Move," says Kate. "I want to sit there."

"Of course, sweetheart," says mother and moves.

It's time for lunch and Kate's mother calls her.

"I don't want to eat," says Kate.

"Well then you don't have to," says Mom.

"NOW I'm hungry," says Kate an hour later. Mom heats up Kate's food.

"Don't talk," says Kate. Mom is obediently silent.

"I want to sleep in your bed," says Kate. "And I want you to go to bed NOW." So Mom goes to bed with Kate at her side.

Kate doesn't make impossible demands on her mother. Her dictatorial tendencies don't create serious problems, but that doesn't make her any less dictatorial. The message that Kate is sending to her mother is "If you don't do what I say, you don't love me." And love like that is not really worth having.

What is happening to Kate? She's is becoming a spoiled little brat, which means that further down the road she will meet the resistance that her mother is denying her. And this resistance will be harsh indeed.

Her mother could have spared her this by assuming the role of "outside world" and offering Kate loving, helpful, manageable resistance that would have prepared her for life outside the home.

Little Robert is a lot harder on his dad than Kate is on her mom.

"Move," says Robert. "I want to sit there."

"OK," mumbles Dad, picks up his paper and gets up. He looks around for another place to sit.

Robert points to a chair. "Sit THERE!" and Dad sits down.

"NO!" screams Robert. "You can't sit there."

Dad is confused. "But you said…"

"Go away! Go away!" screams Robert.

His father tries to object. "But Robert, calm down. I have to sit somewhere. I'm going to sit here."

"Go! Go! GO!" screams Robert, who is now on the verge of hysteria.

His dad moves towards the door, uncertain of what to do next.

"NO!" screams Robert, who is now in tears. "Sit THERE!"

Dad shakes his head. He is at a loss, but he does what the boy says and sits down on the chair Robert is pointing at, only to be told yet again that he can't sit there. Soon both father and son are beside themselves. Dad tries to comfort Robert, but the child just wails like a banshee.

Since whatever he does is wrong, Dad eventually loses his temper. "Oh, make up your mind kid!" he yells. "What do you want?!"

He then gives up on the whole enterprise, stomps out of the room and slams the door behind him.

Out in the kitchen, Dad tries to calm down and finds himself beset by conflicting emotions. He feels confused and helpless, and he fluctuates between guilt over losing his temper and hostile feelings towards his son.

Robert meanwhile celebrates yet another hollow victory. He had tried to take issue with the helplessness experienced by all children going through the terrible twos – the helplessness that results from the paralyzing realization of just how inadequate one's abilities really are. The only way he could do this was by exerting power over his father. Yet Robert could not accept that his father, who should be both leader and protector, seemed to be as helpless as he was. Helpless is not something that dads should be.

Robert's painful but necessary maturation process will not run its appointed course if he is allowed to use his father as a tool to avoid having to confront himself. It will be delayed and derailed.

Dad has to bounce the struggle back to Robert. Our mid-lifer was not able to get his life back on track by using his wife as a punching bag. She had to refuse to play the role. Only then could he do the necessary soul searching and successfully do battle with himself. Making his wife take the rap for his own inner turmoil only made him feel worse. Robert is in the same boat. Robert cannot accept his dad's helplessness, and so he refuses to quit.

Such tantrums, and worse, will be commonplace as long as his dad refuses to take charge of the situation, but rather breaks down and appeals to Robert. He's just pouring fuel on the fire. Dad may start to loathe his impossible child, and such feelings will be hard for him to bear.

And Robert, who can no more accept that he is loathsome than he can accept that his dad is helpless, suffers the tortures of the damned. Who can save him?

Robert is developing a will of his own, and he is not shy about using it. But a strong will is terrifying to children this age because they lack the maturity, experience and judgement to put it to good use.

Robert must be told where the boundaries are in no uncertain terms.

Let's see what happens if Robert's dad takes charge and stands up to his son.

"Move," says Robert. "I want to sit there!"

"No," says Dad calmly. "I'm sitting here."

Robert persists. He wants Dad's chair and that's that.

Dad is not about to give up either. "I'm sitting here," he says. "You can sit on the sofa."

"I don't want to!" says Robert.

"Suit yourself," says Dad.

Robert starts to scream. "I WANT TO SIT THERE!"

"Well, that's too bad," says Dad evenly. "I'm sitting here and I'm not going anywhere. But you can sit on my knee if you like."

"NO!" bawls Robert. "I don't want to."

"Then don't. I'm sitting here."

Robert, who has now decided that this is a fight to the death, starts to pinch his dad's knees.

"Stop that," says Dad. "It hurts. It's not nice." He takes Roberts hands, kisses them and releases them.

Robert starts pinching him again. He's in combat mode.

"Stop it!" says Dad more sharply.

Robert blithely continues pinching.

Dad takes Robert's hands firmly and looks him in the eye. "Pinching isn't nice. It hurts. You can't pinch people. You stroke people gently. Like this. OK?"

With Robert's hand in his, he strokes himself on the knee all the while maintaining eye contact with Robert.

Robert stops pinching and tries to think of something else that might drive Dad up the wall. He catches sight of a vase on the table. A few seconds later, the vase crashes to the floor, and the effect on Dad is immediate and dramatic. He liked that vase, and Robert broke it on purpose.

"What the hell do you think you're doing!" roars Robert's father, who is on the verge of going ballistic. To avoid doing something he might regret, Robert's dad hauls the boy into his room, puts him in bed and closes the door.

Robert howls with indignation. On the other side of the door, Dad waits for silence to descend. When it finally does, Dad opens the door.

"Have you finished?"

Renewed protests.

Dad closes the door and waits. When Robert is quiet, he opens the door and repeats his question. "Have you finished? Do you want to come out now?"

Robert glowers at his dad, but says nothing.

"OK," says Dad. "Let's go pick up the pieces."

He picks Robert up and carries him into the living room. Faced with the evidence of his transgression, Robert starts to protest again.

"No!" he whines. "I don't want to."

"That's too bad," says Dad. "You're going to pick up the pieces anyway. When you break something, you clean up after yourself."

"I don't want to!" screams Robert.

Dad is imperturbable. "Now pick up the pieces," he says.

Dad holds Robert's hand in his and very carefully picks up a piece of the vase and lays it on the table. The action is repeated until the job is done. Robert protests at the beginning, but Dad takes no notice.

"We'll just leave everything on the table, and I'll try to glue the pieces together later."

At which point Dad returns to the chair he was sitting in when this whole little drama began. He goes back to his paper as though nothing has happened.

Robert stands where he is for a couple of minutes. He then wanders around the room somewhat aimlessly, but eventually decides to retire to his bedroom and amuse himself there.

Robert does not try his dad's patience again that day.

Because Dad handled the situation well, Robert received three messages:

• Dad is a man of his word. What he says goes. *Dad doesn't need to be challenged* at a time when Robert's need for change compels him to challenge everything.

• Dad knows the drill. He knows how the world works. (If you break a vase, you pick up the pieces.) *Dad fulfils his role as a leader in the flock* and gives support where it is needed.

• Dad likes Robert just fine. However, he doesn't like some of the things that Robert does. *It's the behavior that receives a failing grade, not the boy himself.* Dad's anger was directed exclusively at what Robert did. He feels no aversion towards Robert as a human being and has no desire to distance himself from his son.

Children this age are not philosophically gifted. They are incapable of drawing general conclusions from one or two concrete actions that adults take. The rules must be reinforced, and children need to reassure themselves that these rules apply to all situations all the time. By challenging and provoking their parents, children are constantly posing new questions. A terrible two needs hundreds, if not thousands, of concrete examples before the penny drops and he is able to deduce a general principle.

Little Robert is a strong willed child, and he pushes his dad to the limit. But whatever Robert does, his father offers resistance and responds to Robert's provocations in a way that satisfies Robert. Thus, Dad lives up to Robert's expectations. He knows he can count on his dad. He can trust him.

The defiant age of the terrible twos is one of the most challenging for both the child and the parent. The child, full of disbelief, distrust, refusals and sometimes violence against you, is constantly testing his confidence in you. And you, the parent, must endure all this in such a way that you prove to him that you are indeed someone he can place his confidence and trust in.

Little Eugene, barely three years old, is getting ready for bed.

"I want another teddy bear," he unexpectedly announces.

His dad is astonished. "Another teddy bear? This is the only one you have."

"I want another teddy bear!" Eugene insists.

"This is your teddy. You've had him since forever. He's yours. Why don't you want him?"

"I want another teddy bear!" Eugene repeats, his voice rising several octaves.

Dad is mystified. He picks up the bear and offers it to Eugene. "Take your teddy and lie down."

"I don't WANT him!" screams Eugene and throws the bear to the floor. "I want another teddy bear!"

"But Eugie…"

"I WANT ANOTHER TEDDY BEAR!" wails Eugene on the verge of hysteria now.

Dad is at a loss. Finally, he decides to try and reason with Eugene. He has learned that you have to explain things to young children. They see the light eventually.

"Listen pal," he says as he tries to put his son on his lap. "This is your teddy bear. He's the only one you've got. Maybe you'll get a new teddy one of these days. Maybe for your birthday. But for now, you'll just have to make do with what you've got. And anyway, I couldn't get you another teddy, even if I tried. It's night and all the stores are closed. There's no way I can get you another teddy. Do you understand?"

Eugene isn't listening, and he's not sitting on Dad's knee either. He doesn't seem to have heard a word his father has said. He's too busy screaming.

"I want another teddy!" he manages to gasp out between hysterical sobs.

What will happen?

The tantrum will come to an end in one of the following three ways.

1. The child will go into convulsions, which will eventually result in loss of consciousness.

2. Eugene will break the cycle himself by rejecting his dad ("Go! GO!"), who seems unable to help him. He will sob in isolation for a long time and console himself as best he can.

3. Dad can break the cycle by speaking to his son firmly but soothingly and *by showing the boy a way out*. This means imposing a solution. ("This is how things are going to be. This is what we are going to do.")

This first alternative obviously leaves much to be desired. Eugene will not physically injure himself and will regain consciousness quickly. He will eventually calm down, sniffle dejectedly and accept comfort from his father. But a person of any age doesn't lose consciousness until he or she has been pushed to the limit both mentally and physically, and I don't believe young children should have to endure that kind of anguish.

The second alternative is hardly ideal either. Even adults have trouble finding their way back to sanity unaided once hysteria strikes. Hysterical persons trapped in a cycle of powerlessness can hardly be left to their own devices if there are loved ones around to help them escape from their own inner chaos. Actually, the afflicted can be reasonably certain of help, even if they are surrounded by strangers. If they are left to fend for themselves, their sense of abandonment grows exponentially.

A terrible two is only a kid, and a little one at that. Parents who expect a terrible two to ride out such a terrible storm and make order out of chaos all alone are demanding a degree of maturity that few, if any, adults possess.

The third alternative liberates the child from an unbearable situation. The fact that the situation is self-imposed doesn't make Eugene's suffering any less intense. The terrible two has to place obstacles in his own path in order to develop and mature.

Hysteria should never be allowed to arise in the first place and is completely preventable.

Eugene's dad can head the whole teddy bear debacle off at the pass with a ruse that is as simple as it is effective. *He can forbid whatever it is the child is refusing*. That way both sides "win".

"I don't WANT it!" screams Eugene and throws the bear to the floor.

His dad picks it up. "Then you CAN'T have it," he says calmly. "I'm taking it away."

"No!" hollers Elias. "I want my teddy bear!"

Problem solved.

Turning the tables and forbidding what the child is refusing is an effective method, since it enables the child to question the order of things without standing the world on its head. Eugene, after all, wants his bear. He doesn't really want to call into question his dear old teddy.

On the other hand, he *has to* because he has to question everything. His teddy has hitherto been self-evident. But why should it be? What if his teddy bear is not self-evident at all? Why should just his teddy bear be self-evident? Why shouldn't he have another one? Why should he have a teddy bear at all?

His father offers resistance by raising the stakes. Not only is Eugene's teddy bear not self-evident, it's not even permitted! At the same time, he sends a message about what will happen if Eugene questions things. They will disappear.

Dad's behavior doesn't say that the teddy bear is self-evident, which is good since Eugene cannot digest facts and experiences that he hasn't grappled with himself. He can't regard his bear as self-evident just because Dad says it is.

Dad's behavior says instead, "No, your bear is not self-evident at all. It could just as easily be mine as yours, which would mean that you couldn't have it. What do you say to that?" Eugene realizes that if he calls the bear into question, he risks losing it. His dad will take it.

Eugene is faced with rather a stark choice: to have his bear or not to have his bear. Either the bear is with his dad or it's with Eugene. The key here is that Eugene decides he *wants* the bear to be with him. He is not accepting the bear because Dad says he should or because it's self-evident that the bear belongs with Eugene. Thus, both sides "win".

Dad's original intention was that the bear should stay with Eugene. He gave it to his son. Eugene defied his father's wishes and rejected the bear. Dad then did a perfect U-turn and forbade what he had been so recently advocating. Eugene in turn defied the prohibition, and now he wants his bear back. Dad "wanted" the bear too, but he accedes to his son's wishes and gives him his teddy.

Eugene went toe to toe with his father and won – but within the framework that his dad had set up. Dad wanted Eugene to have the bear in bed with him. Thus, the world was not turned upside down. Nothing changed.

Eugene's will was put to the test, and he won a victory – within reasonable limits set by his father. Once victory was secured, Eugene could yield. Peace descended without hysteria, humiliation or struggle.

Little Rosita is called to the table.

"I don't want any dinner!" she says.

"Fine," says mother calmly and begins to clear the table. "Then you CAN'T have any dinner. I'll put everything away."

"No!" screams Rosita. "I want dinner."

"So sit at the table," says Mom, "and you'll get something really yummy."

Quite unperturbed, and naturally not the least triumphant, she pretends as though everything is as it should be, which of course it is. Her intention was to get Rosita to eat her dinner. Rosita's outburst was but an aside that changed nothing.

Little William refuses to go to bed. Finally, his dad loses patience.

"OK," he says, "you CAN'T go to bed. Sit on the stool in the kitchen." He puts William on the stool and sets about doing the dishes.

William clambers down after a while.

"Do you want to go to bed now?" asks Dad.

"No, I don't want to go to bed!"

"Well, then you CAN'T go to bed. Get back up on the stool." Dad continues with the dishes.

"I don't want to sit here!" whines William.

"So go to bed then."

"I don't want to go to bed."

"Then sit on the stool."

William climbs down again.

"So do you want to go to bed now?" asks Dad calmly.

"No, I don't WANT to go to bed."

"Then you CAN'T! Sit on the stool."

And so it continues.

Finally, William gets down from the stool and goes to bed in surly silence. Whereupon Dad tucks him in tenderly and lovingly, just as he always does. God is in his heaven and all's right with the world.

William is a stubborn, persistent kid, but as a rule, one prohibition is enough. "You CAN'T go to bed. Sit on the stool." After a few minutes on the stool, which is high and boring, he usually surrenders and hits the hay.

When this happens, Dad naturally doesn't pick another fight by looking triumphant or lording it over his son. "There, you see? Why didn't you just do what you were told? There's no point in messing with me, so you might as well get used to it!"

Parents who react to a tantrum in such an idiotic way are asking for a public flogging – and their children will oblige them.

410

It's just not fair play.

It should be added that as luck would have it, terrible twos can't cope with more than two options. William won't protest against sitting on the stool *and* going to bed. He lives in an either-or universe.

When a sensitive little soul tries your patience – see "Something about personality", where I outline the various personality types – he will do so in ways that differ vastly from the tactics employed by William and his somewhat more robust colleagues.

The sensitive type simply falls apart. He bursts into tears rather than yelling and screaming. If you bang your fist on the table and tell him that this is how things are and if he doesn't like it, he will just have to go to his room, you will crush him. He will sink into bottomless despair. Even a brusque tone of voice can terrify the sensitive type.

But just because you have to tread softly and carefully when dealing with a sensitive type who is having a tantrum, that doesn't mean you don't stick to your guns. You have to stand your ground and achieve your goal, but instead of responding to his challenge with strong, maybe angry resistance, you're aiming for velvet, tender resistance, as though you profoundly re-gretted that you had to resist in the first place.

That said, once you have drawn the proverbial line in the sand, the child can't be allowed to cross it.

"Come on sweetheart, it's time for your bath."

Little Molly stands in front of her mother as though rooted to the spot. Her eyes fill with tears, and she turns on her heel and runs away. Mom gives chase.

"Molly, come back. It's time for your bath. It will be such fun."

She manages to get hold of the child, who is now sobbing loudly. "I don't want a bath!"

"But it's going to be so much fun," says Mom soothingly. She kisses and hugs her daughter, and carries her back to the bathroom.

Molly's sobs are heart-rending, the tears flow in rivers, and she puts her feet against Mom's chest and tries to break free. She's determined to get out of having a bath, and she's getting desperate.

"I don't want to!"

"That's really a shame," says her mother. "You really don't want to have a bath? Well, then you will have to stay in your room for a while. When you're ready to take a bath, you can come out."

Mom puts Molly in bed. She strokes her daughter's cheek, all the while telling her gently that she can come out of her room as soon as she is ready to take a bath. She repeats the message until she is sure Molly has understood. Then she waits by the door.

As soon as Molly falls silent, even if it's only to catch her breath before embarking on yet another chorus of sobs, Mom opens the door and asks softly but enthusiastically, "Do you want your bath now?"

With indefatigable affection, understanding and warmth, she perseveres for as long as it takes. She only relinquishes her post at the door when Molly stops crying and thereby signals that she is ready to take her bath. With great delight, Mom takes her daughter into the bathroom and bathes her.

Forbidding what Molly refuses – "You CAN'T have a bath" – might work if Mom can imbue her words with the right mix of tenderness and regret:

"I'm really sorry, but I'm afraid you can't have a bath. It's a shame, but I'm going to let the water out and put away all the bath toys. No bath tonight!"

There is, however, the risk that sensitive little Molly will be gripped by such deep despair in the face of a direct prohibition that it will overcome her. Gentle but firm banishment – *carefully monitored* – is to be preferred.

The following is a description of how a little eel going through the terrible twos (see "Something about personality") might conduct himself.

"You really do have to clean up your room," Mother tells little Joseph, three and a half years old.

"I will Mommy," says Joseph piously. He disappears into his room, while Mom busies herself in the kitchen.

"Are you cleaning your room?" she calls after a little while.

"Yes Mom," answers Joseph.

Time passes. Then Mom looks in on Joseph and discovers that he is calmly playing with his Tonka truck. The mess is untouched.

"Joseph!" says Mom. "You haven't picked up a thing. Get busy!"

"OK Mom," says Joseph dutifully.

"You'll clean up your room, yes?" asks Mom a little suspiciously.

"Yes Mommy."

Mom goes back to the kitchen and does the dishes. When she's done, she checks to see whether Joseph has done what he promised. She finds him still playing with his truck, not a care in the world. He hasn't budged.

"I'm going to get angry with you Joseph," says his mother. "Clean up your room! I'm not leaving until you're done. Now get busy!"

412

"Actually, Mom, I don't feel like it," Joseph announces and sails serenely out of the room.

His mother can give up on the whole enterprise, sigh over her son's disobedience and clean up the boy's room herself.

Joseph doesn't push his mom any further. He's untiringly sweet and cute.

This is hardly an ideal solution however. Even though Joseph's defiance is relatively civilized, he is showing that he is just as deficient in maturity and judgement as his more aggressive counterparts. He suffers from the need to question everything just as much as any other terrible two does. If his mother lets him get away with not cleaning up his room, he will be forced to come to the depressing conclusion that he cannot count on support and help from her.

And his mother will conclude that she has a disobedient son, which will make her insecure and fearful. What would happen if Joseph were on the point of darting out into a busy street? She would call to him to wait and he would ignore her. The result could be catastrophic.

Joseph's trust in his mother has been shaken, but Mom's confidence in herself, as a leader, protector and nurturer, has also taken a body blow – which is just as serious.

Let's take another look at this situation.

For one thing, Joseph's mother can't expect her son to "clean up" his room. It's too much and too abstract. He is way too young for such endeavours.

For another, he's not yet able to take sole responsibility for tasks that are assigned to him. His mother has to work with him. At the very least, she must be physically present.

If things are going to get picked up, mother and son must do it together, and Mom has a right and a duty to demand that Joseph works *just as long as she does* – which means he has to work until the job is done, but at his own pace and in keeping with his own ability.

If, on the other hand, Mom is prepared to do most of the work herself but wants Joseph to help just a little, she must assign him a specific task i.e. put away *that* particular pile of cars or put *that* puzzle back on the shelf. She then has to make sure that Joseph does it.

Let's assume Joseph's mother said what she said.

"Clean up your room."

"OK Mom," replies Joseph and disappears into his room and calmly sets about playing with his truck.

Mother looks in on him and sees that she and her son have somewhat divergent opinions about what "clean up your room" means. She realizes that Joseph is defying her.

She also realizes that her demands are unreasonable. She has told Joseph to clean up his room and has been met with a flat refusal, but instead of retreating, she modifies her demands.

"Pick up those blocks Joseph," she says.

"OK Mom," says Joseph and studiously ignores the blocks.

"Pick up the blocks," insists his mother raising her voice. Her tone is firm but not hostile.

"No Mom," he replies and makes for the door.

His mother grips him and leads him over to the blocks.

"Pick up the blocks, sweetheart, and put them in the drawer."

Joseph stands silent and motionless in his mother's arms. If anything, he seems absent-minded.

Mother takes his hand and places it over a block. Her hand over his, she picks up one block after another until they are all put away.

She acts as though Joseph was the one who had done all the work.

"Good job! You've done all the blocks – perfect! That's my boy! Well done!"

Now she can either continue cleaning up Joseph's room herself – in which case there is a good chance that he will happily pitch in – or go on about her other chores for the moment. Everything is nice and dandy.

Joseph didn't want to clean up his room. Molly didn't want to take a bath. William refused to go to bed and had to sit on a kitchen stool for his trouble.

All these parents did what had to be done against their children's will – or more accurately their *expressed* will (remember Eugene and his teddy bear). If their actions had involved injustice or humiliation, or had in any way compromised their children's integrity, these children would have reacted with rage, hatred, despair or mute apathy.

On the contrary, the children reacted with relief.

Little Marty is visiting in someone else's house, and he takes a wristwatch off the table.

"Put the watch down please," says the man of the house.

Marty hadn't been in a particularly defiant mood when picked up the watch. He was just curious and wanted to examine it.

But the admonition to put the watch back brings out the terrible two in

414

him. With a you've-messed-with-the-wrong-marine expression on his face, he throws the watch to the floor.

"Pick up the watch and put it back on the table, Marty," says the man of the house calmly.

Marty tries to run out of the room, but his host, who Marty has so energetically challenged, is too quick for him. With his hand over Marty's, he picks up the watch and puts it on the table.

"Good job! Thanks bud."

Marty, who has never been subjected to such treatment in his life, is so chuffed he starts to laugh. He trails devotedly behind his benefactor for the rest of the day.

The reactions of children in the terrible twos will tell you whether or not you are on the right track. Their obvious *relief* is a reliable indicator that they have received a satisfactory (in every sense of the word) answer to the questions that they pose through their behavior.

Explanations, logic, appeals to common sense, indeed verbal communication generally, will have absolutely no effect on a terrible two. It's actions that count. What you say has to be reflected in what you do.

So pick your words carefully! You're going to have to act on them.

"Don't run around with a sandwich in your mouth! And why are you wearing that sweater? Put it back where you got it! Did you find the teddy you were looking for? Listen! The alarm clock is ringing. Go shut it off! Do you have to pee?"

Translating all this talk of sandwiches, sweaters, teddies, alarm clocks and bathroom breaks into actions can take anything from fifteen minutes to an entire afternoon. So, as a wise man put it, don't let your mouth write a cheque that your body can't cash!

In the following situation, a mother tries using logical arguments to persuade her young son to adopt a particular course of action.

Brian, three and a half years old, is on his way home after being picked up at nursery school by his mom. Brian is in his stroller and all is sweetness and light. They pass a convenience store.

"I want a banana," says Brian.

"We're going to eat when we get home," says Mom. "Are you hungry?"

"Yeah, and I want a banana," says Brian.

"But we have bananas at home," says Mom. "After lunch, you can have a banana."

They've left the convenience store behind them, and Brian has left the subject of bananas.

"I want to walk," he says.

"Can't you stay in the stroller? We have to get home and eat lunch."

"No, I want to walk," says Brian and starts to scramble out of the stroller. Mom is afraid he's going to fall out, so she stops.

Brian liberates himself before she can stop him. He takes a couple of steps and then just stands stock still in the middle of the sidewalk.

Mom, who has had time to get a little ahead of him, stops too.

"Come on Brian," she says. "We have to get home and eat."

Brian turns on his heel and heads in the opposite direction.

"Brian," she says, "You're going the wrong way!"

Brian sits down beside a low fence surrounding someone's front yard.

"Come on Brian," pleads Mom. "We have to get home."

"I want to sit here," says Brian.

"If you want to sit down, why don't you sit in the stroller?" asks Mom. She parks the stroller beside him.

"I want to walk," says Brian and gets up.

"Then walk beside me and let's get home," says Mom.

But Brian climbs over the fence into the yard.

"Brian, what are you doing? We're never going to get home at this rate! You said you were hungry. We're going to go home and have lunch. It's what you wanted."

Brian doesn't answer. He's exploring the front yard.

"You shouldn't be in someone else's yard," says Mom. "Stay away from the flowers! Get out of there!"

Brian answers his mother by kicking off one of his boots.

"Why are you taking off your boots? It's so cold!"

She climbs over the fence and picks up the boot. She lifts Brian over the fence and once they are both on the sidewalk again, she puts his boot back on.

"You have to keep your boots on," she says. "It's dangerous to go around in your socks when it's this cold. You'll make yourself sick."

Brian now kicks off his other boot and then, just to make sure his mother gets the point, the one she so recently put back on. There he stands in his socks. It's a raw, wet early spring day.

His mother struggles frantically to get his boots back on, but no sooner is one on than he kicks the other off.

Mother begs, pleads, explains and gets angry, but try as she might, she can't get Brian to keep his boots on or to move in the direction of home. He flatly refuses.

"You have to sit in the stroller," she says at last. "You can't walk without your boots. And we have to get home! Don't you understand...?"

She tries to get Brian into the stroller with his boots in her hand. Brian wriggles wildly. He manages to slide so far down in the seat that his feet touch the ground and get stuck under the stroller.

Mom has to stop walking. Brian sees his chance to escape and grabs it with both hands. He makes a beeline for the yard – in his socks – and stands beside the fence.

"Brian..." pleads Mom, who is nearing the end of her rope.

Brian is nearing the end of his too. Thus far, he hasn't cried, but now the tears well up in his eyes.

Mom goes up to him and bombards him with yet more arguments he doesn't listen to. He's sobbing loudly now.

"I want you to carry me," he finally gasps out between sobs.

"But Brian, you know very well that I'm not strong enough to carry you," says Mom, who is pregnant. "I'm not *allowed* to carry you. Anyway, we have the stroller! All you have to do is just sit in the stroller and I'll push you home!"

She kneels down and tries to hug and comfort him, but Brian sniffles, clings to her and wants up.

"You... have... to... carry... me!" he manages to say.

Finally, his mother picks him up and carries him. No easy task since she has to keep one hand on the stroller.

"You know I'm not supposed to carry you," she reproaches him. "Why are you acting like this?"

Brian has calmed down somewhat, but he's still crying.

They get to a small intersection. One road leads to their house and the other to a playground, which for the moment is deserted.

"I want to go to the playground," sniffles Brian.

"You can go to the playground," says Mom. "Just put your boots on."

"I want you to come too!" sobs Brian.

"But we have to get home and eat," says Mom. "Why are you being so difficult? We have to get home."

Brian is now standing in the road, crying his eyes out. He doesn't seem to want to move in either direction.

"So what do you want to do?" asks his mother. "Shall we go to the playground or shall we go home?"

Brian kicks off his boots again and runs sobbing in the direction they've just come from.

His mother runs after him. She has to carry the distraught child home. At this point, Brian can no longer speak because he's hysterical.

Once they get home, Mom sits Brian down on the porch steps.

"Play … ground," wheezes Brian.

"OK," says Mom. "I'll get your pail and shovel."

She goes into the house, gets the pail and shovel, and holds the door open for little Brian, who sets off for the playground sobbing.

There he sits in the sandbox and digs frantically in an effort to calm himself down.

It's a sad ending to a sad story.

As he sits digging in the sandbox, little Brian is as lonely and abandoned as a human being can be.

He's a tough kid, and he's managed to take control of himself and the situation, but he's paid a high price. He's alone in a cold, chaotic universe. He knows that he can't count on support and help when he needs it most.

It's a heavy burden for a child.

It's a heavy burden for an adult.

Let's take a look at what might have happened if Brian's tantrum had been handled better.

Brian's mother has said that they were going to go home and eat.

"I want to walk," says Brian.

In the scenario described above, his mother answers him with an appeal. "We have to get home. Can't you sit in the stroller?"

This is tempting fate, or at least little Brian. He is allowed to decide for himself, but he is supposed to choose the option his mother wants.

She is placing all the responsibility on her son, instead of either supporting him or resisting him.

Let's assume she says, "No, you can't walk. Get into the stroller. We're going home to eat."

Once she takes a stand, she can't retreat a single inch.

If Brian decides to question what she's saying and defy her by sliding so far down in the seat that his feet get stuck under the stroller, his mother has to pull him back up and if necessary hold him in position until they get home.

If on the other hand she has no problem with Brian walking, as long as he walks beside her and keeps up, she should accede to his request. She should stop so he can get out of the stroller and say, "Of course you can walk."

She's sticking to her original plan. They are going to go home and eat. Whether Brian rides or walks is beside the point.

But now Brian decides to challenge his mother and kicks off his boots.

418

Mother knows a tantrum is on the way.

"If you want to walk, you have to keep your boots on, and you have to walk beside me. If you don't, you'll have to sit in the stroller.

Brian bolts in the opposite direction and heads for the stranger's front yard, leaving his boots where he kicked them off.

"OK," says Mother, "then you're sitting in the stroller."

She picks up the boots, fetches her son, puts him in the stroller and heads for home at full speed. She walks so fast that Brian doesn't dare try to climb out. If he persists, she will have to use brute force to keep him where he is.

"I want to walk!" wails Brian (hypothetically).

Mother can give him another chance.

"If you want to walk, put your boots on and walk beside me."

Again, she has to be as good as her word. *Either* Brian puts on his boots and walks beside her without taking any detours, *or* he sits in the stroller and agrees to passive transportation.

Right from the beginning, the overriding priority has been that they get home and eat lunch.

Brian is a headstrong little boy, and it's probable that he will kick off his boots and make a run for the yard more than once – in which case his mother has to follow the same procedure.

She has to fetch her son, hold him in the stroller and head for home.

She can also avail herself of an effective little ruse that is not unlike the forbid-what-the-child-refuses tactic.

"Fine," she says. "We'll just stay here then. We won't go home. You stay in the yard, and I'll stand here on the pavement. We'll stay where we are."

Ideally, she should have a newspaper or a book with her so she can show Brian that she's more than happy to stay where she is indefinitely. She *likes* standing there reading.

Then it's just a question of waiting for Brian to crack. And he will.

(This ruse is worth remembering if you have the misfortune to be sharing a car with a child who compulsively touches things that are better left alone or a couple of siblings that are into fratricide. When it becomes obvious that your appeals for an end to outright dangerous activities are falling on deaf ears, pull over, turn off the engine and inform the miscreant(s) that the car ride has now stopped for the parking. "We'll stay here, then." An immediate effect won't fail to appear.)

Back to Brian. He and his mother finally get home. Brian has either walked or been held in the stroller.

Lunch is ready, but Brian is still in a defiant mood and of course refuses what the whole thing was all about.

"I'm not hungry," he says.

His mother can't force him to eat, but she can force him to *take part in the meal* and thus make good on what she originally said.

She puts Brian in his chair, sets the table and starts eating herself.

If Brian tries to leave the table, she puts him on her knee and holds him there.

This hardly makes for a world class dining experience, since all Brian's mother can do is take a few symbolic mouthfuls of food, but Brian will at least be physically present at this much heralded meal, however fiercely he resists actually eating.

When his mother has finished her lunch (or at least creates the illusion of having done so), she takes Brian's hand and thanks herself for the meal on his behalf.

Then she clears the table as though nothing out of the ordinary has happened.

Brian's tantrum is history. He has gotten the message. Mother's word is her bond. She is a known quantity in an otherwise unknown universe. Brian can rely on her to be his guide and protector in a world where the only constant is change and nothing is what it seems.

If, contrary to expectations, Brian decides to take things one step further and suddenly announces that he wants his lunch after all – he suddenly realizes that he is in fact hungry and might as well have eaten since he was sitting at the table anyway – Mom behaves as though he *has* eaten. Only a few minutes ago, they were sitting at the table. They ate the meal that had been planned, and now it's over.

"We'll eat again this evening," Mother says cheerily. "We're having hotdogs." Then she goes on about her business without explanations, excuses or apologies.

Once it percolates through Brian's brain that a missed meal is gone for good, it's unlikely that he will make the same mistake again.

His mother can of course move supper forward a little if she's afraid that Brian's pangs of hunger will be too much for him to bear. Telling time is not Brian's strong suit, so if supper is rescheduled for 5.00 p.m., he won't be any the wiser.

Simple *repetition*, which is the hallmark of a clear message, works wonders.

Consider the following classic situation.

"Time for bed," says Sean's mother.

"I don't want to go to bed," answers Sean.

Sean is going through the terrible twos, and there have already been a few

420

outbursts today, all of which have left their mark on Sean's mom. From bitter experience, she knows what's coming.

"Please, Sean, don't start! You know you have to get some sleep if you're going to make it out of bed tomorrow morning. You'll be falling asleep at nursery school. Go to bed. You'll be a whole new person in the morning."

"I don't want to go to bed," says Sean.

Sean doesn't even have to stress his point. He's merely confirming his mother's worst fears. She expected him to refuse. She sighs dejectedly. She has run out of arguments.

"You're driving me crazy! It's the same story every night."

A little later, she tries again.

"You have to go to bed. This is ridiculous! It's nine o'clock."

"I don't want to," says Sean.

It's a dead end. At ten, Sean's mother gives up. At eleven, Sean's asleep on the sofa.

One thing Sean's mother could do is take a page out of her son's book and use his own tactic – endless repetition – against him.

"Time for bed," says Mom pleasantly *and prepares to back up her words with actions.*

She takes Sean by the hand and takes him to his room.

"I don't want to go to bed!" says Sean.

"Time for bed," says Mom as amiably as before. She is unfazed by Sean's protests and acts as though it's the first time she has brought up going to bed.

"I don't want to go to bed!"

"Time for bed," says his mom with inexhaustible good humor.

She gets him into his pyjamas and goes through the bedtime routine and only acknowledges her son's objections with an endlessly repeated "Time for bed."

If Sean goes into tantrum mode and begins to resist his mother physically, she takes him by the shoulders, looks him in the eye, raises her voice enough to sound resolute (but not angry) and repeats "Time for bed".

No matter how long Sean keeps this up, his mother will always go one better. No matter how many times he says he doesn't want to go to bed, his mother will keep telling him he is going to.

Persistently stubborn enough, little Sean may keep up his distrust for hours on end, but he will eventually cave provided that his mother stands firm.

And he will cave when it dawns on him for real that *she* won't, which fills Sean with relief.

This in turn means that he will never again protest when his mother tells him to go to bed. She freed him from having to question that (at least).

The trickster – a close relative of the eel (see "Something about personality") goes to bed without so much as a murmur of protest.

But no sooner does his head touch the pillow than he whimpers, "Mommeeee, I can't sleep!"

"Time to sleep," is the appropriate answer.

Now is the time to throw logic to the winds. "Time to sleep" is hardly a judicious response to the little trickster's pitiful announcement that he can't sleep.

But it works. The child is actually not making a statement. He's asking a question.

"Am I really supposed to go to sleep? Are you sure? Do I have to question this? Can I really just lie back and doze off? Can I take you at your word?"

The answer is yes. "It's time for bed. Sleep well. I'll see you in the morning."

The trickster has the fine art of challenging parents down pat.

"Mommeeee… I feel sick!"

Most kids have parents who are nothing if not solicitous of their children's health. And most parents tend to make far too much of little (often enough non-existing) aches and pains.

When distraught parents rush into the bedroom all set to call 911, little tricksters compliment themselves on a job well done. It sometimes takes parents months to figure out that their kids are winding them up.

Tricksters have an uncanny knack for finding chinks in parental armour.

Once is a coincidence, twice is a habit, three times is a lifestyle!

Don't let things progress past twice. The second time the child protests, you should content yourself with standing outside the door and making it crystal clear that you're not going to take the bait.

"We'll take care of it in the morning. Sleep well."

If you want to make sure nothing's afoot, you can sneak into the bedroom once your little trickster has fallen asleep and make sure he or she is not burning up with fever – a most unlikely eventuality.

If on the off chance the situation is as serious as the heart-rending wailing would seem to imply, the child will not be able to sleep anyway, so the method is as near fool-proof as to make no difference.

"Sleep well. We'll take care of it in the morning."

The trickster's sleeves are deep indeed.

"I have to pee."

"I'm thirsty."

"I can't sleep."

"I'm scared."

"I feel sick."

"I've lost my teddy bear."

"Something is poking me in bed."

"My band-aid has fallen off."

"I have to poo."

"It's so dark."

"I'm cold."

"My pillow is wet."

"What if I have a bad dream... I *did* have a bad dream!"

And so on *ad infinitum*.

Whatever it is, it can wait until morning. At least that should be your default position.

"We'll take care of it in the morning. Sleep well."

Trips to the bathroom, if the urge is genuine, can't really be delayed. You can get around this problem by putting a potty in the child's room.

"You can pee by yourself. Sleep well."

Darkness can't be remedied (nor should it be), and the illogical answer to complaints about it is,

"Time for bed. See you in the morning."

"But it's so dark!"

"Sleep well."

Of course you could explain that usually, nights are dark, and that nights are supposed to be dark, and that even the sun is asleep at night, and so are all the people and all the animals and all the houses... But then the little trickster will ask, "Why?"

Whereupon an endlessly drawn out conversation will take place (all part of the entertainment plan), which is best, as said, left until morning.

Protests about imminent death from dehydration can be nipped in the bud either by placing a cup of water by the bed or by leaving a cup and a stool in the bathroom so the trickster can get water himself.

"Get yourself some water and then go back to bed. Sleep well!"

Take no notice of the child while he's getting his drink and don't follow him back into his bedroom.

To sum up:

• *A defying terrible-two child is suffering from an inner compulsion to question every-thing* in order eventually to become capable of gaining a more profound understanding of "everything".

An analogy can be drawn between a two-year-old and someone who can pronounce the Hebrew alphabet perfectly but is unable to grasp the content of the Torah or that there even is such a thing as "content".

An understanding of the text is what awaits the child on the other side of the terrible twos.

The more tranquil, secure, stable and predictable life and the people around a child going through the terrible twos, the milder the child's necessary but painful development will be at this critical stage.

If, however, the Hebrew text is constantly changing, it will be difficult, not to say impossible, for our little Torah scholar to grasp the content of what he or she is reading.

• *Whatever you've said to a young child, stick to it by action.*

Routines should be kept simple and followed without question. Keep demands to a minimum, but those you do make must be followed through. Your tone should be friendly and your orders specific.

"Pick up the sandwich you threw on the floor please."

Vague reproaches such as "Oh, you know you're not supposed to do that. Clean up after yourself!" are to be avoided.

Children going through the terrible twos want precise and constructive messages in all matters, great and small. The Hebrew text has to be clear and predictable if little scholars are to be able (and willing) to decipher the content.

• *For a little person going through a crisis, Doctor Humor prescribes the best medicine.*

Any ruse is permissible to get a terrible two to crack a smile. A laugh a day is as important as ever (or more). Fun encounters between tantrums with all the attendant hugs, small talk and horseplay (see "Three Years: The Comedian") will work wonders during this difficult transitional stage. The more, the merrier!

• *The word "no" is not dangerous. Quite the contrary, it's essential.*

Terrible twos test, challenge, provoke, demand and refuse. They want answers. Inevitably, you will occasionally have to respond to your child's questions with a NO. It's never easy or pleasant to be tough on those you love, but that doesn't mean it isn't necessary.

Any unpleasantness you spare yourself will eventually come back to haunt your child.

• *You represent the wider world.*

If you accept things that the rest of the society doesn't, your child will reap what you have sown. The velvet glove of loving parental guidance is far more preferable to the iron fist of the harsh, indifferent world outside.

If you react negatively to your child's behavior but fail to back your words

424

up with the appropriate action, you are letting the little one down.

If, for example, your child punches you in the face and you opt to explain it away ("He's so little. He didn't really mean it. He just wanted to make sure I love him"), you are sending a message that rules apply to everybody except him. You are in effect saying, "You can do anything you like just because you are my child."

Your child will not accept this. He didn't come into this world to remain your little child, but to learn how to survive and live his life without you. And he knows it.

• *Hysteria, despair and powerlessness must be put to an end and, ideally, should not come about in the first place.*

A tantrum at the threshold, provide an escape route for the child. By hands-on action, show a way out!

A child who lashes out physically must be dissuaded from doing so with an immediate NO, as immediately followed by action. Take the child's hands. Provide leadership by showing the child what *is* acceptable behavior. ("We don't hit people. We pat or stroke them gently like this.") The goal is not to elicit an emotion, but *to demonstrate the acceptable behavior* in contrast to the unacceptable one.

The methods

1. In general: by action, *stand tall for what you've said* (the outspoken); by action, *stand tall for what goes* (the routines, the rules); by action, *stand tall for what you've done and what you're doing* (remember little Kate: Mother was sitting in a chair. She was in effect "saying" that she was sitting where she was because she wanted to. She has to be as good as her word. She shouldn't move because Kate tells her to; she should only move when she decides to do so by her own will); and, preferably, *stand tall for the person you are and the life you are leading.*

2. *Work hand-on-hand:* With your hand over the child's, make the little defiant angel do what you have told him or her to do – pick up, fetch, put back, pat, touch carefully, put on, take off etc. Shut your ears to protests during the work and follow up with appreciation. Act as though the child had actually done what he was supposed to do all by himself.

Reproachful bullying is strictly forbidden. Appreciation, plain and simple, for a job well done makes the one and only happy ending.

3. *Forbid what the child refuses:* "You don't want your teddy bear? OK. Then you CAN'T have your teddy bear. I'm taking it away."

4. *Turn the child's refusal into your own intention:* "You don't want to go to sleep? OK, we'll just stay up all night then. No one will go to bed. We'll clean the house instead. It needs a good cleaning anyway. Where would *you* like to start?"

"You don't want to go home? We'll stay here on the road then. I have a book with me that I'd love to read."

"You don't want to sit still in the car? Well, I'll stop the car then. We'll stay here. We'll be sitting here by the side of the road."

5. *Repeat your exhortations as many times as the child contradicts them and then once more.* And every time should sound as though it's the first time, regardless of the number of objections.

6. *When absolutely necessary, resort to banishment.*

"If you want to be with other people, you can't bite. If you want to bite, you'll have to be by yourself in your room. As soon as you stop biting, you are welcome to join in."

Banishment has to be followed up. *You must remain at your post just outside the door.* Banishment is revoked the minute the child indicates he is willing to make the concessions required to rejoin the community (in this case, stop biting).

Banishment should be businesslike. It's a clearly delineated behavior that is being condemned, not the child. ("This is not permitted. This is.") Banishment is physical, not emotional.

A child's willingness to make concessions should not be met by triumph on your part, although unfortunately it often is. (Remember what William's father *didn't* say, as William finally left the stool and went to bed.)

You are banishing your child to signal your refusal to accept certain behavior. As soon as the little one shows his willingness to learn the lesson and behave acceptably, things should be back to order with no comments, and you should welcome him back into the fold with a happy – *accepting* – smile.

COMFORT

He walks towards me like a miniature drunken sailor, more asleep than awake. His eyes are hair-thin slits. He hoists his eyebrows as high as he can in a not very successful attempt to keep his leaden eyelids open. It's around one in the morning, and he's on his way to his mother's bed. He moves like a zombie. If there's something in his way, a floor lamp, a chair, a table, he walks into it with unerring precision and knocks it over with a crash loud enough to jolt anyone who is not comatose into wakefulness.

But I'm the one who wakes up, not him. A little bundle, still warm from his bed, crawls down beside me. Bottom well padded from the thick diaper and cheeks rosy, he winds a generous little arm around my neck and drifts back to sleep.

I usually carry him back to his own bed and tuck him in, telling myself that he shouldn't get used to sleeping with me. What's sweet and endearing if it only happens on occasion loses its charm once it becomes a habit, and he has to feel secure enough to sleep by himself at night.

But sometimes I go and get him. I get needy, just as he does. I'm not really stronger than he is, even though I may look it in the deceptive light of day. When the evening darkness closes in, when the silence of night becomes threatening, when doubts and fears and questions swirl around in my mind like malevolent spirits, dawn becomes an object of dread because the day that will follow will be unbearable. At such times, I just want Baby near me. I fetch him without his noticing it, sound asleep as he is, wind his little arm around my neck – and I can sleep.

I can't help but wish that we adults could treat each other like young children treat us – with spontaneous empathy. If I'm sad, I don't have to answer questions. A little hand pats my cheek and wipes away my tears. Two wide, sympathetic eyes look into mine, and I am offered advice as practical as it is simple.

"You need a cup of coffee."

Or, "I'll get you a pillow."

Or, "Did you hurt yourself? I'll give you a kiss and a band-aid!"

It's hard not to say that I really have hurt myself so I can get the kiss. The word soon goes out to the rest of the household.

"Mommy hurt herself, but I made her feel better."

There are few ills that can't be cured by that kind of comfort.

What if half the things we spend so much time and energy worrying about disappeared? What if half the problems, half the unanswered questions, half the obligations, half the ambitions were just tossed to the four winds? Would it really be such a tragedy? In the long run, I think not.

The real tragedy lies in losing the devotion of the people you love.

HELP! RUBY REFUSES TO GET DRESSED!

Question:

I have a daughter, Ruby, two and a half years old. She is a happy little go-getter with a will of steel. The word NO has recently become a fixture in our lives. Some days she has her share of tantrums, while others are relatively calm – which is fortunate since it gives me time to recharge my batteries.

Our biggest problem, no matter what kind of a day we're having, is dressing her. It's items like snow suits, hats, gloves, boots that are the problem, not under clothing. As soon as it's time to get dressed, she screams her head off and runs for her life. If I pick her up, she wails, "Mommy, no! Stop! Stop!" I've tried dressing her on bureaus and chairs, and I've tried to get her to dress herself. (She won't.)

We seem to be locked in a vicious circle. Sometimes we yell at her, "Stop, Ruby! Sit still!" But that just makes a bad situation worse. She yells and screams, and there's bad blood between us for a long time afterwards. We all get depressed and walk around with knots in our stomachs.

We've tried to turn dressing into a game, but we just don't seem to be able to get through to her. The more we hold her, the more hysterical she gets. I've tried talking to her gently and singing to her, but nothing seems to work. What shall we do? We can't confine ourselves to the house 24/7!

Answer:

It looks as though you've reached a dead end as far as getting dressed goes! And once you're stuck in a rut where things just aren't working, you have to go for a totally new approach. (Ever had a computer problem? Turn the obstinate thing off and then reboot!) Here are a few tips on how to get Ruby to listen to you so that she *will* want to get dressed and get out of the house.

• Tell her that everyone is going to go out and describe all the fun things that you're all going to do. Lay out her clothes for her – she can, after all, get dressed herself if she has to – make sure she has seen them, and then declare, "Sweetheart, we'll leave when you're ready!" Behave as though you fully expect her to dress herself. Wait and smile, wait and smile, read the paper, wait and smile. Throw in a cheery "We'll leave as soon as you're ready, sweetheart!" every now and then. If and when she protests, pretend it doesn't register. Simply reply with a cheerful non-sequitur "We'll leave as soon as you're ready, sweetheart!" This may go on for what seems like an eternity. Indeed, evening may come and go, in which case you'll have to shelve the project for that day, but don't reproach Ruby in the least. "Oh dear," you'll say, "look what time it is! It's too late to go out now. It's so sad that we had to stay in *all* day, but we'll go out tomorrow instead. I *really* hope we can go out tomorrow. We have so many fun things planned!" (Which you will of course describe again in great detail). No reproaches, just boundless good humor – a tactic Ruby might find a bit confusing. Then repeat the procedure the next day and that should do it. If she still refuses to crack, confer with your better half loudly and clearly, but without looking at Ruby. "Oh dear, Ruby doesn't want to get dressed. That's so *sad*! I really wanted to get out of the house today. What shall we do? Will you stay home, or will I?" (Ruby's input at this stage is completely irrelevant and should be passed over in silence.) One of you should then wave goodbye to the other and hit the open road – and return twenty minutes later full of stories about how much there is to see out there in the world. You will share all this with your partner so that Ruby hears, but is not a part of the conversation. The point of this strategy is to make Ruby understand how much she is missing by staying at home. The penny will drop, and she will see the connection between outdoor clothes and leaving the house.

• Another effective ruse is to turn the tables and behave like Ruby, only worse – tongue in cheek of course. Put on a show! Make like you, the parents, are trying to dress each other. Chase each other around the house, clothes in hand, shout at each other, but DON'T look at the child. Don't hesitate to pull out all the stops. Don't get hostile, since the goal is not to frighten Ruby, but to confuse her and make her rethink things. You're giving her a demonstration of what happens when people refuse to cooperate and help each other – conflict. She will not want you to argue with each other, and she will do her best to try and end it. Appropriately surprised, you will then show your appreciation for her practical and matter-of-fact efforts to make you understand that everyone has to help each other for the sake of the flock's common interests. Which is, "tells" Ruby, to get properly dressed for the outdoors.

• Alone with the child, you can start wandering around the house when it's time to get dressed, feigning total helplessness. Talk to yourself out loud about how you can't find anything and look in the most unlikely places. "Where is my coat? Is it here? Is it there? I can't find it anywhere! And my gloves! Where ARE they? And my shoes! Oh, dear me! What can I do? I can't find my shoes!" Ruby will be delighted to come to your rescue. You of course will be suitably surprised and grateful. And once Ruby has saved the day, you make it known that you haven't the faintest idea about how people get dressed and your bewildered behavior testifies to the fact. (Ruby will believe you are serious. After all, she understands helplessness only too well. She'll be more than happy to welcome you to the club.) Ruby will again step into the breach, for which you will thank her profusely while you continue to do everything wrong. Tell her how grateful you are that she is around and how lucky it is that there's someone in the house who knows how to get dressed. When you're finally ready to walk out the door, heave a sigh of relief, thank her yet again, and then suddenly you remember! She's coming too! "You have to put on your clothes too! How are we going to manage that?" you wonder. Don't give the slightest indication that you intend to help her. IF she asks for help with something, you plead ignorance but do your best to be of assistance (albeit incompetently), all the while asking her if you are doing everything right. Keep up the helpless airhead routine. "What else have I forgotten? I have to turn off the lights, shut the door… and LOCK it! Of course! But I need keys for that. Where are my keys?" Give her the chance to help you out and feel really good about herself and her abilities. Being *needed* will be very important to Ruby.

When dealing with kids of any age, we should never forget the importance of asking them for advice and help – whether we need it or not. We can never abdicate our parental responsibility, but we shouldn't make the mistake of maintaining a façade of dreary self-sufficiency at all costs. It's very liberating for little children to know that parents don't know much about some things either. This enables them to do a little mental refurnishing and look at things like getting dressed from a completely different angle. Getting dressed is transformed from something obvious into something that isn't obvious at all, to you, to the child or to anyone else.

Humor is never out of place when you are dealing with a terrible two. For all constructive purposes, you can, and should, make the most of it!

THREE YEARS:
THE COMEDIAN

The three-year-old is an accomplished comedian, and as we all know, part of the comedian's stock and trade is to overstep the bounds of good taste.

Bathroom humor is the order of the day, and the three-year-old plays to his audience with unrestrained delight. He will nonchalantly ask complete strangers whether they have weenies too, whether they stand up to pee, and how often they fart. What people have between their legs is endlessly fascinating. Three-year-olds are particularly interested in the male of the species, who unfortunately (or maybe fortunately) is seldom liberated enough to allow themselves to be examined.

The three-year-old is a loving soul who can melt even the hardest heart. When your three-year-old gives you a much needed break from his at times boorish behavior, you almost get the impression he is trying to atone for his sins by indulging in sentimentality that verges on the diabetic. He is perhaps buying some insurance in anticipation of the tribulations that are to come. He senses that if he doesn't cover his butt by building up a reservoir of good will, your already strained patience might finally snap.

There was a time in your child's life when the world ceased to exist the moment he turned his back on it. Now that he's three, he has realized that the world goes right on rocking whether he's around or not. His reactions to this discovery are mixed. He sometimes wishes he were little again, when no demands were placed on him, and he was the only star in the firmament.

As he slogs his way through the maturation process that is the terrible twos, finds his niche in the hierarchy and becomes truly social, his surroundings adapt accordingly. The net result is that he is unceremoniously kicked off his throne.

Since no monarch ever ceded his throne willingly, the three-year-old can be downright dumb in an effort to remain the center of attention. He may revert to the whimpering baby he once was, adopt an air of brusque authority, flirt shamelessly, play the fool... He's got the system figured out. If he's funny enough, everyone will laugh – and that means he's center stage again. And he *is* funny – the first fifteen times anyway.

Sometimes the three-year-old is fascinated by his newfound maturity, which affords him the opportunity to see a world that doesn't revolve around him. People live, work and even love without him.

For the first time in his young life, he's interested in relationships between *other people*. He will pensively observe his mother and father hugging or kissing each other.

He will also intervene in conflicts, "Be quiet you!"

And act as mediator, "Eat your sandwich!"

He's sharp as a razor and can grasp the essence of any given situation at a glance. And if he can't, you can be sure he'll dig until he does.

There's very little you can hide from a little angel this age, so don't try!

The three-year-old is by and large an attentive little buddy who will comfort you in bad times.

The three-year-old is locked in a changing phase. Generally speaking, he is off balance, even though he's granted a two to three-month interlude of harmonious mastery in the middle of the terrible twos so that he can catch his breath.

During this grace period, which usually occurs closer to three and a half than to three for boys (six months earlier for girls), he decides to love the world exactly as it is. He can sit for extended periods playing peacefully with toys that only a month earlier would have been bouncing off the walls at regular intervals. He can wander around the house, his puppy dog eyes radiating love, looking as though he is endlessly grateful to you just for giving him a roof over his head. His tokens of affection can reach such grandiose proportions that even the most chastened of parents begin to get a little suspicious.

A changing phase, with all the demands that go with it, rages at both ends of this grace period, and life can become immensely complicated every now and then. When your child has to wrestle with life's incomprehensible complexities, laughter is a great way to relieve the anxiety. The world can be as contrary and unmanageable as it likes, but laughing at it never killed anyone. Your three-year-old will valiantly seek such relief, and he will be delighted if you keep him company. Make faces, drop things, pretend to walk into doors, and watch how the weight of the world falls from your child's shoulders. He'll laugh until he chokes. If on top of everything else, you pretend to break wind, blow a loud raspberry and look astonished, you will have your three-year-old rolling in the aisles.

Little things please little minds is a maxim that applies to three-year-olds.

If he ever advertised in the personals, one of his specifications for a prospective partner would definitely be "Must be interested in everything that makes life fun."

If you can stand shoulder to shoulder with your child during this period, you can count on having a stout little companion who will stick by you through thick and thin. (Even during tantrums, he will seek out your friendly support.)

"This is my money," your three-year-old might say in a just-between-you-and-me tone of voice as he waves a twenty-dollar bill that he's just lifted from your purse.

"Really?" you reply, and in the same just-between-you-and-me tone you ask, "So where's *my* money then?" – whereupon he will gallantly hand over his ill-gotten gains. "Here! You can have it!"

Three-year-olds are nothing if not generous, just and practical. As you can see, it sometimes pays to appeal to their nobler instincts, especially if what's at stake is a hundred dollar bill, the deed to your house, or your parent's last will and testament.

For information on routines etc., please read "Maintaining good habits" in Part three of *For the Love of Children*.

Here I would like to emphasize that the three-year-old, trapped as he is in an overwhelming development phase, needs his sleep. And he needs food at fixed times. If external existence is stable, the three-year-old's inner life, which is already chaotic enough, is not taxed more than it has to be.

This doesn't mean that a three-year-old should be isolated in the home or that the home has to be completely static. The flock of course can go on excursions – a popular pastime with children this age – but schedules and routines should be observed.

A three-year-old can't cope with being given responsibility for his own routines.

A three-year-old who is temporarily operating outside the flock, whether he's at nursery school or just visiting friends and relatives, needs a human center to serve as his operational base. (See the Part four introduction, "From my life. Theories for comfort".)

This human center should be available in the form of a direct, personal contact that remains constant throughout his visit in the new flock and to which he can always return.

If he is denied this, he will become disoriented, which will lead to insecurity and confusion, and this will make him either angry or sad.

You cannot expect him to do anything on his own initiative. He needs clear and concise information about what you expect of him.

"Have you brushed your teeth?" is therefore not the right question if it implies that simply because he's done it before, it's an established habit. Even if he has done it a hundred times, "habit" means nothing to him.

"Now we are going to brush your teeth!" as though this were a world premier is the proper approach.

And *if* your three-year-old takes it into his head to brush his teeth without being told, you will of course react with the appropriate admiration.

What is obvious for you is not at all obvious for him. In fact, nothing is obvious in his world, and that makes life difficult for him.

(A general tip: if you give your child a toothbrush with a hint of toothpaste on it to play with in the bath tub when he's one, there are seldom any problems with tooth brushing later on. A terrible two can of course question tooth brushing along with everything else. Unfortunately, the only way to get a recalcitrant kid to brush his teeth is with brute force, something you must never resort to. But if the habit is already well established, resistance will be short-lived.)

A three-year-old can make his bed, pick up his toys, put away shoes in the hall and all manner of other chores, but it's important that he's put to work as part of a collective effort. He should not be left to his own devices other than for very short periods, and the tasks he is charged with should be very simple. If you aren't actually working with him, you should at least be physically present to give him fulsome praise, not because he is being nice, but because *he is making a contribution.*

The three-year-old can play by himself outside, and should be encouraged to do so. During this whole period he is broadening his horizons and honing his skills. He has to be confronted with the unknown every now and then so that he can develop his (as yet unsuspected) abilities to deal with the unknown.

Consequently, he needs to be by himself sometimes. He differs little from adults in a changing phase. When we need to do some serious thinking, we have to be alone with ourselves away from the influence of others so that we can mentally feel our way forward. We have to escape from the distractions and the demands, both expressed and unexpressed, of our surroundings.

You should not, however, let a three-year-old be outside by himself for more than an hour, and under no circumstances should you take your eyes off him. *Three is an accident-prone age, as are all changing phases.* Traffic poses a mortal danger, and so do small, seemingly harmless places where water collects. (For information on the ever present risk of drowning, see "The first bath" in Part one of *For the Love of Children.*)

Hollows, deep ditches, wells, pits etc. and three-year-olds definitely do not mix.

Your three-year-old is inexperienced and insecure. In fact, as a two-year-old he was much tougher.

As for the three-year-old's fascination with the unmentionable (which of course isn't at all unmentionable for him), you're just going to have to grin and bear it. This particular interest is cultivated enthusiastically while it lasts, but it will, believe it or not, eventually be abandoned in favor of other pursuits. No matter how cavalierly you react to this pee-and-poo period and however much you play along without blushing or expressing disapproval, the day will come when this little person will ask for a fig leaf.

All children, sooner or later, discover embarrassment. But when this happens and the call goes out for a fig leaf, it's better that it be done with a giggle than with shame and guilt!

The three-year-old absorbs the good things in life like a sponge. He loves to sing, dance and listen to stories. He likes watching TV, even though he finds it hard to sit still for long periods of time. He was made for circuses, amusement parks and puppet shows. Nursery rhymes and children's stories he learns in no time, although the content is quite beyond him.

He is a quick study whenever anything strikes his fancy. Give him a computer with an interesting game on it, and he'll be an expert in no time.

But hi-tech amusements pale into insignificance beside a parent who doesn't mind putting a saucepan on his or her head once in a while, and engaging in a little live theatre. This literally rocks his world. It's the greatest fun there is because it's *liberating*.

And joy is the three-year-old's holy grail.

A FLEETING MOMENT IN THE SUN

Once upon a time, a little man took off for a long, long journey. He ended up in the remote countryside, although he saw the city too. The city was a noisy, confusing place. There was nowhere to pee, and all he could see were people's legs. It was a trying time. He had to be carried. Cawied, as he would say. But people get tired of carrying you everywhere. So Baby with his head of flaxen hair and slightly rounded belly abandoned city life to pursue more bucolic hobbies.

And of course, where such little boys lead, the rest of the family follows.

And what a life awaited him! First, he got to ride a donkey. He sat on the donkey's back, eyes like saucers, and squealed with delight. The donkey bolted with its little charge on its back, and Mother's heart skipped several beats, but Baby was in seventh heaven.

Then he got to clean rice. Little stones had to be sifted out, but Baby extracted the rice and left the stones. He would struggle wildly with his siblings if they tried to stop him. Then the rice had to be washed, but Baby was the only thing that really got clean.

In the afternoon, it was time for a field trip to the stables. Baby took up his position at the head of his delegation. He stopped opposite a buffalo. "Hi cow," he said. The buffalo, which was roughly the size of Mount Rushmore, stared at him solemnly, and the little mite stared back. They gazed at each other for ten minutes. I don't know exactly what passed between them, but they bonded, that I'm sure of.

The sun shone, the birds glided over us, and the women carried pots of water on their heads. Baby staggered after them with an empty jug.

Then he met some gentlemen who were prepared to exchange an orange for a hug. For a little man of warm soft hands and round-bellied beauty, such generous souls are there to be found all over the place.

Back in the kitchen, it was time for dinner. And a fascinating dinner it was too. Three large bowls were set out, their contents steaming hot, and Baby installed himself cheerily at the table and pulled all three towards him. But there were fifteen other people who had to eat out of them too with the help of large flat bread cakes. Seldom had such disappointment welled up in Baby's cornflower blue eyes. Naturally, all the other fifteen had to stand aside for the lone sixteenth and content themselves with crumbs from the rich man's table.

But love is infinite. This little boy who should have been so self-assured from all the attention that had been lavished on him, and in a foreign country too, was in reality a shy and cautious little soul, his cherry lips usually pursed in pensive silence. So when he kissed every one of the fifteen people around the table, it wasn't the result of his mother's nagging but of genuine devotion, of his own serene affection.

How could I not be happy in that fleeting moment in the sun when I have him with me?

In the evening, the crickets chanted. In the morning flocks of birds took wing from the trees, and their song soared heavenward, clear and pure from a thousand throats, each note sparkling like a diamond.

And a little boy hurried out to the stable with breakfast for his buffalo.

1974. Aron in Memoriam (1971–1975).

FOUR YEARS: ON THE RUN

A four-year-old can be summed up in one word: adventure.

The four-year-old is a true adventurer, bold, curious and alert. Life is a never-ending voyage of discovery that encompasses people, life and the world.

His imagination is in overdrive, and he plays fast and loose with the truth. What he sees and doesn't see is anyone's guess (his included). If he says he's seen a blue lion, he's seen a blue lion. And if blue lions don't happen to exist, it's due to an oversight on the part of the Almighty – an oversight that the four-year-old is selflessly volunteering to correct.

The four-year-old is a genial soul, easy-going and good-humored. He is comfortable with his flock – his operational base – his parents, his home and any siblings that happen to be around. He no longer questions everything. He knows what he's got and he likes it.

But now he wants more. He has gone through the ordeal of the terrible twos, and he is mature enough to interact with other people. He can show consideration, put himself in someone else's shoes, step back and wait his turn. Since he now knows he's light years ahead of the competition, he can afford to let other people hog the limelight.

For the first time in his young life, the four-year-old is capable of having a conversation worthy of the name. He can exchange ideas with his interlocutor, air his thoughts, take the opinions of others to heart, and in so doing achieve a more perfect union so to speak. The four-year-old is an accomplished conversationalist, who has mastered the art of imparting his worldview to those who care to take the trouble to listen.

Watching him adapt to unfamiliar environments is a pure delight. Given free rein at an amusement park for example, he will unerringly choose the activities best suited to him, his eyes glistening with enthusiasm and the joy of discovery. Yet, like any prudent voyager adrift in unknown seas, he retains his sense of proportion.

If he is visiting a home for the first time, he will seek out what's most interesting, not only for him but for whoever lives there. He's hungry for knowledge and is a patient listener.

The four-year-old has certain idiosyncrasies. On outings to other people's houses, he will meticulously inspect the toilet facilities.

There's nothing that isn't worth investigating.

"Why can't you walk?" he will ask someone in a wheelchair.

And as rule, people will answer. He doesn't pose these questions to offend, or even to make a value judgement. He is an honest and serious seeker of knowledge.

For the four-year-old, adventurer that he is, a less than five-star day care or nursery school is better than none at all. He now has a need for other children and new worlds to explore that cannot be denied.

He picks his playmates with maturity and insight, and he plays with them on his own terms, secure in his abilities. Most of the time he keeps himself on an even keel and defuses dicey situations before they get out of hand.

In short, he uses his head. He lives the kind of life we all should. He does what he wants, he socializes with people he likes, he withdraws when he feels the need for solitude, and he respects himself.

The four-year-old now leaves the flock on longer and longer excursions. He doesn't return to his human center nearly as often as he did as a three-year-old.

An excursion outside the flock should ideally last approximately three hours – no more – if the four-year-old has anything to say about it.

If you don't let him make his excursions to parts unknown outside the flock, for widening his world on his own, he may well pack a bag and run away from home!

The four-year-old is in the midst of an exploration phase (see "The cycle of life. Something about development"), which means he should be free to roam as much as possible.

Novelties are gratefully accepted. Trips, changes, moves, all these things make his world go round, even though he will be dependent on his human center for a long time yet. If nothing else, he needs to share his experiences – and himself. He needs to inform his surroundings of his noble deeds, of everything he has seen and heard.

And he needs to ask questions. He knows full well the power of the word. Conversations are held in high esteem. For the first time, he can separate words from actions.

The four-year-old can *think*.

"Why is this a blanket?" he may ask, presenting you with a world class philosophical conundrum to ponder.

The four-year-old takes the world as it comes with arms open wide and a soul free from prejudice, and he doesn't step off the pavement for anyone.

Sex education is difficult in a culture where anything sexual is so laden with taboos, but you will just have to soldier through *that* particular mine field as best you can. Whatever you do, don't equivocate. Don't hum and ha for half an hour telling him how much you and your partner love each other. The four-year-old wants the facts straight from the shoulder, so just tell him who puts what where.

Even if you haven't discussed death at all, you may find that your four-year-old has figured out reincarnation all by himself. Perhaps it's not that surprising. After all, a child this age is equipped with a good memory and he is beginning to accumulate experience. He will have observed how nature renews itself year after year.

"When I'm big, you'll be a baby and eat from my breasts," your four-year-old reasons (if you've had a girl). "But first you'll have to die," she adds matter-of-factly, and that's it.

Don't feel obligated to play the omniscient parent when your four-year-old starts to philosophize. You can always answer a question with a question.

"Why are there stars?" the child muses.

"Well, what do we know? Why are there stars?"

"So kids who are scared of the dark can sleep at night, perhaps."

"Yes, that's probably it," you concur.

If you then ask your child to tell you all he or she knows about the stars, you will be in for an unforgettable experience!

The four-year-old is forever rethinking his position, formulating new theories and discarding those that have been found wanting. He is a true intellectual. Unfortunately, his talents are often overlooked because he asks so many questions. You get so tired of the constant stream of questions and words that it never occurs to you to ask *him* something. And that's a shame.

There is no doubt about it: he does get a little tedious when he's stuck in "why" mode.

"Time to go home."

"Why?"

"Because it's dinner time."

"Why?"

"Because we're hungry."

"Why?"

"Because it's a long time since we ate."

"Why?"

And so it goes forever and ever, amen.

Sooner or later, even the most saintly parents snap, especially when it dawns on them that the kid is more interested in exercising his jaws than acquainting himself with facts.

A four-year-old's nagging "why's" in the example above can be an indication that something is missing in his life. That something can be a *connection* outside the routines with you, his mother or father.

There may also be a laughter deficit. A connection with you and a good laugh will bring these interrogations to a merciful end. Squat down, place your hands on the little angel's shoulders, look him in the eyes, smile and answer his thousandth "why" thus:

"You want to know why? I'll tell you why. So you will have something to ask about!"

If he really does want to know something, he will persist. But if he's just running off at the mouth for lack of something better to do, he will laugh, stop asking "why" – and like you for it.

The four-year-old should be given responsibility. He is old enough to work on his own as well as together with you. He should have the opportunity to be his own boss, while you assume the role of admiring inspector when the job is done.

But remember that a good inspector is an observant inspector. A good inspector doesn't just go through the motions of inspecting in order to gush with praise as quickly as possible. Neither adult nor four-year-old workers take such inspectors seriously. A good inspector must be able to justify his assessment. The four-year-old does not want to be appreciated just for existing. He wants to be appreciated for what he's *done*, and the appreciation has to be genuine. This requires more than a cursory glance.

"Look at that! You've made the bed beautifully!"

"I put teddy between the pillows. Teddy is going to sleep there. And I am going to sleep *here*. And Teddy has his own blanket under the pillow."

"Oh, that's really practical."

"And then I closed the curtains."

"So I see. That's great!"

"Then I put the chair back. There's the chair."

"There it is, indeed. That's a really good place for it."

"And now I've finished my job!"

Apart from the social participation – when the little one works with you or the flock towards a common goal – and his own tasks, which should not be too extensive and should *always* be followed up – you should make use of the four-year-old for any little errand outside the flock you can ever come up with for him.

Spy on him discreetly without being seen yourself!

The big problem here of course is traffic, but if you can somehow neutralize that threat, there isn't much that a four-year-old can't be trusted with. In town, he can shop if the store is on the same side of the street. Equip him with money and detailed instructions, and he'll do just fine. The pride he feels after a successful expedition is palpable, and you of course will encourage him to relate his adventures in minute detail.

Before sending him to do anything on his own, explain exactly what you want him to do and question him carefully on what you have said to make sure he has understood.

"And what do you say when you go into the store?"

"What do you say when you leave?"

"And what do you do if you can't open the door?"

The four-year-old is capable of speculating about various situations and of imagining what would be the proper thing to do in them. He can weigh up the odds, make choices and decide upon the better course of action.

Indeed, the toil of the terrible twos has borne fruit.

If you as a parent were passive or even "helpless" (apart from the routines of course) with the brilliant one-year-old, happy with the superb two-year-old, silly with the foolish three-year-old and unshakeably resolute with the terrible two, you will now be business-like, interested and eager to learn with the four-year-old.

If anyone can open up the world for you, it's your four-year-old.

As for himself, he can learn pretty much anything. For example, if you have the time and the inclination, you can teach him the alphabet, and the rest he will take care of himself. Within six months, he will be able to read.

That's the four-year-old in a nutshell: Give him the possibility and he will do the impossible!

THE SMILE OF A SUMMER DAY

It's a beautiful day. As I write, the sun is flooding into the dark little house, putting the shadows to flight and warming both the house and me. Outside the flowers are opening. The air is warm, a harbinger of the summer that will soon be upon us. The children are brand new people. Their summer clothes are too small. Suddenly, everyone has grown. They are a whole year older, and when I look at them, it feels as though I see them for the first time in months. Their cheeks are flushed, and their voices float gossamer light on the sunny breeze. The swing under the apple tree creaks and bare feet pad over the grass. Sometimes, life is captivating – so stunningly close.

And my guilty conscience torments me. So much joy got lost in my neglecting them! So many talks did I never have time for! I grieve over all that I've missed. For one example, did I allow myself to smile over the song my four-year-old sang to her big sister when she was helping her with a recalcitrant puzzle?

I can help with what's so hard for you
Because I can understand you
I'm so big and clever
Poor little you

And this heart-warming little song, which my four-year-old sang with such an enchanting mildness and for a long time, was the soft answer to my five-year old's: "Damned puzzle!"

Other things burden my conscience. My days have had to run like clockwork. Finishing my new book made that necessary. Less than conciliatory words have passed Mom's lips during her appeals for cooperation.

Even my little three-year-old receives more than his share of marching orders. A little hand takes mine as I rummage through the dishes so I can continue my work. "I don't want you to be mad at me. You can't be mad at little boys."

I burst out laughing and his face lights up, although he really has no idea why it's so funny.

Baby and I go out to swing. The sixteen-year-old finds a dazed bird. A friend is building a somewhat lopsided ping-pong table for the older children. Summer is here. All is languorous peace.

Until evening and bath time. There's a squeal of shock from the bathroom and my three-year-old storms into the kitchen, looking like he's just swum the Channel:

"The children have made me drown!"

Baby looks at him thoughtfully and hands him the paper towel roll.

FIVE YEARS:
THE LILY OF PEACE

The five-year-old is a delightful little person, harmonious, balanced, secure with himself and the world.

He behaves as though he *chose* his parents out of comparisons with a thousand others. His loyalty and devotion know no bounds.

He's loving, considerate, obliging, conscious of his responsibilities and really competent. Patiently and methodically he carries out the tasks assigned him. Or that he assigns himself.

If he has younger siblings, he will take charge of them like a seasoned (and slightly over-ambitious) parent. He cares. And he is serious. He is reasonable and sensible.

The five-year-old's lodestar is *moderation in all things*. He knows his world and has mastered it, and since he is moderate in all things, he slots himself into an agreeably predictable groove. He doesn't feel the need to tackle anything he's not sure he can handle. He only puts his hand to what he knows he can pull off, so he always pulls off what he puts his hand to.

He regards himself as well nigh perfect – and rightly so – and as a result he expects the rest of the world to be perfect too.

Should he come face to face with imperfection, he sees it as his moral duty to save the world from itself, and save it he will –and with profound indignation.

He understands that his juniors can misbehave. "They're so little, they don't know what they're doing," he will announce with weary resignation. The last thing he would want to be again is a baby!

The five-year-old has a much harder time accepting behavior he feels is inappropriate for adults. Try as you might to come up with an excuse that will hold even a little water ("I forgot... I couldn't... I didn't have time..."), all you will get for your trouble is a sceptical glare. He thought you were perfect. *He* is, so what's your problem?

But in their capacity as your sons or daughters, five-year-olds are piety itself.

"Mom said I could do that."

"Dad said I couldn't do that, so I won't."

"Mom told me it was true, so it is."

The five-year-old methodically examines his own life, the way it's been and the way it is now. He is accumulating experience.

He remembers things you thought he had forgotten, be it furniture that has disappeared or people who have come and gone. He wants to make sense of it all. He's trying to fit the fragments he has stored in his memory into a context, like the pieces of a puzzle. He wants a coherent picture of his life so far.

"Are you fond of me?" he can ask his mother or father. "Would you be sad if I died? Were you glad when I was born? What did you say?"

Such questions are fairly typical.

The five-year-old exhibits little, if any, of the three-year-old's silliness, and the four-year-old's lust for adventure has largely dissipated. The somewhat reckless buccaneer has been replaced by a perspicacious general.

He has, for example, realized that you can't talk however you like about whatever you like with whomever you like. He now approaches people with tact and consideration. He can be shy initially, but he soon wins hearts with his affectionate consideration and his heartfelt interest in other people.

He also loves to be treated (more or less) as an adult. He understands that younger children cannot be entrusted with the same responsibilities that he can, and he can attest to this fact without being overbearing or cruel.

"You'd get too tired," he might say to a younger sibling. "It's no fun for you. I'm *so* much older. But you'll be big one day."

Like the trooper he is, he puts his shoulder to the proverbial wheel and does his duty, no matter how onerous that duty might be – being quiet for long periods for example.

The five-year-old positively brims with virtue, so much so that he can on occasion be a tad bombastic. He gives the impression that childhood is boring and somehow beneath him. Gone is the four-year-old's wayward imagination. Gone are his swagger and his flat-out falsehoods (in the eyes of adults anyway).

The five-year-old runs a tight ship for the simple reason that he is in the process of forging a moral code for himself and through some mysterious alchemy he thereby develops something called a *conscience*.

The five-year-old knows that you don't take your mother's things without permission. (Well, sometimes you do, but you know it's wrong.) You don't thump your little sister either. (Well, maybe you do, but you're ashamed of yourself afterwards.) The five-year-old is his own worst critic. "I was so bad! But never again…"

All in all, he's a steadfast little fellow, loving and good-hearted, an asset to any family.

The five-year-old finds himself in one of the three most harmonious periods of childhood. It is this mastering, solidly balanced phase of development that the two-year-old and the ten-year-old enjoy.

He is the proverbial rock of Gibraltar. Whatever hardships the family has to go through, the five-year-old will weather the storm and give you his unwavering support.

Like the two-year-old and the ten-year-old, he is responsible and strikingly independent.

As a parent, you can cut the five-year-old some slack as long as his requests are reasonable. You don't have to be rigidly consistent. A little flexibility won't hurt, since by and large his both feet are on the ground. You can bargain with him.

"If you have candy today, you can't have any on Saturday."

"OK, deal. I'll have some candy now, and I won't have any on Saturday."

When Saturday comes, even if you have forgotten, he'll remember that he's not supposed to have candy. A deal, after all, is a deal.

How can you help but admire him?

The five-year-old doesn't ponder metaphysical questions like the four-year-old does. He's practical and down to earth.

While the four-year-old, stone-to-the-bone believer in reincarnation (or whatever) that he is, can look forward to the sweet hereafter quite unperturbed by death, the five-year-old is trying to figure out a way to cheat the grim reaper.

"I'm going to dig my way out of my grave after you bury me. So don't put the coffin lid on too tight."

As you can see, he sometimes gets the wrong end of the stick about certain things, but since he's so mature and knowledgeable, an adult for all practical purposes, he will keep up the façade even when he has no idea what you're talking about.

Thus, it's always a good idea to make sure that he really does understand what you say to him.

"Can you tell me what I just said?"

The account can be fascinating – not necessarily accurate, but fascinating.

Just as the balanced two-year-old shouldered responsibility for the family because he knew that if he didn't, no one else would, the five-year-old keeps a watchful eye on everyone and everything, and in so doing becomes a world class tattletale. As a result, you, his caregiver, may find yourself on the horns of a dilemma.

It's very difficult to explain what a tattletale actually is. (See "Siblings" in Part five of *For the Love of Children*.)

"She hurt herself." Fair enough.

"Little brother hit her." Over the line.

"The doll is broken." Fair enough.

"She broke the doll." Over the line.

The five-year-old, who is so anxious to do everything by the book, can't understand why everyone isn't as law-abiding as he is. Or why it's wrong to denounce evildoers to the appropriate authority. If you criticize him for it, he will feel hurt and misunderstood.

You should from time to time try to explain to him what is right and what is wrong, but you must understand that it will be a long, long time before he really internalizes the knowledge. He doesn't mean any harm, but he won't let other people's transgressions pass without comment either.

He's not out to condemn anyone. He's just looking out for their best interests.

The five-year-old is a diligent little worker who will put in his two cents worth without being asked. He can dress himself, keep his possessions in order, and shop. He is perfectly capable of waiting patiently at a pedestrian crossing until an adult comes along to hold his hand while he crosses the street. He is by no means "traffic proof", but he realises that cars are dangerous and that's a good start.

Since he knows everything, he does everything in his own occasionally idiosyncratic way and doesn't think he needs to ask about anything.

So, if he scrubs the basin with toothpaste or shines your shoes with a hair brush, be tactful and give him the recognition he deserves for having his heart in the right place.

"Oh, it looks great! Thank you! And next time you clean the basin there's some Ajax under the sink. It works just as well as toothpaste. Even better actually. And here's the brush we usually use to shine shoes. The other brush is for hair. This brush will do the job just as well, so you can use this one next time. Thanks again for a great job!"

The five-year-old can handle, and should be given, chores in addition to those he does with you (at mealtimes for example).

"What are my chores for today?" he asks. He seems weighed down by responsibility, buoyed by hope and yet somehow blasé all at the same time. He likes to have his duty sheet read to him each day. He may sigh and bemoan his lot in life, but he will put his best foot forward and get the job done.

Don't be afraid to place demands on him. Insist that he do his chores even if he's not in the mood. You can always appeal to his sense of responsibility and fair play. Just explain that you have to do things you don't like too and that if everyone doesn't pull their weight, the household just won't function.

You can for the first time *expect* him to do what he's supposed to do. You no longer have to clap your hands and look overjoyed as though it's the first time in the history of the world that someone under twenty made a bed or brushed his teeth all by himself.

The five-year-old knows what's right, and his conscience will compel him to do his duty.

Remember that the five-year-old, weighed down by responsibility for absolutely everything as he is, can seem older than he actually is not only in his own eyes but also other people's. He loves to be tickled, to fool around and to laugh at adults who make fools of themselves. He will revel in stories about all the dumb things you did when you were a kid – or that you have done as an adult for that matter.

It's better to be a little too little for a little too long than to be a little too big a little too fast!

Enable him to use his considerable practical skills. If he complains that he can't find his gloves or anything else that hasn't gone his way, don't be too quick to ride to his rescue. A genuinely interested question – "So what are you going to do about it?" – will jump start the five-year-old (and older children) into solving the problem himself.

"I don't need gloves. It's not that cold."

Or: "I'll look for them once more. I wonder where I put them?"

Or: "I'll wear another pair."

Or even: "I'll put socks on my hands. That's OK, isn't it?"

The five-year-old doesn't like feeling helpless, and simple little strategies like this will ensure that he doesn't have to.

The five-year-old is a loving soul. He needs some one-on-one time with you, his mother or father. And this should encompass more than just tender moments. He needs serious heart-to-heart talks as well. Whereas once it was essential to put your child to work within the context of the struggle for survival to develop his practical, concrete abilities (see "ABCs for little people" and "Psychological well-being"), it is now just as important to put him to work to develop his abstract abilities.

The five-year-old is rising through the flock's ranks, so to speak. You don't need to worry about overly intense emotional bonding. That will all be gone with the wind when he turns six anyway...

He's five years old. He doesn't lay claim to all the kingdoms of the world. In fact, he rarely asks for anything at all. That's why I find it so hard to refuse him when he does.

If only common sense and goodwill always came in the same package! One day, he came to me and said, "I'd really like to do Maya's puzzle." Then he smiled, his round eyes the bluest of cornflower blue.

"Where is Maya?" I asked him.

"She's still outside," he informed me cheerily.

I knew a conspiracy when I saw one. Maya was to be kept out of the loop.

I pondered the proposition. "Maya is very protective of her puzzle. She doesn't want any pieces lost. But if you promise to be really careful…"

Oh, did he promise! The puzzle would be returned in pristine condition. He skipped happily away, got the puzzle, plopped himself down on the bed and dumped all the pieces out on the bedspread. His head was bowed in concentration and his tongue was between his lips as it usually is when he's absorbed in a task he likes. A peaceful silence fell.

Since all was right the world, I left him to it and went down to the basement to do some laundry. The peace, alas, was soon shattered. When I came back upstairs, Maya had come home, the puzzle pieces were strewn all over the floor, and a battle royal was raging.

"He took my puzzle!"

"Mommy said I could!"

"He lost some pieces!"

"I did not!"

"It's my puzzle! I got it for my birthday!"

"Mommy said I could play with it!"

"Mommy, tell him to give it back!"

"You're so stupid!"

"Mommy, he's going to hit me!"

"You dumb, stupid…"

It was all downhill from there. Peace, love, tenderness, a soft answer turneth away wrath and all that. Give me a break! It's mothers that need tenderness, not the kids. I bawled something at them, which, roughly translated, meant the conversation should be discontinued forthwith, although the phraseology was somewhat less elegant. I found myself expounding on things that a little boy of five and a little girl of six didn't have an ice cube's chance in hell of understanding. They saw that I was angry, a circumstance which elicited nothing but aristocratic indifference.

The situation was fast spinning out of control, and as my desperation grew, my questions grew more and more ridiculous.

"Why can't you just play with the puzzle without killing each other? Is that really too much to ask? Is it? Is it? Is it?"

The boy, whose cornflower blue eyes had grown as dark as a prairie sky just before a cyclone touches down, answered from the depths of his pragmatic soul,

"I'm not talking to you. I'm tired."

And I understood exactly how he felt.

I wish I had a Solomon on twenty-four hour call to resolve such disputes. And I wish all puzzles back to the woods from where they originally came!

SIX YEARS: IT'S A HARD LIFE

The sensible, balanced five-year-old, master of himself and his surroundings, was a joy to be around. Those days are gone. At six, the same youngster is in a state of total chaos. If you have trouble recognizing him, believe me, he does too.

The six-year-old often goes through a growth spurt, but external growth is matched by internal collapse. He has trouble coping with his gangly new body, an odd contraption that seems put together with parts that were designed for someone else. He stumbles, bumps into things and breaks things, his unruly limbs forever in the wrong place at the wrong time. His inner self is just as out of control as his body. He is a stranger to himself.

He is full of distrust. (No one *really* likes me. No one *really* needs me. No one *really* understands me.) He is desperately searching for fellowship, a place to belong. His friends can tell him he's important, but he doesn't always believe them. His parents can tell him that they love him and need him, but he doesn't always believe them either. The person that the six-year-old finds most difficult to be around is himself. He distrusts everyone else for the simple reason that he distrusts himself.

The six-year-old's eternal quest for affirmation from the people around him – that he doesn't really trust anyway – makes him demanding at times. He can change his mind from one minute to the next. Nothing is good enough. He is about as consistent as a weather vane in a high wind.

He can't take part in games or competitions unless he always wins. If he loses, he falls apart and becomes aggressive, spiteful and generally impossible to be around. He isn't above cheating either.

If he wins, on the other hand, that's no good either. Since he knows that no one *really* likes him, he assumes that his victory just gives everyone all the more reason to hate him. Yet, he *has* to win. That's his dilemma in a nutshell. He has to prove to himself and to others that he's good enough – at any price. And the price is steep.

The six-year-old is slowly breaking free of emotional ties he has forged hitherto. From being a secure five-year-old who was very close to his nearest and dearest, he heads out into the emotional wilderness to mature. He doesn't know that he has several years to accomplish this. Nor does he

450

know what to expect. All he feels is terror over the chill wind of change that is blowing through his universe.

He feels rather like a long-time wife or husband on the verge of divorce who is afraid of losing absolutely everything. The six-year-old has to try and forge a new relationship with his parents and the other people around him, just as a divorcing couple must eventually forge a functional relationship to replace the one that shattered. But the six-year-old is perilously close to help-lessness. He doesn't understand how such a thing is possible. All he knows is what he is losing.

The urge to develop drives him out onto that cold, grey sea that is inde-pendence. Since inwardly he isn't really ready for this, he resorts to external ruses. It's independent to be dirty, ungroomed, and dressed like a homeless person. It's independent to leave his room looking like a disaster area. It's in-dependent to refuse to clear up after himself when he finishes breakfast...

Here the six-year-old has a good deal in common with his colleagues in crisis, the terrible two and the teenager. Like them, he defiantly adopts be-havior that masquerades as power to compensate for the lack of independence he is suffering from.

The six-year-old is a little person in need. Most of the time inner peace and equilibrium are as remote as the outer reaches of the galaxy.

He usually wants a pet to comfort him, although he is incapable of shouldering responsibility for one himself.

As you have no doubt deduced, the six-year-old is going through a changing phase of development, and to make matters worse, it is a period that follows one of the most harmonious phases of childhood – that of the five-year-old.

The six-year-old is driven forward, out of his secure home, to seek an independent ego, an extended ability, an emotional independence, and a base in himself. He is on his way to becoming his own center (see "From my life. Theories for comfort").

The goal is to construct a world around himself – both within and out-side the flock. This world will no longer revolve exclusively around you (or the other flock members). The connection will remain, but it will have evolved into something different.

451

His crisis will culminate in independence, but the road will be long and hard and won't end until the other side of puberty. This is his second preparatory period. The first was the terrible twos.

On the way to independence, the poor child will mercifully get the odd respite – the most delightful of which will come when he turns ten.

If you have a six-year-old in the house, take comfort in the fact that this is one of the most difficult periods there is. Just because you don't recognize your own child, that doesn't mean that anything is wrong. The crisis is not continuous. The worst of the storm will blow over, and what's left will eventually be channelled – through school, the growing importance of friends, and last but not least the six-year-old's own strategies, which he will soon develop for his own relief and peace of mind.

If he wants solitude, back off and give him space. He needs it.

Remember he is still a little boy. Behind the brash, in-your-face attitude, he is in desperate need of love, tenderness and laughter. Just as with the terrible two, try to nab him in his calmer moments and give him the *encounter* he so desperately needs, along with all the inspiring interest you can muster.

Just as you had to give the terrible two support in the form of resistance, you must now be a role model for the six-year-old by conducting yourself with strength, dignity and honesty.

If you don't, he will develop tyrannical habits. And he will assuredly be the one who suffers most if he learns to have contempt for his surroundings.

Beyond the contemptuous verbal abuse and the eye rolling he is so often guilty of, the six-year-old can threaten you and even resort to violence. If he goes too far (and he will), you must set boundaries for what is acceptable (see "How to do it – if you want to" in Part five of *For the Love of Children*).

Just as there are terrible twos of the aggressive variety and those who burst into tears and have tantrums, so are there six-year-olds who react differently to their inner compulsions to challenge everyone and everything (including themselves). A six-year-old who falls silent and seems to step back from conflict perhaps doesn't cry that much, but that doesn't mean he suffers any less. He still feels lonely, abandoned and sad. He may need to be snapped out of it by being given a clearly defined, necessary task.

"Come on, sweetheart, I need help with cooking/laundry/gardening/cleaning. I can't do it alone! You've got to work with me!"

Deep down, he will feel relief and liberation, even though he may seem to be less than enthusiastic about the idea at first.

What the six-year-old has to conquer – at the behest of the inner voice that impels him towards independence – is a sense of security and belief in *himself*. That's why it's so difficult to convince him that he has worth. If it comes from the outside, it isn't enough. It has to come from inside him.

452

It's no easier for a six-year-old than for an insecure adult to conjure up self-esteem. He finds self-worth by being part of a community, a loving community where he contributes and is needed (*the others wouldn't manage as well without me*).

As with the terrible two, you have to distinguish between the six-year-old's behavior and the six-year-old as a person. You can have epic arguments with a six-year-old, but you have to be specific. By all means, set limits and make it clear that there will be consequences if certain standards aren't met, but define all your terms in minute detail. And remember to make it crystal clear that it is the *behavior* that is unacceptable, not the human being.

It's simply a fact of life that you can place more onerous demands on a five-year-old than you can on a six-year-old.

A good strategy for helping a six-year-old in crisis is to treat him as though he were a little younger, a little more wretched, and a little more childish than he really is, or seems, or "should" be.

People have a tendency to regress at times of crisis. They become – they need to become – "little" again.

THE CHILD AND THE GOOD HEART

He's six and he's the youngest child that remains to me. He's the only boy now, and when he was born, after four girls, I lay cradled in the darkness of night and stroked his downy head and pondered the miracle: I'd had a son. Naturally, having a girl after four boys would have been just as miraculous! He cried, as newborns tend to do, so I took him to me and my eyes became moist. A little boy, I thought as I peeked under his diaper.

He has grown into a sunny lad, and now he is old enough to confront the outside world, playmates, and activities of all kinds. But, uninhibited, I still ask him for a hug sometimes. He comes to me after a little embarrassed demurring. And then I get a hug, a kiss and two arms wound around my neck.

"You are my rosin", he says.

Raisins are his favourite food.

His sisters are older and have paired off with each other. He lost his little brother, and now he is alone. It's easy to believe that sorrow is a burden you have to bear alone. No one else can share it or understand how you feel. But it was a hard blow for him.

"I want Aron back! Will he be alive again?" His despair was bottomless.

In the months that followed, he would scour the playground for little boys that reminded him of the brother he no longer had. He spoke to them in the

453

same way he used to speak to his brother and then he would come running to me to tell me how he had "helped".

It's by observing children, especially young children, that we can grasp what "having a good heart" really means. He already knows a good deal about suffering and death, but he can still see his way to putting his arms around everyone who is kind to him. He still laughs his bubbly laugh, and he still draws his beautiful houses adorned with hearts and flowers, blazing with color and surrounded by Swedish flags.

I can't see everything in his soul. But I know there is no evil there. I see only goodness, love and sometimes anxiety over an existence that is pulling him in too many directions at once. Because he is not old enough or competent enough to handle this existence, he is sometimes defiant and insolent against his will. A little while later, he comes to me in tears, soft and little, in need of a hug.

It's a harsh, malevolent world, for little people as well as big ones. We have so little say about what happens to us. Disaster strikes without warning. Rich or poor, wherever and however we live, we can't escape the fact that there is one thing we value above all others: an embrace that is ours, and a place to belong and feel secure in. Everything else is chance, emergency and adaptation. Intimacy and belonging are the things that we can't live without.

SEVEN YEARS: THE SCHOOL CHILD

All parents who send their six or seven-year-old off to school for the first time know that that first day heralds the end of an era that will never return. Early childhood is gone forever.

Two things that will capture the child's attention for many years to come now make their debut in his or her conceptual world: school and friends.

Children who have just started school can very quickly lose all sense of proportion.

After the first day at school, a little boy or girl may be willing to sell Mom and Dad plus any siblings in exchange for a hug from the teacher. A little girl may indicate her desire to move out of the parental home to take up residence at a friend's house without further ado after only one visit. A little boy may be more than willing to trade in his big brother for a better model just because Joey's big brother has an electric train set in his room.

And you will be forced to the realization that you are hopelessly déclassé because you don't own a living room set upholstered in red velvet. Like Veronica's parents.

During his or her first year at school, a child is forced to don a suit of clothes that is several sizes too big. If he has been given the task of writing his name by the next morning – something he has been able to do for a couple of years – he will announce, "I HAVE HOMEWORK", which of course means he is far to busy to help prepare dinner, never mind help with the dishes. The home is a hopelessly petty place, and the mundane tasks essential for its upkeep are beneath the dignity of the newly minted pupil, engaged as he is in activities that have global implications.

And in truth, the new pupil is fully occupied in trying to make sense of the strange new situation he now finds himself in.

He may go on cleaning binges, obsessively organize his possessions, sharpen thirteen pencils at a time, or change his sheets every day. He gives himself strict orders. "I absolutely have to remember this…" or "Every day at five o'clock I will…". You will be given equally strict orders to remind him should he forget.

The seven-year-old's games are highly structured, bound by complicated rules that must be followed to the letter. Anyone who has seen a couple of seven-year-olds playing hopscotch or marbles, lips compressed and brows furrowed in concentration, has trouble believing that they are actually playing.

And when you get down to it, they aren't. They are *mastering*.

If the six-year-old was often depressed – when he wasn't aggressive or provoking – the seven-year-old is often very surly. He can glare at you, his eyes flashing with genuine hatred, and refuse to speak so much as a civil word to you. He isn't always persistent in whatever obligations he's supposed to fulfill, but he can be *very* persistent when he is sulking.

He also has a tendency to whine horribly. He regards his surroundings as nothing but a hindrance. If it weren't for all the obstacles placed in his way, he could be anything he wanted: a latter day Columbus, a millionaire or simply an all purpose genius.

The seven-year-old is sufficient unto himself and never tires of telling you so. But if he so much as falls and scrapes his knee, he becomes very, very little again.

He may be cocky during the day, only to be terrified of the dark when night falls.

The seven-year-old is vain. He selects his wardrobe very carefully before setting off to school. Image matters!

He also falls in love from time to time.

The seven-year-old finds himself in a difficult developmental phase. From the ordeal of a changing phase, over the course of the year he enters an exploring period and becomes easier to get along with, but he is still subject to sudden mood swings.

His tendency to constantly deride his surroundings masks an attempt to cheat his way to an independence that he is not nearly ready for. He will threaten you by telling you he wants to move and may actually run away. The seven-year-old can only accumulate so much bitterness before he has to release it somehow. When it happens, you are dumbfounded. Being in a bad mood is one thing, but running away from home?

The seven-year-old is exiting early childhood, and he is changing.

For a very young child, being loved and needed was enough. The six-year-old's outlook was somewhat more morose. "No one *really* likes me." The seven-year-old asks himself, "Who do *I* like?"

And here he can be very ungracious.

You should interpret his outbursts of ill temper as warning signals – and take the appropriate action. The seven-year-old simply *can't* clear his own air, so to speak, no matter how much he screams and slams doors, and as a rule, he doesn't even do that. He keeps quiet, collects and catalogues every perceived injustice, and glowers at the world ever more darkly.

Another indication that he isn't feeling good about life is the constant restlessness that compels him to exert himself feverishly far beyond the limit of what he wants or is capable of. It's as though he wants to avoid silence and tranquillity, or anything else that might mean being alone with himself.

There are seven-year-olds who are wound so tight they are ready to snap. It's impossible to talk to them without getting them to relax first. And it's getting a seven-year-old to relax that is the crux of the problem.

An effective ruse for seeing how the land lies is to suggest that he sit down with you for a while and simply *do nothing*. If he's in a good mood, he will park himself expectantly beside you and a conversation will ensue that will give you insight into what is really going on in that little brain, bubbling cauldron of new impressions that it is.

If however he is tense or over-extended, he will refuse to sit down. He just isn't capable of it. He flutters around like a nervous bird and behaves exactly like a stressed out adult who has a thousand pretexts to avoid taking the rest he or she needs so desperately.

If nothing else, you can coax him into sitting down by serving the two of you a snack that he can enjoy in peace. He will have to wait at the table until you are finished yourself, by which time he will hopefully have calmed down enough to know how to behave.

Listening to music can work wonders too. The great classical composers knew what they were doing!

A seven-year-old can be so tense that he actually bursts into tears when the tension begins to subside.

As a responsible adult, you have to stand firm against a seven-year-old and refuse to allow yourself to be put down.

"I don't want to live here anymore!" the seven-year-old announces.

"But *I* want you here because I love you and want you with me. So don't even think about it."

Even if your life leaves much to be desired, stick up for yourself and your life, and walk tall.

And make sure your seven-year-old knows you expect him to do the same.

Hanging out with friends should not take up too much of a seven-year-old's time too soon. To consign your seven-year-old to the company of other children and only other children is to tempt fate.

If disaster doesn't strike today, it will tomorrow.

Home and family, the flock, are what the seven-year-old needs above all else. He talks a good fight. But talk is cheap. You shouldn't let him rush out the door in an agitated state. He needs to *connect* with home and hearth first.

You should cuddle a seven-year-old just as you did when he was younger, but be prepared for resistance. He may lash out and refuse to submit to things that are for "little kids". Persevere!

If you stop hugging and kissing him now, physical affection may become artificial and difficult later on. If the idea that physical affection is somehow unnatural takes hold, it may follow the seven-year-old for the rest of his life.

The seven-year-old loves rules and regulations. You can turn this predilection to your advantage as far as his activities in the home are concerned.

For as the seven-year-old's personality becomes more clearly defined – from now on he will be easier to recognize from development phase to development phase – his behavior will get worse, to tell you the brutal truth. It is now that the never-ending nagging comes into the picture and with it the odd necessary punishment. (See "How to do it – if you want to" in Part five of *For the Love of Children*.)

It's better to give him fixed tasks that must be done regularly than to confront him with new orders every day.

If necessary, you can remind him that it's your duty to teach him certain things so that he can manage on his own when he is old enough to move on. This is an effective argument, which also works well with teenagers.

The seven-year-old stands with one foot in the initial stages of independence and it is easy to fall into the trap of trying to bind him to the home and to you by freeing him from all responsibility, coddling him, allowing him to skip school if he doesn't feel like going and so on.

You may even "diagnose" him as over-sensitive, defective in some way, helpless to the point where you renege on your own responsibilities and blame *him* because you want to avoid the changes you should perhaps be making in your own life.

The six-year crisis was the beginning of a liberation process that will only be complete at the end of puberty, and the seven-year-old stands at the threshold of this process. Using himself as his own base, albeit a fragile one, the seven-year-old is trying to explore the world, and he will not be able to avoid running afoul over his own lack of ability and maturity. He will need a sense of belonging, protection and leadership for a long time to come, and naturally, you, as a parent, should nurture a secure connection to the home and to you. But you shouldn't do this by declaring him incompetent or by relieving him of all responsibility.

For example, I would argue that it is *not* appropriate to take care of schoolwork for him through reminders, nagging or supervised homework sessions. Since society has decreed that a normal child of this age is mature enough to go to school, your seven-year-old is presumably mature enough to take responsibility for his own schoolwork.

So let him.

If, on the other hand, you simply want to take a look at his work because you think it is brilliant, that is of course another matter entirely – but in that case you are exercising no control, nor are you in any way taking responsibility for the work itself.

You will gradually become more of a pal than an all powerful parent to your seven-year-old. And you may have to try harder, since his confidence in you is no longer guaranteed. For all that his love and loyalty are strong, you can't take them for granted anymore.

If you betray a confidence, speak as though he were not present, laugh over one of his idiosyncrasies, or relate an anecdote about a weakness or an occasion when he made a fool of himself, this is a stab in the back.

And the seven-year-old will feel deeply wronged. He will look at you with cold, reproachful eyes for a long time thereafter.

In a nutshell, *the golden rules of friendship are in force from here on in.*

OF PIMPS AND POETRY

My son comes to me one day and informs me that his younger brother has gotten hold of some pimps. The boy is clearly upset. "Why don't I get any pimps?"

A veteran parental brain is used to dealing with all sorts of absurdities. Gradually, the situation becomes clear. Nothing sinister is afoot. Nothing unwholesome has breached the walls of the family home. It's not about pimps. It's about shrimp.

I knew another child who was coming up to school age who had a similar talent for mixing up words. After watching a program about astronomy and the planets, he looked at a map of the solar system, put his finger on the large planet with the red spot and announced in Churchillian oratorical style, "According to my copulations, this planet is stupider." I can only assume he meant, "According to my calculations, this planet is Jupiter." What a difference a few misplaced phonemes make!

In spite of the fact that kids this age are still putting the finishing touches on their vocabularies, they are veritable fountains of interesting information. A hopeful little girl rings the doorbell and asks to play with one of my little angels.

"I'm afraid not," I explain.

"Oh. Can she come to my house?"

"No," I say, "I'm sorry, she can't come to your house today."

"Oh. Well, I'm not allowed to bring anyone home anyway. My mom can't take more than one kid at a time."

I know how she feels, I think to myself.

"And my dad," she continues doggedly, "he comes home and he's so tired, he doesn't even take a shower."

I clear my throat, hoping to head off any more indiscretions at the pass, but to no avail. This is not a kid who gives up easily.

"He never showers," she enlightens me further. "I shower every day, but my mom never showers either."

The next day, I see this little girl walking hand in hand with her parents, the people who never shower…

I was once a substitute teacher in a nursery school for a few months. The kids would sleep all afternoon. I tried to find out why they were so tired.

"Because we watch TV," they answered in unison. "We watch TV the whole evening."

"And your parents are OK with that?" I enquired.

"Of course they are," they answered earnestly.

A few weeks later, there was a parent-teacher meeting. Parent after parent came up to me and entreated me to stop lending my seal of approval to habits that were clearly unhealthy – such as spending the whole evening glued to the idiot box. The kids had had the gall to tell their parents that their teacher had said that watching TV all evening was just what they needed.

A philosopher once observed that all children under ten are poets. I suppose the implication is that poets aren't always reliable – we don't talk about poetic license for nothing.

Another somewhat more worldly teacher would periodically send a letter home to the children's parents which said,

"If you promise not to believe everything your children tell you about me, I will promise not to believe everything your children tell me about you."

EIGHT YEARS: THE MAGICIAN

If the seven-year-old would divorce his parents to marry his teacher, the eight-year-old is a bit of a bigamist. (The nine-year-old will return to his mother/father after his short-lived infidelity.)

The eight-year-old is often a very pleasant individual, full of wit, ideas, enthusiasm and imagination. The eight-year-old has a good deal in common with the three-year-old, who took a pause during the terrible twos and could have put an ad in the personals that would have read: "Interested in everything that makes life fun."

Jokes, giggling and general silliness are the order of the day, and although still bound by rules and regulations during play, these strictures are a source of enjoyment and not simply tools to master existence with. The eight-year-old's rules are there to complicate, challenge and fascinate, not to constrain, and he is more interested in pushing himself to his limit than in making sure his playmates don't cheat or do better than he does.

The eight-year-old has rich and varied hobbies.

He saves and collects things. He will turn his room into a veritable empire, and if he isn't collecting stamps, he's collecting dead wasps, shells or something else that's special for some reason. He likes pictures and photos and probably wants a camera.

That's if he hasn't gotten into daddy long-legs, white mice or something even more repulsive... The eight-year-old often has a pronounced interest in insects, whose lives he researches, and if it were possible, he would gladly have an anthill in his room.

The eight-year-old likes himself, and as a result, likes other people too. Interested in anything new, he is great company for a neglected relative. This is a great age for making enriching contact with people. The neglected relative can count on being welcomed with open arms.

You can take an eight-year-old anywhere, sporting events, work places, museums and parties. Wherever he is, he finds something fun to do, and he is immediately liked by the people who come into contact with him for his open, unforced demeanour.

The eight-year-old doesn't shut himself up in his own dark and dismal world like the six-year-old, and he doesn't morosely dismiss his surroundings like the seven-year-old.

On the other hand, he is big on secrecy. He can put a sign on the door of his room that reads ENTRY PROHIBITED. Inside his fortress he occupies himself with things that only he understands the significance of. (Naturally, you would never be so uncouth as to enter his lair without knocking!)

The eight-year-old loves forming secret clubs. He expends a great deal of effort in formulating laws and drafting regulations for this colossally secret organization that is about to be founded.

Then, when everything is ready and the meticulously planned enterprise is about to be launched, he can suddenly lose all interest and devote his energies to something else.

More important than the club itself are the entry requirements. For example:

1. All members shall pay a two-dollar fee.
2. All members must take a vow of secrecy that shall remain in force until death.
3. All members must tell a story that is totally disgusting.
4. All members must have run away from home at least once.
5. No member can have had anything to do with a girl/boy.

And on it goes. What you do is less important than what you are in the eight-year-old's universe.

The eight-year-old is a magician. He beseeches existence itself, and he has a certain power over it.

For example, he will count the books on a shelf to ascertain whether the object of his tender affections loves him or not. Odd number of books: yes. Even number of books: no. Being a constructive optimist, he will always find his way out of a cul-de-sac. If the answer is no, he will count the books again and more or less consciously talk himself into believing that he counted wrong the first time, since he now has the answer he wants!

A magician seldom steps on the lines on the pavement.

The eight-year-old loves to experiment with his environment and test people, preferably people he doesn't know. He can stop a hundred people on the street and ask them what time it is. He can go into a store and wander around the ladies wear department, ask to see various garments, find out how much they cost, and then give the sales clerk his mother's regards.

He is often so convinced of his ability to manipulate the powers that be that he assumes responsibility for everything. If his parents divorce, the eight-year-old knows that he caused the marriage to crash because he broke a plate at Christmas, pulled the head off a doll, or thumped his little sister.

The eight-year-old's conscience doesn't usually bother him too much, but he has none-the-less understood that everything he does has consequences.

And *that* is an insight that can torment him. He will sincerely believe that the house was struck by lightning because he fed his sandwich to the dog when no one was looking.

The eight-year-old is going through an exploring phase that will last until he is ten, when he will enter a sunny haven of mastery.

He can be a tad incoherent, flighty, at times incomprehensible, and his enthusiasm occasionally causes him to go over the top. When he refuses to see his own limitations, he has to be held back.

He seldom reacts by becoming sulky as the seven-year-old would, but instead exhibits physical symptoms. Headaches and stomach aches are common signs of over-exertion.

The eight-year-old still needs twelve hours sleep a night. If he wants to stay up late, it's not hard to get him used to having a nap when he gets home from school, since not much happens at that time of day anyhow.

Little magician that he is, he has a tendency to take everything you say literally. If you tell him not to cross his eyes because they will get stuck, he will believe you.

The eight-year-old dices with the powers that be because he fears them. As a parent, you should resist the temptation to exploit this weak spot. Threats of danger, thieves and murderers, reprisals and punishments frighten the life out of him. He can conjure up images of sudden death all by himself for something as trivial as forgetting to brush his teeth.

The eight-year-old cannot tell the truth. It's simply impossible. The rest of the world just wouldn't understand. Everything has to be doctored, classified, repressed and concealed. Appeals to an eight-year-old's sense of morality will be singularly unsuccessful!

To be sure, he has a moral sense, but it's rather convoluted. He will swipe ten dollars from you and buy himself a ball. When you ask him where he got the ball, he will tell you that he found it. Moral dilemma solved!

He concocts a lie about finding the ball because he knows it's wrong to steal, but it wouldn't occur to him to feel badly because he took your money. After all, balls cost money. You have it, he doesn't. The trick is to make it look as though he hadn't stolen any money.

The eight-year-old isn't deceitful – just ingenious, practical, and, in his own peculiar way, logical.

"How COULD you?!" is not a question that an eight-year-old can respond to.

If you expect him to be ashamed, you will be disappointed. He thinks the whole business is as plain as day. It was just a matter of taking a few dollars from your purse. What else do you want to know?

"If you were at least SORRY!" you continue dolefully, but you'll get more contrition from a pet rock.

Why would the eight-year-old be sorry?

If he's sorry about anything, it's about not having been smart enough to pull the whole thing off undetected. While you wait expectantly for tears of remorse and pleas for forgiveness, he is pondering how he can improve his technique for next time.

You have to appeal to the eight-year-old's common sense. Lectures are effective at this age.

"If you steal money from me, I may have to start stealing things from you. Your cars for example. Or your marbles. Or that knife you like so much. I need a knife now I come to think of it. One day when you get home from school, it will just be gone. And you'll look everywhere for it and ask me if I've seen it, and I'll say no, I haven't seen your knife. And then you'll see a knife that looks just like yours lying on the kitchen table. 'That's my knife!'

you'll say. And I'll say, 'What do you mean *your* knifc! Finders keepers, losers weepers.' Are you with me?"

The eight-year-old won't look ashamed, just astonished. That scenario had never occurred to him.

The eight-year-old is a good little buddy who sometimes walks his own road, but deep down he's a loving soul, and he's still little. He needs to be reassured that he belongs every day, and he needs to really *connect* with you – if ever so briefly.

This connection is as important to the eight-year-old as it is for the rest of us.

He needs fixed daily household chores that he and he alone is responsible for. And he should be involved in choosing them.

The eight-year-old is a born explorer, always up for an adventure, and he should be given as much freedom of movement as possible. However, he will only feel truly free if he has a clearly defined framework within which to operate – times, routines, habits and clear, *very* precise rules.

The time he spends with friends should be limited to a couple of hours a day and only after he's done everything he is supposed to do.

MENTAL GYMNASTICS:
AN EXERCISE IN SELF-IMPROVEMENT

Being a parent is an exercise in self-improvement. It improves you in that it opens you up, so to speak. The scattered remnants of the personality and independence that you might once have had become pathetically inadequate. To look at a photo of yourself from your pre-kid days is to look at a being from another planet. "Was that really me?" you think to yourself. "Was there ever a time that I lived for me and me alone? How simple life must have been."

It's not that being a parent breaks you down. Quite the contrary, it lifts you up. Everyone knows how beneficial problem-solving is for the human brain, and if constant problem-solving sometimes makes you feel like you're spread a little thin, well, keep your sense of humor! A sense of humor is a blessing. The funny thing about a parental sense of humor is that it only kicks in after the event. Once the kids are asleep, the fact that they decorated the broadloom with chocolate syrup can seem amusing.

I remember math problems at school. If Mr. Smith has to drive from New York to Los Angeles, a distance of 3,246 miles, and he travels at a speed of 55 miles an hour for eight hours a day, how long will the trip take? Parents have far more interesting problems to solve. And what makes real life problems interesting is that there is no answer key to fall back on.

You have six kids. Two want to have a bath, one wants to change his clothes, one wants to pee but can't get his pants undone, two want to play video games, and dinner is getting cold. Solve that equation. Answer…

You are making breakfast with four kids. Three want to pour the milk, one wants to stir the cereal, and all four want to butter the same piece of bread. Answer…

You are doing housework with five kids. Two don't want to make their beds, two don't want to vacuum the rug, and one doesn't want to do anything. Answer…

You are trying to get six kids to help you clean up the yard. One says, "Why does it always have to be me?", one says, "I'm too tired", one says, "Do I have to?", one doesn't answer, one wanders off, and one has locked herself in the bathroom. Answer:

You have seven kids and six cookies… Maybe we shouldn't go there.

That's I what I mean by mental gymnastics. And very rewarding they are too. Exhaustion and the absence of a solution are guaranteed. But then, one day, as you sit gaunt and hollow-eyed contemplating your life and wondering what possessed you to take on this impossible task of child rearing, a young child suddenly pats your hand and hugs your knees and whispers "You're so nice, Mom!" You have your answer. And when an older child spontaneously tells you, "You're like a pal", you would walk to the ends of the earth for her.

Until, that is, you accidentally overhear the five-year-old say, "I told Mommy she was nice so she won't get mad when she finds out I drew on the table…" To which big sister replies hopefully, "I think I've swung us a trip to the movies this Sunday."

It's an exercise in self-improvement. It's wonderful. It's impossible.

It's love, I suppose!

NINE YEARS: THE SEEKER

The nine-year-old is a seeker. He is looking for himself, his friends, the meaning of life, a tolerable existence, his parents, understanding, respect, love, integrity, and something fun to do.

At the very least this last item can be a problem.

The nine-year-old is a world-class brooder. He can also be something of a kill joy, brilliant at complaining about everything, less so at actually doing something about it.

He will bestride the barricades with the glowing intensity of the revolutionary firebrand, prepared to defend to the death his right to be who he is – the nine-year-old often gets into fights – but after an inflammatory speech he stands alone none-the-less, the expression on his face suggesting that he really wasn't expecting anything else.

The nine-year-old has learned to appreciate the qualities of his family and the flock he belongs to. At least, he has realized how dependent he is on his very belonging.

There is an element of prestige in his loyalty. He and his friends will endlessly analyze and compare each other's families, houses, cars and peculiarities. ("Your mom has fake nails!" "She does not!") Passionate disagreements are common. The nine-year-old's rhapsodies about his family can reach epic proportions. There is not now, never has been, and never will be a family on God's green earth quite like his. Nor is he above inventing mega-rich uncles who own half of Silicon Valley just to sweeten the pot.

In this regard, the nine-year-old is rather like a husband who is forever singing his wife's praises in public – but only when she's not around. Eyes moist, he will wax poetic about how lucky he is, and his audience knows that they are in the presence of a man who loves his wife as no woman has ever been loved. But when this same man gets home at the end of the day, the transformation is total. Not a word of appreciation, not even a cursory caress. He whines, complains, groans and sighs over his lot in life.

The parents of a nine-year-old who is forever complaining about the wretched state of affairs at home would be stunned to hear how they are described out there in the world.

The nine-year-old does not struggle against authority. He annihilates it.

The nine-year-old can see right through people – parents as well as teachers – with cold, penetrating, indifferent eyes. Freezing people out of his life is a hobby that the nine-year-old cultivates assiduously. Silent, systematic terror to attain a certain end has become his speciality.

The nine-year-old can be a serious bully. Nine-year-olds are masters at making each other angry, and children who have hitherto managed to get through life without ever resorting to violence do a U-turn when they hit this age.

Sooner or later the nine-year-old is forced to defend himself physically. It's not at all unusual for a nine-year-old to run home from school in floods of tears. At the very least, he wishes he could.

The nine-year-old has a sharp tongue.

"I'm more bigger than you are," says the first nine-year-old.

"More bigger? Why don't you learn to speak English? Or didn't your parents ever go to school?" sniffs the second nine-year-old (heart pounding).

The first nine-year-old is devastated, which of course requires revenge.

The nine-year-old thinks ahead. What happens today interests him less than what is going to happen tomorrow.

He contemplates the next day with mixed emotions. Part of him hopes it will be better. Part of him is afraid that it won't be. He has a tendency to assume the worst case scenario is inevitable and panics over the possibility that he might forget something or lose something. He doesn't greet the new day with the eight-year-old's bold-hearted confidence but rather (if he's lucky) with a strange combination of hope and suspicion.

The nine-year-old is so convinced that he will fail he is incapable of feeling joy when he actually succeeds. If he has a test coming up at school, abysmal failure is a given. Should he against all expectations ace his test, he assumes it was pure luck. The gods are lulling him into a false sense of security so that they can nail him when he least expects it. He sinks even deeper into a slough of despondency, much to the delight (he thinks) of the capricious powers that govern his existence.

It is not uncommon for the nine-year-old to exhibit aches and pains that seem to strike just as he is about to start a household chore or do his homework. He has to go to the bathroom frequently, especially at inopportune moments.

He is lonely, misunderstood and insecure.

The nine-year-old is going through an exploring phase of development, and it is a bleak journey. Depression and anxiety dampen his exploratory fervor and his zest for life founders on the reefs of real or imagined disappointments.

He delves into life, the world and himself, all the while tottering on the brink of that chasm called loneliness.

What the nine-year-old needs is his own company in the shape of his former eight-year-old self. He is caught between the eight-year-old's happy-go-lucky, ingenious lust for discovery and the ten-year-old's peaceful equilibrium. The path that leads from one point to the other is far from straight.

The nine-year-old simply has to pull himself up short and stop looking inwards and downwards instead of outwards and upwards in order to claim his rightful place on earth.

If the eight-year-old wanted to see the world, the nine-year-old wants the world to see him. He has to *be somebody*.

He doesn't have to be as bitter, unhappy and complaining as described here, but one thing is certain: the nine-year-old gets *noticed*. There is no happy medium for the nine-year-old. It's one extreme or the other.

He can for example be best friends with someone one day only to replace the person with a new best friend the next. A good number of tragedies are played out among nine-year-olds who abandon each other at the drop of a dime. They are less than eager to investigate the whys and wherefores of any given situation. The perceived sinner is left to his own devices, a despised outcast beyond the pale of human compassion.

Thus, nine-year-olds should not be allowed to hang out with friends outside school hours for more than an hour or so a day. They can't cope with the harsh world that they have created for themselves.

He is sensitive, the little seeker, and his discontent and anxiety take him to the brink of despair sometimes. He feels he has to make the grade, but fears he never will.

It's not uncommon for the nine-year-old to enhance his prestige among his contemporaries by resorting to less than honest means to supply them (and himself) with money, candy etc. You should not tempt fate by leaving money lying around, and don't have any illusions about your little angel! At this age, kids don't steal for profit or excitement but to prove that they have street cred.

The nine-year-old is made of stuff considerably less stern than the tough, courageous eight-year-old. Mistakes should be recognized for what they are: mistakes.

"Did you happen to take that five dollars? You mustn't do that. I need my money, OK?"

You will get further with tact, sensitivity and matter-of-factness than with fire and brimstone tirades about morality. If you do punish a nine-year-old, the punishments should be simple and logical. (See "How to do it – if you want to" in Part five of *For the Love of Children*.) The nine-year-old is down on himself enough already. If he has to hear he's a thief, a liar, a slacker or whatever sin he's being accused of, it may break him. Without much fanfare, he will conclude that there's no point in even trying, since failure is preordained.

If you expect the worst of him, he may well live down to the expectations you place upon him.

For example, instead of telling him how lazy he is for neglecting his chores in spite of your exhortations to smarten up, just let the kitchen or the living room go to hell in a hand basket. If dirty laundry obscures the TV or the hall becomes impassable, so be it. It takes nerve and grit to stay the course, but eventually the nine-year-old will start to complain. You can then, with an air of complete innocence, pose the question,

"We agreed to stop cleaning the house, didn't we?"

The message gets sent, and sermons lamenting the decline and fall of western civilization are unnecessary.

A flat-out lie is a vote of non-confidence, so instead of coming down hard on the nine-year-old and branding him a liar, you should try and find the root causes of this lack of confidence. The nine-year-old isn't hard to get along with if you can get him to understand that you are in fact on his side and that you will stand by him no matter what. A solid attachment, tenderness and a daily laugh will do wonders for his confidence.

Humor is a universal cure-all.

The nine-year-old is a seeker. You can't give him all the answers. But you can be his friend.

THE JAWS OF THE BLACK DOG

There are times when we are afraid. We feel like we've been slapped in the face, we feel humiliated, we feel bitter – and we feel that we can't fight back because there is nothing to fight against.

Common sense tells us we are overreacting. Yet our emotions burn and smart and tear us to shreds. We don't like making our innermost feelings public if for no other reason than to do so would only bring more torment, more humiliation, more ridicule.

Nothing actually has to happen to provoke emotional turmoil, at least nothing that means anything to anyone else. Alone and terrified, we are locked away in our own emotional prisons. No earth shattering injustices are necessary to bring any of this about. All it takes is a mundane little fear that the rest of the world finds laughable. A fear of going to the dentist, a fear of thunder, a fear of being alone in the dark, a fear of going out, a fear of coming home, a fear of speaking in front of more than one person, a fear of just not being able to measure up. And the fear doesn't call forth any hidden inner strength to fight the good fight. We have nothing to fall back on but feeble common sense that basically parrots the message that the people around us are constantly throwing our way. "There's nothing to be afraid of."

Of course there's nothing to be afraid of. It's simply a question of rolling up your sleeves, throwing yourself into the fray of life and being optimistic. Everything will work out! But loneliness has its own language beyond words and logic, a numbing silence that begins as vague uneasiness and eventually becomes paralysing despair. We're caught in what someone once called the jaws of the black dog. And there's no outlet for the pain, no outstretched hand to grasp, no kindly voice to soothe, no kindred spirit that offers, if not a way out, at least a modicum of understanding.

But how can we stand up in public and plead for understanding when we know we don't have any reason to be unhappy? And even if we did have our reasons, who would we tell? We can turn to TV and shopping malls for distraction, but it's a one-sided conversation. And even if TVs and shopping malls could talk, what would they say back to us?

I suspect their response would be brief and to the point. "Everyone else can manage their lives, why can't you?"

TEN YEARS: A LIFE ON TRACK

The ten-year-old is wonderful company – a little miracle of a human being. Bursting with parental pride, you will wonder how you ever managed to create this fantastic person. But you did, and, as incredible as it sounds, the child that stands before you wouldn't have come into existence without you.

Obviously, you have accomplished *something* worthwhile during your time on earth!

The ten-year-old's good qualities are legion. He is dependable, responsible, calm and competent. He has a cheerful disposition and a positive attitude towards life. He's patient, meticulous, sensible and independent. He is a valuable resource indeed.

And on top of everything else, he is his parents' best friend. You can count on his understanding, and reality no longer has to be air brushed.

Should calamity strike and you break down, you don't have to shield the ten-year-old from the harsh truth as you would with a younger child. If you are worried about not having enough money to pay the rent this month, you can tell it like it is. He will ponder the problem and come up with constructive, well thought out ideas on how to deal with the situation that can range from a list of things that you both can save on to offers to walk the neighbour's dog to earn a little extra money. When the chips are down, the ten-year-old has your back.

Like the harmonious five-year-old, the ten-year-old likes himself and devotes a lot of thought to the future. His imaginings on what the future will bring are realistic. If he was dead set on becoming an astronaut when he was eight, he now realizes that it's a profession that requires a lot of work, and he can also grasp that he may change his mind as the years go by.

None of this will necessarily cause him to abandon his goal however.

The ten-year-old has judgement. Just as he has realized that one day he is going to have to earn a living at something, he has also realized that he should find himself a partner to lean on when the going gets tough. He falls in and out of love fairly frequently, and doesn't hesitate to swear eternal love and fealty while the relationship lasts.

His affairs are serious and profound, and they follow their own particular pattern. The ten-year-old has perhaps never hugged the object of his affections or even looked her in the eye – he may not even be sure of her name – but his love for her is as deep as the sea.

If he can't work up the nerve to tell her in person, he will write her a note. If he receives a positive response, he is *with someone*. The young couple will spend a few minutes a week with each other, during which time a cryptic conversation will take place. They will refrain from touching each other or even looking each other in the eye, and then they will part abruptly and head off in different directions. But they are a couple.

Until they break up that is, whereupon a singularly nasty invective will be conveyed via a third party.

The ten-year-old's love life (which includes skin mags and masturbation) doesn't consume him completely however. He has many more strings to his bow.

Above all, he feels secure in his everyday life, and he creates a contented little world of his very own. What's happening around him doesn't affect him much, even though he registers it all very well. Because he can respect himself, he can respect others.

He has a good sense of humor, but it's tempered by common sense, so he rarely steps over the line.

The ten-year-old is a loyal fellow and devoted to his friends. He is a balanced realist who by and large sticks to the middle ground between the extremes of blue-eyed naïveté and anxious neediness. He gets down sometimes of course, but he doesn't get demanding.

The ten-year-old is well on the way to becoming truly independent. He has left a large slice of childhood behind him, and he still has a way to go before he reaches adulthood, but in some mysterious way he manages to combine the best of both worlds.

The ten-year mark, like the five and two-year marks before it, is one of childhood's most harmonious periods.

It's an age to be savored – especially since a storm is gathering. The storm will hit with gale force winds when the child turns eleven, and his equilibrium will be but a memory.

Your ten-year-old is a steadfast friend, and you can be yourself in front of him. You can open your heart. He's not fazed by complexity, nor is he easily frightened. For the first time in his young life, the ten-year-old can handle anxiety and insecurity in you (the flock) without getting the wind up himself.

However, the fact that the ten-year-old can understand and even accept things like divorces and moves does not mean that he doesn't *react*.

When, after much agonized soul searching, parents get up the nerve to give their ten-year-old the bad news, he seems to take it in his stride. Mother and father heave a sigh of relief.

But after a week or so, their well-behaved child suddenly begins to skip school, steal or in some other way show that his equilibrium has been thrown off kilter. (Physical symptoms are rare. He expresses his discontent through his actions.)

The ten-year-old's reaction comes, but it's delayed and disguised. The reason he disguises it is that his deductive powers are so well developed.

His rational side won't allow him to show sorrow or disappointment over something he can grasp and accept intellectually. His reason won't even allow him to *feel* sorrow or disappointment.

Thus, the sorrow and disappointment find their expression in protest actions that are directed at things that have nothing to do with the issue at hand.

This is why follow up is so important.

However well the ten-year-old takes news of impending disaster, a more profound conversation should take place in private a few days later. If he is skipping school, stealing etc, you should condemn the behavior in no uncertain terms, which will hopefully cause the dam to break. You can then get him to express his true feelings about whatever it is through patient, thorough questioning. The placid ten-year-old seldom needs much coaxing.

In this well-balanced mastering developmental phase, the ten-year-old's abilities are growing by leaps and bounds. His sense of responsibility is stalwart and his judgement is sound.

Put him to work! Like the five-year-old, he must be allowed to feel as grown-up as he actually is, and if you can make him feel indispensable, so much the better. Teamwork with you (the flock) is ideal.

If you set to work with a ten-year-old, you can count on him to pull his weight. He's a great comrade, especially if you have fun with him too.

He's a playful soul, a cheerful loser and a gracious winner. When playtime ends, he doesn't sulk, but as long as it lasts he gives it his all.

The ten-year-old understands that material possessions cost money, and you can pamper him without spoiling him.

He's very adept at doing as the Romans do. The fact that people are different bothers him not one whit. He's adaptable and finds his feet quickly even under the strangest of circumstances.

He is sensitive however. Low blows, ridicule and ironic comments wound him deeply. (Irony is largely wasted on kids under ten anyway. It goes over their heads.)

Any confidences about his love life should be considered on a par with state secrets.

Just as the five-year-old doesn't want to be treated like a baby, the ten-year-old doesn't want to be treated like a "little kid". As a parent, you must take pains to be fair and honest with your ten-year-old. You will be repaid many times over.

You should also be careful about not appearing to do things out of simple force of habit. If you hug or kiss a ten-year-old, you should do it because you really want to. If he feels that you and the flock are treating him like a package to be disposed of as you see fit, you will hear about it. He is not sensitive, but he does possess, as well he should, a sense of dignity.

This is the year when the ten-year-old will begin to reject the parent of the opposite sex and gravitate towards the parent of the same sex.

The opposite sex comes to represent just that: *opposite.*

The ten-year-old is slowly preparing for a new and sexually determined set of behaviors. If you feel rejected, try to swallow your disappointment, loosen the emotional ties and rein in your nurturing parental instincts.

Content yourself with being an attentive, caring friend – to the best little buddy on the planet.

THE CLASSIC QUESTION

"Will I be as old as you some day?" asks the five-year-old.

Keeping my composure – since I don't feel I'm that ancient – I answer in the affirmative.

"You'll be as old as Grandma," I say. "Older even," I add in an effort to make myself somewhat more youthful in my child's eyes. "And I have been as young as you."

"Oh no," the child laughs. "Not as young as me!"

I decide to raise the stakes. "I've even been a little baby. And been in my mommy's tummy."

The child falls silent and ponders this.

"Have you?" she says thoughtfully. "But I've never been a baby," she continues with conviction. "I've always been big."

So that was that. A mother can be born at any age. A child is always as big as she is now. Children are either big or small. The rest of us are just old.

After I assured her that she was once a baby and that she was really tiny when she was still in my stomach, she popped the classic question.

"How does a baby get into your stomach?"

Now I fell silent. All parents worthy of the name have been emphatically taught the importance of initiating their offspring into life's mysteries. It's not good enough to fall back on clichés like "You wouldn't understand" or "We'll talk about it when you're older" or "Your Aunty Britt can explain that to you. She's a teacher..." No, you have to strike while the child's interest is piqued and give her a simple no-nonsense explanation in order to avoid difficulties later on.

Unfortunately, in this particular case, it happened to be very late, the five-year-old should have been in bed a long time ago, and she was not the type to be satisfied with short explanations. However, I bowed to the wisdom of the psychologists and cleared my throat.

"Well, in Mommy's stomach there's a tiny egg, so small you can hardly

see it, and in Daddy's… uh… (How am I going to put this, I ask myself desperately.) Here the lesson was interrupted by a laugh so raw, it was faintly pornographic. Ten-year-old big sister, who was in the adjoining room with the door ajar, had collapsed in a paroxysm of inappropriate mirth, and the five-year-old, thirsting after knowledge and sensitive to ambience as she was, immediately figured out that there were a lot of bodies buried in this particular field and she was going to dig up every one of them.

It was a remarkable lecture, punctuated at regular intervals by half concealed reprimands directed at the ten-year-old saboteur, all as the five-year-old followed her mother's blushes and stammering explanations with glowing eyes.

The net result was that the three kids, two girls and a boy, who had always bathed together in the most natural way imaginable and who had never paid more attention to body parts than to anything else in the world, now developed an idiotic obsession with one particular body part. They would chase each other around the house red cheeked, giggling wildly and shrieking, "You can't look at my bum! You can't look at my bum!"

At bath time, they wrapped towels around themselves. In the water.

That's what happens when theory and reality collide.

ELEVEN YEARS: THE TRICKSTER

After his harmonious days in the sun as a ten-year-old, the poor child falls head long into a new changing phase with all the accompanying disharmony, insecurity and confusion.

The eleven-year-old employs various strategies to cope with his problems, several of which are less than endearing. The eleven-year-old has a broad repertoire. He can be irritable, sulky, mouthy, depressed, angry, insolent, ironic (he's seen the light!), flat out nasty and even cynical.

And he can play the martyr better than anyone you will ever meet.

The eleven-year-old is brilliant at suffering the tortures of the damned in aggrieved silence. With a single venomous look, he can indicate that he is only putting up with his family because he doesn't have a choice. As soon as he gets next week's allowance, he is going to invest it in a firearm of some kind. If he doesn't wipe all his relatives off the face of the earth, he'll off himself. Then won't everyone be sorry when they gather round his coffin!

The eleven-year-old has quite a lot in common with the six-year-old, although, naturally, you should not tell him so...

The eleven-year-old manages his body just as badly as he manages his soul. He is often lanky and uncoordinated. He bumps into things and has accidents, he breaks anything breakable and tears down anything vertical, he stumbles and takes spectacular falls – metaphorically as well as literally.

He is so anti everyone and everything that extracting even a shred of affection from him is like pulling teeth. Everything he's learned, all the trust he has given or received he can abuse now. He schemes and manipulates by any means necessary.

Honesty and loyalty are definitely not his strong suits. Everything he held sacred a year ago is now tossed on the scrap heap of the profane. He bosses his nearest and dearest around, and he is superb at laying guilt trips on people. A single mother who feels guilty because she has a lover, is taking courses a couple of nights a week, or stoops to picking up McDonald's because she is too tired to make dinner can be sure that the eleven-year-old will zero in on the soft spot in her conscience and drive the knife in with unerring accuracy.

And if she's worried about how schoolwork is going for her beloved offspring, the eleven-year-old will not lift a finger to relieve her of her anxiety.

In fact, he will do everything in his power to make her feel worse.

The eleven-year-old is not totally devoid of sympathetic traits. He has genuine sympathy for the underdog, since he feels like such an underdog himself.

He can be movingly tender towards young children, loving with animals and generally protective of the weak, all of whom he will defend often at the price of his own prestige. Let the rest of the world laugh if it pleases. He doesn't care as long as he has something worth fighting for.

What the eleven-year-old lacks in joy he makes up for with dreams. He finds life tough and he feels unjustly treated. He can fantasize that the people he calls Mom and Dad aren't his *real* parents.

In affairs of the heart, he searches for the kind of romance that's unattainable in this world. As a result, he has a tendency to fall in love from a distance, which of course condemns him to relationships that are doomed to failure.

The eleven-year-old raises the object of his affections to the status of the saints and the angels. On the day when the truth is revealed and true justice done, this exalted being will realize what a paragon of virtue he the eleven-year-old is and will love him accordingly.

One can't help but feel sorry for him, locked as he is in his lonely fantasies, but they help him.

As does masturbation. The eleven-year-old masturbates, and it relaxes him and (hopefully) brings him a little joy. *Occasionally* at least, his body is his friend. Even though he may not ejaculate yet, the eleven-year-old experiences an intense orgasm, and this is as true for boys as it is for girls.

The eleven-year-old is a trickster, but not all his manipulative techniques are nasty. He can use charm to his advantage, and eleven-year-olds have been known to wheedle better grades than they actually deserve out of unsuspecting teachers.

The eleven-year-old puts together crossword puzzles, enters competitions, composes riddles, persuades clueless little old ladies to part with their money, finds usable gadgets that people have put out with their trash, and is generally a world class inventor.

He's a person who can change the external world, but he would probably feel a lot better if he could somehow avoid changing himself.

The eleven-year-old is stuck in a changing phase and feels as wretched as he did when he was a terrible two or a six-year-old, if not worse.

This is the third big step on the road towards real independence. The road is long and strewn with thorns. This third step is particularly difficult now that the child has experienced several long, stable periods – between one and two, at five and at ten – during which he has gathered the strength and acquired the maturity to walk this road with all its obstacles and trip wires, most of which challenges, consciously or not, the child made up himself.

Like his partners in crime, the terrible two and the six-year-old, the eleven-year-old can be difficult not to say insufferable. He desperately wants resistance and he won't quit until he gets it.

Before the days of "disorders" and "syndromes", kids this age were simply referred to as scamps and rascals – with good reason!

Eleven-year-olds should be taken aside and given a good dressing down from time to time. It's not a pleasant task, but if you don't do it, someone else will.

The unpleasantness you spare yourself will sooner or later be visited on your child.

An eleven-year-old who behaves unacceptably towards his parents or his siblings should be taken down a couple of rungs immediately. He should not be permitted to express contempt, swear or bark orders at people. Get in his face and remind him forcefully that *you* refrain from treating *him* that way.

You can also remind him that you have the same right to personal integrity and respect that he claims for himself. If that tactic doesn't bear fruit today, it will eventually.

Loving a contrary eleven-year-old isn't always easy, but you have to try. Do as you did with the unbearable (at times) terrible two and the six-year-old. Take full advantage of every occasion when the kid *is* easy to love.

And try to make that all important *connection*, create that sense of belonging that can be affirmed with a pat on the head, a kiss, a caress on the cheek, a smile or even an affectionate look.

The worst thing you can do to an eleven-year-old who is going through a crisis is to ignore him. If he can't connect with you and his nearest and dearest through regular, peaceful interaction, he has to be difficult just to be noticed.

The eleven-year-old is prey to flights from reality of all kinds. The most innocent variety manifests itself in obsessive TV or video watching and compulsive computer game playing.

Eleven-year-olds who are out and about downtown with money in their pockets and their parent's approval will sample anything, and, as we all know only too well, there is quite a lot on offer. You have every reason to be on guard.

The eleven-year-old should be kept at home as much as possible, and his freedom of movement should be curtailed far more than that of the sensible ten-year-old. Time spent hanging out with friends outside school should be strictly limited. An ounce of prevention is worth a pound of cure.

You keep an eleven-year-old at home partly by making it worth his while to be there, by which I mean creating a convivial atmosphere where adults and children are not segregated, and partly by pointing out what he's hopefully known for a long time: he is *indispensable*. He may moan and whine, but it is just as important (probably more) for the eleven-year-old to know that he is needed in some concrete, practical way as it is for everyone else.

He should participate in choosing the chores that will eventually be assigned to him, and these chores should be performed daily. The nagging and the arguing that come with the territory are easier to deal with in the content of a previously negotiated contract that the eleven-year-old has agreed to in a rare moment of lucidity.

Without this contract to fall back on, you will find yourself stuck in no man's land facing an angry, contrary kid who will oppose you on everything as a matter of general principle.

While we are on the subject of nagging, remember this rule. *Show your appreciation as often as you show your displeasure!*

You should put just as much effort into praising him when he does something well as you put into tearing a strip off him when he does something badly (or doesn't do it at all).

Not all chores should be done alone. Nothing promotes contact between adults and kids like teamwork, even if all you do is prepare meals together. It gives a child a sense of being part of a community. Household tasks should take precedence over everything else. Their overriding importance should be self-evident to all concerned.

The eleven-year-old is *contributing*. His input is *needed*. He is not doing what he does to be "nice", earn money or kill time.

When human beings work together towards a common end, they value the fruit of their labors. There is no better way to make a child feel secure and satisfied in his home and family than through social participation.

Thus, dinner is not the only time everyone gets together if ever so briefly. Dinner is strained anyway because people are actually expected to say something. Conversation around the dining table is not the eleven-year-old's forte.

"How was school?"

"Fine."

"What did you do?"

"Nothing."

"You didn't do anything?"

"Nope. Can I be excused?"

CHANGE

We all strive for balance in life. No one should be given a burden that he or she is not strong enough to bear. The crises we go through are not always characterized by panic, despair or the need to make decisions instantly. Some crises are drawn out affairs that little by little grind us down and hollow us out. Our room for manoeuvre is limited, but even if it were infinite, we still wouldn't know what to do. Limits are often an advantage. Perfect freedom would paralyse us.

Virtually no one avoids these drawn out crises where there are never any dramatic emergencies that demand a direct decision. Indeed, for some people they seem to be a permanent state. "I know something is wrong, but I don't know what." "My life is trickling away. The days go by and I don't really know why I am alive."

These feelings are not necessarily the result of a depression. There may not be anything "wrong" in any accepted sense of the word. There is just this feeling of slowly dissolving, a feeling that things can't go on the way they are. But they do go on, month after month, year after year. What do we do?

Who offers us a guiding hand, points the way and says, "This is the road you will travel. It's the right one for you."

The answer is no one. No one leads, no one shows us the way. We wander further, no destination and no place to belong, as empty days and silent nights accumulate.

Maybe what's most debilitating is living what seems to be one long lie. Maybe that's why we try so hard to gloss over what is happening. Who wants to stand up in public and say, "I don't know how to live my life. My whole existence is wrong, but I keep putting one foot in front of the other anyway." If we did, we would be forced to make changes.

So we lie to ourselves. "I'm no worse than anyone else," we say, and then we put our fingers in our ears when the lie rings so patently false. What can we change? And what's it going to cost us?

I think it costs us more to live a lie, to not even try to live in accordance

482

with what we know is the truth. That's the only thing I'm utterly convinced of: that this honesty, this inner voice of truth that comes built in to every human being is what we should listen to for the sake of our self-respect and dignity. Every human being can afford dignity, but none of us can afford to sell out our principles.

But years pass and habits form like layers of ice, one on top of the other, and what's right and wrong is no longer clear. What are principles? Self-examination, where does that fit in? We hurry off on our errands. We all have so much to do. As for examining our lives, well, we'll find time for that later.

And the day comes when we've forgotten completely and forever all that we once held sacred.

TWELVE YEARS: THE RELATIONSHIP RESEARCHER

The twelve-year-old does the impossible. He takes the hopelessly fragmented shards of the eleven-year-old's psyche and welds them into a coherent whole.

The twelve-year-old is no longer at war with the world. Quite the contrary, he contemplates it with calm curiosity. His main interest is human relationships with all the term implies.

The twelve-year-old is marvellous company and his maturity is truly astonishing. He seems to age several years in the blink of an eye.

As a parent, one understands that the antics of the eleven-year-old, however trying they were at the time, had a higher purpose.

The twelve-year-old is responsible, stable, open and positive: a person of substance. He is reliable and trustworthy, and, if you will make the journey with him, he will show you a hidden world, a world of profound feelings, desires and dreams.

The twelve-year-old is beginning to try to fathom people's relationships with each other, with him and with life. His intuition is remarkable. He senses how people feel about each other. He can walk through a room where adults are sitting and having what they think is a neutral and amicable conversation and afterwards comment, "That can't have been easy. You guys don't like each other much, do you?"

If you have divorced, your twelve-year-old will want to know why. He will also want to know who you were with when you were young, what your hopes and dreams surrounding friendship and love were, what went wrong and why, what your parents' relationship was like and so on. The twelve-year-old recognizes his own emotional life in yours and no longer thinks that adults are from another planet.

Feelings and relationships are complicated, and the twelve-year-old has realized with both dread and fascination that human beings are sometimes

484

the victims of uncontrollable, self-destructive, agonizing forces that rage within them. He is slowly but surely beginning to learn humility, and he can now look at his parents with forgiving, even admiring, eyes.

The twelve-year-old is so sensible and full of insight, and seems to see the world so clearly that it is easy to come to regard him as an advisor. Yet if you ask him a direct question before taking a difficult decision, "Do you think I should marry Eric?" or "Do you think I should take this job?", he will become coldly defensive. "Do what you want. It makes no difference to me."

Of course it makes a difference to him. What he is really defending himself against is the responsibility. The twelve-year-old is philosophically sophisticated enough to sense that people have to act in accordance with their convictions. If they haven't figured this out, there is really no helping them. If they can't make up their own minds, no one can do it for them.

The twelve-year-old's solid intuition and self-respect enables him to choose the right friends, that is people that he really likes and that he gets something out of spending time with. He doesn't need to have his significance constantly reaffirmed by others. He knows he matters, so he is not vulnerable to peer pressure. He seldom loses his head and doesn't allow himself to be pressured into doing things he doesn't want to do. He can say no if he has to, and his judgement is sound.

This is a happy time for you as a parent or caregiver, since you can loosen the leash somewhat. You don't have to be everywhere at once to monitor everything. You no longer have to micro-manage, predict, plan, and organize. The twelve-year-old can do most of that himself. You will think you're on vacation! The twelve-year-old is his own boss. He guards his independence jealously – because he likes it.

If you like going on excursions to museums, historical sites, exhibitions and the like, the twelve-year-old is the best travelling companion you could wish for. His primary interest is people, their roots and origins, their potential and their future.

The twelve-year-old is going through an exploring developmental phase.

This will last until he approaches the end of puberty at around seventeen.

At this point he will find his feet and his balance during a mastering phase, which in many ways is comparable to the two-year-old's, the five-year-old's and the ten-year-old's.

Within the general framework of puberty, he will pass through all the developmental phases: the mastering phase at thirteen, the changing phase at the sensitive age of fourteen (this sensitivity will linger until he is well into his fifteenth year), and finally the exploring stage at fifteen and sixteen.

The twelve-year-old is going through puberty. The head start that girls have is very clear now. The boys will be kids for a while yet. It's only around fourteen that it becomes apparent that they will be men one day, while girls often start menstruating at eleven and take on the physical characteristics of fully grown women.

Just as the body readies itself for procreation, so does the mind. Whether they are conscious of it or not, twelve-year-olds are preparing themselves for sex. This can find expression – especially among girls, who develop earlier – in the belief that everyone else is inordinately interested in sex.

A father who gives his daughter an innocent goodnight hug and pats her on the back while he is hugging her would be stunned to discover how his behavior is dissected behind closed doors.

"It was awful! Dad was feeling me up! What if he…"

And all kinds of diabolical scenarios are envisioned.

Then again, diabolical scenarios occur. Incest happens. Children are violated.

These children remain silent out of loyalty and guilt. People, big or small, who have "only" been the victims of physical abuse are not enthusiastic about telling the rest of the world about it. Only people who believe themselves to be perfect are immune from guilt, and how many of us can lay claim to being perfect?

Children can't.

Sexual and physical abuse is a fact of life. And it is always the children who suffer most.

There is always someone who knows what's going on. And that someone has to come to the child's defence.

I believe that it is not the child, the victim, who should be punished by being wrenched from her or his home – taken into care, as it is euphemistically called. It is the adult who has betrayed the child's trust and committed a crime who should be punished.

Sexual and physical abuse are forbidden by law. *By protecting the criminal, you condemn the victim.*

The twelve-year-old who misinterprets her father's innocent goodnight hug has nothing to worry about. If the truth came out, the father would be less than thrilled to discover that his child thought him capable of sexually molesting her. Naturally, he has noticed that she is developing, but she is still his little girl. He would feel maligned in the most horrible way.

But the fact is that the twelve-year-old isn't maligning him. She honestly *believes* that the hug he gave her had a sexual overture. Consciously or not, she interprets the world as sexual. Both mentally and physically, she is preparing herself for sex whether she likes it or not.

Fathers of daughters and mothers of sons can't be too careful! No touchy-feely hugs, and keep kisses relatively indifferent. Generally speaking, the less physical contact, the better.

Discretion is important too. If you come upon your child when he or she is naked or half-dressed, leave the room at once! The parents of all twelve-year-olds should heed this advice. Not heeding doing so could result in your being labelled as somehow sexually deviant in your twelve-year-old's eyes, or, even worse, you might seriously frighten your child.

The twelve-year-old assigns a new role to the parent of the opposite sex. You become a representative of man or womankind. You are an ambassador for your sex. The responsibility is so enormous that it's hard to wrap your mind around, but it's a responsibility that has to be shouldered.

How you do it of course is your business. My somewhat cowardly strategy was simply to circumvent the whole problem. For there is a way for a parent to "de-sex" him or herself, and that is to be the child's friend.

Friendship implies rules that speak to the twelve-year-old, even across the sexual divide. Friends listen to each other, friends don't slander each other, and friends stick up for each other. Friends are honest and straightforward, and in the face of an external threat, the ranks always close.

Friends can *count* on each other.

What the twelve-year-old likes is to be treated fairly and respectfully by someone who is independent and has a good track record on dealing with the problems that life throws at us.

What he doesn't like is irritability and sour looks, nagging, interrogations, threats, underhandedness, mood swings and general insecurity on the part of those around him.

The twelve-year-old can sense the mood of the household the second he steps in the door. If you *connect* with him, the rest will look after itself. If you don't, he will turn his back on you and storm out of the house like a disgruntled husband who is fleeing to the pub to seek solace with his mates.

In an atmosphere of peace and tranquillity, the twelve-year-old will thrive, and he will quietly pursue his own interests.

This is a time of chess and endless games of Monopoly. Keeping diaries becomes popular with girls. The twelve-year-old will be enchanted if you stay up all night playing canasta with him. His intellectual hunger knows no bounds, and he devours non-fiction books on every conceivable subject.

He is also the world's keenest tourist.

The twelve-year-old is going through an intense growth spurt and needs at least ten, preferably eleven hours sleep a night. He doesn't always agree. There is no shortage of chronically exhausted twelve-year-olds (and teenagers for that matter), and that's a shame, since their zest for exploration – which is vast – wilts if they can never recharge their batteries properly.

Siestas are not part of the culture in our part of the world, but it's not that hard to persuade a twelve-year-old to take a little nap in the afternoon, and a nap will do him good. It's worth a try at any rate. After a few days of sleeping like a log in the afternoons because of accumulated fatigue, things will stabilize. He will be able to sleep for twenty minutes or half an hour and wake up on his own without disrupting his nightly sleep pattern. This works for kids either side of twelve as well.

The twelve-year-old is logical and precise. He values clarity. If you want his input, you should tell him exactly what you expect of him. "Can't you just lend a hand?" and similar vague appeals will fall on stony ground.

He should be consulted before you assign him chores, and this agreement should be preventive – rather than of the *ad hoc* variety, which has to be struck when things are already falling apart.

These chores should be carried out daily. Don't restrict him to things that only affect him such as his own laundry or his own room. Put him to work in ways that benefit everyone in the flock.

Working a little every day is better than working a lot once a week, and he should take responsibility for adhering to the agreement that both of you have come to.

Naturally, he should not be paid, since his contributions are essential (or at least should be presented as such) to the family's survival. His work should give him the feeling that he is needed. (*The others wouldn't manage as well without me.*)

If you pay him, you will turn him into an expert little haggler, and one doesn't haggle over survival. Staying alive is not negotiable. The flock looks after its young, just as the young, in so far as they are able, put in their two cents worth and take care of the flock.

All through puberty, social participation is of paramount importance in the form of teamwork and cooperation with you (the flock). An activity that offers the opportunity for social participation should be part of the twelve-year-old's daily routine. You can shop together, prepare meals together, clean up the living room together, anything from the very simple to the very complicated, as long as it's done every day.

The twelve-year-old wants to know exactly what you expect of him, and if you are not satisfied once he's done what he's been told, you have no one to blame but yourself. He is not going to put himself out just to make you happy. Appeals of the can't-you-and-me-be-friends variety will only tick him off.

On the plus side, he won't expect you to put yourself out just to make him happy.

All in all, if you play fair with the twelve-year-old and treat him with interest and respect, as though you were meeting him for the first time every day, he is a pure joy to have in the house.

WARMTH

It's a wet and dreary day. The children pass the time baking bread. A little seven-year-old is with us for a visit, and my brood swarms around her like flies around honey.

"How often have you been sick? I am going to tell you about all the stuff I've had." The interest is enormous, but my children's listening abilities leave much to be desired. Our little guest's account of all her various illnesses gets lost in the shuffle before she even opens her mouth. My six (five I should say. As usual, Baby is serenely indifferent) have to give their accounts first. Their imaginations soon run away with them.

"I nearly died from small pox!"

"And I nearly had PLAGUE!"

The little girl munches her sandwich pensively.

"You hear what they're saying?"

Oh yes, I hear what they are saying. I hear their voices rise, fall and merge into a symphony that I never tire of listening to. I'm thankful. I don't want them to be quiet or to grow up or to ever disappear from my life. My days are like pearls, each one more beautiful than the last. For me, the future is now. This is as good as life ever gets, and that knowledge helps me put things in perspective, and I can rise above those little daily frustrations. I need the children, and they need me. That must be the most glorious thing that can befall a human being: being needed. Nothing makes human beings lonelier than feeling that they're somehow superfluous.

I wish we could remember that. We're helpless without each other. Just knowing that we need each other confers tremendous strength. It's not just about needing and being needed. It's about seeking others out and meeting them with open arms without worrying about what they will think of us. It's about not being afraid of getting too close.

Now Baby is protesting. He's fussing a little. He doesn't say "mama". He says "maaamaaa". It sounds a little whinier.

He's quite a comedian like all one-year-olds. He can play peek-a-boo and tag on all fours for hours. It doesn't take much to amuse young children. It doesn't take much to amuse adults either. Or maybe I'm just speaking for myself. I never get tired of getting kissed on the cheek by lips smeared with blueberries, or of being patted by fingers sticky with mashed potatoes, or of being offered Pablum. If only someone else could clean the same blueberries, mashed potatoes and Pablum off the floor and the furniture! I smile at Baby and commiserate. Oh, life is hard when you're that little. This contents him and he crawls off about his business.

There are things I must have said ten thousand times over the years I have been a mother:

"Oh, what a shame!" (With infinite sympathy.)

"Oh, that's awesome! Look what you can do!" (With boundless admiration.)

Not to mention,

"Be careful!"

Then my words come back to me when one of my children adopts my role. At the moment I can hear my four-year-old remonstrating with her little brother.

"Careful! Careful! You'll break the baby! Then he can't be fixed! There'll be blood! We only have one baby!"

What more can one ask of life than to be close to so much warmth?

THIRTEEN YEARS: THE IMPORTANCE OF BEING EARNEST

The thirteen-year-old is a thinker. His approach to life is more serious than the twelve-year-old's, but his attitude is constructive and positive.

The thirteen-year-old, who has learned so much about relationships, says what is on his mind, and if the air needs clearing, he is more than up to the job. But while he doesn't hesitate to start an argument (he's actually quite good at it), he doesn't argue just to get things off his chest. He genuinely wants to find solutions.

While the twelve-year-old simply avoided people who affected him negatively, the thirteen-year-old really wants to try and create a good atmosphere. He is meticulous about his relationships, and if there's one thing he finds utterly baffling, it is indifference.

The thirteen-year-old is a homebody. The worst thing that can happen to him is being driven out of his home because the atmosphere is so negative that he doesn't like being there. He is very dependent on a stable base camp in which to stake out his territory.

The thirteen-year-old reads and thinks. Things that strike him as interesting, he wants to discuss *right now*. In this respect, he is like a young child or an overly eager adult. Thoughts tumble into his head and he wants to have a conversation about them as they occur to him. By evening, however, he will have forgotten all about them.

The thirteen-year-old is fascinated by the past. He wants to know whom he takes after and where he got his various talents from. He loves hearing what you think of him. "What do you think I am going to be? What do you think I'm suited for?" are common questions.

He is secure in himself. He feels more or less like a finished product, even though he knows – and relishes the prospect – that he has a lot more to learn and experience.

Still, his independence is on the fragile side. As an adult, your opinion of him carries a great deal of weight. Since his identity is still germinating, you should be careful not to tie him to a perception of his identity that is not really his own. Don't "pigeon-hole" him by taking him at his word and telling him what you think he will be.

And remember he is certainly not mature enough to hear anything but positive things about himself!

The thirteen-year-old's memory is an interesting resource to draw on. He has the ability to use his own experiences to draw conclusions of a more general nature. If you talk to him about something that has happened to you, you may be astonished at how clearly he understands your predicament because he has been through the same thing himself – a fact you were blissfully unaware of.

The thirteen-year-old is dependable and responsible to a fault, especially when there is a job to be done that requires every man to do his duty, so to speak. He is sensible and reasonable, and always willing to help out if someone is having problems or there is some kind of emergency. He knows very well what consideration means, and he is a steadfast friend – provided that he is treated with loyalty, and not forgotten, railroaded or treated like a little kid.

He will react with visceral indignation if something happens in the household, and he is left out of the loop.

"Aunt Elsie is coming today," you announce.

The thirteen-year-old is completely uninterested.

"Did you hear me?"

"Yes," he mutters and disappears from the room.

The next time Aunt Elsie comes over and you either forget or don't bother to tell him, once she's gone, the thirteen-year-old may comment acidly,

"It's good to know what's going on in this house." (The thirteen-year-old has gotten the hang of irony and has dirty looks down pat.)

"But you didn't seem to think it was such a big deal the last time," you say defensively.

"I happened to have been thinking about something else," comes the aggrieved reply.

And he means what he says. When the thirteen-year-old thinks, he *thinks*.

One of the thirteen-year-old's many endearing traits is his love of order. He doesn't keep his environment tidy *all* the time, but he is bitten by the neat-freak bug at regular intervals.

"I feel like cleaning today," he announces. And clean he does.

Not only does everything have to look clean, it has to smell clean too.

(This is not an obsession that's restricted to girls.)

Unless you have given him the impression that he is living in a hotel with 24-hour-a-day room service, the thirteen-year-old is only too happy to create an orderly environment for himself.

And his domestic aspirations extend beyond himself. They encompass you, the rest of the family (the flock) and the common living areas.

The thirteen-year-old often has impressive talents, although how he comes by them is unclear.

He can, for example, without ever having had a single lesson, teach himself to play a musical instrument. When he cleans a large window for the first time, you would swear that he had been doing it professionally all his life. He can successfully repair household appliances that he has never even used, never mind disassembled. His abilities are nothing short of stunning.

The thirteen-year-old's personality is solidifying. He regards his body with both interest and anxiety.

A girl develops complexes at this age, and she won't be comforted by parental assurances that she is pretty. Far better to regal her with stories about how awful you looked when you were her age. Go on to describe all your various defects in lurid and convincing detail with special emphasis on how you *felt*.

Boys regard the prospect of becoming men with little enthusiasm. They would rather skip puberty all together. When the thirteen-year-old catches sight of that first pimple, it makes him nauseous. He is embarrassed over his body generally, and the very idea of getting naked in front of anyone fills him with horror.

If you are the mother of a son, you will have to restrain yourself when showing physical affection, and if you are the father of a daughter, you can no longer put her on your knee, and you must be *very* careful about how and where you touch her. (See the previous chapter on the twelve-year-old.)

Romance blossoms at this age.

Girls are more advanced than boys. Generally speaking, matriarchy rules. The girls initiate relationships and break them off – as well as controlling the intervening course of events. The boys just go around and wait for the phone to ring.

Thirteen-year-olds are so serious and reflective, and so desirous of being in control of themselves and their surroundings that they wouldn't be human if they didn't go to the other extreme every now and then. And this they do! This is an age marked by giggling and horseplay.

Girls can giggle for hours. Since stopping them is impossible, the only course of action open to the rest of the family is simply to flee when the giggling finally becomes unbearable.

Boys can hurl the most awful insults at each other and get into wild fights. They claim the fights are friendly, and they are until someone really gets hurt, at which point the injured party takes time out and licks his wounds – or flies into a frothing rage and starts to fight for real.

The thirteen-year-old is enjoying a period of mastery within the framework of an exploratory developmental phase that he entered after the eleven-year crisis and that will continue until the end of puberty.

He likes himself and life. Unless you as a parent make it impossible for him to feel at peace with, and at home in, his flock, he won't cause you any problems.

If problems do occur, you have already lost control of the situation. Don't despair though. Stay calm and look at the situation objectively, and you will see how hard the thirteen-year-old is trying to make things right.

His preferred method is to think things through in peace and quiet, which is always a good start.

A good guideline for dealing with younger teenagers is to behave every day as though you had met them for the first time.

This point of departure can help mothers, fathers (and even teachers) become aware of their own deficiencies – nagging, irritation, negative expectations, expressions of displeasure – all the things that are guaranteed to raise a thirteen-year-old's hackles.

If you meet a person for the first time, you are courteous, interested, respectful and generally positive. You show your best side in other words. You don't stomp into someone else's home (in this case the thirteen-year-old's room) and tell your host how awful the décor is. Nor do you interrogate your host aggressively and ask him what he has done that day and why, and then proceed to tell him how you could have done it better.

Meeting the thirteen-year-old, one human being to another, friend to friend, should set the tone for day-to-day life.

494

Remember that an ounce of prevention is worth a pound of cure. Try to stay a step ahead of the game, foresee and prevent.

"How could you *do* that?!" is definitely the wrong question to ask.

"It was easy," the thirteen-year-old will calmly inform you.

State where you stand and what you expect calmly and respectfully *before* the situation gets away from you.

"You can invite one friend home from school today, but only one. I'm not comfortable with a whole gang of people in the house when I am not around. Are we agreed?"

The implication being that it's one friend or none.

"If you are going out tonight, do all your chores before you leave. And I want you home by 9.00 p.m. at the latest. I'm going to start to worry if you are not home at the stroke of nine."

The implication being that if the chores aren't done and he doesn't guarantee he will be home by nine, he's not going anywhere.

By acting preemptively, you are in effect entering into an alliance with your thirteen-year-old, which makes him feel secure since he knows that you know what's going on in his life, or at least you're trying to. You are not standing on the sidelines watching and waiting, and hoping that nothing goes too seriously wrong.

You are with him, not literally perhaps, but in spirit at least.

You are not making value judgements, but you are providing a framework for his life. You are the one who puts together the routines and sets the boundaries. (For information about the thirteen-year-old's contribution to household chores and social participation, see the previous chapter.)

The thirteen-year-old knows a great deal about relationships, and so do his friends, but that doesn't mean he is always competent enough to cope with them.

In a group, peer pressure can force children in directions that they really don't want to go in.

For this reason, time spent with friends should be limited to weekends or an hour or so on weekdays until he turns sixteen.

Sleepovers should be strictly rationed, especially if the thirteen-year-old's friend is of the opposite sex. The thirteen-year-old can swear up and down that sex is something he would never get involved with. He concedes that he is far too young, and his protestations of virtue make him sound as though he would not be out of place on The Old Time Gospel Hour.

But events get away from him.

"It just happened... I never meant it to..."

The problem is not morality or even the risk of early parenthood. The thirteen-year-old simply lacks the emotional maturity to handle sex.

He seldom suffers physically from a sexual debut, but it can throw him into emotional turmoil. The aftermath can be catastrophic. The thirteen-year-old can reject a sexual relationship (established or newly begun) because he can't handle and therefore doesn't want a sex life – and this more often than not entails rejecting his sexual partner in the most heartless way imaginable.

He vilifies, betrays, torments and ridicules.

In this context, his sense of fair play is conspicuous only by its absence.

If your thirteen-year-old starts smoking, you must use all your authority to dissuade him. Don't hesitate to use any means at your disposal to make it *impossible* for him to smoke.

If you smoke yourself, you can tell him that one moron who was dumb enough to give in to peer pressure is enough for any family.

Tell him that you, as his mother or father, have a duty to stop him in time. Few thirteen-year-olds can hold out against such a frontal assault because deep down they don't *want* to smoke – just as they don't want to leap headlong into the adult world in other ways.

The thirteen-year-old is a peaceful soul, content to be who he is. He knows very well what lies ahead of him, and he often wishes he could somehow get out of becoming an adult. You can help him "get out of becoming an adult" by not fobbing him off on his contemporaries. Make sure he knows he's needed at home, talk to him, and work things through with him.

A long walk with a thirteen-year-old can be quite an experience.

He feels what amounts to a duty to pretend he's older than he actually is. Oppose it!

Be grateful for his presence and respect him as a person, but establish routines and set boundaries.

DAYS FILLED WITH LAUGHTER

Those wonderful days, those days filled with laughter, when I realize what a blessed gift to humankind a good belly laugh is – not to mention those giggles that start by causing my stomach muscles to tighten so delightfully and then rise to my lips like the bubbles in a glass of freshly poured champagne. It's the healthiest, most beneficial cure-all there is, and once I've laughed to my heart's content, my body and soul seem to vibrate with new life. Oh, if I could only experience that at least once a day every day of my life.

Keeping company with two girls in their lower teens who raise sheer silliness to the status of art can push parents to that well known limit where the furniture can start to fly unless it is nailed to the floor. But it can also cause the corners of your mouth and your stomach muscles to start twitching, sure signs that a laugh is on the way. In spite of yourself, you are suddenly doubled over, howling with laughter at sublimely idiotic jokes, double entendres and slips of the tongue, and this takes you back to a long forgotten time when you would sit around a table crimson-faced, trying to control your laughter. What you were laughing at could have been a morsel of food stuck to an adult's face, a lampshade that reminded you of an unmentionable body part, not to mention the woman who managed to drop a false eyelash into her soup. How many times did you have to go to your room, shaking with hysterical laughter! You would giggle so hard, you eventually became unmanageable, and once the worst of the giggle attack was over, you could hardly walk. Your legs were like jelly and your diaphragm ached.

Having reached that stage of life where I am mature, boring, respectable and on occasion even well behaved, I sit listening to my two eldest daughters who have been known to conduct themselves like a two-person girls' school. They tell jokes, and before they even get to the predictable punch lines, everyone is close to falling off their chairs.

"Why do Norwegian cars have windshield wipers on the inside?" The ensuing raspberry has the desired effect.

Question: "What did the Newfie woman say to her daughter when she found out the girl was pregnant?" Answer: "Are you sure it's yours?"

Both open the sluice gates, and thereafter nothing is too hopelessly stupid to laugh at.

There are some things that we shouldn't forget when we become adults and social conventions become so rigid that they threaten to stifle us. We shouldn't forget to seek out opportunities for a good laugh.

We can get therapy for virtually everything today. Why not make laugh therapy a part of our daily lives?

FOURTEEN YEARS: LONELINESS

The stable, robust, constructive thirteen-year-old has changed. Now that he is fourteen, he is, or will become, *sensitive*.

The world seems to be closing in on him, and he feels fragile and alone.

For the first time in his young life, he knows what loneliness is. From birth until death, we are all alone, no matter how many people we have around us. There's a part of the human soul that is forever condemned to the darkness, there's always a cry from the heart that goes forever unanswered.

Even in happy times we are alone, and perhaps that's when loneliness hurts the most.

Solitude was once something that the child actively sought and took comfort in because it gave him peace, but for the fourteen-year-old solitude has metastasized into loneliness – and it's inescapable.

As a twelve and thirteen-year-old, he felt relatively at ease in the adult world and took a realistic view of his surroundings, but as a fourteen-year-old he has been knocked to his knees by a feeling that he just doesn't belong.

This feeling is so intense, he genuinely fears for his future. He knows that one day he will grow up, find his niche and live his life, but he's beginning to wonder if there's any point.

A fourteen-year-old is susceptible to serious depressions.

Dejected, he will toss all his hopes and dreams on the scrap heap. If, for example, he has always been convinced that he will one day be a musician and have lots of children, he now wants to retire to a cave, live out his life as a hermit and have no children at all.

The fourteen-year-old has acquired so much knowledge and insight that, along with the great philosophers, he has come to the conclusion that everything is nothing. He has a soul mate in the preacher who thunders to his congregation, "Vanity, vanity, all is vanity!"

The fourteen-year-old ponders the meaning of life. He is open to the supernatural and wrestles with religious questions. Horoscopes fascinate him. Perhaps he hopes to somehow avoid the difficulties that lie ahead. If he can somehow "know" what is waiting around the corner, he can relax.

The fourteen-year-old will often pore enviously over old photographs of himself. He understands that not only was he little and ignorant of life's mysteries, but he was also happy because life was simple then.

It is not uncommon for a fourteen-year-old to retreat behind a wall of silence and shelve any plans he might have made for the day.

For the first time in his young life, an element of indifference that has its origins in the frightening realization that perhaps everything is pointless creeps into his consciousness.

The fourteen-year-old is often misunderstood – and he almost expects it. He talks too little and thinks too much, convinced that no one understands him. Over time, his morose contemplations accumulate and become too much for him, and cause him to explode into fits of hysterical sobbing or temper tantrums, leaving the people around him slack-jawed in astonishment.

Suicidal thoughts are common at this age. One would be hard pushed to find a fourteen-year-old that hasn't experienced them or at least toyed with the idea of ending his life.

"I wanted to kill myself, and I tried... but then I got scared," he will announce, thereby sending his parents into cardiac arrest.

Death is closer than any of us think.

The fourteen-year-old is sensitive to the reactions of his environment. He cannot cope with the thought that someone might be displeased with him. Criticism from a teacher he likes, for example, will wound him to the core. Being told he will never amount to anything can mark him for life.

On the other hand, since everything is pointless anyway, the fourteen-year-old will give a project everything he's got when the spirit moves him. If he plays sports, he can excel one day and fail abysmally the next.

In a true spirit of existential indifference, he relishes rebelling against authority. "Why should I worry about making myself impossible when everyone thinks I'm impossible anyway?"

One fourteen-year-old I know was learning German. When it was his turn to read aloud, he decided to demonstrate his dislike of both the teacher and the language by butchering every word.

To his utter astonishment, his teacher was delighted and informed the class that that was how German should be read. From then on, the fourteen-year-old embraced both the teacher and the language with great enthusiasm.

Such things happen when the fourteen-year-old sees things with new eyes, even though a fresh take on whatever it is was the furthest thing from his mind.

The reverse is also true. Admiration for someone or something can turn into scathing contempt over the course of a coffee break. Two fourteen-year-olds can go from being fast friends to sworn enemies without either of them lifting a finger to save the friendship – which a thirteen-year-old certainly would.

The psychologically fragile fourteen-year-old is physically fragile too.

A fourteen-year-old girl's budding breasts are extremely tender, and a fourteen-year-old boy lives in terror of being hit in the testicles.

Boys usually get a growth spurt at around this time, and this elicits mixed feelings. As adults we can imagine how confused we would be if we grew six inches and suddenly acquired voices that could rise or fall three octaves without warning. It's the body's relentless and tangible *presence* that makes the fourteen-year-old so fragile and self-conscious.

The fourteen-year-old finds himself in a changing phase within the framework of the exploratory period that began when he turned eleven and that will continue until the end of puberty.

The change that he is defending himself against, after his comfortable stint as a well-balanced thirteen-year-old, is comparable to the change the nine-year-old experiences; he is embarking on a transformational quest. Who am I? What does life hold in store for me?

But the fourteen-year-old philosophizes more profoundly than the nine-year-old and goes way beyond musings of a purely factual nature. He ponders the meaning of life itself.

He may stray into the danger zone. Suicidal thoughts are a distinct possibility, and, as a parent, you must factor them in, no matter how unfounded you think they might be.

If you ask a bunch of fourteen-year-olds why they might consider suicide an option, you may receive answers like the following:

"You get so tired of school or a summer job that you just don't want to show up."

"You might want to get back at someone who has been mean to you."

"You want to get noticed. You can go to the zoo and get ripped apart by a lion. There was a man who actually did that. It made the front pages of all the papers the next day."

The last fourteen-year-old in the group may chime in, "Can you think of a way to kill yourself that would cause a bigger splash? Right, you can't!"

And there you sit with your adult common sense, shaking your head in disbelief, thinking that human life has a higher purpose than exacting revenge or making the headlines.

But, as is painfully clear, fourteen-year-olds don't see it that way.

There are three remedies to counteract suicidal tendencies, depressions, melancholy and hypersensitivity:

1. Laughter, amusement, childish diversions and just plain silliness.

2. Make a fourteen-year-old feel needed. Make him feel that he is indispensable emotionally *and* practically.

3. In acute cases: a survival cure. This cure will have to be cobbled together by you and your child in the form of a period of primitive living. Go camping for a couple of weeks or take a trip on a really skimpy budget.

The goal is to re-ignite the fourteen-year-old's *joie de vivre* by tapping into his instinct to survive.

Needless to say, the fourteen-year-old doesn't have to be the rather morose figure that has been described here, and even if he does succumb to his inner demons, it is temporary. Generally speaking, however, he is vulnerable and sensitive – hypersensitive. Common sense is not his forte. What he laughed at yesterday, he regards with disdain today, and will threaten to leave home over tomorrow – only to laugh at it again the day after that.

Since his ability to clear up misunderstandings is minimal to non-existent, his interests must be guarded from time to time.

I have dragged my share of fourteen-year-olds into the presence of those who have humiliated them (the offenders of course had not so much as an inkling that they had given offence) and demanded that the guilty parties explain themselves.

"Geez," they reply, "I didn't say a word!"

"Yeah, right!" says the fourteen-year-old through clenched teeth. "You know what you did. You *looked* at me in a really insulting way."

Naturally, laughing is not an option in such situations even if you do feel the corners of your mouth start to twitch.

"So don't look at him like that!" I admonish. "If you must look at people at all, be civilized about it!"

When fourteen-year-olds are in a dark place, they need such assistance. They need a touch of loyalty. They need you to show the flag. This will enable the odd ray of light to penetrate shadows of their lonely souls. (The fact that the hapless individual who "looked" at someone the wrong way will regard both the fourteen-year-old and his parent as hopelessly insane is collateral damage that cannot always be avoided.)

The fourteen-year-old is a grateful conversation partner if subjects of a metaphysical nature come up.

His thinking is both down-to-earth and sublime. He exemplifies and seeks support from his own experience for his questions and musings, but he also digresses into the unknown, plays with theories and hypotheses, and never gives an inch.

If nothing else, he is stimulating company in that he will force you to look inwards and shake some of the dust off your own soul.

His company is a spiritual breath of fresh air. If you are willing to stick your neck out and talk to him about the meaning of life and the sweet hereafter, subjects beyond the mundane, you will delight him. The little kid who used to be so fascinated by Lego and Meccano sets will emerge. And perhaps that's fitting because life after all is a bit like a Meccano set – enigmatic at times yes, but exciting and ultimately doable.

For information about the fourteen-year-old's activities in the home, contact with peers, sexual debuts etc., see the preceding chapters on the eleven, twelve and thirteen-year-old.

THE LIGHT

There's an old proverb:"There isn't enough darkness in the whole world to extinguish the light from a single candle."

And what lights up the world more than the smiles and eyes of children?

"I love you more than you know," says the little girl who has just turned eight. And it's love that permeates everything pure, heals the sick and banishes pain.

"I like this place!" exclaims the little boy of six as he sits down at the table in the restaurant. When he can't finish his meal, he offers me his leftovers. "Do you want some bean pork?" (He had ordered Pork'n' beans.)

A little girl is about to turn seven, and we are away on a trip. Her big sister asks her if it would be alright to postpone the party until we get home. "OK," says the birthday girl cheerfully, "just don't post me!"

As we drive through the Swedish countryside one early summer morning, the mist is lying heavy on the fields. I tell them a story about the elf who got lost in the mist, and when the sun came up, she realized that the other elves had gone and she was all alone. I tell them that the lost elf still wanders the earth, crying bitterly and trying to find her way home through the mist. Three pairs of eyes, round as saucers, stare at me from the back seat and then the questions come, all lyrically sympathetic to the plight of the poor lost elf. The two older children smile condescendingly but keep silent. They remember what they believed when they were little.

The world will lose its magic soon enough. Soon enough, little children grow up. Soon enough, elves aren't real anymore, mist evaporates in the sunlight, and the wonder with which children look on the world evaporates with it. Soon enough, children grow up and are faced with questions that have no answers. There's no enlightenment – only endless darkness. That's when I would like to be there for them. That's when I would like to say, "There's not enough darkness in the whole world to extinguish the light from a single candle."

It's a shame that all those who are sick or tired, lying on a bed that gives little rest, can't feel a child's hand, light and playful, on their cheek and forehead. It's a shame that everyone can't hear a child's voice reasoning and speculating about love, life and death, about whether the moon has brothers and sisters, about what sort of music Jesus would have liked and whether He ever danced. It's a shame that everyone can't hear the whisper of little children's naked feet as they run through a meadow, kissing the grass with every step and leaving a trail of light behind them.

FIFTEEN YEARS:
AN ADULT?

The fifteen-year-old is not an adult yet, but he is well on the way.

In many ways, Swedish society regards him as an adult. He can buy himself a moped and consent to sexual activity, and he is legally responsible for his actions. In a few short years, he will take his place in society and assume all the rights and duties of a citizen.

The fifteen-year-old wrestles with almost being an adult. Since he knows he is deficient in both maturity and experience, he relies on appearances to fill the gap.

If, for example, he starts to smoke (which you *must* discourage at all costs – see the previous chapter), he will puff on his cigarette in front of a mirror to make sure it looks "natural" – i.e. worldly – and he won't budge from the mirror until he has his act down pat. When the fifteen-year-old does something, whatever that something might be, he has to look as though he has been doing it for years – or at least since he became, well, an adult. (Just lighting a cigarette with the right blend of spontaneity and sophistication requires hours of dedicated practise.)

Fifteen-year-olds in certain social circles will arrange dinner parties at which they are almost pathetic in their efforts to seem adult. They will seat their guests at elaborately set tables complete with name cards, smoke, drink wine and give after dinner speeches.

They would probably have more fun playing tag, but of course they would die rather than admit it.

504

(In my opinion, hard liquor should be off limits, and beer and wine consumption should be restricted to the very occasional sample, but only in the home and not before the age of sixteen.)

Like the fourteen-year-old, the fifteen-year-old carries within him feelings of loneliness and exclusion. On top of that, he lacks the social support that we adults can count on.

He is bitterly aware of his shortcomings in many areas. He is inexperienced, not to say naïve. He simply doesn't know enough.

And he feels so alone. There is no one on the planet that is quite like him – or so he thinks.

That is why he is so pleasantly surprised when he finds someone who *is* like him. A fellow traveller who has the same idol or interest, or has had the same experience and drawn the same conclusion is a precious commodity indeed, and the fifteen-year-old seizes eagerly on any indication that he has at last found a soulmate.

The fifteen-year-old has learned to weigh his words. He adapts his behavior so as to appear shrewder and more experienced than he actually is. There remains a great deal of input that hasn't been processed yet, but he is anxious to give the impression that he has cracked life's codes and has fully matured. His efforts to this end can be dramatic!

Neither patience nor prudence is his strong suit. Image is everything.

The fifteen-year-old is terrified of making a fool of himself. If ridiculed, he will retaliate by making everyone around him understand that he didn't make a fool of himself at all. Quite the contrary, everything he did, he did on purpose.

Just to make sure everyone has gotten the point, he will push whatever he is doing to the outer limit in a spirit of "If you thought that was bad, get a load of this!"

The fifteen-year-old stands in a netherworld somewhere between how he wants to be perceived and what he knows he really is. He believes that the more effectively he hides the truth, the more difficult it will be for the people around him to figure out who he really is.

And of course he is right, but it's a Pyrrhic victory.

The fifteen-year-old can harbor serious complexes, and the more he has to hide his insecurities, the worse they get.

In his heart of hearts, he may feel like a frightened little kid who would like nothing better than to hide behind Mommy's skirt, but if someone gets too close to what he is really feeling, no matter how empathetic and understanding this person is, the fifteen-year-old can turn on his heel and storm out of the room. Being little is no longer an option.

All of us can recall times when we have been misunderstood. It hurts. The fifteen-year-old collects and assiduously cultivates such moments – and the harvest is bitter. The happy times don't count. Any light they might have shed has long since flickered and died. All that's left are painful, bleak memories of being misread and abandoned.

The fifteen-year-old is a mental tenderfoot. His most characteristic trait is *not* distance.

Dream interpretation interests him, as does psychoanalysis.

Existentialism is not without appeal if he is exposed to it.

And if he gets hold of a Bible, he can find confirmation of his own situation in every description of suffering in the name of a noble cause.

The fifteen-year-old is exceptionally receptive to philosophy. He will read works on the art of thinking, living and loving with an interest that will not return until his mid-life crisis – if then.

His dreams are grandiose. He wants to be somebody. He wants to be great, famous, foremost in his field. His name will one day be on everyone's lips. He will succeed!

The fifteen-year-old has a strong sex drive, and it can take him places that he doesn't really want to go.

A sexual debut at this age is not unusual.

Furthermore (since fifteen is the age of consent in Sweden), he finds it more difficult to abstain from something the law permits than to indulge in something that is illegal.

Fifteen-year-olds, especially young girls, often feel an unpleasant pressure "to get it over with", and they think that everyone has – except them.

But the fifteen-year-old is seldom (if ever) mature enough to handle a sexual relationship. Anyone involved in sex education can testify to the lukewarm interest that purely physiological accounts of the sex act elicit in fifteen-year-olds. (We all remember those painful penis-is-inserted-into-vagina speeches delivered by mortally embarrassed teachers.) What they are really interested in is the emotional aspects of sex.

Coloring, streaking and blow-drying your hair so that it *looks* "natural" is relatively easy, but learning to *feel* "naturally" is of course an entirely different proposition.

Fifteen-year-old girls are attracted to boys who are somewhat older. They find boys their own age dull and childish.

Boys on the other hand have wild sexual fantasies about very much older women – their mothers, a teacher, the mother of a friend.

And advanced fantasies they are too, and fantasy can make the leap to reality more easily than one might think if the opportunity arises.

506

The fifteen-year-old is going through an exploratory developmental phase, but he also has to contend with agonising change.

What he is exploring is his own fast-approaching adulthood. He has studied the adult pattern. Now he is trying to put theory into practice. He is preparing to leave the flock he has lived in all his life and start his own.

This is why the fifteen-year-old can no longer give his parents (or parent) his seal of approval as the undisputed leader in the flock he still belongs to. He competes with them and rebels against them. Conflicts are simply unavoidable.

It's impossible for the fifteen-year-old to accept that other people have the power to decide his fate – not when he is so close to being able to decide his own.

Authoritarian demands for absolute obedience will inexorably lead to revolution. Pressure from adults, whether it takes the form of heavy-handed control or emotional blackmail, will yield the same result – dissociation, protest and, ultimately, revolt.

Indifferent silence will also sow the seeds of rebellion.

A fifteen-year-old will shy away from emotional dependence because he knows he will one day have to move on. Conflicts can be minimized and, if you're lucky, can even be kept constructive if you bear in mind that your fifteen-year-old really *does* have to move on and find his own way in life.

Emphasize your fifteen-year-old's right to shape his own life when he becomes an adult at the age of eighteen (or at which point he will be expected to move away from home. See "Marry your child or prepare the child for a life without you?" in Part three of *For the Love of Children*). Send a clear message that you not only approve of his taking charge of his life but that you are also fascinated by the prospect. Be enthusiastic about all the changes that are going to take place. Tell him how exciting you think it is that he will one day have his own place, his own career and perhaps a partner in life.

Encouraging him to prepare for his new life as an adult is diametrically opposed to the "My house, my rules" approach. The more you rely on the former, the less you will have to resort to the latter.

The fifteen-year-old is adept at wedging the entire household in between a rock and a hard place. He can make up his mind to refuse to accompany his family to the cottage, on vacation or to dinner with Aunt Elsie before he's even been asked.

Arguments to the effect that it would be in his own best interests to come along will fall on deaf ears. You're better off telling him that you really *want* him to come because his presence will make everything so much more fun for *you*. If you can also convince him that he is *needed* in a concrete and practical way, he will concede defeat.

Once you convince a fifteen-year-old that he is indispensable to the flock in which he lives, he can stand shoulder to shoulder with the flock's leader(s). He is no longer just a camp follower.

Admittedly, convincing him that he is *needed* at Aunt Elsie's dinner party is a bit of an uphill climb. The fifteen-year-old will ask, not illogically, why he can't visit her another time. His parents can plead all they want. If he doesn't want to go, he won't. The fact that he is needed emotionally rather than practically at Aunt Elsie's doesn't carry much weight with him.

Convincing him that he is indispensable at the cottage or on a trip, however, is another story. Don't be shy about being underhand.

"You have to come to the cottage. The plumbing has to be redone. You've got to help me! I can't do it alone!"

"Connecting pipes is no big deal," says the fifteen-year-old (who probably doesn't know a U-pipe from a bubble gum machine).

Proudly – and a little vainly – he will shoulder his responsibilities as a leader if you are obstinate enough to convince him that he qualifies for the role.

In my opinion, a fifteen-year-old should not be left alone for more than 24 hours if the rest of the family has to be somewhere else.

For information on social participation i.e. the essential teamwork and cooperation with you and the flock, and the youngster's household chores, see the chapters on the thirteen-year-old, the twelve-year-old and the eleven-year-old.

In Part two of *For the Love of Children*, there is an in-depth analysis of the importance of social participation.

For the fifteen-year-old, relationships with peers are essential.

He should be encouraged to treasure true friendship as opposed to love with all its dreams and disappointments.

Friendship endures and it will reassure the fifteen-year-old that he is not alone. There are others just like him. They feel like him, they think like him, and they love the same things.

He and his contemporaries find being members of a clearly marked group, such as punks, Goths or any other extreme subculture, deeply satisfying because it enables them to pretend that they share leadership in a new flock.

This new flock must of course clearly distinguish itself from the flocks of parents, teachers, the middle class generally or whatever authority figure needs to be rebelled against.

(Remember Marlon Brando's famous line in *The Wild One*. "What are you rebelling against?" he is asked. "What have you got?" he replies.)

Parents are, as a rule, less than thrilled by the offspring's new allegiance, but I believe that adults should content themselves with controlling the *form* this allegiance takes, not the *content*.

If, for example, you suspect that your fifteen-year-old might experiment with marijuana now that he wants to spend the weekend with friends that you suspect of using drugs, you should not let him go.

You thus remove the prerequisites for experimenting with drugs. You are deciding the *form*.

If, on the other hand, you give him permission to go, but you admonish him not to smoke any marijuana, you are putting all the responsibility on the fifteen-year-old. All the prerequisites for drug use will be present, but you expect him not to exploit them.

You are deciding the *content*.

The latter alternative is not really fair. An unfortunate by-product of this approach is that since the fifteen-year-old will in all likelihood succumb to temptation sooner or later, you are burdening him with guilt. He knows he wasn't supposed to, but he did anyway.

The former approach is better because it is always easier for him to say, "I can't" than it is for him to say, "I don't want to".

Just as the freedom can give rise to coercion, a prohibition can be liberating.

We adults cite circumstances beyond our control when we want to get out of a social obligation. We resort to excuses like "I have too much to do", "I have to be up early tomorrow" or "I'm a little under the weather". Very few of us have the nerve to say flat out, "I don't want to". What would our friends and relatives think of us? We would have made it abundantly clear that we really don't care about them.

A fifteen-year-old who can truthfully say, "I can't" is spared having to say, "I don't want to."

Once you grant the fifteen-year-old permission to do something, however, let him get on with it. No restrictions and no guilt. The *form* is a given, but the *content* is all his.

If, for example, you find your daughter locking lips with her boyfriend on her bed in her room, simply say, "In five minutes we are going to eat dinner, so Mark will have to go home." Then shut the door and come back in five minutes.

Don't try and decide the content by saying, "If Mark is going to be in your room, you have to leave the door open."

Supply the framework and set boundaries, but within the framework that you supply, let the child decide the content.

You are not restricting your child's freedom. Quite the contrary, freedom is made possible by setting boundaries for children who are not yet able to set boundaries for themselves.

Fifteen-year-olds have strong sex drives. Nocturnal emissions and masturbation are not only normal; they are necessary. Otherwise, the sexual tension would be unbearable.

Very often, the fifteen-year-old wishes he could sink through the floor. He gets erections at the most inopportune times, and he has no control over it.

Thoughtless allusions and jokes mortify him, as do strained efforts to affect a prejudice free attitude towards sex.

Sexuality is a sensitive subject, and the adult world would do well to acknowledge this. This does not mean that adults should be indifferent or passive when they have to contend with fifteen-year-old boys set on asserting their sexuality and identity, both of which rest on very insecure foundations.

Boys have a penchant for degrading invective, and girls who are harassed and insulted should be believed and supported.

Boys should be censured, sympathetically but firmly, for unacceptable behavior. And it will take more than one rebuke before they get the message. (See "Your adult word is law" in Part five of *For the Love of Children*.)

You should of course ensure that your fifteen-year-old son doesn't think that the mass-produced pornography he consumes, openly or in secret, provides an accurate portrayal of human sexuality (or, even worse, a normative one).

Let him ponder why pornography isn't computer generated, since it's a social construct anyway. The answer is that the only thing that's real about pornography (and which must be real for pornography to have the desired effect on its insecure public) is female degradation.

And that is hard to generate.

Scrutinize your own attitudes. If you find sex difficult to talk about, you're better off giving your young son or daughter a good book on the subject – and there are good books; ask at your local bookstore – than trying to fake a "natural" attitude towards sex.

A fifteen-year-old girl is often more concerned about her physical development and her periods than she is about a sex life that she seldom initiates anyhow.

That's not to say that she will be able to abstain once desire is awakened.

Fifteen-year-old girls can develop early or late. Female puberty can be spread over many years. Some girls start to develop breasts at eight or nine, others don't start until fifteen or sixteen.

Early budding breasts don't necessarily mean early menarche.

For a fifteen-year-old girl who feels isolated anyway, physical characteristics that set her apart from her peers make matters much worse.

You will have to try and convince your big little girl that everything will fall into place eventually. You can draw parallels with your own early or late development. Exaggerate if you have to, and read up on the subject so that she feels understood. After all, you can argue, you went through the same ordeal and you turned out all right in the end. Chances are she will too.

Humor will soothe the worst of her fears, but humor must be accompanied by a certain amount of understanding for her plight. However trivial her fears seem to you, they are deadly serious to her, so you must try to take her problems as seriously as she does – at least as long as the conversation lasts.

A young girl's periods are seldom regular for the first two years. They can be heavy one month and almost non-existent the next. She may skip a period altogether only to experience two almost back to back. She may suffer terribly from cramps and nausea, or she may feel nothing at all.

The differences are as great as they are normal. The body's machinery has not yet hit its stride.

Boys usually experience ejaculation before the age of fifteen, but it is around this age the seminal fluid begins to resemble that of a grown man in terms of sperm count and general appearance. The formerly clear liquid becomes more opaque, thicker and more abundant.

For advice on the fifteen-year-old's social life with his peers, sleepovers, and possible sexual debut, see the chapter on the thirteen-year-old. These guidelines can just as well be applied to the fifteen-year-old.

The only difference is that you should actively encourage your fifteen-year-old's friendship with one or two members of the same sex while at the same time actively limiting time spent with larger groups.

If things go askew and negatively affect the fifteen-year-old's relationship with family, friends, school and society in general, he may be engaging in activities that border on the criminal or experimenting with drugs, and this can very well have lifelong consequences. If he is drawn into criminal circles at this tender age, he will soon forge bonds that are very difficult to break.

Do whatever is necessary to get him away from these destructive influences and back on track.

As soon as you realize that something is wrong, you, mother or father, should leave your regular environment to rally around the fifteen-year-old. This sojourn may last a week or a month, but the new environment he is removed to should be one in which the two of you have to work hard to survive.

A road trip in an RV that has seen better days, a camping trip in a harsh environment, a journey to the middle of nowhere where living conditions are so primitive that cooperation is the only guarantee for survival – this is what really welds people together. A fifteen-year-old at risk will be brought back down to earth. His zest for life will reawaken. The instinct to survive will become paramount, at least for a while, and he becomes *indispensable* for himself and everyone else.

The fifteen-year-old will once again be an asset in his own eyes, an asset that is worth preserving, worth defending and worth developing. In short, an asset that's worth living for.

Sometimes, when the fifteen-year-old takes you into his confidence, you will wish he hadn't. (You remember the fourteen-year-old who was planning to kill himself but got cold feet at the last minute. He then told his parents about the suicide attempt as nonchalantly as you might talk about getting caught in the rain.)

In his efforts to be the adult that he isn't, the fifteen-year-old is less than angelic. His behavior covers the spectrum from remorseful confessions and despair to cocky insolence and warped pride over behavior he knows full well is wrong.

You must *not* use what he tells you in confidence against him. Don't brand him as untrustworthy for life (or even for the next 24 hours). Once you deal with the issue, whatever it may be, it should be tossed into the oubliette and never mentioned again.

If you have misgivings about something, which all thoughtful parents sometimes do, have a little preventive talk with him. Don't pre-suppose anything, but do calculate the odds of his getting into a difficult situation.

Then give him clear, simple, friendly instructions.

"*If* people are drinking at the party and you don't think you can say no because everyone is doing it, just leave. Say you have a headache and come home."

Don't condemn his friends, whatever you might think of them, so the fifteen-year-old doesn't feel pressured to condemn them too. Like you, he can think what he likes, and he has the right to express his opinion. Your only task is to distance yourself from certain types of *behavior* and show some leadership for his sake. Should trouble loom, you have given him an exit strategy.

For information on the fifteen-year-old's sleep needs and input in the home, please see the chapter on the twelve-year old.

IT'S OUR CHILDREN THAT MAKE US TRULY RICH

The day comes when your eldest child can look you in the eye without having to stand on anything. She's nowhere near your age of course, and (hopefully!) you still have the edge in life experience, but she's as tall as you are. You no longer look down on her when you make your wishes known; you just look straight ahead. And I can promise you that a child's height and a parent's authority vary inversely.

Clear eyes, dead level with your own, stare back at you. She has become a teenager. She has suddenly sprouted, and she is no longer a little person that you lug around or drag by the hand. She walks by herself – in more ways than one. And I feel as nostalgic as all mothers in all times and places have felt when their children outgrow them and begin their journey out into the world.

I remember her when she would sit on the kitchen counter with her feet in the sink pretending plastic mugs were boats. I remember when she would pull the cat's tail in one of her countless attempts to drown it. I remember when her father got home one night and came rushing into me and said, "My God, she's been eating cat food!" I remember when she took me by the hand and said, "Come with me." She took me out into the garden and up a little hill, which for her was like climbing Mount Everest, and led me to a little patch of ground where the pine needles pricked and the ants bit. "Sit down!" she said. And I sat.

She had long, brown tresses and eyes big enough to drown in. She would phone people day in and day out, and listen intently to all the exciting un-familiar voices. She once managed to bounce her crib across the bedroom to get close to her baby sister so that she could slather her with the contents of an economy size jar of moisturizing cream. She was so chubby that her legs almost buckled under her, and no ready-made clothes could accom-modate her tummy.

Now she is tall and willowy, she throws basketballs instead of baby bott-les, and when she moans, it's not because she has a full diaper but because her mother is playing the stereo too loudly. Adults! Can't live with them, can't shoot them!

And when tragedy struck the family, she was the one who stayed strong. It's impossible not to be proud of a child who can give love and support, who suddenly goes from making demands to carrying her share of life's burdens, and with distinction too.

I think way too little is said about the happiness children bring us. I think it should be said loud, clear and often that our children enrich our lives more than anything else. They leave the competition in the dust. And what's remarkable is that we don't really deserve it. No parent is so good that he or she is worth the love and devotion that a child bestows. Human beings, as a species, are just not made to be so loyal, so dependable, so strong and so generally wonderful that they can ever live up to the image a child has of his or her parents. No human being can claim to have an inalienable right to absolute loyalty and unconditional love. Nevertheless, that is precisely what our children give us. They place demands on us, yes, but what would a life without demands look like? What we invest in our children is a pittance compared to what we get in return.

There she stood, long ago, my little girl with eyes so wide, pulling at my skirts. "Come on," she said and I let myself be dragged off for a walk in the forest, even though it was the last thing I had time for. She gave me a memory of love and closeness that I have carried with me ever since.

Now she's tall and strong, and she says, "Everything will work out."

And it will. Wherever there is love, there is always a joyful life force that enables us to move forward.

SIXTEEN YEARS: INTEGRITY

The sixteen-year-old has high self-esteem.

If there's anything wrong (and there usually is), it's not with him. He is seldom, if ever wrong – a fact that he will draw your attention to more often than you might wish.

As someone once inscribed on a coffee mug, "We'll get along fine as soon as you realize I'm God."

The sixteen-year-old knows where the bus is going. Everyone else is just along for the ride. He will not put up with being told what to do, but he is not shy about giving orders to other people.

The sixteen-year-old sleeps the sleep of the just. After all, insomnia is for people who don't happen to be perfect.

In many ways, he is mature enough to rely on his own good sense – and this he does, most of the time successfully. His personality has fully solidified, and the traits he has now will not come out in the wash.

Life will smooth off the rough edges, but apart from that, little will change. If he is strong-willed and outgoing, he will stay that way. If he is the low-key shy type, he will stay that way too.

If he is sensitive and abhors violence in any form, these traits are fixed. Whatever his forte, be it music, literature, writing, water polo or running marathons, he will most likely pursue it all his life. If he doesn't, he will wish he had.

If the fifteen-year-old was feeling his way towards adulthood, the sixteen-year-old feels he has arrived and he is at peace with his adult self.

Actually, he is more than at peace with himself. He is rock solid sure of himself. "Compromise" is not part of his vocabulary. The sixteen-year-old will never sell out. His integrity is sacred.

He will never be truer to himself than he is now.

Such incorruptibility can pose a threat to adults, since most of us have crossed lines that deep down we know we shouldn't have crossed. Sixteen-year-olds that are subjected to physical or psychological attack rarely crack under the strain. When Nietzsche wrote, "Whatever doesn't kill me makes me stronger," perhaps he was musing about how he was at sixteen.

Disappointments can leave permanent scars, just as everything else that "takes root" does at this age.

Let me give you an example.

A sixteen-year-old boy was making himself impossible at school, where he felt misjudged and misunderstood. Eventually, he refused to go. The father, who lived in another town and who was definitely of the old school, was sent for. The assumption was that he would knock some sense into the boy.

The father's new wife witnessed the physical abuse, but what she reacted to was the fact that the sixteen-year-old didn't cry or apologize.

The boy was eventually branded a hopeless case and sent off to a psychiatrist who was well known for affixing all manner of pathological labels to people. The parents informed the psychiatrist of their fears concerning the boy's mental stability (or lack thereof), while the sixteen-year-old eavesdropped outside the door. When it was time for his consultation, he refused to so much as give his name to the psychiatrist, who was poised to start writing prescriptions for antipsychotics.

The upshot of it all was that the sixteen-year-old felt distrust and hatred towards his mother, who he felt had betrayed him, distrust and hatred towards his father, who had beaten him, distrust and hatred towards his stepmother, who had been outraged that he hadn't burst into tears of contrition for having caused trouble at school, and distrust and hatred towards the psychiatrist, who had taken the parents' side and was prepared to label him mentally ill.

It took twenty years for the hatred to mellow into indifference and into something even approaching reconciliation.

Distrust is devastating.

A sixteen-year-old is perfectly capable of living down to negative expectations out of sheer spite.

Another adolescent was attending a boarding school. She went to a school dance, laughed a lot and generally had a good time. When the dance was over, she went back to the dorm to go to bed. At this point, the principal stormed into the dormitory and demanded to know how much alcohol she had consumed. The girl protested that she had not been drinking at all. The principal insisted that people just don't laugh the way she did if they are sober.

From then on, despite the fact that this sixteen-year-old girl disliked alcohol and was perfectly capable of having fun without it, she saw to it that she was thoroughly intoxicated at every school party she went to.

The sixteen-year-old is in the final phase of the exploratory period that is puberty.

In his own eyes, he is more or less perfect, while his surroundings are pretty hopeless. His world is exciting and rich, and he gladly does what he can to enlighten the benighted heathens who stumble around in the dark by bringing them the one true faith i.e. his own insights. He is rather charming in his efforts to spread the Word by explaining technological advances and musical innovations that will ultimately be humanity's salvation.

Adults are of course expected to be duly grateful for the sixteen-year-old's condescension.

The sixteen-year-old's burning commitment to a particular cause does not mean that his opinions are immutable. He can cheerfully switch sides on a political question from Saturday to Monday, depending on whom he talks to on Sunday.

If he goes from atheist Democrat to God-fearing Republican in forty-eight hours, you will have to take it in your stride.

"You don't know what you want!" is a crude observation that will elicit nothing but consternation in a sixteen-year-old. You confirm his suspicion that adults are hopelessly stuck in their dreary little ruts.

The sixteen-year-old is embarking on the most important of all journeys: that of life experience. The experience of others holds little interest for him. He must acquire his own.

We have all heard pearls of wisdom in the form of proverbs. "It's always darkest before the dawn", "Honesty is the best policy", "He who fights and runs away will live to fight another day", "Better to light a candle, however small, than curse the darkness" and so on. We believe them, but without really reflecting over the content.

Then something happens that enables us to understand what they really mean. What was just another cliché suddenly takes on a profoundly personal dimension.

So it is with the sixteen-year-old. If he is really to understand something, he has got to experience it himself.

For this reason, he has a tendency to dismiss out of hand everything that he doesn't know much about.

You, his loving parents, may have to endure the odd interrogation. How can you live the way you do? How can you drag yourself in to your pathetic job every day? How can you associate with such hopeless people? How can you gawk at such terrible TV shows every evening? How do you stand the narrow, petty little world you live in?

I don't think you should allow him to condemn your way of life. His reaction will be utterly contemptuous if you don't stand up for yourself. You must try to be proud of your life and who you are, whatever your failings might be, without trying to shift responsibility onto someone else.

For the sixteen-year-old, life is a station where many trains are poised to depart. He wants to get on all of them.

You may feel that, as far as your life is concerned, the last train has come and gone, which makes it difficult not to be wounded when a sixteen-year-old gets the bit between his teeth. He doesn't understand that you have suffered too and that you haven't always been able to choose freely or even act in your own best interests.

It's worth being frank with him and demanding respect. It's possible (even probable) that you will get a less than sympathetic hearing, but he will at least listen, and what he hears might lay the foundation for the humility that the sixteen-year-old so sorely lacks.

One thing you can and should demand of a sixteen-year-old is a work ethic.

His personal moral code is his and his alone, and thus none of the adult world's business as long as he doesn't hurt himself or anyone else. He is, however, duty bound to discharge his obligations at home, in the work place and at school.

A recalcitrant sixteen-year-old will not respond to emotional arguments of the do-it-for-my-sake variety. Appeals to his need for integrity and autonomy, however, will hit home.

"However you decide to live, you will have to attend to your home and person, and your job. It's only when you have done what you should that you are free to be who you are."

This line of reasoning works with a sixteen-year-old precisely because he is mature enough to understand that anarchy and freedom are not the same things, that caring for the spirit is not synonymous with neglect of the body, and that a human being's worth is not necessarily reflected in the amount of power he wields.

As far as he is concerned, he is the leader now (see the preceding chapter on the fifteen-year-old who is competing for leadership within the flock), and he has nothing against taking sound advice as a leader – but he will never take advice to heart if he feels like a subordinate.

In the home, he should have set duties that have been mutually agreed upon. You have every right to expect him to deliver on his promises.

Your genuine surprise over the fact that he hasn't delivered should be expressed in the form of an interested question:

"How are you going to manage two years from now?" (or whenever he is supposed to move out).

This will provide him with food for thought.

Since the sixteen-year-old expresses himself intensely (and his intensity sometimes tips over into vitriol), he is rarely depressed, but, for better or worse, he never compromises.

Inevitably, you will have to take issue with his behavior. When you do, be as concrete as possible. Specify exactly what's unacceptable and exactly *what you expect instead*. Justify your demands as clearly, as objectively and as logically as you can without becoming emotional.

A single mother I know had difficulty letting her son go out in the evening. She was so emotionally dependent on him that she got "sick" whenever he wanted to go out.

When he got home he would find an apple on his pillow with an affectionate note from his mother telling him how much she hoped that he had had a good time.

The sixteen-year-old can't stand such contradictory messages. They may give rise to guilt that will stay with him his whole life, and I think he has every right to reject such messages.

Back to the sixteen-year-old's less attractive characteristics! They are nothing if not conspicuous.

If he is prone to sulking, he will sulk for days. If he is hot-tempered, his rages will raise the roof. If he has a flare for melodrama, he will play the role of martyr to perfection, tearfully threatening to throw himself out the window so his family can dance around his mangled corpse, which he knows full well is what everyone secretly wants to do.

Generally speaking, the sixteen-year-old can be very provocative if he feels his integrity is being compromised.

You should condemn *behavior* you find offensive without for a moment condemning the sixteen-year-old as a human being.

The sixteen-year-old is fully capable of handling his sex life and his social life, so leave him to it unless you have good reason to believe he is at risk.

He knows his own worth, and he is mentally strong. For the first time since he hit puberty, he is capable of resisting peer pressure if he feels he is being pushed into something that he is not comfortable with.

This is why the age of sixteen was such a milestone in my house. When my kids turned sixteen, we celebrated the occasion ritually, just the two of us, in a restaurant over a good meal and a glass or two of wine.

We discussed sex, love, adulthood, freedom, responsibility and morality among other things, and I solemnly made the following promise:

"From now on, you make your own decisions. For one thing, you decide when, where, and with whom you go to bed. I am your friend, not your capital M mother who tells you what to do."

I had of course alluded to this freedom, this shining city on the hill, often over the years, when I said "no" to virtually everything my kids nagged for permission to do in their early teens.

"But when you're sixteen, *then* you can do what you want," was my constant refrain.

I thus avoided endless discussions, and my children, who were counting the hours until their sixteenth birthdays, accepted my edicts with minimal grumbling.

Under normal circumstances, you can give your sixteen-year-old a great deal of autonomy.

If you have reason to believe that he is getting involved in something sinister, you may have to remove him from his normal environment for a while (see the preceding chapter on fifteen-year-olds at risk).

The sixteen-year-old wants to improve the world. If you stick by him but still give him the space he needs, he has much to contribute, and he is a fascinating, if self-appointed, little guru.

You don't need to yank him back to earth. Life – and the sixteen-year-old himself – will do that eventually.

A SONG TO A SON

Hi, little fellow, my little guy,
There's nowhere anyone like you.
Snugly wrapped in your blanket you lie,
Thinking of where you will hike to.
Look at you run,
A boy full of fun,
Across the fields you will venture,
The lush, grazing lands,
Invite you to dance
Enjoy your cradle adventure!

Look, little buddy, capture the dream!
Open your sapphire eyes!
Look how the trees, so tall by the stream
Await you where blue mountains rise.
The fleet horse he rides,
With galloping strides,
Carries him under the birches.
The evening air mild
Tells the young child
Of adventures for which he searches.

Wide is the world, the boy wants to roam,
The air weighs heavy around him.
Now fully grown, he's leaving his home,
Cutting the ties that have bound him.
Life isn't long
But his yearning is strong,
To see what lies over the ocean.
His love sheds a tear,
And begs him, "My dear,
Return to my arms and devotion!"

Come little fellow, my little guy,
The world your Daddy will show you.
Safe and secure in your blanket you lie,
Thinking of where you will go to.
Now, get some sleep,
Not too long nor too deep.
Beware of threatening danger;
Your Dad like before,
Will lead you ashore.
Come stay where you're not a stranger!

BOYS WILL BE BOYS… WON'T THEY? SOMETHING ABOUT SEX ROLES

OF BOYS AND HUMAN BEINGS

Once upon a time there was a mother who believed in sexual equality. Or, more precisely, she believed in sexual similarity. She thought that men were men and women were women solely because they possessed certain physical characteristics. "No sexism in this house!" she said. "Boys or girls, my children are going to be raised the same."

And the children came. She had daughter after daughter. But that was fine. No one ever heard her say that she longed for a boy. After all, gender didn't really exist. Only people did. The girls played with dolls, but they also played with cars. They got footballs to kick around and Meccano sets to put together. They did dishes and laundry, but they were handy with drills and screwdrivers too.

The years passed, and she gave birth to her first boy. The mother would cradle the little boy in her arms at night when the rest of the house was asleep and murmur ecstatically to herself, "A boy! Finally I have a boy!"

And life went on. The newborn got dolls and teddy bears to have with him in bed, but as soon as he was physically capable of it, he tossed them onto the floor.

"He'll grow out of it," the mother said to herself.

He began to crawl. He puffed and groaned and labored. His sisters tried to provide him with pleasant distractions but to no avail. It was crawl or die. Crawling was his career and vocation.

Until he caught sight of a toy car. It was a blue, plastic dinky toy that came

522

with a box of cereal. He literally pounced on the car and pushed it ahead of him with an energetic, unmistakeable, "Brrrrmmmm..." And this baby, who was only seven months old, had never so much as seen a car let alone ridden in one, unless you count the trip home from the hospital.

From that day on, the boy and his cars were inseparable.

In time he learned to walk. For support and encouragement, he was given a baby carriage to push, and his mother and sisters put dolls in the carriage. They were instantly tossed out. The only passengers allowed in the carriage were cars. And they were not to be tucked in! He systematically banished from his life everything that was warm and soft and cuddly.

When the boy turned two, the mother gave up. Since there was only one thing on the planet that interested him, she decided to go with the flow. She bought him twenty-five cars at ninety-nine cents apiece and gave them to him for his birthday.

Then the boy got a little brother. It was a chastened mother who introduced the two brothers to each other. She had no great expectations when she put the first doll in the new baby's crib. But, miracle of miracles, as time went by it became plain the new arrival liked dolls and *cars!*

Here the story ends. Almost. There's a moral in there somewhere, although I'm not sure how I should express it. It has to do with the people around us and their right to live they way they want to and to be who they are. The rest of us don't have to "approve" of them, and we shouldn't be forever comparing them and finding them wanting.

As far as the male/female divide goes, there are differences, both internal and external. But beyond all that, aren't we all striving to become human beings?

Nature has decreed that it is women who will carry and bear children. Women's bodies have been designed with this end in mind.

A newborn baby girl carries within her body all the physical prerequisites for eventual motherhood, and evolution has also equipped her with psychological responses that coincide with her functions as a sexual being. Little girls *are* nurturing. They like to play with dolls and take care of things. Naturally, this doesn't mean that caring and nurturing are the only things that girls are interested in or that they should be *forced* into a nurturing role. It simply means that this aptitude for nurturing is probably an expression of a woman's essential nature.

It is, after all, the woman who has ovaries. It is in her body that the eggs are produced and, when the time comes, fertilized. It is her body that protects and nourishes the fetus as it grows. And once the baby is born, it is still the woman who, as a breastfeeding mother, takes care of her infant and literally keeps it alive.

Physical nurturing is not part of the masculine function. A man's body has no space for a fetus to gestate. He has no eggs awaiting fertilization. His task is to fertilize, and he does his duty with commendable dedication. Sperm literally *gush* out of him by the millions, but whether they land on fertile soil or stony ground is of no particular interest to him. It's just not part of his universe. He plants the seed; someone else tends the garden. *Nesting* does not come naturally to a man.

It's a much attested-to fact that it is more difficult to train little boys (and big ones) to take responsibility for household chores than it is little girls. (There are of course exceptions, but we are going to permit ourselves the luxury of guilt-free generalizations!) Only a man can stand in a room that looks like a hurricane just blew through it and say, "Mess? What mess?" Only a young man can tidy the living room and leave dead flowers in the vase and an overflowing ashtray on the coffee table and say, "OK, Mom, we're ready for the guests!"

Sorry to have to say it, but guys need to be walked through everything. A curtain can hang askew for years before a young man notices, whereas a young girl will fix it instantly without even thinking.

The guys are prone to cleaning frenzies however. They suddenly get the urge to clean absolutely everything. They empty the whole house, and the rest of the family has to take refuge at a neighbor's. These cleaning frenzies have to do with all the *gushing* men do. It's creative but fleeting. It's the same story with cooking. Men will prepare elaborate feasts (provided the woman takes care of the kitchen afterwards), but they are not so keen on providing the family with sustenance on a day-to-day basis.

Men *do* something – *gush* – and then it's on to the next project. They're just not into all that regular maintenance stuff. (The big exception of course is cars, but that is a symbol of masculinity that facilitates *gushing* anyway. The car stands for freedom of movement.)

If you think I'm kidding then just test the men in your life. Do you know any man who can mop a floor and talk at the same time?

Those who have to *care* for other people have to be able to multi-task. A mother can mop a floor, plan dinner, talk to a child, scope out a neighbour

524

who looks sick, and wonder what is wrong with him – all at the same time and without even breaking into a sweat. Those who *create* have to concentrate on one thing at a time. A guy will stop mopping if you speak to him!

We all suffer because of misconceptions surrounding sex roles. Because of their nurturing side, women should be chained to hearth and home, raise the kids and deny the masculine or androgynous aspects of their body and soul. Women should not do heavy physical labor, participate in "masculine" sports, or attempt to break into creative (gushing) fields. They should keep quiet, breed and nest. Period.

And men of course are denied the right to express the feminine or androgynous aspects of their body and soul.

Now these boundaries are dissolving and few people will miss them when they are gone. It is now more or less respectable for a man to cry, show tenderness, take care of children and clean. Admittedly, the so-called "new man" is not always regarded as a potential jack-hammer in the sack, but a woman who admits she likes to have sex just because it feels good is not regarded as completely respectable either. No doubt these bones of contention will eventually be resolved.

Another unfortunate misconception is that men will somehow discover their hidden nurturing talents all by themselves. Why should they as long as they have women to take care of them and their children? Many mothers of sons sin in this regard. Logic dictates that if women want men to shoulder their share of the burden for housework and childcare, they are going to have to train their own sons to rise to the occasion. Mothers must step up to the plate. There are many male chauvinist pigs out there who have ruled the roost since they were in their terrible twos.

Many women dodge their responsibilities and fail to demand respect for themselves for so-called women's work.

Spoiled little boys who never have demands placed on them grow into spoiled big boys who are *always* placing demands on other people.

We are all androgynous. Men have feminine traits, and women have masculine traits. Nature hedges her bets.

A few thousand years ago, women stayed in the cave with the kids, and the men went out to hunt. If the man died, the woman had to fend for herself and her children. The latent hunter in her would come alive. If "he" is needed, he will emerge.

The man can also lose his woman. If she dies and leaves him alone in the cave with the kids, he must function as "mother" and his latent maternal talents will also emerge. (Men's nipples are not simply for decoration. There is at least one documented case of a breastfeeding male.)

While sexual differences bind us to certain physical functions, all of us have the ability to transcend these differences and perform the functions of the opposite sex if we really have to.

At the end of the day, human beings do what has to be done. What enables our hidden latent talents to come to the fore is not parental pressure or fashion but need.

Just as girls today have to be taught how to earn a living – they are probably not going to be able to sit around at home nesting while the man brings home food for the family – a boy has to be taught how to look after a home. He is going to have to live somewhere, and he is going to have to provide ground service for himself. He can no longer count on someone providing it for him.

Cultural patterns and living conditions are changing. Gender roles are becoming amorphous, and this is more due to necessity than enlightenment. People change because they have to not because they want to.

Perhaps the day will come when men and women have adopted each other's characteristics to the point of becoming behaviorally indistinguishable from each other. Upon meeting, two people will have to ask each other,

"Excuse me, are you a gusher or a nester?"

A LITTLE BOY LEARNS GROUND SERVICE

This is the story of a little boy who got training in ground service. Ground service means all those household chores that are as boring as they are essential.

Needless to say, these chores are performed by the woman of the house because there are certain things that men just don't see. ("Dust? What dust? Dirty dishes? I'll do them next week. Look, I vacuum the carpets once every three months whether they need it or not!")

The little boy, who had just turned five, was to be given practical exercises in the art of seeing. He was to learn to take responsibility for his share of the ground service. "You're never too young," said the mother.

The boy was put in charge of cleaning the kitchen for a week. "You take care of everything," said the mother. "You'll get help with the cooking, but you're doing everything else. I don't want to hear you complain, and I don't want to have to remind you. We'll see how you manage."

The boy, who was a) adorable and b) utterly convinced of his own superiority, was only too happy to accept the challenge if only to prove that he could do anything his older and more accomplished sisters could do and then some.

The boy also expected to be accorded divine status by his little brother, who was appointed kitchen assistant so that he could sing his older brother's praises at regular intervals.

As per the agreement, day one unfolded behind closed doors. The boy bore sole responsibility for the kitchen. By dinnertime, however, a confrontation was unavoidable. The mother somewhat apologetically opened the kitchen door only to see the boy and his little brother playing battle ships with tea saucers in the sink while the suds from the detergent threatened to engulf the whole room. They were singing in unison, "Oh the big ship sailed on the alee-alee-yo, the alee-alee-yo, the alee-alee-yo, oh the big ship sailed…"

On day two, the boy walked brusquely into the living room and announced that the kitchen was "ready". The mother found the plates from the last meal in the cupboard, unwashed and with the leftovers still stuck to them.

On day three, the boy dispensed with his little brother's services in the interests of leaner management. At around noon, he rushed out of the kitchen with the cutlery drawers, which he planned to rinse off in the bathtub. "They're so filthy!" he said. The water flowed in rivers, and might still be flowing to this day, if the mother had not scuttled this new fleet that was re-enacting the Battle of Trafalgar in the bathtub with sponges and tubes of toothpaste doubling as the French.

On day four, the boy had been in the kitchen almost continuously for half the week without so much as catching a glimpse of the sky, let alone seeing any of his friends. The mother's conscience began to bother her. Then he stepped out of his prison and said, "Now, this time the kitchen is ready!" And it was. The walls and floors sparkled. Everything was in its place and no corners had been cut. The mother was moved and impressed.

On day five, the boy said, "You mean I have to clean the kitchen again*?"*

On the sixth and last day – even God got the seventh day off – the boy worked silently in the kitchen, brow furrowed in concentration and teeth clenched. The clinking of plates and the rattle of pots and pans could be heard all over the house. Eyes on the prize, the boy cleaned the kitchen strategically, section by section. He wasn't playing. He was working with great precision and taking each task very seriously. He was shouldering his responsibility like a man, if you'll pardon the expression. He accepted the praise heaped upon him gracefully with the air of one who is happy to accept what is rightfully his.

Finally, the job was done. The boy had completed his ground service and received an honourable discharge.

One might have expected that he would banish the memories of his Babylonian captivity from his mind and savor his newfound freedom. But such was not the case. He sat down outside the kitchen with a Donald Duck comic book, balefully monitoring the movements of the other members of the household. As soon as someone entered the kitchen, he would stand in the doorway and watch them suspiciously. And then it came:

"What are you doing here? Why are you opening the cupboards? Don't touch! Put that back where you found it! Why does everyone have to mess everything up!"

Apparently, ground service wasn't the only thing he had learned...

PART
FIVE
Upbringing

HOW TO DO IT – IF YOU WANT TO

Raising children is a job. As with any job, there is a good way and a bad way.

You can make things easy for yourself today and difficult for yourself tomorrow, just as someone who works in an office can clear his/her desk by tossing everything from the in-tray into the wastepaper basket. To all intents and purposes, the in-tray is empty, but come tomorrow, the work is still there and more work has piled up. So, our office worker has to root around in the wastepaper basket, physical or virtual, and if it's already been emptied, the proverbial chickens come home to roost. Of course with e-mails from irate customers, angry queries from co-workers, warnings from the supervisor, and perhaps the impending bankruptcy of the company, our office worker may possibly resolve the problems, but trying to repair the dam after it has burst is hardly the best of strategies.

The same logic can be applied to raising children. There are two alternatives. You can goof off today, patch and fill tomorrow, and maybe find yourself drowning the day after that. Or you can accept that every day is going to be a little on the trying side, but as long as you keep your bases covered and you have a long-term plan, the job will get well done.

Many years ago, poor Prince Henry of Denmark found himself in very hot water indeed when he publicly stated that raising a child was like training a dog.

Nonetheless, there are many parents who agree with him. Children – like dogs – have to be house broken. They should know how to behave. There are kids who take hammers to pianos, cut up seats on buses and subway cars, vandalize schools, blanket public places with graffiti, threaten people with knives and tell adults to fuck off. Very few people would interpret such behavior as a hallmark of freedom, security and independence.

A young child's "I don't want to!" doesn't have to be the harbinger of an older child's "Screw you!".

Let's take a closer look at Prince Henry's analogy. How should a dog be trained? With a whip? What kind of a dog will he become? An obedient dog to be sure – but also one full of dread, anxiety and fear.

What if the dog is not trained at all? What kind of a dog will he become? At best, an uninhibited dog, but also an unreliable, insecure dog. And an unreliable dog poses a threat to others, if not to himself.

Less than 125 years ago, Swedish parents were required by law to punish their children physically. Today corporal punishment is illegal and has been for some time. Authoritarian child-rearing methods inevitably involve corporal punishment and are therefore out of the question. They are criminal, pure and simple.

And rejecting authoritarian methods isn't hard, since very few of us, if we are honest with ourselves, really want a child to obey us out of fear. However, rejecting laissez-faire, non-existing child-rearing methods is not difficult either, since such an indifferent approach encourages children to grow up to be tyrants, "free" to injure others (and themselves).

There is a happy medium, and I like to think that most parents today are searching for it. I eventually managed to find it by making a distinction between *loving* my children – comforting them, hugging them, understanding them, protecting them, offering them a sympathetic ear and a shoulder to cry on – and *teaching them social norms* – showing them, guiding them, sometimes forbidding them, and generally providing leadership.

A parent's task is to love *and* to lead. It's a package deal.

You can own a dog, but you can't own a child. You raise your children to enable them to lead a life *without you*. You raise a dog to stay with you forever. There's a big difference.

That said, most dog owners and most parents do have something fundamental in common: They want their dogs and their children to obey them out of trust, not out of fear.

Do you have to put your foot down and forbid? Yes.

Every society has its norms. People cannot just help themselves to whatever they want in stores, shoot each other at bus stops or toss tiresome relatives off cliffs. Social norms are a fact of life, and everyone has to follow them.

What is to be gained by following them? Membership in society. What happens to people who refuse to follow them? Exclusion from society.

Every individual who aspires to membership in society is required to internalize the norms deemed valid by that society.

In addition to societal norms, most people have a parallel set of personal norms. A mother might blanche at the thought of her child playing with its food. A father's blood pressure might skyrocket at the thought of a kid sitting itself behind the wheel of his new car and playing with all the high-tech gadgetry.

As a parent, you must try to be true to yourself and abide by your own personal code. If you don't, you may find yourself punishing your child for your own transgressions.

A child is not damaged by not being allowed to treat food like a toy. After all, there are other things to play with. A child who isn't allowed to play with the controls of an automobile isn't damaged either. Dad can doubtless find an adequate substitute with all the requisite bells and whistles.

The outside world may object to your personal norms, which you demand that your children follow, but the children will accept anything you deem necessary, precisely because the children are hungry for knowledge about the norms of the society (or rather those of the family within a larger society, the flock) into which they have been born.

The children seek knowledge about the society in which they live – be it an Inuit community in the Yukon or a Bedouin tribe in the Sahara – because that's where they have to survive.

Children are constantly asking for information, and they usually ask through their actions.

Children are by no means unique. If you or I wanted to learn how to drive, we would have to ask the instructor as well as the car.

When it comes time to take the car into traffic, the questions would come in a never-ending stream: "Can I drive against a red light? Can I drive before he does? Do I let him in first? Can I park in the middle of the street? Who has the right of way at an intersection? What does that sign mean?"

If the instructor blithely told us, "It's a free-for-all. Do whatever you like," there would definitely be a few fender-benders and possibly a serious accident. We might survive, but it would be touch and go.

Many children are brought up with just that message: "It's a free-for-all. Do whatever you like." Most of them probably survive without hurting themselves or anyone else too seriously, but growing up takes them a long time and such laissez-faire attitudes make it unnecessarily difficult for them to absorb and internalize social norms.

How would you like learning the rules of the road by trial and error?

The happy medium might be described as *mutual trust child rearing*.

Every child is born with built-in trust. This trust does not have to be won; it just has to be confirmed. It can, however, be forfeited.

One could draw a parallel between the trust that you or I would feel for a driving instructor at our first driving lesson. He would be a stranger to us, but we would automatically assume that he would teach us to drive. That's his job after all. We would be very surprised if he taught us to drive dangerously or if he suggested that we just sit around and drink coffee, and not bother with the lesson at all.

For his part, the driving instructor must have unwavering faith in us. He must believe that we have it in us to learn to drive one day. If he doesn't, why accept us as students in the first place, however much we pay him for his trouble?

The goal of both instructor and student is that you and I will one day be able to operate a motor vehicle *without* the instructor. No one has any illusions about the instructor being a permanent fixture.

The laissez-faire driving instructor – if you can imagine such an animal – says, "It's a free-for-all. Do whatever you like." Then he gets out of the car, repairs to the nearest café and reads his newspaper.

The authoritarian instructor, on the other hand, would probably refuse to let us drive at all. He drives or no one does.

Since we have to learn to drive sooner or later, we would probably "borrow" the car when he wasn't looking and try to teach ourselves – or we would have to confront the authoritarian instructor and try to force him to teach us to drive. In both cases, the punishment would be harsh. Authoritarian people don't like having their authority questioned. Our instructor might even go so far as to arrange a little accident to convince us once and for all that there was no future in trying to secure ourselves a place behind the wheel and that we would never be able to drive a car without him.

- *Authoritarian* child rearing is based exclusively on – and exploits – the child's trust in the adult.
- *Laissez-faire* child rearing (the much misunderstood "free" child rearing) is based exclusively on the adult's trust in the child.
- *Mutual trust* child rearing is based on the mutual trust between an adult and a child.

Free child rearing was a reaction against the authoritarian variety. The goals were freedom, respect and trust. The parents would regard a child as a person, not a piece of property. They would listen without condemning. They would be always understanding.

The method was misunderstood because parents somehow got the idea that free child rearing involved an abdication of their responsibility to provide the leadership that the teaching of social norms requires.

Not only did they not have the *duty* to provide leadership, they didn't have the *knowledge* either. To go back to our analogy with the driving instructor, he not only says, "It's a free-for-all. Do what you like", he also tells us, "I don't know how to drive any better than you do."

We probably wouldn't believe the last assertion.

If he continued to insist that he didn't know how to drive, we would most likely call his bluff and floor the accelerator as we approached a pedestrian crosswalk where a little old lady was laboriously making her way across the street. Inevitably, our instructor would crack, take the wheel and slam on the brakes.

"You can't run over little old ladies!" he would admonish us.

That's more or less how children behave when their parents refuse to lead.

Whether you like it or not, you, as a mother or father, are an *authority figure* for your child – which is very different from being *authoritarian*.

It is plain for the child to see that you can cope with life out there in the world and that you know and obey all the rules and regulations that make coping with life out there in the world possible. You *know* things. You can *do* things – just as the driving instructor can handle himself in traffic. At the end of the day, it's about the art of survival.

When a child is born, it is incapable of surviving all by itself. A child expects leadership from its parents, just as you and I expect leadership from our driving instructor.

We all know that children cannot always take responsibility for their own actions. We all have a responsibility to protect children, but also to lead them, show them and teach them – just as the driving instructor has a responsibility to keep his pupils out of harm's way while at the same time teaching them how to survive in rush hour traffic.

So, if the son – let's call him Matthew – is doing one thing, and his dad – who we shall call Frank – thinks he ought to be doing something completely different, then Frank has to take responsibility for that.

"I don't want to," says Matthew.

"Well, you have to," says his father.

Frank may sound authoritarian both to his son and to himself. Hopefully, he knows what he is doing and has made the right call, and can therefore stand by his decision. If this is the case, the price of appearing authoritarian and unpleasant has been worth paying.

If however Frank does *not* want to take responsibility, if he is *not* prepared to stick to his guns and ensure through his actions that what he says goes, then he should keep his opinions to himself. He should refrain from interfering, which in effect means that he wholeheartedly endorses his son's right to decide. Matthew can do as he sees fit with his father's blessing.

If Frank opts not to shoulder his parental responsibility, but thinks his son should respect his wishes anyway, he will choose a third strategy, a strategy that is neither authoritarian nor laissez-faire, but is based on negotiation. Frank will appeal to his son's common sense and instinct of self-preservation.

"Think about your own best interests," says Frank.

Negotiated child rearing has its rewards, which is why so many parents choose it. If Frank can convince Matthew by logical argument to obey him, he can avoid being authoritarian (and perhaps unpleasant). If a father can actually persuade his son to *want* to do what he is told, no one can say that the father has forced him. The child takes the responsibility and the parent is off the hook.

This is not really negotiation, however; it's *manipulation*. (Compare this situation with little desperate Brian and his negotiating mother in the chapter "The terrible twos: I want to, I don't want to!" in Part four of *For the Love of Children*.)

The son has been shamelessly manipulated. His father, because he is afraid to take charge, has laid all the responsibility on his offspring's fragile shoulders.

As a result, Matthew may very well put his father in a situation where he has no choice but to protest. "Stop! You can't run down little old ladies on pedestrian crossings!"

What are the chances of things coming to such a pass?

It's hard to say. Authoritarian upbringing breaks some children for life. Others recover. They bend with the wind when they have to, but they snap back without breaking.

By the same token, a good many children who are left to themselves and reach adulthood without ever having heard the word *no* don't grow up to be tyrants or terrorists. They hurt neither themselves nor others.

At the other extreme, the laissez-faire approach can produce kids who will pillage as they please until the driving instructor/parents/society draw a line in the sand and say, "Stop! This far and no further!"

With all the means at their disposal – including hurting others as well as themselves – these children require leadership in the form of resistance.

Often enough, leadership means taking personal responsibility.

Often enough, abdicating the responsibilities that leadership entails constitutes a refusal to accept any personal responsibility.

Some children can bear and handle deputy responsibility. Others can't – or won't.

Some children can learn to drive by themselves. Others can't – or won't.

Parents are legally responsible for their children's actions until these children reach the age when they can be charged with a criminal offence. Do parents have a moral responsibility as well?

Do they have a responsibility to lead, a responsibility to say, "This is right and this is wrong"?

Does the driving instructor have a moral responsibility to provide leadership by telling his pupils, "There is a right way and a wrong way to drive a car"?

Or is his responsibility limited to a purely legal sphere in which all he has to do is pay the fines if one of his students hits the old lady on the crosswalk?

Let's take a look at a common – and inevitable – situation.

Matthew – our case in point of manipulation – has grown up and is going to move out of the parental abode. His father has always known that this day was coming. He never thought that his son would live with him forever. Kids eventually make their way out into the big wide world. It's part of Nature's plan, and no one questions it, least of all this particular father.

So what does Frank do? In his heart of hearts, he is less than enthusiastic about Matthew moving out. He wants him to stay, but he can't come right out and say it. If he did, it would take the form of an authoritarian prohibition:

"You're staying here! You're not moving anywhere!"

Or, it would take the form of a plea:

"I want you to stay here with me!"

"So I'm never supposed to move out?" Matthew would burst out.

"No," his father would say. "I don't want you to."

Both Frank and Matthew know that Matthew's *invocation* is to be his own man, independent of his father's protection and leadership. His goal is to be the captain of his own soul and his own protector.

(Both driving instructor and student prepare for the day when the student will be able to drive without the instructor.)

Now, Matthew does not just walk out the door without further ado. The world is a confusing place, and he is not sure he will make it out there.

(Just as our driving student would be apprehensive about the road test.)

Frank decides not to help his son move. He is not about to take responsibility for that. Why would he help his son walk out the door? He wants to keep him at home for as long as he can.

(The driving instructor refuses to take responsibility for booking the road test. On the contrary, he wants to delay it as long as possible.)

Since Matthew is naturally a little insecure, his father milks this insecurity for all its worth.

"You have nowhere to live," says Frank. "You'll be homeless. It's best to wait."

("Look how nervous you are," says the driving instructor. "There's no way you're ready for a road test.")

Frank lays the blame for the move that never was at his son's door. Matthew continues to live at home, but whose will is he conforming to, his own or Father's?

It's probably a little bit of both. On the surface at least, it looks as though Matthew has a sweet deal. He doesn't have to find himself an apartment, he gets his meals cooked and his clothes washed, and he only pays a symbolic rent.

The years go by. Frank is happy and Matthew is grateful, but both are in denial about what Matthew, in his heart of hearts, really wants. Sooner or later, something snaps.

("I'm taking my road test whether you like it or not!" the pupil tells his driving instructor, who has managed to delay things for a whole year.)

Matthew tells his father that, for one reason or another, he has to move. He has found a place to live, he is planning to move in with his girlfriend, or he has found work in another town.

("I've taken forty lessons. It's time. I've booked the road test myself.")

Matthew organizes the move himself. Frank realizes that he has to bow to the inevitable and wishes Matthew luck, but he has done nothing to help his son come to decision.

What if Matthew hadn't had a place to live, a girlfriend or a job in another town? What if he decided to move out just because he wanted to move out and simply presented his dad with a *fait accompli*? Frank would probably be less than pleased.

"Is living here that bad? You have things pretty good at home."

"I know," counters Matthew. "It's not that…"

"Oh, so I'm the problem?" says Frank. "You just can't stand living with me."

Matthew still has to take responsibility for his move, but now the only way he can do it is by rejecting his home and his father. He can't count on his father for support. On the contrary, the move is interpreted as a betrayal. He is "leaving" his poor father and "abandoning" his home.

Father and son are now at odds, and Matthew is made to feel that he is the villain in the piece.

(After a successful road test, our student might feel that he had "betrayed" the instructor.)

Some species of birds will push their chicks out of the nest if they refuse to fly. Faced with the choice of flapping their wings or crashing to earth, the chicks pick the former. They have to fly, and so they can do it. (See "Marry your child or prepare the child for a life without you?" in Part three of *For the Love of Children*.)

Frank should have acted in accordance with his son's invocation, which he never directly questioned anyway. He should have said, "At such and such a time, you are going to move out." In so doing, he would have expressed confidence in his offspring's ability to manage on his own (fly).

If Matthew, because of his understandable insecurity, had doubted his own ability – "But where will I live and what will I live on?" – Frank would have stepped into the breach by showing faith in his son. "You'll be fine. You don't think so, but you will. I know you can do this." (You will be able to fly when you have to.)

Thus Frank would have been a great help to his son. He would have shared or even taken over responsibility for his son's move, and Matthew would not have had to question the life he was leaving. He would have been able to move away from home as though it were perfectly natural because it was simply time to move on. There would have been no recriminations or guilt.

And he would have had to rely on his own resources. He would have survived because it was necessary.

Dad would have been an enabler rather than a hindrance if he had shown faith instead of distrust, and he would have spared his son all that guilt.

The so-called free upbringing was supposed to give the children freedom, respect and confidence. It was supposed to equip a child with all that was necessary to live an independent life – a life solidly founded on self-reliance and unconstrained ability. It was supposed to free a child from guilt and fear. Its goal was freedom not ownership. Central to a free upbringing was the parental responsibility to help and guide in the interests of the *child*.

It was gravely misunderstood.

NORMS, MODELS AND CONSEQUENCES

Instilling norms requires leadership. "Drive this way" instead of "Drive however you like".

Certain norms are universally valid. Those who conform to them are inducted into society. Those who don't are excluded.

The first community to which your child belongs is the family – you and the flock in other words. This first community stands in for the larger society. It is a *preparatory* community. Norms teach your child how to live in the community into which he/she has been born.

And *the world has to be small before it gets big*.

It is in this first community, which comprises you and the flock, that the norms that you personally embrace, as well as those that are valid for the larger society, are instilled. So when you permit something that is permitted in a larger context, you are instilling a norm. When you forbid something that is forbidden in a larger context, you are also instilling a norm.

However, if you permit something that is forbidden in a larger context, you are making it that much more difficult for your child to acquire a norm that the larger society deems valid (whatever that norm might be).

If, for example, you espouse a norm that says *it is wrong to fight*, then you must not let your child hit you.

If you espouse a norm that says *you don't take all the cookies on the plate* (we won't flinch in the face of moral dilemmas of less than earth-shattering proportions!), then you must not allow your child to take all the cookies on the plate while you go without.

Our feelings betray us however, steeped as they are in the guilt that seems to be such an integral part of parenting today. Does it really matter if little Justin hits you? He's so tiny after all. You can grin and bear it.

He just wants to make sure you love him. And if little Jenny eats all the cookies, is it really that big a deal? She likes cookies so much, and you can always buy some more.

Yes, our feelings betray us. But feelings have nothing to do with norms, just as routines have nothing to do with love. (See "ABC's for little people" in Part three of *For the Love of Children*.)

Allowing your kids to hit you or eat all the cookies on the plate, contrary to the norms you claim to embrace, is rather like our driving instructor saying to his pupil, "Sure, drive against a red light. There's no one else on the road anyway".

Instilling norms requires *leadership*. Violation of these norms necessitates *consequences*.

In this first society, this preparatory society, consequences don't have to be particularly unpleasant. You simply put a stop to unacceptable behavior and show the child the right way to do whatever it is. You take the little hands that are hitting you and show the child how to pat gently. You take the last cookie away from the child, put it back on the plate, tell him (let's say) that you want a cookie too, and then you eat it.

If you *don't* stop your child from violating the norms you live by and the norms endorsed by the larger society, he will eventually be punished in a wider context.

If, through your actions, you don't tell your child "no" when he fights in the sandbox, other children will say "no" to him by ostracizing him. They will refuse to play with him. If, through your actions, you don't say "no" when your child takes all the cookies on the plate when you are at a friend's or relative's house for coffee, the friend or relative will say "no" by labelling the child spoiled and badly brought up, and disliking him.

As a mother or father, you have to be on the lookout for "norm forming" situations. They are everywhere!

All societies have norms because without them, societies could not function, and those who violate society's norms have their membership in society revoked.

A variation of this system operates in virtually all walks of life. A driver who does not obey the rules of the road loses his license. He is no longer a member of the car-driving community. He is ostracized.

Violent people are put in prison. They are not allowed to mingle with other members of society. They are ostracized.

An employee who steals company property is fired and is unlikely to find other employment. He is ostracized.

A child who violates the norms of the playground will sooner or later find himself with no playmates. He is ostracized.

It's said that children are cruel. So are adults, although we're more sophisticated about it. The net result is the same however: ostracism.

Children are born to survive and to learn how to live in their societies. Survival depends on community, membership in a flock. A human child that is abandoned or ostracized by the flock doesn't live for long.

Children allow themselves to be reared in order to avoid ostracism.

Children make compromises and concessions. They accept constraints. They may *want* to fight, but they refrain from doing so. They may *want* all the sweets in the store or all the cookies on the plate, but they choose not to take them. They may *want* to scream "no", but they opt to say "yes". They are willing to pay the price that inclusion carries. If they don't, they risk ostracism from the family, the workplace, the roads, and ultimately society itself.

We adults are forever making concessions too. We refrain from yielding to our impulses a hundred times a day. We don't tell the boss to drop dead. We don't punch rude bus drivers. We don't stab our spouses. We don't throw our kids out the window. We don't send letter bombs to the IRS. In short, we behave in a way that is acceptable to the society in which we live. The penalty for not doing so is swift, certain and harsh: ostracism.

The family, the flock is society writ small. Even if it only consists of one adult and one child, it is society in miniature, a preparatory community.

As a parent, you cannot give your seal of approval to behavior that is unacceptable to society. If little Lisa bites her father, Dad must show his disapproval in word and deed so that Lisa understands that biting will not be tolerated. He will make it more difficult for his daughter to internalize social norms if he says, "Well, it doesn't matter if you bite *me*. I know you love me anyway." Who Lisa loves is irrelevant. It's what she does that counts. If biting is not accepted by society, then Lisa must not be allowed to do it. As the representative of the flock/society and the instiller of society's norms, Lisa's father is responsible for teaching her those norms.

We have seen that society punishes those who fail to abide by the prevailing norms by ostracizing them. Therefore, you, as society's representative, must do likewise. If your child fails to abide by the norms of the flock, he/she must be ostracized.

Before laissez-faire childrearing took hold, this was the justification behind the classic parental admonition, "Go to your room and don't come out until you are ready to behave!"

An interesting development occurred during the latter part of the last century. A socio-political spanner was tossed into the works. It was decided that the rules that governed the relationship between parents and children should be completely different from the rules that governed society at large.

Let me give you an example. In a well-known book about children, which has been in circulation for about three decades, the writer gives parents advice on how a child's room should be set up. The author refers to the child's room as a *mini-home*.

"The point of all this effort," the child-rearing expert explains, "is to create an environment in which the child will enjoy resting, playing or sleeping. But if you send a child to bed or to his or her room as a punishment, you will ruin everything. Children should never be sent to their rooms or to bed just because they have been naughty."

So there stands Lisa's father with the book in one hand and Lisa in the other. And Lisa just keeps on biting. The child is behaving in an unacceptable way, and Dad, as parent and a representative of society, has an obligation to indicate disapproval and to correct unacceptable behavior. But the book has told him that he cannot do as society would when confronted with unacceptable behavior. Ostracism is not an option. ("Children should never be sent to their rooms or to bed just because they have been naughty.")

Lisa bites and Dad is doing a slow burn, but he cannot spank his daughter either. If he did, he would be committing a criminal offence. He has to get Lisa to stop biting but *how*?

Lisa's father, parent, society's representative and instiller of social norms though he is, cannot say through his actions, "If you behave in a way that is unacceptable to society, you will be ostracized." According to the latest trend in child psychology, he has to say, "If you behave in a way that is unacceptable to society, society will tolerate it."

Which is a flat out lie. Unacceptable behavior may be tolerated in the home, but in a wider social context it most definitely will not.

Lisa is being lulled into the comfortable but utterly erroneous belief that unacceptable behavior has no price tag. She is being placed on a collision course with society and with reality, and her inevitable awakening will be a rude one indeed.

Let's take a closer look at this socio-political spanner. Why is it so im-

544

portant that you, a mother or a father, must never, under any circumstances, send your child to bed or to his or her room? "... if you send a child to bed or to his or her room as a punishment, you will ruin everything."

What exactly is meant by "everything"? What is going to be ruined?

Why do people advocate one set of rules for instilling norms out in society and a completely different set for instilling norms within the family?

Because children must be manipulated as early as possible into stifling their need for social participation, which in practice means renouncing their place in the community.

An industrial society like ours ostracizes its non-productive members. They are on the outside looking in. They are not allowed to participate in the struggle for survival. Children, like the elderly, the sick and the disabled, are banished to the margins. They are unproductive, a drag on growth. With much altruistic fanfare, children are expelled from the flock and the community. Their instinct to participate socially is denied, not with regret as one might reasonably expect, but with acclamation, the sole purpose of which is to cloak crass economic considerations in the garb of virtue.

Children must be made so comfortable in their little children's world that their demands for social participation are killed with kindness. They must be manipulated into voluntarily suppressing one of the attributes that makes us human – our need to participate in the flock's struggle for survival, our need to be put to work for the common good, *our need to be needed.*

Children allow themselves to be reared to avoid ostracism, just as we adults make concessions to remain part of our communities. However, in contemporary society, which makes a virtue of sidelining the non-productive, ostracism must not be regarded as affecting children negatively for ideological reasons. Indeed, children must endorse their own ostracism. They must agitate for it themselves.

Thus, children are to be raised (or rather manipulated) to embrace ostracism rather than to avoid it.

Little people (and not so little people) are to be so cosseted in their own rooms – their little *mini-homes* – that the outside world will pale by comparison. They are to be brainwashed into loving their gilded cages already within the walls of their own homes. They are to be so deluged with toys that they prefer the splendid isolation of their mini-homes to attempting to break into the adult world, where they could have meaningful lives, social participation and a purpose to fulfil in the common struggle for survival. They are to have so much fun in their therapeutically constructed child worlds that they will deny a fundamental human trait: the desire to explore, master and eventually change their world.

545

- Ostracism as a consequence presupposes children's social participation.
- Ostracism as manipulation presupposes the opposite: children's exclusion from social participation.

Let's make a traffic analogy:

Mr. Anderson is a seasoned driver, a fully-fledged member of the driving community, and he is out fighting the traffic with everyone else. If he commits a serious breach of the rules of the road, ostracism will be the result. His driver's licence will be revoked.

This is *ostracism as a consequence*.

If Mr. Anderson wants to be a part of his community again, he will have to sharpen up and obey the rules like everyone else. When he has done his time on public transit, his driver's licence is reinstated, his ostracism is rescinded and he can drive again.

Mr. Lundstrom is also a driver, but he is not allowed to drive in traffic with the rest of the driving community. He never has been. He gets a parallel road system all to himself. There are others who use this parallel road system, but, like Lundstrom, they are not allowed to stray outside it.

Lundstrom's driving doesn't really have a point because he's not actually going anywhere. He just drives around aimlessly because he thinks it's amusing. He can't use his car as a means to get from A to B because the only road he is permitted to drive on is cut off from everything. But he has fun anyway. The road is well maintained, and if he endangers himself or other drivers (which happens on occasion), no one is going to blame him.

The only drawback is that he never actually gets anywhere.

Lundstrom lives in a democratic country, so there's no barbed wire lining the side of the road. Instead, Lundstrom is seduced by various means into preferring a purely recreational highway system devoid of destinations over the real-world highway system that will actually take him somewhere – a highway system with a purpose in other words.

This is *ostracism as manipulation*.

Lundstrom doesn't need a license, and even if he did, it would never occur to anyone to take it away from him, no matter what he did. He can drive however he likes, but he is not allowed out into the regular traffic.

- Ostracism as consequence says that if you don't behave in a socially acceptable way, you will be ostracized from your community. If you do, you won't.
- Ostracism as manipulation convinces you that you actually *want* to remove yourself from your community. Ostracism as consequence doesn't apply in your case, *since you have been ostracized already.*

Just as today's modern parents have been taught that ostracism as consequence is strictly forbidden, they have also been told in no uncertain terms that letting a child help out around the house is highly inappropriate. Kids should not be put to work. If they make themselves useful, they should be paid.

To this day, I have never met a parent who has not at some time or other resorted to ostracism. Their child's behavior was so unacceptable there was just no alternative. (Lisa's dad finally lost patience with his little girl's biting rampage, put her in her bed, banged the door after him, all the while trying to retain at least a shred of his sanity.)

Nor have I met a parent who has not at some time "forced" his/her child to help out around the house. Sins must be atoned for and guilt alleviated – with money, for children shouldn't have to work.

But children should at least clean their rooms and make their beds, shouldn't they? Of course they should. That is not work however. That is merely personal ground service. That is not something that parents have to feel guilty over "forcing" their children to do, according to the Friend of Order. *What is forbidden is social participation*, which, practically speaking, means that children should never have to do anything that benefits the other members of the flock in the common struggle for survival.

Children must not be *needed*. If they are, the parents must pay for the service and feel guilty about it afterwards...

The lunatics have taken over the asylum.

So send Mr. Lundstrom out into the rush hour traffic with everyone else, even if it's only for an hour a day, and let him actually get somewhere! Close the therapeutic highway system where driving is amusing but utterly pointless!

And if he doesn't obey the rules of the road, ostracize him from the driving community until he learns his highway code!

The home is still a work place – one of the very few that children are allowed to enter. The home is a place where people drive because they want to arrive at a particular destination.

That is where Mr. Lundstrom belongs. The work carried out has a purpose: survival. Food has to be cooked, clothes have to be washed, floors have to be mopped, and repairs have to be made. These things are *necessary*. This is life, not therapy. The members of the community are struggling to survive, even if the struggle for survival is more hi-tech than it used to be.

When Mr. Lundstrom is just three weeks old, he gropes for the "wheel" for the first time. In connection with the true birth, after the trauma of the physical birth has subsided, the child's instinct to participate socially manifests itself. At only three weeks of age!

We put Mr. Lundstrom on his blanket, and he is a part of the community. This is *passive* social participation.

At four months, Mr. Lundstrom is reaching for something. It's the "wheel" he wants to grab hold of naturally. Of course, he is allowed to hold it.

But how does the driving go? Just fine. We discreetly hold the wheel too so that he doesn't end up in the ditch.

At eight months, Mr. Lundstrom can sit on the kitchen counter and put sausages in a pan. That is *active* social participation.

At a year, Mr Lundstrom can vacuum. He is making his contribution, and for this we thank him.

How long does he vacuum? About five minutes. Was there a point to it? Clearly he thinks so because now he plays contentedly by himself for fifteen minutes. Mr. Lundstrom is taking a break after a job well done.

At two, Mr. Lundstrom helps his dad shave. But Dad makes sure his son doesn't end up in the ditch. Dad holds the "wheel", his hand over his helper's. Dad has his hand on his son's, his son has his hand on the razor, and the razor is on Dad's face. That's teamwork indeed.

Dad thanks Mr. Lundstrom for his help.

As usual, Mr. Lundstrom takes a break. The cycle of work and rest comes naturally to human beings, even very small ones.

At three, Mr. Lundstrom is ready to come along on shopping expeditions. He lugs a bag of flour all the way down the aisle. He is thanked profusely for his trouble. Shopping is so much easier with him along. Mr. Lundstrom is an essential part of the operation.

At four, Mr. Lundstrom is ready to go solo. He walks all the way down to the corner store, fifty yards from his house, and buys an evening paper for the family. The clerk kindly holds the door open for him. After all, Mr. Lundstrom has his hands full! His family is happy. Thanks to him, they have a newspaper.

At five, Mr. Lundstrom sets the table for breakfast and gently wakes the rest of the family. Someone has to make sure they all get up on time.

At six, Mr. Lundstrom can handle spring cleaning. Oh, there's so much to do. Mr Lundstrom tackles the hall and the bathroom, while the other members of the family tend to the rest of the house. Co-operation is the word!

At seven, Mr. Lundstrom makes dinner. Spaghetti is on the menu – with ketchup on the side. À table! Grub's up!

At eight, Mr. Lundstrom is his own interior designer. His room is definitely in need of a coat of paint. He sets about the task and the rest of the family is only too happy to help him. They do a good job, and Mr. Lundstrom is more than pleased with the result. He lavishes praise on his deserving assistants.

At nine, Mr. Lundstrom is in charge of packing for the family vacation, a job that he takes very seriously indeed. What will everyone need?

At ten, he can take care of his sick grandma. He spends the whole weekend cleaning her house and doing her dishes. Poor grandma can't get around too well. Lucky Mr. Lundstrom is around to step into the breach.

At eleven and up, Mr. Lundstrom is a big boy. How does he spend his days? His agenda is full. He has three permanent jobs that he, and he alone, is responsible for. On one day he cleans up the kitchen after dinner, the next day he's responsible for keeping the living room tidy and on the third day he does the vacuuming. His routine runs like clockwork, which is not surprising since he was involved in setting it up.

In addition, Mr. Lundstrom co-works with the other members of his family. He likes being involved in food preparation. Mashing potatoes and airing worries. Forming meatballs and telling jokes. Rinsing salad greens and discussing the events of the day. Baking breakfast rolls and asking questions. Cleaning pans and telling secrets.

And what else? Whatever is necessary. The others wouldn't manage nearly as well if Mr. Lundstrom wasn't around. There is no doubt in his mind on that score.

One day, he will drive his car, all by himself, on his own, out into the wide world. And he will know how to do it.

And Mr. Lundstrom will be able look the world square in the face. He knows he has always been useful. He knows he has always been needed. He's never been in anyone's way.

Little Mr. Lundstrom was never a hindrance.

Ostracism is the price people pay for unacceptable behavior out in the real world. The only thing ostracism "ruins" is a strategy for manipulating children.

That said, remember that ostracism is reserved for serious offences. We adults don't lose our licences because our parallel parking isn't what it should be, nor are we sent to jail for jaywalking.

Nevertheless, children are sometimes guilty of clearly inappropriate behavior for the simple reason that *children ask questions about society's norms through their actions.*

If you, as a parent, think that your child's behavior is intolerable, you should send a clear message to that effect. If words get you nowhere (and they seldom do) and physical resistance fails, then ostracism is your only option.

Let's go back to Lisa's poor father who was driven to the brink of a psychotic episode by his daughter's biting and committed (he thinks) a cardinal sin; he has put his daughter in her bed and confined her to her room.

He did the right thing – but too late. Things should not have been allowed to progress to the point where Dad was on the point of losing his temper. This sets the stage for child abuse. Parents should never allow themselves

550

to be pushed that far by a recalcitrant child.

Let's see what Lisa's dad could have done if he had not let the situation get away from him.

Lisa is biting her dad.

"No," says Dad. "It hurts, so don't bite."

Lisa bites him again. Dad takes her little head in his hands and stops her. He looks her right in the eye.

"You must not bite," he says. "It hurts and you are to stop it right now!"

Lisa keeps biting him.

"Lisa, biting is not allowed," says Dad. He takes her hand and holds it, puts it on his face and pats his cheek.

"You pat people. You don't bite. Patting feels nice. Biting hurts. You pat, like this. Oh, that's nice!"

He releases her hand and looks happy, but Lisa is not about to give up. She bites him again.

An edge creeps in to Dad's voice.

"Lisa, stop that NOW!"

Lisa bites like it's going out of style. She is consciously pushing her father to the limit. She has no plans to stop biting.

"OK," says Lisa's dad. "You are going to your room. I am going to put you in your bed, and you will have to stay there until you stop biting."

He carries his struggling, screaming and still biting daughter to her room and puts her in her crib.

"You can come out when you stop biting," Dad calmly informs her. He then leaves the room and closes the door behind him.

Lisa shrieks with indignation.

As soon as she stops screaming, even if it's only to pause for breath, Dad opens the door and asks, "Do you want to come now?"

His voice is friendly and matter of fact, but it is loud and clear enough for Lisa to hear.

Lisa resumes screaming, and Dad closes the door again. As soon as there is another moment of silence, he immediately opens the door.

"Are you done? Are you ready to come now?"

Lisa lapses into surly silence. Lisa glares at her dad, but she doesn't scream, thus indicating her consent.

Dad happily lifts her out of her crib and kisses her on the cheek. They go back into the living room and resume what they were doing before Lisa started to bite.

Dad gives no indication that anything was ever amiss.

Lisa's relationship with her dad, her flock, is preparing her for membership in a wider community.

If, a few weeks later, Lisa suddenly starts pushing the children who have come to her birthday party, and verbal eye-to-eye warnings and discreet physical resistance don't work, her father will ostracize her again. Without, of course, humiliating her in front of the other children.

Not being able to play with the other children is the price she will pay for her unacceptable behavior. She is welcome back into the fold on the condition that she stops pushing. If she starts pushing again, she will be ostracized again.

It will eventually dawn on Lisa that pushing means not being part of her community. And she wants to be a part of her community.

When she changes her behavior or indicates she is willing to change her behavior to avoid ostracism, Lisa will have learned her lesson. She will have internalized a norm: *You don't push.*

Because she is willing to change her behavior in order to be readmitted, she should be welcomed back with open arms because her behavior is now acceptable.

If the other children reject her and complain that they don't want to play with her because she pushes, Lisa should be defended. Her dad should tell the other children in no uncertain terms that Lisa does *not* push any-more and that they should all play together.

Ostracism was a consequence and served a purpose: instilling a norm. It was not a punishment.

If Lisa's dad had used ostracism as a punishment, he would have angrily dumped Lisa into her crib and left her to her fate. The only thing Lisa would have learned from the experience would have been that her father was angry with her. She would have felt rejected and abandoned, ostra-cized for no good reason. She would have been unhappy and/or even more defiant, and nothing would have changed when Lisa's father eventually let her out of her room. Lisa would not have internalized a norm. She would merely have been punished and made to feel like an underdog.

She might have felt guilty, but she would have learned nothing and her behavior would have remained unacceptable. She would have continued to bite her father and push her playmates. And she would have done so not just to see what the reaction would be but also to take revenge and exculpate herself.

Raising young children well means offering them calm and loving leadership. They should never be humiliated, degraded or oppressed.

552

THE CURSE OF GUILT

As a child, I somehow knew that I was the author of, not only my own, but everyone else's misfortune. It was my fault that I existed, and my existence was nothing but a misery to those around me. I even felt guilty about the money that my parents had to spend just because I was alive.

Any psychologist will tell you that children often feel guilty over their parents' divorce. Divorcing parents often make the following optimistic declaration: "Mom and Dad don't like each other as much as we used to. We argue too much. We will be happier if we live apart, but we both still love you as much as ever."

This little homily is completely incomprehensible to any child under the age of twelve. Children think in concrete terms, and very often there aren't any concrete reasons for a divorce. "You argue?" the child thinks. "So what? I argue with my friends at school. Does that mean I change schools?"

I sometimes think it might be better if parents just made something up. Any white lie will do, as long as it's concrete. "This place gives Daddy a bad cough. He is going to live somewhere else, a place where he won't cough so much. And you can go visit him there..."

During all my years as a parent, not least during my years as a single mother, I have tried to avoid burdening my children with guilt. This is paramount, not only in a relationship between parent and child, but in our relationships with people generally.

Guilt paralyses. Guilt makes true freedom impossible.

"Why are you sad?" one of my children asked me.

I told the truth. "Because I feel so alone."

"Well, you have us!" she said.

She comforted me tenderly, but there was real fear in her voice. This fear said not only, "Aren't we enough?", but also "We're the ones making you unhappy, aren't we?"

I tried to explain that adults feel lonely sometimes, even if they have great kids around them... Adults sometimes need other adults by their side to love them... and so on. I could see that my explanation wasn't having the desired effect. She didn't understand me.

Later I learned that it is only at the age of twelve that a child *begins* to glimpse the individual behind the parent/leader/protector. And it takes many more years before children, having become adults themselves, can look beyond "mother" or "father" and really see an individual.

My little one's anxious voice – "Well, you have us!" persuaded me to separate my "private life" from my "mother life" from then on. I became more business like. I avoided venting. I avoided saying things like, "You are all impossible. Why can't you help me? I can't stand this." Instead, I tried

553

to think in concrete, practical terms. What was it that I really wanted? Did I want them to be quiet? Did I want the house to look as though reasonably civilized people lived there? Did I want to be left in peace for a while?

After all, I didn't expect the children to make me happy, give my life meaning, or give me therapy. That would be unreasonable. So I did my best only to make demands that *were* reasonable, and if the kids delivered, I would be happy for them and with them, and keep my private anguish to myself.

I resolved to take responsibility for my own well-being (or the lack thereof). I felt I had no choice, since obviously, the children blamed themselves for my unhappiness.

The father in our example about the son moving out of the house used guilt to get his way by remaining passive. Both father and son knew that the writing was on the wall and that the son was eventually going to leave, but the father put his own interests above his son's. The son in our little parable must have had good reasons for moving if he could do it with a good conscience.

Genuine love is about liberation not guilt!

Why is guilt so effective as a tool of oppression? Why do children so easily fall victim to it?

Perhaps it is because people are born *dependent*. We all have someone to thank for our very existence, be it parents, God, or fate, since we can't spring into being all by ourselves. Life is given to us – with love, but also with obligations. We are indebted if you like. We have an obligation to try and do the right thing, to be worthy of the gift that has been given us. That is the immutable human imperative.

The debt we owe is forever. We carry it with us for as long as we are on this earth. But to be indebted to life, love, God is not a punishment. The gift of life does not make us guilty of anything. The debt we owe for the gift of life is evolution's loving yet demanding challenge. It is a debt that we make our payments on with honor and gratitude.

To be guilty of something, on the other hand, is to be deficient, unworthy or wrong. Human beings, big or small, who are burdened with guilt are automatically underdogs. Without self-respect, they cannot claim what is rightfully theirs. They cannot make demands. They are not free.

Those who can be persuaded to bear the burden of guilt – and children are easy marks – become locked in a cycle of victimization, and thus give the person, or persons, wielding power room to manoeuvre.

A man once told me about his marriage. His wife had her own definite ideas about sex within marriage: the less, the better. After appealing to her in both word and deed in every conceivable way, the husband had an affair. He never told her, and she never found out, but because of his infidelity, this man felt guilty from then on. The guilt made it impossible for him to ever make any demands on his wife, at least as far as their sex life was concerned, so sex pretty well died.

Underdogs are always at the mercy of others. Underdogs also fight furiously to free themselves from their tormentors. We are all familiar with words like "exonerate" and "redress". The wrongfully accused fight to clear their names, and perhaps demand compensation. Who is indifferent to having their good name dragged through the mud?

In many places in the Western world, child rearing based on traditional authority has been replaced by child rearing based on guilt. And guilt-based child rearing is just as soul destroying.

Children will fight frantically to free themselves from guilt. They will only put up with being the underdog for so long. Guilt tripping children may be effective, but that doesn't make it any less contemptible.

"You're going to babysit?" says Dad. "You can't even take care of yourself."

The son turns out to be an outstanding babysitter because he wants to prove to his father that he can indeed take care of himself and others.

"What do you need a clock radio for? You'd sleep all day if I didn't wake you!" says Mom. "Why did I even give you your own room? You never clean it."

Mom will have achieved her purpose. The child will get up on time and keep his room clean – but only because he has been humiliated and made to feel guilty.

Guilt tripping soon morphs into real cruelty.

"The way you carry on, it's no wonder your father doesn't want to live with us anymore!"

The child will feel terribly wronged, and the need for redress is as strong as any instinct, and when instinct takes over, all sense of proportion flies out the window.

A woman told me about something that happened during a party at a friend's house. Suddenly, one of the guests accused her of being an alcoholic. She was deeply offended and protested loudly.

"You know perfectly well you aren't an alcoholic," said one of her friends. "Why did you let that guy get under your skin?"

Of course, that reassurance didn't stop her from spending the rest of the evening trying to persuade the man who had called her an alcoholic to retract his accusation.

"I don't know why I reacted the way I did," she told me. "I knew everyone else was on my side, and I knew what he said wasn't true. But I had to hear it from *him*."

Since he was the one who had falsely accused her, he was the only one who could make it right.

"You're chicken!" Huey tells Dewey.

"Am not!" says Dewey.

"Prove it!" says Huey. "Walk blindfolded on a tightrope over the Niagara Falls."

"That's impossible!" says Dewey.

"So you *are* chicken then!" says Huey, and from that day on he never misses an opportunity to throw Dewey's lack of intestinal fortitude in his face.

It is entirely possible that Dewey, furious and defiant, decides that one day he will walk a tightrope over the Niagara Falls blindfolded. He then undergoes extensive training, spending a lot of money and the next thirty years of his life, to prove to Huey (and himself!) that he is not chicken.

I remember having a teacher who said that I would never graduate from high school. All the other teachers thought I would do fine, but I didn't care about them. After changing schools and going through much tribulation, I sought out the one teacher who didn't believe in me, proudly showed him my high school diploma and prepared to enjoy my moment of triumph.

Alas, he hadn't the faintest idea who I was.

Guilt is a means to power.

To be burdened with guilt is to be the underdog.

Shame, ridicule, false accusations are all weapons that can be used to burden an adult or a child with guilt, and the need for redress is so powerful that it can drive human beings in directions they really don't want to go.

WHAT YOU MUST NOT DO

1. Abandon your child.
2. Burden your child with guilt.
3. Hit your child.
4. Refuse to answer your child's questions.
5. Emotionally dump on your child.
6. Humiliate your child.
7. Ridicule your child.
8. Look for faults in your child.
9. Fail to understand your child.
10. Deceive your child.

To Abandon Your Child

An abandoned child is a rejected child. The child just wasn't good enough.

The damage can be controlled to some extent if you can convince the child that the separation is necessary for *you*. You are leaving because you are genuinely convinced that this is the right thing to do. It is impossible, however, to convince a child that the separation is best for *the child*.

Children love their parents, not because they don't know any better, but because they belong with them. Parents are the flock, and to be with the flock is to belong. Without a specific belonging, a true connection, no living creature can survive for long.

If children are abandoned by their parents, they become disoriented (see the theory of the fixed center in "From my life. Theories for comfort" in Part four of *For the Love of Children*). Abandoned children need as much tenderness, patience and love as the abandoned young of any species do. Adults who take on the task of caring for these children would do well to remember that.

For a long time, sometimes all their lives, abandoned children long for the flock that they originally belonged to. They yearn for the person or the people to whom they first gave that innate primordial trust and to whom they so faithfully turned.

To Burden Your Child with Guilt

Guilt does so much damage because it is the proverbial self-fulfilling prophesy.

Eric, 28, knows full well that he didn't steal the company check book that everyone at his work place is looking for. But he blushes and starts to stammer whenever anyone asks him if he has seen it, and in the end he starts to wonder if maybe he really *did* take it.

Agnes, 34, wanders through life with a vague feeling that she is a fake. Everyone is going to see through her one day. They will realize that she is trying to be something that she's not, and when they do, they won't want anything to do with her.

Children are an impediment in our society. In spite of all our fine words to the contrary, children deep down know the truth about themselves, and they are afraid that the truth might get out. They aren't needed. They make no contribution. They don't take part in the struggle for survival. They are a burden.

They have trouble justifying their existence, and we adults do precious little to help them.

We have turned children into fashion accessories.

Few children grow up free from guilt. They can't look at themselves in the mirror and say, "The others wouldn't manage as well without me" and believe it. The sad truth they have to contend with is, "The others would manage just fine without me. Actually, they would probably manage better…"

To Hit your Child
To hit a child is to admit failure.

This is not about self-control. If you hit your child, you are, in effect, giving your parenting skills a failing grade.

Ostracism to the child's bed or room, with the aid of physical restraint, is infinitely preferable to corporal punishment. Gently but firmly restraining a child is sometimes necessary, just as restraining an intoxicated adult in a bar is.

Restraining a child is not the same as hitting a child.

There is always a non-violent way to solve a problem. If you truly have the courage to listen to your own inner, genuine convictions, then you will find the solution – in time.

To Refuse to Answer Your Child's Questions
"We'll talk about this when you're older," you find yourself saying, either because you are embarrassed, irritated or angry.

"You wouldn't understand!"

"Stop asking so many questions!"

But – *every question has an answer.*

You can furrow your brow and look like you are really concentrating and say, "Let me think about that" when the truth is "Actually, I have no idea, and I don't have the strength to talk about it right now anyway."

(The next day, your child comes to you and asks expectantly, "Have you thought about it?" Since you have forgotten what the conversation was about, you feel a bit like Icarus must have done when the wax holding his wings together melted, but you try to keep flying anyway. "Uh, yes, of course, I have. But before I make a decision, I'd like a few more details.")

A clear, convincing answer (convincing because you are convinced yourself) means security and leadership. Faced with a bawling little one-year-old, you can actually say, 'BEANS WITH GLUE AND BOOKSHELVES!' and the child will fall silent, content. Your tone of voice and your body language send the message.

It's not the words, but the conviction that gives the answer, sends the message and communicates guidance and leadership. And there's always an answer.

To Emotionally Dump on Your Child

You have no doubt met them – guys who are forever pulling their forelocks and kissing up to the boss when they are at work, but when they get home they treat their wives like the ancient Romans treated their galley slaves. The wives become punching bags to compensate for all the humiliations that their husbands have to endure at work.

Then of course there is the other extreme – men who rule the roost at work, but once home their backbones turn to jello, and they accede to their wives' every whim.

Not dumping on your children doesn't just mean biting your tongue when you feel like yelling at them when you are in a bad mood. It also means not using them as compensation for what's lacking in your life – as do the men described above.

It's not your child's job to make you happy. It's your job to prepare your child for a life without you.

To Humiliate Your Child

If you humiliate your children, you are robbing them of their dignity and sense of self-worth. Such disloyalty is tantamount to a failure to protect.

In my opinion, complaining about a child, even in jest, is a mark of moral deficiency, whether you are talking to your therapist or to family and friends.

(It's something I have never done – which of course never stopped my kids from complaining about *me*...)

To Ridicule Your Child

Contempt and taunts corrode the soul like acid. Resorting to contempt and taunts is as low as you can sink.

"You're so stupid! You always manage to do the exact opposite of what I tell you!"

What's stupid about that? It may be wrong, but it's not stupid.

Contempt, even when it's disguised as humor, never does anyone any good.

You can get irritated with a child for a thousand reasons, just as you can get irritated with an adult for a thousand reasons. There will always be a reason.

So deal with the reason objectively, and leave the child out of the firing line of ridicule!

To Look for Faults in Your Child

Children are classified as disturbed, abnormal, deviant, dysfunctional, and a host of other things. Kids are graded, evaluated, labelled and branded according to the DSM or a doctor's profitable whim.

Remember Mr. Lundstrom, who had a highway driving system all to himself? Let's look at another example.

Little Peterson, who is a child, weaves mats in a workshop that is just as cut off from reality as Mr Lundstrom's highway system.

"I don't want to weave any more mats," says Peterson one day. "I want to do something that makes sense. I want to do something that has a *point!*"

There must be something wrong with Peterson, the workshop supervisor concludes. Because there is nothing wrong with the mat-making materials. And the work environment couldn't be better. The air is clean and the décor attractive. Peterson gets three meals a day, and he is surrounded by people who are specially trained to help little Petersons weave mats.

Since Peterson has nothing else to do – unless of course he intends to wander the streets and cost society money – why would he wail and gnash his teeth about having to weave mats that no one will ever use? He must be suffering from some form of mental illness.

The staff give him exciting new materials to weave mats with. They also administer appropriate amounts of anti-depressant and/or tranquillizing medication to prevent him becoming violent.

If that doesn't fix him, the next step is to cut his brain open and take a look inside. What's wrong with Peterson?

To Fail to Understand Your Child

Over the years, you will come to hear many things from your child, some painful and others hair-raising, but *understanding is more important than evaluating.*

If your children want you to evaluate any given situation, they will ask you flat out what you think. If they don't, you should content yourself with trying to understand, even at the cost of your own pain.

People always have reasons for the things they say and do. Children do not have the self-knowledge or the experience to analyze why they do what they do or say what they say, but they always have a reason.

A child who is not understood is a child who has been rejected, and rejected children clam up.

To Deceive Your Child

If you have said that you will wave goodbye to a child who is watching you from the window, you must do it, even if you can see neither child nor window.

If you made a promise without forethought, you will have to try and keep it regardless.

It's better to let common sense come to the fore immediately – "No, this just won't work" – than to hide behind it after the fact – "It just wasn't possible (because of this, that or the other)."

RESPECT

"Hold me," says Dick to Jane one evening after they have gone to bed. "I feel so sad."

"Why?" says Jane, looking at him over the top of her book.

"I don't know. I just do."

"You don't have anything to be sad about!"

"No, perhaps I don't, but... Can't you hold me anyway?"

"You're being ridiculous," says Jane and goes back to her book.

Respect is permitting and believing.

Respecting a person means permitting him to be who he is, feeling what he feels, and not rejecting him. Respecting a person means believing in his ability to think for himself and to do the right thing. It means according him dignity and respect.

Does Dick have a reason to feel sad? It doesn't matter. This is not a question of objective truth. The point is that *Dick* thinks he has a reason to feel sad.

Jane could have let Dick be himself and feel what he was feeling. Because she loves him, she could have met him in whatever emotional space he found himself and treated him with respect. She could have given him a hug.

Little Leo has broken a vase. His mother tears strips off him.

"I liked that vase! It can't be fixed! Pick up the pieces! Why can't you be more careful?"

Leo bursts into tears. His mother hugs him and comforts him.

Does Leo need comforting because he broke a vase? No, he needs comforting because *he is sad*.

His mother lets him feel what he is feeling and respects it. She doesn't reject Leo. She only rejects what he has done.

It is the *action* that is the problem, not the child. Mom accepts Leo for what he is: a sad little boy. His action – breaking a vase – is still unacceptable, and she tells him so, but Leo is as loved as he has always been.

"You have to be careful. You have to watch your step. Things can break. You mustn't do that."

"I will, Mom", sobs Leo. "I will try to be careful."

A man says about his wife, "She would never manage without me."

The wife, in turn, says of her husband, "He won't take responsibility for himself."

"She just can't be alone," says the husband.

"He is way too dependent on me," says the wife.

That is what a relationship in which neither party believes in nor respects the other looks like.

If no one believes in your ability, sooner or later you find yourself incapacitated. Negative expectations are just as self-fulfilling as positive ones.

Children operate the same way. Parents who don't believe in their children's abilities, sooner or later will incapacitate them.

"Phil can't be away from me for five minutes."

"Lisa will never dare to dive."

"Ann can only sleep in my bed with me."

"Oh no, Mike is way too sensitive for that."

"Mark could never manage such a thing. He wouldn't even try."

But who knows what might happen if *necessity* entered the picture?

Isadora, two years old, is visiting a large playground with her mother. In the playground there is a slide that is higher and longer than anything the little girl and her mother have ever seen. Children of all ages are crowding around the base, waiting their turn. Isadora of course wants a turn too.

But once she gets to the top of the steps, she is suddenly terrified. She leans forward onto the slide, lies on her stomach, and hangs onto the railings for dear life. Below her, the steep slide seems to go on forever. She is so frightened that she starts to cry.

She wants to climb back down the steps, but the children behind her are blocking her way and yelling impatiently for her to hurry up and take her turn.

Her mother rushes to the rescue, but the top of the slide is too high and the other kids are blocking the steps, so she can't get a hold of her daughter and lift her down. She has to clamber up the slide. Finally, she reaches her daughter, but she can't carry her down that way, since she has to hang on to the sides of the slide to keep her footing.

She manages to get Isadora into a sitting position. Even though her mother is holding her securely, Isadora is paralyzed with fear, but the only way to get back down is to slide down.

Isadora's mother gently eases her daughter forward and lets go.

Isadora shoots down the slide, flies off the end and lands on the ground with a thump. Shocked but unhurt, she scrambles up. Meanwhile, her mother has made it back to earth, and she hurries over to comfort her. But Isadora doesn't cry, and when Mom has satisfied herself that her daughter isn't hurt, she heaves a sigh of relief and sits down on a bench.

Then Mom notices that Isadora is circling the slide and watching the other kids, and before she has a chance to intervene, the little girl has climbed up the slide again.

Pale but collected, she sits down at the top of the slide, takes hold of the sides with her little hands, and launches herself down. She again flies down the slide and lands on the ground with a familiar thump.

When Isadora gets to her feet, the expression on her face is one of radiant happiness. She runs over to her mom as fast as her little legs will carry her.

"I did it! I did it!"

It was necessity rather than her mother's faith that enabled Isadora to conquer the slide.

But at the end of the day, the victory was Isadora's and Isadora's alone.

ON BEING SPOILED

Who is spoiled?

Anyone who takes the good things that life has to offer for granted, demands them and yet doesn't appreciate them, is spoiled.

Uncle Tom comes to little Jerry's birthday party to wish him many happy returns.

"Where's my present?" asks Jerry.

Uncle Tom hands over his present.

"You mean you only bought me *one* present?"

Jerry opens his present. It's a toy car.

"You can take it back. I have lots of cars that are a lot better than this one."

Spoiled children are not born; they are made. Spoiled children have been badly brought up, a fact that all parents are painfully aware of. That's why parents monitor each other so meticulously.

"You're spoiling the boy," a father is informed. His sin was giving his son three Christmas presents instead of just two.

"You're spoiling the girl," a mother is informed. Her sin was refraining from replenishing her own wardrobe so she could pay for her daughter's designer clothes.

However, as long as children *appreciate* what they receive, whether it's in the form of material goods or plain old-fashioned consideration, they are not spoiled.

David's dad is out shopping with his brother.

"Grab some baked beans," Dad says to his brother. "David likes them."

"You shouldn't cater to his every whim the way you do," says the brother. "You'll spoil him."

"Why?" asks David's father. "He likes baked beans."

"My point exactly," says the brother.

Is the brother right or wrong? He's wrong, provided that David appreciates the fact that his father tries hard to buy things that David likes.

A good measure of whether or not a child is spoiled is your own attitude. If your little (or not so little) boy likes to eat McDonald's in front of the TV on Saturday nights and you are happy to buy it for him, then everything is as it should be. If, on the other hand, you buy him McDonald's because you are afraid that if you don't, your life won't be worth living, then something is amiss. You are in effect being blackmailed. You have taught your child that the good things in life are a right, not a privilege.

If I cook dinner for the love of my life 364 days a year, but on the 365th, when I have either no time or no energy, I ask if we could just send for pizza, and his reply is "No way! I want my bloody dinner!", then I have spoiled him. Because I am dealing with an adult, I can just go on strike. Hopefully, we would talk it over, and I would have the opportunity to tell him that it's no fun cooking him dinner if he doesn't appreciate it.

That is not an approach you can take with children, however, since it entails burdening them with guilt – one of the deadly sins.

The only strategy for dealing with a spoiled child is withdrawal of privileges.

Let's go back to Uncle Tom and Jerry. Uncle Tom's feelings have been hurt, and Jerry is telling his dad that he doesn't want some cheap knock-off in his car collection.

His father calmly starts gathering up all Jerry's cars.

"If you don't want the car that Uncle Tom gave you, I don't suppose you want any of your other cars either."

"Yes I do!"

"But you don't want the car that Uncle Tom gave you?"

"No. It sucks."

"If *you* don't want Uncle Tom's car, then *I* don't want you to have any cars at all."

So Jerry has to go and thank Uncle Tom profusely for the car.

More often than not, it's only when people are faced with the prospect of losing the things they really value that they realize that the good things in life are not guaranteed, and they are certainly not a right.

A simple life is the best safeguard against spoiling a child.

If you take a little boy to Disneyland every Sunday, where are you going to take him on his birthday? If you give a little girl a soda with every meal, what is she going to drink when you throw her a birthday party? Champagne?

One of your jobs as a parent is to draw a distinction between the necessities of life and conspicuous consumption.

Treats should be presented as what they are: treats.

When David's dad gets home with the beans, he makes a production out of it. "You know what I got for you today? *Baked beans!*"

If Dad just hands David the beans like it's no big deal, David will take his cue from his father – and demand baked beans every meal.

You can't *talk* a spoiled brat into being a good citizen.

If your child isn't thrilled by being given a treat, all you have to do is stop giving them – without reproaches of course – and wait for the reaction. It will come, believe me.

"Why don't we have pancakes anymore?"

"You want me to make pancakes?"

"Yeah, I'm *dying* for pancakes!"

"Then I'd be glad to make some for you."

"I want to go to the movies," says an older child. "Everybody in my class goes to the movies a couple of times a week. I want to go too. So you'll have to give me the money."

"Really? Well, if I give you money to see a movie, it's not to make the kids in your class happy. It's to make *you* happy. Going to the movies is not a human right. It's a privilege. Until you figure that out, you're not getting any money from me."

I once knew a divorced dad who had a relationship with a single mother. She thought he was spoiling his son because he brought him a new toy every time he visited. The mother travelled a fair amount on business, and whenever she came home from a business trip, she always had an expensive piece of designer clothing for her daughter.

When the divorced dad gave her a dose of her own medicine, she replied, "But this is different. My daughter is very fashion conscious!"

The boy was probably toy conscious, so it's not an argument that holds any water.

The important question is whether these kids *expected* toys and designer clothes as a matter of course.

How would they react if their parents came home empty-handed?

Anything that is not a necessity is a privilege, and when privileges are conferred, they should be met with genuine gratitude.

Let's say you take your little angel to the fun fair. He rides the rides, sees the clowns, and eats cotton candy like it's going out of style. No expense is spared.

The next outing is somewhat less pretentious. You take the child to the local petting zoo to show him the animals.

Your offspring is less than pleased. He was expecting the fun fair again. The day, which began so promisingly, is ruined. Your child is disappointed, and you are in a foul mood.

The trick is to set limits in advance.

"We're going to the fun fair today. We can do anything we want! The sky is the limit! I have a little money for once! But we can only do this today. It's all I can afford."

Or:

"We're going to the local petting zoo today. We can look at all the animals, but we can't buy anything and we can't eat out today. So, we'll take sandwiches with us."

Admittedly, setting limits isn't always fun. But a child who is used to restrictions is overjoyed when the restrictions are lifted.

Here's a tip: Get your child used to saying "thank you" when something is finished! Say "thank you" on your child's behalf, and you'll avoid those endless, whiney, but-I-want-some-more scenes. The happy "Thank you" has a magic effect. It reminds the child of the pleasure of whatever it was, that is now finished: it was great while it lasted.

"I want more ice cream."

"All gone. Thanks for the ice cream!"

"Thanks for the ice cream."

LIMITS

Setting limits is essential, although it's tempting not to. As a mother or father, you can't avoid being unpleasant sometimes (or even oftentimes). You will have to put your foot down. And being unpleasant to those you love is not easy.

If human beings didn't need to acquire knowledge of life through their own personal experience, kids could set their own limits, and we adults could sit back and relax. Unfortunately, that is not the way the world works.

A father once asked me if I had a fourteen-year-old daughter. I told him I did. He then asked me what her curfew was on weekdays.

"She doesn't have a curfew because she doesn't go out," I answered. "None of my kids are allowed out of the house after dinner on weekdays. If it's a very special occasion, I might let her stay out until nine. Otherwise, she is allowed out on weekends, but not by herself, and only until eleven. If she doesn't have someone to bring her home, her brother goes and gets her. Why?"

He proceeded to inform me that his fourteen-year-old daughter was out until two in the morning a couple of times a week. She would go to a club with her friends and stay until closing time. He wanted to know if I thought staying out that late was acceptable. My answer was an emphatic "no".

"Would you be able to stay out until two in the morning twice a week and still make it into work?" I asked him.

"No, I wouldn't," he replied.

"So how do you expect her to?" I said angrily. "You're letting your daughter down!"

What diplomats delicately refer to as "a frank exchange of views" ensued. I didn't know what I was talking about the father informed me. For one thing, the club didn't close until two. For another, all the fun stuff happened in the hour before the club closed, and his daughter had told him that if you don't stay until the end, there wasn't much point in going at all. And in any case, all the other kids stayed until two.

"Well, if you're fine with all this, why are you asking my opinion?" I said.

Obviously, he wasn't fine with it at all. The fact that he brought the subject up at all indicated that he was worried. He didn't like his daughter staying out that late and would have been overjoyed if she had volunteered to come home a couple of hours earlier.

"Listen, Dad, I think I'd better come home by midnight from now on. It's a bit too much for me to stay out until two. Am I right or am I right?"

Unfortunately, that is not how the world works.

I would have given the girl a clear choice: "Either you'll be home by eleven, or you can't go there at all."

"But everything fun happens so much later!"

"Well, then don't go. It's your choice. Either you go, or you don't go. Whatever you decide, you'll be home by eleven. That's it."

If she had tested my resolve and stayed out until two in the morning anyway just to see what would happen, she would have faced the consequences: she would not be able to go there at all the next time she wanted to go clubbing.

If the girl had interpreted my actions as a violation of her integrity, she would have found a way to go the club anyway – for example, she could have knocked me down. But the fact is that children, even teenagers, will accept directives from their parents because, deep down, directives are what they want.

When you give directives, set limits, and stand up for community and personal values, you are in effect telling your child that you care. You are providing leadership and protection by virtue of your love and experience. And kids pick up on this.

The father was caught on the horns of a classic dilemma. He believed that one course of action was the right one, but he allowed himself to be talked into supporting another. He lost confidence in himself. Was it right or wrong for his daughter to stay out so late? And since now all her friends were out so late...

If you feel the least bit uncomfortable about a situation, you should have faith in your own judgement and hold your ground for your own sake and the sake of your child. Listen to your inner voice of conviction and act accordingly! It's soft but it's there. Listen to it and obey it!

If you respect yourself, you win the respect of others, and respect is the soil in which trust germinates.

"I can depend on my dad. He knows what he's doing, and he stands proud because of it."

One productive little ruse is to set limits by offering a choice.

"You get home by eleven, or you don't go at all."

Compared to not going at all, being home by eleven sounds pretty good to most kids.

But if you say, "The club closes at two? Well, I want you home by eleven," then the choice is between eleven and two rather than eleven and nothing – and of course two sounds a lot better than eleven. Protests will follow.

"I want the whole bag of cookies!"

"You can have two, or you can have none."

"I want a whole bottle of soda!"

"You can have one glass or nothing."

"I don't want dinner! I want to watch TV!"

"You can watch TV until 6.00 or not at all."

And if the child decides not to watch TV at all, that is of course fine with you. Don't have an attack of conscience and cave in: "Oh, alright, watch TV as long as you like. I'll hold dinner."

Even if you don't exactly effervesce with good will, you don't have to lose your temper. All you have to do is explain clearly and concretely what you will not tolerate and what you expect instead. And of course it is the unacceptable *behavior* that you are condemning, not the child.

Here are some possible scenarios:

"I'm sorry, but since you haven't been keeping up with your chores, you are going to have to make up for it somehow. If *you* don't do what you're supposed to do, someone else has to, and that's not fair. So, I want you to clean the oven. I hope that you will take your responsibilities a little more seriously from now on. Call me when you're done with the oven."

"You are two hours late, and, as I'm sure you realize, I can't let that go. You are grounded for the weekend. I'm sorry to have to do this, but we had a deal. Please make sure you get home when you say you will in future."

"It has come to my attention that your grades are slipping and that you've been getting to school late. That is not acceptable. I have allowed you to go to bed more or less when you like and to decide how much TV is appropriate, but you are not holding up your side of the bargain. So, here's what's going to happen. You are going to go to bed earlier and TV is going to be rationed. During the week, you are to be in bed by nine, and the television set is off limits. When your grades improve and you start getting to school when you're supposed to every morning, we can negotiate, but until then, this is how it's going to be."

And with a regretful smile, you turn off the TV if your little (or not so little) angel has somehow contrived to park himself in front of it anyway.

Children don't bite – at least not so hard that you have to be afraid of them!

PUNISHMENT

Human beings allow themselves to be brought up because they want to be inducted into a community and allowed to stay there. We are herd animals. We are not constituted to live alone, and we don't survive very long if we are forced to. That's why just having our physical needs satisfied isn't enough. We really don't live by bread alone.

It takes children a long time to internalize the norms, rules and values of whatever society they happen to land in. Explanations aren't enough for them. They have to learn these norms through hands-on experience.

When children try their hands at something, they are in fact asking questions, and these questions require answers. These answers have to be accurate and satisfactory to the child, and they are best expressed through *actions*.

More often than you would like, as a parent, leader and guide, you will have to give answers that break your heart.

My son, who had always been a punctual lad, suddenly started arriving late for things, sometimes by as much as an hour. In developed countries, there is a societal norm that places great value on punctuality. I happen to approve of this particular norm, so I found his behavior unacceptable.

Pleas and admonitions had no effect at all. Finally, I had to show him that violating a norm that was endorsed by his society, his siblings and his mother had *consequences*. One day, he found himself in the unenviable position of being home alone by himself while the rest of the family was out eating dinner at a restaurant – which was one of his favorite pastimes. He had been told to be home by four. He wasn't, so we all set off without him at a quarter after.

I didn't enjoy dinner much that evening, but it did the trick. From then on, you could set your watch by him.

A friend of mine told me about how he had stolen something in Egypt when he was a teenager. Theft is regarded as an extremely grave offence in Muslim countries. The Koran stipulates that a thief's right hand should be cut off.

The theft was discovered. The boy's father took his son into the kitchen where a little fire was burning in a clay pot on the table. He held his son's hand over the flames.

"I can't allow my eldest son to become a thief," he declared. "I would rather burn your hands myself than allow you to grow up to be a thief and have your hand cut off by someone else."

But the tears were running down his father's cheeks.

Children are not saints, any more than adults are. As a mother or father, you naturally want to believe that *your* child will always stick to the straight and narrow and never stoop to stealing, lying, vandalism, slander, etc. Unfortunately, this isn't how life usually works.

If you can bring yourself to regard your child's less attractive tendencies as questions that require answers, you won't feel obliged to react with outrage. "How could you do something like that?" (Remember how a thirteen-year-old interprets such questions literally? "It was easy!") If you regard your child's poor behavior as a question "Is this acceptable?", you can give a business like answer, "No, it isn't." "And what happens if you do it anyway?"

the child asks through his actions. Through your own actions, through consistent consequences and/or punishment, you provide the answer, "This is what will happen."

Just remember that it is always the *behavior* you are condemning, never the child.

Child psychologists have told us that all children shoplift at some point. The fact that such behavior is common does not mean it is acceptable. Shoplifting is never acceptable. A child who shoplifts is asking about a societal norm, and this norm can be formulated as follows:

"Shoplifting is theft. Theft is taking things that don't belong to you, and that is unacceptable. Therefore, shoplifting is unacceptable."

A mother I know got a call from the police. Her teenage daughter had tried on a dress, put her own clothes on over it and was on her way out of the store when she was nabbed by an observant sales clerk. Since the girl had no ID, the police were called. The police then phoned the mother, who was told to come down to the station, identify her daughter and take her home.

Understandably, the girl's mother was very upset.

"What were you thinking? You know you don't have to steal! Take this money and go buy the dress!"

That was kind of the mother, but it was wrong. She was in effect rewarding her daughter for shoplifting. She tried to steal – and got a dress for her trouble. The mother made it impossible for her daughter to internalize a societal norm.

The message the girl was given was that stealing is acceptable. Either you steal and get away with it – in which case you get to keep what you have stolen. Or you steal and get caught – in which case you get to keep what you have stolen anyway.

Children rarely, if ever, steal because they really need something. They steal for excitement. They know they are doing something that is forbidden, and they want to see what happens if they don't conform to a societal norm.

If the consequences or the punishment is to have the desired effect – acceptable instead of unacceptable behavior – the child must not be humiliated. Many of the punishments meted out by society are humiliating. Humiliation produces fear and submission, but it also breeds hate, thus making the punishment completely pointless.

Humiliating punishments never produce the desired result.

Laura, twelve years old, is in a store and she puts a watch in her pocket. No one sees her, but a couple of days later, her mother spots the watch on her wrist.

"Where did you get that watch?"

And Laura is busted.

Her mother forces Laura to take the watch back to the store and admit that she stole it.

That is a humiliating punishment. No adult would stand up in public and admit to being a thief. No adult would hand over a stolen watch to a shopkeeper or a salesclerk and say, "I stole this."

Adults, like children, can steal, regret what they have done and try to make amends. But their explanation would go something like this: "I don't know how this happened... I must have gotten this watch with me by mistake... Anyhow, here it is... I'm terribly sorry." The shopkeeper or the salesclerk would of course react with astonished gratitude at such honesty.

One of my daughters, at the tender age of seven, stole a Barbie doll and a Barbie outfit from a toy store. I received an irate phone call from the outraged clerk. Her indignation knew no bounds. I thought the tirade would never end...kids today... budding criminal... crafty little devil... walked out of the store bold as brass, and on and on.

I wasn't happy, but I tried to contain myself. Finally, I interrupted her. "Just send her home. I'll give her the money and she'll be back to pay you."

She arrived home, and I saw what she had stolen. A doll she had always wanted and an expensive outfit to boot. I couldn't have afforded to buy it for her.

We went to the bank and raided her bank account. Her accumulated fortune matched the price of what she had stolen almost to the cent. She went back to the store and paid.

Then she had to throw the doll and the clothes into the garbage. She lost the doll, the clothes *and* the money that she had been saving for so long.

She had to pay her debt, but she did *not* have to stand in front of a self-righteous salesclerk and declare herself a thief.

I took no joy in punishing my little girl, but it had the desired effect.

A teacher catches a student urinating in a wastepaper basket. He punishes the boy by emptying the contents of the basket over his head.

That is a humiliating punishment. Think what you will about the student's escapade, which admittedly was distasteful, but the punishment was an exercise in futility. The student will probably make it his business to urinate in every wastepaper basket in the school.

A punishment that isn't designed to humiliate would have the opposite effect.

The teacher catches the student in the act and says: "What the hell do you think you're doing? Get a bucket of water and a cloth and clean the basket. And just for good measure you can clean those other two baskets as well. Get busy!"

Another teacher happens by and stops to see what's going on.

"You the janitor now Peter?" he asks. "Why are you cleaning the waste baskets?"

Before Peter has a chance to answer the first teacher says, "They were pretty grubby. Peter was good enough to clean them."

The teacher makes sure that Peter isn't unnecessarily embarrassed.

Preserving people's dignity is the opposite of humiliating them.

The teacher is not out to humiliate Peter, nor does he want to give his colleague the means to humiliate the boy. His purpose is to express disapproval and to correct unacceptable behavior – which peeing in a wastebasket most definitely is. Because the teacher shows Peter a way to atone for his sin – he not only has to clean the wastebasket he dirtied but two others as well – he gives the boy a shot at rehabilitation.

And Peter takes the opportunity precisely because he is allowed to maintain, or rather restore, his dignity.

As a result, Peter's days of urinating in wastebaskets are gone forever.

He also thinks his teacher is a pretty cool guy and would probably walk the plank for him, but that's another story!

MASTURBATION AND SEX

A person who is not understood inhabits a desolate no-man's land.

I once lived in another country whose language and customs were so foreign to me they were utterly incomprehensible. My identity started to dissolve because I was so isolated from other adults who understood *my* language and *my* culture.

In the end, it seemed as though my body was dissolving as well. A day came when I could no longer write my name. The letters were just wrong somehow. Try as I might I couldn't form the four symbols that made up my name.

Towards the end of my exile, I would sit for hours in front of a mirror staring at my reflection. To prove to myself that I existed, I would move my body in the exploratory, concentrated way that young children sometimes do. I catalogued the odors that emanated from my own body: the smell of my sweat, breath, skin, hair, feet, vagina, anus. Smell is one of the five senses necessary to fully experience reality.

All that staring into the mirror enabled me to understand why people make small talk when they meet. Every day, we all need confirmation that we exist, that we are visible, that we have bodies. This makes superficial connections just as important as profound ones.

Touching and exploring my own body, and contemplating its various scents made me wonder if masturbation for a young child is really about sex. A child's world is concrete. The self must be concrete too – tangible. Diligent contact with the sex organs and the anal region provides comfort, self-awareness, and the warmth of familiarity.

Children going through a changing phase, children who are frightened, confused or anxious about something, children who are under stress and who seek to confirm the tangibility of their bodies and themselves should not, in my opinion, be denied the help that they can give themselves.

If what your child is doing makes you uncomfortable, tactfully extol the virtues of solitude.

"Touching your body is something you do when you are by yourself," you can point out. "When we want to pee or poo or burp, it feels good too, but we go into the bathroom and close the door."

Masturbation and budding sexuality in children is a problem not only for many families but also for day care centers. How parents and caregivers should react to masturbation and children's sexually colored games is debated regularly. And, just as regularly, the experts file into TV studios and solemnly pontificate on the questions that are vexing everyone. Should we provide sex education to young children? Why do we expect kids to fall in love at three and pair off at five? Have we in effect rationalized the concept of childhood out of existence?

Young children don't need instruction in sex, anymore than infants need instruction in *their* innate sensuality. Children do not have a problem with sex. Adults do. I'm not sure who should be educating whom!

For better or worse, children are both easily deceived and easily led. So, if you find your children engaged in games of a sexual nature that you don't think are appropriate, just find something better for them to do. Don't overreact and don't reproach them. That just makes the whole business that much more interesting. Distract them enthusiastically and ignite their interest in something else.

Even if you have a positive and natural attitude towards sex and are comfortable being naked in front of your children, even if you shower and bathe with them, talk openly about sex to them, and allow them to examine themselves and you, bear in mind that children in the end learn embarrassment. At around the age of three, all kids demand the proverbial fig leaf. This shyness isn't necessarily consistent or permanent, but when little children decide that they want to cover up, respect their decision and spare them those cheery little naked-as-nature-intended sermons.

A young man of twelve for example is perfectly capable of having sophisticated sexual fantasies about his mother. It would hardly be humane for the mother to insist that the son regard her nakedness as "natural", since the feelings the boy harbors towards his mother are anything but.

A teenage girl might be perfectly comfortable exposing her body to both her father and male acquaintances, but whether she regards nakedness as natural or not is hardly the point. She is sending out sexual signals, but she is not emotionally or socially mature enough to deal with the consequences.

I have often shooed my girls off to their rooms in various states of undress with the admonition, "Get dressed! There are men in the house!" It wasn't that I thought the men would have trouble controlling their urges. I was simply protecting my children's interests.

Many parents think that they should conduct their sex life in such a way that their children think they don't have one. If a child peeps into the bedroom and catches his parents in the act, Mom freezes up harder than Hudson's Bay in January, Dad pulls out of her like a pilot ejecting from an F-16, and it's red faces all round. Both adults feel the weight of original sin come crashing down on their shoulders, and there's no more sex that night.

It's not dangerous to ask a child to leave you in peace. "Mommy and Daddy want to finish hugging each other. We'll be with you in a minute. Close the door on your way out please."

Two adults who fly apart as soon as a child opens the bedroom door are indicating by their actions that what they are doing is shameful, disgusting and wrong. They can talk lyrically about how much they love each other all they want. In a child's world, when words go up against actions, actions win every time.

If you are "caught" in the act, the trick is to look as though you haven't been caught at anything. Stop what you're doing, but don't fly apart. Ask calmly and affectionately to be left alone, and when you are, resume doing whatever it was you were doing.

It is a sad reality that the majority of children and younger teenagers believe – or at least want to believe – that intercourse is something that adults engage in for reproductive purposes. Exclusively. That it might actually feel good doesn't occur to them.

Young children are easily frightened. If Mom is moaning and squealing, she must hurt somewhere. If Dad is on top of Mom thrusting for all he is worth with a doggedly determined expression on his face, he must be angry or crazy...

If your child is too young to follow simple instructions, try to finish your love-making softly and tenderly with as little movement as possible and cast an occasional affectionate glance the child's way.

Young people lead a solitary existence. They may look as though they are securely connected to their cliques and friends, but that's deceptive. Each of them must walk a very lonely road towards a mature, clearly defined identity.

Young people think that they are unique. The idea that there is such a thing as shared experience does not enter their minds. A boy who masturbates five times a day is convinced that everyone else only masturbates once a week. A girl who masturbates once a week is equally convinced that everyone else masturbates every day or once a month. "I" am *different*.

Just as a very young child is fascinated by the realization that Mom was little once, a teenager is fascinated and relieved to discover that Mother and Father once felt left out, lonely and geeky. Admitting to your teenager that your sex life left a lot to be desired when you were young helps ease the pain – as does anything else that says *you are not alone!*

In Part four of *For the Love of Children* I touched upon the subject of sexual debuts at various ages. Here is a good guideline. *Don't interfere in whatever is going on, but limit what is going on.*

Not: "So you're playing doctor? Put your pants on!"

Rather: "So you're playing doctor? Dinner is in five minutes. I'll call you as soon as it's ready."

Not: "If you're going to dance cheek-to-cheek, keep the light on."

Rather: "Nice music! Two more songs and then we're going to watch a video."

Not: "If you are going to lie on the bed, keep the door open and leave the light on."

Rather: "Oh sorry. Didn't mean to barge in. But X has to go home in five minutes because we have things to do tonight."

Whereupon you shut the door, come back in five minutes (or sooner!), knock and bid X a fond farewell.

TRUST

All successful childrearing is based on trust.

Who do we choose to trust? The people who understand us, or at least try to, and who, once our trust is given, don't betray it.

We all know the importance of communication. We all need someone to talk to. We're told that we should talk to our children extensively and correctly thereby stimulating their linguistic development. Children's language skills have to be honed. But what is the purpose of language? Why do human beings talk to each other? What is communication?

What does it matter if I have a million-word vocabulary and speak thirteen languages if I feel that no one understands me?

The purpose of language is to understand and to be understood. Understanding can be expressed in many ways: words are one. But gestures, posture, a sympathetic glance, and all those other wordless connections we make with each other matter too. Perhaps understanding is most clearly expressed through our actions.

For children, actions always speak louder than words. If there is a discrepancy between your words and your actions, it is your actions your child will pick up on.

"I want you and me to be friends," Lavinia's mother tells her one day because it pains her that she and her daughter have drifted so far apart.

But her actions do not match her words. One of Lavinia's friends comes over to visit, but Lavinia's mother ignores her completely. She serves Lavinia dinner, but doesn't eat with her. When Lavinia changes her clothes, she casts a disapproving look at her daughter's outfit. Finally, she leaves the house on an errand but doesn't say good-bye or tell Lavinia where she is going. Through her actions she is saying to Lavinia, "We're different you and I. You live in your world and I live in mine. You don't understand me, and I don't understand you. There is no common ground."

Children, quite rightly, distrust people who declare their desire for mutual understanding in words but demonstrate nothing but disdain for mutual understanding through their actions.

"I am going to take the train to see Daddy," little Adam tries to tell a friend of his mom's.

Unfortunately, what comes out of his mouth is a tad garbled. "I gonna tay tainsee Daddy!"

It's not always easy to understand a young child's idiolect if you don't know him well. The woman is perplexed. What is the child saying?

"I gonna tay tainsee daddy!" Adam repeats obstinately.

"I don't understand," says the woman. "What do you mean sweetheart?"

"I GONNA TAY TAINSEE DADDY!"

"I'm sorry, sweetheart but I don't understand what you're saying."

Angry, sad and disappointed, Adam realizes he's fighting a losing battle and withdraws.

But was the content of his message really that important? What did Adam want to do with the woman? Did he want to share information, or did he want to share a bit of himself?

Whether she understood or not, the woman could have said, "Oh, that's wonderful! Good for you!"

Or, if the child had looked unhappy, she could have said, "Oh dear, that's awful! I'm so sorry!"

Even if we find the message being conveyed utterly incomprehensible, we can try to understand the feelings behind it, and this is as true for older children and adults as it is for toddlers.

It's easier to talk little children into a frenzy than to understand them without resorting to words. And this is worth remembering if one is not particularly articulate or intellectually gifted – or has a child that doesn't talk much (see little Aron, page 394).

The words intelligence and intellect both come from the Latin verb *intellego*, which means "I understand".

To meet children on common ground is to see them. *To see children is to recognize their significance and joyfully confirm their existence.*

You cannot convince children – or adults – that you are according them the significance they deserve if you literally don't see them.

You acknowledge your child when he walks into a room. You look at him. You look at him when you talk to him and when he talks to you. You acknowledge what the child does – the bad along with the good.

"You were so good in the store. You didn't take any candy off the shelf. I could see you wanted to, but you didn't."

That daily *meeting* is of tremendous importance, both for the infant who is searching for that vital connection and for the teenager who flies by you in the hall on his way to God knows where.

"There you are! Let me look at you! I haven't had a hug today. How are you anyway?"

In Part four of *For the Love of Children*, I explained the importance of *meeting*, particularly during changing phases.

As adults, we know this. When we feel out of sorts, off balance, depressed, confused and insecure, we want other people to care about us, to be kind to us, and to acknowledge that we exist and are important. But we also know that we very quickly shut ourselves up in our own little worlds when we feel down. We think we are so defective as people that there is no way that anyone could like us, since we dislike ourselves as much as we do...

Even older teens express their wish for someone to be around when they get home from school. They are searching for that all-important *encounter*.

YOUR ADULT WORD IS LAW

Parents who pass judgement on their children are entering a minefield. All the positive things you say will be remembered – all the negative ones too.

"What do you think I'll be?" your daughter asks you.

"Hm... I don't really know."

"Come on, you must think something. What do you think I'd be good at?"

"Well, you're really good with kids... maybe you'll be a kindergarten teacher."

Five years later, the same kid announces with some chagrin that she wants to study engineering.

"That's fabulous!" you say. "But why the long face?"

"Well, you said I should be a kindergarten teacher."

You expressed an opinion – just to be friendly and polite – and then forgot about it, but your child interpreted it as a prerequisite for your good regard.

Children are forever plying their parents with questions. They want to know what their parents think about them, their appearance, their future.

I have learned *never to express a negative thought*.

And as for their musings about their future professions or looks or lifestyles, I learned to answer: "You will do just fine, but you have to do it your own way."

One day, a couple of my daughters were sitting talking to a friend of mine, a woman named Monica. They were complaining over the fact that I was devoting so much time to a man I was in love with. Did my friend also think that I was spending too much time with him?

My friend hummed and hawed and did her best to dodge the question.

When Monica had left, my children gave me their version of what she had

580

said about how I was conducting my love life. I was spending way too much time with this person!

Needless to say, I was less than pleased. I called Monica and told her that if she had something to say about me, she could damn well say it to my face. Monica was appalled. She had gotten the impression that the children had thought I was spending too much time with this man, but she had just nodded and bobbed and tried to stay above the fray.

Kids, big and small, ask questions. From the time your children are old enough to talk, you, as a mother or a father, have to understand that kids usually ask questions by making assertions. And whether you like it or not, your pronouncements about your children and what they do carry the authority of Holy Writ.

Children who slander a friend, a parent or a sibling should be contradicted as though you were providing an answer to a question. (I need hardly point out that *you* must never speak ill of anyone your child is attached to!)

Show understanding for your child's criticism of whoever it is, but your job is to provide a solution.

"I understand why you are unhappy with so-and-so for doing such-and-such. I really do. But believe me, it's fixable. You two will find a way to patch things up and everything will turn out for the best."

Things may look bad now, but they won't always be that way. That's your message.

Children get frustrated and need to vent periodically, just like we adults do. But just because kids have to vent sometimes it doesn't mean they are chronically miserable. People have a tendency to jump to conclusions. If a young child says he hates his parents, that doesn't necessarily mean that Child Protection Services should put the boy in foster care. We judge adults by a different standard. Society would hardly advise a husband and wife to file for divorce because they had one argument.

All parents have expectations for their children. It would be strange indeed if they didn't. However, if parental ambitions become excessive, the result can be tragedy.

Sport is an area that is particularly treacherous. Parents can put tremendous pressure on their kids for all the right reasons. Playing a sport keeps a child in shape and off the streets. The kids travel and compete and always have something to occupy their time. With the best will in the world, loving parents are prepared to sacrifice everything... and an investment is made.

Children who do their best and train hard but in the end fail to make the grade will naturally disappoint their parents. The parents gave the children their whole-hearted support. They invested time, money and effort – and their investment did not bear fruit.

A not insignificant number of children who never managed to achieve super star status have destroyed their lives through drug abuse and criminality.

I heard of one young man who was being groomed to take over the family business. Rather than admit to his parents that he had made a complete hash of his studies and failed all his exams, he decided to poison them.

Children who cause their parents disappointment regard themselves as not really fit to live. After all, parents take care of their offspring. They provide them with protection and leadership. Day and night they work to make the children fully-fledged members of the flock so that one day they can leave and live dignified, productive lives. Then the child realizes that he is never going to be a fully-fledged member of the flock. He just doesn't have what it takes. And the parents' disappointment, whether it is expressed or not, becomes the child's. The child bitterly brands himself a failure and gives up. The strong survive and the weak die. It's the way of the world.

You, as a mother or father, have expectations, hopes and ambitions for your child. That is as natural as it is inevitable. But try to turn these expectations into joy for what is. Don't let them sour into disappointment over what isn't. Support, encourage, but be open to everything.

"Things change. A lot can happen in the next year or so. You don't have to decide anything now. It's your life and you decide over it. You'll be fine, but you have to live your life in your own way, and I will always support you in that."

As far as sport is concerned, or any activity that is going to require an investment from you, look before you leap. Are you prepared to sacrifice time, money and effort, and then be philosophical if your children decide that a particular sport is not for them?

My rule was one recreational activity per term, but once my children committed to something, they had to see the term out. This meant that my *children* were responsible for their commitments.

THE VOICE OF CONVICTION

If you, as a mother or father, are going to provide leadership, make decisions and set limits, you have to know where you stand.

Children are singularly adept at spotting inconsistency. Your child expects you to shoulder your responsibilities as protector and leader – even if you have never made a decision of any importance in your life.

Naturally, passing the buck and asking someone else to make all the tough decisions is tempting. If, in my book, I could simply decree that all ten-year-olds shall have an allowance of five dollars a week, all twelve-year-olds shall be home by 8.00 pm, and no one under the age of eighteen shall watch more than seven hours of television a week, a lot of parents would heave a sigh of relief. But that is not going to happen.

There are parent meetings, as we all know, where everyone tries to find some common ground, and there is nothing wrong with a support network. When the children hit their moms or dads with the perennial refrain "But everyone else does!", the parents can reply, "Oh, no they don't!"

The only problem is that *your personal convictions* can get lost in the shuffle. You still have to know where *you* stand on certain issues, have the courage of your convictions and demand that your child respect those convictions.

What are you going to do if your child violates a generally accepted norm? You can call another parents' meeting – but that puts the child's dignity at risk (remember the wastebasket incident and the teacher's reaction on p. 574).

There is a voice within you, a voice that tells you what is right and wrong, what you believe in and don't believe in, what you want and what you don't want. That voice can be drowned out by common sense (so called), expertise, admonitions, fear and general insecurity, but it's always there. It's the voice of your own conviction. Listening to it means living by it as far as you can.

It seems perfectly obvious to me that children listen for and listen to this parental voice – this voice of conviction that transcends circumstances and words, subterfuge and insecurity, seemingly airtight arguments and strained "common sense". This voice transcends everything that hides the truth.

Who are you?
What do you believe?
What do you really want?

"I don't want to visit daddy," says little Anthony bitterly.
"Why not?" Mom wonders.
"Because all he does is study."
"He does?"

"Yeah, study, study, study," sighs Anthony and rolls his eyes.

Anthony's mother is concerned and gives Dad a call. Doesn't he have time for the boy when he visits? According to Anthony, all he does is study.

"But I never so much as open a book when he's there!" says Dad. "How can he say something like that?"

What Anthony "hears" when he visits his father is that Dad *wants* to study – and has a bad conscience because he doesn't. Dad's desire to put himself at his son's disposal is not authentic. And it never will be as long as there is something else that he deep down wants to do.

He would serve both himself and his son better if he were honest enough to give his desire to study the respect it deserves and say to his son, "I'm going to study now. You do your own thing, and then we will go out," or whatever it is that's on the agenda once business is out of the way.

But this particular father is a so called Weekend Dad, and he feels he should put his entire existence to one side so he can devote himself to Anthony – with the apparently paradoxical result that Anthony doesn't want to have anything to do with him.

This is one of many examples that show how even infants can put their parents on the spot to find out how they really feel about things.

Ben and Karen were an item and Karen became pregnant. That wasn't what Ben really had in mind, but Karen was adamant about keeping the baby, and anyway they had been living together for so long that it was probably time to get married anyway. Or so Karen reasoned.

Ben hummed and hawed, but eventually the date was set. Ben had a panic attack. It was the end of the world as he knew it. Now he would be just another married drone and a father to boot.

"Oh, sweet Lord," he said to himself. "How am I going to get out of this?"

Ben bit the bullet and married Karen. But on the very day of the wedding, he had a tête-à-tête with a former girlfriend.

Eventually the baby was born. From day one, the baby was a problem. She had colic, exotic skin rashes, inexplicable fevers, sleep problems, allergies; the list went on and on. There was so much wrong with this kid that Ben was on first-name terms with the staff at every children's clinic in town. There was even talk of the child being developmentally handicapped or afflicted with a disease that was equally serious.

In the end, the sleepless nights and the worry took their toll on them both, so much so that Ben decided to take a leave of absence from his job. *Then* the baby was fine.

As soon as Ben went back to work, however, the baby's problems returned with a vengeance. The doctors put their heads together and dispensed their wisdom. Ben trudged wearily to GPs, then to specialists, then to hospitals and then back to GPs again. If referrals were ten-dollar bills, he would have been a very rich man. Worry piled on worry.

Until Ben took a vacation.

Then the baby was fine.

So it was.

Ben had not had the time for assignations with former girlfriends since the baby was born. He hadn't had time to go drinking with his male friends either. He went to work and came home. That was his life. He certainly never had the chance to forget he was a father!

I would argue that it was the baby that drew him home. She forced him to embrace the life he had chosen and the baby he had sired. She made sure that her dad thought about her, worried about her and spent as much time at home as he could. But she never got so sick that she had to be put in hospital. If she had, someone other than her parents (who were by now joined at the hip because of all the trials and tribulations their daughter had put them through) would have had to take care of her...

Ben, I'm sure, did a great job of being a father.

We can't always live the way we would like. But through their actions, children stubbornly persist in sending their parents the following message: *Either take pride in the way you live your life or change it.*

"Going out again?" asks a somewhat hostile father as his son hurries by him on his way out the door. "You think I ever have any fun?"

"That's not my problem!" replies an equally hostile teenage son.

"Go out and have fun. Don't worry about me," says an unhappy mother as she puts her hands to her temples. "It's only a migraine."

"Do you have a problem with me going out?" William asks his mother. "Louise and I thought we would go to the movies."

The mother starts to cry.

"Are you going to be all right by yourself?" William asks.

"Oh yes, I'll be fine. I just get lonely sometimes."

When he gets home, William finds a freshly ironed shirt on his bed with a note. "Wear this the next time you take Louise out. You look so handsome in it."

A visible enemy can be fought, but guilt is insidious. Fighting with people who don't take pride in the way they live their lives is like punching the air.

The teenage boy's father can't very well say, "You're not going anywhere. You are going to stay home and be miserable like me. If I don't have any fun, you aren't going to either, so wipe that smirk off your face."

And William's mother can hardly say, "I'm lonely, bitter and afraid. I hope everything goes to hell in a hand basket for you and Louise because it sure has for me!"

Would it be the truth? Not really. Deep down, parents don't begrudge their kids fun and happiness, but dissatisfaction with life leaves its mark, and since misery loves company, it spills over onto other people.

"What do you think is the one thing that parents should never do to their children?" I asked my thirteen-year-old daughter. She thought for a long time before she answered.

"They should never dump their emotional problems on their kids," she answered. "Kids can't help it if their parents are unhappy," she continued.

"That's the most important thing?" I asked.

"Yes," she replied.

These parents we have described have to decide whether or not to let their kids go out. They have to see beyond their own unhappiness and look deep into their own souls. What do they really feel?

They can react in one of two ways. Either: "I don't begrudge my children some fun. It's not their responsibility to solve my problems. Only I can do that."

Or: "I don't want to be alone tonight. I want us to be together this evening. I really need it. I'll ask my son or daughter to stay home so I can talk to someone about what's on my mind."

Whatever you say or do must reflect your own inner truth. Our lives are our own, and our truth is our own.

However, human beings are indolent and occasionally cowardly animals, and if parents see an opportunity to manipulate someone else – like their children – into taking the fall for their own frustrations, they sometimes take it. Thus, they avoid having to listen to that oh so demanding inner voice, avoid rolling up their sleeves and changing the things about their lives that they don't like.

When I was sixteen, I wanted to save the world – or at least my mother, with whom I was visiting at the time. She was complaining about the dishes one day.

"Don't do anything you don't like," I said. "Human beings shouldn't do things they don't like. It's wrong."

"Really? I don't *like* doing dishes, but if I don't do them, who will? You?"

I thought she was numbingly petty-minded and limited. I was reading Sartre at the time, so I of course knew everything. Applying existentialism to washing dishes was problematic. But is it really?

If I think doing dishes is necessary, I should have the courage of my convictions and do what has to be done with a smile on my face and a song in my heart.

If I don't think doing dishes is necessary, what stops me from just leaving them in the sink? Dirty dishes don't go anywhere of course, but if I am going to give my convictions the respect they deserve, maybe I can do something for someone else and have them do the dishes in return. I can also wait out my distaste for doing dishes. I might change my mind and get the urge to do the dishes later. I could also invest in a dishwasher. I'd have to come up with some money, but I could prioritize. I could forego a new sofa, a winter coat or a vacation.

Children are good at putting us on the spot. What do we want *really*?

Whether you like the idea or not, you are the authority figure for your child (remember the driving instructor on pages 534–536). As such, you have to be confident – or at least look as though you are. You have to be able to take pride in your life, your actions and the values you believe in – and that extends to dishes.

"You're never here," says little Daniel to his mother, who is taking a course. "I don't want you to go! I want you to stay here!" he whines.

His mother thinks hard. Should she drop out of her course? It wouldn't be difficult. All she has to do is not show up. Does she *want* to drop out? No, she doesn't. If she didn't want to take the course, she wouldn't have registered for it. Does she *have* to take the course? No, the course has nothing to do with her job.

So why is she going? Because she wants to. But is that a good enough reason if her son wants her to stay home? Good mother that she is, guilt kicks in. If Daniel wants her to stay home, and she wants to take her course, why do her wishes carry more weight than Daniel's?

Daniel's mother creates a little scenario in her head. Suppose she decided the course wasn't really that important and stayed home. She imagines herself sitting on the edge of Daniel's bed and telling him with or without words, "OK, you win. I'm staying home, even though I really wanted to take that course." The scenario is not a pleasant one. She knows she would not be very happy that evening.

So what does it all mean? She is beset with conflicting emotions. Does Daniel mean so little to her that she leaves him, even though he asks her to stay? Does her course mean more to her than her child?

If she stays home, she would certainly not be the first woman to bow to her young child's wishes. On the other hand, if she goes, she would certainly not be the first woman to wonder if she were doing the right thing. (She can still hear Daniel crying when she's half way down the street.)

In my opinion (and actually in little Daniel's too), if she really wants to go, she should. Of course Daniel would like her to stay home, *but only if she wants to*.

If she stays home against her will, Daniel would probably not be very nice to her. He would either turn his back on her, literally and figuratively, and his mother would wonder why on earth she let herself get talked into staying home, or he would place other demands on her, which over time would grow evermore capricious and unreasonable. Why? To force her to have the courage of her convictions and to take pride in who she is and what she does. To force her to shoulder her responsibility as a leader and role model.

Daniel cannot respect his mother if his mother does not respect herself. Nor will Daniel be able to respect himself as an adult if his mother, his role model, doesn't comport herself like a self-respecting adult.

Daniel's protests are really a question. "Do you really want to take this course?"

He is trying to figure out a norm. "Are people supposed to do what they want?"

And just for good measure, he poses another question. "Are people supposed to do what they want, even though other people don't like it?"

And his mother answers him. "If you really believe in what you're doing, you should do it, even though other people don't like it."

That Daniel's protests aren't an expression of what he really wants is demonstrated by his behavior if his mother stays home against her will. He might seem content (or at least neutral) for the moment, but the next time there is any talk of his mother going anywhere without him, the scene will be repeated. Daniel got what he wanted – or so it seemed – but he won't reward his mother with calm acceptance if she leaves him again. On the contrary, he will pose the same question because no one gave him an answer when he asked the first time.

More precisely, Daniel had to content himself with the wrong answer: "Even if you really believe in what you're doing, don't do it if other people don't like it."

Daniel wants his mother to be a good leader, a free leader who is honest with herself (and therefore with her son). He is searching for a role model he can depend on. Daniel doesn't want his mother to work against her own best interests or allow herself to be pushed around. He wants her to walk tall and believe in herself. He wants her to have the courage of her convictions so that he can too – at first vicariously through her and then, when he has acquired enough life experience, on his own.

If his mother stays home, it must be because she really wants to. She must be able to say to herself and to Daniel, "I don't really care about the course. It's actually not that interesting. I was going to drop out anyway. I'd much rather stay home and do something fun with Daniel." And she has to mean it. Her authenticity will not be lost on Daniel.

If she decides to go, she must have the courage to stand by her decision, courage which, through his mother's example, Daniel will one day claim as his own.

She must be able to say, "No, sweetheart, today is Thursday, and I am going to class. It's not true that I am never around. I am only gone when I really want to be or really have to be. And tonight, I really want to be. So why don't you do something that you think is fun, and we'll see each other when I get home."

"No! You have to stay home! You can't go!" we can imagine Daniel screaming.

"I can and I am. I'll see you when I get home." Daniel's screams can be heard half way down the street. He is asking a question. Does his mother really believe in what she is doing?

But in all likelihood, he will only react this way once because he will get the answer to his question the first time around. More to the point, he will be *content* with the answer he has been given.

A child's reaction – satisfaction or dissatisfaction – will indicate whether the answer was right or wrong. Satisfaction ensues the moment you, as a mother or father, express in word and deed the courage of your convictions and act in accordance with what you genuinely believe to be right.

It's the children who bear the love, and they seek it stubbornly in all of us.

"If I had children," said a friend of mine, "I'd either be happy and affectionate when I was around them or I'd be in a frothing rage."

I laughed and had to admit he was right. Affection and joy, or (controlled) rage – it's a choice that works for me too. But *irritation* is not an option.

As a writer, I've learned the value of time out. If you sit on a hard chair for long enough, you get a sore butt. Irritation is the existential equivalent of a sore butt. It's low-grade pain that infects and corrodes your daily life, it causes you to make mountains out of molehills, and in the end it gets you absolutely nowhere. Its only purpose is to make happiness impossible.

You *can* take time out. Lock yourself in your bedroom for ten minutes. Have a lie down. Just sit quietly for a while with your eyes closed.

You can and should say to your children, "I need time out. I'll be with you in a minute."

Children will always go along with whatever is necessary for adults.

For better or worse.

MAN'S ONLY DUTY IS TO BE HAPPY.

Albert Camus

CHILDREN'S VIOLENCE

Children use violence. They use it to find things out, to guard their territory, to get respect, to exact revenge, to defend themselves and to break the cycle of powerlessness.

Even children who have never been the victims of violence can start using violence early. They bite, they shove and they slap. They start using implements as weapons at around three. They rarely, if ever, have evil intent, but young children act (and react) to promote their own interests. A one-year-old explores the world, people, animals and things by trying to taste them. A three-year-old who bangs his younger colleague on the head with a plastic hammer enjoys the resulting sound. It's fun!

But regardless of intent, children who behave in a way that endangers or might endanger others must immediately be dissuaded.

You can err on the side of tact and regard the first assault as an accident.

"Oh, did he fall? Then you've got to give him a hug."

"Whoops! Did you bite her? Kiss it better."

Repeated provocations from a brutal little street fighter must be met with unequivocal opposition in both word and deed.

Here it is not the child who is being condemned – "Naughty, naughty!" – but the behavior is. Violence is not acceptable behavior, and ostracism will be the consequence if the child persists.

"You can't do that, you mustn't do that."

And this is to be followed by *a way out,* by which I mean clear instructions that juxtapose acceptable behavior to unacceptable behavior:

"You don't hit. You hug people. That's what you do."

The hugging makes peace.

The perpetrator is not keen at first, but I usually persist and wrap the young fighter's arms around the victim and hold the two of them close to each other for a good little while. (Watch out, so that the little warrior doesn't grab the chance to bite the hurt party during the hug!)

Children who are encouraged – through words *and* actions – to hug each other after a fight will soon do it of their own free will. It's rather touching to see a young child who has knocked his companion off his feet rush over to his crying victim and put his arms around the unhappy one.

The habit of hugging after a fight gives children a rule of thumb for making things right again. They don't just remain standing there, ashamed.

I enforce this hugging-after-discord rule with children until they are well into their teens.

Unfortunately, it is all too common that peaceful children fall victim to bullies when they start school.

If you are faced with this situation, advise your child to ignore the bullies as best he can.

"Don't look at them, walk away and make like you don't care about or even notice what they do. Hopefully, they'll get bored with you and find someone else to bug that pays off better. Try not to be sad. And try to be kind to others yourself. Stick to nicer playmates and be really good to them."

You must, as must we all, teach children, big and small, that violence should be met with love – or an imitation thereof.

"I'm not saying you should love people who make you sad or frighten you, but for your own sake avoid them. When you get older, you will be able to treat people who behave like that with kindness and sympathy. That's what disarms them. Because inside every violent, hateful person there is a lost, sad, frightened soul."

Just as important, if you come to the conclusion that the bullying is becoming chronic, you must shoulder your parental responsibilities. Go to the principal and make sure the school is aware of the problem. If the school authorities can't or won't solve it, change schools. There's no law that says a child has to remain in a school where he/she is obviously suffering.

The powers that be may try to dissuade you with the argument that the problem lies with the child, not the school, and that the problem will follow your child wherever he goes. I can assure you that this is not true. Stand firm. You would never leave a baby or a toddler in the care of an abusive babysitter, so don't leave an older child in an abusive school environment.

People who run day care centers out of their own homes often agonize over violence. A new arrival exhibits violent behavior, and more often than not it's the caregiver's own child who is being harassed.

Day care providers know all to well that little fighters are often unhappy. Their sympathy for the child gets the better of their common sense. They hesitate to intervene and point out the error in the child's ways because they know that it is the violent children that need love and understanding the most. Nevertheless, day care providers must take a stand against violent behavior. Children have been known to strangle, suffocate and stomp other children to death. Terrible things have happened and serious accidents occur every day, not least in day care centers.

It may be necessary to take the little offender aside and remonstrate.

"You are fighting. I have told you to stop. You keep fighting all the same. So this is how it's going to be. Either we fight in this house, or we don't fight. You decide. If you think we should fight, remember this. I can fight a lot better than you can. I'm bigger than you, I'm stronger than you, and I can hit a lot harder than you can. So if you want us to fight in this house, just say the word, and I will go fighting!"

Children who continue to provoke after a declaration like that are few and far between, but naturally they exist. If the violence persists, you have to show the offender that you mean business. That doesn't mean you actually have to become violent yourself. Just take a firm hold on the child's chin and look him right in the eye.

"If you want *me* to stay calm, you'd better stay calm too!" Then you turn your back on the child without trying to make up or giving the child the opportunity to object.

The child will get the message, not just because of the threat, but because you, an adult, have shown that you are made of the same stuff the child is and that you have violent impulses too – but you refrain from acting on them. This indicates that you don't condemn yourself. What you do condemn is *violent behavior* in yourself.

The child can take your message to heart without feeling that he is being condemned as a person.

This may seem paradoxical, but the fact is that taking such an approach gives the child confidence. He feels he is understood.

An aggressive little six-year-old named Agathe once visited me with her father. I had three younger children in the house, ranging in age from two months to two and a half years. Agathe immediately began attacking them in various ways.

Agathe's dad would periodically tell his daughter to calm down, but he didn't see to it that Agathe took his exhortations seriously. He buried himself in his newspaper, while I followed Agathe around with my heart in my throat. Agathe had armed herself with a carving knife she had found in the kitchen and an extension cable she had pulled out of the wall. I was afraid she might actually wrap the cord around one of my children's throats and pull it tight. The last straw came when she took my two month-old out of her cradle and walked towards the balcony door – we lived on the eighth floor – loudly announcing to all and sundry that she was going to toss the baby over the railing because the baby was so ridiculous.

I took the baby away from her and told her to follow me out into the kitchen. Behind closed doors, I put my hands around her neck and said, "If you don't behave yourself sweetie, I'm going to wring your neck. You hear me?"

Agathe realized that I was serious. At least she thought I was. She ran screaming to her dad for protection. But the interesting thing is that she didn't tell his father what I had said to her. Behind her screaming and yelling, she was actually relieved. And she didn't harass my babies anymore.

This little girl was at war with just about everything. I knew her background, and it was tragic. A sad life, however, is not a carte blanche to behave like a barbarian. We all carry baggage, and we all have reasons for what we do. But the fact that I might empathize with another human being's pain does not mean I have to excuse contemptible behavior.

Children should of course be given an outlet for their pain, their feelings of powerlessness, their bitterness, but *not by hurting others* or by hurting themselves.

Children, like adults, have to realize that you fight with words, not with fists. They have to learn that, regardless of the reason, if they must hit something, it had better be a wall not a person. It's that simple.

And it is our responsibility as adults to teach them, through our words and actions, from day one.

Logically, this means that we can't supply young children (or not so young ones) with movies and computer games that glorify murder.

If there's a particularly violent fight in a TV program don't hesitate to cover your child's eyes. If protests ensue, offer your child a choice: accept the censorship or the TV is turned off.

It is my heartfelt conviction that access to computers and the internet should be both *limited and monitored*.

I also think that children should not be given toy weapons of any kind.

Some things never change. Violence is a fact of life. It always has been and it always will be. But we don't need to actively seek violence out. We don't need to open the door to the nursery and invite it in!

IN OUR HEARTS WE CRY

It happened again. A five-year-old little girl was murdered by her playmates. According to police, three six-year-old boys jumped up and down on her until she stopped screaming and then finished her off with a rock.

"This is one terrible but single incident," a psychotherapist commented.

"I've never seen a case involving such excessive violence," said a child psychologist. "It is highly unusual."

But is it?

Violence among children has increased dramatically since the 1980s, and there is no sign of the trend turning.

So far, the USA is in the lead. There was one case of a couple of ten-year-olds throwing a five-year-old from a fourteenth floor balcony because he refused to steal candy for them from the local convenience store.

There was another in which a handicapped six-year-old boy lost his life because he didn't want to share his potato chips.

And what did little Jamie Bulger, the two-year-old British boy, do to deserve his fate? His murderers, children themselves, found Jamie's screaming irritating. They just "felt like" bombarding him with bricks and putting his broken little body on the railroad tracks. Shortly thereafter, a fifteen-year-old, "inspired" by Jamie's murder strangled a six-year-old.

Children murder children. That's what we have to learn to live with.

Society of course blames the parents. They must be alcoholics and responsibility dysfunctional. At the very least, they are guilty of not providing adequate supervision. Pious accusations are levelled against the film and computer game violence, which everyone claims to despise but no one attempts to curb.

If nothing else, we sentimentally bemoan the omnipresence of evil. Human beings are just bad through and through.

But in our hearts we cry. Children were always good. Children were innocent. Children never had any evil intent. Children are born pure. They cannot be burdened with any responsibility, because they shouldn't have to take responsibility; we adults are the ones who should take responsibility for them.

And that is exactly what we have done. More accurately, that is what we have *neglected* to do.

We have abandoned our children. We don't live with them anymore. We fob them off on each other and on other people. Child rearing is carried out by a collective security firm employed by society.

We parents are a part of it. The minute we hand over our parental responsibility – our child rearing responsibility – to others, we reduce ourselves to rent-a-cops.

The security company's job is making sure the children don't disappear. Preferably, it should also make sure that the kids don't kill each other. A crash weekend course in murder prevention has only recently become part of the training.

"Where were the adults?" asked the child psychologist when the five-year-old was murdered.

The security guards were looking the other way or on coffee break. They weren't around at that moment.

What we find even more horrifying is that children who kill don't seem to realize what they have done. They show no remorse, no empathy. They only show emotion when they realize they are going to have to pay for what they have done.

They seem to be devoid of inhibitions when they beat playmates or toddlers or infants to death. No warning bells go off in their brains. No failsafe mechanisms kick in. No inner voice says, "Stop! Don't hit people! Don't hurt people!"

But how many parents have said these words to their young children over the last three or four decades?

How many parents have been physically present when those words needed to be said?

How many parents have been around to grasp the hand that is hitting and prevent it from hitting again?

How many parents have implacably taught the owner of the hand that hits to gently stroke instead, so that a kind caress replaced the violent touch?

How many parents have nurtured the implantation of *good inhibitions*?

"Day care takes care of all that," say the parents.

"The parents take care of all that," says the day care center.

The buck is passed to the schools, to the social services and to society. In the middle of all this buck-passing stand our children – children who have basically been told to go away and raise themselves, children who have been consigned to a Darwinian sandbox.

Someone has to live with children while they are little.

When I say "live with", I don't mean "look after" or "be with" or "supervise". I mean LIVE WITH because nothing less will do.

It is only by making children a part of our lives in our daily struggle for survival that we can fulfil our task as parents. It is in the midst of this struggle that we teach our children how to live with other people. It is here we teach them to cooperate with other people without hurting them and without losing themselves so that they can eventually live rewarding lives on their own.

Every mammal knows this. The young walk alongside their parents in the common struggle for survival to learn how to live in the world and live well.

But human beings have created a new set of rules. When they go out into the forest to hunt, their young are placed in an enclosed pasture.

"You can't come with me, little children, but I'll be back as soon as I'm done ensuring our survival for today. Now, have great fun! You won't kill each other, will you?"

It is only by sharing in this struggle for survival that young children learn to be moral, considerate, helpful and empathetic. They don't learn these things in the sandbox, no matter how well it is designed.

It is only by sharing the trials and tribulations of everyday life that people learn to depend on each other practically and concretely. This mutual dependence is the soil in which deep relationships germinate and flourish. And deep relationships are what take us beyond the superficial.

Superficial relationships produce superficial, emotionally cold people: If your neighbors get on your nerves, so kill them. Who cares?

Someone has to live with children when they are little.

VENI
VIDI
VICI
The Pill

PROBLEMS? FOOD

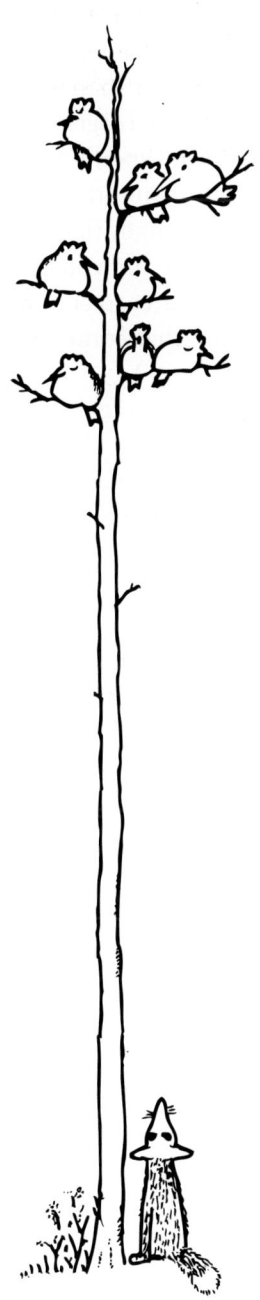

No child has ever starved to death voluntarily. There is a significant amount of manipulation behind the rather bizarre, sugar-laden food culture that so dominates the Western world. Food, its production, distribution and sale, is hardly a small-scale enterprise. Oceans of money flow into the coffers of the food industry, and, as we all know, dieting off the surplus that collects on our bodies isn't cheap either. They get you coming and going.

There are many ways of separating people from their hard earned cash. Children are taught to consume rather than to eat. Young children must be "stimulated" to eat with the aid of added sugar in meals and child-friendly presentation, complete with clowns and cuddly animals on the cups and plates. The aim is to ensure that children at an early age embrace a food culture that is less than healthy. They are also taught that food represents not only survival, but also friends, fun, comfort and conspicuous consumption...

Eating is one of life's great pleasures to be sure. But the greatest pleasure of all is the feeling of satisfaction that comes when real *hunger* is stilled.

Without real hunger, there can be no real satisfaction. If a child is never really hungry, that feeling of satisfaction has to be contrived somehow.

Hunger has disappeared from western culture. People just don't get hungry anymore. We get "peckish", and that peckishness has to be satisfied with a burger, a donut or a candy bar. As a result, portions served at meals today have changed. They are rich in protein and therefore expensive. When I was a child, a meal consisting of a chicken leg and seven potatoes was the norm. Nowadays, a typical meal consists of half a chicken and two potatoes.

Very young children have not yet discovered all the other things food stands for today. They still think food is a means to survive. A hungry child eats whatever is put in front of him and doesn't care whether his bib matches his cup.

Food problems occur when children no longer feel hungry. Children who are already full when they sit down at the table aren't going to pay much attention to the meal. No matter how much the cook begs and pleads, coaxes and "stimulates", the kids won't eat. It's hunger that makes the difference.

But no matter how empty those little stomachs are, you can't expect your child to eat as much as you do.

In "Something about personality" in Part four of *For the Love of Children* different body types were discussed. The little asparagus – the ectomorph – by and large enjoys excellent health, but it is usually children with this body type that are branded as hunger strikers.

The asparagus may look a little frail, but he isn't. The asparagus is relatively uninterested in food and can stay that way until he is a teenager. The asparagus is a kid who "eats like a bird".

600

Let's look at what little Michael, three years old, eats in a typical day – a day on which his mother claims "he barely eats a thing".

In the morning, he gets a serving of Pablum. He barely eats half of it.

A few hours later he eats half a small sandwich. He is given a glass of juice to wash it down, but he leaves half of it.

Later on in the morning, he is given an apple, but he only takes a few bites. All told, he eats perhaps a quarter of it.

Then comes a lunch of wieners, potatoes and peas. Michael eats one potato, half a wiener, and a spoonful of peas.

He didn't want anything to drink at lunch, but in the afternoon he gets a glass of milk, which he almost finishes, and three crackers.

A little later, when he's out for his walk, he gets a popsicle.

Evening falls and it's dinnertime. Michael eats two meatballs and two level tablespoons of mashed potatoes, and drinks half a glass of milk. He eats half a pancake for dessert. And that's dinner.

When it's time for bed, he gets a bottle and drinks two deciliters of rosehip soup.

Michael weighs fifteen kilograms. His mother weighs sixty, which means she is four times heavier. Would she survive on the following diet?

• Early morning:

Two bowls of Pablum

Two sandwiches and two glasses of juice

• Late morning:

An apple

• Lunch:

Two wieners, four potatoes, four tablespoons of peas

• Afternoon:

Four glasses of milk

Twelve crackers

Four popsicles

• Dinner:

Eight meatballs

Eight tablespoons of mashed potatoes

Two pancakes

Two glasses of milk

• Evening:

Almost a liter of rosehip soup.

She would definitely survive on such a diet and may even put weight on!

I had food problems with one of my children in the days when I didn't know any better.

This little baby, who had the lowest birth weight of all my children, ate like a horse. I remember visiting friends when she was nine months old and my hosts were wide-eyed in disbelief. The baby's plate was piled high with food: a large baby food jar with ham and vegetables, a small mountain of mashed potatoes and a whole jar of puréed vegetables. She practically inhaled it.

A few months later, her eating habits had gone from the gluttonous to the ascetic. During her second year, every meal was a pitched battle. At the time, I didn't have the experience to realize that her diminished appetite was nothing to worry about.

This child turned out to be an asparagus, a typical ectomorph. (Nowadays, she is back to loving her food!)

Eating problems in my family came to an abrupt end when we moved abroad. The six months my children and I spent in a tiny village in Egypt exposed me to a way of life that was light years away from what I was used to. It forced me to re-evaluate things I had taken for granted my whole life.

In this village, where life hadn't changed much since the Middle Ages, people ate three times a day. Breakfast was served around seven and consisted of a thin piece of flatbread with a spoonful of fried mixed vegetables instead of butter. The adults drank black tea with sugar, and the children drank water.

Lunch was served five hours later at one o'clock. Nothing was consumed between meals. Even water was in short supply, since it had to be fetched from a well on the outskirts of the village.

During that last hour, between twelve and one, our Swedish stomachs were rumbling loudly enough for the whole village to hear…

Rice was the mainstay of the midday meal. The mother of the house (who had eight children) served up the rice on everyone's plate in generous but carefully measured portions. The rice was accompanied by a sauce made from onions and tomatoes, to which was added whatever was available: peas, carrots or nothing. Once a week, twice if we were lucky, we might get a few scraps of stringy meat swimming in fat.

After lunch we were almost delirious. We were literally "high". No buzz from alcohol or anything else comes close to making human beings feel as euphoric as when real hunger is satisfied.

The evening meal was at six. The last hour before dinner was as hard to bear as the last hour before lunch. For dinner we were served the leftovers from lunch and a piece of flatbread each. The rice was cold but that didn't make it any less divine. If the buffalo cow had milk we could sometimes break our bread into the warm milk and eat the mixture with a spoon. Occasionally, dessert was offered in the form of one or two oranges or a couple of small, sweet bananas apiece.

Before coming to Egypt, I had never really understood what the words *hungry* and *full* meant. It was with stunned disbelief that I watched my picky Swedish children fill their faces with cold, greasy meat scraps and equally cold rice, delicacies they wouldn't have touched with rubber gloves and a barge pole at home.

When we got back to Sweden, we ate ourselves silly, ecstatic that we could again eat as much as we wanted of whatever we wanted, whenever we wanted. But by the third day already we were back in the familiar rut: no real hunger, no real satisfaction, and no real joy in eating…

Again, like before, we were left with that stubborn craving for something that was even tastier, more exciting, easier to swallow, more expensive and quicker to prepare.

I made a resolution to try to find a happy medium, and so I did. We stuck to it from then on.

Food is a big thing, a vital thing. Food is essential for life itself – but food is not self-evident. Food should never be taken for granted. This was the attitude I wanted to instil in my children.

The food supply is limited. What we have has to feed all of us. You can't just run to the store and buy more and more.

Milk is not water. If you're thirsty, quench your thirst with water.

Fruit is not free. Fruit is no impulse snack between meals. It is real food and should be regarded as such.

Meals are not religious services, but they become so if everyone is hungry enough. Conversation stops automatically as the food is put on the table – only to reach withering heights after the meal when everyone is full and feels blessed because of it.

Meals should not be trivialized. To be able to eat – and thereby survive – is something we should rejoice over and be thankful for. But without good wholesome hunger, all that is impossible. Without good wholesome hunger, there will always be food problems.

With good wholesome hunger, and its attendant satisfaction, all food problems are eliminated at a stroke.

Such hunger doesn't have time to develop if we eat between meals, which means more frequently than approximately every four hours. Even moderate snacking can throw the rhythm that human beings seek from early infancy out of sync.

Obviously, once the meal is over, any remaining food should be put away. (See below.)

Knives and forks are not the easiest things to eat with. Nor are chopsticks. As with potty training – or the lack of it – all you should do is give the child the tools (the potty or the knife and fork), and then sit back and watch as he/she learns to use them. The skills will come!

Little two-year-olds, for example, already know that they are supposed to sit at the table until they have finished eating because that is what the grown-ups do. But where does it say that they must always and only sit at the table until they have finished eating? (Remember the account of the stove researcher, who knows how to use a stove, but not *exclusively* for what it was designed for!)

Five-year-olds know how to use a knife and fork very elegantly, but they are not above stuffing food into their mouth with their fingers.

Table manners will come in their own good time. You don't have to nurture them along. Setting a good example is more important than constantly intervening. Take a tolerant and positive attitude and your patience will pay off.

A common complaint about little people is that they are constantly leaving the table to engage in various activities. Even if you had the patience of a saint, it would start to get on your nerves after a while.

One year old Ollie is placed in his highchair and eats three spoonfuls of his dinner. He then hits upon the idea of turning around in his chair, standing up and balancing himself precariously on the seat. Or he tries to escape from the highchair altogether.

Two years old Tootsie leaves the table and sits down somewhere to play. At your request, she obediently comes back to the table and eats another spoonful of her meal – and then returns to her projects on the floor.

Three years old Tim pushes his plate away, dumps his milk on the floor, braces his legs against the table, pushes his chair out and says, "Bad Mommy!" Or he smiles sweetly and "drops" his spoon fifteen times.

Four year old Frances decides she wants to utilize what is in the fridge and the larder to plan the menu herself. She disappears from the table, is out of your sight and is nowhere to be found.

Five years old Fredrick eats all the peas, thinks the rest of the food on the plate is yucky, gets a stomach ache, needs to throw up, but nothing comes.

You probably can make up a list of your own... Much of it looks funny when written down but is not nearly so amusing to cope with in your own reality.

It's not really fair to demand table manners before your child turns five. And then you can exploit the fact that your little one is going through "The Lily of Peace" stage, and your parental word is law.

Unfortunately, the same child can behave appallingly at the table when he turns six (see the chapter on the six-year-old in Part four of *For the Love of Children*).

If you feel you can't stand it anymore, don't. Lay down the law: "Either you behave like a human being at the table, or you eat by yourself."

By this you are not making threats or meting out punishment. You are simply pointing out the consequences (admittedly unpleasant for all concerned) of a certain kind of behavior. If the child is behaving unacceptably, you should not have to put up with it.

But as long as little children aren't hurting anyone, there is nothing wrong with permitting them to engage in their unacceptable behavior by themselves.

Even if you can't demand that your child master the intricacies of etiquette before he turns five, you can of course express your appreciation when the little angel makes an effort.

A parallel can be drawn with (non-existent) potty training. If your little one manages to use the potty properly, that's wonderful. But the child has not done anything altruistic or clever. Managing one's bodily wastes is something that all human beings are expected to do. It's the same with eating. If a child eats properly, or more accurately in the way that the adults in the prevailing culture *think* a child should eat, then the child is eating "properly". However, the child is not exhibiting a talent that merits praise. Chewing with one's mouth closed, for example, is not the same as doing a good deed.

Hunger is still the best guarantee of good table manners.

Hungry young children sit still at the table and eat neatly – even if they do eat with their fingers – and don't spill, dribble or talk. Moderately hungry young children eat what they feel like and then play with the food rather than eat it. Food is more fun than a lot of toys. There are so many interesting consistencies, tempting colors and fascinating mixings and combinations. The possibilities are endless...

If watching your child play with the food is more than you can bear, just lift the child down, say thank you for the food on the little one's behalf and clear the table.

And try to make sure your child works up a better appetite before the next meal!

If on the other hand it doesn't bother you, let your child play – it will do no harm. Table manners will come automatically in their own good time.

As you know, how adults react to little people at the dining table is very individual. You won't know your own limits until you have been exposed to mealtimes with children on a daily basis for a while. When your patience is exhausted, act accordingly. It's the only way to communicate your limits to your child.

Paul, eleven months, is being fed on his dad's knee. Paul is in a contrary mood. He squirms, spits the food out, turns his head away and refuses to open his mouth.

Dad is patient and uses every trick he knows to get Paul to eat. "Here comes the airplane, brrrrummmm... Right into the mouth!"

When mealtimes draw out for one, sometimes one and a half hours however, Dad runs out of patience. He lifts Paul into his highchair and wedges him in with small cushions front and back, since the boy still sits a little unsteadily, and leaves him to his own devices.

The food is interesting. Paul puts his little fist into it, while Dad gets a spoonful in edgeways. Paul also has his own spoon and uses both spoon and fist to treat himself to some tastings.

He eats for a while and then turns his plate upside down. Dad turns the plate right side up again, scoops the food back into it and holds it in place with his other hand.

At regular intervals, Dad tries to feed Paul a bite, but only as long as Paul feeds himself as well.

When Paul stops, Dad decides the meal is finished. He takes away the plate, cleans Paul's mouth and hands with a damp cloth, says thank you for the food on Paul's behalf and lifts him down.

Julia, eighteen months, sits steadily in her highchair and feeds herself. After a few spoonfuls she gets bored and wants to get out of her chair, an operation that looks a little precarious to her mother. Mom holds her hand close to her daughter but doesn't touch her. She and Julia's dad continue eating.

Julia sits down in her highchair again – but backwards. Since she is facing away from her food, she can't eat. Dad turns the highchair around, with Julia back to front in it, but says nothing.

Julia takes a few more spoonfuls – and fistfuls – of food. She tries to drink her milk, but spills some. Her mother doesn't reproach her, but she moves the cup out of reach. Julia protests angrily. Mom gives the cup to Julia so she can drink but she keeps her own hand on it. When Julia is finished, she places the cup out of reach again. The third time, Julia is allowed to hold the cup all by herself. After she takes a drink, she elegantly puts the cup back on the table without spilling a drop. "You did it!" says her mom. "Good for you!"

Now Julia gets up again and sways ominously, but sits back down back to front, so she is facing the right way again. Dad turns the chair again so that Julia is facing the table. The meal continues. As long as Julia can eat under her own steam, even if she engages in extracurricular activities between rounds, the meal continues. When she can no longer eat by herself and doesn't want to be fed by anyone else either but is *only* interested in things that have nothing to do with food, the meal is over.

Julia is allowed out of her highchair, her parents say thank you for the food on her behalf and the plate is taken away.

But now Julia comes back to the table a couple of times. She is *not* allowed to sit on the lap of either of her parents but like a little puppy, she is fed a little taste of what they are having – straight in the mouth.

When everyone has finished, no more food is given.

Robin, two, isn't content with twisting and turning in his highchair. He climbs in and out of it five or six times in a row.

He eats well enough, but he has food all over his mouth and hands, and he leaves his mark wherever he goes on his little expeditions away from the table. The rest of the family is less than enchanted.

Two-year-olds are pretty big, very charming and undeniably competent in many ways. It is easy to believe that they can be taught such things as table manners. Should you try to do this with your two-year-old, the result, alas, will likely be that you kill half, or all of his charm.

A two-year-old is a free spirit – man as a *free* human being. It is you, the mother or father, the adult, who must skillfully adapt the environment to accommodate the child's (necessary) freedom of movement.

That doesn't mean you should allow the routines to be called into question. The child eats when food is served. There is no discussion about that. Even two-year-olds have to stick to meal schedules, and, since it is in their own interests, they do so. *How* they eat, however, is quite another matter. In my opinion, it's one of those parental socialization projects that had better be left for another day!

Robin's parents now arm themselves with a damp cloth at the dining table. Every time Robin climbs down from his highchair they wipe his mouth and hands somewhat clean. Robin happily submits to being cleaned up as long as no restrictions are placed on his freedom of movement.

When the meal draws to a close – for the adults – mother or father informs little Robin of the fact (if he happens to have gone on an excursion).

"Do you want anymore? We are clearing the table now."

If he doesn't come back to the table, he is full. If he does, he can eat until he is.

If Robin just roams around the apartment during a meal, his parents draw the conclusion that he hasn't been able to work up a real appetite since he was last fed. They therefore see to it that all crackers, buns, fruit or anything else that's edible is kept well out of reach of the little "hunger striker" until the next meal.

For more information about children in the terrible twos, who question everything, food and eating included, see "The terrible twos. I want to, I don't want to!" in Part four of *For the Love of Children*.

Emily, three, is in the habit of wandering from the dining table to various other locations in the house, but her parents have decided to demand that she stay in her chair.

The first time she leaves the table, her parents treat it as a one-off occurrence and, in friendly tones, they call her back.

"Come and eat your dinner, sweetheart!"

Excursion number two provokes a question.

"Are you finished? Are you sure you don't want anymore?"

Emily returns to the table and continues with her (so called) meal.

Watching three-year-olds eat is a fascinating experience. Their ingenuity is astounding. All peas are skewered on three of the fork's four prongs in geometrically straight lines, a process which takes a good five minutes. Mashed potatoes are sculpted into complex works of art that would not be out of place next to a Henry Moore. Rice is carefully arranged in a perfectly symmetrical snowdrift around the edge of the plate. Meatballs are regarded as finger food, and tomatoes have to be sucked hollow. The skin can then be placed over the teeth, producing an effect that three-year-olds find endlessly amusing.

Food is important, but that doesn't mean you can't have fun with it. I don't think children should not be allowed to treat food with a little contempt. Throwing food on the floor, imitating Old Faithful with milk, or confusing meatballs with cannonballs should of course be discouraged, but I waited until my children were at least four before coming down on them for even these transgressions.

Emily now embarks upon her third voyage of discovery. And she gets a clear warning that there may be rough seas ahead. "Sit at the table if you want to eat, honey," says Mom. "If you don't come and sit down Emily, I'm going to clear the table and put away the food. Last chance Emmy! Going, going, gone!"

Emily has been given a choice. Either she eats more or she doesn't. Because she didn't immediately come back to the table, she chose the latter. Her parents ratify her decision by saying thank you for the food on her behalf.

Now dessert is served.

At three, little Emily is too young to be able to choose between something she can see and something she can't. Telling her that she won't get dessert unless she finishes her dinner is therefore a strategy doomed to failure. Emily lives in the moment, and what she can't see doesn't exist. Only when dessert is in plain view can Emily react to it.

Thus, denying Emily dessert once it is in front of her because she didn't finish her dinner is a tad cruel. Emily will protest vigorously, since she feels betrayed.

However, Emily can be given a smaller helping of dessert. How much smaller depends on how much of her main course she left on her plate. She will not have too much trouble putting two and two together.

If she wants seconds, she is of course out of luck. Her parents tell her that the meal is over and she can have more dessert another day. They then go through the ritual of saying thank you for the food on Emily's behalf.

Milton, four, is complaining.

"I don't want this... I can't eat that..."

His dad starts dividing up the food on Milton's plate.

"If you eat this, you can leave the rest," he says. "Come on, just two more spoonfuls."

Milton, who most of the time whines his way through his meals with his "I don't wanna eat that...", or even worse, "I'm not gonna eat that...", now has to learn to say, "I'm full, thank you!", which sounds a lot better, especially to his grandma.

"I'm soooo tired," Milton whines when he is having a particularly bad food day.

"If you're that tired, then you should go to bed," says his father calmly. He starts to get up to show Milton that he is quite prepared to take him by the hand and put him to bed, but Milton has by this time decided that discretion is the better part of valor and is eating diligently.

The next day, Milton doesn't touch his main course. He won't even eat the two or three spoonfuls that his father has scooped to one side. Dessert is put on the table, but Milton isn't offered any. His untouched meal is still in front of him. Milton howls with indignation.

"Sorry," his father says, "but if you don't eat your main course, you won't get any dessert. When people don't eat, it means they're not hungry."

"But I *am* hungry!" Milton whines.

"Really?" says Dad. "Eat what I've scooped to the side then, and you'll get some dessert."

If Milton starts to scream out his rage over what he regards as a stab in the back, his father will stick friendly but firmly to his guns.

"Too bad, but no dessert."

At school, where children have to eat quickly under conditions that are less than spiritually uplifting, much falls by the wayside. Children who have learned exemplary table manners at home can forget everything from one day to the next.

If, after numerous pleas and admonitions, your school-aged children persist in slurping down their food, faces virtually on their plates, in an eerily accurate impersonation of Al Pacino snorting cocaine in "Scarface", you might want to try mimicking their behavior – and then going one better. This usually has the desired effect. Just make sure you do it with a twinkle in your eye!

Table manners are a bit like migratory birds. They come and go. With time and habit, they eventually settle down for the duration, but discreet reminders will be required for quite a while.

Five-year-olds, for example, will take off their boots and place them neatly in the closet day after day without being told to. Then a day comes when mother finds her beloved offspring's boots in the middle of the living room floor.

Nagging goes with the territory. You just have to grin and bear it.

But make sure the nagging is considerate and sensitive. Don't sigh and roll your eyes. Don't let yourself succumb to *irritation* in other words. Effective nagging conveys information as though it was never said before. Good nagging is a friendly reminder.

Saying "Can't you even cut your food!?" in an irritated tone of voice won't get you very far. A smile and a friendly offer of assistance, "Would you like me to show you how you cut food?" is far more likely to have the desired effect.

Mom poses this question to Patrick, six years old, and puts her hands over his as they hold the knife and fork. She starts to guide his hands, which Patrick is none too keen on.

"I can do it myself!" he bursts out, and so he demonstrates.

"You sure can! That's amazing! I didn't know you could do that!"

Mom looks as though she had no idea her son was so well versed in the art of cutting food.

Table manners are no different from any other aspect of child rearing. You, as a parent, will be far more successful in attaining your goals if you rely less on making demands and more on providing leadership.

The spectre of obesity haunts many parents of infants today. This is perfectly understandable. The fact that children are now contracting diabetes 2

before they even start school is a terrifying development.

Children, like adults, have their ideal weight, and obesity isn't fun for anyone. But the first year is never the villain of the drama.

The foundation for obesity is not laid by breast milk or sugar free formula. Mass produced baby food poses no risk either. I would argue that it is the second year of life that is make or break. All kinds of foods with added sugar enter the picture. Cookies, cakes, pop, artificially sweetened fruit juice and condiments, chocolate milk, white pasta... this list of foods available in western countries that are really nothing more than candy in a misleading wrapper goes on and on.

And since children's appetites diminish so drastically during their second year, parents are tempted to take the attitude that eating sweet stuff is better than eating "nothing". The fact that human beings are hard wired to seek pleasure and avoid hunger doesn't help. If I had to choose between a fresh and warm lemon meringue pie and cold cabbage pudding, it wouldn't take me long to decide... The preference for sweet things seems to be innate. Or, it is acquired very early. Breast milk is utterly sweet.

In the old days, people usually weaned off their sweet tooth in favor of more fiber and energy rich foods (protein, non-refined carbohydrates), which, from what I understand, human beings are designed for anyway. The food industry, however, makes a great deal of money out of our propensity to eat like breastfeeding infants, metaphorically speaking. Swedes, for example, are world leaders in the consumption of small pieces of candy.

Be wary of the sugar coated (pardon the pun) propaganda that the food industry bombards us with from the day we are born! The more "real" food, chemical free and made from non-refined products, you give your children the better they will feel – for now as well as for the future.

Some child psychologists tell us that three year-olds that refuse to eat are common. Obviously, however, this phenomenon does not occur in countries where food is in short supply. For this reason, I don't think labelling certain ages and certain stages of development as "food refusing" is justified. Food equals survival. All the other things that food and mealtimes have come to stand for are artificial constructs that we force on our children because the prevailing culture in the Western world tells us to.

That it takes time for a young child to accept the prevailing food culture is nothing strange. It takes adults a good while to adapt to alien, sometimes incomprehensible customs too. (Remember the Bedouin camp allegory in Part two of *For the Love of Children*.)

Whatever problems you are having with children above the age of one with regard to food can be solved with the following program. Use it as a "cure" or as a permanent family food policy!

• Plan the day on the assumption that children, like adults, should eat about every four hours. There should never be less than three whole hours between meals. Put together a schedule and try hard to stick to it!

• Snacks are now a thing of the past. Fruit can be served as an appetizer or a meal in itself. Squeezed juice can also be served as an aperitif right before eating. A sandwich can accompany Pablum, yogurt, soup – whatever you are serving, all as one proper *meal*. So, instead of giving your child snacks between meals augment meals with the snack.

Friends of Order say we should eat a little frequently rather than a lot infrequently. When it comes to young children I couldn't disagree more. Their hunger will vanish before it even starts to make itself felt. The constant munching will increase the risk of both cavities and obesity.

• De-dramatize mealtimes! Meals are not status symbols. If you set the most beautiful table and compose the most elaborate meals, of course you won't be very happy if your offspring don't even look at it, let alone eat it. If you keep everything as simple as you can, you will find it much easier to sit back and let your child eat his fill in peace. You will also spare yourself all those dark feelings of rejection.

• Simplify the menu! You can serve the same meal day after day. You don't need to serve foods from every food group at every meal. Nor do you need to "stimulate" your child to eat. Remember that hunger is the best stimulus! Children are creatures of habit. Take advantage of this and offer the same two, or even three, nutritional mainstays every day.

• From one year of age and on, your child can eat anything and should be offered the same things to eat that everyone else does. (No pressure should be applied of course.) Your little angel can survive handily on the mainstays, so let the choice be the child's! One-year-olds who are freely given the chance to taste everything can develop a passion for herring, onion, olives, oysters... I do not recommend baby food after the age of one.

• Beware of jumping to conclusions and seeking remedies for problems that may not exist. If you think there may be certain foods that your child cannot tolerate, listen to your gut rather than to other people's speculations or the fad of the day! If your instincts repeatedly tell you there is something amiss, seek medical advice, and the doctor will in all probability confirm what you already know. Until then, put all anxiety aside and assume that everything is as it should be.

• Parental anxiety does more damage to a little baby than most physical ailments.

• Babies are prone to loose bowels. Blueberries in any form and weak tea with a little honey can be substituted for dairy products and formula. Otherwise, serve what you always do, but keep your child generously supplied with water.

Fasting, which is sometimes prescribed for babies with diarrhoea, does more harm than good in my opinion. Children who are suddenly confronted with food they are not used to or who are put on liquid diets become confused and anxious. And emotions such as confusion and anxiety can trigger diarrhoea without there being anything physically wrong in the first place.

Stubborn cases of diarrhoea can sometimes be caused by tap water. In acute cases, switch to bottled water.

• If your child suffers from constipation, give him or her prunes and fruit, crisp bread rather than regular white bread, and stay away from cow's milk.

• Learn to say no! The kitchen is closed between meals.

A young child complaining of hunger pains is of course a heart-rending spectacle. However, a child who doesn't know what real hunger is – and very few people in our well fed part of the world do – thinks that a hint of a craving to munch something is the same as being hungry, which it isn't. A glass of water will silence the "hunger". Real hunger is a precious gem that should be hoarded and then joyfully satisfied by a real meal.

Teenagers and infants have more in common than you might think. They sleep like logs and they eat like horses.

A teenager's eating habits can be exotic to say the least. In my opinion, this is not a problem as long as the rest of the family doesn't suffer.

It's often impossible to dictate rules about eating anyway. Your teenager will simply ignore or "forget" them. As usual, the best course is to try to think preventively and work out a mutual agreement with your teenager.

"Give us this day our daily bread" goes the Lord's Prayer. Easy enough to say if you're not the one doing the baking. There is no reason why the household should revolve around a constantly ravenous teenager who is perfectly capable of devouring an entire loaf of bread at a single sitting. A child who participates socially bakes his own bread and shares it with the rest of the family.

Your teenager should also participate in everyday meal preparation or take his turn at preparing a meal from scratch according to a weekly work schedule. This includes doing the dishes afterwards!

We live in a culture that is morbidly obsessed with physical perfection. As a result, many a teenage girl, and even the occasional teenage boy, fall victim to anorexia or bulimia, two sides of the same depressing coin. Teenage girls become fixated on dieting as a result of a distorted image of their own bodies. If the self-imposed starvation is allowed to progress beyond a certain point, it results in death.

Be on the look out for warning signs. When a teenage girl starts volunteering to cook for the rest of the family, but then finds all kinds of reasons to avoid eating anything herself, alarm bells should go off in your head.

Children's neurotic fixations say a great deal about how sensitive they are about the adult bodies they are in the process of developing. We adults look at teenagers and envy them their youth, their glowing skin and their beauty. But we are on the outside looking in. A teenager looks at her body and sees something incomplete, unknown, alien. An anorexic teenager also sees something frightening. Her body is an enemy that must be fought.

You can take preventive measures. Tell your growing daughter (or son) that dieting is totally inappropriate before the body has even nearly finished developing, that is before they turn eighteen. Point out in no uncertain terms that you, as a parent, will not go along with it.

Also, remember that the worst thing you can do is make negative comments about a teenager's body. Your word carries far more weight than you think, so be careful. Your teenager will zero in on the faintest negative vibe and take it to heart. Trying to make amends after the fact is a waste of time. The damage has been done.

Your teenager's own wildly self-critical observations must, however, be accorded the respect they deserve.

"God, I've got fat calves. It's unreal. Everyone calls me Miss Piggy."

"You really think you have fat calves?"

"Well, yeah! Don't you? Be honest. Don't you think they're fat?"

"No, as a matter of fact I don't. You're very well proportioned. I think your calves are perfect." (Scrutinize the offending body part meticulously as you say this. Study her calves as though they were of crucial importance for the advancement of medical science even if you can't for the life of you figure out why she is so worried.)

And be convincing: "No, really I think your calves are great. You should have seen me when I was fifteen. I looked like the Michelin Man. I'd wrap my calves in cellophane and do ballet exercises to get them smaller. In the end, I quit wearing short skirts. And short skirts were in back then. But when I turned eighteen and had finished growing everything was fine. I never think about my calves now."

Should serious problems arise with regard to your older children's eating habits (or lack of them), there is always the tried and true remedy that rekindles the instinct to survive, cures complexes and banishes the spectres of self-absorption and indifference.

Take time out with your child. Leave the familiar environment you are both so used to and seek out an environment that is simple, primitive and harsh enough to ensure that the struggle to survive is not an abstraction. On the contrary, the struggle you both share should be palpable and immediate. You can camp, live in a trailer, or perhaps rent a cottage that is off the beaten track. The fewer modern conveniences you have access to and the more isolated the location, the better.

By focusing on the common struggle to survive, the little flock forges together. The child is distanced from her/his problems and is imbued with a unique joy and satisfaction achieved by meeting the elementary needs of human existence.

To eat is to live. To want to eat is to want to live.

Anyone who is deeply depressed doesn't have much appetite. Kids are sometimes profoundly unhappy. A love affair gone wrong, for example, cuts a teenager's soul to its very core.

And in your role as the responsible adult in the house, there isn't a whole lot you can do. Even very young people have to learn to cope with life's disappointments and somehow soldier on. A parent can't do much besides be there for the children in their hour of need, empathize and hopefully make their pain a little less unbearable.

Laughter is a wonderful cure for just about everything that can afflict a human being. Anything that causes your child to laugh or even crack a smile is worth the effort. When your crestfallen teenager walks through the door, long faced, weighed down by burdens not of her own making, and trudges up to her room like Marie Antoinette on her way to the guillotine, you *can* actually sit in your chair silent as a mouse with a false mustache under your nose. Whoever can laugh, can also eat!

Fresh air is also good medicine. Children, big and small, should be outside and moving.

Unfortunately, kids can be as sluggish as adults. Depressed adults aren't outdoor enthusiasts either. They literally have to be dragged out the door, and my hat goes off to friends who are devoted enough to make it happen.

Your depressed teenager may have to be lured out of the house. "Come with me please. I need some help out here!"

Never lose sight of the fact that kids, especially depressed ones, *need to be needed*.

Sound sleep and lots of it works its magic too.

Sleep becomes better if the room is cool. Air it out for a couple of hours before bed time, and/or leave the window open at night, making sure the bed is out of any draft.

Sad children, like sad adults, have a tendency to sit up far too late and brood, more hollow-eyed and more off their food with each passing day (and night). Don't let it be that way! Even older children have to be graciously helped to sleep sometimes.

And as always, *anxiety* is the villain of the loss of appetite drama. Take action!

PROBLEMS? KEEPING BUSY

Little angels who can't seem to find anything to do with their time can be described in one or several of the following ways:
1. They're not allowed to make themselves useful.
2. They've been over-stimulated into passivity.
3. They've been physically bound to the parents, who, by constantly carrying them around, have basically declared them handicapped.
4. They've had their freedom of movement curtailed.
5. They're over-tired, stressed to pieces and listless – life has lost its lustre.

1.

It takes so little to make a child feel needed.

"Can you please hand me my shoe?"

It sounds so trivial, but don't be deceived. Such little requests give a child the feeling that *the others wouldn't manage quite as well without me*. And feeling useful is just as essential for a young child's well-being as it is for yours and mine. Children are made of the same stuff that adults are.

A child who has trouble finding something to do is almost always a child who is never allowed to be useful.

No one can endure a vacation that never ends. No one can endure a lifetime of rest, recreation and "having fun". Most people are glad to get back to work after a long period of inactivity. After a hard day's work, kicking back and relaxing comes naturally. If we put in our time at the office or factory and make our contribution to society, be it ever so humble, we don't need a course in how to relax. We don't need an army of leisure time experts to

618

pick out hobbies and activities in order to make our free time meaningful. Children who are put to work don't either.

What can your child do? What does your child like doing?

The tasks you set your child don't have to be remarkable in and of themselves. The point is that *the child works at your side, and that what's done is (or at least seems to be) necessary. It's essential work, not a game.*

The tasks you set, no matter how miniscule the child's input, must be done every day at least twice, and they must be part of a schedule so that they don't get forgotten.

Social participation should be the rule, not the exception. In addition to this schedule, there is also all the social participation that the child initiates. All kids want to help out. They want to be included. All you have to do is strike while the iron is hot!

After every contribution to the flock that makes the common struggle for survival just a little bit easier, the child takes some time off for R and R. People who know they have done their bit can amuse themselves just fine.

If you think that it takes an eternity to do the dishes with your child beside you on a stool sloshing a sponge around in the water, if you think that making a bed turns into a tug of war with your child pulling on one end of the bed spread while you pull on the other, if you think it's a drag to have a sopping wet kid throwing water all over you when you wash the windows, then ponder this. The investment in time and patience you make now will be returned to you tenfold. *After the successful completion of a joint venture, your child will be able to play happily all by himself,* and you will not have to endure the dreary, clingy whining that is the hallmark of a child who knows he's not needed.

From the terrible twos on, you must try to ensure that your orders are followed. As the years go by, stick to this rule.

Once you give an order, make a demand, or assign a task, the mission must be accomplished.

The child's input must be – or at least seem to be – *necessary.* Choose your words carefully and don't bite off more than your child can chew. "Pick up those blocks!" is infinitely preferable to "Clean up your room!"

If, however, you ask a question instead of giving an order, you will have to learn to take no for answer. "No" is a perfectly logical response to "Would you like to pick up those blocks?" A question is a good alternative to an order, but the terms are not synonymous.

Daily life teems with situations where no parent has the strength to always do what should be done. If you ask a child to perform a task instead of demanding that the task be done, you can – if your child says no – drop the subject without losing face.

"Do you want to pick up those blocks?"

"No."

"Fine, we'll do it later."

The work that is being performed – even if the child's input is insignificant, or hinders more than it helps for that matter, must be seen through to the bitter end. This means that you and your child work together for the same length of time until the task is completed.

The tasks you assign your child do not have to be, indeed they shouldn't be, particularly grandiose. Think through the tasks carefully and set the bar low, but insist that whatever it is be seen through to a successful conclusion.

This will make your child feel self-reliant. "I did it! The others wouldn't manage quite as well without me."

Twins Edward and Elisa are painting a wall with their dad. The kids are eight years old and fully capable of painting, as long as they are given some elementary instructions before they get started. They're painting and having fun.

But their interest flags after a while. There are other distractions, and the job is taking longer than they thought it would. They leave their rollers and paint trays on the floor and scamper off.

Dad is left with a vague feeling that things aren't as they should be, but he's been told that you can't force children to help you. So, he continues working, but he's a little ticked off.

Here's where he went wrong. *If painting the wall was really necessary for the flock's survival, Dad should have shouted for his children to come back.* Without a shred of hesitation, he should have reminded Edward and Elisa that the project they were engaged in was essential for the family's welfare and had to be seen through to the end. The kids would just have to put off playing until later.

Of course, painting a wall is not a question of life and death. And that no doubt is why Dad hesitated. He allowed the children to regard painting as a game, something they only had to do for as long as they found it amusing. Thus, Edward and Elisa didn't feel that they were *needed*. They were allowed to paint because Dad was just being nice. This was not about doing their bit for the flock's survival. Dad should have demanded that they continue working with him, protests notwithstanding, so that the kids would know in their bones that they were needed. (*The others wouldn't manage as well without me.*)

The story of little Mr. Lundstrom on pages 548–550 will perhaps inspire you!

The over-activated, over-stimulated child sits passively and waits for the manna to fall down from heaven, and each batch of manna better be a lot more fun than the last if it is going to rock the child's world.

Take an inventory of your child's toys. Better a pile of Lego or some wooden blocks and nothing else, or a pencil and paper and nothing else than a wildly expensive array of pedagogically correct toys so technologically sophisticated they put NASA to shame. If you child's room resembles Houston's Mission Control Center, gather everything up and throw it into a closet.

Then sit back and do nothing. Don't find fun things for your child to do, don't buy new interesting toys, and don't set up any stimulating (supposedly) activity programs. You will find that something I call *empty time* creeps into the picture.

"What am I going to do? I have nothing to do!" says the child – your son, let's say.

"Good question. What are you going to do?" you ask.

Your demeanour is patient but genuinely interested. Things will start to happen.

A passive child needs a little push to kick start his imagination, so he is then able to take the initiative. You administer this little push simply by having faith in him.

Take your child to a playground and just park yourself on a bench and read a newspaper. Don't help him slide or push him on the swing. Don't talk to him or look at him (except discreetly over the top of your paper). *Empty time* enters the picture and your child will activate himself. He'll look around for things to do – and passivity is broken.

Simply turn your child loose in your backyard or on a beach, anywhere outdoors, where you can keep an eye on him without being seen yourself. He may be clingy and sad, and he may protest against being left to his own devices, but if his protests don't result in your coming to his "rescue", he will take matters into his own hands. He will start to do things and will soon find that he is perfectly capable of amusing himself without any outside interference.

The important thing is to make sure that you take your child back into the house *before* he starts to get bored (see "Solitary play" on page 337). You want him to quit while he's ahead.

If, however, you wait until your child starts to cry and complain before you take him home, your actions are saying that you made a mistake. It's dangerous to be alone: "Anything can happen! The wolf may come! We should never do this again!"

Interrupting him while he's still playing happily says, in effect, that every-thing is as it should be and that another solitary excursion can be put on tomorrow's agenda.

Children under four should never be left unsupervised. An enclosed back-yard is relatively safe, but you should still keep a watchful eye on your child without being seen yourself.

Empty time cures clingy dependence by giving the child's own initiative a chance to come to life. If your little one, whiny and discontented, toddles up to you and starts to tug at your skirts (or pants!), you can, as a stop-gap measure, include him in whatever you are doing.

You can also sit on the floor so your eyes are level with his and hug him. Look happy – you're not comforting him or feeling sorry for him – and stay sitting with him for as long as he wants. Sooner or later, he will hit upon something to do and will be on his way.

He will probably be back before too long, start to whine again and want up in your arms. Sit down on the floor again and place yourself at your child's disposal until he decides he has had enough.

What happens on the floor, while you are just there for your child (rather than carrying him around) is *empty time*. He is getting that all-important connection by having his mother or father to himself for a while. And after that, things happen.

3.

"You are helpless. You need my constant protection. Without my body as a shield, you will fall prey to the wolf."

That is the message you are giving your child if you constantly carry him around and forever seem to be commiserating with him about something. This can easily solidify into a rather depressing habit.

Solitary play in the morning is convenient for parents who want to sleep in a little or start the day gently and eat breakfast in peace. But solitary play is also marvellously beneficial for children who have become so physically attached to their parents that they have been reduced to a state of fearful, helpless dependency.

As previously mentioned in "Eleven months to one year: maintaining good habits", these solitary play periods test children's abilities and inspire them to act on their own initiative, to confront problems and to use their increasing capacity to solve them in their own good time and without outside interference. They learn to believe in their own talents and rejoice in them. (Naturally, you must be careful not to jeopardize the beneficial effects of solitary games by allowing them to become something that the child might even remotely perceive as ostracism.)

Most parents come to regard these solitary play periods as essential institutions. Babies are a lot cuter at five in the morning if everyone gets to go back to sleep. One-year-olds are cute too, but they don't go back to sleep. Two-year-olds are charming little people – except at 6.00 a.m., when even the most loving parents would gladly auction them off in exchange for another hour in bed.

At three or four months, children will initiate solitary play periods themselves after a good night's sleep, so *carpe diem!*

But even if you didn't take the chance when it was offered, it's not too late.

• Give your child his own room, or a room that can be used for solitary play. If you are short of space, screen off a corner in the living room. Arrange things so that you can see your child, but he can't see you.

• Ensure that social participation is a part of the routine. During the day, put the child to work on two or more occasions. And don't go overboard with toys. Let everyday objects double as toys. If you use your imagination, you might be able to avoid the toy store completely.

• Set aside a week when solitary play will be introduced. It should be a week when you will be able to get up early and be reasonably chipper.

• Put together a battery of five or six interesting, age-appropriate pedagogical toys. Include something that makes noise. Don't show the selection to your child!

• Here are some toy suggestions for children who can sit up in their cribs.
A wooden shape sorter toy
A hammer nails pounding bench
Large Lego pieces
Dinky cars with doors and hoods that can be opened and shut
A toy trumpet or a xylophone
A mouth organ (of good quality)
A music box that the child can wind up
A doll that makes a sound when you poke it in the stomach
A doll that can be dressed and undressed
A pad and some crayons (only if you are not too particular about your walls!)
A comic book or a magazine that can be ripped apart or cut – in which case include a pair of blunt kiddie scissors that can also be used for self-administered haircuts. (Older children only!)

623

Small items you no longer have any use for e.g. curlers

A deck of cards with a rubber band around them

A little grab bag, paper or fabric, properly sealed. It should contain things like old curtain rings, photos of the family that no one looks at anymore, little Christmas bells, a whistle, a small flashlight, maybe a little bribe in the form of sugar free crackers… Use your playful imagination! (Oh yes, it's all there.)

When D-day arrives, it's best *not* to pick the child up (unless you are breast-feeding of course, in which case this is the only thing that happens outside the child's crib). The idea is that the day starts with solitary play – no other entertainment than what the child gives himself.

Give your child a bottle, change his diaper, and remove the bedclothes and stuffed animals, draw the curtains and/or turn on the lights.

Present the toy collection with great fanfare and put them in the crib. Don't look at your child or wait for expressions of gratitude.

Smile encouragingly, "See you soon! Have fun!" Then wave goodbye and leave the room, and let your child's curiosity do the rest.

Bring solitary play to a close *before* he begins to complain. Fifteen minutes the first day is more than enough.

Put away all the toys. They are for solitary play only and should not be available for the rest of the day.

Gradually lengthen the period allotted for solitary play over the course of the week, and always call time when your child is still playing happily.

Spy on him! If there are signs of frustration, resist the urge to help. Let him find his own solution.

Anger and disappointment when your child is in the midst of trying to figure his way out of an impasse are permitted.

What you have to be on the lookout for is genuine sadness. Then you can intervene to help, and re-ignite enthusiasm, but you are not there to "rescue" him. Once the problem is solved, leave immediately.

Keep an eye on the clock. Go in and fetch him at a pre-determined time at a stage of his play when he is still in a good mood.

Make your reunion cause for much celebration to send the message that everything is as it should be, that solitary play has been a part of every child's life since the dawn of time and how wonderful it is that he is now old enough to participate in this hallowed tradition.

Even a trace of anxiety in your tone of voice or facial expression will send the message that danger threatens and that the wolf is close behind you.

Children who are old enough to get out of bed by themselves but still too young to show consideration for their under slept parents can play with their interesting toys – and eat their breakfast while they're at it – at a table.

The table should be low and round (children like round shapes) with lots of room to spread out. Young children are perfectly happy to stand or kneel while they work, so chairs are unnecessary.

The toy collection can be complemented with simple puzzles, spinning tops (very popular) and perhaps a paint set with a jar of water and two large pieces of paper. The same availability rule applies; these toys are only brought out for solitary play periods.

The toys should be presented with appropriate enthusiasm. Lay them out carefully as though they were brand new. Toys that have been randomly dumped in a drawer are singularly uninspiring.

Once everything has been presented and neatly arranged, tell your child that you are going back to bed and that you will see him over breakfast/coffee/lunch or whatever is next on the agenda, then wave and disappear.

If the child trots into your bedroom after a while, pretend to be fast asleep. Don't answer if he speaks to you, and don't feel you have to jump out of bed and entertain him. He is perfectly capable of entertaining himself.

Just remember that children become frightened if their "fixed point" in the world is completely immobile. They suspect something bad has happened. So sleep so you can be heard. Breathe audibly, turn over, snore a little, but don't open your eyes or say anything. Don't "wake up"!

It won't take him long to get bored watching you "sleep", and he will soon go back to what he was doing.

End the solitary play period at a pre-determined time, and don't wait until your child starts to show signs of feeling abandoned and bored. That will sabotage everything, and you can kiss late mornings goodbye.

If you think you might really drop off to sleep, set your alarm.

It is very important to inspect the room carefully before you leave your child alone. Make sure there is nothing that can injure him. Always assume the worst.

Accessible electrical outlets, drawstrings on Venetian blinds, bookcases that have not been bolted to the wall are just a few of the things that are potentially life threatening.

4.

Young children whose freedom of movement has been restricted, who are constantly bombarded with NO, DON'T TOUCH and BAD, and who are imprisoned in play pens and harnesses, literally or figuratively, eventually lose that innate urge to try new things and explore the unknown because they know that any attempt to do so will somehow be foiled.

And it's not just their initiative, originality and creativity that are stifled. Their *joie de vivre* is snuffed out as well.

As soon as infants can grip and hold things, their hands should never be empty.

Unfortunately, all a lot of infants get is a pacifier stuck into their mouths while their hands remain idle and the light in their eyes flickers and dies.

Young children should not be hindered in their explorations (unless, through their actions, they ask to be). They should be allowed to roam the world freely. That is, after all, what they came into it for.

In the chapter on the five to six-month-old and the crawler in Part three of *For the Love of Children,* there are tips on how you can familiarize your child with the world he has been born into without restricting him or raining on his parade.

These suggestions can also be used to teach older children too so that initiative, originality and creativity is fostered.

If you have been wanting in this area, you can always make up for lost time if you know what you're doing and why. Young children are much easier to deal with than many people think, as long as you have a goal.

Kids don't suffer from being treated as though they are younger than they actually are. On the contrary, it's good medicine if something has gone wrong.

Human beings regress in times of crisis. When we're sick, in despair or just unhappy, we feel small, weak, helpless and inadequate. We want someone to take us by the hand and show us the way. The same goes for young children, who really aren't that different from adults.

Problems with young children can often be solved by starting afresh; by doing now what you should have done before, or by retreating from what you should not have interfered with before.

You let the child "go back" and start over, seriously and carefully, cheerfully and tenderly, decisively, methodically, and lovingly – all the while focusing on a very specific goal.

If, for example, you finally succeed in teaching your child how to deal with things and people – after perhaps years of restricting, forbidding and blaming him – you can very soon give him the freedom of movement that is so essential for developing the ability to operate independently.

5.

A little person who is suffering from a chronic lack of sleep – a disorder that has swept through the nurseries of the Western world like a forest fire – is no more able to amuse himself on his own than an adult who is suffering from chronic sleep deprivation.

Children have to develop. They have to grow. Nature's merciless imperative compels them to, no matter how tired they are. Unless we adults help, they don't get even a moment's rest. Sleep is the pause that refreshes young children, for it is only when they sleep that they find a respite from the imponderables that the world is constantly throwing at them as well as their own innate, relentless urge to develop.

An exhausted child who gets up and walks for the first time – compelled by this imperative – would far rather fall down and bang his head on the floor than refrain from trying to stand upright. He doesn't have a choice. (Suggestions from the experts about baby helmets are so absurd I don't know whether to laugh or cry. The simple truth is that the child is too tired.)

This urge to develop has pushed humankind forward for millions of years, and it cannot be stifled even by chronic sleep deprivation. There is only one possible outcome: burn out. Today there are children who burn out before they even try to learn how to walk. In general, our kids are stressed to bits. They don't even get the sleep they need when they are infants, and therefore never get the chance to build up the reserve they need to maintain their immune systems and physical stamina.

If and when you see the roses fade from your child's cheeks, his eyes lose their lustre or stay blank as if filled with tears, and dark circles form, *job one is to make sure he gets enough sleep*. Don't let the fact that he is so bravely perky during the day fool you.

It is your duty as a parent to learn how to help your child to find the peace he needs, just as you learn how to help the little one to eat and get dressed.

You can't do your child's sleeping for him, any more than you can do his eating for him. That's why you have to help him dare to sleep *secure in himself*, rather than always being disturbed by you. (Yes, I know that hurts!) Your physical presence benefits your child wonderfully – but not at night. It disturbs his rest. (See "The Safari. An Allegory".)

At night, *sleep is more important to your child than you are*. It has to be.

In no culture on earth, do children who eat well and sleep well (assuming they are lovingly protected by their flocks and they get their quota of social participation) have trouble playing by themselves.

For them, life does not lose its lustre.

It's the little things that give life its lustre. A beautiful tree, a leaf in autumn, a black ant crawling over a chalk white stone, the feeling of rain drops on your face... Everyday miracles.

It's all too easy for stressed adults to take these miracles for granted.

Don't give your child an ice cream cone with an irritated sigh after he's been bugging you for one all morning in the hope that he will leave you alone for a few minutes. Turn it into a celebration and say, "Look what I have for you! An ice cream cone!"

If you never rejoice in your child, your child will lose his capacity to rejoice in himself. What's mundane and a little dull for you, Mom or Dad, will become just as mundane and dull for your child.

People, big and small, very quickly get used to the good things in life. What we never get used to are the bad things. The bad things anger us, worry us and churn around inside us ceaselessly. They rob us of our peace of mind. A splinter in the finger can be enough to erode even the most solid happiness. Only for what is bad and wrong do we seem to have perpetually new eyes.

What's bad demands bettering. Bad things need changing, and change requires a different, courageous way of thinking.

It would be unrealistic and unfair to expect you to always be happy, en-thusiastic or in "top form" when you are with your little (or not so little) one. But listen to that inner voice, the one that persistently tells you to make changes and to forge structure into the day – and night! If you think differently and courageously – and make change, both joy and enthusiasm will abound in a way that an ice cream cone from an irritated, stressed par-ent could never come close to giving.

And a joyful, enthusiastic little person is supremely confident at amusing himself.

628

LITTLE JOYCE AND HER MOTHER

Joyce's mother regards herself as a professional playmate.

When three year old Joyce comes to her and hangs on her skirts when she's washing the dishes, she stops what she's doing, sits down at the table and helps Joyce do a puzzle. In her irritated moments she says, "No, I don't have time to play now. I have work to do!"

She doesn't include Joyce in the household chores. When she's doing the dishes, she doesn't lift Joyce up on to the counter, give her a brush and a cup and let her help out.

Joyce's mother makes guest appearances in Joyce's world, a children's world, carefully screened off from the adult world.

Joyce is a clingy, generally discontented child who can't amuse herself for long. She has no work to rest from. She is not part of the reality that her mother has to contend with – the flock's struggle for survival – and so cannot model her playing on that. She can play without her mother's help, but she can't participate socially without her mother's help.

Although her parental leave is over, Joyce's mom, a single mother, has decided to stay home with her daughter. She believes that Joyce needs to be around her mom and her home for the first few years of her life.

Society has punished Joyce's mother for the sin of staying home with her child by, practically speaking, ostracizing her. Joyce's mom has to live on social assistance, which is relatively generous in Sweden, but what's interesting is that society has decided that there is no place for someone like Joyce's mother because she won't *opt not to share her everyday life with her own child.*

Joyce's mother has a duty to provide her daughter with opportunities to participate socially. Because she refuses to deny Joyce the social participation she needs (and is born to relentlessly seek), she has been forced to sacrifice her own.

She lives isolated from her own adult community, and is more or less a permanent guest star in a socially segregated children's world.

Her own activities, necessary for the survival of her family of two, are tended to as quickly as possible, preferably when Joyce is asleep.

Otherwise, Joyce's mother devotes all her time to her daughter. She plays with her, takes her out, buys her toys and takes her to all the children's activities that are offered in the suburban community in which she lives.

She walks the floor with Joyce in her arms until late into the evening, rocking her and comforting her.

Joyce sleeps in her mother's bed.

Joyce's mother has sacrificed her integrity and her social life for her daughter. She never sees other adults privately. She never goes out in the evenings. She is at her child's beck and call twenty-four hours a day, seven days a week.

Little Joyce is still not content however.

"Are all children this demanding?" Joyce's mother asked.

"Yes, this is what you accept when you have kids," was the perennial refrain at the children's clinic throughout Joyce's first year.

Why is Joyce's mother so miserable? Why does she think her life is so hard? It was what she wanted after all. She chose to stay at home with her child, just as she chose not to have Joyce's father in her life. She didn't want to live with him. She wanted to live with her much longed for child.

She constantly asks herself how things could go so wrong, and she is her own harshest critic. She is not doing right by her daughter, she tells herself. That must be it. She just doesn't love Joyce enough. She isn't doing enough to make her daughter happy. She's a bad mother.

She has to do more, love more, play more, and stimulate more. She's a glorified day care worker, an employee with one child in her charge. And that child is not happy.

Then, one day, Joyce's mother has one of those eureka moments and reassesses her life.

She decides to structure her day the way *she* wants. She isn't a mere employee at a day care center. She will create a life for herself based on *what is necessary for her* and in which little Joyce will have a place.

She sits down one evening and ponders her options. Two things are certain.

First, she wants to be home. She wants to share her daily life with her daughter.

Second, her mothers' allowance covers her basic expenses, so if she is frugal, she doesn't have to earn any extra money. But whatever she decides to do with her time must be – or at least seem to be – necessary.

She decides to take up painting. She has always wanted to draw and paint, but she somehow never got around to it. As she sits making her plans, her enthusiasm grows. (She also could have decided to sew clothes, make mobiles, knit little Santas for Christmas or learn to play the violin... – as long as something is *produced,* surpassing the merely re-productive nature of household chores.)

She decides that she will paint at a specific time each day, and she will stick to that schedule regardless of whether she has the inclination, the time or the inspiration.

Whether or not anything makes it onto the canvas, she will stand in front of her easel for a set period of time every day and try her best to paint. In so doing, she will convince herself and Joyce that painting is not a hobby that she potters around with when she feels like it, but an activity *that is necessary for the family's existence.*

What else does she want to do?

See her friends and perhaps meet some new people.

Where? How often? One evening a week? Two?

How does Joyce figure in all this? She should have the opportunity to get together with other children, one or two at a time, in a nice and easy, safely controlled home environment, rather than playing with a lot of unknown children at the somewhat chaotic children's events organized by the municipality.

How would these play days be organized?

Joyce's mother ponders and schemes, and finally puts together something that resembles a plan for the life that will be hers. And Joyce's.

She reasons the way she would have if she had lived alone.

Daily life starts to take shape. Joyce's mother comes to a quid pro quo arrangement with two old friends who are also single mothers. The net result is that all three women end up with two free evenings a week.

What's remarkable is that little Joyce, who was once unwilling to let her mother out of her sight, takes all this in her stride. Her mother goes out in the evenings and sometimes stays the night at a friend's, and Joyce doesn't protest – because these activities are – or seem to be – *necessary for her mother.*

The day begins with Joyce and her mother eating breakfast together. Breakfast is followed by a period of solitary play. This is the only time during the day that Joyce plays with toys.

Joyce's mother gets a couple of hours to herself.

Mother and daughter reunite over a meal in the late morning at a set time, after which they go out – every day, regardless of weather.

This walk is Joyce's time. Her mother is at her disposal as a tool and as a companion. They climb hills, splash through puddles and take turns pushing each other on the swings at the playground. They look at the trees, the gravel, the snow, and they get acquainted with any dogs that happen by. Joyce, who walks the whole time, sets the pace. The world is hers.

Her mother holds the keys to the kingdom. She unlocks the gates for her daughter and lets her explore.

They are out for an hour and a half.

When they get home, it's time for mother to get to work. Nothing is allowed to interfere with that. Painting is necessary for this little family's existence. Under no circumstances can it be called into question.

Joyce has to learn to respect this and give her mother space for her work, which must get done.

Sometimes Joyce puts her head around the door to watch, and sometimes she wants to help. She might help by holding the easel for example. Mother looks as though having the easel held steady during moments of extreme concentration is very important.

She thanks her daughter profusely when Joyce decides her job is done.

Joyce might also wash a brush, in accordance with all the rules that govern such things, with her mother's hand over hers. This is an important task and a tremendous responsibility, which mother would not have been able to manage nearly as well without Joyce's input.

At the appointed hour, the work session ends.

Mother's work was interrupted briefly only once, when she put Joyce down for a one-hour afternoon nap. While Joyce slept, Mom finished her quota for the day.

"Now I'm done!" Joyce's mother announces, which clearly indicates that one activity is over and another is about to begin.

It's time to eat. But the food has to be prepared first. Joyce helps. She sits on the counter and hands her mother things.

Mother encourages her contributions, takes them very seriously, and thanks her daughter profusely.

Then they eat. When the meal is over, mother starts clearing up, and as soon as Joyce shows signs of wanting to participate, she is given a job.

Once her allotted task is done, she plays by herself for a while.

Joyce is given the task of cleaning a whisk. She cleans it and puts it carefully back in the drawer in its assigned place. Mother thanks her for her help.

Joyce then takes the whisk out of the drawer again, pulls a stool over to the kitchen counter, and asks for help to turn on the water, which Mother gives her. She then starts whisking. Using the whisk, the dish brush, the dish cloth and a cup, Joyce proceeds to amuse herself for a whole half hour, whereupon she climbs into the sink herself.

Her mother leaves her alone. Joyce is pleased with herself, and Mom is pleased with Joyce.

The important thing is that the whisk *did* get put back in the drawer where Joyce was asked to put it. Joyce completed her task. When she then took it out again to play with it and process reality the way children must, she kept busy all by herself. She played in her own way and in her own time, fulfilled from finished work and free from interference.

Now comes social participation.

Joyce's mother lifts her soaking wet child down, dries her and dresses her.

"You know what we are going to do now?" she asks her daughter. "Laundry! Have you ever seen such a dirty sweater? *Here* it's dirty, and *there* it's dirty... Joyce has to carry it down to the laundry room!"

There follows an expedition down to the basement. Important work awaits, and Joyce will take part. Joyce does her job beautifully, carrying the sweater down to the basement and carefully putting it into the washing machine.

Joyce is needed. *The others wouldn't manage quite as well without me.*

Towards evening, Joyce and her mother call it a day, kick back and relax. They watch TV, read stories, cuddle and play. Often they take a bath together.

Mother doesn't devote this time to Joyce because she feels she will be a bad mother if she doesn't. She spends this time with her daughter because she genuinely enjoys it.

Some evenings they spend apart, depending on the babysitting schedule Joyce's mother has negotiated with her two friends.

Other afternoons, they might eat somewhere else, visit friends or have guests themselves. When guests come to visit, Joyce and her mom take care of the evening together.

Joyce's mother puts her daughter to bed in another room now. She does it with an attitude that says, "At night we all sleep. It is the way things are now, always have been, and always will be."

We sleep and we sleep well so we have the strength to work the next day and like it.

We sleep so we can do what is necessary, whether we do it alone or with others, and what is fun, pure and simple.

The last thing little Joyce does before she goes to sleep is laugh, the harder the better.

Each and every day, Joyce's mother makes sure that her daughter's world shimmers with the stardust of laughter.

Does a woman belong in the kitchen with her children?
Yes.
Does a man belong in the kitchen with his children?
Yes.
But above all, work belongs in the family.
The whole family.

PROBLEMS? SLEEP

When night falls, every child's cry is a question. "Will I survive or will I die? Do I dare fall asleep, or will the wolf come for me?"

A young child will continue to cry at night and to ask these questions until you, mother or father, answer these questions in a way that reassures the child. Your child will not accept anything less.

Like all of us, young children need to know that they are secure in the sense of *physically safe* to be able to sleep at night.

Babies know that they are helpless. They cannot pick up a gun and shoot the proverbial wolf that lurks at the door. They cannot ensure their own survival. Your baby needs you, his guarantor of survival, for absolutely everything. Without you to keep the perils of the night at bay, he will never be able to sleep. He needs to know that you will be walking the battlements until the day comes when he can guarantee his own survival and ensure his own physical security.

Your duty as the adult is to give answers. "Yes, you are going to survive. You are not going to die. The wolf will not come for you. I will stop him. You can sleep."

A healthy two-month-old of normal weight is fully capable of sleeping through the night without a feeding. This is the rule of thumb:
- One month old: 6 hours per night
- Two months old: 8 hours per night
- Three months old: 10 hours per night
- Four months old: 12 hours per night

The rule of thumb for any given twenty-four-hour period is:
- One month old: 16.5 hours
- Two months old: 16 hours
- Three and four months: 15.5 hours
- Five and six months: 15 hours
- Seven and eight months: 14.5 hours
- Nine, ten and eleven months: 14 hours
- Twelve to twenty-four months: 13.5 hours

The variations are few and far between.

I don't think that a sound, unbroken night's sleep is desirable for the sake of the parents. A sound, unbroken night's sleep is desirable for the sake of the children.

I have heard more than one doctor say that babies sleep as much as they need to, which is utter nonsense. Infants can no more sleep as much as they need to without help from their caregivers than they can eat as much as they need to without help from their caregivers.

If they cry because they are tired, they need help to calm down. If they cry because they are hungry, they need help to eat.

There is also a good deal of misleading advice in circulation on how to reassure infants so that they are indeed protected from the archetypal wolf at the door. Parents are told that they must walk the floor with their babies, comfort them, and if necessary allow them to sleep in the parental bed, preferably at their mothers' breasts twenty-four hours a day.

I don't think it is wrong to let newborns sleep close to Mom or Dad – provided Mom and Dad constantly check the child's breathing (see p. 65) and take precautions to avoid smothering the child. But this is only acceptable during the *honeymoon*, that is, up to what I call the true birth. The honeymoon passes quickly, and once it is over, a baby is no longer a newborn. A three-week-old baby will no longer drop off into that sleep of total oblivion, but will begin to ask questions.

However, parents continue to pick up and comfort their infants, sleep with them and feed them around the clock until neither parent nor child can take it any more. No matter what they do, the parents don't seem to be able to make their infants feel secure enough to go to sleep and stay asleep.

What has perplexed me for the last forty five years is that a baby's constantly repeated question so often draws an incorrect response.

Human beings, big or small, cannot handle fearing for their lives night after night, and that is why babies stubbornly persist in demanding a reassuring answer. If the constant attention, comfort and nursing at mother's breast were truly reassuring, the little one would go to sleep, sleep sound, go on sleeping – and stop asking questions.

So why doesn't the constant attention of doting parents make infants feel safe? *Because the parents' actions are diametrically opposed to the message they are trying to send.*

Their actions say, "Danger threatens. You aren't safe here. Poor you, you may not survive. Probably you will succumb. I feel so sorry for you. I know how terrible you must feel. All I can do is try to protect you as best I can. I will have to protect you with my body, for without that protection you are helpless. Without my bodily protection the wolf will come and take you."

Not only does this "answer" defeat the parents' purpose. It's not even true.

Little Oscar is five months old. Oscar has never slept through the night in his life. Mother's breast is his pacifier. He sleeps for twenty minutes to forty-five or, at best, two hours, and then wakes up, cries, nurses, falls asleep again, wakes up, cries, nurses, and on it goes. His mother has been wound as tight as a watch spring ever since Oscar was born.

Both Oscar's parents are starting to crack under the strain. They are also very worried about Oscar. They know he is made of the same stuff they are. Because they have gone without sleep so long themselves, they have an inkling of what their son must be feeling.

They decide that these unbearable sleepless nights have to stop. They pick a date on which to begin the Three-Night Cure. They feel a bit guilty about hatching this villainous little plot behind poor Oscar's back, but desperate times call for desperate measures.

Oscar gets a splendiferous last meal on D-day. The boy is nothing if not predictable. He usually falls asleep at 7.00 only to resurface at 9.00. From then on, he holds court at regular intervals for the rest of the night.

His mother has brought in the baby carriage, and she puts Oscar in it on the stroke of seven. He obediently drops off.

Mom and Dad are trying to keep their sense of humor through all this, and they have devised a written duty roster.

Oscar, punctual little soul that he is, comes to at nine sharp. He lifts his head, astonished at the absence of his mother's breast, and starts to cry immediately. Dad has the first watch, and he starts to push the carriage back and forth. His motions are vigorous and he extends his arm fully each time he pushes the carriage forward. Each movement finishes with a noticeable jerk, the tempo is high, and the rhythm is steady. Oscar is so stunned that he stops in mid-scream, but the silence is short-lived. He tries to raise himself on his arms, but he can't keep his balance because the movement of the carriage is too rapid.

Oscar's father doesn't say a word. He just pushes and pulls tirelessly. Oscar can't see him, since the room is dark. The only light is the little that comes under the door from the hall.

Oscar protests lustily for twenty minutes. He is sad and angry, but he also seems to be wondering what is going on. Intriguingly, his protests are not continuous. Sometimes he puts his head down and falls silent, and his little body relaxes. As soon as this happens, but *before* Oscar drops off, his father's movements slow and then dwindle away completely. At which point Oscar resumes screaming.

Dad again swings into action. The cycle repeats itself until Oscar finally falls asleep, instead of starting to cry again as soon as the carriage is still.

Oscar's parents have decided not to give him a pacifier. Oscar is used to being constantly nursed, and his parents are afraid that he would be disappointed if he were given something to suck that didn't produce milk. Better to make a clean break.

Oscar stops crying and goes back to sleep after about twenty minutes. He sleeps for just under an hour. Now it's Mom's turn to answer the call.

By this time, Oscar is beside himself. His mother feels sorry for him, but she hears the force he is putting into his crying. She can almost hear him asking furiously, "What do you think you are doing?!"

Mom says nothing and resists the urge to touch him. She just keeps pushing the carriage back and forth. She keeps a steady, rhythmic pace, and jerks the carriage noticeably at the end of every movement.

All told, her shift lasts forty-five minutes. Oscar falls silent every now and then. He puts his head down, and the little body becomes still. As soon as he shows signs of wanting to sleep, mother slows down and stops pushing – and Oscar starts up again. Mother sighs and follows suit.

Oscar is no pushover, however. He finally manages to roll over onto his back. Mom stops pushing the carriage back and forth and quickly puts Oscar back on his stomach. Quickly and firmly, she puts his arms up, straightens out his legs, and turns his head to the right. She then resumes pushing the carriage back and forth.

Finally, peace reigns. By ten past eleven, Oscar is mercifully asleep. Mother has been hard at work for three quarters of an hour, and her arm is tender. She leaves him with a soft good-night jingle.

The truce lasts until 1.00 a.m. Dad is sound asleep, but his wife gives him an elbow in the ribs. It's his watch. Dad's a zombie, but he does his duty. This time things go faster. Oscar is out in fifteen minutes and sleeps until 2.30.

Mom pushes the carriage back and forth for twenty minutes. Barely conscious herself, she exercises her still tender arm for a couple of minutes at a stretch, and dozes between rounds.

The next reveille is around four. Oscar is now ticked off rather than demanding, faint rather than angry. His father is tempted to stroke him over the cheek, but he resists the urge. He doesn't want his son to get any associations to food or his mother's breast. Dad stays at his post pushing the carriage until 4.30, but Oscar falls silent several times during that half hour before he finally dozes off.

Peace reigns until 8.00 a.m. Oscar is happy as a lark, and his guilt-racked parents are astonished. They were expecting weeping, wailing and gnashing of teeth.

The second night is much easier. Oscar wakes up at nine as usual and expects his mother's breast. He's reminded of the recent regime change by his father, who is at his post pushing the carriage. Oscar gives up after twenty minutes and sleeps until 1.00 a.m.

Mother's shift begins just as she falls into a deep sleep. She drags herself out of bed and pushes the carriage on and off for almost half an hour, but then Oscar sleeps until 4.00 a.m. Dad takes the third watch, but it's a walk in the park. Just a few short rounds, and Oscar is asleep in ten minutes.

The rest of the night is uneventful. Oscar greets the new day with boundless good humor at around seven – exactly as his parents had planned.

On the third night, the peace is shattered only once. Oscar asks the all-important question, and his parents give him an unequivocal answer through actions. Their actions say, "At night people sleep. You are going to sleep now. There is nothing to be afraid of. You can sleep and sleep well. You are safe."

Apart from this one wakeful period lasting only twenty minutes, Oscar sleeps for twelve hours. If and when he wakes up, he can go back to sleep all by himself.

On the fourth night, the house is silent. Parents and child sleep soundly. The carriage is placed outside the parents' bedroom, and there it will stay for the next week just to make sure that the cure has had its desired effect. But Oscar does not wake up, at least not so as anyone can hear.

When the week is over, Oscar moves into a crib in the nursery, and there he soon becomes a secure little sleeper.

But three weeks later, he has a relapse. Dad quickly puts him into the carriage and reminds him of the new regime. Ten to twelve minutes later, when Oscar is asleep, Dad puts him back to bed, closing the business with his reassuring good-night jingle. And that does the trick.

For Oscar and his decisive, goal-oriented parents, this sleep-through-the-night cure only took three nights. It can of course take longer to establish a healthy sleeping pattern for little children who have slept badly and/or insufficiently their whole lives, but it rarely or never takes less.

Patience and confidence in your child are essential if this cure is to work as quickly and effectively as possible. The other indispensable ingredient is an attitude that conveys the message that *everything you do is as natural and self-evident as breathing*. This last element is the bulwark of all good childcare.

Lena, nine months, has an unpredictable sleep pattern. Sometimes she sleeps and sometimes she doesn't. Her poor mother never has any idea what to expect once night falls. She has never dared leave her daughter with a babysitter. She has carried and comforted, hoped and lost faith. At eight months, the situation deteriorated, and since then there has not been a single calm night.

Lena's crib is in her mother's bedroom, but she usually sleeps in her mom's bed.

Lena's mother decides that it's time Lena learned that at night everyone sleeps – and nothing else. She picks a date to begin the cure.

On the morning of D-day, Lena's bed is placed in the little guest room. Lena is given some time to familiarize herself with her new environment. She plays on the floor beside her bed with an interesting new toy, a drawer with hitherto unexplored contents.

During the day, Lena gets more than her quota of fresh air and exercise, and copious amounts of food, especially in the evening. The evening bath is a lavish affair. The last thing her mother does before she puts Lena down for the night is make her laugh until she almost chokes. Then it's time to say goodnight.

"Good night," says Mom. "Here's your teddy. Time to sleep. Nighty-night! See you tomorrow!"

And then she's gone while repeating her last reassuring words in a happy tone times four.

It suddenly dawns on little Lena that she has been set up. Mom is actually going to *leave* her here! She immediately starts to cry. She manages to pull herself up into a standing position with the help of the crib's slats and wails like a banshee.

"Time to sleep," says mother in a loud, firm voice. She goes over to the bed and holds Lena, but *she does not pick her up.* "There, there, now it's time to sleep, sweetheart. Everything is going to be alright," she says in a voice loud and confident enough to be heard over Lena's cries. "Nighty-night. See you tomorrow."

She puts Lena down again. And Lena protests again. Her cries are a question. "Am I really supposed to sleep here? All by myself? Isn't it dangerous? Won't the wolf come for me?"

Mom tucks Lena in firmly. She holds the little body in place with both hands without speaking for perhaps ten seconds. She then gets up and leaves the room, and as she does so, she half sings her reassuring goodnight jingle. "Time to sleep. Nighty-night! See you tomorrow!"

She gives no indication of the worry she is feeling over Lena's renewed screams. She has turned off the light, but she leaves the door ajar. Lena screams. "Time to sleep. Nighty-night! See you tomorrow!" says Mom reassuringly from outside the door.

Then Mom makes a little noise. She puts on some music and potters around in the kitchen, opening and closing cupboards and drawers, and rifling through them. Lena continues crying, but her crying isn't continuous, nor is it quite as piercing. Every now and then, Lena shrieks in utter despair. Mom positions herself outside Lena's door, but makes sure little Lena cannot see her. She then repeats her reassuring but firm goodnight jingle. "Time to sleep. Nighty-night! See you tomorrow!"

Like little Oscar before her, Lena needs three nights to understand that her question (*Is it safe to sleep and do you guarantee that the wolf won't come for me?*) is being answered with an unequivocal, reassuring "yes".

If, like Lena, your child protests vigorously, it is of the utmost importance that you don't doubt your doings and hang around the child. *Your own anxiety feeds your child's fear of the wolf.*

Your words and actions should send a clear message: "At night we sleep. At night, that is what all people do!" Your words and actions should radiate serene confidence.

If, however, you have a child who doesn't cry but just lies there, abandoned and alone, looking at you with puppy dog eyes, a gentler transition may be indicated.

Put the child to bed and then wander around the room looking efficient. Pull the curtains, tidy up, arrange toys, and talk as you work. "This goes here, and that goes there. Teddy belongs up on this shelf." Don't look at the child. Just behave as though nothing is amiss. Everything is as it should be and always has been.

Finally, take a last look around, look happy and give the child a last goodnight kiss. "Sleep tight. See you in the morning. Sleep tight!"

Don't wait for a reaction, and don't seek approval – you are the one who provides answers after all, not the child.

It's hard I know, but don't let your heartstrings be tugged too hard by a little human cub who looks at you so entreatingly. Once you've said your goodnights, just leave. And even if the baby's room is absolutely silent, make a little noise and once in a while repeat whatever goodnight jingle you have made up.

A "cure" of this kind usually takes no more than three or four nights to work its magic. (Unless of course the child has been misled into severe sleeping problems – then I would highly recommend my book *GNS. A Good Night's Sleep*. www.annawahlgren.com.)

The formula for success is of course consistency. Keep your eyes on the prize. At long last, your baby is going to sleep well – finally!

It's not an easy road, however. The first night is especially difficult with the constantly repeated *calming* in the form of pushing the carriage back and forth or buffing (see "Sleep" in Part two of *For the Love of Children*). Obviously, it is hard to keep your resolve when faced with a crying, seemingly heart-broken child. It might help you to rationalize what you are doing thus: *Your child is crying because you have taught him that it is dangerous to sleep without your bodily protection*. And after all, that isn't true, is it?

Also, it might help you to consider the choice you are facing. Which is worse, three difficult nights now or three hundred later (to say the least)?

The Three-Night Cure provides an excellent context in which to bid the pacifier farewell forever. Believe me when I say that your child will forget about the pacifier in one single night (if *you* do).

The cure will be jeopardized if you run into the child's room every fifteen minutes to reinsert the pacifier. Pacifiers do not facilitate little babies' sound sleep at night. On the contrary, they disturb it.

In new situations such as this, babies produce new types of cries, and parents of course become worried. Understandably, they think something is seriously wrong. Try to steel yourself and do *not* enter the child's room until the little one has fallen silent as a result of your reassuring jingle outside the door, and you are sure he is sleeping soundly. After ten minutes (not twenty, mind you), you can go in and check for any possible problems without disturbing or worrying the little one.

Changing a sleeping child's diaper in the bed can be done. So can giving a feverish child a water bottle, whether the little one is sleeping or not. You can also tend to the clothing, tucking the baby in and so on.

Should the child wake up, just put him in place quickly and silently and leave the room. Time the goodnight jingle, times four in a row, so that you complete and finish it outside the door.

The same procedure applies if the child manages to stand up in bed and can't lie down again. When you hear him really ask for help, sounding tired and sad (not angry), you'll have to put him in place again, and finish and leave with the same old reassuring goodnight jingle.

Calming the child is what's most important. And *little children should be calmed where they are lying.*

Otherwise, you could just put the infant to bed, shut the door, put in your earplugs and leave the baby to scream.

I think that method, however, is inexcusably cruel. Moreover, this cruelty is completely unnecessary. Because what gives an infant peace is the *immediate answer* by word and deed. Your efficient calming, the familiar noises of the household going about its business and the secure, reassuring voice outside the door are what gives your child a sense of peace worthy of the name – not *fear*.

Leaving little children to their own unanswered screaming, hoping that they will eventually fall asleep by themselves (from exhaustion in other words), in the belief that all the parents have to do is appear every five minutes to tell them that they are there – all according to the so-called Controlled Crying Method – is, in my opinion, indefensible. No research results can ever "prove" to me that no damage is done if young children are left to firstly succumb to despair and then to remedy the more or less hysterical situation all alone.

The Controlled Crying Method does work. That is, sooner or later the children realize that asking all those questions is pointless, since the questions receive no reassuring answer or no answer at all. In time, they learn from experience that the wolf *probably* isn't going to come for them... So they sleep, but uneasily. It's a sleep that even mild stress can throw out of sync. A new tooth or a cold can be the catalyst. It is not the peaceful sleep that the children themselves seek.

Children who do sleep peacefully like going to bed, and they will even ask to go to bed if they need parental assistance. They drop off quickly and wake up happy. They are secure in themselves. No worries about the wolf there!

Some children are blessed with sound-making equipment that may result in complaints from the neighbors. I know one father who felt it better to head up to his cottage for the first two nights of the cure.

The Three-Night Cure will work in an unfamiliar environment, provided it is administered *by the mother or the father*. If however the parents fear they may not have the confidence or possess the necessary determina-

643

tion or enthusiastic decisiveness to see the project through in a reassuring way, then the cure will also work with someone other than the mother and father as long as it is done in the child's home environment.

Children who have been sleeping well can suddenly start to wake up night after night. This is especially common around eight and eighteen months. The rule of thumb is: *Once is an exception, twice is a habit.*

An unhappy little person who has had a bad dream must of course be comforted. Don't wait for the crying to subside! Go to the child at once!

However, *after* you have comforted the child, even if the crying continues or starts anew, don't go in. Stand outside the door and reassuringly repeat what you said when you went in.

When you do go in, remember that the goal is to soothe the child, not upset the little one even more! Your baby has been frightened somehow and needs to know that you are there to hold the wolf at bay. Take a deep breath and try to summon up all the *sang froid* you can muster. Adopt an air of confidence (which of course you don't feel) that says to the child that everything is as it should be. Soothe the baby in his bed.

If on the other hand you overreact, pick the child up, turn on the lights and overdo the (anxious) comforting, you are basically telling the already terrified child that he's right. Danger lurks everywhere, the darkness is to be feared, the bed is not safe, and the child must be whisked away to somewhere that is!

If you stay calm, leave the child in bed and the room in darkness, you convey an entirely different message. Just because you don't make a huge affair out of his fear, that doesn't mean you don't take it seriously. "I know you were afraid," you're saying, "but don't worry! Nothing is going to happen to you. The wolf won't get by me. I won't let it. You can sleep. You're safe."

By going to the child immediately, instead of hoping that he will stop crying of his own accord (which he well might, but the next time he will probably wake up screaming as well), you are also saying, "I am always close by. I am always watching over you. The wolf won't get by me. You can sleep peacefully."

Once is a coincidence. But if your child wakes up the next night, cries and exhibits the same level of anxiety, think twice before you go in. Repeat your reassuring good-night jingle outside the bedroom door. When the child drops off, wait ten minutes and then you can make sure all is well. The little one won't notice.

On the third night, you should definitely hold your horses. But as quickly as you went to the child's room to calm the little one down on the first night, take your post outside the (open ajar) door and say the magic good-night jingle times four.

Sooner or later – usually as soon as they are able to get out of bed (so keep the crib as long as possible, ideally until your child is through the terrible twos) – most children toddle into the parents' bedroom to see what they are (not) up to. There are a lot of families where Mom and Dad fall asleep in their bed and the kids fall asleep in theirs, but come morning, everyone has changed places, and no one can remember how it happened.

How you handle these little visitors is of course up to you. But if you feel the least bit uncomfortable or you feel that your personal well-needed rest is at jeopardy, you should do something about it. It is dishonest to harbor resentful feelings towards your child. Kids don't volunteer to be a nuisance or to make life difficult for their parents.

If you have decided that the family is going to stay put once everyone has gone to bed, a little therapy for your nocturnal wanderers is in order. Stay awake for two or three nights so that you can nab your children as soon as they come sleepily trotting into your bedroom. *Wake* them gently and, as you lead them back to their own bed, tell them kindly but firmly that they are going to sleep where they belong at night and that you will see them in the morning.

The odd nocturnal visit is, of course, bearable. There is a risk though – unless you immediately lead your children back to their own beds – that you may be asleep the next time, noticing nothing. A habit will be established in no time. Then you might hear, as you walk in the door after a late evening out: "I couldn't sleep because you weren't home."

At the end of the day, you can't do your children's sleeping for them. They have to feel secure enough to fall asleep and go back to sleep on their own, if and when they wake up, knowing that *at night, nothing happens.*

Your child's nocturnal sleep should not be connected to you or your bed.

Your child's nocturnal sleep should be connected to the child and to the child's bed.

A not uncommon problem is a seemingly endless ritual around going to bed. Parents who have been schooled to believe that children take the sleep they need all by themselves, which is not usually true, don't dare provide leadership but wait until their kids fall over from exhaustion.

These elaborate, time-consuming rituals can take hold as early as the age of two, but in my experience this only afflicts kids who *are not needed* – kids who are denied social participation in other words.

A young child who is not allowed to make a contribution to the common struggle for survival within the flock suffers from a feeling of meaninglessness and frantically tries to compensate. These anxiety-ridden nightly rituals give the child a sense of control.

You should therefore not encourage these rituals, but rather regard them as warning signals.

Try to put your little trooper to work during the day, be the tasks ever so humble. Do it regularly and take it seriously! Show your children every day that you *need* them, not just emotionally but practically and concretely within the common struggle for existence. Just like all of us, even very young children need to know deep down that they are useful. *The others wouldn't manage quite as well without me.*

Many so-called experts recommend a soothing, drawn-out winding down before bedtime, and the parents' cooperation in going-to-bed rituals is strongly encouraged. The same stories must be read, the same ceremonies performed hour after hour, night after night.

I am skeptical to both these recommendations, to the latter for the reasons just cited, and to the former because I think it is manipulation (as well as an abdication of parental responsibility). A so-called winding down puts a damper on the day. The assumption behind this winding down is that the children will go to bed of their own accord.

Naturally, it is easier for you, as a mother or a father, if your child takes responsibility for going to bed. But you will make life easier for your child if you do the honorable thing and take responsibility for it yourself.

A happy little person sleeps better than a "wound down" little person. Young children, in my opinion, should be positively joyful before they go to sleep, rather than soothed or "tranquillized". Play, tickle, joke, make faces, anything you can come up with to get the child to *laugh*! Thus the day has come to a good end and accordingly sleep will be good too.

Adults don't much like going to bed after a dull, monochrome day, memorable only because nothing memorable happened. After a boring, "empty" or frustrating day, it is difficult to jump into bed looking forward to another day of more of the same. But if before bed we leave the day behind and engage in something fun or interesting, then the day wasn't completely meaningless and we are able to look forward to tomorrow.

It's far more satisfying for you as parent to wave goodnight to a happy little soul than to a whiny, morose one – although waving goodnight to whiny children doesn't happen much these days, since so many parents lie down with their kids and end up falling asleep themselves.

I don't think it's fair not to trust little children with the ability of – and the need for – falling asleep on their own.

Some slightly older children who are extremely persistent but who realize that their ruses and complaints won't get them anywhere, are adept at keeping themselves awake on purpose. While there are others who struggle with real problems falling asleep.

"I can't sleep!" they announce.

You can sit on the edge of the bed and suggest the following: "Think of something nice. Then you'll sleep. You know what I used to think about when I was your age? (Pick your story!) I'd like to know what you think about when you go to sleep. You can tell me about it in the morning."

Then get up and leave the room without giving the child a chance to object. (Just don't forget to follow up the conversation in the morning!)

For significantly older children and teenagers who have sleep problems, a good talk or a folk remedy can help. Warm milk with honey or a little valerian goes a long way.

The most important thing is to have an explanation at the ready. "You're too tired. It is as simple as that. You need to give your mind a rest. Think about something – or someone – that you really like!"

A tender caress, a stroke on the cheek, a kiss on the forehead, a hand in the hand – is good medicine for people of all ages. Tenderness is the world's best sleeping pill.

Or at the very least, it runs a close second to laughter!

MARIE AND SAMUEL, SIX WEEKS OLD
– AN E-MAIL CORRESPONDENCE

January 3, 2004

Dear Anna:

Honestly, is the idea to breastfeed 23 hours a day?!

I'm puzzled about this demand-feeding method. I was told that after four-to six weeks, some sort of an eating pattern would be discernable, but so far I haven't seen an inkling of it.

Little Samuel will soon be six weeks old, and his appetite has been amazing ever since he was born. I feel like I'm breastfeeding him incessantly. Occasionally, he sleeps two hours in a row during the night – what a blessing! What I'm getting more and more concerned about is his turning so restless while eating. He lets go of the nipple, arching his back and working himself up, and at the same time he's unhappy because the nipple disappeared! This tends to occur toward the end of the meal, not in the beginning, when he's usually concentrating and eats well. I'm starting to believe that he suffers from tummy ache. Is it colic, maybe? Would you have any advice on what I can do to help him? I keep away from milk and other foods that might affect my (and his) stomach negatively.

Another thing: he seems to prefer placing his head to the right. Do you have any experience of that?

Now I have to rush and save Samuel from the end of the world.

Sincerely,
Marie.

January 5, 2004

Dear Marie:

Oh no, the idea is *not* to breastfeed 23 hours a day! The 'honeymoon' is over, and it's about time to structure the days (and nights). Now little Samuel is supposed to eat more at fewer feeding sessions, and so be it!

My so-called Standard Model looks like this: a meal of one and a half hours – including food, refill, change, conversation and other entertainment; breast number two, burp, and refill – to be followed by a sleep of two and a half hours. That's the principle.

Presumably, little Samuel now has the strength to stay awake for two hours at a time, at least sometimes. Hence, between certain meals, he could be allowed to sleep two hours instead of two and a half.

At night, he's supposed to sleep not two hours in a row but six, or six and a half hours! He'll manage just fine, as long as you see to it that he's awake for long enough periods in the daytime, and that he gets all the food he can ever take. By the time he's eight weeks old, his night's sleep should last for eight hours, and he'll be well capable of that. (And ten hours by three months of age, and twelve by the time he's four months old.)

The requirements for this are, 1) a full-weight, healthy baby, 2) parents who take the lead and, when need be, help the little one to relax in bed.

So, forget about colic! I promise you that no such thing is troubling him. It's just that no longer is he as newborn as you may think... As long as you offer him your breast and nipple all around the clock, he won't be hungry enough to suck properly (except for the first few minutes, as you can see), which is why various kinds of objections are bound to follow. Only hunger can make him concentrate on eating. Alas, structure! Write down a schedule – mealtimes should *start* approximately every four hours – and from now on, make the clock your best friend!

You put him to sleep on his back, I suppose? A personal tip I would very much like to give you is to purchase an apnea monitor and put him to sleep on his tummy instead. He will sleep deeper then, 'better' – longer. This is the case with the vast majority of little babies – they both need and like this sleeping position.

To help him sleep through those two and a half hours, or two, between the 'meals' (all included), roll the carriage back and forth, rapidly and steadily, until little Samuel is quiet and calm, ready to doze off.

As for your question about your little one putting his head to the right: If you look around you will see that instinctively most parents carry their infants against their left shoulder. It seems that little ones' instinct is to lay their heads to the right. Why? Well, who knows?...

Love,
Anna

January 7, 2004

Dear Anna:
Oh my God, I'm so happy that you replied! I felt as though a big block of concrete dropped from my breast (!) when you wrote I should start to structure things. Many thanks for telling me how!

Two questions: our baby carriage is not really designed for sleeping flat in it, nor for heavy rocking. Would it be totally wrong to take him in my arms and try to rock him to sleep while holding him tight? Or else, I'm afraid there will be screaming beyond imagination!

And could you please tell me more about the Standard Model? Is there any chance you would help me come up with a schedule?

Love and thank you,
Marie

January 8, 2004

Dear Marie:
Holding him in your arms and trying to lull him to sleep is *not* a good idea,

since as soon as you pick him up, he'll believe that it's nursing time. To him, you're not associated with sleeping. Your presence means eating and being 'up' and awake.

A flat and roomy baby carriage would be your best investment! Rocking is invincible; with the right technique, you can make even hysterically screaming little babies turn quiet in less than two minutes.

My second best tip is this: place Samuel on his tummy or side on a bed (even in the daytime), spread a blanket over him, make the room as dark as possible, and sitting next to him begin buffing him. This means that you find a way of rocking him with your one hand, whereas you keep him in place with the other. The little body should rhythmically jerk a bit at every regular buffing, which should *not* be rigid, hard or violent but soft, firm and decisive. (Sitting down, you could practice buffing on your own thighs, imagining the side of your right thigh to be Samuel's little diaper bottom, the top of the left to be his back.) Soon you'll find out what makes him calm and find peace, and thus be able to go to sleep. The point is that he can't see you while you do this (preferably, he should see nothing at all) and of course, that you do not talk to him.

Here's a schedule suggestion for you to consider:

5–6.30 a.m. the first Standard-Model meal. Food (no interruptions whatsoever), burp when he refuses to have more, and then a refill from the same breast; 20 minutes altogether. Diaper change. Conversation: you hold him against you, his head in your hands, and make eye contact. This is *not* about eating (and at this point, he won't be very hungry anyway). Talk to him, see him imitate you ... Make sure that light falls on your face, and try to keep his attention! He is *not* allowed to fall asleep. Keep going as long as you can make it (change included, you ought to manage about 45 minutes). Naturally, you are free to carry him around to show him the world. Mind you, there must be no 'consolation' in the air! Let him look at lamps, windows, the outdoors... Colors, flowers... you know. When he no longer shows any enthusiasm, sit down where you breastfeed him and serve the other breast. This should invigorate him and make him eat fairly well. Burp; he's still not allowed to fall asleep, so don't be too 'kind' when you burp him! Offer the same breast one last time. Now, after one hour and a half, the meal is over, and he's been fully awake this whole time – beware of the slightest dozing! Sleep to follow: 2,5 hours. If need be, you have to help him continue sleeping, but don't pick him up until the next meal is on the scheduled doorstep. By then, put him at the breast whether he's awake or not.

The second meal: 9–10.30 a.m. As above. Sleep 10.30–1 p.m.

The third meal: 1–2.30 p.m. Ditto. Sleep until 5 p.m.

The fourth meal: 5–6.30 p.m. Ditto. Sleep until 9 p.m.

The fifth and final meal of the day: 9–10.30 p.m.

Such a structure would mean calling it a night from 10.30 p.m. till 5 a.m., which makes six and a half hours. Due to all that food in the daytime – four rounds at every meal – and all that waking time – 5 x 1.5 hours a day = 7.5 hours – little Samuel will be perfectly capable of managing six and a half hours without food. (Little people of his age need to sleep 16–17 hours in a 24-hour day.)

Indeed, the idea is not that you nurse 23 hours a day! Launch this kind of a schedule, and you'll be granted 4 x 2.5 hours free time during his daytime sleeping sessions, and 6.5 hours nightly. You can live very well with that! Particularly as in three weeks or so, his nights will be eight hours long.

As you understand, little Samuel won't be the one to establish such a schedule. You will have to do it for him. He will gladly accept it though, since little children – just like everybody else – need to know what counts. All human beings in this world (one size fits all!) want to be confident with a somewhat stable routine. In order to learn what's up, Samuel will have to ask, and since he has no words for his questions, he will ask in the form of screaming. That's why you should regard his screaming as *questions* in need of your immediate and proper answer (through your actions), *not* as worrying signs of his being sick or sad. Because there's nothing wrong with him. He simply wants to know. He's programmed to learning how to make it in this world. Ultimately, it's a matter of survival.

If and when you decide to take the lead, start with a three-day 'cure' during which you follow the set hours in a stalwart manner, allowing a margin of no more than fifteen minutes at both ends. This will put *you* in charge of when Samuel is supposed to sleep, to be awake, and when to eat. By the third day, you'll notice him clearly responding to the cure, and during the week to come, as everything is falling in place, he'll astonish you by turning into your own personal little timekeeper!

January 9, 2004

Dear Anna:
Can I bottom-pat also when Samuel is on his side, or is it best to have him on his tummy? I tried the tummy style, and it worked well the first time. I even managed to turn him over onto his side without waking him up. It seems quite obvious that he's the most comfortable on tummy.

Anyway, here's the big news: we got started! We took off yesterday, struggled through the night and are just about to start a new one. I have been consistent and haven't diverged a bit from the schedule.

I must say, though, it's a bit hard at times, when he becomes sad. I do the buffing, trying out all kinds of rhythmical treatment... It isn't easy! I feel barbarian not being able to make him quiet right away, but I'm doing the best I can. I cradle him in the bed and keep my hand on his back, and I'm careful not to let him see me, and I keep totally quiet. It works fine – but only for a little while. In a few minutes, his little arms go startling and twitching; he wakes up again, and there we go again. This is how we went through some of the daytime sleeping sessions, and I do hope that things will improve.

He likes to be awake when he's supposed to sleep, and to sleep when he's supposed to be awake... By the time we're done with the breastfeeding (and during my nursing him), he's almost unconscious, and I really have a hard time to get him alert. You wouldn't have any tips at hand?

This morning at 5 a.m. he was asleep, so I had to wake him up!! Didn't feel too happy about it, but I realize that it has to be that way.

January 10, 2004

Dear Marie:
Good heavens, you got the Standard Model under way already? That tells me you are motivated enough! Because, as you can see, it's hard work to bring order to chaos. Such an enterprise calls for both doubtless determination and doubtless consistency! But rest assured: as soon as little Samuel gets the hang of it, he will start to 'respond' in the most beautiful way. Along the road, how-

ever, he will have to ask you some hundreds of 'questions'...

As I understand it, you've figured out a buffing technique that works. Well done! The idea is to make him quiet in less than two minutes. Be patient with yourself! In the beginning, you can't expect an immediate, and everlasting, result! After all, two minutes is quite a long time. He needs this period of time to allow himself to listen to your message. That's why you mustn't change it too quickly (or at all). There always *is* a rocking or buffing strategy that brings forth peace; it's just a matter of figuring it out and patiently making use of it – and you seem to have come that far already. That's my girl!

Little Samuel awakened soon after because he needed to pose a new (same) question, and the only thing to do, which you did, is to give him a new (same) answer. Repeatedly, until he accepts it. And the message is, translated from words to deed, 'Go back to sleep, sweetheart, you're supposed to sleep a little longer (i.e. until I take you out of bed, not until you scream yourself out of it). I'm guarding your interests here, I guarantee your safety, I promise you that you can sleep peacefully, nothing bad will happen to you, no beast will come to snatch you! Everything is in perfect order.' Moreover, he scares himself with his own screaming; he can be after himself simply because he's after himself. That's why it's so important that you manage to quieten him quickly.

If you can't make it happen instantly, you are no barbarian. People (even little babies) must be allowed to react, and, quite frankly, to be in a bad mood sometimes. Your scrupulously following the schedule will help you *know* that at each 'meal', he's getting everything he needs. If all the same, he starts whining, grumbling and expressing disappointment because he can't fall asleep immediately, so let him (for a little while)! Such dissatisfaction you can't deny people. The point is that if and when he screams, he shouldn't do so because of the *lack* of something. Because of your continuously satisfying his every need at every meal, this can't happen. And that's why you'll feel sure enough to 'demand' that he calm down and be quiet in order to be able to fall asleep.

Almost unconscious – well, he's been used to short little naps and short little slurps, all around the clock... That's a pattern that may suit little honeymooners (during the first three weeks of life). It's true that on their own accord, most three to four-week-old babies do prolong the meals – they eat more and more, and less often – and, in response to that, they sleep longer in between the feedings. But not all babies do. Like Samuel, lots of them keep on going *staccato* 24 hours a day, believing that this is how it should be! Which soon creates misery, because in the long run, no more do they have the strength to cope with unpredictable chaos than their tender parents do.

So, when he's supposed to be awake, try to keep him conscious with all possible tricks of the trade! He'll soon get used to the new order. Next time, the next meal, he'll be hungrier and eat better, which will bring him strength and energy, which will keep him both conscious and alert. In no time, he'll end up in a good cycle! Hold him high and walk around, keeping him in an upright position, not like a rag doll over the shoulder. Entice him to look at things, speak to him in a loud voice, and insist on his attention! (If he starts crying, drown the cries with even louder, even happier talk. Beware of consolation here – he mustn't feel that something is wrong.)

Put him flat on his back and be silly with him: splatter and blow air on his tummy and cheeks, nibble his little hands, 'bite' and tickle his feet... Go for it as if you were competing in a sport: make him laugh, at all costs, and victory is yours! Find out new activities to reawaken his curiosity: listen and dance to music, let him watch his mirror picture, make funny faces for him to imitate, sing, talk, make the lights go on and off, swing him in your arms – anything you can come up with that tickles his joy. It's tough work, I know, but trust me: in just a day or two, your toil will be but a memory.

Thanks to his regular sleeping those two hours, or two and a half, between the meals, the 'unconsciousness' will disappear, and your little Samuel will be pure sunshine.

January 10, 2004

Dear Anna:
Could anyone be more motivated after having had no more than two hours of continuous sleep for six weeks, plus an odd half hour every now and then? Don't think so!

Obviously, I got started in the nick of time for the sake of all three of us. In the beginning, my husband was a little dubious, but now realizes the advantages of having a rested wife. Samuel didn't cry a lot these first six weeks, because as soon as he opened his mouth, he got food. . . I suppose this is why my hubby thought there was a bit too much hassle the first night.

Last night, Samuel slept from 11 p.m. to 4.30 a.m.! Five hours and a half. Absolutely fantastic! It proves we're on the right track. At the end of meal one, all included, both of us fell asleep and slept like logs for two hours and fifteen minutes! After meal two, however, he wasn't that easily convinced, but all I had to do was rock the cradle a little, and so he went back to sleep. Didn't even have to lay my hands on him. Now we're getting close to meal three, and after two hours and 20 minutes, he's still sound asleep!

It goes like clockwork! Isn't he doing wonderfully? I must say, I was prepared for something much worse. Anna, I will be forever grateful for this!

Now it's time to wake him up. (Reversed roles, it used to be Samuel waking me up!)

January 12, 2004

Dear Marie:
Now I'm terribly curious! A full account, if you please!

January 12, 2004

Dear Anna:
We are doing fine! The third night, he slept for four hours and 45 minutes in a row. Last night, he fell asleep by 10.30 p.m. and woke up 3.30 a.m. – only to go back to sleep, and all by himself! He was never hysterical, and now he does manage to fall asleep on his own. Unbelievable but true!

In the daytime, he's doing fine as well. It's just that for some reason, he has set his internal clock fifteen minutes before the scheduled waking time and thus often anticipates me, the little villain. But since this occurs within the allowed margin of a quarter of the hour, I suppose it's OK. Now I also feel confident about him really sleeping (when he should be) as we leave home to go grocery shopping, for example. And it's so good to know that he can't possibly be hungry.

From that unconscious after-eating state he's now passed on to being *extremely* tired. That, too, may indicate an improvement, I guess. We just got home from grocery shopping (during his sleeping time) and I lifted him over to his bed; so far he hasn't uttered a sound. Yet you should know that his eyes were open when I moved him.

Anna, I'm totally happy with this already!

February 6, 2004

Dear Anna:

Just want to let you know that everything is fine around here. Samuel is doing swell, and I'm really proud of him. I met a couple of mothers, one of them of a four-month-old baby, and one of a nine-month-old. Both babies used to wake up several times every night and, exactly as I did earlier, their moms used to nurse them all around the clock. How proud I was to tell them about my good little two-month-old Samuel, who sleeps a whole six hours every night (*and* fifteen minutes!). Now I suspect you think it's time to make those six hours into eight? If his bedtime is at 10.30 p.m. and he sleeps for eight hours, it will take us to 6.30 a.m. How do we continue from there?

One of the mothers said she read your book and tried your buffing method, but with her little son, it didn't work. It made me wonder if she failed because she wasn't motivated enough. I remember one occasion – I think it was during the second night – when I was just a minute away from giving it all up. Then I reminded myself of what I would have to return to, and I realized I had no choice. All I could do was keep on buffing for dear life!

February 7, 2004

Dear Marie:

Oh my, is little Samuel terrific or what! And so are you. You listened to your common sense, you took over the responsibility for his well-being – the well-being that is now your reward. I'm so proud of you!

Right; people read (or hear) about the Standard Model and give the buffing or rocking a half-hearted try. Their mistake is precisely what you say. You have to be properly motivated. Experimenting a little, expecting the baby to take on the responsibility for success, won't do. There is a dieting comparison which I use to light-heartedly get the point across: 'The banana diet, a-ha! Okie-dokie, I'll eat a banana and see if I get any slimmer. See? It didn't work at all.'

If you want to stick to today's bedtime at 10.30 p.m., and add two hours of sleep, just as you wrote, it will take you to 6.30 a.m. It is time to make up a new schedule. Go for five meals over the day, when he will be awake for at least one and a half hours at a time, perhaps two. In between, sleep will last for two and a half hours, or maybe only one and a half. You know the general times he tends to get tired, as well as the times when he is more alert, so make up the schedule using what you know about the habits he has already. For example, mealtimes could begin at 6.30 a.m., 10 a.m., 2 p.m., 5.30 p.m., and 9 p.m. You have to think your way over carefully! Once you have written down the new schedule, you mustn't be tempted to start changing it, if and when something troubles you. Samuel will need his time – one week – to get what the news is all about and to cope with it, and every now and then he will have to ask questions.

I assume he is not using a pacifier? If he is – discard it! He'll forget all about it in one single night. In times to come, you'll have one worry fewer. That's all there is to it.

February 12, 2004

Dear Anna:

I made up a new schedule, and we put it into effect this morning. Sweet little Samuel woke up a quarter to five, as usual, and wondered if it really wasn't time for a new day. Eventually, I managed to convince him that he'd love to sleep until half past six! The first daytime sleeping session I've set to last for two hours and a half, and the others for two hours each. Usually, he sleeps like a log after the first morning meal, all included, and so he did today as well.

Hi! It's me again, one day later, and so far, everything works super. He fell asleep at 10.30 p.m., woke up at 5.45 a.m., went back to sleep and kept on sleeping till 6.35 a.m. Daytime sessions also went well.

P.S. Don't know what to do with myself – can't stop kissing him, because he's such a sweetheart!

February 18, 2004

Dear Anna:

How right you are. Everything runs exactly as planned. Samuel sleeps and is awake when he should be, and obviously, our schedule suits him fine. He's always happy. Now he's discovered a new entertaining hobby in nibbling and tasting his hands. They seem to be yummy!

Last weekend we were off to the beach, enjoying ourselves immensely. Samuel was behaving wonderfully. No problems whatsoever. However, I watched a mother with two children, one a few months older than Samuel, the other maybe two years old. Holding the little one in her arms, the mother cradled the baby to sleep (it took her ages). Then she lifted the other, bigger child, into her arms, and did the same thing with him!!! I feel sorry for her back, is all I can say. All I had to do was put Samuel in his carriage and shake the handle a couple of times. In no time, he was asleep.

My husband noticed the trouble the other mother was having and said to me, 'How lucky that you got in contact with Anna, because if you didn't, we would be doing that same thing.'

Gee, I'm dying to read your book!

Yours forever grateful,

Marie.

THE SAFARI. AN ALLEGORY

Imagine you are on safari. You have been dreaming about going on safari for several years. Now you are doing it!

You are in the middle of no man's land. It's only your first day and you have already seen scores of wild animals. Early tomorrow morning, you are going bird watching.

You are part of a small group that is eagerly seeking grand close encounters with Nature.

And your guide is fabulous. He is knowledgeable and confident, and he adores his work. You have complete confidence in him. He has porters, cooks, scouts and all manner of experts to help him. This is truly a world-class operation!

From day one, you have been very professionally looked after.

This enterprise is not cheap, but it's worth every penny. It has surpassed your wildest expectations!

You set up camp and night falls. You enjoy a hearty dinner around the campfire. The conversation is exhilarating. You even got to see a lion earlier in the day. A large male, close enough to touch, was indolently stretched out in the sun.

What an experience! Your travelling companions are as excited as you are.

You are given your own tent to sleep in out there in the bush. There are one-person tents for solitary sojourners, and you appreciate that. You want to be left in peace with no disturbances. It makes for a better night's sleep.

The guide provides you with a blanket and a pillow, and wishes you good night. Before he goes, he takes you aside and gives you a friendly word of warning.

"Make sure you stay on your travel bed during the night. Scorpions and poisonous spiders sometimes get into the tents."

You scramble up onto your travel bed and try to draw your knees up to your chin.

No need to be nervous, you tell yourself. It has been a long, somewhat overwhelming day. Your poor brain has been bombarded with new impressions, and you are tired. You're dying to sleep.

You lie there in the dark, vaguely aware of the light from the campfire, listening to the jungle's nocturnal symphony. Your eyelids feel heavy.

But what was that? What was that sound? Wasn't that a lion roaring right outside your tent?

You sit bolt upright on your travel bed. There's a lion out there! You heard it roar! And there it is again! A lion is roaring for all he is worth right outside your tent!

Your heart is pounding. Frozen with fear, you stare into the darkness towards the entrance to the tent. The material is flimsy. Thin canvas. It offers no protection. You realize in horror how easy it would be for the lion to rip through the tent flap and pounce on you in the darkness.

Oh God, it's roaring again! Wasn't it closer this time? Your heart is beating so loudly it all but drowns out your terrified thoughts.

You try to pull yourself together. You have to do something. But what? You are all alone in this pathetic little tent out in the middle of nowhere, and you won't have a chance if the lion decides to attack.

The roaring again! You are awash in icy sweat.

You don't scream. You are an adult after all, and even if you have never been this petrified in your life, you are going to conduct yourself with decorum.

You clear your throat nervously.

"Hello!" you cry timidly towards the tent flap. "Is anyone there? Hello...?"

What an indescribable relief! The tent flaps part and in the campfire's feeble light, you see the barrel of a rifle. And who is holding the gun? Your guide, your wonderful, splendid, glorious guide!

Now you see him clearly, and he is truly a sight for sore eyes.

"No problem," he says with a reassuring smile. "I'm standing guard out here. You can rest easy."

You are so relieved, you want to throw your arms around him. But there's that business with the scorpions...

"I thought I heard a lion," you manage to gasp.

"No lion would dare get this close," the guide reassures you. "And if one were stupid enough to try, he'd only do it once, believe you me."

He leaves. The tent flaps close. Reassured, you lie down again. Your heart slowly descends from your throat and assumes its customary position. You fall into a sound sleep.

But what was that? You heard it again!

You sit up on the bunk with a start, wide-awake. Your heart is going like a jackhammer. Now you hear not just one, but *several* lions. There are at least three of them out there roaring like it's going out of style. You could swear that there is one on each side of the tent and one behind you.

How long have you been asleep? You don't know. If only this were a nightmare, but no such luck. You can see the lions skulking around the tent, casting their ominous shadows on the canvas. They are all around you! Their roaring engulfs you in the dark jungle night.

Frantically, you try to get a grip on yourself. The sweat trickles down your face, your heart pounds. You try to think…

The guide said that he would stand guard. He told you that you could rest easy. If the lions came, he would take care of them. He promised.

But what if he doesn't stay at his post? The guide needs to sleep too, doesn't he? What if he doesn't hear the lions? Maybe he has a girlfriend out here in the bush somewhere and he is sleeping with her in some distant tent. He might not have the faintest inkling that your life is hanging in the balance!

Now the lions are roaring again. You are convinced that one of them, or two, or maybe all three are going to storm the tent at any moment, rip it to shreds and sink their blood-thirsty fangs into your flesh. They are going to tear you limb from limb!

"Hello!" you whimper again, and now you sound every bit as terrified as you actually are. "Hello? Is anyone there? Hellooo?"

Do you dare hope for the same wonderful sight as last time? No, you don't! The lions are roaring in the darkness. Can the guide hear them, even if he is standing just outside? Maybe they've got him too!

But thank the Lord, there he is!

The gun barrel parts the tent flaps and the guide enters. He stands before you, large and confident, rifle at the ready.

"There's no danger," he assures you. "I'm here. You can rest easy."

You would throw yourself at his feet in blissful gratitude if it weren't for the scorpions.

You're still afraid, but doesn't the roaring of the lions seem a little more distant now? Maybe they weren't as close as you thought. Maybe they weren't anywhere near the tent. You know how hard it is to judge distances in the dark. And the shadows? Maybe it was only the flames of the campfire playing tricks on you.

But common sense doesn't allay your fears. You are still so terrified you can hardly breathe.

"They sound awfully close," you manage to get out.

The guide sees how frightened you are. He puts down his rifle and comes closer.

"There are several of us out there," he says soothingly. "No one's life is in jeopardy on this safari!"

That was what you wanted to hear. You stretch out again on your narrow bed and try to swallow the lump in your throat.

The guide looks dismayed.

"Poor you," he says and comes a little closer. "Were you really that scared? But you don't have to be scared. I'm here. I'm with you."

That's the problem, you think to yourself as the lump in your throat starts to grow again. The guide *is* with you. He isn't outside the tent, his rifle at the ready. His gun is out of reach. He put it down at the entrance to the tent. He is standing beside your cot looking down at you, instead of standing guard outside.

That's hardly reassuring.

You are beginning to feel nervous. This professional guide, who radiates confidence, who is security personified, is hovering over your bed looking worried.

And now you hear the lions again! They're here! They are overrunning the camp! You can hear all three of them! And they're getting closer and closer...

Panic-stricken, you stare at the guide. Doesn't he hear them? Why doesn't he do something?

You're on the verge of cardiac arrest you're so terrified.

"Dear heart," says the guide sympathetically. "You're so frightened! I feel so sorry for you!"

Now he comes right up to the bed, as you lie there paralyzed with fear.

He tilts his head and looks at you comfortingly.

"I can lie down you with you for a bit if you like. I can pat you."

Pat you? You are so petrified you don't know which end is up. That's very kind of him, but... the lions are roaring outside. Three of them. Their roars are so ear splitting they might as well be inside the tent.

How can the guide think that the lions will go away just because he lies down beside you and pats you?

You try to think straight. He must know what he is doing. After all, he is an experienced safari guide and he knows the bush. What would happen if your cowardly side accepted his offer to lie down beside you and pat you?

He would be lying on the side nearest the entrance to the tent. He would be the one to get eaten first if the lions were to get in. That would mean at least some protection for you.

But it would be fleeting! There would still be two more lions! One would gobble down the guide, but the other two would still be hungry. You would be easy prey. Your final hour would be delayed but not by much.

No, you don't think this lie-down-and-pat stuff is a very good idea!

The guide looks worried. Then he brightens up and comes up with another suggestion.

"We can dance! Wouldn't that be nice and soothing?"

He opens his arms invitingly to take you into his embrace for a slow waltz.

Nice and soothing? You're not too sure about that. You don't think it would be particularly soothing to put your feet down among the poisonous spiders and scorpions and dance a waltz with the guide. What's more, you don't understand how dancing around the tent is going to stop these lions from launching a deadly attack at any moment.

No, you don't think this is a good idea at all.

"Shall we have a cup of tea then?" asks the guide. "Tea for two and a nice chat, just you and me! Wouldn't that be fun? And a cakey-wakey maybe?"

Cakey-wakey? What's with the baby talk?

The guide, the man to whom you have entrusted your life and your security is smiling so tenderly at you. He seems to really want you to have a good time there in the tent.

Out in the bush.

At night.

With lions roaring just outside.

What are you supposed to think? You wonder if you are losing your mind. You are in mortal danger, and your guide is cooing at you like you were a little baby at your mother's breast!

Just at that moment, you hear a roar that is so close you don't dare straighten your arm for fear of having your hand bitten off. Your blood runs so cold it congeals in your veins. You realize that the lion has advanced to the spot where the guide should have been standing guard.

Your nerves, already stretched to breaking point, finally snap.

"Shut up and shoot something!" you howl, abandoning any pretence of decorum. "I paid good money for this trip and I want the security I was promised. And another thing! I want to go bird watching tomorrow, and I need my sleep! Sleep! As in unconscious! So stop bothering me! Do your frigging job! Get your butt out there and stand guard!"

"Don't you like me?" asks the guide.

"What?"

You can't believe you're hearing this. And speaking of hearing, you suddenly don't hear any lions roaring.

"I thought you liked me," says the guide.

He looks at you as though you should be worried about *him* instead of a bunch of lions and all the other things you are so scared of. He seems to be implying that you should be feeling sorry for him because you've been so mean to him. After all he has tried to do for you, all you do is yell at him!

"What does that have to do with anything?" you say. "This isn't about *feelings*! It's about me being able to sleep and you keeping the lions away."

"There are no lions around here," the guide says sulkily. "At least no dangerous ones. At least no dangerous ones that come very close to the tent. At least no dangerous ones that come very close to the tent that you have to be afraid of. At least no dangerous ones that come very close to the tent that you have to be afraid of because they might eat you. At least…"

"Don't talk so much!" you interrupt. "Prove it."

You're starting to wonder if the guide and his assistants, who are supposed to function as a reliable security force after dark, are really qualified for the job.

Do they really think that cooing, patting, comforting, dancing, cakeywakeys and all this talking will guarantee the *security* of the people on this safari?

At last the guide gets the message. He picks up his gun and leaves. Finally! The tent flaps close silently behind him and you feel at peace.

The lions have fallen silent. And that is pure heaven because now you are absolutely exhausted. It won't be long before it's time to get up and go bird watching and you want to be able to keep up.

And not just keep up. You want to enjoy it!

You came along on this safari because you wanted a once-in-a-lifetime experience, not a nocturnal circus like the one you have just been through.

You stretch out on the bed fully conscious of the fact that a new threat can materialize at any time and frighten you half to death. But at least now you dare to believe that the guide is at his post, armed and at the ready.

You can sleep soundly! He is not going to hang around your cot and babble about feelings.

But what was that? Was that a gunshot?

Or was it something else, one of the myriad wilderness sounds that you don't recognize?

Or are you just imagining things?

Anyway, now you can sleep in peace and that is going be sheer ecstasy!

IT TAKES TWO TO TANGO

It is a fact of life that it takes two people to make a child, and in most cases it is these same two people who parent the child.

As long as these two parents can sit down together, talk things through and agree to a common course of action then all is well and good. But if the communication between them is not ideal, or if one or both refuse to compromise, then there are a thousand details on the road to raising a child which can lead to a head-on collision.

Dad perhaps thinks his little girl (let's say) should be able to sit at the table and eat properly, while Mom thinks it's not that important. Mom nags the child and demands obedience, while Dad takes the child's side. Before the poor kid knows what hit her, she is the rope in a tug of war.

If the relationship crashes, the child may end up living with her mom and visiting her dad every so often. (And comes back: "Totally changed! How is the man caring for her?!")

Soon enough, a new man may come into Mom's life and house – and so Dad number two makes his entrance.

Whether he has vague or precise ideas about how children should behave in this world, he certainly has ideas.

And then Mom and her new man perhaps make a baby of their own. Dad perhaps also remarries and also starts a second family. It is becoming

662

more and more common for children to have two moms (of which one may be honored with the prefix "step"), two dads (ditto) and one or more "half" siblings. Two sets of maternal and paternal grandparents may also be around to watch their interests – with *their* ideas about child rearing.

And in the middle of this turbulence stands a mainly responsible mother or father who has learnt that the A to Z of child rearing can be summed up in one word: consistency.

In some cases instead of living with one parent and visiting the other, both parents have agreed to equal custody where the child ends up staying with each parent for the same length of time – one week on, one week off.

In either scenario, how can the child be given a consistent upbringing if all the time one parent allows what the other forbids, or disregards what the other parent feels is necessary?

If there are new partners and relatives who have entered the picture who are also "contributing" their ideas and opinions on how the child should be raised then it would be no wonder if poor Mom or Dad – or both, crack under the strain.

Two parents living together must obviously have some principles in common.

If Dad puts his daughter to bed at 7.30, Mom can't pick the child up again: "She doesn't have to go to bed until she gets tired."

Let's say that Dad, who has been at work all day, thinks that his little girl should go to bed at 7.30 just as usual. But Mom, who has been home all day, knows that the little one had an exceptionally long afternoon nap and didn't wake up until 5.00 p.m. She is bright as a button at 7.30.

Such potential sources of disagreement should be aired *before* anyone brings up going to bed. Once Dad has started putting his daughter to bed, Mom can't pull the rug out from under him. It's too late. They should have had a little conference beforehand.

For all sensible purposes, the child should *not* be a witness to these conferences, since she would easily take them for signs of parental insecurity.

A situation that involves two parents living under different roofs naturally requires an entirely different approach.

Believe me, however, when I say that a consistent upbringing is a bigger problem for the parents than for the child.

Children have a very practical approach to life. Once they have been around for a year or two, they quickly pick up on what rules are in force where.

Little Cyril, for example, knows that just because he can stay up as long as he wants at his dad's, that doesn't mean he can do so when he's with his mom.

These differences strike the child as no stranger than the fact that Dad might have short hair and drab furniture, while Mom might have long hair and brightly colored furniture. Different strokes for different folks.

The same child can behave as though he is attending a Buckingham Palace garden party when he's with his strict Grandma but roll around on the floor like a wild man when he's with his somewhat more mischievous Grandpa.

"He's never like that when he's with me!" an astonished mother may exclaim on learning that her son is constantly on the rampage when he visits his dad. Naturally enough, the mother wonders whether her son is unhappy when he is with his father and thinks his unruly behavior might be some kind of protest. But the more likely explanation is that this kind of behavior is *permitted* at his father's house.

In fact, the little boy may be genuinely puzzled by his mother's questions.
"Are you unhappy when you're at your dad's?"
"No, it's great."
"Why do you misbehave then?"
"Do I?"
A child's personality follows the child, so to speak, but a child's behavior is totally adaptable and follows the environment.

What parents fear with regard to an inconsistent upbringing is that the child's personality might suffer. But the child's personality is his or her own, and I don't think that it allows itself to be substantially or permanently influenced by upbringing (or lack thereof).

Behavior is determined by the conditions that prevail at any given time. The behavior won't follow the children around, unless they think they need it.

Aunt Bernice sings the praises of her niece Phyllis, who has come to visit. She gravely shakes hands with her aunt and greets her very courteously.

"What beautiful manners you have, sweetheart. Don't see that very often today," she gushes.

But after dinner, Aunt Bernice demurs when Phyllis tries to thank her for the meal.

"Dear heart, you don't have to thank me for feeding you!"

The result will be that Phyllis will stop saying thank you. Here people don't say thank you when they finish eating, she will reason, and soon Aunt Bernice won't have any reason to praise Phyllis for her beautiful manners.

664

Phyllis isn't polite because she has learned to behave politely. She won't become impolite if politeness is no longer demanded of her. She will simply stop behaving politely.

The dim idea that behavior somehow would be built into a child – be a part of her personality – causes many adults to refrain from any kind of child rearing at all.

"Mom/Dad/day care/school can take care of all that" (or let the child take care of it herself). They neglect to declare what the rules are *in this particular place*.

Children find out what rules apply where in their own way. And their methods are not always overly pleasant. ("What happens if I spit on the floor? Am I allowed to feed my sandwich to the dog? Is it OK to call her a bitch? Can I disobey him and get away with it? Will anything happen if I call Mary a slut?")

Whereupon the adults brand the child as ill mannered and unpleasant, without responding to the child's questions and/or provocations; without instructing her about the rules that apply in this particular place.

Naturally, if you have the primary responsibility for raising, say, your little Cyril, you should not allow yourself to be steamrollered by your ex-partner or by a newly arrived "parent" to stand back and just rely on his ability to adapt his behavior. Children are to be protected as well, and your little Cyril's happiness should be your primary concern. His zest for life depends on it.

But the problem for the single mothers that I have had contact with (as well as for myself in the old days) is not that the children are unhappy or depressed when they return from visiting their fathers. It's the broken routines that are pissing you off (excuse my French). Your little Cyril is over-tired, at the end of his rope, screams for candy – and you draw your own conclusions: the kid has had a lot of candy from his dad. He eats like a horse (hasn't had any food), has no clean clothes (Dad didn't do the laundry), was too late for school (Dad has thrown his responsibilities to the wayside). The routines have flown out the window, and that does not amuse you. Over-tiredness, for example, takes a toll over several days.

But broken routines *per se* are no reason for distrust.

Children adapt themselves to the prevailing norms – or the lack of them. *The other parent must be trusted with the ability to take care of his or her child and with his or her own responsibility,* however critical and perhaps worried you feel as the main caregiver.

It is only if the child shows clear signs of anxiety, sadness or depression that you have a reason – and a duty – to intervene. (Refer to the chapters on children's psychological well-being in Part two of *For the Love of Children.*)

A little Cyril who screams, "I don't want to go to Daddy's house!" is really asking a question.

"Do *you* want me to go to Daddy's house?" is the question behind the protest.

If our little Cyril acquiesces when Mom smiles to him, joking a little, "Oh yes you do, you just don't know it yet!" – or, when she calmly and sweetly contradicts him, "Of course you do! It's going to be fun, you'll see!" then the question was a mere formality and there's nothing to worry about. Mom has confirmed.

A little Cyril who stubbornly persists in asking the same question in the same telling format, "I DON'T want to go to Daddy's house!" senses Mom's resistance and the parents' conflict. He is demanding a response that will *liberate* him.

Then the question behind the protest is far more serious.

If Mom is against her child visiting his dad, or even just somewhat negative about it, she is putting little Cyril in an impossible conflict of loyalty. No children want, in their heart, to lose one of their parents. It's unsporting, not to say cruel, to directly or indirectly demand that a child pick a side in a conflict involving the parents.

Whatever Mom feels about Cyril's visits to his father, she must at any cost appear positive – *for the child's sake.*

The child who persists won't stop protesting – questioning, that is – until Mom succeeds in convincing the child that she really *wants* him to go to his father's and is a hundred percent behind it.

"Sweetheart you're going to visit your dad. It's all been arranged, and I really want it to happen. It's going to be lots of fun! And I am going to do what is fun for me, while you are there, and we'll see each other again when you get home. Say hi to Daddy."

Children who persist in complaining are seldom, if ever, satisfied with arguments that appeal to the child's – or the father's – best interests.

Archie, four, is squealing like a stuck pig. There is no way he is going to visit his Dad.

His mother takes him onto her knee and talks to him about this and that. She suspects that he has seen too little of her today, and that's why he doesn't want to be separated from her.

After a few minutes of talking and cuddling, which end with both of them having a good laugh, Mom says, "It will be fun to see daddy, won't it?"

"Yeah," says Archie. "And teddy is coming too."

Archie was suffering from a mommy deficit, and it had to be paid in advance. Now the books balance, and he is ready to embark on new adventures.

Maya, also four, is genuinely apprehensive about visiting her father. The night before she wets the bed. She sobs whenever the subject comes up and screams her head off when it's time to get dressed and leave. When her father arrives, it soon becomes apparent that just getting her to come with him is going to require physical force.

Faced with a protest far too intense to be interpreted as a question, the parents must unquestioningly act to protect their child.

Dad will have to come back another day, and thoughtfully. He will have to try to persuade her into taking a walk with him to begin with. Then he can gradually lengthen their (short) meetings, until she finally consents to visit him at his home.

Divorced fathers (and mothers) whose child is living with their former partner are at a terrible disadvantage in one very important area. They lose the everyday contact with their child.

Daily life encompasses membership in the flock and the common struggle for survival. The family member who moves away to establish a permanent domicile somewhere else no longer belongs to the flock, and his or her status is downgraded from member to visitor.

As a visitor, the erstwhile flock member may even be regarded with suspicion. We are all territorial, and trespassers are monitored carefully and sometimes flat out rejected.

It is therefore vitally important that non-custodial parents induct their children into the new flock they now belong to – or are in the process or creating – rather than visiting their children in the flock to which these parents once belonged.

The reality faced by these new flocks can then be offered to the children, and since the non-custodial mothers and fathers are not visitors but fully-fledged members, their children will naturally gravitate towards them in this new environment and "belong".

No child, however, can "belong" to a visitor. (For more on the theory of the fixed center, see "From my life. Theories for comfort" in Part four of *For the Love of Children*.)

What children need in their second homes is not necessarily a room of their own or a sea of their own toys, but *a reality that is valid for the parent* in which the children can participate as fully fledged flock members. Along with the other members, they must be allowed to share in the joys and sorrows of daily life and make their contribution to the struggle for survival.

Fathers usually bridle at the idea of being "weekend dads", who take their children to the zoo, to the movies, or out to dinner at substantial expense whenever they see them. This reticence is no doubt rooted in the knowledge that the time they spend with their children is not part of their *reality*. There is no struggle for survival and therefore no flock.

If children of divorced parents who live with their mothers are still to look to their fathers for leadership and protection in this world (at least in Dad's world), these fathers must induct their children into their own reality.

"Why didn't you say anything to *me* about this?" is a question that many a father has posed to his child when something terrible has happened and Dad is the last to know.

The answer is that children, like all of us, virtually always turn to members of the flock that they belong to and interact with on a daily basis.

For children to reach out outside the flock, constant reminders are required from the former flock member that the child can count on leadership and protection even in the new flock. These constant reminders are necessary as it seems to be hard for the child to take to heart and utilize all that the new, other flock may dearly want to give.

Children seldom safeguard interests outside the flock spontaneously. This is not the result of indifference or a lack of love, but the child's existential sense of belonging to his or her own flock. Therefore, it's up to the parent who has moved out to strongly and consciously maintain the connection without expecting the child to do it and without being hurt when the child doesn't.

This holds true for older children and teenagers too. You, the parent who has moved out, must constantly remind your child of your existence. A daily phone call, if ever so brief, a letter of only a few lines delivered regularly a few times a week or, if the child has access to a computer, a daily email will ensure you a place in your child's day-to-day consciousness.

In all your dealings with your child, predictability and regularity are what's most important. Even if contact is seldom, make sure it is regular! Even very young children note regularity and quickly learn to know what they can count on.

Irregular contact may be rewarding in the short-term, but it is regularity that will enable the relationship to grow and develop.

Contact should be scheduled and not questioned, and it should be realistic. One weekend a month is better than three weekends one month and none the next. But if three weekends one month and none the next is what you are stuck with, make sure the cycle repeats itself: three weekends every other month, no weekends every other month.

Being a parent is a commitment. If contact diminishes and eventually ceases, the child can't do much else but draw the conclusion that he/she has been discarded. The child wasn't good enough.

Many and animated are the discussions about what is best for children. The needs of the parents, the flock, are rarely mentioned.

Naturally, it is as rewarding, joyful and uplifting for a child to hear the simple words "I WANT YOU WITH ME" as it is for you or me.

Instead, custody battles revolve around what is supposedly best for the child, whereas the inflicted parties rarely stand up for what the battle is really about: "I want you with me. That's why I want custody."

Marrying one's children is not an option so the analogy is not entirely appropriate, but I must say I would much rather a man proposed to me with the words "I WANT YOU WITH ME" than listening to his long explanation on why it would probably be much better for me to live with him than with the man I was married to before!

Children that arrive in the nest with your new love sooner or later create problems, just as your new love creates problems in terms of his or her role as an extra parent to the children that are already there.

There are no one-size-fits-all solutions. As a rule, collisions are inevitable and you will have to cope with them as best you can.

Smart people let things take their time.

You cannot force yourself to love someone you don't know and don't "belong" to. Children are human beings, and as strange human beings they are strangers – to start with and perhaps for a long time to come.

By the same token, you cannot force a child to love someone who suddenly appears and takes up residence in the place the child calls home.

It takes time for a flock to regroup its members and become homogeneous. And it doesn't always succeed as well as everyone hopes – if it succeeds at all. Love comes or it doesn't. It can't be manufactured on demand.

What can come, quickly and relatively easily, is the living terms and community of friendship, provided that you, as an adult, make it possible and work for this friendship (as opposed to being passive and perhaps critical). This is best achieved by having children work alongside you – be the work ever so simple – so that every child who arrives in a new flock feels needed (*the others wouldn't manage as well without me*).

Being needed emotionally isn't enough, especially in a relationship which neither adult nor child chose, and which therefore doesn't have an emotional foundation anyway.

A custodial parent who has successfully formed a new family with a new partner may experience loyalty conflicts with his or her ex. Divorces usually happen because the parties concerned don't see eye to eye on a range of issues, and one of these issues may well be the kids.

If you marry or move in with someone who shares your views and principles and on top of that is more loving, playful and responsible than your ex could ever hope to be, it's only human nature to harbor less than loving feelings towards your former spouse. More often than not you wish he would just disappear. Ken, your new partner, is the perfect parent you have dreamed of. Your little Thomases love him. They even call him Dad. Life is as good as it gets this side of heaven, and you have finally got the family you have always wanted, but life would be even better if the biological father got hit by a truck.

Instead, he is lurking in the background and bugging you for visitation rights – or not bugging you for visitation rights, which under certain circumstances can be even worse.

Whatever your situation, your first loyalty, as a parent, is always to your children. For the sake of your children, whatever you might think of your ex, you must make contact between your children and their biological father *possible*. You must see to your children's interests until they can do it themselves. It just goes with the job.

If your children are prepared to "trade in" a biological parent for a better model, you must recognize that this is *temporary* and is the result of a loving atmosphere in the home and the flock's restored completeness, which was obviously compromised when your ex-husband left.

It may also be the result of your own attitude. You obviously prefer the new partner to the old. The children's enthusiastic acceptance of your choice may seem moving, but you cannot permit them, in word or deed, to distance themselves from their absent biological parent. Children lack your adult experience and your ability to step back and look at the big picture. Bear in mind that the choice you made is yours and yours alone. Your children had nothing to do with it. *Children in their heart of hearts do not want to lose either one of their parents.*

By enabling them to maintain contact with the other parent, you are caring for them. No one is suggesting that you, as a mother, should have to nag an uninterested father. He is not the person you are a mother to. His are not the interests you are safeguarding. Your goal is to ensure that maintaining the connection is never more difficult than it absolutely has to be. Any attempt to hinder or prevent contact by not sticking to agreements or deceiving your children – for make no mistake it is your children you are deceiving, not your ex – is an infringement on their right to have contact with the other biological parent.

Maintaining contact between your children and an uninterested father – or worse an absentee one – means having a thousand explanations up your sleeve when your little Cyril wonders sadly why Daddy never calls. These explanations, which should reassure your child that Daddy would of course come if only he could ("Poor Daddy is very sick." Or, "Daddy works so far away from here that he can't come") demand infinite ingenuity.

Supporting a father who can't even be bothered to send a birthday card isn't much fun, which I can attest to from personal experience, but it is necessary.

It's necessary to *protect your children from the knowledge that their father has written them off.*

To keep contact possible (at least for the future) means you do not slander your former partner, no matter how bitterly you hate him (or her).

It also means you do not even concur if and when Cyril himself slanders his other biological parent.

"Mommy is mad all the time. All she does is yell at me."

"I'm sure it's not you she's mad at. I'm sure she's upset about something else."

You must try to adopt an attitude that everything is as it should be, even though you are absolutely steaming with fury. It's not the angry mother or father you are being loyal to – it's your children. They can't cope with having to trash their own other parent, however uninterested she/he is.

Even if the other parent totally refuses any contact, you have to try to keep the opportunity for contact open and clean, until your Cyril one day all by himself can form his own opinion.

That is the goal.

When the day comes, it's a good thing to be able to stand free from guilt and say, "I have never denied you contact with your father/mother. I never told you what to think or feel about him/her. I left it up to you to decide."

In Sweden, as in many parts of today's world, joint custody – "shared" custody – has become commonplace in the event of divorce or separation.

In practice, this means that the child (our little Cyril, for example) divides his time equally between both parents. He is to have two sets of clothes, two sets of toys, two toothbrushes and two addresses. Both parents are to be equal parents and take on as much responsibility for Cyril, who is alternating between them on exactly the same conditions.

The only problem is that the child cannot be cut in half...

I am reminded of how King Solomon resolved a dispute between two women who both claimed to be the mother of the same child. King Solomon lifted his sword to cut the child in half and divide it between the two women. One woman begged for the child's life and promised to withdraw her suit if only the child were allowed to live.

Solomon deemed her to be the real mother, since she cared more about the child than herself.

Among joking – or bitter – parents, it's often said that joint custody works just fine, as long as the parents don't need to divorce.

Worked out, formal written agreements still seem to be necessary.

With joint custody, the parents have certain legal and moral obligations towards each other. One parent can't emigrate to the other end of the world with the child without the other parent's permission for example.

But joint custody does not mean an exactly evenly divided living, and I would be surprised if people did not soon realize that such a solution serves the parents better than it does the child. There aren't many adults who would even consider alternating between two homes and families, two flocks, every other week.

We need our fixed point. We seek our place on Earth. So do children.

So, if we really have our children's best interests at heart, joint custody agreements should designate one of the parental abodes as the child's *primary residence*. For the sake of little Cyril's basic belonging, he is utterly dependent on the leadership and protection of *one* flock.

From this primary flock, he can make his excursions, both numerous and long lasting, but there can only be one fixed point to depart from and return to.

This in effect means that he spends more time in his primary residence than at his second home.

The closest two parents can come to a reasonably equitable joint custody agreement that doesn't leave the child dangling in mid-air, a perpetual tourist with no place to belong, would be for example two weeks with Mom, one week with Dad, or vice-versa, and once negotiated, the agreement must not be changed. There can only be one *primary residence*.

It's only around the age of twelve, when children begin to find their feet and acquire the ability to survive on their own, that their need for the leadership and protection of their *one* flock begins to ebb. Older children can therefore alternate between flocks to which they have an emotional and practical attachment – some form of common origin – as long as they are allowed to return to their own flocks, their fixed points, and have their sense of belonging confirmed.

Beyond the age of twelve, spending more time in their primary flock is no longer essential.

WHO DO YOU LOVE THE MOST?

"Think now, sweetheart. What did Daddy say?"

"Nothing."

"Didn't he say that you and him were going to live with Minnie?"

"Don't know."

"Well, he's told you we are divorcing, hasn't he?"

"I don't know."

"Dear God, do you go deaf when he talks to you?"

"What?"

Mom grits her teeth.

"Once he said that I could take Minnie's dog for a walk," says the child. "But when we got there, I wasn't allowed to."

(Oh, so she's got a dog too...)

"Do you like Daddy?" mother asks.

"Sure I do."

"Do you love Daddy?"

"Sure I do."

"Do you love Mommy?"

"Sure I do."

"And Minnie? Do you love Minnie?"

"Sure I do."

"Who do you love the most?"

"What?"

"Most. Who do you love the most?"

"Lisa," says the child.

Mom looks blank.

"Who is Lisa?"

"The guinea pig I have at daycare," says the child.

YOU CAN'T BE TOO CAREFUL
IN YOUR CHOICE OF PARENTS.

Henrik Pontoppidan: *Lykke Per*

SIBLINGS

**If God were to bestow on me one power,
I would give all children siblings.**

A friend of mine, herself a mother of several children, was at a little get together at my house one evening.

A young man in the group said that he really wanted to have a child with his much beloved girlfriend.

"Don't have *a* child," said my friend. "Have two."

She was an only child, and she told us about her childhood.

"Everything revolved around me. The pressure was terrible. I dreamed of having a sibling. If I had had one, maybe I would have been able to relax once in a while."

"Everything I didn't understand," she continued, "everything I wondered about and worried about I could never talk about in my own way. You can't talk to your parents about everything! But who else was there? People outside the family understood me even less. The constant attention was a terrible strain. Attention isn't the same as love."

No one can stand being the center of the universe for very long. When does love, which we all want and need, metastasize into a ball and chain? When do interested questions start to feel like an interrogation? When does attention start to feel like surveillance?

It's both intriguing and frightening to note that tranquillizers are prescribed more frequently for only children whose parents are together than for children with siblings, even if the children with siblings live in single parent households.

"You can't help but feel sorry for her children," people often said behind my back when they commented on my brood. "She can't possibly have time for all of them. Each of them needs *all* her attention."

My friend with her seven kids was constantly asked the same question when her children were growing up. "Do you really have enough love for all of them?"

675

But love is not a cake that's cut up and portioned out until there is no more. Love grows with each child that's born.

Parents may tremble at the birth of their second baby and wonder how they can possibly love this child as much as they love the first, but you don't take half of the love you feel for your first child and give it to the second. On the contrary, love grows exponentially, and brand new feelings awaken. The new baby opens a door in your heart that has never been opened before.

And there are many doors in the human heart.

If you had twenty children, you would meet each new arrival with a wellspring of love that would never have come into being had not that particular child been born. These wellsprings exist within you. You just don't know it until this special miracle of a newborn child calls them forth.

In this age of over-heated love demands, when "love", i.e. the overly concentrated free time attention, is supposed to compensate the children for their being expelled from social participation (see "The best laid plans…" in Part two of *For the Love of Children*), child psychologists have trumpeted the following:

1. Sibling rivalry is inevitable.
2. Presenting a sibling to your child is tantamount to presenting a new spouse to the one you already have.
3. The first child is deprived of the love she or he has the one and only copyright to.

Indeed, the Western world is facing a difficult socio-political dilemma! On the one hand, people shouldn't have children at all, but should devote themselves body and soul to production and consumption. On the other, the population has to be replenished to finance pensions and elder care, and people (of the desired kind) are having far too few children…

There are more only children than ever today. The pressure on the parents of these children is tremendous. They are expected to sacrifice their nights, walk the floor and comfort their children ceaselessly, feed them round the clock ("A baby belongs at its mother's breast!"), volunteer at their children's day care center or school, devote their already non-existent free time to endless meetings, read, learn, take parenting courses, buy thousands of dollars worth of toys, and last but not least ferry their children around to countless "extra curricular activities" to ensure that they get the "stimulation" they need – all to prove that they are *involved parents*.

All I can say is: it's better to give your child a sibling!

A sister or brother is a life's asset comparable to nothing. Someone of your own generation is there who shares your background, biological origin and basic experiences in life.

No love is as strong and lifelong as the love between two siblings who are close to each other.

As a parent, your main task is to prepare your child in the very best way for a life without you. One of the best ways to do that is to give your child a sibling.

NO, NO JEALOUSY!

For a long time now, sibling rivalry has been regarded as more or less axiomatic. Siblings must argue and fight, and begrudge each other life's bounty. Whether they express it or not, each wishes life out of the other. As the term implies, to be siblings is to be rivals.

In my opinion, one could just as well argue that married couples will invariably argue and fight, friends will invariably begrudge each other life's bounty, co-workers will invariably wish life out of each other, and neighbors will invariably be rivals. Misanthropy rules, and to expect anything else is naïve.

But throughout history (at least up to now) people have regarded siblings as a blessing. And no matter how often parents are told that sibling rivalry is inevitable, they do all they can to counteract it. Obviously, they believe, whatever they are told to the contrary, that sibling rivalry isn't inevitable.

They're right. It isn't.

There is always more that unites siblings than divides them. The most important thing that unites them, apart from their shared biological origins, is the fact that they live in the same community. They belong to the same flock.

One or more of the adult members of the flock provide them with leadership and protection in the collective struggle for survival. One day the children will leave the nest, the flock and survive by the sweat of their own brows.

As everyone is aware, great effort has been put into dissolving the (nuclear) family, but people stubbornly persist in forming families, even though there are significant financial penalties for doing so. This stubbornness is not the last gasp of bourgeois morality. It is a biological necessity.

Human beings are hard-wired to live in groups. It is their flocks that give human beings their sense of belonging. The flock also constitutes a territory. Solidarity within the flock is rooted in a *common origin* and a *common goal*, the struggle for survival, which everyone contributes to.

One or both of these elements are essential if the flock is to constitute a territory that all its members guard. (A collective, where the members lack a common origin and a common goal, does not constitute a flock and usually dissolves quickly.)

So, siblings belong to the same flock and guard its territory.

Parents find civil wars between siblings hard to tolerate despite what the "experts" say about the inevitability of it, and this intolerance stems from experience as old as the human race itself: The flock has to stick together. Solidarity is essential if danger threatens from outside. If danger does threaten, the ranks close, and the flock members form a united front.

Paulina, who grew up in a rough area of Stockholm, talked to me about her childhood. "We lived in a clearly defined neighborhood. All the kids knew each other. Sometimes we would get into wild fights. But if ever kids from another neighborhood came into ours, our differences were forgotten in a second, and we stood shoulder to shoulder, ready to fight to the death!"

Even if danger doesn't threaten, the flock members have to be ready for it. It is to maintain this readiness that the flock members seek and give each other confirmation that everyone is on the same team.

The flock does periodic head counts. They keep an eye on each other. Members cannot disappear without saying where they are going. And excursions from the flock cannot be too long. ("You're never home!") Everyone must be ready to mobilize on short notice as and when it's necessary.

Originally, the struggle was for physical survival and territory, but the struggle can also be for a meaningful life.

Basically, conscientious parents oppose internal disputes between their children because they want their little flock members to survive not only today, but also tomorrow and on into the future. Conflicts within the flock weaken its members at both the collective and individual level.

In light of all this, it is not hard to see that siblings are ill served by not only the fights, but also the presumption that siblings are somehow predestined to fight with each other just because they are siblings.

Actually, it's the exact opposite.

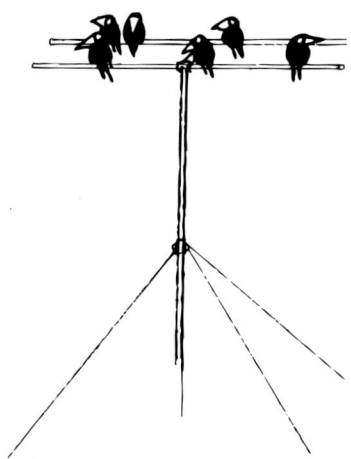

Membership in the flock is confirmed in two ways.

1. Common origins and solidarity are emphasized by the marking of territory in diverse ways. WE BELONG TOGETHER.
2. The common purpose (survival, the collective struggle for existence) is emphasized by everybody's social participation. WE NEED EACH OTHER.

We belong together. I see you. I worry about you. I touch you. I protect you. You are mine. I am yours.

We need each other. I use you. I accept help from you. I count on you. I wouldn't manage as well without you. Your abilities are mine. My abilities are yours.

The more clearly and reliably the belonging is confirmed among the flock members, the more strong and intense they will experience their togetherness, and the more positive – *life forceful* – their community will be.

And the less their rivalry.

Rivalry is a symptom of insecurity about belonging. Confirmation is insufficient or misdirected.

If the eldest child has had his sense of belonging to the flock confirmed by the constant physical presence of his mother, and the arrival a new baby causes this constant presence to diminish substantially – or, God forbid, disappear entirely (if the child is shunted off to day care or relatives) – the eldest child in all probability will attack this threat to his sense of belonging, namely the new baby.

Constant physical proximity, in and of itself, does not confirm belonging. A husband and wife can spend all their days and nights with each other without necessarily feeling solidarity with each other. If they have ceased to touch each other, they have also stopped marking their territory. Each knows what the other is doing because they live under one roof. There's *control* but it is unsupported by solidarity.

This control is quite rightly regarded as surveillance by both parties, and neither feels free. (But jealousy can certainly flourish!)

A sense of belonging between parents and children is acknowledged and confirmed by actively connecting rather than by passively just being present. These connections confirm belonging in no uncertain terms, and most parents seek them too.

Kirstie's mother says, "Hi darling!" every time she bumps into her daughter in their spacious house, even though she saw her only a couple of minutes ago.

Marvin's dad is barely in the door before he calls Marvin, hugs him, and tosses him in the air.

If Marvin doesn't come when Dad calls, Dad knows that something is wrong. Nothing is more important to him than getting hold of Marvin and confirming his son's sense of belonging, which Marvin seems to doubt for some reason. When he eventually finds Marvin sitting quietly in a corner, the little boy tells him in words or body language that he feels abandoned, sad and alone – all signs of a sense of *non*-belonging. Dad then does everything in his power to really connect with his son and confirm that he really belongs. He doesn't quit until Marvin is happy again.

Bill, fifteen, cannot be accused of having too tender feelings for his parents. The fights are frequent and bitter. On those rare occasions that he speaks to them, it's usually to tell them to F-off. His parents have no redeeming features in his view.

Naturally, he neither gives nor accepts tokens of affection.

But when he brings a friend home, a visitor to his flock, he wants the fact that he belongs confirmed. Suddenly it's very important that his mother or father, or whoever is home *receives* him. Under these circumstances, Bill accepts a kiss and a hug as a means of marking his territory. He would be extremely put out if his parents just kept their eyes glued to the TV set and didn't get up to greet him when he had a friend with him. (Normally, he doesn't even say hello to his parents when gets home, but just disappears to his room.)

I happened to witness how his parents ignored him when this boy came home with a friend. We had been talking about his behavior, and they had said that they had given up. They didn't have the strength to care anymore. "I'm so tired of being sad all the time," as his mother put it.

Then Bill stepped into the living room with his friend and stood there waiting. He gave his parents, who had not even acknowledged his coming through the front door, a second chance. Maybe they hadn't noticed his friend?

When he got no reaction from his parents, he turned on his heel to lead his friend up to his room, but I heard the other boy's sarcastic comment. "Do you know those people...?"

The parents had refused to acknowledge and confirm that Bill did indeed belong to this flock, and his friend was quick to needle him for it. Bill was made to look like an outsider, inadequate and rejected. His flock was in effect saying that his membership had been revoked.

The struggle for survival no longer involves all the flock's members. Children's instinct for social participation is denied in a society like ours; even within the home, children are excluded from activities that are necessary for the adults.

If all the flock's members don't struggle for survival under the same conditions, even within the walls of the home, then the sense of belonging is weakened and solidarity is diluted. Whoever doesn't participate in the struggle for survival is a liability rather than an asset.

Rivalry, therefore, often manifests itself in families in which the children feel that their only purpose in life it to provide emotional satisfaction to their parents. They are not needed for any practical reason, and they can never tell themselves that *the others wouldn't manage quite as well without me.* They are more likely to think the opposite. *The others would probably manage better without me.*

Social participation, even on a small scale, confirms belonging like nothing else. A two-year-old who is allowed to put a sausage in a frying pan, who is allowed to participate in making dinner, who is put to work according to his/her abilities, and who is really *needed* is far less likely to be jealous of a sister or brother than a child who *isn't* allowed to put a sausage in a frying pan.

Children in so-called developing countries, who take care of their younger siblings don't do so because they are kinder, cleverer, more obedient, or better disciplined than kids in the so-called developed countries; they do it because it is necessary. *If everyone is to survive, everyone has to help out.*

If they were ever afflicted with the inevitable (according to the experts) plague of sibling rivalry, they would be tossing the babies to the rats, or at least leaving them to their fate as soon as the parents were out of sight. But they don't.

Even on excursions outside the flock territory has a way of getting marked. Study yourself or other people in a restaurant. People have a way of rearranging the place settings in a very particular way. They are making them *theirs.*

In stores too, people have a way of marking things that they don't even intend to buy. They handle various items and examine them from different angles. The classic adult admonition to children, "Don't touch!" is preached far more than it is practiced!

Tokens of affection between parents and children are of course expressions of love and devotion, but also of belonging. They are in effect putting a brand on each other, and this brand says, "You are mine."

They hug, kiss, stroke and confirm. "We belong together."

When people meet on the street and walk together, they mark the people they belong with by walking beside them.

But belonging is confirmed most clearly inside the home, not outside.

"I want to be there when my kids get home from school," is something parents still say today.

"I want Mom or Dad to be there when I get home from school," is a sentiment expressed by virtually all children.

Why is that? Because the members of a flock want the most unequivocal confirmation of their sense of belonging when they arrive home after an excursion.

To come home means far more than simply arriving somewhere. It means far more than just walking through the door of the building you live in. To come home means to seek and find security; it means to return to the one place on earth that you can call your own.

This is where you belong. This is where you connect. We are your flock, and we are always here for you.

In Bill's case, coming home, regardless of the feud between him and his parents, would have meant his parents confirming, in front of their son's friend, that this is the place Bill belongs. It would have meant his parents rushing out into the hall to greet Bill and then standing at his side as a visitor is received.

Ideally, it would have meant touching Bill and confirming physically that this is indeed where Bill belongs.

And after that, his parents could have gone back to whatever it was they were doing.

And the comment from his friend would have been, "You have cool parents!"

Little Peter, two years old, is going to get a sibling.

His parents aren't making a big deal out of the situation. Babies are born every now and then, and it's the most natural thing in the world, is what their attitude says.

One day, Mom pats her stomach in front of Peter.

"Have you seen how big my tummy has gotten? There's a little baby in there."

There's no insecurity in her voice. ("What do you think about this? Will you be jealous?") There is no hint of an appeal in her voice either. ("I have a baby in my tummy, and there's nothing I can do about it. Please be happy! It would be such a relief!")

If Peter asks a question, his mother answers it, but his mother doesn't expound on things he doesn't seem to be curious about. She only wants to give him a little guidance.

Since two-year-olds don't know much about how babies get made, being suddenly confronted with Mom's huge stomach is a little daunting. Peter can be forgiven for needing a little time to make sense of the situation.

Towards the end of the pregnancy, Peter's parents start making preparations for the newcomer. Peter watches. When the carriage or crib is placed in the bedroom, he might wonder, "Is the baby going to sleep here?"

"Yes," answers Dad. "Is this the right spot? Or should we move it a little further into the corner?"

Peter gives his opinion (in his way), to which his father defers. Dad then thanks son for his input.

"Good suggestion! Thank you!"

Zero hour strikes in the middle of the night. When Peter's mother leaves for the hospital, she wakes him up and says her goodbyes. She tells him that she has to go to the hospital because the baby has decided to come out and she needs a little help. She is only going to be gone a couple of days and then she will be home again with the baby. While she's gone, a couple of her friends, and Dad of course, are going to look after him. She kisses him tenderly and leaves.

Peter's dad works outside the home, and his sister, Aunt Anna, who is a student, takes care of Peter for the few days that his mother is in the hospital. She looks after Peter in his home and doesn't take him away from there. Thus, little Peter, while his mother is gone, can guard his territory.

He has his mother's things around him, which confirm that this is where she belongs. He knows that she will come back. In her absence, he stands watch. The flock, the nest, remains as it has always been and awaits his mother's return from her excursion.

If, however, Peter was placed somewhere outside the flock during his mother's stay in hospital, he would be the one on an excursion, and he would be the one coming home. Under these circumstances, Peter would be faced with two possible scenarios. If he got home before his mother, his mother would not be able to receive him and confirm that he belongs, which would confuse him. Where's Mom? Why isn't she here?

If, on the other hand, he got home after his mother, there would be a new little baby in the house, which would also confuse him. The flock would have a new member, whom Peter was not there to receive, and that would not do much for Peter's sense of belonging either.

If Peter were to go to the hospital with his parents to see the new baby, it is very probable that he would not show the delight and enthusiasm on meeting his little sister or brother that his parents had hoped for. He might find the baby mildly intriguing, but his primary interest would be his mother. He would want to investigate *her* new environment.

He is visiting her away from home. They are both on an excursion.

During his visit to the hospital, Peter is away from his flock and outside his territory. There is nothing for him to mark. Therefore, he cannot "annex" the new baby. Indeed, he might well regard the hospital as the new baby's flock. (See below.)

The younger the eldest child is, the more important it is that the "annexation" process take place at home. If Peter goes to the hospital at all, his meeting with his mother should take priority. The baby could simply be out of the picture for the time being!

When it's time for Mom and Baby to come home, if I were Peter's father, I would not take the boy with me to the hospital. He is only two. I would leave him at home and ask Aunt Anna to babysit.

The new baby is not something to be fetched from somewhere else. (When will it be put back where it belongs? It must have a flock somewhere. Where does the baby belong? At the hospital?)

The baby should be *received* into the flock. The baby has never been anywhere else (except inside its mother), so it can't very well belong anywhere else.

This is what would happen the first day home:
- Mommy comes home from her excursion.
- The flock gathers. The members' *belonging* to it is confirmed.
- A new little member is received into the flock.
- All its members get to know, examine, and "annex" the new arrival.
- The new flock member is inducted into the family community.

The last point should perhaps not be on the list already, since being fully inducted into the family community takes longer than a day. But "annexation" expresses a willingness to welcome and accept.

To accept is to receive.

Dad goes to the hospital to bring Mom and Baby home, while Peter stays home with Aunt Anna.

Aunt Anna makes a great fuss over the imminent home coming. Together Aunt Anna and Peter make Mom's bed, they lay out her dressing gown, and they carefully arrange her prize possessions. Thus, Peter is prepared to receive his mother, and his mother's membership in the flock (which is also Peter's) is confirmed.

As soon as Mother, Father and Baby arrive, even if the baby is screaming loud enough to shatter the windows, Mom immediately goes to Peter and has a glorious reunion with him, a real *home coming*.

Dad and the baby stay discreetly in the background for now. The unforgettable moment when Peter will meet his little sister will come soon enough – but not yet. (Ideally, the newborn has been fed as late as possible at the hospital or in the car on the way home and is now fast asleep.)

Peter's reunion with his mother is joyful and untainted by anxiety, expressed or hidden. ("*Now* everything is all right! Mom is home again!") There was nothing wrong with Mom being away. The flock members go on excursions sometimes, and then they come back. There's nothing unusual about that.

Either Mom sees or Aunt Anna recounts that Peter has helped make his mother's bed, lay out her dressing gown and arrange her things. Much is made of his sterling service. Now his mother really feels like she's home! Everything is back to normal. The flock is gathered.

It's now time to introduce Peter to the little newcomer. Mom squats down, looks Peter in the eye and tells him that she has something to show him, something really exciting!

She goes and gets the baby. Without saying a word, she lays the newborn on a blanket on the floor in front of Peter.

The time has come for Peter to "annex" his little sister, and this time is his and his alone.

There may be quite a crowd gathered in the room, but everyone should be very quiet. This is a sacred moment, and nothing should disturb it. It would be prudent of Peter's parents to make sure in advance that Aunt Anna and whoever else is in the room understand the importance of silence at this point.

For Peter to take the baby to him, "annex" her and make her his, he must touch her, examine her and become familiar with her. And he must do it in his own way without outside interference.

A very young child will begin his inspection of a new baby by sticking his finger in the baby's eye. The eyes are the windows to the soul... The onlookers need nerves of steel to stay passive through all this, but the baby has the ability to blink instinctively. Newborns are not as fragile as they look!

Next he will place the same finger in the baby's mouth. Peter pushes his finger in fairly far – nerves will again be tested – and the baby reacts violently. Peter immediately withdraws his finger, but soon puts it back in. He probes and lets himself be tasted.

There's a pause. Then they look each other in the eye. What are they saying to each other?

Further examination follows. The baby's hands and feet are interesting, as is what is underneath her clothes. Peter starts to loosen the baby's clothes or rather roughly pull them off. His dad helps him. There are no recriminations or comments, just smiles and encouragement.

After a thorough investigation, the moment arrives when the older child takes the brand new person to him – literally.

Peter tries to lift his baby sister onto his knee. Mom discreetly intervenes. The "annexation" takes place on the floor with Peter on his knees, so the risk of the baby falling and hurting herself is minimal, but a supporting hand is needed.

Peter is motionless with the baby in his arms. An angel passes through the room.

I have never seen anyone witness the scene with dry eyes.

Now it's necessary to keep your eye on the ball – and the baby. Once Peter has given the baby his seal of approval as a new member of the flock, he heaves her off him quickly and carelessly. He's got other business to attend to!

The sacred moment has passed, and life goes on. Membership in the flock has increased by one. And there's nothing strange about that!

Daily life resumes.

During the baby's honeymoon, it's best if Dad or Aunt Anna is around to tend to Peter's interests when his mother is otherwise occupied. Crises can erupt when the interests of both young children collide, and they do every now and then, since it's impossible to organize the day until the baby gets into a routine.

It is *not* a smart move to send the older child to stay somewhere else. (See above.)

Mom can be replaced within the flock (the nest), but if she is available, Peter will seek her out. It's when she isn't available that Peter willingly accepts her replacements. It is therefore better if Mom disappears into another room with the baby, thereby making herself unavailable, than if she nurses in the same room and tries to direct Peter to someone else if he needs something. If his mother is absent, Peter will go to her replacements of his own accord.

Mom always announces her departure, looks Peter in the eye, waves good-bye to him, and tells him that she'll be back soon. On her return, she has a grand reunion with Peter to show him that she is available again.

Dad or Aunt Anna can take Peter out. He may be clingy and whiny when he's leaving, but once out, he will be just fine. Outside the home, he cannot run to his mother and have his sense of belonging confirmed.

The other adults can also provide Peter with opportunities for social participation.

Peter will work intensely, helping with food preparation, loading the washing machine or anything else that is necessary for the flock's welfare – until his mom shows up, whereupon he will immediately stop whatever he is doing and run to her.

A classic dilemma. Mom is disappointed and says, "But Peter, you were working so well. Why have you stopped?"

But Peter wants to take his mother to him. She has "returned", and he wants to confirm that he belongs with her. Every time they meet, they should *connect*. Then life can resume its course.

If you have recently had your second child, you might not always be able to call on another adult to help you with your first. Paddling your own canoe under such circumstances is not easy, but you will manage.

Necessity is the mother of invention, and inventiveness (along with a certain knack for bribery) is a quality that you will definitely need.

Sometimes, the older child will have to wait, and sometimes the baby will.

You will learn to breastfeed and tend to the needs of your older child simultaneously. You arms will extend, and you will grow an eye in the back of your head.

It is important to try to rise above the chaos, stand by your older child and maintain your bond with her. It should be emphasized that the whole flock should be looking after the new arrival.

The baby is not only Mom's business. The baby is everybody's business.

The baby is the flock's newest member. As veteran members in good standing, Peter and his mother are equals, and they will take care of the newcomer together. The baby has become a part of something that existed long before she came into the picture.

So, Mom should not flutter between baby and older child as though they were separate smaller flocks that had nothing to do with each other.

Little Peter has "annexed" the baby. He has accepted her. The baby is now a part of his everyday consciousness. She can't be hidden from him. He can't pretend that she doesn't exist.

Mother is the one with nourishment in her breasts and therefore guarantees the baby's survival, but in every other way, the other members of the flock interact with the baby under identical conditions.

Peter and his mother have both been confronted with an unknown entity: a new baby. Caring for the new baby should be approached in a spirit of equality. No one knows better than anyone else (in theory). Mom can ask Peter, and Peter can ask his mother, "Is the baby asleep?"

"Your little sister is crying again!" Mom might say to Peter. "She's such a mischievous little thing! Always hungry! Just eats and eats. But where's her dinner?"

"There!" says Peter and points to his mother's breasts.

"Oh, of course! Thanks for the reminder!"

You should not come across as helpless, but try to share your older child's curiosity, surprise and occasional puzzlement. You are both in this together and you should help each other out.

You will then be able to experience your older child's delighted and astonished reactions over your new baby's developing talents.

"She can *sit*!"

"She took it, look, she can *hold*!"

These are touching moments, as far from rivalry as it's possible to get.

And you of course must react with the appropriate surprise and enthusiasm at the status reports from your older child, even if you've seen the baby sit up and hold things many times before.

The older child will try to lead – help and teach – and protect his little brother or sister. Your first child is demonstrably more competent at handling his environment and has accumulated an impressive store of experience.

If you confirm the older child's sense of belonging clearly and daily through physical contact, emotional connection and social participation, there will be no jealousy directed at the new baby.

The older child will shoulder the heavy responsibility of leadership and protection in his role as an older more experienced member of the flock.

Older children can go overboard however. More often than not, I had to remind my five-year-old daughter, big sister to a two-year-old and a three-year-old that they were in fact *my* children – or we were joint owners at least!

In this connection it should be said that a pre-school aged child must *not* be left alone with the responsibility for a younger child. Within the flock, yes – meaning that you are still there – but not if you leave the nest.

(Personally, I have drawn the line at ten. A ten-year-old is capable of looking after a baby while the adults are gone. Detailed instructions are required however. You should also question ten-year-olds in depth about what they would do in case of emergency.)

Children possess a strong protective instinct, and there is no reason why you should not appeal to it.

"The poor baby! She can't reach her rattle. Oh, look how hard she's trying!"

That's all it takes to get your older child to ride to the rescue.

Three little boys got a new baby brother. The atmosphere was tense, since the family had to live in cramped quarters.

"We don't have room," said the brothers.

"Well," said the parents, "we'll have to put him in the attic."

The attic was draughty and cold, and the brothers knew it. There was a silence, and then the tears started to flow.

"No, not the attic!" the little brothers cried. "He can be with us... We DO have room for him!"

A workable solution was quickly found, and the new little boy was one of the crew.

You can inspire an older child to do things for your new baby (things which admittedly you could do better and faster yourself) by appealing to his ability.

There is a big difference between saying "Would you get me a diaper please?" and saying "CAN you get me a diaper?" *Can* will always get you further than *would*.

To be *able* to do something, to possess skills is just as good for a child's self-confidence and inner strength as it is for an adult's.

At the end of the day, it's a question of survival ability.

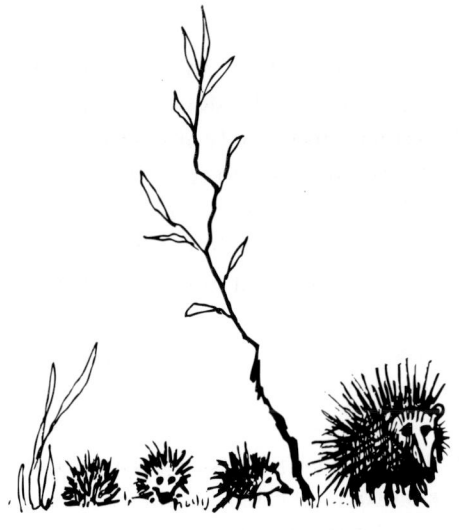

The older child is put to work according to his or her ability in the collective struggle for survival.

The new baby is the flock's responsibility, which means all activity that involves the baby is social participation for the older child. The older child is needed.

Children that are needed do not live on the love of their surroundings alone. They matter in their own right.

The others wouldn't manage quite as well without me.

A sense of belonging is kindled, and this strengthens the child's protective instinct.

Simon, ten, has a father in the navy. His dad is only home sporadically. His mother is often lonely, worried and irresolute. She is not up to the task of assuming leadership of the flock when her husband is away. (In fact, she doesn't shoulder her share of the burden when he's around. She prefers to let him take over.)

Simon can clearly see that his mother needs protection. He literally tries to replace his father. He sleeps in the double bed in his dad's spot, he sits in his dad's chair at the dining table, he watches TV sitting in his dad's armchair, and he spends very little time with friends or outside the house generally.

But when his dad comes home, Simon takes a break from his self-imposed responsibilities and resumes sleeping in his own room, cedes the various chairs to his father and plays outside with his friends as often as he can.

An older child's leadership and protection vis-à-vis a younger sibling is an expression of flock-belonging. The little sister in turn confirms her sense of belonging through small kindnesses and signs of appreciation for the older sibling's protective leadership.

Mom encourages little Suzy to do what she can for her big brother

Patrick. She sets the table for him sometimes, gives him his clean sweater, or puts something that is his on the desk in his room.

If Patrick doesn't notice what Suzy does for him, his mother tells him so he can show his appreciation to Suzy.

"Suzy poured you a glass of milk Patrick," says Mom.

"She did?" says Patrick. "Thanks Suzy. That was very nice of you."

If Patrick hurts himself or is crying, Mom sends Suzy to comfort him first of all.

"Look Suzy, Patrick is sad! Go comfort him! He'll be so glad."

The members of every flock, large or small, guard the flock's territory against outsiders.

In families where siblings argue, fight and compete, they guard their territory against each other. There is no sense that the territory is held in common and belongs to all of them.

Like neighbors who are always feuding, they are constantly drawing petty demarcation lines.

"This spot is for *my* bike! Put yours somewhere else!"

"This is *my* room! You can't come in here!"

The obsession with creating a special world for children, which is more or less universal today, creates ideal conditions for sibling rivalry. (See "The best laid plans…" in Part two of *For the Love of Children*.)

Once you set up a screened off children's world within the walls of your home for your first child, where the child is not needed, does not participate socially, and is in effect condemned to live with his toys, you probably do the same for your second child. You create two separate "mini-flocks" and you alternate between them, a perennial visitor in both.

Your guest appearances in their worlds fuel the rivalry. You have to divide your "visiting time" equally, or the "mini-flock" that feels short-changed will take it out on the other.

And that's where the absurd "fairness" disputes enter the picture.

So do arguments and fights. "He started it!" ("He attacked my flock. I have to guard my territory.")

I used to answer, "What's interesting is not who started it. What's interesting is *who is going to finish it.*"

The most important thing among members of the same flock who share the same territory is that peace is made – regardless of who was right or wrong.

Maintaining solidarity within the flock is every member's responsibility. Lives may depend on it. Competition and rivalry between siblings reduces the flock's chances of survival.

Siblings should live, work, cooperate and depend on one another within one and the same territory. They belong to each other within the flock until they leave to enter a new one or to form their own. You should encourage anything that strengthens that solidarity and combat anything that threatens it. You and any other adult members are the leaders and protectors of the flock to which you all belong.

As you may have gathered, I am not a big fan of the idea that siblings should all have their own rooms with their own furniture and possessions (although from eleven on children of different sexes should have separate sleeping arrangements).

These little "mini-homes" can easily morph into territories.

Hence, a younger child should not be given a separate room when she moves out of the parents' bedroom but should be placed in the room of an older sibling.

Sooner or later, the younger child will investigate the older child's possessions, thus provoking a territorial reaction.

"She's breaking my things! She's taking my things!"

You can then fall back on a tried and true little ruse to promote some constructive thinking. Rather than challenge, or even worse, reproach the older child, ask with genuine interest, *"So what do you intend to do about it?"*

The older child will find a solution. (Which of course cannot be exclusionary. That the siblings continue to share a room is a given.)

Sibling rivalry is above all a consequence of separating family life from work life and emotional life from the business of survival.

The adult members of the flock struggle for survival outside the flock, so the children cannot participate.

Even within the home, children's need for social participation is denied. Today's parents are strongly influenced by a socio-political ideology that states that children are not needed in our society – anymore than the elderly and the unemployed are – and indeed *must not be needed* other than emotionally.

Children are hobby accessories.

Children shall not help out, this ideology states. They shall not put in their two cents worth and contribute to the common good. They shall not be of service to others in the collective struggle for survival. Their only purpose in life is to be happy and feel good (nevertheless).

And to this end, the parents become their children's service staff.

Child psychologists who claim that sibling rivalry is inevitable and must be accepted are, in my opinion, approving and defending a profoundly un-natural social order that is very damaging to children.

Sibling rivalry can and should be prevented.

And as far as I know, all parents combat it, regardless of what they are told – because they are instinctively conscious that it is *wrong*.

To give a child a sibling is to give that child a friend.
It is an act of love.
The eldest child is enriched by the love that siblings call forth.

A LITTLE ADVICE FOR EVERYDAY LIFE

How siblings live together in their first flock, the first little society that they are exposed to, may be not be decisive in determining how they live when they form flocks of their own, but to some extent it sets the tone.

Siblings who resolve conflicts with violence can grow into adults who resolve conflicts with violence.

Siblings who jealously guard their turf within their first flock can grow into adults who jealously guard their turf within their own families.

Siblings who refuse to make even the slightest concession can grow into adults who do likewise.

A brother who hits his sister – "sibling rivalry is normal" – can grow into a husband who abuses his wife.

A sister who refuses to let her brother hug her, go into her room or touch her things can grow into a wife who won't allow her husband to get close to her.

Siblings who are allowed to begrudge each other the good things in life can grow into adults who can't bear to see their friends lead a happy life.

MEAN ZEKE

Once upon a time, there was a little boy named Zeke.

He was born mean. He screamed and screamed, and mostly he screamed at night.

"If only we knew what to do!" his parents sighed.

Little Zeke grew, and the bigger he got, the meaner he got. He broke glasses and plates, and had hysterical temper tantrums. He wouldn't let his mom go to the bathroom in peace. He pulled the dog's tail and hit his poor father over the head with a broom handle. There seemed to be no limit to how mean he could be.

"If only we knew what to do!" his parents sighed.

Little Zeke was put in day care. There he kept right on yelling and screaming, true to his mean streak. He couldn't bear to lose. He always had to be the winner, the best, the one in charge. The day care staff were at their wits' end, but Zeke kept fighting with everyone, and his parents kept sighing.

"If only we knew what to do!" they sighed.

Then little Zeke started school, where he managed to get even meaner. He refused to sit still, sabotaged the lessons, and pushed a TV set off the teacher's desk. He snuck into the cloakroom, poured water in his classmates' boots and tied the sleeves of the jackets together. He tore up books and called his teacher a bitch.

The poor parents sat in the Principal's office and wrung their hands.

"If only we knew what to do!" they sighed.

Little Zeke grew and grew. He was put in special ed classes – on those days when he showed up at school at all. He was examined by doctors and psychiatrists, and was diagnosed with all sorts of exotic conditions, Hyperactivity, ADD, Obsessive-Compulsive Disorder, to name but a few. His parents soon knew the APA's Diagnostic Manual by heart.

In desperation, his parents turned to a radical child psychologist, who said, "Just let him act out."

The family home soon resembled Coventry during the Blitz, and Zeke's parents considered seeking psychiatric treatment themselves, but Zeke got to act out.

The years went by, and Zeke met a girl. Suddenly, he was all sweetness and light. His parents were beside themselves with joy.

But the happy couple barely had time to get home from the church before Zeke slipped back into his old habits. He yelled and screamed, and treated his wife like the maid.

"If only I knew what to do!" his wife sobbed.

Zeke's elderly parents were fading fast. Even though they were close to death, Zeke, true to form, refused to visit them.

"They never cared about me. Just like you!" he said to his wife.

But his elderly parents happened to hear this remark and said, "But we've done everything for you Zeke!"

"You never did anything for me!" said Zeke, meaner than ever.

"What is it that we haven't done?"

Then Zeke outdid himself.

"YOU NEVER TAUGHT ME HOW TO LIVE WITH OTHER PEOPLE!"

To strengthen	*To prevent*
Solidarity	Territoriality
Protection and help	Fights
Responsibility	Envy
Cooperation	Arguments
Tenderness	Tattling
Consideration	Disloyalty
Honesty	Begrudging
Respect	Ruthlessness

• *Territoriality* can be prevented if you avoid setting up screened off children's worlds within the walls of your home. Such segregation makes it impossible for your children to participate in activities that are necessary for the flock's welfare.

Put your children to work according to their abilities. You need each and every one of them every day, and you need them for practical rather than purely emotional reasons. Siblings who know they are needed and that they benefit others – be their contributions ever so humble – do not compete with each other.

Have your children share their sleeping space. If you refuse to permit locks on the doors and "No Entry" signs (unless they are for your own use!), you will put a stop to any exclusionary tendencies before they even get started.

1.

"She's not allowed in here."

"Oh yes she is. If your sister isn't allowed in here, then neither are you."

"But she's taking my things!"

"So what are you going to do about it? Your little sister has got to be allowed to be in here, and you don't want your things broken. Solve that problem! You can do it."

2.

"He can't be in here when we're playing."

"Oh yes he can. If he can't be in here while you're playing, then you can't play. You don't have to play with him, but you can't kick him out."

3.

"I don't want to eat breakfast with her. She's such a sloppy eater."

"Then don't eat breakfast."

4.

"If he tries to swipe my pencils once more, I'm going to sock him."

"Let him have one of your pencils and put the rest away."

"No way! He's not getting *any* of my pencils."

"Then I guess you can't have any either. I can take them."

"No!"

"So give him one pencil. Share. Then you can keep the rest for yourself."

If the child is stubborn, you have to be stubborn too and really take the pencils away from him, so everyone knows you mean business.

Cracking your metaphorical whip is an unpleasant but necessary art that you will have to master as a caregiver.

Any unpleasantness you spare yourself will eventually come back to haunt your child.

• *Fights* between siblings must never be condoned.

It's sometimes implied that fighting is acceptable as long as you don't hit someone smaller or weaker or fight dirty. I disagree. Fights between siblings are *never* acceptable.

"Don't fight! It's not allowed! Stop it right now!"

"He's a …"

"She's just as…"

"I don't care. You can't fight!"

"She started it!"

"He's crazy! He…"

"I don't care about that either. You can't fight. Hug each other."

"No!"

"I'm not hugging him! No way!"

"Oh yes you are. You're brother and sister and you belong together. You love each other and you need each other, and you know it. Hug each other and feel that you belong together. Then you can talk the problem over. But you can't fight."

Then wrap the children's arms around each other, or at least put the aggressor's arms around the victim and hold them there.

But does a forced hug really do any good?

Yes, it does. It confirms the children's solidarity with each other. It breaks the hostility. It makes peace.

A hug is far more effective than a forced apology because it involves touching.

A hug is a way of marking territory and saying *we belong together*, and the contact is not just physical. There is a positive emotional connection as well.

A blow is negative physical contact. A hug is positive physical contact. The hug cancels out the blow; the positive cancels out the negative.

A hug also provides the combatants with an alternative. It gives them a way out. The admonition, the prohibition "Don't fight!" isn't left hanging in the air, and hostility dissipates. A hug is compensatory and restorative.

Even children who are unaccustomed to hugging after altercations can be persuaded to hug each other. The relief they feel afterwards is palpable.

Children want peace. Love is the antidote to violence – even if it is a little forced at first – and a hug is a token of that love.

All siblings love each other because they belong to each other. All siblings want to live in peace with each other.

• *Envy* is a poison. Common sense and an ability to step back and look at the big picture are the antidotes.

I asked one of my children, who was then thirteen and had three older siblings and four younger ones if she had ever been jealous of them.

"Yes, sometimes," she answered. "But then I think of the things that I have that they might envy me for. If I put myself in someone else's shoes, I can always find a reason to envy myself."

Children think in very concrete terms, and their common sense is only influenced by concrete examples.

You can talk about the things you envy people for and what you think is unfair. People who are envious can rarely step outside themselves. Try to get the children to look at their situation from a different angle. Don't find fault with them, but try to broaden their horizons.

"I understand why you're envious. I would be too. But there isn't much that's fair about the world. There are millions of people who don't have enough water to live on, and the little water they do have is not even clean. There are millions of people who starve to death, just because they happened to be born in countries where others rob them of their means to survive. And then there are people who never work a day in their lives but they have money to burn."

"I do the best I can, but life is never completely fair. You two are not identical. Everything can't be exactly the same. Could you make the two of you identical?"

"I'm envious of *my* brother. I'd like to travel as much as he does. But then again, I have things that he doesn't. I have you guys for example."

Point out that justice is an ideal. We all have a duty to strive for it, but, precisely because it is an ideal, we never quite reach it.

You can also point out that envy isn't one of the Seven Deadly Sins for nothing. It blights people's lives and kills joy like nothing else does.

"Instead of feeling envious of your sister because she got a new coat and you didn't, try being happy for her. It will make the coat that much more precious to her. Then, when you get something that she doesn't, you will be that much happier over what you've been given because she will be happy for you."

Do ut des – I give so that you will give – as good a justification of mutuality as any – was enshrined in ancient Roman law.

• *Arguments* are like the rows that adults have. Sometimes they clear the air and do some good, and sometimes they just rub salt in an already painful wound. Arguments between children hurt, just as rows between adults lacerate.

Arguments between siblings that change things for the better should not be discouraged, but arguing well is an art. A beneficial argument is actually not an argument at all but a negotiation.

Arguments between children often revolve around a Thing.

You can exhort older children to lend the Thing to younger children and vice versa.

You can exhort children to take turns playing with the Thing.

You can also run out and buy another Thing, but this is a bad solution. Once children get the idea that they are all entitled to their very own edition of each Thing, the situation quickly dissolves into a litigious quagmire. Sooner or later, your children will become territorial towards each other and lock themselves up in their own little fortresses.

A good way of activating the flock instinct is to refuse all disagreements over the Thing.

"If you can't agree about the Thing, I'm taking the Thing away."

The result will be instant unity. Confronted with the threat of the Thing being taken away, the children will quickly find a solution. If the choice is between a shared Thing and no Thing at all, it's not much of a contest. (See page 565 on how to avoid spoiling children.)

Your children might also unite against *you*. They can be movingly supportive of each other when they are angry enough at the boss...

Personally, I would much rather my children were angry at me but supportive of each other than fight among themselves and think I was fabulous.

"Either you sit still in the car, or I am going to pull over and stop the car. No one will be going anywhere."

"I've made a cake for you because I wanted to make you happy, not start an argument. If you argue about the cake, I'm taking it away."

"Instead of devoting all that energy to arguing, why don't you do something useful? You clean the oven, and you go scrub the toilet! Don't feel like it? So, come up with something better. I'm listening."

Arguments between siblings should be followed up.

"You're still in a bad mood. Haven't you made up yet?"

"Yeah, but..."

"But what?"

"She's so mean."

"Go and tell her then. Tell her what you think is mean that she has been doing. *And tell her what you think she should do instead.*"

• *Tattling* can be a serious problem. For what is tattling? Can a brother tell on his sister because she has started smoking? Can a sister tell on a brother if he falls off the roof where he wasn't supposed to be in the first place?

You have to learn to distinguish between tattling that is meant to help and tattling that is meant to slander.

The brother who fell off the roof needs help. Whether or not he should have been on the roof in the first place is beside the point. The sister who has started smoking is damaging her health. She needs help too.

If someone needs help, children should be encouraged to report what has happened even if the person in question has done something wrong. Tattling for other reasons should be discouraged.

1.

"Brother surfs on your computer at night!" says Sister.

"That's none of your business."

Sister should not be rewarded for tattling. Keep a closer eye on your computer at night, but you don't have to say anything to Brother about it. He can be allowed to believe that you noticed his nocturnal activities yourself but that you are too sensitive and understanding to censure him over it.

If you decide to move the computer to a more secure spot, have a reason ready. You need it in the bedroom, the table it was on was too low, you have to reformat and it's going to take time, or whatever comes to mind.

Sister must not be allowed to celebrate having her brother nicked.

2.

"Sister threw away her sandwich."

"Don't snitch on your sister."

"You're going to let her throw away her sandwich?!"

"I'm the one bringing her up, not you."

"But you don't notice the things she does!"

"I don't notice everything that you do either. Do you want your sister to snitch on you?"

3.

"Brother hit Sister!"

"You can tell me that your sister hurt herself, but not that her brother hit her."

"But he did!"

"That's tattling. You can tell me what happened but not who did it."

• *Disloyalty* can be discouraged by setting a good example. You are your children's role model.

Never speak badly of one of your children in front of the others. Never complain about one of your children to the others.

You shouldn't complain about any of your children *in front of other adults* either, and especially not when the children are within earshot.

Young children have great difficulty accepting adults laughing when they unintentionally do something funny because they feel they are being ridiculed. They hadn't meant to be funny, so they can't understand why everyone is laughing. To ridicule is to show contempt, and showing contempt for your children is about as disloyal as you can get.

"We're not laughing *at* you darling. We're laughing *with* you," you can say. It's not the most truthful line in the world, but it works better than nothing.

Last but not least, always defend family members in front of the children. Negative statements should never be passed over in silence.

Disloyalty must be balanced through the process of discouragement – understanding – reconciliation.

"That boy of mine living in here is just weird," said an acquaintance of mine as she showed me around her new house. "He just doesn't belong." Indefensible.

Children who are *needed* always belong with their flock – regardless of personality clashes, and regardless of the flock members loving each other or not.

1.

"She's so stupid. I'm going to tell her boyfriend."
"I forbid you to talk about your sister that way. I wouldn't dream of talking that way about you."

2.

"It wasn't me! It was him! He took it!"
"You're not going to convince me that you didn't take it by trying to pin it on your brother. It's up to *you* to convince me that *you* didn't take it."
"Maybe I can't."
"But you can blame your brother? Don't do that again!"

3.

"She's such a drag. She's always arguing. No one else likes it either. We decided not to have anything to do with her."
"If you have a beef with your sister, then tell her to her face. But you can't talk trash about her with your other sister, and you can't decide to freeze her out behind her back."

• *Begrudging* is a spiritual stinginess that is best fought under the banner of *shared happiness is double happiness*.

Again, the adult example that you set is decisive.

If you, as a mother or father, can rejoice over and with your children when they succeed at something – even if you wish they had succeeded at something else that you think is more important – or when they did something nice, even though it could have been done much nicer in the way you would have done it yourself – or dressed themselves with care and enthusiasm, even if the result is awkward – or lovingly refurnished their room, even if it looks terrible – or spent all their money on something you think is crazy – then your children too will be able to rejoice over and with each other.

"Why does she always get such good marks? It's not fair."

"It's great that she got good marks, isn't it? It's great for her. That's why I'm happy, not because of the marks themselves. I'm happy for what you do as well. I'm happy because you're happy."

"I wish she'd failed everything."

"I don't think so. If she had failed, you wouldn't be any the happier for it."

This is perhaps a suitable juncture for a loving sermon.

"If you are eating a meal with someone, and the person you're dining with doesn't get enough to eat, you wouldn't be happier and feel more satisfied because of the other person still being hungry. What makes you feel full and satisfied is the good food you had. You would want your fellow diner to rejoice with you, preferably that you were happy together – even if he wanted more to eat. It's perhaps difficult for the other person to be happy that you are full if he is still hungry, but he would not think it particularly pleasant to be full if you were still hungry either. Do you see the mutuality? Try to be happy for the person who is full even if you are still hungry, indeed because you are still hungry. You can understand the pleasure that satisfying one's hunger brings. If you are hungry, you become no less so just because someone else is even hungrier. You have to try to satisfy your hunger with the food that is available *without taking food from other people*. There is enough happiness to go around, and I want to be happy with you."

• *Ruthlessness* is often pure thoughtlessness.

Big sister snatches something out of her little brother's hand. "You can't have that!" she says.

"Thank him nicely and give him something else instead."

Big brother slams the door in his little brother's face. "You can't come in now!"

"Tell him gently that you will be out in a minute and smile. Make it clear to him that you are closing the door because you need to be alone right now, not because *he* has done anything."

Big brother wants to drink all the soda.

"What about your sister?"

"She's not here. It's her problem."

"Show some consideration for your sister and save some for her. She'll do the same for you when you're not around."

Big sister is teasing little brother.

"You can't dive! You're afraid to dive! Scaredy cat! Scaredy cat!"

"Teach him then. You're a good diver. Since you're so brave, teach him to be brave too! Or else, stop teasing him for being scared."

• *Solidarity* between siblings is strengthened by anything that emphasizes the ties that bind them. These ties spring from their common background and the fact that they belong to the same flock.

They all belong – regardless of how "suited" they are to each other and regardless of how much they love each other.

In many cultures siblings sleep in the same room in one large bed, which makes the territory they hold in common immediate and literal.

Siblings can share everything that it's possible to share – from furniture and toys to bikes and clothes. Even if you can afford to buy them separate sets of everything, you should perhaps refrain and ponder the effect on sibling solidarity.

Even among siblings who seem to be constantly at loggerheads with each other, I have never met a child who would willingly trade a brother or a sister for material possessions – at least not after giving the matter a little thought.

The recurring theme – *whatever is done is done together* – does not have to be reiterated that often to take the edge off any possible protests. Either together, or not at all, is the underlying message.

"Yes, you can have it together – you can buy it together – you can do it together."

Don't apologize for any belt-tightening measures you may have to take: "There are so many of you. I can't afford it." The children might get the idea that of course you/the flock would have had more money and survived better if they hadn't come into the world.

Try to emphasize the positive side of any given situation because there always is one.

"Everything that money can buy can be had if you really put your mind to it and go for it until you get it, but you can never buy yourself a sister or a brother or a friend from birth and for life."

People who don't believe in the essential goodness of human beings have reason to change their minds when faced with a brood of siblings who are close to each other.

Siblings show each other tenderness, consideration and empathy. They help each other and protect each other.

They seek the truth, and they don't want to lie, deceive or betray each other.

They teach each other – with or without an adult seal of approval! And they stick together, even against adults if it's necessary (and sometimes it is).

They take responsibility for each other. They think about each other. They ask about each other. They care.

The dealings that young siblings have with each other are marked with infinite helpfulness and tenderness.

Older children need to be reminded sometimes, since they are subject to outside influences (most of them negative). We parents have to expect and encourage them explicitly, by words, to treat each other the way people who love each other do.

But we also have to show our appreciation when they do – even if we consider it self-evident.

Try to encourage mutuality so that it is not always the older kid who knows and can do everything!

"Wait! Let her try!" you can say when a young child tries to "help" an older one.

Even the smallest gestures of consideration and concern that you can inspire and/or help the children to show each other bring siblings closer together and make their sense of belonging together stronger.

Flock solidarity and the territory it holds in common must be maintained with some effort. Siblings should know where their brothers and sisters are and when they are coming home, say goodbye to each other when they leave, and greet each other when they get back – all to confirm the *belonging* together.

What is good human beings get used to and soon expect as their right. We never get used to what is bad. The good between siblings must be given as much – if not more, attention than the "bad" so that the children really *see* how much more value the good has.

Children in large families rarely feel neglected, however paradoxical that might seem to the outside world.

What do their parents have in common?

• *They touch* each and every one of their children every day – a hug, a caress, a pat on the cheek.

• *They encourage* each and every one of their children every day – by giving praise, showing appreciation, expressing gratitude, and by giving every contribution and every attempt to assist the recognition they deserve.

• *They show interest* in each and every one of their children every day, by focusing on something that involves that particular child exclusively.

"Let's have a talk," doesn't always have to signal that a sermon is imminent. Just as often, or more often, it can presage an affectionate, intimate chat.

"How did it go with that project you were planning?"

"What did he say when you talked to him about that?"

"You were worried about that. How did it turn out?"

• *They "keep hold"* of their children with a special engagement with each and every child and let no day pass without that vital connection.

• *They need* their children and make use of them, each and every one of them in some way every day. As a rule, the children's duties are mutually agreed upon and often involve teamwork. The work is carried out under the banner of necessity, which in large families is a beautifully positive force, free from complaining and irritation.

• *They laugh.*

THE GIFT

The year is drawing to a close, and Christmas is fast approaching. Christmas candles light the winter darkness, families gather round the fire, and children, eyes shining with anticipation, look longingly at the presents piled under the tree. It is a holiday for children and families, a time of peace and togetherness, love and belonging.

But it is also a time of bitter loneliness for those who have no families, who belong nowhere.

Let me relate a little story.

One year, I was in town with my four youngest children doing my Christmas shopping. The store was ablaze with lights, stuffed to the rafters with every conceivable ware and mobbed with people. My Christmas list was long, and, since I have trouble choosing, Christmas shopping was the usual purgatory. It was several hours before we finally got out of the store, laden with shopping bags.

We sat down on a low parapet to catch our breath before the long journey home. In front of us was a little park. In the summer, the fountain would have been bubbling merrily, the flowers swaying in the summer breeze and the benches occupied by people soaking up the sun, but now it was frozen and desolate.

In spite of the cold, a small crowd of people had gathered there. They were scruffy and looked as though they had not been in contact with soap and water for some time. Most of them had been drinking. But they gave my children friendly smiles.

After a few minutes' hesitation, a man approached.

"You have nice children!" he said.

His breath was white in the chilly air and billowed around his ravaged, mottled face. He was drunk. He squatted down in front of my children.

"Let's sing!" he said. "Baa-baa Black Sheep!"

And he started to sing. He got a little confused over what came first, the wool or the three bags, but he managed to get through the song a couple of times. My children looked a little reticent, but they joined in. They stood with half bowed heads looking down at the man, who, because he was squatting, was shorter than they were.

"Now let's dance around the Christmas tree. Everyone hold hands! It doesn't matter that it's not Christmas yet. We can use the lamppost! It will make a fine tree!"

The children held hands and formed a circle with the man. They were still a little wary, as they always were with strangers, but they danced obediently around the lamppost with the man, who was trying to drag the song that we usually sing around the tree on Christmas Eve out of his somewhat befuddled memory. My children didn't really remember it either. Their uneven, thin voices rose in the cold night air, but the man smiled and stamped his feet every so often to mark the rhythm.

Then he got tired and sat down on the parapet. My children stood in a group a little way from the man looking at him doubtfully. I got up and said we should be going.

Then my children went over to the man and, one by one, gave him a hug.

I was surprised, but the man was overwhelmed. He looked from one to the other, and his eyes filled with tears.

"God bless you!" he cried. "God bless you little children!"

STORIES FOR LONELY SOULS

THE LITTLE TAILOR

Once upon a time there was a little tailor who lived in the Kingdom of Capitalia. The Kingdom was ruled by King Prosperitus.

One day King Prosperitus visited the little tailor. And what a remarkable visit it was!

"Now my good tailor," said King Prosperitus, "I have tidings of great joy for all my subjects. I have built a factory in Consumerville. There you will work making suits, and in this factory you will be able to make suits a hundred times faster than here in your shop."

So the little tailor went to work at the factory, and he saw that the King was right. The suits literally flew off the conveyor belt.

The tailor worked from morning till night and was well rewarded for his labor.

"Now you can afford to live better!" said King Prosperitus. "Did you know that houses are manufactured in Consumerville too? Beautiful modern houses that would suit a man who works as hard as you do."

So the tailor bought a house and moved in with his wife and children, and his elderly mother, who was a little hard of hearing.

The tailor worked at Consumerville in joy and contentment, for if a beautiful house isn't worth working for, what is?

"Now I think you should get some new furniture for your house," said King Prosperitus. "Have you seen what fine furniture is made in Consumerville?"

Bless me, how beautiful the house was! The tailor's wife and mother were delighted, and the children sat almost reverently on the edge of the brand new sofa.

"Now you can afford to eat a little better," said King Prosperitus. "Have you seen what fine food is produced in Consumerville? Better than the finest restaurants and as good as the food that is served in my castle."

But living had become very expensive. The tailor worked as hard as he could, but he never seemed to have enough money, which was strange.

"I'd better start working too," said his wife. "Then we'll have more money."

"But who is going to look after the children?" the little tailor asked.

"And who will look after my mother, who is as deaf as a post?"

"I'll fix that," said King Prosperitus. "Don't worry!"

And King Prosperitus gathered up the little children and put them in a day care house, and he put the tailor's mother in an elder care house too, so everyone had everything they could possibly want.

"Now that both you and your wife are working in Consumerville, you should get yourselves a car," said King Prosperitus. "Have you seen what fabulous cars are made in Consumerville?"

"But we don't need a car," said the little tailor, who thought paying for all the things he already owned was too expensive.

"Don't you need a car when you go to visit your mother?" asked King Prosperitus. "And think how easy it would be to pick up your children if you had a car."

So the little tailor bought a car.

He worked and sweated and slaved, and his wife worked and sweated and slaved. The days became ever longer and harder, and only sleep brought relief.

But one day, the little tailor sat down and started to cry.

"I do nothing but work," he cried. "I never have time to talk to anyone, and when evening comes, I'm so tired that I wish I didn't have to go and visit my mother or take my children home. I just want to sleep. It shouldn't be this way!"

King Prosperitus was very concerned.

"But my good tailor," he said, "aren't you happy? Look at the great life you have!"

Then one day the little tailor got sick. There he lay on his bed, alone and sad. He missed his deaf mother and his rowdy children, and he missed his wife, but she had to work day and night as well because the house, the furniture, the clothes, the food and the car all had to be paid for.

The little tailor got sicker and sicker. Finally, he became so sick, he lost his mind.

"You tricked me King Prosperitus!" he yelled. "My house can't talk to me, and my furniture can't hug me, my car can't comfort me when I'm sad, my clothes can't read to me, and my food can't hold my hand. You tricked me. You have taken all the people I love away from me, and I have worked myself into an early grave for THINGS!"

And with that the little tailor died.

And maybe it was for the best, for now his wife could marry someone with more sense...

TWO LIVES FOR KARL

In society A, there are good day care centers for all children. From the time he is born Karl is cared for by committed professionals.

Karl's mother actively discourages his dependence on her in order to foster his independence.

Karl is devoted to all his caregivers, but these people are not available to him privately.

When he starts school in society A, Karl is given a great deal of individual attention. Psychologists and social workers are on hand to help with every conceivable problem. Karl is devoted to these people too, but they are not available to him privately either.

One day, it dawns on Karl that none of these people actually *care about* him. The only reason they have anything to do with him is because it is part of their job.

Karl's mother is politically active and agitates for:

1. The dissolution of the nuclear family

2. All children's right to night and weekend day care

She encourages Karl to strengthen his independence and concentrate on getting an education that will lead to gainful employment.

Karl learns that in society A:

• People are valued in terms of their profession.

• Involvement and responsibility are reserved for the workplace.

• Freedom is synonymous with economic and emotional independence.

If Karl passes a person dying on the street, it's someone else's job to intervene. When Karl realizes that a third of the world is starving, it's someone else's responsibility.

Karl finishes his education and looks for a job. He is vetted minutely by eighteen human resources departments, who look into his background, evaluate his qualifications and administer aptitude tests.

Karl is politically active too and agitates for higher pay.

The nuclear family has been eradicated in society A.

Karl's emotional needs are satisfied by:

1. Professional exercisers (engagement for a price, emotions for a business, love for sale).

2. Consumption (cocooning furniture, pleasuring clothing, mood-altering substances.

Karl pays his way through life.

Karl's circle of friends is narrow. In society A, people don't depend on each other for practical help in everyday life (everyone is independent), and people don't depend on each other emotionally either (there are experts for that).

Karl becomes a dutiful consumer however. He buys everything he thinks he needs: house, car, TV, clothes, washing machine, stereo, DVD, plush sofas, garden and kitchen pots.

When he retires from his profession, which gave him his sole worth, he ends up in a severe loneliness. He tries to alleviate it by:

1. Going to stores where people know him.

2. Seeking medical attention so he can have a conversation that centers on him.

As an old man, Karl is slotted in at an elder care facility, where he is subjected to recreational therapy.

Karl quietly dies in the institution.

Karl's objectives in society A have been:

• Independence, i.e. loneliness (material goods as compensation).

• Freedom, i.e. freedom from responsibility (it's always someone else's job).

• Official commitment, i.e. personal indifference (talking the talk, rather than walking the walk).

THE LESS REALITY THE MORE PEDAGOGY.
THE LESS DEVOTION THE MORE PSYCHOLOGY.
THE LESS PEOPLE NEED EACH OTHER
THE MORE THEY NEED THERAPY.

In society B, Karl is his parents' responsibility.

Karl's parents are divorced. They regard Karl's dependence on them as self-evident. They feel themselves to be dependent on him.

Society B values life above everything else.

Karl's neighbors in the apartment building where he lives include a pensioned widower, a single mother of three, and a young student. Karl's parents ask them if they could take turns looking after Karl.

During the day, they worry about Karl a good deal. Worry is a part of responsibility. Worry is also, they think, a part of love.

In the pensioner's apartment, Karl hears all about times gone by. He looks at old pictures, goes on walks and visits old ladies. Under the pensioner's supervision, Karl also amuses himself both inside and outside the apartment.

At the single mother's apartment, Karl plays with the other children, learns to do dishes, make meals and look after babies. More often than not, these kids don't play with toys. They invent games, have competitions and sing songs.

At the student's apartment, sometimes Karl sits quietly reading or drawing, and sometimes he roughhouses with the young student. He meets other students, goes running in the woods, and hangs around the coffee table listening to philosophical debates.

All the adults in Karl's world are available to him privately, and Karl is available to them.

In society B, looking after children is not an industry. Money does not change hands. In return for looking after their son, Karl's parents help out their three neighbors.

Karl's dad gives the pensioner a lift when he needs it. Karl's mother makes him Sunday dinner, and on weekends she and Karl clean the pensioner's apartment.

Karl's mother does the student's laundry, and Karl's dad lends him his car. These services are supplemented with food and company.

Both Karl's parents babysit for the single mother on evenings and weekends, and when she goes on vacation, her children live in Karl's apartment.

Karl learns that in society B:

• Cooperation is more important than profit.

• Loneliness is self-imposed.

• Responsibility and involvement, whether at a private, societal or global level, are highly personal matters.

In society B, schools are educational institutions and nothing else. Knowledge is power.

Parents and friends are trusted to look after Karl's psychological well-being.

In society B,

• Work is regarded as a necessity and a source of personal satisfaction, but it does not define people.

• The obsession with profit is regarded as a cancer on the human soul and the body of society.

• Children are regarded as society's most precious treasure.

Karl grows up to be a bad consumer. His neighbors and friends are more important to him than possessions. He borrows chairs when he has a party, he car pools with four other people, he exchanges apartments for vacation, he shares cooking and dining with ten other people and watches TV with fifteen.

Karl will probably be a bad capitalist too, convinced that he is that all human beings are every human being's personal concern and responsibility, and knowing that within all human beings is the possibility to fulfil all human needs without a financial profit being any part of the equation.

IN REMEMBRANCE OF A LOST CHILDHOOD

She is little and fair with very large, round, trusting eyes. Her lips could have been chiselled by Cupid himself. With her waist length hair and elfin features, she is a fairy tale come to life.

She gives me a confident smile.

"I'm *leally* a boy!"

Really isn't the right word. Leally is.

She is full of insights. She is five and knows almost everything already. The sun goes to sleep behind the lake after the trees have made its bed. The moon follows us when we drive at night and keeps a watching smile at us.

She knows this too:

"When you die, you turn into a baby. Then I'll take care of you."

"Do you know what's the meanest thing someone can do?" she asks me one day.

I don't exactly, although I have my theories.

"The meanest thing to do is *fight*", says Isadora.

"And do you know what's the most meanest thing you can do?"

No, I don't know that either.

"It is to *liar*", says Isadora summoning all the indignation she can muster. And then it comes.

"But, do you know what's the *veryest* most meanest thing you can do? It is to STOLE!"

I try hard to stop the corners of my mouth from twitching.

"You are absolutely right," I say. "Taking something that doesn't belong to you is the most horriblest thing in the world." (In certain company, my language skills are somewhat flexible.)

Two minutes later, she calls to me from the yard.

"Mom, mom! Look what I've stoled! A ball!"

"Sweetheart, give it back right now!"

"But it's mine!" she lies blithely. She liars, I mean.

"Isadora...!"

Now the upset owner of the ball arrives on the scene full of righteous wrath. Isadora dispatches him handily with a well-placed kick to the shin.

In less than two minutes she has thus managed to commit the three sins she claimed were the deadliest in the world. She comes in and gives me a hug.

"Do you know what's the *veryest* most meanest thing you can do?"...

We've been driving for a long time on our way to our home in northern Sweden. Isadora discovers that the moon is up even though it's day, which surprises her mightily. A pale crescent in a blue sky has been following us ever since we left town.

"I only sing the moon a lullaby when it's dark," Isadora announces.

She waits for dusk, and as the sky fades to black, the moon shines ever brighter, and the stars twinkle slowly to life (peepholes for the angels according to Isadora), she starts to sing.

"Little moon, you're so kind, you follow with us, all way home, I like you so, you're so kind, and say hello, to little budgie, for he was tired, and sick and died, and say hello, to little froggie, who wouldn't eat, and also died, and when you're cold, I can warm you, you can come, to Isadora, and I will hold you, and I'll sing..."

Isadora sings to the moon for all of an hour, moving her head from side to side, the tenderness in her eyes as luminous as the moonlight itself.

When she's finished, she says, "That's it!"

We arrive at our destination and get out of the car.

And of course the moon stops with us.

"We're here!" says Isadora. And she starts to greet her surroundings. "Hi lake, hi forest, hi house..."

She yawns and looks so little and tired, but she doesn't forget to go into her bedroom and get her big white Snoopy, who has waited longingly for her on her bed, and hold him up to the moonlight.

"Say goodnight to the moon, Snoopsie! He followed us all the way home."

A FINAL WORD: TO MY BELOVED CHILDREN

These last lines of *For the Love of Children* I want to direct to you – you who are my beloved child, one for all and all for one.

No one knows what the world will be like when a child, so little now, eventually steps out into it. No one knows what kind of a world your children and grandchildren will experience. No one knows what those who survive this era in history, when the human species appears to be in such terrible, self-imposed danger, will be like.

But there is hope. Human beings themselves are their own strongest hope. In times of crisis, in times of necessity, human beings rise to the challenge. They marshal their capability and that capability is limitless.

To think freely, to act and live according to your inner conviction, is the highest goal. That is freedom.

Selling your soul is death.

And the greatest sin, with a word from Jesus, is to torment your brother in body and soul.

The way I believed in you, I want you to believe in yourself, and armed with that belief you will move mountains. Fearless, devoid of illusions but brimming with love, you will conquer the mountain deemed insurmountable.

Cultivate your zest for life! It's the foundation you stand upon. It's what powers your life.

Cultivate your joy and your laughter! That's what kindles love in the human heart. Strive ceaselessly to be happy, even in those times when happiness seems but a distant dream. For it's really beside you and within you.

Hard times aren't bad. They motivate you to struggle, to wrestle with life and win by growing spiritually and becoming more than you were.

Don't let yourself be lulled into submission, labelled or silenced. Don't sell your soul!

Love. Take what life has to offer. Live!
You have a right to a place in this world. Fight for it with love!

Your Mom,
who thanks to you, and for the love of children,
could give birth to this my tenth child.

THE EARTH

The Earth and its people
Tumbling through the infinity of space
The sickle moon in tow
A glistening speck of dust
So tiny, so silent, so insignificant
Do you hear the sound of life?
The strength and despair
The hope and disappointment
The thronging joy
Of life on Earth
Here the fragrant forests, intractably green, grow and stretch
Here the enticing birdsong rises heavenward
Here animals flock to the water's edge
Here the sun sears the fields to ashes
Or caresses them to fertility
Here the rain hammers the soil to liquid
Here the oceans rage and the flowers glow
Here dwell people locked in a battle for life!
The Earth and its people
Tumbling through the infinity of space
The sickle moon in tow
An Earth of joy and sorrow
An Earth of comradeship and loneliness
The Earth and its people
Here must you dwell and here must you live
Here must you toil and here must you suffer
Here must you bear all your silent longing
This is your home, you, earth's people,
You, child,
Born to live on the Earth.

INDEX